W9-BDI-498

America Remembers

Our Best-Loved Customs and Traditions

America Remembers

Our Best-Loved Customs and Traditions

EDITED BY

SAMUEL RAPPORT and PATRICIA SCHARTLE

HANOVER HOUSE
Garden City, New York

LIBRARY OF CONGRESS CATALOG CARD NUMBER 56–12126

PRINTED IN THE UNITED STATES OF AMERICA

Acknowledgments

Thanks are due to the following publishers, publications, authors and their representatives for permission to reprint selections from the volumes listed below:

American Heritage—*Holiday Time at the Old Country Store* by Gerald Carson.

The American Mercury—*Smith Street, U.S.A.* by Elizabeth Hughes.

Appleton-Century-Crofts, Inc.—chapter *Christmas on the Prairie* from *A Lantern in Her Hand* by Bess Streeter Aldrich. Copyright 1928 D. Appleton & Company, condensed by permission of the publishers.

A. S. Barnes & Company—*My Greatest Day in Baseball* by Lloyd Lewis as told to John P. Carmichael. Copyright 1945 by A. S. Barnes & Company.

Mr. Richard Barnitz—*How Dear to My Heart.*

Mr. Lucius Beebe—*Nob Hill* from "Holiday Magazine," January 1950 issue.

The Bobbs-Merrill Company, Inc.—*Abe Martin's Broadcast* by Kin Hubbard. Copyright 1930, used by special permission of the publishers and *One Man's Life* by Herbert Quick. Copyright © 1925, 1953, used by special permission of the publishers.

Brandt & Brandt—*The Gentleman from Indiana* by Booth Tarkington. Copyright 1926 by Booth Tarkington, published by Doubleday & Company, Inc. and *Morally We Roll Along* by Guy MacLaren. Copyright 1938 by Little, Brown and Company, published by them.

Curtis Brown, Ltd. and David L. Cohn—*The Good Old Days* by David L. Cohn. Copyright 1940 by David L. Cohn.

Mrs. Everett Case—*White Commencement.*

The Estate of Irvin S. Cobb—*Ken-*

tucky Derby Day from *Kentucky* by Irvin S. Cobb. Published and copyright 1924 by George H. Doran Company, renewed by Laura Baker Cobb, c/o Buhler, King & Buhler.

COWARD-MCCANN, INC.—*But Look, the Morn* by MacKinlay Kantor. Copyright 1947 by MacKinlay Kantor.

ROBERT L. CRAGER COMPANY—*Fabulous New Orleans* by Lyle Saxon.

CROWN PUBLISHERS, INC.—*One Thousand and One Afternoons* by Ben Hecht. Copyright 1927 by Pascal Covici, Publisher, Inc.

DODD, MEAD & COMPANY, INC.—chapter 1 condensed from *How Dear to My Heart* by Emily Kimbrough. Copyright © 1944 by Dodd, Mead & Company, Inc.

DOUBLEDAY & COMPANY, INC.—*920 O'Farrell Street* by Harriet Lane Levy. Copyright 1937, 1947 by Harriet Lane Levy, *Great Possessions* by David Grayson. Copyright 1917 by Doubleday & Company, Inc., *That Reminds Me* by Alben W. Barkley. Copyright 1954 by Alben W. Barkley and *The Rosebowl Game* by Rube Samuelsen. Copyright © 1951 by Doubleday & Company, Inc.

DUELL, SLOAN & PEARCE, INC.—*FDR, His Personal Letters, 1905–1928* by Sara Delano Roosevelt, edited by Elliot Roosevelt. Copyright 1948 by Elliot Roosevelt, *Town Meeting Country* by Clarence Webster, *Mormon Country* by Wallace Stegner and *Corn Country* by Homer Croy. Copyright 1947 by Homer Croy.

MR. JOHN GOULD—*New England Town Meeting.*

HARCOURT, BRACE & COMPANY, INC.—*Prairie Town Boy* by Carl Sandburg. Copyright 1952, 1953 by Carl Sandburg.

HARPER & BROTHERS—*The Horse and Buggy Doctor* by Arthur E. Hertzler. Copyright 1938 by Paul B. Hoeber, Inc. and *You Can't Go Home Again* by Thomas Wolfe.

MR. MACKINLEY HELM—*Angel Mo' and Her Son: Roland Hayes.*

HOLIDAY MAGAZINE—reprinted by special permission—*Brooklyn* by Irwin Shaw. Copyright 1950 by The Curtis Publishing Company—*Nob Hill* by Lucius Beebe. Copyright 1949 by The Curtis Publishing Company—*Fifth Avenue* by Silas Spitzer. Copyright 1951 by The Curtis Publishing Company—*American Folkways* by Duncan Emrich. Copyright 1955 by The Curtis Publishing Company—*The Pennsylvania Dutch* by Fredric Klees. Copyright 1947 by The Curtis Publishing Company and *State Fair* by Phil Stong. Copyright 1948 by The Curtis Publishing Company.

FRANZ J. HORCH—*"Sap's Startin' "—Sugaring Off* by Walter Needham as recorded by Barrows Mussey from "Saturday Evening Post."

MR. HENRY BEETLE HOUGH—*It's Thanksgiving Because It's Homecoming.*

HOUGHTON MIFFLIN COMPANY—*A Time to Remember* by Lloyd C. Douglas and *Raintree Country* by Ross Lockridge.

MR. FREDRIC KLEES—*The Pennsylvania Dutch* from "Holiday Magazine," June 1947 issue.

ALFRED A. KNOPF, INC.—Condensed version of chapter *Brief Gust of Glory* from *Happy Days* by H. L. Mencken. Copyright 1939, 1940 by Alfred A. Knopf, Inc.

LITTLE, BROWN & COMPANY—*The Late George Apley* by John P. Marquand. Copyright 1936, 1937 by John P. Marquand and *Melville Goodwin, U.S.A.* by John P. Marquand. Copyright 1951 by John P. Marquand. Copyright 1951 by John P. Marquand and Adelaide H. Marquand.

LITTLE, BROWN & COMPANY AND ATLANTIC MONTHLY PRESS—*From the Top of the Stairs* by Gretchen Finletter. Copyright 1943, 1944, 1946, 1948, by Gretchen Finletter and *Country Kitchen* by Della T. Lutes. Copyright 1935, 1936 by Della T. Lutes.

LIVERIGHT PUBLISHING CORPORATION—*The Vermonters* by Dorothy Canfield Fisher from *These United States* edited by Ernest Gruening, published by Liveright Publishing Corporation, copyright 1925 Boni and Liveright, Inc. Copyright R 1952 by Ernest Gruening, copyright 1956 by Dorothy Canfield Fisher.

MRS. JULIAN LONGLEY—*Red Hills and Cotton* by Ben Robertson.

THE MACMILLAN COMPANY—*Son of the Middle Border* by Hamlin Garland.

HAROLD MATSON COMPANY—*State Fair* by Phil Stong from "Holiday Magazine," August 1948 issue.

MCA MANAGEMENT, LTD.—*My Son Johnny* by John McNulty.

McGRAW-HILL BOOK COMPANY, INC. AND THE AUTHOR, MR. BELLAMY PARTRIDGE—*Big Family*, copyright 1941 by Bellamy Partridge, published by McGraw-Hill Book Company, Inc. and *Country Lawyer* by Bellamy Partridge. Copyright 1939 by Bellamy Partridge, published by McGraw-Hill Book Company, Inc., also *Country Flavor* by Haydn S. Pearson. Copyright 1945 by McGraw-Hill Book Company, Inc., published by McGraw-Hill Book Company, Inc. and *Get Thee Behind Me* by Hartzell Spence. Copyright 1942 by Hartzell Spence, published by McGraw-Hill Book Company, Inc.

MR. THOMAS E. MURPHY—*New England Orgy* from August 28, 1943 issue of "Saturday Evening Post."

THE NEW YORK TIMES—*Easter Parade* by Anne O'Hara McCormick, from April 18, 1949 issue.

THE NEW YORKER—*Savage Homecoming* by Clifford Orr, *The Figgerin' of Aunt Wilma* by James Thurber and *Farewell My Lovely!* by Lee Strout White.

OXFORD UNIVERSITY PRESS, INC.—chapter *Chores* (condensed) from *The Land of the Crooked Tree* by U. P. Hedrick.

RANDOM HOUSE, INC.—Condensed version of chapter *A Third Ward's New Year* from *Grandfather Stories* by Samuel Hopkins Adams. Copyright 1955 by Samuel Hopkins Adams.

RINEHART & COMPANY, INC.—*The Age of Confidence* by Henry Seidel Canby. Copyright 1934 by Henry Seidel Canby and *The Wabash* by William E. Wilson. Copyright 1940 by William E. Wilson.

CHARLES SCRIBNER'S SONS—Excerpts from *The Spirit of St. Louis* by Charles Lindbergh. Copyright 1953 by Charles Scribner's Sons; excerpts from *Early Memories* by Henry Cabot Lodge, copyright 1913 by Charles Scribner's Sons, 1941 by John Ellerton Lodge and excerpts from *The Family on Gramercy Park* by Henry Noble MacCracken. Copyright 1949 by Henry Noble MacCracken.

SIMON AND SCHUSTER—*Father of the Bride* by Edward Streeter. Copyright 1949 by Edward Streeter and Gluyas Williams.

SOUTHWEST REVIEW—*Barbecue Day* by F. M. Kercheville and *Cow Country Theatre* by Winifred Johnston.

SOUTHWEST REVIEW AND MR. WILLIAM A. OWENS—*The Play Party in Texas.*

MR. SILAS SPITZER—*Fifth Avenue* from "Holiday Magazine," December 1951 issue.

MISS RUTH SUCKOW—*Iowa Interiors.*

TAYLOR-POWELL PRESS—*A Hill Farm Year* by Lansing Christman. Copyright 1956 by Lansing Christman and The Taylor-Powell Press.

TIME, INC. AND INTERNATIONAL COOP. PRESS SERVICE, INC.—*Memoirs* by Harry S. Truman.

VANGUARD PRESS, INC.—*It's an Old Wild West Custom* by Duncan Emrich. Copyright 1949 by Duncan Emrich.

MR. W. L. WHITE—*The Ethics of a Country Editor* by William Allen White.

PART I

"Where the Heart Is"

HOME AND FAMILY

PART II

"Down on the Farm"

COUNTRY DAYS

PART III

"Back Where I Come From"

HOME TOWN

PART IV

"Me and Mamie O'Rourke"

CITY SIDEWALKS

PART V

"From Maine to California"

ACROSS THE NATION

Preface

America remembers best those customs and traditions that lie close to the heart. Such memories are inclined to be homebred, homegrown, and homespun. We remember what we have experienced ourselves, or what our parents have taught us to cherish. For good or for bad, it is the nostalgic and the heart-warming memories that endure.

Historians who record the American heritage must consider the bitter hardships of pioneers, the roughness of our frontier tradition, the rawness of backstreets and slums. Yet there are happier bonds that hold Americans together: the simple, unpretentious traditions of home and community that democracy has fostered. Although the memories of bad times have often strengthened us, it is the happy times Americans remember best and longest. These too belong in the record. This volume, then, is not intended to be a survey of our political or social heritage. For this the reader will turn to more formal history. Here, instead, are the informal recollections, the memories of people and places, of joyous celebration and festival.

Our selections have been drawn from the recent past, a period with which most of us can identify, and which continues as an integral part of the present. They have been assembled around home, farm, big city, and the well-defined cultural regions of the nation because this grouping affords the greatest possible reading pleasure. It also reveals the similarity and the variety of America's best-loved memories, and the environments that sheltered them.

The reader will find many selections from serious or popular autobiography. Such accounts, because they are not self-conscious about "making" history, reflect its meaning in human terms. Fiction sometimes captures a character or an event with even more immediacy, and for that reason an occasional work of fiction has been chosen.

It is not, of course, possible to include in one volume all of our favorite memories or customs. Because of the restriction of length, some have had to be sacrificed in order that those included might be more fully and fairly presented. By avoiding a potpourri of bits and samples, we have attempted to gather a unified and readable volume of America's most treasured traditions.

SR, PMS

PART I

"Where the Heart Is"

Home and Family

Home is the place that comes first to mind when America Remembers. It has been sung in saccharine melody; it has been attacked in bitter prose as the breeding ground of repression and frustration. But for all its imperfections, it remains for most of us the ultimate symbol of security and stability. The loving care we received there instills the confidence with which we face the problems of adult lives.

For all the universality of its appeal, every home is unique. Home means people, and those in any one home are unlike those in any other. Perhaps it was one parent whom we loved best. There may have been an uncle who took us fishing. We may remember our own growing pains or those of some younger member of the family. There was sure to be a grandma or a grandpa who "knew best;" often a devoted maidservant. Our family album is composed of all of these. And we love them all—their faults diminish, their virtues strengthen with the passing years.

But while personalities differed, the events in which they took part remained very much the same. And these events, shared by everyone under a single roof, forged bonds which were often more powerful than those of blood. Only by hindsight can we measure their effect on our character and growth. The arrival of a new life, the marriage of a son or daughter, or the heartbreak of final bereavement are major happenings in a procession which, in the words of the song, has made us what we are today. In cumulative effect, the minor scenes, perhaps only dimly remembered, have been equally strong—a wonderful family excursion, a commencement day, or a reunion with loved ones after years of separation.

All of us join in sharing certain well-loved annual occasions—the Thanksgiving bird, the song and sentiment of Christmas. From them our families have gained strength and cohesion. They are America; and they are recalled to us in the selections which follow.

God Bless Our Home

By Henry Seidel Canby

In the days of youth, home was the center of our world. Clubs, hot-rods, and movies were remote or nonexistent. The parlor, used only for company, the golden oak furniture, the hat rack in the hall may be laughable by contemporary standards. But they were the outward trappings of a family life whose serenity and solidity has all but vanished.

"God bless our home," which I can just remember in worsted tapestry, framed in jigsaw walnut, and hung on a spare-room wall, never meant "God make our home a happy one." The blessing was asked upon virtues which were often more conducive to moral conduct and material success than happiness. And indeed it was not a superior quality of happiness that distinguished the pre-Ford, pre-radio, pre-boarding school home from our perches between migrations. . . .

It was confidence, not happiness, that made the great difference between then and now, a confidence that reached down below comfort or pleasure into stability itself. My cousins, who tiptoed around the chair of an old-fashioned, self-willed father, never knew from day to day what his authority might require of them. Their manners and their careers were both whipped into them. Yet they had this same confidence, and would be sure as I, with a memory of a happy and easy-going home, that something solid and valuable has been lost by our children.

In our town, and I think in the American nineties generally, home was the most impressive experience in life. Our most sensitive and our most relaxed hours were spent in it. We left home or its immediate environment chiefly to work, and neither radio nor phonograph brought the outer world into its precincts. Time moved more slowly there, as it always does when there is a familiar routine with a deep background of memory. Evening seemed spacious then, with hour upon hour in which innumerable intimate details of picture, carpet, wallpaper, or well-known pointing shadow were printed upon consciousness. When bicycles came in and flocks of young people wheeled through twilight streets past and past again the porches where the elders were sitting, it was the first breakaway from home, a warning of the new age, but then more like a flight of May flies round and round their hatching place. . . .

The home of the nineties . . . had a quality which we have lost. We complain today of the routine of mechanical processes, yet routine in itself is very persuasive to the spirit, and has attributes of both a tonic and a drug. There was a rhythm in the pre-automobile home that is entirely broken now, and whose loss is perhaps the exactest index of the decline of confidence in our environment. Life seems to be sustained by rhythm, upset by its changes, weakened by its loss. An apartment house with a car at the door, though comfort summarized, has no rhythm, except for a broken, excited syncopation, or the spondaic movement of boredom. . . . It was this familiar movement, this routine with a certainty of repetition, that inspired a confidence in a patterned universe missing today. . . .

Most of us in the late eighties and the nineties still lived in squarish houses of red or painted brick, heavily corniced with wood at the top, or mansarded, with porches at front and back, and painted iron fences between the lawns and the brick sidewalks with their rows of buttonwoods or Norway maples. There were a few old houses of lovelier lines, and many bizarrities of Italian, Greek, Queen Anne, and Egyptian inspiration, or of bastard Gothic pointed with gray slate. All, except the very oldest, had spacious, high-ceilinged rooms, hung with chandeliers recently converted to electricity, and trimmed with dark, polished walnut which also spiralled down giant stairways, and were upholstered wherever possible. Golden oak in the very latest houses relieved the gloom by substituting the frivolous for the dignified.

It is possible to describe what that generation would have called, say about 1890, an ideal home. The hall was broad and deep, a waiting place hung with steel prints and furnished with benches, stiff chairs, and a hat rack. It was Main Street, meant for traffic. On the right the parlor, on the left the sitting room. The parlor was for decorum. It was the largest room in the house, and the least used, with the most massive tables, the biggest pictures, and the showiest chairs. Mirrors at each end gave it an illusion of still greater spaciousness, and between them the piano which, when used for practising, admitted the only disorder allowed in that room. On the center table were the more pretentious gift books, for show, not reading. . . .

Across the hall was the sitting room, smaller, cozier, with easier chairs, bookcases, a tall brass lamp, a gas stove in the corner (fireplaces had not yet come back except as tiled ornaments for the hall where of course no one ever used them), and an air of comfort and usability. Here the family sat and friends were entertained (company went into the parlor). Here were the magazines, the books to be read, the cat, the dog, and the children studying after supper. This was the heart of the home.

The dining room, again, was formal, family portraits on the wall, a china cupboard out of which glinted what never was used even on the grandest occasion. Morning sun in the dining room was one of the specifications, as important as the sideboard and the serving table. The pantry was built up to the high ceilings in tiers of shelves and closets on and in which were kept that incredible clutter of household china and glass which every family seemed to accumulate. There was a drawer labelled "cake," another "bread," and a lead-lined sink with cockroach poison on the edges. The kitchens sprawled—coal stoves, laundry tubs, tables for baskets, tables for rolling dough, hooks and closets for a forest of tinware, and so on out into the shed with its tables and bins and closets. And in the cellar more bins, more shelves, a cold room, and a bricked in furnace as big as a funeral vault.

The main stairs followed a curving serpent of black walnut to a long upstairs hall off which opened vast bedrooms. The bath room was here (often the only one) with doors in at least two directions, accessible to all. The parents' room would be an upstairs sitting room also, with a desk somewhere spilling with small change and account books, and at the further end a vast walnut bed whose back rose to the ceiling, a cliff of polished veneer topped by a meaningless escutcheon. Other monumental pieces of black walnut flanked it at either side, and at the foot was a crib for the smallest child, or a green plush sofa for naps.

Across the hall would be the spare rooms, usually "blue" and "red," as in the White House, very bleak and usually shrouded in sheets. On their walls the outmoded pictures collected: "Old Swedes' Church," by Robert C., "Scene on the Brandywine," "Pauline" on glass. Guests in those days usually went home at night.

The stair banister to the third floor was scratched by children's slidings. This was where freedom began. There was the boy's room and the girl's room, indistinguishable in furnishing (cast-offs mostly) but differing in the kind of disorder, and an alcove at the end of the hall for doll houses, and mineral or birds' eggs collections. On the other side of the hall, last relic of the self-contained age of our grandparents, a "lumber room," with its bench, tools, oddments for repairs and plumbing, the rest of the floor space carrying a mass of family trunks piled up on each other in buttes and mesas. Last of all a cubicle where the visiting seamstress slept and some drawers for her scanty clothes. (She came of the good "plain people," and kept up her tiny remnant of gentry by gifts of big red apples to the children.) Here freedom ended, since the next door led to the servants' quarters . . . . and no one, not even a parent, was supposed to trespass there except on monthly inspections of the sanitation. . . .

Our house, with the tall two-hundred year old clock ticking at its heart, sank into the subconsciousness and became a sense of stability and permanence. It was a proof of a friendly universe, to which memory could always return. When a home was closed on our street, its shutters flapping, its blinds pulled awry to show empty floors and bare walls, we pitied the family that had lost their external self. The homeless, like the landless men of the Middle Ages, seemed to have no country.

The family made the home, yet the home, when it was made, had its own laws. Thus while the relaxing of family ties in the present era has had its powerful effect upon the home, the auto, the radio, commuting, boarding school, and apartment life have struck direct at the laws which made the laws of the home and on through to the family. It is the latter cause which seems more fundamental. Confidence is a habit which must be acquired young and from an environment that is constant and rhythmically continuous. The kaleidoscopic patterns of life today are more exciting and probably liberate the intelligence when there is an intelligence to be liberated; but the pattern they make is seldom realized by youth which turns and twists and darts in an environment which to its seeing never once makes a whole. Home life in the nineties could be very sweet, and often profoundly dull, and sometimes an oppressive weight of routine inescapable; security was often bought at a ruinous price; yet what conditioned reflexes it set up! The peace movement of the early nineteen hundreds, naively confident amidst a world in arms, was an attempt to make that world our home, our American home. Nor was heaven exempt from the home-making activities of the American family. We sang lustily in church—

There we shall rest,
There we shall rest,
In Our Father's House,
In Our Father's House.

The Age of Confidence got the habit of security in its homes.

Family Album

By Kin Hubbard

How could any young man ever "git up nerve enough to marry into a home after lookin' through its family album"? Abe Martin asked. Perhaps the answer lies in the fact that the swain was familiar with a similar album in his own home before he popped the question.

A loan exhibition under the auspices o' the ladies o' the Western Star wuz held in the Model Skatin' Rink lately. Ther one could see ole Civil War swords an' guns an' canteens, together with candle snuffers, spinnin' wheels, flint lock eskipets, stuffed owls an' jay birds, sword canes carried by Democrats at the close o' the Civil War, primitive household implements, ole books an' chromos, an' scores o' other relics, some hundreds o' years ole. All are interestin' an' have histories, but the one thing that constantly has a crowd around it is a big, fat, squeaky, faded blue plush family photergraf album belongin' to the ole Bentley family before an' durin' the dark days o' the Civil War, an' now treasured by our own Farmer Jake Bentley. In this ole musty repository o' whiskers, wens, an' retreatin' chins may be seen early likenesses o' Mr. Bentley's forebears an' relatives. One may see a strikin' likeness o' the first Jake Bentley seated on a fringed plush stool with his cornet restin' on one knee. Thrown carelessly across his chest like a fin is his left hand, on which may be seen three rings. The first Mrs. Jake Bentley is shown jest as she appeared at the photographer's studio at Fostoria, Ohio, in 1851. Her hair is combed back to the time of Marie Antoinette, an' the expression on her face makes her look like she was holdin' in till she passed a skunk nest. Ther's a peculiar somethin' in the expressions of all pioneer mothers. Owin' to bears an' Indians an' motherhood an' plowin' they were little given to lookin' pleasant. The ordeal o' havin' a photo struck in the early days wuz a thing to be dreaded. Only when the sun wuz shinin' wuz it possible to git a photo took. The early photographer an' his Windsor tie an' yeller, fluctuatin' windpipe, only attempted full front views. He strived to give one his money's worth by showin' both sides o' the face. He steadied the head with clamps screwed to the skull jest behind the ears. Then he would arrange the arms an' legs, even up to the coat lapels, powder the cheek bones an' nose, bend the ears in place, an' tell you to concentrate on a figure in the wallpaper fer about five minutes. The thing wuz to have photos of all the family connections, cousins, aunts, an' first, second an' third husbands. Sometimes a feller would be took with his favorite gun or croquet mallet. Uncle Milt Bentley's photo shows a snare drum hangin' at his side. He wore long, trailin' side whiskers that looked like live oak moss. Ever'buddy in the album looks sad an' resentful, like they'd been photographed agin their will. But the ole album tells a wonderful story, an' it's remarkable how people dressed the way they did an' lived. Ther's a strikin' family group showin' a band stand, or summer pavilion, in the background. The elder Bentley is in the center with his legs crossed an' his left forward foot is three times bigger than his right foot. His whiskers have evidently been pinned down an' his lapels glued to his coat. The photo proves at least that his wife an' family wuz intact an' available. Early photographers knew nothin' about touchin' out moles, extra chins, hair lips, warts an' scars. On the contrary they emphasized 'em, played 'em up, in other words they made real likenesses. The curious thing is how any young man or woman ever used to git up nerve enough to marry into a home after lookin' through its family album.

Papa, Mama and Uncle Worth

By Lloyd C. Douglas

Of a winter's evening, the whole family would cluster around Papa as he read the current installment of the serial in *The Youth's Companion.* Mama was a crusader—her courage and zeal were the stuff of martyrs. But it was Uncle Worth who made new toys for the boy and showed him how to fish. He was the one whom young Lloyd loved best.

My father, Alexander Jackson Douglas, was fifty when I was born. He had lived longer than most men of his years, having been a farmer, a schoolmaster, a college student, a lawyer, a State Senator; and, when we first met, a rural preacher.

He had also sired a large family and was a grandfather to children older than I, so that by the time we of the second crop came along little kids were no novelty and certainly no treat.

My younger brother and I were taught by our mama to call our father Papa, which we did, and continued to do until the end of his days.

Mama, too, who was his junior by more than a score of years, called him Papa, except on infrequent occasions of brief but brisk annoyance when she addressed him as A.J. Mama was sincerely devoted to Papa but when she called him A.J. we all—including A.J.—took to cover.

When I was a small boy all men in their fifties were elderly. It was not to any man's advantage to appear youthful. The world had always been operated by and for old men and my papa had been brought up in that tradition. . . .

My papa had a clean-shaven upper lip but the rest of his face was bearded and his beard was long and white. I once asked my Aunt Nancy, Papa's much younger sister, how old he was when he began to let it grow, and she couldn't remember having seen him without it. . . .

He was five feet, eight and a half inches in height and carried an average weight of two hundred pounds, some of it worn around the middle. He never owned a leather belt; but, had he used one, it would probably have measured about forty-four inches. Papa liked good food and took very little physical exercise; and, as has been remarked earlier, he had spent several years in the Indiana State Senate, an ideal place to acquire rotundity.

Papa was a good mixer and made friends quickly. He had quite a talent for remembering names. His rather florid face was easily lighted with an infectious smile. He had a winning voice and people listened when he talked. He was a gifted storyteller with an inexhaustible repertory of yarns appropriate to any occasion. Even as a little boy I was one of his most appreciative fans. No matter how often he repeated a well-remembered tale, I sat spellbound, for it was never told the same way twice. Papa had an active imagination and could have been a successful novelist.

Among the most cherished memories of my childhood is the recollection of our small family clustered close around Papa's favorite rocking chair, of a winter's evening, listening intently to the current installment of an adventure story serialized in *The Youth's Companion*. This enchanted weekly arrived on Friday. By common consent, nobody tore off its wrapper until supper was over and the dishes had been put away. Then, in an ecstasy of anticipation, we waited while Papa deliberately opened the magazine and prepared to read. But there was always a torturing delay, for Papa would make a big thing of polishing his spectacles.

At the time, so urgent was my eagerness to get on with the story, I felt that Papa, having had no responsibility for helping with the dishes, might at least have wiped his glasses. Many years later it dawned on me that his maddening tardiness to come to our relief was a calculated ruse to whet our appetite for the feast in store. Papa must have had an instinct for precision timing. He knew intuitively the priceless value of suspense in any form of dramatic entertainment. . . .

In those days the typical American family of modest means was held together by the fireplace or the huge coal stove in the living room. All the other rooms were cold. The conditions were not ideal. The family was huddled together: those nearest the heat were too warm, the others had cold feet. Frequently there was only one lamp fit to read by. About half past eight the little kids undressed before the fire and scampered off to bed exhaling clouds of steam as they climbed the stairs.

When central heating came in and the whole house was made habitable in winter, revolutionary changes were wrought in family life. Everybody agreed that the invention was a godsend. Instead of being bunched together uncomfortably through the entire evening the family promptly scattered after supper. Now everyone had his own room, his own lamp, and could amuse himself in his own way. It was a long step toward the freedom of the individual.

But there's something to be said in defense of the fireplace and the dirty old coal stove. They kept the family intact. The arrival of the furnace in the cellar was the first hard blow struck at the American Home.

Throughout my childhood and youth we never lived in a house heated by a furnace in the cellar, nor did we ever have a cellar. Most of our better-off neighbors had cellars for the winter storage of potatoes, beets, parsnips, onions and canned fruits and vegetables, but evidently it was not considered necessary for the village parsonage to be thus equipped. . . .

By the middle of March, every house with a cellar reeked of decaying apples. Not even the attar of sauerkraut could compete with the apples. In most households it was customary to use first the apples that were farthest advanced in their decomposition, but the people never quite caught up with this relentless disintegration and were forced by their own theory of economy to eat rotting apples all winter.

My papa often said that it would be more sensible to sort out the ailing apples and throw them away. He was a firm believer in taking one's losses manfully and promptly before they grew to disaster proportions. He was no spendthrift but he saw no sound economy in supporting lost causes or in saving rotten apples by eating them. I never knew anyone who spent less time fretting over misadventures, and I have my papa to thank for bequeathing to me, either by blood, precept or example, the effortless incapacity to worry very long over something that failed to come off as I had hoped. In my youth there was much made of the virtue of perseverance. Hang right on, shouted the orators. Never let go! See it through!

My papa was not so imprudent as to debate this matter in public but he had a private belief that perseverance involving sacrifices that stood no chance of ever paying their own way was no virtue at all. Of the old adage, "If at first you don't succeed, try, try again," Papa once remarked to me, "Well, *twice*, maybe: after that, let somebody else try it." I still believe that Papa had something there. The stirring challenge of the dauntless poem "Excelsior!" always left me cold as the youth who bore the banner with the strange device. Onward he went, through snow and icc, passing up all creature comforts, not pausing even when his girl begged him to come in and thaw out his frozen toes; and at length, completely spent, he arrived at the tipmost, topmost crag where he planted his banner. So what? In the spring the dogs nosed him out of the slush, and that was that.

Of course my papa was all of sixty-two before I was old enough to take much notice of his principles. It may be that when he was a youth he, too, was willing to come at life the hard way; but I doubt it.

In his attitude toward me and my little brother he was always kind and just, but he never played with us, never tossed a ball in our direction, never helped us fly a kite. Sometimes, in summer, when Mama suggested driving down to the river for an early evening picnic, Papa cheerfully consented, but ate his supper in the back seat of the surrey while we spread our tablecloth on the grass near by. He didn't like to sit on the ground and he detested ants. When supper was over, he was for going home. Supper was what we had come to do: having done it, we might as well go home. Mama wanted to linger until dusk, but made no protest. I feel sure that Papa never meant to be inconsiderate. He just couldn't see any sense in our sitting out there on the riverbank, fighting mosquitoes, when we would be so much more comfortable at home. So we would drive home, for it would be no fun for Mama to insist on our remaining longer if Papa was getting restless.

Now if this were all I had planned to say about my father, it would be an incomplete and cruelly unfair portrait of this quite remarkable man who—had he stuck resolutely to one trade—might have gone far. But I feel that the time has come for me to talk about my mama.

My mama, née Sarah Jane Cassel, eighth child in a compact family of ten, was born a little more than a century ago in the then small village of Mount Eaton, Ohio, where her father, Samuel Cassel, owned and operated a sawmill, a gristmill, and what was vaguely remembered as a "woolen mill."

As a tot Mama was called Sam, she told us, not only because she was her father's favorite but because she was always at his heels, though she did not resemble him in any way, as he was reportedly a quiet, well-balanced man of few words and no gaudy enthusiasms. She was the spit and image of her mother who, in her middle years—according to the legend—was known to have a very low boiling point.

To any fair evaluation of my mama's distinguishing attributes it is necessary to brief her background and the circumstances in which she spent her early years, for she was a peculiar character, resourceful, ambitious, dynamic.

As for these Cassel mills, with which our story begins, my mental picture of these various enterprises, drawn for me by my mama when I was but a lad, is indistinct, for when she was only twelve a fire broke out, one stormy night, and swept the entire establishment away, including their house and most of its contents.

All we ever knew about the catastrophe was reported from the confused memories of a badly frightened little girl who had been gifted with an utterly reckless imagination. Just how big, how flourishing were these mills is anybody's guess. But it is a solid fact that after the fire had died out, Samuel Cassel—together with his numerous heirs and assigns—was completely washed up; and when one loses *everything*, an accurate inventory of what one previously had may be considered unimportant.

The Cassels had salvaged a team of horses and a big wagon. Into the wagon they tossed their few remaining articles of household furniture and took off for "the West." Mama always loved pioneer stories and thought and talked of this migration as a pioneering adventure, which wasn't far from the truth, though the journey ended in Noble County, Indiana. There, in the deep woods, my grandfather cleared a few acres of sandy soil, hard by a pleasant little stream, built a sawmill, and reportedly made a go of this industry until the quarrels between the Northern and Southern states, which had been simmering and bubbling on the fire for many years, came to full boil; and Sam Cassel was drafted. . . .

My Uncle John was only a kid and he had never been rugged. He left his soft young bones in the National Cemetery at Chattanooga. Mama's favorite uncle, Saul Cassel, a bachelor who lived with them, was buried at Antietam. Grandpa Cassel plodded home with little to show for his experience but a well-developed taste for corn liquor.

"Yes," Mama used to murmur, sadly, "he often broke down and cried about it; but, somehow, he couldn't quit, though he was a good man."

Unhappy old Sam, from there on out, contented himself with odd jobs as a carpenter, helping to build barns and small mills. He put up a little shop, not far from the house, where he mended broken farm tools and various household tackle. . . .

Now that my grandfather's little shop is on my mind, perhaps you will be patient with me if I say something more about it; for I'm afraid that if I don't tell you now I may forget to do it later.

When I was a small boy (about nine, let us say) and we visited

Grandma Cassel, the shop was still there and in active operation. My bachelor uncle, Worth Cassel, had fallen heir to it, which was quite right, for he was the only child left at home to look after his mother. He had also inherited his father's talent for skilled carpentry.

When we visited there, usually in midsummer, Uncle Worth, whom I adored, would take an afternoon off and devote his time to me. After dinner at eleven-thirty, he would unlock the trim little shop with a big iron key while I waited beside him, quivering with excitement. The place was dominated by a frighteningly large wooden flywheel overhead, high above the lathe on which my tall, curly-headed, soft-spoken uncle would turn out beautiful little tops and cups and saucers and napkin rings from selected pieces of oak and walnut.

There is no aroma more heady than the scent of hot walnut shavings. The sharp chisels squealed and turned blue as they bit into the hard knots that were to furnish the completed product with its exquisite graining.

(Ah—those irrecoverable scents that distinguished "the old home" from all other places in the world; the peculiar fragrance of the tortured walnut ribbons in the enchanted shop, the perfume of the little beds of mint and anise in the garden, the pungent smell of the old smokehouse, behind the kitchen, where many a ham and side of bacon had hung for days on end over an open barrel of smouldering hickory coals. Yes, and if you will believe it, the half-elusive aroma of the long-abandoned stable; it, too, was of the fragile fabric that summer dreams are made of.)

I often wished that Uncle Worth would let me help push the treadle that operated the big flywheel. Once I ventured to ask him but he shook his head.

"You don't want to get your foot mashed, do you?"

And, of course, I didn't. So we left it at that. I did not debate the matter. It was not customary with us to tease for things. When any of our elders and betters said No, we never objected; much less persisted by inquiring whether our objection was sustained or overruled.

There's still something to be said in favor of this Mama-knows-best technique. It certainly saved a lot of time and temper. We kids never had tantrums, never howled and bawled with the hope (born of experience) that if we made enough racket something would have to give, and we would emerge not only with a splendid victory but the firm assurance that whenever we wanted anything we had only to keep on yelling and kicking until our folks capitulated from sheer exhaustion. It should also be said of such juvenile victories that they probably account for the crowded docket of our present-day Juvenile courts. Had I ever talked back to my papa or my mama in the same tones and terms commonly tolerated today by indulgent parents, there would have been a prompt laying-on of hands.

After an enchanted hour in the little shop, Uncle Worth and I (with my small hands filled with the new toys) would come blinking out into the bright sunshine.

On the shady porch, Grandma and Mama would be seated, Grandma quite frail and wan, sitting placidly with empty hands folded on her lap, her deep-set, half-open, inattentive eyes leveled at the far horizon, Mama rocking vigorously, discoursing on whatever issue happened to be of urgent interest to her.

Mama was an indefatigable crusader. Maybe that's why I never headed a parade. Crusading was a tiresome trade. It took too much out of you. Loud talk always distressed and confused me. And I distrusted it, too. My childish instinct told me what experience much later confirmed: when people have to shout their opinions they are usually on the wrong side; and they suspect that you know they are.

I would be for running over at once to display my pretty gifts, but Uncle Worth would veer off toward the old stable.

"We'd better not interrupt them," he would explain. "We'll go out behind the stable and dig some worms."

The truth was that he didn't want to be drawn into an argument: a very quiet fellow, was Uncle Worth. Perhaps, you may surmise, he got his complacency from Grandma. But that's a bad guess. The old volcano had burned out now but once upon a time it had been active.

When I was a grown man my papa told me that old Sam Cassel had once told him, in a hush-hush consultation, that when Grandma was in her rip-roaring forties she would go out to the far end of the potato patch and yell "till they heard her clear down to Ryder's mill!"

There was more than a touch of this excitability in the distaff heritage. Mama had all the relentless courage and zeal that martyrs are powered with. She lacked only some wide-open opportunity to have become a great leader. I mean that! Even after this long lapse of years I am persuaded that this is so. Mama could easily have been a Florence Nightingale (though the books say that Florence was mighty hard to live with after she came home from the Crimea). One is reminded of Mr. Churchill's remark about one of his top generals, "Indomitable in defeat; insufferable in victory."

One of my mama's older sisters was also high-geared, startlingly precocious, and anxious to beat the drum. But she couldn't find a drum, and—at middle age—went completely off her rocker, and spent several years in an institution; though there were special reasons for her crack-up. Uncle Henry, who was said to be a competent and conscientious physician when sober, lay sprawled in a drunken stupor while their three-year-old twins were dying of scarlet fever in my Aunt Amanda's arms. When dawn came, the babies were dead and their mother was hauled away to the madhouse. . . . Not much wonder my mama used to tighten her small fists and grit her teeth when she sounded off about hard liquor. . . .

With our tin cans alive with bait, Uncle Worth and I would cross the potato patch and slither down the grassy slope to the river. Then we climbed into the big, flat-bottomed boat that was tied to a stake under a clump of graceful "weeping" willows (the kind they used to carve on gravestones) and drifted slowly past the lily pads until we reached what Uncle Worth thought might be a favorable place to lower the old anvil. He did this gently, so as not to scare away the perch and blue-gills and rock bass. Hooks would be dropped into the water and presently the red bobbers would be hopping up and down and under.

I am quite aware that this is not a sportsmanly way to catch fish, but it was effective. Our tackle was crude and our methods were primitive, but what we were out there for was fish and plenty of them to fry in a pan, and this was a good way to do it.

In more recent and more prosperous years I have been occasionally inveigled into fishing with much better (certainly much more expensive) instruments, but I never caught so many fish as I did with Uncle Worth's homemade equipment. But I never was much of a success as a sportsman. Perhaps I entered the field of sports too late in life to have any real enjoyment of it.

If there were any fish-and-game laws in operation at that time, we didn't know about them. We caught all we thought we could eat for supper and breakfast. . . .

When the fish had stopped biting and a huge dragonfly was perched impudently on my motionless red bobber and the late afternoon shadows were slanting toward the east, Uncle Worth would row us back home, the oars clattering in their locks. The experienced navigator rarely glanced over his shoulder to plot his course for he knew this friendly river by heart.

Now we were at the shaky little wharf, had tied up the boat, put on our shoes, scrambled up the bank, trudged through the sandy potato patch, and were (Uncle Worth was) dexterously cleaning our catch.

"Want to go with me to prayer meetin' tonight, son?" Uncle Worth would inquire, rather diffidently, without looking up.

Of course I wanted to go anywhere, so long as I could be with Uncle Worth, though prayer meetings were not my favorite form of entertainment. My idol would draw a slow smile of appreciation. He couldn't help knowing that I worshiped him, and it may be surmised that not many candles shone on his lonely shrine.

Soon the flour-coated fish would be sizzling in the big iron spider (skillet to you, no doubt). Grandma would be tending them, with an eye on the country-fried potatoes in an adjoining pan. Mama, an excellent cook, would be at the kitchen table, crafting an appropriate salad made of tender lettuce leaves to be served with a warm, sweet-sour dressing well loaded with slices of hard-boiled eggs and diced bacon. Uncle Worth would be tenderly nursing a little kettle of freshly picked peas.

I would be pacing about like a tiger at feeding time.

"You might fill the wood box," Grandma would say, to get me out from under her feet.

And now—at last—it would be time to eat, almost. We suddenly became silent and sad. Uncle Worth would glance inquiringly toward Grandma; and, getting no response, would murmur, "Jen, will you ask the blessing." Mama, propping an elbow on the table and shading her closed eyes with her hand, would clear her throat and offer a brief prayer, thanking God for our blessings, "both temporal and spiritual," asking for an extension of our good health, putting in a friendly word for "our absent loved ones."

Now the gloom lifted as Mama whispered, "For Chrysake—Amen." Now we could eat. Everything was on the table, ready to be passed, all but the strawberries and cream, which would come on in due time.

Never, at least never in my experience, did fish taste like these.

Ummm-mmm! Good! . . . Uncle Worth would chuckle happily over my applause. Blue-gills were an old story to him. He concentrated on his peas. . . . *Ummm! Good!*

Just now I ejaculated these words aloud so I might type them at their full value, and my *Ummm-mmm! Good!* startled me back to the present moment, for I sounded precisely like the typical commercial plugster, in an agony of ecstasy over his merchandise. I wonder what my gentle, long-gone Uncle Worth would think or say if some strident voice had shattered his quiet little world with:

"*Ummm-mmm! Good! Our Peas!* Garden-fresh! Mouth-wateringly de—licious! . . . After a nation-wide survey! . . . Endorsed by medical profession! Our Peas! Get 'em tomorrow! Get 'em tonight yet! Our peas! That's spelled O-u-r P-e-a-s. Coast to coast! Three out of four! Nine out of ten! Prefer Our Peas. Remember! Get *O-U-R* Peas!"

Doubtless the soft-voiced old bachelor would suspect that he had been misdirected to another world than the one he had left behind.

But we can't stand still, Uncle Worth. We have come into a new era, an era of progress. You'd do well to get back to wherever you were. You wouldn't like it here. It's pretty noisy now.

But now, without further digression, we must return to my mama. When she was only fifteen, her eighteen-year-old sister Mary (my Aunt Molly, one of the happiest and most lovable of all the women I ever knew) who was the teacher in a country school a couple of miles from the Cassel home, fell ill in midwinter, and Mama volunteered to take over until they found somebody.

Apparently the trustees were satisfied with the way things were going; and because Aunt Molly's bad cold was followed by a siege of malaria, a pernicious disease which for many years was endemic in the undrained swamp lands of Indiana, Mama finished the term. Her education was limited to what she had received in that same ungraded school over which she had now presided. But that elementary education was not as inadequate as you might suppose.

Mama was quick to learn. Besides whatever she absorbed in school, she read everything that came to hand. There were not many books to be had, certainly not by the Cassels who were "poor as Job's turkey"; but Mama was able to borrow a few old books and magazines from newly come neighbors who had brought them along on their trek from Pennsylvania.

By the next fall, Aunt Molly had married Uncle Paul; and Mama, having acquired a license, continued to teach in the school where she had so ably substituted. The chief qualification of a country teacher, at that time, was courage. It was no trick to maintain discipline when school opened in early September, for only the younger children put in an appearance. But when the crops were in, and the corn had been husked, and the winter wheat had been sowed, a dozen or more man-sized farmer boys in the middle and later teens would stroll in, to squeeze themselves between the rear desks and benches, resolved to give the teacher a rough job.

Mama became known throughout that area as "a good disciplinarian," which was one way of saying that she would, at the first sign of insubordination, grab a six-foot, one hundred and seventy-five pound yokel by the hair, drag him out of his seat, and "whale the daylights out of him." She was more terrible than an army with banners, and quickly won the respect of any and all who were foolhardy enough to dispute her authority. Yessir, Mama "made the fur fly." Not only did we learn of this from her own testimony. We believed it, and could furnish corroborative evidence if called upon.

But Mama's prowess as a schoolmarm was not based entirely upon dauntless bravery and skill in battle. She was an excellent pedagogue. At least she taught the youngsters how to read and write and spell and do problems in simple arithmetic, which is ever so much better than is being done in our progressive schools at present. Maybe Mama did it the hard way, but the kids—when she finished with them—were literate and knew the multiplication tables. . . .

After a couple of years as teacher of her home school, Mama was elected to teach a larger country school in Whitley County, many miles to the south, where she boarded around in her pupils' homes.

Then she made the adventure of accepting a teaching position "in the far West," in the then small village of Watseka, Illinois. Returning, after two or three years, she again taught in Whitley County, faithfully attending the summer Teachers' Institute at the County seat, Columbia City.

One day, in July of 1876, when Mama was twenty-nine, she volunteered to help the hard-pressed County Superintendent in grading the examination papers, for she had come to idolize this genial widower who always had a warm smile for her—and had given her a rating with the young hopefuls by publicly calling her "Jennie." I can imagine the flush on her cheek and the quick bounding of her heart when he singled her out for this conferment of distinction. He was prompt to accept her proffered help.

When the Institute was over, Superintendent Douglas married Jennie at the old Cassel home and took her back with him to Columbia City and his houseful of children. . . .

I was born on a hot August afternoon in 1877. A year and a half later a baby sister arrived, but soon died of whooping cough. It was in midwinter and the snow was deep. Mama was for burying the baby in the Salem cemetery, a half-mile from "the old home," but because she was far from well and the roads were deep with snowdrifts, they talked her out of it and buried little Mabel in the well-filled Douglas family lot in Columbia City where there was room for just one more alongside the graves of Grandfather and Grandmother Douglas and Mary Douglas (Papa's first wife) and three children of the first family who had died in infancy.

When spring came, Papa yielded to Mama's tearful pleadings and the little white coffin was conveyed to the Salem graveyard. It rained all that day. I was taken along on this journey, and claimed later that I remembered being held in Papa's arms, while somebody sheltered us with an umbrella, as the white coffin was lowered to its final resting place; though I couldn't have been more than two and a half years old, and Mama thought my precocious "recollection" of this event was the memory of it as told to me when I was at least four or five. But I still have a distinct remembrance of the little white coffin as it sank into the ground; and, for many years, every time I saw the corrugated white enameled inside of the screw-on top of an old-fashioned Mason fruit jar, I was reminded of it. If Daniel Webster could conjugate Latin verbs at four, I see no reason why I should not remember a shockingly impressive scene that had rocked my little world at two and a half.

When my father entered college, after three years as teacher of a country school near his home in northern Ohio, he discarded the redundant *s* which, until then, had adorned the family name.

On the flyleaf of the only book preserved from my grandfather's small library, a leather-bound, pocket-size volume entitled *Comstock's Philosophy* (an elementary treatise on Physics) published in London, in 1782, appears the faded signature of William Douglass, the final *s* resembling a dissipated *f* in a perilous heel-skid on an icy street.

Papa, when asked—a half-century later—what had moved him to omit this second *s*, lamely explained that as a student he had been forced to practice the most rigid economies, that he had hoped some day to be wealthy enough to resume it, but what with small salaries and heavy expenses he had never felt able to afford anything but bare necessities.

And then Papa was likely to repeat the old story about Abraham Lincoln when he was courting Mary Todd. The Todds, who were aristocrats (without portfolio), bitterly resented the intrusion of this uncouth, un-pedigreed rail-splitter into their family circle. On the defensive, Lincoln attempted to teach the uppish Todds their proper relation to other natural objects by addressing his letters to Mary "Tod." Brought sternly to task for this sacrilege he replied that there was no good reason for the Todds to spell their name with two *d*'s when God needed only one.

Of my grandfather, William Douglas, I know practically nothing beyond the sad fact that at thirty-six he was suddenly crippled by rheumatism of such severity that he never walked again, though he lived until he was nearly sixty. I cannot remember ever hearing him quoted: if he had any opinions they must have been benign rather than malignant or militant. Nor have I anything to report of Grandmother Douglas who quietly spent her declining years in my father's home.

Papa was only twelve when Grandfather Douglas was stricken with rheumatism. A tenant farmer was engaged but was so neglectful of his duties that Papa and his younger brothers were soon doing most of the work; so the lazy tenant was dismissed and the Douglas kids took over. They toiled mightily through spring, summer and fall, attending their country school in winter. Bent on acquiring a good education, Papa read everything available; and at eighteen turned the farm over to his brothers while he set forth, first as a country schoolteacher, then as a student at Ashland Academy, and on to college. . . .

A legend has it that Papa and a boon companion at the Academy had decided to attend the same college. As Papa was descended from a long line of Presbyterians, he would naturally have gone to the young college at Wooster; the other fellow was a Lutheran and had expected to attend Wittenberg College, then fighting for its life at Springfield. They flipped a coin and went to Wittenberg. Because he was practically penniless, Papa found a job as hostler, coachman, gardener, dishwasher and errand boy in the home of the college president, the Reverend Doctor Samuel Sprecker, a warmhearted scholar and seer, who was to become his man Friday's idol and hero.

The main business at Wittenberg, in those early years, was the production of Lutheran preachers. Although it had been my father's intention to study law, Doctor Sprecker needed only to suggest the ministry as a profession for his young disciple. But when Papa had finished his college training and applied for a license to preach he failed to answer the Examining Board's questions correctly.

For one thing, he did not believe that unbaptized infants went to hell; adding, to his inquisitors' horror, that he wasn't sure there was such a place as hell; that he couldn't fit hell into his belief in a God of infinite Love. And, furthermore (as if these heresies weren't sufficient to blackball him) Papa went on to say that he didn't believe in the Devil; for if God had created all things He surely wouldn't have rigged up that kind of competition to dispute His Own authority.

At the noon recess, when the outraged Examining Committee were at dinner in the President's home, kindhearted old Doctor Sprecker pleaded with them to be mindful of the rash young man's inexperience in solving such philosophical riddles; and, having been comforted with their host's fried chicken, mashed potatoes, gravy and warm apple pie, promised to have another go at my papa in the afternoon.

They asked him to tell them how he felt about Martin Luther, for surely he had been properly indoctrinated on the life of the great reformer. But here again my papa froze them by replying that while a general clean-up of the old Mother Church was clearly in order, Martin Luther loved a good fight and was lucky to come out of this one with a whole skin.

This was the wrong answer. The Committee wanted a little more reverence shown for the man who had courageously risked his future, and they said so. But my papa was unimpressed. Considering how firmly the Church handled apostates, the good Doctor had done very well to escape a bonfire and die of natural causes, in bed, with his boots off. And then Papa added that he had often wished Luther had kept his vow of celibacy, and had avoided the criticism of those who thought he broke from the Church primarily because he wanted a wife and children. If he had remained single, said Papa, it would have added much to his stature.

With this, the Examining Board gave up and left the room without the formality of a motion to adjourn.

It having thus appeared that Alexander Jackson Douglas was not geared for the Lutheran ministry, he resolved to pursue his earlier intention to become a lawyer.

On my desk, as I write, there is a copy of a "whosis," entitled *Representative Men of Indiana* (1880) containing the log of Papa's rather rugged journey, teaching part time in an Ohio academy while reading law, of his marriage to the youthful Mary Jenner, of his migration to Columbia City, Indiana, where he was progressively a Prosecuting Attorney, a State Senator; and, to fill a vacancy, Superintendent of the Whitley County Schools. After a while this was made a permanent position.

Papa seems to have traveled far and wide visiting schools. The Lutheran Church in Columbia City, temporarily without a minister, asked him to preach for them until they found a regular pastor. Apparently they didn't hunt for one with any zeal, for Papa continued as their Sunday preacher while attending to his duties in the county schools. He must have been a busy man.

My papa was an excellent public speaker. He often talked to me, in my youth, about the importance of voice cultivation, no matter what profession one practiced. If you wanted to make yourself attentively heard, either in public address or private conversation, you should pitch your voice in the lowest register at your command. High-keyed shouting would earn you nothing but the other fellow's suspicion that you were in doubt or insincere. You should be careful to enunciate your consonants clearly: the vowels would look after themselves. No matter what he talked about, when my papa spoke, his audience listened. You could hear a pin drop. . . .

In the early autumn of 1881 our family unexpectedly bundled up its somewhat harried lares and penates, and moved into the northern rim of Kentucky.

Papa had begun to feel the weight of his anxieties and increasing cares. Mama was unhappy and begging to have a home of her own. Not only was he the superintendent of the county schools, requiring long drives in all weathers, but he had been preaching every Sunday at the Lutheran Church in town. Many old clients, whose legal affairs he had handled, still came to him with their problems, and his wide acquaintance throughout the county brought urgent pleas from long-time friends to conduct the funeral services for their loved ones. It must have been a heavy load.

The funeral business was mounting. It was on such an errand, one hot July morning, that Papa was driving past the Morrison homestead a few miles to the north. The old farmer had been ailing for a long time. Papa saw the three husky, lumpish Morrison sons sitting in a row on the front porch. He drew up and called, "Good morning, boys. How is your father feeling today?"

"Guess!" replied Bill, the eldest, after some delay.

"Better, I hope," said Papa.

"Nope," crowed Bill, for it was the wrong guess. "He's dead!"

With that, the trio ambled down to the picket fence and arrangements were made for Papa to "preach the funeral" on Friday, which he did. . . .

When the committal service had been read at the grave, and the neighbors were busily shoveling, Bill Morrison handed the officiating clergyman a half-dollar, and said, "Thanks, Reverend. Mebby we'll be a-callin' on yuh again sometime"—for their maw was poorly.

One day in the later summer of 1881 a fine old Kentuckian named Benjamin Strickland came to visit some relatives who had recently moved to Columbia City. On Sunday they brought him to the Lutheran Church. Next morning he called on Papa and told him that a group of three country churches, a few miles apart, and to one of which he belonged, badly needed a resident minister. They hadn't had one, he said, for a long time now. It seemed like the preachers all wanted to live in big towns.

There was a comfortable, well-furnished parsonage, he went on, not too far from a friendly little town, and only twelve miles south of Cincinnati; but out in the country. If a man had a mind to, he could almost make his living from the four fertile acres belonging to the place. One acre was in blue grass. There was a good barn, a high-wired chicken run, and a pigpen at the far end of the pasture field. . . .

To my parents, the quiet spot to which we had come was Paradise. The neighbors, riding by and seeing signs of life, dismounted from their horses or climbed out of their antique "rockaways," and strolled in to get acquainted. Stringy little Mrs. Manning, from a near-by cottage, came to the kitchen door with a warm blueberry pie. The autumn days passed swiftly; halcyon days. . . .

A partially grass-grown, graveled lane led from the wide front gate, which was never closed, past the south side of the house, and on to the weather-beaten barn. Beside the lane, and opposite to the spacious side verandah, was a small wooden platform, about three feet high, with a few steps attached. This was a mounting block, intended mostly for ladies who rode on sidesaddles.

When Papa went down to the crossroads store for the mail and *The Cincinnati Enquirer* and perhaps some groceries, he would lead Flora to the mounting block. I do not know whether he could have hoisted himself into the saddle without this assistance; probably not.

He always wore his second-best frock coat and a high topper, known at that time as a "plug" hat. I surmise that an equestrian who turned out in such a rig today would draw a crowd. And, even then, Papa's erect, august figure, riding in formal attire on a lonely country road, must have brought the neighbors to their front windows.

But however much the farmers may have viewed the majestic newcomer at first sight with awed amazement, they were soon to learn that he meant to be one of them. He would lift the dignified plug hat and wave to the countrymen in their fields or lounging in their barnyards. I doubt whether they returned his salute on the first occasion but it was not long until they were waving back to him. Sometimes they would be on the lookout for his return and he would find them busying themselves at their front gates. He would pull Flora up to the fence. Perhaps the farmer's wife, with a gingham sunbonnet loosely tied under her chin and dangling down her back, would stroll out to join them; and their boys and girls too.

Papa soon became the chaplain for our whole neighborhood. He visited their sick, married their grown sons and daughters, buried their dead. They came to the Hopeful Church, only four miles away where, it was said (for I was too little to be interested in that), they felt at home, regardless of the religious denomination with which their fathers had been affiliated.

My papa's sermons, then and always thereafter, were not dogmatic. They effortlessly avoided the polemic issues that had so frequently made otherwise kindhearted people despise their neighbors who militantly stood for tweedledee but stubbornly rejected tweedledum. As I remember my papa's easily understandable homilies, when I was grown old enough to think seriously about them, they were strangely reminiscent of the hillside sermons which attracted great crowds in Galilee. They were illustrated with parables taken from everyday life. "A certain man had two sons, and the younger of them said unto his father, 'Give me the portion that falleth to me.'" The people could see that picture clearly. If either of the two sons was restless to get away from the old place, it would be the younger. They had known such cases. My papa, instead of beginning a sermon with a quotation from Martensen's *Systematic Theology*, would be likely to say, "Last Thursday, while we were waiting at a blacksmith shop in Florence for our horses to be shod, a few of us were talking about James Blodgett, and the friendly way he had with horses. One man said the horses seemed to know that Jim wouldn't hurt them by carelessly paring a hoof too far. Jim knew his business, another man said. And as I rode home, it occurred to me that a man so mindful of his duties that even the horses of the community were on his side, is giving as good an account of his stewardship as any man can in a public office." Then would follow a beguiling talk about making the best use of our talents, whatever they were.

The next time Papa rode into town to have Flora's shoes reset, Jim said when the job was done and the customer had brought out his well-worn coin purse, "I reckon that won't cost you-all anything, Reverend. . . . Here: let me give you-all a leg up. . . . Thanks, Reverend; come again."

Dear Mamma & Mary

By Harry S. Truman

Even in the White House he was a typical American father. He remembered always that he was the head not only of the great family composed of all the people in the United States, but of his own, a family of three. And he never failed to write home the news he knew would interest Mama and Mary back home in Missouri.

I was up before six on the morning of Sunday, April 29, and before breakfast I wrote Mama and Mary. It had been more than a week since my last letter, but I had found a little spare time now.

Dear Mamma & Mary:–Received your letter with the one from Dr. Graham in it and was glad to get it. Hope you and Mary have not been bothered too much. It is terrible–and I mean terrible–nuisance to be kin to the President of the United States. Reporters have been haunting every relative and purported relative I ever heard of, and they've probably made life miserable for my mother, brother and sister. I am sorry for it, but it can't be helped.

A guard has to go with Bess and Margaret everywhere they go–and they don't like it. They both spend a lot of time figuring how to beat the game, but it just can't be done. In a country as big as this one there are necessarily a lot of nuts and people with peculiar ideas. They seem to focus on the White House and the President's kin. Hope you won't get too badly upset about it.

Between the papers and the nuts they surely made life miserable for the Roosevelt family. Maybe they can have some peace now. I hope so.

I must caution both of you to take good care of your health. Don't let the pests get you down. I'm writing this before breakfast–before anyone is up.

Love to you both.

Harry

Savage Homecoming

By Clifford Orr

The small savage has returned to her family after a summer in camp. She's different somehow. We tell ourselves she's lovable —underneath. But her standards have changed. For the first time her mother senses with disquiet an outside influence vying with that of home.

Frieda came back last week from her first summer at Camp Conomo, and her mother isn't sure whether it will be quite wise to send her another year. She's different somehow, her mother says.

First of all, right in the station, there was that little incident about the berries. She came down the platform followed by a porter with her bags, still shining new, and let her mother kiss her with what seemed to be a bit of sufferance.

"How are you, darling?" her mother cried.

"*Mokka-lo-cakki,*" said Frieda. At least, that's what her mother *thought* she said.

"What, darling?" asked her mother.

"That means 'The-health-spirit-is-smiling,'" said Frieda. "It's Indian. It's what you say when someone says '*Wo-manni-no?*' to you."

"I see," said her mother.

"That means 'How-sits-your-stomach?'"

"Hush, darling!" said her mother.

"It's all right," said Frieda. "It's Indian. Miss McClintock says it. She used to yell it right across the lake. Sound carries on the water."

"Well," said her mother, "you're certainly looking well. You're brown as a berry."

"Name one," said Frieda.

"What, dear?" her mother asked.

"Berries," said Frieda, "are red, blue, black, white, and green. They're seldom or never brown, and if you say that anything is brown as a berry, you could never be an Eagle in Elementary Nature. You'd be lucky if you even got to be a Nuthatch."

"I see, dear," said her mother.

Nothing really untoward happened during dinner. Frieda talked, her mother said, in a rather strange sort of jargon, but her mother refrained from any leading questions. She did, however, notice the frequency with which Miss McClintock's name came into the conversation, and finally she got up sufficient courage to ask about her.

"Miss McClintock is Head Counselor of the Otters. Those are the girls who live between the basketball court and the Grand Canyon. The girls on the other side, over near Yosemite and the cookhouse, are Beavers. The Otters are much the best. I wouldn't be a Beaver for anything. The Beavers haven't won Woodcraft for three years."

Her mother clucked, disparagingly.

"Miss McClintock goes to Wellesley," Frieda continued. "I've decided to go to Wellesley."

"But Frieda, dear," said her mother, "you always wanted to go to Vassar, and Father and I registered you when you were just a little thing. Mother would like to have you go where she went."

"Wellesley is best," said Frieda. "Miss McClintock can chin herself nineteen times."

"I'm sure that Miss McClintock is very nice," said her mother, "but we shouldn't let things like—"

"There's a Vassar girl who's one of the counselors of the Beavers," Frieda interrupted. "Miss Fellows. She teaches Basketry."

"Well, she's nice, isn't she?" her mother asked, a trifle timidly.

"She can't clean fish," said Frieda.

Somehow, her mother thought, Frieda's standards had changed. So, it became apparent at bedtime, had her habits. It had always before been a bit of an ordeal to get her upstairs at the appropriate hour, but tonight she discovered that it was eight-thirty all by herself.

"*Kama-bo,*" she said, standing in the doorway.

Her mother guessed that this meant "Good night," so she said it herself, "*Kama-bo!,*" and was rewarded by a smile of understanding as Frieda lifted three outstretched fingers in what was evidently a gesture of benison. She disappeared, but in a moment she was at the door again.

"Mother," she asked, "in case you need anything in the night, do you know the Cry of Distress?"

"I'm sure I shan't need anything, Frieda. Thank you just the same."

"Well, this is it, anyway," said Frieda. "If you cry '*Conomo!*' just once, why that's just a greeting or to let people know you're in the neighborhood, and friendly, see?"

"Yes, dear."

"If you do it twice—'*Conomo! Conomo!*'—that means that you've found a new Specimen or have located the next Cairn, and the others should try to come where you are. Is that clear?"

"Perfectly, dear, but I doubt very much if tonight—"

"But if you cry it three times, with a note of alarm," Frieda went on, "like this—'*Conomo! Conomo! Conomo!*'—that's the Cry of Distress, and I'll come at double-time with a first-aid kit and, if possible, a hand axe and a piece of rope."

"I see, dear," her mother said. "I'll try to remember, and I'm sure you'll be of great help if Mother calls."

"The rope, of course," said Frieda, rather ominously, "is in case of Quicksand."

It was eleven o'clock when Frieda's mother went up to bed. It was after twelve-thirty when she woke up with a dry throat, a tickling in her nostrils, and a slowly reached conviction that she was smelling smoke. In less than a minute, after rushing from her room and halfway down the stairs, sniffing, she had thrown open Frieda's door and had been greeted by a cloud of it rolling out.

"Frieda! Frieda!" she called. "Frieda!"

"Tent Number Eight," said Frieda's sleepy voice from the bed. "All present."

Pawing her way through the smoke and finding the light switch, her mother eventually discovered that there was a small and sullen blaze in the fireplace, and that was all. The fire had been laid and unused all summer and the chimney draught evidently kept closed. But the smoke was almost unbearable. By practically main force, she dragged Frieda from the room and closed the door behind them. She would wake Annie and send her in to open the draught. Frieda was coughing and choking a bit, too, if sleepily. She was coherent enough, though, when her mother had put her into her father's bed and opened the windows wide.

"I was making a smudge," said Frieda.

"You certainly were," said her mother. "What on earth did you light the fire for, and why didn't you open the draught?"

"I felt a mosquito," said Frieda, "so I closed the draught and made a smudge."

"But Frieda, dear, there couldn't have been any mosquitoes. We haven't had any all summer. The screens are brand-new."

"I opened the screens," said Frieda. "Screens are symbols of civilization."

Her mother sat there, pondering this for a while, and finally Frieda spoke again.

"I used a match to light the fire, though," she said, more slowly and more faintly. "I didn't have any tinder. I might have scraped the furniture, only it's maple. Ash is best for tinder."

Her mother sat for another moment, and then rose and switched off the light.

"Good night, Frieda," she said.

There was a long pause.

"*Kama-bo*, Miss McClintock," said Frieda.

Mama Knows Best

By Sara Delano Roosevelt

Her son was a rising young light in American politics. She may not have foreseen that he would become president, but his mother would have taken him to task anyhow, if she'd felt like it. She was confident that the older generation knows best. It's a rare family that doesn't have a member like her.

New York
October 14, 1917—Sunday

Dearest Franklin and Dearest Eleanor,

I feel too badly that I let you go without your pearl collar, too stupid of me! Do wear the velvet one Aunt Doe gave you! I think of you almost in New York and I am sorry to feel that Franklin is tired and that my views are not his, but perhaps dear Franklin you may on second thoughts or third thoughts see that I am not so far wrong. The foolish old saying "noblesse oblige" is good and "honneur oblige" possibly expresses it better for most of us. One can be democratic as one likes, but if we love our own, and if we love our neighbor, we owe a great example, and my constant feeling is that through neglect or laziness I am not doing my part toward those around me. After I got home, I sat in the library for nearly an hour reading, and as I put down my book and left the delightful room and the two fine portraits, I thought: after all, would it not be better just to spend all one has at once in this time of suffering and need, and not think of the future; for with the trend to "shirt sleeves," and the ideas of what men should do in always being all things to all men and striving to give up the old-fashioned traditions of family life, simple home pleasures and refinements, and the traditions some of us love best, of what use is it to keep up things, to hold on to dignity and all I stood up for this evening. Do not say that I misunderstood, I understand perfectly, but I cannot believe that my precious Franklin really feels as he expressed himself. Well, I hope that while I live I may keep my "old-fashioned" theories and that at least in my own family I may continue to feel that home is the best and happiest place and that my son and daughter and their children will live in peace and keep from the tarnish which seems to affect so many. Mrs. Newbold's theory that children are "always just like their parents" is pretty true, as example is what really counts.

When I talk I find I usually arouse opposition, which seems odd, but is perhaps my own fault, and tends to lower my opinion of myself, which is doubtless salutary. I doubt if you will have time dear Franklin to read this, and if you do, it may not please you. My love to our fine little James, and to you two dear ones.

Devotedly
Mama

The Figgerin' of Aunt Wilma

By James Thurber

Everybody has an aunt—or an uncle or a grandfather—who insists on acting slightly "teched" in public. What agonies of embarrassment we suffered in their company! Young James Thurber was tolerant enough, but his Aunt Wilma was typical of the breed. Her figgerin' simply wouldn't come out to match the grocer's.

When I was a boy, John Hance's grocery stood on the south side of Town Street, just east of Fourth, in the Central Market region of Columbus, Ohio. It was an old store even then, forty-five years ago, and its wide oak floor boards had been worn pleasantly smooth by the shoe soles of three generations of customers. The place smelled of coffee, peppermint, vinegar, and spices. Just inside the door on the left, a counter with a rounded glass front held all the old-fashioned penny candies—gumdrops, licorice whips, horehound, and the rest—some of them a little pale with age. On the rear wall, between a barrel of dill pickles and a keg of salt mackerel in brine, there was an iron coffee grinder, whose handle I was sometimes allowed to turn.

Once, Mr. Hance gave me a stick of Yucatan gum, an astonishing act of generosity, since he had a sharp sense of the value of a penny. Thrift was John Hance's religion. His store was run on a strictly cash basis. He shared the cost of his telephone with the Hays Carriage Shop, next door. The instrument was set in a movable wooden cubicle that could be whirled through an opening in the west wall of the store. When I was ten, I used to hang around the grocery on Saturday afternoons, waiting for the telephone to disappear into the wall. Then I would wait for it to swing back again. It was a kind of magic, and I was disappointed to learn of its mundane purpose—the saving of a few dollars a month.

Mr. Hance was nearly seventy, a short man with white hair and a white mustache and the most alert eyes that I can remember, except perhaps Aunt Wilma Hudson's. Aunt Wilma lived on South Sixth Street and always shopped at Mr. Hance's store. Mr. Hance's eyes were blue and capable of a keen concentration that could make you squirm. Aunt Wilma had black agate eyes that moved restlessly and scrutinized everybody with bright suspicion. In church, her glance would dart around the congregation seeking out irreverent men and women whose expressions showed that they were occupied with worldly concerns, or even carnal thoughts, in the holy place. If she lighted on a culprit, her heavy, dark brows would lower, and her mouth would tighten in righteous disapproval. Aunt Wilma was as honest as the day is long and as easily confused, when it came to what she called figgerin', as the night is dark. Her clashes with Mr. Hance had become a family legend. He was a swift and competent calculator, and nearly fifty years of constant practice had enabled him to add up a column of figures almost at a glance. He set down his columns swiftly on an empty paper sack with a stubby black pencil. Aunt Wilma, on the other hand, was slow and painstaking when it came to figgerin'. She would go over and over a column of numbers, her glasses far down on her nose, her lips moving soundlessly. To her, rapid calculation, like all the other reckless and impulsive habits of men, was tainted with a kind of godlessness. Mr. Hance always sighed when he looked up and saw her coming into his store. He knew that she could lift a simple dollar transaction into a dim and mystic realm of confusion all her own.

I was fortunate enough to be present one day in 1905 when Mr. Hance's calculating and Aunt Wilma's figgerin' came together in memorable single combat. She had wheedled me into carrying her market basket, on the ground that it was going to be too heavy for her to manage. Her two grandsons, boys around my own age, had skipped out when I came to call at their house, and Aunt Wilma promptly seized on me. A young'un, as she called everybody under seventeen, was not worth his salt if he couldn't help a body about the house. I had shopped with her before, under duress, and I knew her accustomed and invariable route on Saturday mornings, when Fourth Street, from Main to State, was lined with the stands of truck gardeners. Prices were incredibly low in those days, but Aunt Wilma questioned the cost, the quality, and the measure of everything. By the time she had finished her long and tedious purchases of fresh produce from the country, and we had turned east into Town Street and headed for Mr. Hance's store, the weight of the market basket was beginning to pain my arm. "Come along, child, come along," Aunt Wilma snapped, her eyes shining with the look of the Middle Western housewife engaged in hard but virtuous battle with the wicked forces of the merchandising world.

I saw Mr. Hance make a small involuntary gesture with his right hand as he spied Aunt Wilma coming through the door. He had just finished with a customer, and since his assistant was busy, he knew he was in for it. It took a good half hour for Aunt Wilma to complete her shopping for groceries, but at length everything she wanted was stacked on the counter in sacks and cans and boxes. Mr. Hance set deftly to work with his paper sack and pencil, jotting down the price of each article as he fitted it into the basket. Aunt Wilma watched his expert movements closely, like a hostile baseball fan waiting for an error in the infield. She regarded adroitness in a man as "slick" rather than skillful.

Aunt Wilma's purchases amounted to ninety-eight cents. After writing down this sum, Mr. Hance, knowing my aunt, whisked the paper bag around on the counter so that she could examine his addition. It took her some time, bending over and peering through her glasses, to arrive at a faintly reluctant corroboration of his figgerin'. Even when she was satisfied that all was in order, she had another go at the column of numbers, her lips moving silently as she added them up for the third time. Mr. Hance waited patiently, the flat of his hands on the counter. He seemed to be fascinated by the movement of her lips. "Well, I guess it's all right," said Aunt Wilma, at last, "but everything *is* so dear." What she had bought for less than a dollar made the market basket bulge. Aunt Wilma took her purse out of her bag and drew out a dollar bill slowly and handed it over, as if it were a hundred dollars she would never see again.

Mr. Hance deftly pushed the proper keys of the cash register, and the red hand on the indicator pointed to $.98. He studied the cash drawer, which had shot out at him. "Well, well," he said, and then, "Hmm. Looks like I haven't got any pennies." He turned back to Aunt Wilma. "Have you got three cents, Mrs. Hudson?" he asked.

That started it.

Aunt Wilma gave him a quick look of distrust. Her Sunday suspicion gleamed in her eyes. "*You* owe *me two* cents," she said sharply.

"I know that, Mrs. Hudson," he sighed, "but I'm out of pennies. Now, if you'll give me three cents, I'll give you a nickel."

Aunt Wilma stared at him cautiously.

"It's all right if you give him three cents and he gives you a nickel," I said.

"Hush up," said Aunt Wilma. "I'm figgerin'." She figgered for several moments, her mouth working again.

Mr. Hance slipped a nickel out of the drawer and placed it on the counter. "There is your nickel," he said firmly. "Now you just have to give me three cents."

Aunt Wilma pecked about in her purse and located three pennies, which she brought out carefully, one at a time. She laid them on the counter beside the nickel, and Mr. Hance reached for them. Aunt Wilma was too quick for him. She covered the eight cents with a lean hand. "Wait, now!" she said, and she took her hand away slowly. She frowned over the four coins as if they were a difficult hand in bridge whist. She ran her lower lip against her upper teeth. "Maybe if I give you a dime," she said, "and take the eight cents . . . It is *two* cents you're short, ain't it?"

Mr. Hance began to show signs of agitation. One or two amused customers were now taking in the scene out of the corners of their eyes. "No, no," said Mr. Hance. "That way, you would be making me a present of seven cents!" This was too much for Aunt Wilma. She couldn't understand the new and preposterous sum of seven cents that had suddenly leaped at her from nowhere. The notion that she was about to do herself out of some money staggered her, and her eyes glazed for a moment like a groggy prizefighter's. Neither Mr. Hance nor I said anything, out of fear of deepening the tangle. She made an uncertain move of her right hand and I had the wild thought that she was going to give Mr. Hance one of the pennies and scoop up the seven cents, but she didn't. She fell into a silent clinch with the situation and then her eyes cleared. "Why, of *course!*" she cried brightly. "I don't know what got into me! You take the eight cents and give me a dime. Then I'll have the two cents that's coming to me." One of the customers laughed, and Aunt Wilma cut him down with a swift glare. The diversion gave me time to figure out that whereas Mr. Hance had been about to gain seven cents, he was now going to lose a nickel. "That way, *I* would be making *you* a present of *five* cents, Mrs. Hudson," he said stiffly. They stood motionless for several seconds, each trying to stare the other down.

"Now, here," said Mr. Hance, turning and taking her dollar out of the still open cash drawer. He laid it beside the nickel and the pennies. "Now, here," he said again. "You gave me a dollar three, but you don't owe me a dollar three—you owe me five cents less than that. Here is the five cents." He snatched it up and handed it to her. She held the nickel between thumb and forefinger, and her eyes gleamed briefly, as if she at last comprehended the peculiar deal, but the gleam faded. Suddenly she handed him his nickel and picked up her dollar and her three cents. She put the pennies back in her purse. "I've rung up the ninety-eight cents, Mrs. Hudson," said Mr. Hance quickly. "I must put the dollar back in the till." He turned and pointed at the $.98 on the indicator. "I tell you what. If you'll give me the dollar, I'll give you the nickel and we'll call it square." She obviously didn't want to take the nickel or give up the dollar, but she did, finally. I was astounded at first, for here was the penny-careful Mr. Hance knocking three cents off a bill, but then I realized he was afraid of losing the dollar and was willing to settle for the lesser of two evils.

"Well," said Aunt Wilma irritably, "I'm sure I don't know what you're trying to do."

I was a timid boy, but I had to plunge into the snarl, if only on behalf of the family honor. "Gee, Aunt Wilma," I told her, "if you keep the nickel, he's giving you everything for ninety-five cents."

Mr. Hance scowled hard at me. He was afraid I was going to get him in deeper than he already was. "It's all right, son," he said. "It's all right." He put the dollar in the till and shoved the drawer shut with a decisive bang, but I wasn't going to give up.

"Gee whizz, Aunt Wilma," I complained, "you still owe him three cents. Don't you see that?"

She gave me the pitying glance of a superior and tired intelligence. "I never owed him three cents in my life," she said tartly. "He owes me two cents. You stay out of things you don't understand."

"It's all right," said Mr. Hance again, in a weary voice. He was sure that if she scrabbled in her purse again for the three pennies, she would want her dollar back, and they would be right where they had started. I gave my aunt a look of disenchantment.

"Now, wait!" she cried suddenly. "Maybe I have the exact change! I don't know what's got into me I didn't think of that! I think I have the right change after all." She put back on the counter the nickel she had been clutching in her left hand, and then she began to peck at the coins in her purse and, after a good minute, arranged two quarters, four dimes,

Mr. Hance's nickel, and three pennies on the counter. "There," she said, her eyes flashing triumph. "Now you give me my dollar back."

Mr. Hance sighed deeply, rang out the cash drawer by pushing "No Sale," and handed her the dollar. Then he hastily scraped up the change, deposited each coin in its proper place in the till, and slammed the drawer shut again. I was only ten, and mathematics was not my best study, but it wasn't hard to figure that Mr. Hance, who in the previous arrangement had been out three cents, was now out five cents. "Good day, Mrs. Hudson," he said grimly. He felt my sympathetic eyes on him, and we exchanged a brief, knowing masculine glance of private understanding.

"Good day, Mr. Hance," said Aunt Wilma, and her tone was as grim as the grocer's.

I took the basket from the counter, and Mr. Hance sighed again, this time with relief. "Goodbye, goodbye," he said with false heartiness, glad to see us on our way. I felt I should slip him the parsley, or whatever sack in the basket had cost a nickel.

"Come on, child," said Aunt Wilma. "It's dreadfully late. I declare it's taken hours to shop today." She muttered plaintively all the way out of the store.

I noticed as I closed the door behind us that Mr. Hance was waiting on a man customer. The man was laughing. Mr. Hance frowned and shrugged.

As we walked east on Town Street, Aunt Wilma let herself go. "I never heard of such a thing in all the born days of my life," she said. "I don't know where John Hance got his schooling, if he got any. The very idea—a grown man like that getting so mixed up. Why, I could have spent the whole day in that store and he'd never of figgered it out. Let him keep the two cents, then. It was worth it to get out of that store."

"*What* two cents, Aunt Wilma?" I almost squealed.

"Why, the two cents he still owes me!" she said. "I don't know what they teach you young'uns nowadays. Of course he owes me two cents. It come to ninety-eight cents and I give him a dollar. He owed me two cents in the beginning and he still owes me two cents. Your Uncle Herbert will explain it to you. Any man in the world could figger it out except John Hance."

I walked on beside her in silence, thinking of Uncle Herbert, a balding, choleric man of high impatience and quick temper.

"Now, you let *me* explain it to your Uncle Herbert, child," she said. "I declare you were as mixed up as John Hance was. If I'd of listened to you and given him the three cents, like you said, I'd never of got my dollar back. He'd owe me five cents instead of two. Why, it's as plain as day."

I thought I had the solution for her now, and I leaped at it. "That's right, Aunt Wilma," I almost yelled. "He owed you a nickel and he gave you the nickel."

Aunt Wilma stabbed me with her indignation. "I gave *him* the nickel," she said. "I put it on the counter right there under your very eyes, and you saw him scoop it up."

I shifted the market basket to my left arm. "I know, Aunt Wilma," I said, "but it was *his* nickel all the time."

She snorted. "Well, he's got his precious nickel, ain't he?" she demanded. I shifted the basket again. I thought I detected a faint trace of uneasiness in her tone. She fell silent and quickened her cadence, and it was hard for me to keep up with her. As we turned south into Sixth Street, I glanced up and saw that she was frowning and that her lips were moving again. She was rehearsing the story of the strange transaction for Uncle Herbert. I began to whistle. "Hush up, child," she said. "I'm figgerin'."

Uncle Herbert was sitting in the living room, eating an apple. I could tell from his expression that he was in one of his rare amiable moods. Aunt Wilma grabbed the basket away from me. "Now, you let me explain it to your uncle," she said. "You wait till I get back." She sailed out of the room on her way to the kitchen.

A little breathlessly, I told Uncle Herbert the saga of Aunt Wilma's complicated financial quandary. He was chuckling when she came back into the room.

Uncle Herbert's amusement nettled her. "The boy got it wrong," she said accusingly. "He didn't tell it right. He was ever' bit as mixed up as John Hance." Uncle Herbert's chuckle increased to full and open laughter. Aunt Wilma glared at him until he subsided. "Now, Herbert, you listen to me," she began, but he cut in on her.

"If Hance ever gives you that two cents he owes you, Wilma," he said, "I tell you what you have to do to square accounts. Someday you're going to have to give him a dime for three cents." He began to laugh again.

Aunt Wilma Hudson stared at each of us in turn, with a look of fine, cold scorn, and then she raised both her hands and let them fall helplessly. "I declare," she said, "I don't know how the world gets along with the men runnin' it."

The Family Retainers

By Harriette Levy

They used to remain for decades and sometimes for life; and they were often as much a part of the family as proper relatives. The Levy retainers were a motley crew. An Irish cook, a German baker, an Italian fish man and a Chinese vegetable vendor waited on the Jewish mistress of the house. A truly American mixture in the days when America was the melting pot of the world.

Coming into the kitchen from the shadow of dining room and hall was like stepping into sunshine. A stripe of brown wood, then a stripe of yellow, then a stripe of brown, then a stripe of yellow, on and on, all the way to the wall. Glossy golden: that was our kitchen floor, our inlaid floor. The steel top of the big range shone; I could see my face in it. It was so clean that we fried pancakes on it. We lived in a wonderful house, cooking pancakes on our stove instead of in a frying pan!

The kitchen was the temple in which Mother was priest and Maggie Doyle, Levite. When Maggie first came to us to do general housework, Mother explained to her the custom regarding diet and the use of kitchen utensils. Not only was there a gulf between animal food, including all that had its origin in flesh, milk, and its derivatives, but the distinction also applied to the utensils with which they came in contact. No butter must touch meat of any kind nor be served at table when meat was a course; no meat pot must know the contact of milk. The distinction held to the least knife and teaspoon. So Moses had decreed, and so Mother explained to the tall, gawky, bobbed-haired Irish girl come to take service.

Maggie Doyle smiled the amused, red-gummed smile that was destined to elude us for more than a decade and said, "I know. I've cooked Jews before."

In the tall dresser that stood between the two large closets were two drawers and two small cupboards. Milk knives, forks, and spoons were kept in the right-hand drawer; in the right cupboard below it were milk pots and pans. The meat cutlery and tins were arranged in the left compartments. Between them lay a gulf as deep as that between ancient Jew and Philistine. The distribution in the closet was more intricate. The lower shelf held the milk dishes, the second shelf the meat dishes. On the two upper shelves, undisturbed for fifty weeks of the year, the Passover dishes waited for the spring observance of the feast of the unleavened bread, in commemoration of the days when Israel, hastening from pursuit of Pharaoh, dared not wait for the dough to rise. As the Bavarian Jew and the Polish Jew became Jew under a common persecution, so the meat and milk dishes, individualized during the ordinary flow of circumstances, united as leaven under the taboo of the Passover, and were thrust into the shadow of the upper shelves during the week of holiday celebration. The lower shelves were dusted, washed, purged of dishes and of any leaven that they may have contained, even in memory, and they were as if they had never been.

All through the year, like a searchlight, the eye of Mother ranged over the kitchen. Woe to the lovelorn cook who stirred the mutton broth with a milk spoon, or to the brazen one who basted the turkey with a lump of butter. Woe, woe to the waitress who, breaking the plate, hoped to fill the gap with another purloined from the upper Passover shelf. Triple her guilt if she dared to return it after the contamination. A Passover vessel, once deflowered, though passed through flame, could never recover its native purity.

Temptation to delinquency lay ambushed in cupboard drawer and closet bin. To possess one's self of a slice of bread and butter without committing a Mosaic offense was a feat. No movement was too slight to stir a sense of danger, as feet felt for safe ground between the taboos; and always present was the zest of an unpremeditated transgression undetected. If a sudden contraction of my heart gave warning that I had cut into the butter with a meat knife, I turned toward Mother, bent under the effort to cut stars into the cookie dough, and over her back I intercepted in Maggie Doyle's eyes the gleam of amused complicity. Nowhere was my fear of Mother so great as in the kitchen, where her native capacity for anger was reinforced by her priestly office. Awe of His agent, rather than dread of the displeasure of the Lord, secured my faithful obedience. When I heard the tablets crack, I fled beneath her wrath.

As a little girl, and when I grew older, I loved the kitchen. So much had happened, was happening, and would happen again. There was this that you must always do, that which you must never do; here were punishments threatening if you did; there, retribution if you did not. Preparations were always going on for something new: cleanings, purifications, dishes that were personalities because they came into view for occasion from dark shadows into which they returned. There was exotic food that never appeared except upon holidays—beet soup, hard-boiled eggs eaten with salt water, home-brewed raisin wine, epicurean dishes made of Matzoth meal and the soaked Matzoth. So many people were about—God, Moses, Mother, tradespeople, and Maggie Doyle.

Maggie worked thirteen hours a day and ended the day with a dance. General housework included care of the sidewalk and outside steps, the back yard and garden, the alleyway between garden and fence, the floors of the basement and kitchen, windows, cooking and serving at table, washing and ironing of small pieces and flannel underwear—everything but the starched pieces, which were sent to the Chinese laundry. Before dinner Maggie went to her room to wash and put on a fresh dress. Sometimes she remained in her room half an hour or more. Mother never solved the riddle of how a maid could take so long to wash and to change her dress. If Mother complained, Maggie smiled but did not answer. Her reserve never yielded, and after ten years of service her private history, including the details of her approaching marriage, remained undivulged. To a question, she answered with an oblique glance or an open smile, and she told nothing.

"Did you have a good time at the party last night?" I asked.

"Why wouldn't I be having a good time?"

"What did you do?"

"A little of everything."

"Did you dance?"

"What would I be doing at a party if I wasn't dancing?"

That was all. I wondered what she talked about when she was out at night. I was always wondering what girls talked about when they were alone with their beaux.

"What did you talk about, Maggie, you and your beau?"

"Oh, we just talked."

"I know, but what did he say?" I persisted.

"Oh, he said nothing and I said the same," answered Maggie, adding, gratis, a side glance of amused insolence.

The kitchen offered the social potentialities of a ballroom, and Maggie missed none of them. Twice a day the tradesman or his emissary knocked at the kitchen door. In the morning he took the order, in the afternoon he delivered it. The grocer, the baker, the steam laundryman, the fish man, the chicken man, the butcher boy, came twice a day proffering a salty bit of conversation or a flashing glance of fire. Bent over the sink, Maggie Doyle aimed a shaft of repartee over her left shoulder in invitation, or she buried her scorn in a bowl of dough, or she leaned lightly against the jamb of the door in coquettish intimacy with the man who pleased her. His footsteps running down the back steps were gay as laughter. I wondered what she said to the men that made them linger at the open door. If I came near, she stopped talking and returned to her work.

Between us and the tradesmen who came to our door an equality existed. Not the butcher boy, perhaps, but that was different, for he brought meat wrapped in heavy brown paper through which blood trickled. It was a curious rule, I thought, that butcher boys had rosy cheeks and whistled as they drove their horses and wagons. I observed them as they clattered over the cobblestones and found no exception. Laundrymen, on the contrary, had long, serious faces and large families. You could ask a laundryman how his children were, and he would tell you that two were down with chicken pox or mumps. The men who came from the big markets were harder to classify. Our chicken man was on the Board of Education.

I liked the social life of the kitchen better than that of the parlor. The men brought the wind and the rain into the house on their faces and hair, and they bore the smell of fish and vegetable and meat. They were young and noisy and hurried. They were quick-tongued, with a joke upon their lips and a challenge in their eyes. They ran up the steps, burst into the room, scattered raindrops upon the floor, flung packages upon the table, joked with Maggie Doyle or Mother, and the door slammed behind their retreating footsteps. My fancy followed them into the street, and I could see the horse start with a run before they jumped into the seat and caught the reins.

When Christmas came, the tradesmen brought presents. Gifts, in kind, were expected of them, and we should have been shocked at the omission of the bottle of cream or the basket of fruit, which came with the holidays. The most welcome offering was that presented by the baker, a huge yellow cupcake hidden under a coat of heavy white icing with Merry Christmas outlined upon it in crinkly pink sugar letters.

Mother examined the gift with critical approval. "Shrunk!" she said, if the diameter showed the slightest diminution from the standard size.

The tradespeople were subject to constant toll. No glass protected their wares, and while we lingered in cordial conversation, unconscious fingers automatically dipped into box and barrel. Nothing was bought on trust; everything was sampled.

"How about the apples today, sour?"

"Try one," came the certain answer, and the fruit was proved before bought.

To market with Mother was a regaling experience; at each stall a tidbit was handed to me, and I returned home, my stomach filled with pickles and gingersnaps, tomatoes and picked shrimps, with perhaps a sliver of sausage. "Soup greens"—celery, turnips, parsley, and onions—were a straight tax on anything bought of the vegetable man.

"Do you call those soup greens?" Mother demanded if the donation were not generous, and the tradesman, abashed, added recklessly.

Many nations and races united to furnish us with our supplies. The baker was German; the fish man, Italian; the grocer, a Jew; the butcher, Irish; the steam laundryman, a New Englander. The vegetable vendor and the regular laundryman who came to the house were Chinese. The Chinamen were the high note of color and piquancy in the kitchen traffic of the day. Chung Lung was fruit and fish man. He carried the combined stock, suspended in two huge wicker baskets balanced upon a long pole, across his shoulders. He did not come to the kitchen door, but remained outside in the alley. We heard the back doorbell and hurried down, Mother, Maggie, and I. The uncertainty of the contents of the baskets—today only apples and cauliflower; tomorrow, cherries and corn; today, shiny silver smelts; tomorrow, red shrimps with beards and black-beaded eyes—made a delight of his coming. Such laughter at the weighing: Mother adding a potato to the scale, Chung, his eyes screwed into slits, removing it; Mother scowling in indignation, Chung showing three black fangs in merry insistence upon his rights—all of us knowing all the while that we were playing a game. Such arguments and noisy disputes! Chung talked and talked a language, unintelligible to any of us but himself, his cadences rising high and falling again into murmurs.

"Yes, yes," cried Mother, red in the face with determination.

"No, no," cried Chung, grown suddenly solemn as if in defense of a religious conviction. Anger, indignation, resentment, an impasse; then the concession of a head of lettuce here, the withdrawal of an apple there, laughter, good humor, Maggie carrying the fruits of victory to the kitchen and I remaining outside so that Chung might teach me how to twist the tail of the shrimp to make the meat pop out, unbroken. I loved Chung Lung, and when, with a straining of muscle, he lifted the bent pole to his shoulders and trotted off, a little bowed under the heavy baskets, I called out to him, "Good-by, Chung, bring me a big peach tomorrow."

"All light, all light," he called back.

No bell announced the coming of Hi Lo. His name was Hi Lo, but we called him John, our generic name for all male Chinese. Hi Lo did not come. He was there. He moved about as one who had long enjoyed the freedom of the house. We would hear a noise upstairs and, to a questioning look, the answer came, "It's the Chinaman with the wash."

The wash left the house a huge soft white ball upon the high bony shoulder of Hi Lo; and returned, starched to the breaking point, in a great heavy wicker basket. Hi Lo mounted the backstairs and deposited the wash neatly, in classified stacks, upon the bed of the back bedroom. Torn hems of sheets hung frankly between the piles. The wash gave out a strong human odor of a Chinese laundry and called forth a picture of a long cue and a shaven head bent over the ironing board, sprinkling the sheets and pillowcases with a mouthful of water, blown and vaporized by some delightful ingenuity.

We looked up from the pan of sugared cookies, which Mother was drawing out of the oven, and saw Hi Lo standing at the door.

"What you want?" Mother asked.

We talked pidgin English to Chinamen. Hi Lo grinned, revealing a yellow tooth perched high on a gum like a village on a cliff.

"Want money?"

Hi Lo nodded and grinned again. "Yep, want money, this time, last time." He held up two fingers.

"We no got money," said Father who had come downstairs. "All money gone." This was Father's weekly joke.

Hi Lo laughed loud. "You got heap money."

Mother grew serious. "There was a towel missing last week, John."

"No towel missing."

"I tell you there was. My list fifteen, and you bring fourteen."

"No, no."

"Did you ever hear such a thing?" This to us.

"My list fifteen, you understand?"

"No, no, eberyting right, fourteen."

"Your list"—Mother's voice was rising—"your list"—she hesitated for a word—"your list no good."

"My book velly good. I write it in book. Fourteen towel. You give me money."

"I give you money when you bring towel," said Mother. "You look in book."

"Book, book," shrieked Hi Lo. "I no come more," and, in a noisy fury of sound, he rushed from the house.

On the following week, while we were at dinner, he was in the doorway again.

"You give me money?" He grinned engagingly, as if the subject had never before been broached.

"You findee towel?" from Mother.

"Towel, towel! All time towel. No towel. I look book. You give me money."

It was useless to argue further. The lost towel, like the torn sheet, was the price we paid for cheap Chinese service.

"You pay him," said Mother to Father, saving her face by disengaging herself from the whole transaction.

Hi Lo was in the room now, standing over Father, laughing and pointing a long, bony finger at Father's trouser pocket.

"He got him," he confided to the table.

"How much?" asked Father.

"Four dollar-hap. I make him for four dollar quarter," he conceded grandly. And the contest ended with honors even.

Smiling, Development of

By John McNulty

The new baby is born—miracle of miracles! The baby smiles—an event without parallel in human history!

We have a new baby, my wife and I; the cellophane is hardly off him yet. And like most people in our fix, we have to have Doctor Spock's book around the house. It costs only thirty-five cents, and we have two copies. One copy is mine, and one is my wife's.

When anything happens in Johnny's room—noises, that is—we both start running. My wife runs for Johnny, and I run for the book. She's playing this thing by instinct, and I'm playing it by the book. I don't know which of us is wise, but between us Johnny should make out okay. Hope so, anyway.

A couple of times the noises in the night were gruesome. One night I jumped up and ran for the book, and Faith, my wife, ran toward Johnny. It was two in the morning. I flicked on the light and turned to the index of the book. I was looking for "Strangling," because that is what he sounded as if he were doing.

No "Strangling" in the index. Nearest to that was "Strangers, baby's attitude toward." I was not interested in that at the moment. I ran to Johnny's room. "She," as I often refer to my wife, had the light on by then. Johnny was looking up at the two of us, and he was smiling. He was about two months old, and I had never seen him smile before. I said, "I guess the guy is all right." Then I went back to the living room and got the book, and, as long as my wife had gone back to bed, I thought I would read a few things here and there. I turned to the index. To where "Strangling" would have been if there had been any "Strangling." What I was thinking was that Johnny had not strangled this time, but maybe he would start to strangle some night and I'd better be ready. Still no entry under "Strangling."

But right on the opposite page of the index, page 498, there was an entry that caught my eye. It said, "Smiling, development of."

Oh, boy. He had just smiled! It was so marvelous a simple happening that I had not even dared to speak of it to my wife. He had smiled at me.

The index said the smiling stuff was on page 141. I turned to that. It said there: "He smiles early, because he is a social being. Somewhere around two months of age your baby will smile at you one day when you are talking and smiling to him. It's an exciting moment for you. But think what it means about his development. He knows little at this age, he can't use his hands, or even turn his head from side to side. And yet he already knows that he's a sociable being, that it's nice to have loving people around, that he feels like responding to them. And if he's treated with plenty of affection and not too much interference, he'll go on being friendly and reasonable just because it is his nature."

While the dim morning lay outside the window in Manhattan, where I live, I read that twice. Gee whizz! It had happened to other people before. Otherwise, Dr. Benjamin Spock would not have had it in *The Pocket Book of Baby and Child Care*. A few minutes before, my Johnny had smiled at me, and there it was, exactly right, under "Smiling, development of."

No fooling, I had foolishly thought that what had happened to me—Johnny's smiling up at me—was the first time anything like that had happened in the history of the world.

I put the book down, turned out the light, and went back in to sneak a look at Johnny. He was sound asleep, with his hands, which look as if Benvenuto Cellini had made them, spread out in the crib. He sleeps on his belly.

White Commencement

By Josephine Case White

For the son of the family, commencement means the beginning of a new life. Usually the ceremony takes place in a springtime setting. But many of us remember a more poignant commencement, when young men graduated in wintertime in order to hurry off to war. Yet innumerable details remained the same. Best girls bought new dresses for the festivities. Mothers burst into tears when their sons won special honors. In the following selection, the wife of the President of Colgate University helps us relive the occasion.

Some of the seniors thought it would be a good plan not to have any Commencement at all. They were of the class of 1943 although they were to graduate in December of 1942, and in the general spirit of sacrifice and business-not-as-usual that swept the country as the first anniversary of Pearl Harbor came round, a petition was gotten up to urge upon the administration the sacrifice of Commencement too. It seemed a good idea and many signed. But later when the Dean, a veteran of World War I, talked to them, the majority decided that they might be cheating themselves and their fathers and mothers; so they voted to hold Commencement not as usual but in a simplified way.

The date was first set for December 20, but soon the college received notice that the boys who had enlisted in the Marines would be called before that time. In a hastily summoned meeting that provoked a warm debate, the Faculty decided that Commencement could and should be moved ahead to Sunday, December 13. After this announcement the telephone and telegraph offices were swamped with calls. Parents in fifteen states were notified by anxious sons that if they were coming to Commencement they would have to hurry.

At the Inn the few remaining maids who had not yet left for war jobs scurried to get the place ready and the rooms made up. The vacuum cleaner ran continuously. And all over the town housewives who rented rooms cleaned house in haste.

At schools, in sorority houses, in homes, girls tore open special-delivery letters and remade their plans for the weekend. Hairdressers were called to the phone for new appointments. The dress shops did a good business. And all through the many heads busied with these affairs ran the undercurrent of thought like a somber refrain: "This may be the last time I shall see him—for a long time, anyway."—"This is the last of his college life, of peace, of youth."—"This is the end."—"This is the beginning."

On Saturday the 12th, the seniors began to pack. The accumulations of three and a quarter years were thrown away or stuffed into the already gaping bags and trunks. The underclassmen were mostly gone for the holidays, and all over the campus hung the air of untidy desolation and impending finality that is usually associated with the warm air and still sunshine of June.

But on this day the snow fell lightly from fast-moving broken clouds. The yellow sun peered through, then disappeared. The wind carried the snow into little drifts at the corners of the fraternity houses, and the boys wore their ski boots as they clattered in and out.

At the President's house the children had put up a Christmas tree and were hanging dozens of ornaments upon it. The older ones gave loud directions continually and the younger ones, in their eagerness to help, dropped ball after ball until the rug was covered with little glittering fragments. The daughter hung the mistletoe in the doorway and wondered secretly in her ten-year-old heart what the result would be. The President's wife hurried about town collecting the food and drink, the paper napkins, the red candles necessary for the coming party, while in the kitchen the butler and cook exchanged a few sharp words.

The Dean and the President conferred in the latter's office. There were fewer casualties than usual in the graduating class this year. Either the Faculty, impressed by the imminence of war's demands upon their pupils, had been kind where kindness was possible, or the boys had earnestly applied themselves to their final civilian duties. There were some, however, upon whom neither grace had fallen, and no amount of re-adding could possibly bring their credits up to the necessary number. The Dean left unhappily to notify them, and the President went on signing the 185 diplomas of the more fortunate ones. The heavy parchment paper curled in waves over the desk as the India ink flowed from the pen above the engraved *Praeses* and the attentive secretary carefully removed each one to dry without blotting.

At the chapel the Marshal drilled the class in the procedures of Commencement. They shambled across the platform in their plaid shirts, learning the proper place to stand to receive the diploma and when to tip the cap, thinking all the while of boot training or parade grounds at dawn.

The parents began to arrive. The Inn was filled with the sound of greetings and the smell of snow on fur. The strip of carpet across the lobby was covered with heel-shapes of snow melting in little pools of water. The harassed room clerk tried to disentangle his reservations. The waitresses served coffee and doughnuts in the Tavern Room and the porter said the second bus from the city was an hour late on account of the bad condition of the roads. Mothers secretly but eagerly pressed the firm flesh of their sons' arms, fathers shook hands long and hard, young sisters and brothers made a nuisance of themselves.

The boy from Iowa looked at his father who had traveled a night and a day to reach him and wondered desperately if the President would feel it necessary to tell of that escapade at Tony's Bar. Thank God the judge had been kindhearted and let them off without a record; thank God the President had done the same—though after what a talking-to! They had understood he had meant no harm; but Dad would never understand.

In the afternoon the seniors brought their fathers and mothers and relatives, and girls if they had them, to the reception at the President's house. The late sun was golden on the little drifts of snow, the dark trunks of trees threw blue shadows, the campus had never looked lovelier. Inside, the house was warm and bright, the lights on the Christmas tree were gay and welcoming. One by one the seniors brought forward their families, some shy, some eager, all proud, all serious. Fat mothers, small mothers, pretty mothers, plain mothers, fathers of all shapes and descriptions, went by. How the boys show their origin, thought the President's wife as the long procession passed; in each one you can see the parents over again; they are one, these families, they are units, indivisible. "I am so glad you could come," she said over and over again; "we were so afraid the difficulties of travel, the change in date, would keep you away. We are so happy to have you here. We shall miss your boy so much." It was true. Who would not miss them and they going God knows where? The

President took pains to speak at some length to each father and mother. He hoped that each one left with a special feeling.

The little sisters and brothers with shining faces shook hands softly, their little fingers limp. The grandmothers' eyes shone brightly behind their glasses; this is an old story but somehow each time more dear.

In the dining room the cider and Christmas cookies disappeared. The seniors introduced their families to each other, the little brothers and sisters made a beeline for the gingerbread men. The daughter of the house noticed with disappointment that no one made use of the mistletoe.

While more guests were coming, others said good-by. Chicago, Westchester, Texas, Detroit, Long Island, Salem, Syracuse—all gathered together for this brief moment in common cause, spoke of the beauty of the college, its gift to their sons, its future. The parents now felt with the boys a rush of enthusiasm and sentiment for the old stone buildings on the lovely hill. At last everyone was gone, the children ate up all the cookies that were left, the butler swept up the crumbs, and the dog was released from his prison in the cellar.

After supper everyone hurried to the level space by the lake in front of the Union. A fire burned brightly on the ground, and to the seniors assembled round it in their caps and gowns the professor of philosophy spoke briefly. The wind blew the flames, blew the black gowns, blew away the serious and tender words. Then the seniors lit at the fire their kerosene-soaked torches and marched single file down the path at the edge of the lake. Overhead the interlacing willow branches leaped to view, the snow gleamed pinkly all around, the thin ice on the water reflected sudden gleams. Beneath each torch the face of its bearer stood out boldly, the nose jutting from eye-wells of shadow, the mouth firm and determined. Soldiers on some strange night attack, savages at some grim celebration, young priests at the altar of an ancient god . . . In long line at the water's edge they sang the "Alma Mater," the song sounding low and distant across the water; one end was slightly out of time with the other and the effect was one of weird melancholy and sadness. At the last the flaming torches hissed in the lake, went out with a splendid steam, and the seniors came running back to their silent audience, boys in caps and gowns once more.

For the evening, the local movie theater was taken over by the Dramatic Club, and every seat was filled. It was a melodrama with the murdered body right on the stage and a circle of ghoulish criminals and innocent bystanders around it. The senior from New England played the cynical and melancholic poet who at last laid bare the crime. His mother looked on with amazement. In reality he was fresh-faced, sweet-natured, clear-eyed. His father was thinking of what the boy would learn at Parris Island.

When the curtain went down, the audience, pleasantly horrified, clapped loudly. The grinning cast appeared for a curtain call, and the chattering audience slowly departed. The President and his wife congratulated the actors. On the way out a group of seniors waylaid the President and asked if something couldn't be done about one of the boys who could not graduate. The others no one defended; but this one had been popular, and almost good enough to get by. The President, feeling sad, said no to the anxious faces around him. "It wouldn't be fair," he said, "to him or anyone."

Downstairs at the Inn the taproom was filled and the young voices went on and on. In some of the fraternity houses there was dancing, and some drinking, but not so much as at other Commencements. The boy from Iowa refused to take a drink and thought of the abysmal hell of the morning when he woke and remembered what had happened at Tony's Bar.

Very early Sunday morning, long before the late dawn of wartime winter, the superintendent of grounds climbed out of bed and peered out the window. Seeing the snow whirl thickly and the new layer of several inches on the sill, he went to the telephone. "Dan, you better get Harold and the other men right away. Get out both plows—every road on the campus must be cleared. Clean out a big place around the chapel. It's snowing like the devil."

The President, hearing the plow go by, looked at his watch and rolled over with a groan, thinking with a sudden stab of his Commencement address, on which he had worked so hard and which he felt was so inadequate. What could one say to boys setting out upon such errands as these; boys for whom one felt such affection, such apprehension?

At the Inn the mothers and sisters dressed carefully in their best, soon to be hidden under fur coats and galoshes. At the fraternity houses the boys dug their cars out of the snow, threw in their last belongings, ready for a quick getaway after the ceremonies were over. At the chapel the men were clearing the steps of the soft, light snow that endlessly drifted back. Inside, the student marshals were looping long streamers of ribbon along the reserved pews.

Half an hour before the ceremonies were supposed to begin, the cars started coming up the long hill, and warm-wrapped cargoes were delivered at the chapel steps. "What weather!" they said to one another. "What weather for Commencement!" In the hall next door the seniors were donning their caps and gowns, making fun of each other, secretly serious. Across the way the Faculty were decked in hoods of all colors; the President was wearing his new hood, gaudy with orange and purple.

The organ began to play. Everybody stood up. The heavy silk flags came down the aisle. The crowded chapel was enlivened with bright colors, with an access of vitality and warmth, as though the entrance of the long file of teachers and students generated a strong current that vibrated in every breast. Families looked eagerly for their darlings; the boys—though endeavoring to appear not to be looking—searched also and small secret smiles were exchanged.

Outside, the snow sifted on the roof, on all the gray stone buildings, catching in the cornices and window frames, in the old trees that had seen so many Commencements but none like this. Inside, the President spoke gravely, looking very young in his gold-tasseled cap. The long rows of faces looked up at him. The black-gowned seniors sat very still, their faces showed nothing. The veils and feathers on the women's hats jiggled slightly. The children shifted in their seats, trying to count the stars in the big service flag behind the platform.

Now the Dean was reading the list of names; whenever he came to a *cum laude* a small fire of clapping ran through the room. A *magna* rated more prolonged applause. And when he came to the one *summa cum laude*, the roof reverberated and the boy's mother burst into tears. One by one the seniors came to the platform to receive their diplomas and their dark-red-lined hoods. The audience watched fascinated to see each roll handed out, each hood put on, each man received with a few words by the President. One fellow tried to leave before his hood could be put over his head, and laughter ran lightly as the President held him back.

There was clapping for each one, and no lessening of it throughout; for each one his friends and family made a special little claque, to whom he was the central performer of the day. When the long list was finished they sang with a great outpouring of relief, regret, pride, sorrow, and gladness the "Alma Mater." For its brief span the whole congregation was knit into one; for now these many hearts were one, this never-to-be-again-united assemblage was united in a moment without a name, the epitome of the end and the beginning which was this day.

The attendant minister pronounced the benediction, the organ played the recessional, the academic procession slowly withdrew. Little by little the families and friends followed, speaking softly, laughing lightly, some eyes shining, some shadowed, some merely tired. Outside in the portico in the snow they joined their sons; the black gowns flapped in the snowy wind, the new hoods were handsome against their black and the snow's white. Cars drove up, cries of farewell began to be exchanged. Group by group the crowd departed, seeking shelter from the wind, from the snow, from the chill in their own hearts.

Father of the Bride

By Edward Streeter

The family chronicles describe no more important event than the marriage of the daughter of the house. At the reception, all is confusion, at least in the mind of the bride's father. Is there enough champagne? he wonders. Does she really love her new husband? Why doesn't the reception line move more swiftly? How will he feel as he continues to live in a home without his little daughter?

It is traditional that, between the church and the house, wedding guests are free agents. This is the one period in the schedule where they can express their own individuality.

The majority appreciate this unsupervised interlude and are apt to turn it into a kind of hare-and-hound race in which the bride, groom and immediate progenitors are the hares, the guests assuming the role of hounds.

The latter are held in check briefly by a few yards of satin ribbon and a rear guard of ushers whose hearts are no longer in their work. Scarcely have the hares disappeared down the striped tunnel of awning than the pack is after them with lolling tongues.

Gone the little pre-wedding courtesies when one car waited politely for another to pull in to the curb and friends exchanged genial words of greeting while trying to crawl out of underslung sedans. Now it is every man for himself, *sauve qui peut*, and devil take the hindmost, for the last man to arrive at the house knows that he must spend the balance of the afternoon standing in the reception line watching his more active neighbors guzzling free champagne.

Mr. and Mrs. Banks arrived at 24 Maple Drive a few minutes behind the bridal party. During their absence Mr. Massoula had taken over completely in accordance with his promises. His Buckingham Caterers were darting about like Walt Disney gnomes.

Mr. Massoula met them at the front door. "Everything is in hand," he said. "Don't worry about anything. Go right into the living room. They're taking pictures of the bridal party."

In the living room Mr. Weisgold of Weisgold and Weisgold was perspiring freely and photographing the bridal party in various combinations. Those not engaged in being self-consciously photogenic stood about making wisecracks about those who were, between deep draughts of Mr. Banks' champagne, which had already begun to flow. A Buckingham representative approached with a tray full of glasses.

Mr. Banks took one. He felt like those men in the whiskey ads who go through nerve-shattering experiences in jungles or on mountain precipices, then, their job well done, settle down calmly with friends in the last picture to a glass of their favorite grog. He had also gone through his own private ordeal and, he thought complacently, not without distinction. Now it was all over but the shouting. "Don't go away," he hissed to the waiter.

The bridesmaids were being photographed. Finally the Bankses and the Dunstans took their places before the flash bulbs. Mr. Weisgold's ability to produce an endless supply of bulbs fascinated Mr. Banks. The man must have been a hand grenade thrower in the war.

Over Mr. Weisgold's shoulder he suddenly noticed a cluster of faces in the doorway of the living room. Behind them were other faces. Faces jammed the front doorway. Through the window he could see them stretching in close formation halfway down the walk. Mr. Massoula blocked the entrance to the living room with firm urbanity, like the headwaiter of the Persian Room on a busy night.

The faces that peered at him were not of the happy, laughing type traditionally associated with wedding feasts. They were, rather, the glum, frustrated faces of those who had broken their fenders to get there early and were now denied the fruits of their sacrifices. They were the faces of citizens who definitely wanted to get this runkydunk over with and proceed with the main business of the afternoon.

Mr. Weisgold stopped flashing. The receiving line suddenly snapped to attention as if at the bark of a phantom drill sergeant. Mr. Massoula stepped aside nimbly to avoid being trampled. Mr. Banks never had a connected memory of the next forty-five minutes.

No one had told him whether or not he was to be part of the receiving line. For a moment he decided against it. Then it occurred to him that if he just stood in the middle of the living room he might be mistaken for the caterer. He slid quietly into place between his wife and Mrs. Dunstan as the first guest began to pump Mrs. Banks' arm.

It became immediately apparent that one of his duties was to introduce the guests to Mrs. Dunstan. Introducing one old friend to another had always been enough to give him complete aphasia. On ordinary occasions when guests arrived he disappeared into the pantry and busied himself with the refreshment department, leaving to Mrs. Banks the task of making people known to one another.

Those who were now so eagerly pushing forward to shake his hand were, for the most part, lifelong friends. In spite of this he fell immediately into his accustomed groove and could not remember anyone's name. Occasionally he would recollect their first names, but he couldn't very well say to Mrs. Dunstan, "This is Joe and Booboo." For once his retreat to the pantry was blocked.

Mrs. Banks felt herself jabbed from the rear with a thumb. She jumped slightly and turned toward her husband with the injured look common to all people when jabbed unexpectedly from the rear. "Sing out the last names," he whispered desperately.

Mrs. Banks glanced at him anxiously. She knew he had been going through a considerable strain, but she had hoped with all her being that he would hold together for another couple of hours. "Why, Jack and Nancy *Hilliard*," she cried gaily. "My dear, you look adorable. Yes. Wasn't it. I am so glad you thought so. And Grace *Lippincott*, I am so glad you could get here."

"Mr. and Mrs. Lippincott," mumbled Mr. Banks uncertainly in the general direction of Mrs. Dunstan. "I mean—that is to say—Mr. and Mrs. Hilliard."

He gave it up. He found that, by turning to the next pair of guests before they left Mrs. Banks, it was possible to pass up the whole business and let Mrs. Dunstan rock along as best she could. After all, she would probably never see any of these people again. Maybe she had something there.

Mr. Weisgold struggled through the line. "Look-it," he complained. "You told me you was goin' to have somebody with me to tell me who to shoot. I can't shoot no specials if I dunno who they are."

Mr. Banks looked despairingly around for Ben and Tommy. He had covered this point with the greatest care. Both had assured him that they would not leave Mr. Weisgold's side come hell or high water. Now they had disappeared. "Good God," he said. "Find one of the boys. Find one of the ushers. I've got my hands full here and besides I don't know who these people are any more than you do. Shoot anybody for all I care. Shoot them all. How do you do. So nice to see you. Wasn't it? Yes, she *is* a grand girl."

"O.K.," said Mr. Weisgold. "You'll get what you get. I ain't no mind reader."

A battle-ax of a woman was wringing his hand. "Buckley is my sweetheart," she was saying. "I have known him since he was a little boy." She released his hand to indicate how very tiny Buckley was. "He used to visit us at North Deering, you know. I expect he's told you all about me. I am Mrs. Butterton. Mrs. *Matilda* Butterton. Buckley was a darling little—" Mr. Banks took her great hand in both of his and transferred it to Mrs. Dunstan.

If only people wouldn't stop and talk. There should be a law requiring them to pass silently in front of receiving lines the way they did before the biers of statesmen. They were still pouring in the front door. Glancing through the window, he could see the line extending beyond his field of vision. God knew where it ended. Had someone issued a general invitation by radio?

"Well, well, well." It was Joe Bludsoe and his diminutive wife. Joe was exuding good-fellowship and looking as if he might have apoplexy at any moment. "So you're on your way to joining the grandfather's club, eh? Well, well, well, I'm glad you lived through the wedding. God, you certainly looked awful when you came down that aisle. I said to Martha, 'Let me go out and drag him off the course. He's never going to make it.' You don't look so good now either. Still look green. When Mary was married—"

He continued to pump Mr. Banks' arm rhythmically. Mr. Banks transferred him to Mrs. Dunstan without causing him to miss a beat. "How do you do, Mrs. Karp," he said. "It was good of you to come. Oh, excuse me. Of course. Mrs. Park. Why, of course I knew it. Yes, we couldn't be happier about the whole thing."

It was over at last and not a minute too soon. If another person had injected himself into the living room the receiving line would have been squeezed into the fireplace.

Something was wrong, very wrong, with Mr. Massoula's "circulation." Theoretically the guests were supposed to slither off the end of the reception line, through a French door, and into the marquee where Mr.

Massoula had set up his bar and buffet tables. It was all laid out like a pinball game.

The first few couples to come off the line, however, had chosen the French door in which to hold a long, eager conversation. Those who followed had merely rebounded from this obstacle back into the living room. The pinball idea still held, but it was not working according to plan.

Mr. Massoula's gnomes were so efficient that no one needed to go to the bar anyway. They slid like eels through the melee, mysteriously carrying trays full of champagne glasses where no amateur could have transported an uncorked bottle.

It seemed to Mr. Banks that these busy little figures must be paid on a piece basis—so much per glass dispensed. Never had he seen men more devoted to their work. The moment a person tilted his glass they were at his elbow waiting eagerly with a fresh supply. It was true that he had told Mr. Massoula to keep things moving. He had merely been thinking of other weddings where he had stood around for hours with an empty glass talking to someone whose name he did not know. It was one thing to avoid that and another to hurl the stuff down people's throats every time they opened their mouths.

The sickening idea occurred to him that at this rate it would be all gone in half an hour. For thc third time that day he felt damp and clammy. His emotions were beginning to set up a distasteful system of hot and cold running perspiration.

He decided to go to the marquee and investigate. As he started for the door he tripped over a dog which, he noted, was being followed by another dog. To the best of his knowledge he had never seen either animal before. However, even if they had been his two favorite canines this did not seem a proper place for dogs.

A lovely young creature approached.

"*Mr.* Banks," she cried. "What a darling, *darling* wedding. Kay looked too, *too* beautiful. You should be so *proud*, Mr. Banks. And Buckley's just *divine*. We are all crazy for him. And Mrs. Banks looked too, too—"

"Where the hell are all the dogs coming from?" interrupted Mr. Banks. He had just noted a brown and tan number entering the room through the legs grouped in the French door. It was apparently in search of some friend. "Is this a Bide-a-Wee Home or a wedding?" He wondered if the Buckingham Caterers were beginning to pour his champagne into the neighborhood crossbreeds.

His unknown companion gave a silvery laugh. "Oh, Mr. Banks, that's *cute.* The place does seem to be getting filled up with pooches, doesn't it."

"Listen," said Mr. Banks. "Do me a favor. Get hold of Tommy or Ben, if they haven't left town, and tell them that part of an usher's job is to throw out livestock."

"Oh, I will, Mr. Banks. I will. That's darling." She gave him a look that might have meant anything—but didn't—and disappeared into the crowd. He made another start for the marquee, but the impromptu reunion in the French door had grown to such proportions that he gave it up for the moment and pushed his way about the room at random.

Later he could remember a roar of voices—and people making faces at him—and making faces back at people—but it was a scene which would remain forever out of focus in his memory. Eventually he felt a tug at his sleeve. Kay and Buckley were standing behind him, Kay holding her crumpled train over her arm and grinning.

"Hi, Pops. We're going to get ready now. Don't you want to see me hurl my bridal bouquet?"

He followed them to the front hall while the wedding guests whooped noisily after. Kay and Buckley were already looking down from the landing.

Mr. Banks was astonished to discover an entirely new expression on Kay's face. Vanished the ethereal look she had worn as they started down the aisle. Now of smug possessiveness that sent an unexpected wave of irritation down Mr. Banks' spine.

The maid of honor was jockeying for position under the landing. Kay was waiting for her with the bridal bouquet poised. Small chance for the eager virgins clamoring with outstretched arms, their faces expressing in half-light what glowed so brightly and unashamed in Kay's. It struck Mr. Banks that the accepted belief that men married women was a colossal hoax—they were merely married *by* women.

There was a shrill yelping as the bridal bouquet came sailing over the rail and fell, with its usual precision, into the outstretched arms of the maid of honor. Then Kay and Buckley disappeared around the corner of the stairs followed by the bridal party.

The crowd began to spread out again and Mr. Massoula's walking dispensaries, apparently refreshed by the pause, went into action with renewed enthusiasm. Again Mr. Banks was struck by the need for taking inventory and he turned once more toward the marquee. Ralph Dixon collared him at the French door. He was a lawyer who took two things in life seriously. One was Ralph Dixon, the other the law.

"Hello, Banks," he said.

Mr. Banks wished Ralph Dixon wouldn't call him "Banks." He considered himself equally successful as a lawyer and they were the same age. He realized that the English all addressed one another this way, but he wasn't English and when addressed as "Banks" he always felt like a stage butler.

He should, of course, have said, "Hello, Dixon." Instead he said, "Hi, Ralph."

"Nice wedding," said Mr. Dixon and apparently considered that he had thereby paid his tribute to the amenities. "Got a minute?"

"Well, the fact is—" began Mr. Banks with a sinking heart.

"It's about that Shatton matter," said Mr. Dixon. "I don't like to be on the other side of the fence from you, Banks, and I think in this case you're all wet. Now just take the facts."

Mr. Dixon then took the facts and laid them out in orderly rows for Mr. Banks' appraisal. A waiter appeared with champagne and as Mr. Banks drank it he suddenly realized that he did not have the slightest idea what Ralph Dixon was talking about. Perhaps this stuff was getting him. He decided to hold his glass quietly and not touch it for a few minutes.

It was all the same to Mr. Dixon, however, whether Mr. Banks understood him or not. He was marshaling his facts and he would have marshaled them with equal gusto if Mr. Banks had been stretched out insensible on a window seat.

"Heidee-ho, heidee-ho. This *is* a party." A pasty-faced gentleman with jowls like a bloodhound injected himself into the summation. It was Uncle Peter, who had come all the way from Sioux City and was obviously not going back empty. Although Mr. Banks had always privately considered Uncle Peter an old bum, at the moment he was delighted to see him.

"Peter," he said. "I want you to meet a friend of mine, Mr. Dixon. Ralph, this is Peter Quackenbush—he's related to my wife," he explained parenthetically.

Mr. Dixon glared silently at Uncle Peter and gave evidence of being about to move away. This would have been merely a transference of evils for Mr. Banks. Danger made him alert. Within the bat of an eye he had disappeared through the French door.

Judging by the crowd in the living room he had expected to find the marquee half empty. On the contrary, it was also jammed with people. The temperature was midway between that of a Turkish bath and a greenhouse.

Mrs. Banks had hired a push-and-pull man to circulate among the guests. Mr. Banks discovered him standing unnoted by one of the tent poles, dressed in his intrepretation of a Neapolitan costume, obviously bursting his lungs and his instrument in the public weal. The din in the tent was so great, however, that he might have been squeezing a blacksmith's bellows and gargling his throat. Mr. Banks wondered why, from an economic viewpoint if no other, his wife had considered it necessary to pay someone to add to a confusion which was contributed gratis.

In spite of the Buckingham boys, who were getting rid of Mr. Banks' champagne just as eagerly here as in the house, there was a crowd of eager customers in front of the bar table. He shouldered his way in and tried to get the attention of one of the sweating men behind it. They were engrossed in snatching bottles from huge tubs of icewater, uncorking them and dividing their contents between massed glasses and the tablecloth.

A strange man next to Mr. Banks watched them with the tense concentration of a bird dog. "Lousy service," he said finally to Mr. Banks in what was obviously meant as a friendly opening.

"Terrible," agreed Mr. Banks.

"About on a par with the champagne," said the stranger.

"I thought the champagne was pretty good," said Mr. Banks defensively. "For American champagne, of course."

"Bilge," said the genial stranger. "Sparkling bilge. I regard all champagne as bilge, but some comes from a lower part of the hold than others. This comes from just over the keel." The young man took two dripping glasses and backed away.

Mr. Banks beckoned to one of the barmen.

"How is the champagne holding out?" he asked.

The barman looked at him coldly. "O.K., O.K.," he said. "Don't worry, mister. You'll get plenty." Mr. Banks found himself blushing, then he remembered the old Chinese proverb and decided to relax and have a look at the garden. It would be interesting to find out if it were also filled with people.

His progress through the tent was slow. Near the entrance he spotted Miss Bellamy talking to a group from the office. She detached herself and came toward him balancing a glass of champagne without too great success. He had never seen Miss Bellamy dressed like this before and it rather startled him. He didn't know just what to say, but she was obviously quite at ease.

"Boss, we certainly put on a wonderful wedding. Yes, sir. If I do say so, it was beautiful. I want to drink a toast. I want to drink a couple of toasts. First, to the bride. Say, you were swell coming down the aisle. No one would ever have known you were scared."

"Thank you," said Mr. Banks. Somehow or other this was not the self-effacing Miss Bellamy he had left at the office yesterday afternoon. They drank solemnly.

"And now I want to drink to the best boss in the world. Yes, sir, the finest boss in the world." She had certainly never looked at him quite like that before.

"And I'll drink to the finest secretary," said Mr. Banks, embarrassed.

"Oh, you're just saying that," said Miss Bellamy, her large brown eyes searching his face intently. "You're just making that up, I know you are. Got a cigarette?" As he lit her cigarette he wondered if the world could ever again be forced back into its comfortable old normalcy.

"You got to watch this stuff," said Miss Bellamy, gazing thoughtfully into her glass. "You got to watch it every minute. If you don't—it'll get you. No question about it. Want to know something?" She leaned toward Mr. Banks' ear. "That Miss Didrickson's plastered. She's the new one with the dyed hair. Come on over. The bunch will want to see you. She's a silly ass, though. I didn't like her from the start. She was saying—"

A young man in a cutaway approached. "Mrs. Banks is looking for you, sir. She sounds as if she wants to see you right away."

Relieved to have some objective, Mr. Banks began to fight his way back to the house. He had almost made the exit from the marquee when an enormous woman blocked his way. She was accompanied by a gangling young girl with a mouthful of braces.

"Oh, Mr. Banks, it was such a heavenly wedding. I want you to meet my daughter Betsy. This is Kay's father, dear." Betsy tittered as if she found the idea grotesque. "Humphrey couldn't come." Mr. Banks cast vainly about in his mind for anyone by the name of Humphrey. "He wanted me to tell you how sorry he was. You were *so* nice to ask us. I said to Humphrey, 'That was *so* nice of the Bankses to include us. And to the reception too.' I brought Betsy. I didn't think you'd mind. She adores Kay so and she's been so excited about the wedding. Haven't you, dear?"

Betsy's excitement seemed to have died down since the ceremony. At the moment she looked like a captured German prisoner brought to headquarters for questioning. "Kay looked perfectly beautiful," continued the large woman. "Simply ravishing. And the bridesmaids' dresses—Well, my dear, they were out of another world. I think the whole thing—"

A second young man in a cutaway approached. "Mrs. Banks is sort of tearing her hair out, sir. She said for me to tell you that Kay and Buckley are getting ready to go and where are you."

Mr. Banks made a mumbling noise and forced a passage between the stout woman and Betsy. Mrs. Banks pushed toward him through the crowded room. "Stanley Banks, where have you been? I'm almost crazy. I suppose you've been in that tent telling stories. Now come. Kay and Buckley will be coming down any minute."

Again there was a dense crowd in the front of the house. Mr. Massoula's henchmen moved through it bearing salad bowls filled with confetti. At least they were distributing something inexpensive for the moment. People were self-consciously grabbing handfuls, most of which they immediately let slip through their fingers to the floor. Everyone was watching the stairs tensely as if they expected a couple of whippets to come streaking down and out the door before they could get rid of the balls of damp paper in their clenched fists.

This was the scene that Mr. Banks had visualized so often during the last twenty-five years; the moment when his first-born would come running down a broad staircase on the arm of a muscle-bound stranger, to disappear from his life forever—at least in the role of his little daughter.

When he had stood at the foot of other people's staircases waiting to throw damp paper at their daughters, his heart had been warm with sympathy for the fathers of the brides, who strolled with such brave nonchalance among their guests. He had hoped that he would have equal courage when his time came.

Now that it was here he only felt numbness. He had rehearsed it all so often in his mind—he had hugged his private sadness to his bosom so many times—that its fulfillment was less real than its anticipation.

A bridesmaid peered around the corner of the stair landing, grinned sheepishly and disappeared. Someone cried, "Here they come," as if it were a horse race. Then Kay and Buckley, conspicuously new in every detail, were tearing across the landing and down the final flight of stairs with that hunched, headlong look of charging moose that Mr. Banks had observed in all brides and grooms coming downstairs.

They were on the front walk now, their shoulders covered with confetti, their heads still lowered between their shoulders. Mr. Banks was right behind them, running in form, the ushers and bridesmaids bringing up the rear in full cry. Buckley's car stood at the end of the walk. It was amazing how these details fell into place against all odds. They were in. Kay leaned through the open window while Buckley fought off ushers on the other side.

"Good-by, Pops. You've been wonderful. I love you."

The car lurched forward. Mr. Banks revolved off the rear mudguard into the arms of a bridesmaid. "Good-by, good luck." They were already half a block away.

Golden Wedding

By Ruth Suckow

A Golden Wedding is a summing up of two life experiences. Husband and wife have done their share of the world's work. Children have departed. The old folks wonder whether they have been forgotten. Then their day arrives. Golden Wedding is one of the greatest of family days.

"You ought to change your clothes, pa."

"What you in such a hurry to get my clothes changed for?"

"Well, you want to be ready when George comes in, don't you?"

"Aw, he won't get in to-day. How can he get the car through all this snow?"

"He will, too. Didn't they invite us out there?"

"Yeah, but they didn't know it was goin' tuh snow like this."

"You go now and put your other clothes on."

He grumbled, but finally obeyed—which was just like him.

Yes, but why did he always have to act this way? He had been doing it ever since they were married. He went through just so much grumbling first before he would do anything that he knew he must. It was the same thing over again every time they went anywhere; and all her prodding hadn't done any good that she could see.

"Won't get in to-day." That was just like him, too. If he knew that she was counting on anything, he had to hold out and belittle it, raise objections. He never wanted to admit that anything was going to turn out right. He always had good arguments to oppose to her faith, which he declared didn't take any account of the facts. But she still held to this blind faith of hers, and he to his objections. Sometimes things worked out her way; sometimes his. She pulling ahead, he pulling back. But the pulling had amounted to this much in fifty years—that he usually gave in in the end; and that she was a little worried in spite of her hopeful assertions that things were going to justify her belief.

So that now she did have to admit to herself that it was snowing hard. She was sure that George would come . . . but her eyes screwed up anxiously as she looked out over the plants at air thick with misty flakes. It looked as if it wasn't going to stop all day. The covered plants and peony-bushes just outside were big clumps of whiteness. Fine dark twigs stuck out from the snow humped over the bending raspberry-bushes. When she peered down the street, she could barely see the willow-trees at the farther end, bluish and dim. Few passers-by came down this little side street where the old Willeys lived. The glimmery softness of the white road showed only two crooked tracks from a morning milk-wagon that were already nearly filled, and as white as all the rest of the world. Just the same, she believed that George was going to get in somehow.

Mr. Willey came back into the room.

She looked up sharply, and cried in despair: "Oh, pa, why did you have to go put on that old necktie?"

"What old necktie?"

"Oh, you know what I mean! That old thing that I should think you'd be ashamed to wear around the place any more, let alone where we're going to-day. Go and put on your nice one—the one Jenny sent you for Christmas."

"Whatta I wanta put that on fur! To ride out in the snow?"

"Snow!" she scoffed. "How's the snow going to hurt it? Can't you cover it up? Now you go and put that on. Try and look decent for once, to-day. You don't know who may be there to see us."

"Yes, you keep talkin' about that. Who do you think's goin' to be there?"

"Well, pa, you know the dinner's for us."

"Oh, I guess they ain't such a whole grist of folks comin' out in all this snow jest to eat dinner with us."

"You go and put that other tie on."

He went. But her small frail hands, bluish and veined, shook a little at the crocheting with which she was trying to fill in the time. Her eyes moistened, and her mouth tightened into a childish grimace of weeping. Why did pa have to be so mean—and just to-day? They knew each other with such terrible intimacy that each had an uncanny perception of just what tiny things could hurt the other. Pretending this dinner wasn't going to amount to anything; depreciating her proud glory as a bride of fifty years; bringing up the sense of all the intimate, dingy happenings to tarnish the splendour of this occasion. Putting on that old tie to-day was a blow at her importance as his wife, at their marriage. He was always insisting upon their age and insignificance . . . and the silent, ghostwhite street, the meagreness of their little yard with the few bushes, the bleak lines of the storm entry, those half-filled wheel tracks—all bore him out. Two old people, out of things, living in a little house off the main road. Denying the significance of their one achievement of continuity.

It made her bitter, too. What did it amount that they had been married fifty years? Pa was so mean. Sentimental thoughts with which she had begun the day—unconsciously framing themselves in her mind in the grandiloquent terms of the town paper—were stringently checked by the terrible familiarity of his attitude. Just then, she didn't see why she *had* been such a fool as to have lived with him fifty years—why anyone should celebrate it.

Oh, well—but then, that was pa. After all, she knew how much the grumbling amounted to. Why did she let herself be so riled by it every time? Her best dress of dark-grey silk, shimmering so nicely in the light from the window, raised the occasion, would not let her feel harsh. She knew that all those objections were partly a defence against the ill fortune of which they had had enough—he was not going to admit that things might turn out well, so that he wouldn't be disappointed again. He had had to make an assertion with that old tie to conceal a sneaking hope that this dinner might be a big affair, with people met to celebrate. Their long years together stretched out before her inner vision. . . . He'd been a pretty good husband after all, had worked hard, hadn't spent his money for drink or run after other women. She supposed you couldn't have everything.

She cried excitedly: "Pa! Here comes George! Now you hurry up and get yourself ready."

But she was the one, after all, who had to scurry to the dresser for a last hairpin to stick into her neat little knob of hair, to refasten her brooch in her lace collar, search for another handkerchief. He was ready, tie and all, and she was still in the bedroom when George, their son-in-law, came stamping in, scuffing the thick soft snow off his big overshoes.

"Ain't you ready, folks?"

"Ma, hurry up! Well, what in thunder's she doing? Thought she was ready an hour ago."

"I didn't know as you'd get here, George."

"Yep—oh, there's lots of ways of gettin' in."

"The old bobs still come in pretty handy, I'll tell ye," Mr. Willey said. "Wrapped up good, grandma?"

"Oh, yes, I know how to bundle." Her voice came muffled through the fascinator that she had wound around her head over a knitted hood. She stepped along blindly behind George, down the covered walk, squinting against the misty flakes, trying to keep hold of the coarse brown hair of George's fur coat . . . feet making soft cavernous dents in the thick snow . . . "Why, there's Reverend and Mrs. Baxter in the bob, ain't it?"

"Yeah, they're going along with us. Can yuh get in, grandma?"

George lifted her over the side of the bob, and with a little scramble she managed to get in. The Methodist minister and his wife were tucked snugly into a corner. Mr. Baxter shouted jovial greetings. Mrs. Baxter smiled and nodded, only glints of eyes showing between squinted eyelids, two little hard red cheeks and a ruddy blob of nose let out of the big scarf tied over her head.

"Get in. Lots of room."

Four ministerial feet in heavy, shining rubbers were hitched awkwardly over the thick robes covering the floor of the bob, through little holes of which stuck bent yellow straws. The old people squatted down stiffly, and Mr. Baxter drew the fur robe over them.

"Well, how's the wedding party?"

"Oh . . . I guess they're all right," Mrs. Willey said with shy pleasure.

"Looks more like a silver wedding than a golden wedding to-day."

"Yes, ain't the snow bad!"

"All fixed back there?" George called.

"All fixed! Let 'er go!"

"Gid-dap!"

The two big horses gave a plunge forward, the bob rocked, tilted up on the edge of the road . . . They passed the snowy willows and got out on the main road, where there were already silvery-smooth bob tracks above the gravel, no ruts to make the women give little shrieks and put out their hands blindly. The horses settled into an even trot.

"Isn't this nice, though?" Mrs. Baxter exulted.

All felt the exhilaration. The strangeness of the snow made the day a festival.

They stopped trying to shout things at one another, getting the wet small flakes in their mouths. They snuggled down on the straw under the fur robe. The bob went softly through the new, pure whiteness. Snow kept falling, gentle as mist—tiny flakes, and big tufted splotches. The road ahead and the road behind were lost—there was only a place of dim white silence, and they moving in it.

"Are we there?"

"Why, I guess we are!"

"I didn't hardly know where we're getting."

The bob trundled over the wooden planks across the ditch and into the drive between the willow-trees that were blue-brown through the snow . . . misty, dreamlike, strange. The place had a festive air, too, because of the magic difference the snow made—the big barn roof white against the shrouded sky; the old wagon standing out there softly covered, rounded, all its stark angles agone.

"Well, I guess I didn't spill anybody out," George said.

They plodded to the house. George had let them out near the back door. They went up the steps, with a great stamping and scuffing—Clara in the doorway urging them in, they protesting that they must "sweep themselves off."

"Aw, it's just the kitchen—won't hurt this floor—come on in."

They went in, brushing and shaking. At once they were enveloped in warmth from the big range, with scents of chicken browning, biscuits, coffee, that their nostrils breathed in with a sharp deliciousness . . . snow melting on their wraps, shaking off in a fine chill spray, making pools on the linoleum. They had a glimpse of Darlene, the youngest girl, at the stove, her face flushed a deep hot rose under the brown hair. Many dishes about. . . .

"Oh, don't stay in here!" Clara was urging. "No, your things won't hurt anything. Ain't the first time there's been snow in this house to-day."

Mrs. Baxter and Mrs. Willey found themselves pushed into the chilly downstairs bedroom, where they unwrapped scarfs and fascinators, and where Mrs. Baxter—with apology and an alert glance at the door—yanked up her skirt and revealed black woollen tights which she tugged off her portly legs.

"Didn't know but what the snow might get in," she panted. "So I thought I'd come prepared. I guess I won't shock you ladies getting these off—hope none of the men'll look in here—might see a sight—"

"They ain't around," Clara said comfortingly. "That's just all right—just the thing to wear."

Clara stood until the wraps were off. She was heated, so that her greyish-brown hair looked dry and sheeny above her flushed face. She wore a bungalow apron. And yet she looked festive, too. Extra clean, her mother thought, with her fat arms bare to the elbow, her perspiring neck.

"Well, if you've got everything you want—"

"Oh, yes! Don't pay any attention to us, Clara. I'll come out and help you just as soon as I get my things off."

"No, now, ma. You go in the parlour and visit with Mrs. Baxter. I don't want either of you in the kitchen. Minnie'll help me."

"Oh, is Minnie and John here?"

"Yes, they're here. Minnie's here and the rest are coming."

"Well, I guess we'll have to obey," Mrs. Willey said with a pleased flattered laugh.

They went into the parlour and seated themselves nicely. Mrs. Willey bent down to pick off a tiny straw clinging to her grey silk dress. Then she folded her hands and rocked.

She had half expected all along to find people here. And she saw no one but Clara and Darlene, and her daughter-in-law Minnie, who peeped in a moment. But the minister's family being here made it all right to have worn the grey silk—justified her in having ordered the necktie. Mrs. Baxter had on a dark-blue taffeta that rustled as she rocked.

All the same, the old lady could sense an air of preparation. The odours in the kitchen, that quick, half-realized glimpse of dishes . . . Even the bedroom had been specially clean; a glossy white scarf on the dresser, and the tatting-edged pillow shams. Clara had her best things out. The dining-room door was closed. Yes, and in the parlour too the chairs were set so neatly. The perfect order of the mission table suggested something beyond the everyday. As they rocked, Mrs. Willey was alert for every sound. There was a shrill excited tone in the noise and laughter in the kitchen, abruptly stilled, and then breaking out again; a tramping, a going back and forth that suggested more people in the house than were apparent; children's voices in some upstairs room.

The realization of the occasion brought back heightened memories. As she looked about the parlour, with its new Victrola and Davenport and miscellaneous chairs, Mrs. Willey was on the point of saying to Mrs. Baxter: "This don't look much the way the place did when Mister and I first came here!" But she could not communicate that poignant memory of the old rooms, that was somewhere deep in her mind . . . small, bare, the few walnut furnishings, the feeling of raw openness all around. . . . She rocked. Her eyes had a distant look.

She was excited by the scents from the kitchen, the subdued bustle there.

Shouts came from outside. Mrs. Willey turned quickly to the window —the shouts an answer to her expectation.

A great bob load was coming up to the house, rocking as it turned into the drive—people shouting, waving. Mrs. Willey's hands felt trembling, her heart beat sharply, as she rose. The two old people stood blinking, she gratified, he sheepish, as a confused lot of people came tramping in, and crying:

"Where's the bridal couple? Look at the blushing groom! Well, well, well—many happy returns of the day!"

The dining-room door opened—

"Go in, ma."

"Yes, the bridal couple must lead the way."

The old people protested, as a matter of duty, but inwardly pleased to be pushed in ahead of the others, to sit at the head of the long table. Old Mr. Willey looked sheepish—all this splendour for an old couple like them. But Mrs. Willey was exalted. She saw the room in a heightened dazzle of bright confusion—glitter of tumblers, plates and silver, shine of white and yellow. Laughing, calling, appreciative murmurs . . . and then all of them standing there, suddenly and uncomfortably grave, Mrs. Willey still tremulous with excitement, while the minister gave the blessing, appropriately solemn and loudtoned . . . only one high, unconscious piping from the children's table in the corner.

The company seated themselves. The laughter, the murmurs broke out again.

"My, isn't this lovely!"

"Well, grandma, what do you think of it?"

"Well, I . . . I don't hardly know what to say," the old lady quavered.

The others laughed delightedly.

But as she sat at the head of the table, waited upon, getting served first, gradually things began to emerge out of that first shining confusion. She had known that this would happen, marvellous as it was. She recognized her daughter-in-law Minnie's best table-cloth, pieced out at the farther end (where George sat) with one of Clara's—that table-cloth with a crocheted border, that had been laid away in a chiffonier drawer to be peeped at by admiring women, that had been used only at the weddings of Minnie's daughters. The granddaughters must have brought their best wedding silver in carefully packed baskets. Clara and George had never accumulated any silver. But even more thrilling than this was the festive look of the room, with its decorations—the yellow crepe paper drawn from the centrepiece and tied in bows at the four corners, the yellow tissue paper flowers (Gertrude was the one who had made those) at every place . . . and all the decorations converging significantly toward the centre of the table where a huge cake frosted in yellow, frilled about with paper and flowers, stood under a hanging, ruffly, yellow wedding bell.

She looked about the long, crowded table. They were all there—all the people whose lives were bound up with hers and pa's. Clara and George, Minnie and John, grandsons and grandsons-in-law, "connexions" from Prospect and the country around; even Nels Olson, a prosperous merchant in town now, but years ago the Willeys' hired man. The children at the square table were gleeful, and in their best.

And it was for them—for her and pa. She felt that exalted swelling in her breast, and tears stayed just behind the surface glisten of her eyes. Let pa say again that they were old and left behind, that no one thought of them, their day was over! No, this occasion was as glorious as she had been imagining it, in spite of his pessimistic objections. After all these work-filled years—fifty years—that had seemed at times to be petering out into a small meagre loneliness, to sit here, honoured, receiving again the delicious food and wine of personal recognition. All her people met to do her honour, to show that her life work had counted. . . . There was just one little twinge of disappointment. Robert had not come from Seattle. She had thought against all reason that when she opened the door, she would miraculously find Robert. She was glad she had mentioned it to no one. Pa's scoffing would have been justified.

It showed the grandeur of the occasion that Clara was "sitting down to table" beside George; although she gave hasty uneasy glances toward the kitchen. She had changed her apron, at the last minute, for her best dark green taffeta, above which her fat neck and face were flushed hotly. The granddaughters were waiting on the table, squeezing in between the chairs and the wall with their great platters of fowl, and bowls of gravy, and shining coffee-pot. The meal was like an old-time harvest dinner in abundance—beside the chicken, two big platters of goose that Minnie had cooked at home and brought over warm, and covered, to be heated in

Clara's oven; potatoes, baked beans, escalloped corn and peas, three kinds of bread and biscuits, relishes and jellies and pickles. But there were, beside, the special dishes that marked the importance of wedding and reunion dinners in Prospect and the country around—perfection salad, made the day before by the married granddaughters, great biscuit pans full of it; mayonnaise; and the women guests at the table had already discerned that the huge, yellow-frosted cake was Golden Companion, for which Lottie Disbrow had the community recipe.

The first absorption in food was giving way to a chatter. The children at the small table were yielding pieces of chicken that they had snatched, consenting to wait for "something *awful* good" promised by mothers in a deep whisper. Faces shone and glistened with warmth and food . . . and past the window-panes drifted the last aimless flakes of the big snowfall.

There were satisfied, admiring comments on the food. . . . "Ain't these biscuits just fine! You make these, Clara?" "Yes. I was afraid they wasn't going to come out good." "Oh, they're lovely!" . . . "More chicken? Well, sir, I've had a good deal already. Do you let folks have their third piece?" A worried "Oh, now, Henry, you want to be careful. You've had enough." "Aw, go on and take it, Reverend. You need that drumstick."

John said expansively: "Don't pay any attention to the womenfolks! This is the time when a fellow can eat all he pleases. Can't have a golden-wedding dinner every day."

"Yes, but then you'll expect your wives to run around for you maybe half the night because you eat too much again," Minnie put in smartly.

All the wives murmured: "I guess so!" And laughed significantly.

But the men said: "Time enough to worry about that afterwards. Anyway, I can't see but you're eatin' plenty yourself."

Talk, clatter of dishes, shrill voices of children, babies waking and wailing in the bedroom. Mrs. Baxter said: "It seems a shame to eat, and spoil this lovely table." But it was spoiled now—littered—the hand-painted jelly dishes messy, the salad bowls nearly empty, some of the crepe paper torn and pushed askew. The dinner was ending. The girls brought heaping dishes of home-made ice cream with chocolate sauce.

"Oh, my! Look at this! I don't know where the room for it's coming from, but I'll have to find some."

Mr. Willey muttered: "What's this stuff on here?"

Mrs. Willey nudged him. "Pa! That's choc'late."

"Huh! Well, I dunno—"

"You rather have yours without, grandpa?"

"No, no!" Mrs. Willey protested, shocked. "He'll eat it this way. It looks lovely." She gave him a look.

The women perceived—felt in the air—what was about to come. But some of the men took up their spoons, began to eat, were reprimanded by their wives, and looked about, belligerent and then subdued. Mrs. Willey knew what it meant. Her small, faded mouth quivered. Clara was getting ready, half apologetic, to make the people listen. Gertrude stood behind her grandmother's chair, smiling.

"Sh! Sh!"

Clara got up with difficulty, squeezed between the table and her chair. Her voice had the toneless quavering of one unaccustomed and half ashamed to speak before others.

"Friends . . . and—a . . . As long as this is our mother's and father's golden-wedding day, maybe now we better ask mother to cut the wedding cake."

Mr. Baxter relieved the silent moment that followed by a loud, cheerful, "That's right—let the bride do it." There were repetitions of "bride"; and they all laughed and murmured. Gertrude handed her grandmother the large knife; and the old lady, her hands trembling slightly, cut through the Golden Companion. The first wedge came out, moist, rich and yellow. They applauded. There were shouts of laughter when Mr. Baxter found the old maid's thimble in his piece. Lottie Disbrow had marked the location of the ring, and Gertrude gave that piece to her grandmother.

"I'm gonna be rich—look, mamma, I'm gonna be rich!" one of the children cried, holding up the coin.

The wedding cake was passed about the table. The groom's cake—a dark, spicy fruit cake—was brought in already cut. Plates of angel food were passed about—"Better eat this, girls," the women told the unmarried girls, "and save your wedding cake to sleep on!" Now all the table relaxed into a warm, easy, chattering exhilaration. Even old Mr. Willey had dropped his defences, carried along by the spirit of the hour.

How did everyone feel it now? But those still talking relapsed into startled silence. Throat-clearings. The men looked down, rigid, embarrassed. The children turned with round, bright, fascinated eyes. Mrs. Willey's heart pounded. Clara's eyes began to water.

The Reverend Mr. Baxter rose, tapped on his glass with his knife.

"Sh—sh!" to the children.

Silence.

Mr. Baxter began to speak. Although he spoke in the slow, portentous voice that he used for the texts of his sermons, only significant phrases stood out, echoed and diminished in the minds of the listeners . . . "met together to-day . . . do honour to these two people . . . long journey together . . . achievement . . . God's blessing on this couple . . ." Words irradiated by the winter sunshine that came through the windows now, sparkling off the snow, and striking iridescence from the silver and glass, the glossy table-cloth, the warm shining heads of the listening children. The old couple at the head of the table took on a deep significance into which a lifetime of meaning was compressed, brought to a sudden realization. . . . "And now I have been asked by all these good people to present this token of the occasion. And may it always bring to your minds, Mr. and Mrs. Willey, the memory of the affection of your children and neighbours, and their appreciation of your having reached this day."

He took the package that Gertrude handed him. Old Mr. Willey had to receive it—unwrap it—show to everyone the silver loving-cup. There were applause, hand-clappings, nose-blowings. A telegram from Robert was read. The sun shone warmly on the silver cup with its gilt lining, flashed off the two handles. The old lady could only murmur that she "thanked her dear children and neighbours." But the old man was flushed, carried beyond himself. He saw everything heightened . . . and his vision, like his wife's, stretched back and back to scenes so long ago that he scarcely knew how to communicate his sense of them. But he had to say something if she didn't.

He remembered when he first came out to Ioway, he said. The bob ride had brought back old times. Things that the children had thought old stuff, the tales that old men tell sitting on benches in front of the hotel—they listened to now with a sense of drama and event, of time passing. When he talked about the wedding day fifty years ago, the children heard him with delighted appreciation.

"In them days, we didn't go to all this fuss we do now for weddings. When folks wanted to git married, they just hitched up and drove into town, and that ended it. Well, sir, I was thinking what kind of a day that was. Not snowy—one of them real muddy days—and I tell ye, there *was* mud in those times! You fellers talk about roads, but you don't know what roads can be. Well, sir, we'd fixed on that day—and I was willing to put it off—but *she'd* got her mind set on it and of course it had to be. . . . We took my brother Luke's team, and him and me and her and

Luke's girl—girl he had then, name of Tressy Bowers, she went out to Dakoty later—we started, with the horses all slicked up and their manes combed out, to drive into Prospect. Well, good enough goin' for a ways—and then jest out here beyond where Ted Bloomquist's place is now, we run into one of them mudholes about three foot deep. Mud splashes up—girls screeches—and them two horses gits stuck so they can't pull out. Well, then the womenfolks had a time! They don't want us to git out in the mud because it'll spoil our wedding clothes, and they ain't nothing else for us to do but set there until somebody comes along. Well, a fellow did, and he helped us, and we got out.

"But then me and Luke's about as muddy as the team, and the women thought it was awful to go into town to the preacher's that way. So before we reached town—right down there by the crick, in what's Hibbert's pasture now—they made us fellers git out; and the girls they took sticks and whatever they could find handy, and tore a big chunk out o' their underskirts—women wore plenty o' clothes them days—and they made us fellers stand up and hev the mud scraped off our pants—and then when we's cleaned up a little, we went along to the preacher's and got married."

"And it's lasted quite a while!"

"Yes, sir. He done a good job of it."

Mrs. Willcy was flustered, protesting— "You know it wasn't near as bad as that! What do you want to go and tell such things for?"—blushing when the underskirts were mentioned. In the warm, relieved, easy glow that followed, the loving-cup was passed about the table and admired. The names of all the givers were engraved upon it; and beneath the names of Asa Willey and Angie Pilgrim Willey, the two dates: 1874–1924.

Finally it was time to leave the table. The granddaughters would not let the older women into the kitchen. Carrie Gustafson had been called to help out with the dishwashing. The others went into the parlour, all the women urging one another to take the best rockers; looking out of the windows and commenting that the day had "turned out nice" after all. They were moving still in that warm, easy exhilaration that came from food and coffee and that high moment at the table. "Tired, grandma?" "Oh, no, I ain't tired." The sun glistened on the snow. Mrs. Willey sat in an ease in which it seemed that she could never know what fatigue was—strangely free, her spirit exulting, doing what it pleased with her body. The great dinner was over, but the day was not ended yet.

There were things to come. And then there would be the afterglow lingering for a long, long time.

"Guess we'll have a little music, folks," George said.

They listened, sentimentally gratified, when a mellifluous barytone with an overdone accent sang *Silver Threads Among the Gold*. But the murmuring and chatter, the pleas and shouts of children, sounded above the music—George's few "good" records, conscientiously played: *Il Trovatore, A Perfect Day, The Last Rose of Summer*. George began to yield to the children's pleas for "This one, grandpa," "Play this one, Uncle George"—*Morning in the Barnyard* and the "Uncle Josh" monologue. The room was filled with a high noise of chatter, laughter, resolute music, sounds from the kitchen . . . and outside, the sun sparkling off the great, untouched spread of snow across the yard and fields.

Shouts from the road, and then a running to the windows. Charlie, one of George's boys, came tramping into the house, ruddy-faced, in his sheepskin coat . . . from somewhere a jingle of sleigh-bells. The girls followed him from the kitchen, dish towels in their hands.

"Well, grandma and grandpa, do you want a sleigh-ride? Team's out here ready."

The others urged, laughing, excited, pushing toward the dining-room windows from which—through a blinding sparkle—they could see the sleigh. The young men were out there, patting the horses. They had got the Tomlinsons' old two-seated sleigh, that had been packed away in a musty, cluttered barn corner for years. It was furbished, decked with sleigh-bells the boys had found somewhere; John's big horses stamping, shaking and turning their heads to see where the jingling came from, letting out clouds of silvery vapour.

"It ain't cold—just grand! Better go, grandma."

"Take your wedding journey!"

The bedroom was full of women laughing, encouraging, helping to bundle her into heavy wraps—shouting to George to get his fur coat for grandpa. There was discussion as to who should have the place beside Charlie. "You go, Clara," "Oh, no—some of the rest of you." "Mr. and Mrs. Baxter—" "Oh, no, no! Let some of these little people." "Me, mamma! I want a sleigh-ride!" "No, you children can have lots of fun here." "I think Clara'd ought to go. She's the only one ain't had a ride to-day." Clara would not go without Minnie. The two plump women were packed into the front seat, with Charlie squeezed between them. The old Willeys had the place of honour in the back of the sleigh.

All the company flung on wraps, shawls, whatever they could pick up, and hurried out to the back steps to watch the sleighing party leave. The women hugged their arms in their shawls, squinted against the sharp flash of sun from the drive and glistening shed roofs.

"Look-a there! Ain't that great?"

They pointed to the placard that the boys had fastened with a white streamer to the back of the sleigh—

JUST MARRIED

"Get back—get those kids back. These horses are rarin' to go."

The clustered company waved, shouted, as the sleigh started with a jerk and frosty jingle of bells; watched it out of sight around the turn; then went back to the house, away from the white emptiness in which the new sleigh-tracks had left steely marks.

Bobs had been along this road since it had stopped snowing, making the going easier. The jingling bells, the sky a dazzle of blue after the snowfall . . . The world they were passing through was as shining, remote, as those ethereal, silvery hills and thickets drawn on frosty window-panes. The sunlight glittered on the horses' smooth-curving backs. The sleigh runners left narrow, hard, flashing tracks. The low rounded hills were crusted deep with sparkling white. Corn stalks, humped with snow, shone stiff and pale gold. They had to close their eyes against that blinding radiance.

They drove into Prospect—not down that little street where the old people lived, but "right through the main part of town." People halted at the sound of bells, laughed at the placard, waved and called out greetings. The sleighing party, warmed still by the happy intoxication of the wedding dinner, responded hilariously.

"What's this—an elopement?" Judge Brubaker shouted.

"We've got to stop for you to have your pictures taken," Clara turned to say.

"Oh, no!" Mrs. Willey protested.

But she liked it—even grandpa liked it.

They climbed the sloping wooden stairs to the gallery, covered with thick soft snow. The photograph would be in the Des Moines paper. "Prospect Couple Celebrate Golden Wedding." It would have their names—tell about the loving-cup, and Robert's telegram. The long room of the gallery, filled with snowy light, had the same dazzle as the street to-day.

The old man was lifted above his gloom and forbodings. He raised his wife's hand clasped in his, and shouted back at people. A crowd of little boys swarmed out into the road, making for the sleigh with ludicrous determination. "Hop on, boys!" he called jovially. They clung until a jerk at the corner threw them off the runners; and they still trailed the sleigh for a block or two.

"Well, was the ride nice, grandma?"

"Oh, it was fine!"

"Get cold?"

"Not a bit cold. . . . I guess I am a little chilly now, though."

And as she trudged up through the heavy snow to the farm-house again, she realized that the afternoon was late, the best of the sunshine over. When she went into the house, too, there was a different feeling. The big bob-load of people had left during the sleigh-ride. Now there were only the family themselves—the granddaughters sitting wearily in the parlour after their long siege in the kitchen. "Oh, children, be still awhile. You make such a racket." Carrie Gustafson was plodding about in the kitchen doing the last of the cleaning up.

Standing in the bedroom, taking off her many wraps, Mrs. Willey realized that the chill of the winter day had sunk into her. Her eyes were reddened, her small faded lips were blue. Her thin frail hands felt stiff and chilled.

"I guess you did get kind o' cold, grandma."

"Oh, not so very. It was awful nice."

They sat about in the parlour, where the grandchildren were playing with undiminished liveliness, even wilder than at noon. The older people were tired. The men talked, and the women, in two camps. Then some of the women went out to the kitchen to "set out a few things for supper."

"Now, don't go to a lot of trouble. We don't really need a thing after all we've et."

"Oh, the men'll want something. We'll just put on what's left."

But when they went to the table, the cold goose and chicken, the warmed-over potatoes, the different bits of salad, tasted good after all. There was a revived cheer, an intimacy in gathering around the remnants of the great meal after the outsiders had left. The glossy table-cloth had spots of jelly. The yellow bell still hung there; but the flowers and crepe paper and wedding cake were gone. Plates of angel food and fruit cake, a little crumbled, were put on. The coffee tasted better than anything else.

Under the old woman's smile lay tremulous fatigue. She could scarcely sit at the table. As soon as the meal was over, George hitched up the bob to take the old people and some of the grandchildren home.

"Well, sir, it's been quite a day!"

Now they had seen too much to notice the whiteness of the fields that they passed, the willows dim and motionless. The straw was warm under the robe on the floor of the bob. The plop-plop-plop of the big horses' hoofs was magically soothing . . . and the slight jolt and sway of the bob, going over rough places in the road, turning corners. . . .

They were all surprised when the bob stopped.

"Are we here?"

"Sure. Where'd you think we was?"

"Why, I didn't hardly know."

"Wait a minute, grandma, I'll lift you out."

George lifted her over the side of the bob. When he put her down, her legs felt stiff and queer, and she could scarcely make her feet move. She looked with a kind of wonder at the house standing bleak, silent, no shine from the windows, no smoke from the chimney. She entered it with the feeling of a traveller from splendid scenes who still carries a trace of their radiance with him to shed upon the familiar home. The little entry was cold.

"Wait a minute," George said. "I'll get your fire going for you."

"Oh, you needn't to bother, George."

"Sure. Only take a minute."

The sound of his heavy boots, the crackle of wood and rattle of coal, made a cheerful bustle. "There! I guess she'll warm up now." Then he was gone. Shouts of goodbye from the bob—it trundled off down the snowy street, around a corner.

It seemed as if the day could not be over. But they were in the house together. There was nothing for them to do, after all, but to go to bed.

Their bedroom was chilly.

It took the old woman longer to put away all her cherished best things—her silk dress and lace collar and brooch. He was in bed long before she was, and impatient. She wanted to linger. The silk dress kept the feeling of occasion. There was still a sense of exaltation—a jumbled memory of the dinner, the shining table, the jangle of bells and the sparkling snow, the greetings along the street.

But the old pieces of furniture, set with a meagre exactness in the chilly room, exerted the long-known influence of the everyday. After all, it was this that they must come back to. The day had been fine, but the day was over and would not come again. Now, when they were alone, they had so little to say. Their room was too close, too familiar. Their knowledge of each other was too intimate for their speech to go outside its daily boundaries—they were afraid of that. They fell so quickly into the old ways with each other. She struggled against admitting this. "The cake was nice, wa'n't it?"

"Hm?"

"The cake. It was nice."

"Um. Yeah. Ain't you nearly ready?"

"It was nice of the children to plan it for us that way, a surprise like that."

. . . But it was no use. He would never talk about things. He was pulling her down to the old level again. She folded away the lace collar, put the brooch in the small jeweller's box with her watch chain and an old ring. She would have liked to go over the whole day, picking out and holding up the intimate and significant details—but he wanted the light out, wanted to get to sleep. She was softened toward him, thinking of that moment on the snowy street when he had lifted their two hands. She was not ready to let the day go. Why couldn't pa ever talk things over with her? He'd talk more to anybody than to her.

She felt the still, frosty wonder of the night, as she stood a moment at the small window. And because she could not share this—felt so helpless—a little old, thin bitterness seeped through her proud exaltation, tincturing it with the familiar quality of every day. . . .

He turned over restlessly. "Well, ma! Ain't ye ever comin' to bed?"

"Well, can't you give me time to put away my things?"

"Hmp . . . 'time'!" And other mutterings, half intelligible.

But when she put out the light and climbed into the creaking bed beside him, he was at ease. He soon went to sleep. She lay beside him, awake for a long time.

The irritation died away into calm, and she lay holding in the solitude of her own mind deeply felt, wordless things . . . as she had done in countless other nights; holding quiet both the beauty and the bitterness, encompassing them in the tranquillity of her comprehension . . . not so ill content, after all, that hc should drop off childlike to sleep, and leave her and those incommunicable thoughts alone.

Funerals

By Lloyd C. Douglas

For all its sadness, a funeral was a recognized family occasion. Relatives came from afar. The services took place according to ritual. After it was over, friends brought baked chicken and refreshments to the family residence. In this selection Lloyd C. Douglas, a minister and the son of a minister, draws on his memories of many typical midwest funerals.

My papa was in great demand for funeral services; and, if the weather wasn't too bad, he would take me along. Nearly all funerals, at that time, were held in a church, and the graveyard was always an important part of the church property; an appropriate place for it, I think. The "funeral parlor" and the secular, commercialized, noisily advertised cemetery were yet to appear.

Well within the scope of my lifetime there have been fundamental changes in our general attitude toward the dead. I hope it will not depress you if I speak of them.

Today, if there is a death in the family, by natural causes, the physician or the nurse or a neighbor phones a mortician who arrives in an ambulance with a promptness exceeded only by the Fire Department. The family, still upset emotionally by their bereavement (for, no matter how long the loved one had been ill, the immediate relatives are never quite prepared for the shock), have been herded into a room where they will be unaware of proceedings. The mortician's men quickly and quietly tiptoe out of the house with the so recently vacated tenement of clay; and by the time the family strolls back to the bedchamber, everything has been put to rights. It is as if father or mother or sister Mamie or little Jimmy had never lived there.

And that night, and the next one, sister Mamie (we will say) who had been sick so long that she dreaded to meet strangers, shares communal lodging with a dozen or more in a sort of public dormitory for the dead.

Now I fully agree with you that the real Mamie, who was Mamie, is gone; and that her frail little body is not our precious Mamie at all. But this modern practice of permitting our dead to be grabbed up, while still warm, by total strangers, and hustled at top speed to a place of business, to be impersonally operated on by embalmers and beauticians, is the most cold-blooded performance that our era of efficiency and assembly-line production has achieved.

Of course the old way of handling these sad affairs was immeasurably worse. There were a couple of days when mortality had much the best of it over any calm consideration of the spiritual Life Eternal. The home was full of the confusion of distant relatives, friends of the family, neighbors, and comparative strangers who had come out of curiosity, expecting to be shown the corpse, preferably by the next of kin, who was thoroughly worn out before the torture was ended.

I think it would be a good thing if every church had a little chapel where the remains of our departed could be taken, after having been embalmed in the privacy of the home. That might help to solve the dilemma. As the matter stands today, the Church, which should be prepared to offer the physical equipment and spiritual counsel so urgently needed on such occasions, is missing a great opportunity to be of service.

The typical country funeral of sixty years ago was an event of general public interest.

Papa and I would drive first to the bereaved home and head the long procession of buggies and carriages to the church. Usually the remains of the deceased would be conveyed in a hearse provided by an undertaker from a neighboring town who was primarily a furniture dealer. In that case he would have brought a coffin with him.

At the church door, everybody but the drivers would disembark. Papa would get out and I (feeling very important) would drive to the first vacant hitching rack; and, having made sure our horse wouldn't get into trouble, I would slip into one of the rear pews. The church would be full; and in one of the "Amen corners" (a group of about four pews on either side of the pulpit platform) a choir of twenty or more adults, mostly young farmers' wives, would be ready to go into action at the appearance of the funeral cortege.

It would be entering now, Papa leading; and the choir would shrilly blast the peace of the countryside:

Uh—sleep in JEEZ—ZUZ—Bless—ud sleep,
From which none EV—VER wakes to weep.

By now the coffin, in the hands of a half-dozen husky farmers, is squeezing through the narrow aisle, followed by the close relatives, in the order of their relationship, the men leaving their hats on. I do not know why the men kept their hats on. Papa thought the custom might have originated with the idea that the male relatives were so stricken with grief that they forgot to take their hats off.

I know that my papa never wilfully tried to make these sorrowing people cry. What he had to say was spoken in calmness and reassurance. But it was obvious that the choir would be contented with nothing less than an emotional storm. In their opinion, that's what funerals were for; to give the bereaved a chance to cry it all out.

Indeed it was common practice, in the country, for an officiating minister to stress the family's loneliness and "the vacant chair" until the whole congregation would have lost all control of its emotions, and would be howling like dogs.

Papa used to tell us of an old "Pennsylvania Dutch" preacher who specialized in such performances. Once, according to Papa's recollection, the good old man, while "preaching the funeral" of an octogenarian, said, "Now ven you get home, vadder vill not be dere. You vill set down to dinner, and vadder vill not be dere. You vill go to vadder's bedroom to see dat he is comfort—able, and vadder vill not be dere. Everywhere dere vill be a lackancy!"

But I must get on—and out of this gruesome subject. I'm half-sorry now that I ever got you into it, though I do think it is of quite important psychological interest.

Now the funeral sermon is ended and it is time to "view the remains." Beginning with the rear pews, presumably occupied by those farthest removed from the close neighbors, long-time friends and the relatives, the audience marches slowly forward to pass the coffin; mothers lifting up bewildered three-year-old tots for their last (and probably their first) look at the deceased.

This seems an endless business. The tension mounts as the procession begins to draw upon the forward pews containing cousins once or twice removed. Now, at last, the immediate family huddles about the coffin, in a complete breakdown. More likely than not, the cold face is kissed. I have seen a mother tuck a warm shawl around the throat and shoulders of the departed.

There is more singing: "Shall We Gather at the RIV—VER?"

We are out in the cemetery now, at the graveside, where a great heap of black soil and yellow clay is held back by a pile of fence rails. Leather lines, borrowed from some farmer's team, are looped under the coffin, and strong arms lower it into the flimsy pine rough-box, the lid to which quickly follows. Papa reads the conventional "Forasmuch as it hath pleased Almighty God . . . we commit this body to the ground: Earth to earth."

A neighbor, with a shovel heaped high with dirt, would dump it onto the lid of the rough-box, and an anguished cry would burst forth from the family.

"Ashes to ashes."

Another shovelful bounced and rattled on the rough-box, and another wail came from the bereaved.

"Dust to dust."

More dirt and more crying. Then the shovels really went to it with a vim. At least a dozen men joined in the prompt filling of the grave. The fence rails were tossed aside; and, in less time than it takes to tell it, the grave would be shaped to the age-old pattern.

Then everybody grew quiet and Papa would be ready to pronounce the benediction. But before he did that, he would say, "Friends are invited to return to the family residence for refreshments."

Now that it was all over, the community felt an immediate sensation of relief, and made no bones about it. The men, amazingly cheered, strolled out to the hitching racks, discussing their crops on the way. The women, who had barely spoken to one another, ambled out in groups, lightheartedly exchanging news of their families.

At the residence of the bereaved, a dozen or more of the women living in the neighborhood had set long tables in the dooryard, under the trees, loaded with heaping platters of fried chicken, cold baked ham, potato salad, pickled beets, deviled eggs, homemade bread, fruit preserves, every known variety of pie, and beautiful cakes with white icing and glamorized by little red cinnamon drops.

Naturally the women of the family received tender attention. They could smile now. It was a wan, weary little smile, but it was a smile; for they had cried until they could cry no more. And the men of the family, who had been out in the barn, were patted on the shoulder by the neighbors who had put the team away in their stalls and filled their feed-boxes with the right amount of oats. Then the men would gather around the table. They were hungry. Within an hour, you wouldn't have guessed that any of these people had attended a funeral. They had cried it all out. I used to cry, too, even when I had never seen a member of this family before. Some kindhearted woman, seeing the Reverend's little boy with swollen eyes, would bring him another drumstick.

During the thirty years of my own ministry, great changes came to pass in the conduct of funerals. Now, at the appointed hour, a limousine calls for the family. At the mortuary, the casket, surrounded by floral gifts from friends, is already waiting for the service.

The officiating clergyman is ready, too. Perhaps he pauses, before entering the small chancel, to shake hands with the mourners who are tucked away, out of the view of the friends who have come to pay their respects. The funeral service is brief and usually impersonal. When it is ended, all the friends of the family go their way, and the relatives are quietly sneaked out a rear door and into the limousine for the ride to the cemetery. There the earth has been carted away. Rugs, in imitation of green grass, cover all the raw spots on the ground. The grave is lined with some green fabric. The casket is waiting on a mechanical chassis, well covered with flowers. If it is an inclement day, a commodious tent has been erected to keep the weather out.

The minister reads from a little black book, and the casket, almost imperceptibly, apparently of its own volition, begins to descend. (When these gadgets first came in vogue, they frequently got stuck, refusing either to complete the job or back up. On these embarrassing occasions, a male relative would remain to see the matter through, while the rest of the family was packed off home at 30 mph.)

But, assuming that everything is working properly, the casket begins its descent while the minister reads from his liturgy. When he arrives at "Earth to earth," the mortician lets a handful of rose petals flutter down.

Everybody is spared the shock of seeing shovels in action. The bereaved may have wept quietly, but there has been no emotional release; much less emotional collapse.

That is still to come! They take all their unrelieved grief home with them. They take it to bed with them. It may darken their days. It may make them a perplexing problem to their best friends. It sometimes takes them to the psychiatrist.

No; I'm not recommending a return to the old way of dealing with this most painful of all the dilemmas faced by lonely people who have survived their best-beloved. I am sure the old way was much too heart-rending. But the modern way, which refuses to permit any measure of relief and hides away the sorrowing ones from so much as a handclasp and a sympathetic pat on the shoulder, is wrong; all wrong, and nothing less or else than wrong.

The first funeral I ever conducted was held in our church, but the interment was to be in a country graveyard many miles from town. As I had very few country parishioners, I did not own a horse and buggy. The bereaved family was poor. We wanted to spare these good people any unnecessary expense; so the undertaker drove the hearse and I sat perched high beside him.

It was a very hot day. The graveyard, evidently not used much, was overgrown with tall timothy hay. The old caretaker, who apparently hadn't cared very far beyond the call of duty, met our little cortege at the open gate.

"I don't know jest how yer a-goin' t' make out," he 'lowed. "The boys ran into a yallerjackets' nest; and they's a-buzzin' around right thick like at the grave."

But this was no time to abandon the business that had brought us here. We drove on to the graveside. I firmly intend to spare you the details of this event. The committal service was brief and to the point. If I left anything out, there were no complaints. The relatives were too busy fighting yellowjackets to pay much attention to what we had come to do. Nobody lingered.

As boy and man, I think I have seen about everything happen to disturb the orderly procedure of a funeral.

Once, during the early days of my ministry, on the half-mile trip from the church to the cemetery, the team attached to the pallbearers' large conveyance, frightened by the band, ran away.

The deceased, prominent in county politics, had been an incorrigible "jiner." In the procession, far ahead of clergy, hearse, pallbearers, family, etc., marched, in full uniform, the Knights Templar, I.O.O.F., Modern Woodmen, Junior Order of American Mechanics, Elks, Moose, and more.

The frightened horses took off for the country by the shortest route which lay straight ahead. At full gallop they plunged through the long files of marching men who scurried to the fences making no effort to defend themselves with the axes and swords with which they were armed.

At a funeral I conducted, some twenty-five years ago, a belated family of relatives arrived at the cemetery after the casket had been lowered to what had been referred to as its last resting place, and firmly insisted on seeing Auntie. Everybody but the protagonists of this idea thought that it was an immensely foolish thing to do; but the late-comers held their ground. It took a long time, but we did it. A lot of relatives weren't on speaking terms when they left for home.

In that same cemetery I once quite unintentionally lost a whole procession of out-of-town people. In Akron, Ohio, there is an old cemetery, far out in the country when it was established, but more recently encircled by the rapidly growing city. Akron is a hilly place, and this cemetery is an ideal spot to get lost in unless you are familiar with its winding roads. Customarily the undertaker sent a car for me, so I had never paid very close attention to the geography of that burial ground. On this particular occasion, an interment was to be made here by people living some fifty miles away. I was to have the committal service at the grave, and I had phoned my friend the undertaker that I would drive my own car as I had another errand to do immediately afterward.

Someone from the undertaker's establishment met me at the gate and piloted me to the grave. The out-of-town people had already arrived. After the committal service was over, and I had said good-bye to my new friends from a distance, I climbed into my car and drove away. As I proceeded, it began to occur to me that I couldn't recognize anything but the half-dozen cars I saw in my mirror.

Around and around we went, over little hills and through unfamiliar valleys, my pursuers relentlessly keeping up. I indecorously gave my engine more gas and so did the hapless strangers who had a right to believe that I could be trusted to lead them out of their predicament.

Now, to my horror, we began racing through tortuous roads which I recognized! Surely we had been this way before; maybe a couple of times before! Then, to my immeasurable relief, my pursuers left me. I had taken a right turn and they had gone straight ahead. So I turned around quickly and followed them. Eventually they found an exit. If the strangers hadn't become suspicious of my leadership, we might all be driving around in that cemetery yet. I never met any of these people afterward: I never wanted to, though they had impressed me as being well worth a further acquaintance.

Late in my papa's life, one of his old cronies told him a story that amused him very much, apropos of the odd situations which occasionally turn up in the course of a clergyman's life.

There was to be a home funeral service for an elderly person whose church, at the time, was without a minister. A retired clergyman, living in a city some distance away, had promised to come and officiate; but, at the last minute, when the house was full and running over with relatives and friends, a telegram was received, stating that the minister had missed the only available train that would get him there in time.

One of the neighbors remembered that a young clergyman, of another denomination, had just moved into the community; so somebody was dispatched to request his immediate attention to the predicament. The young man cheerfully consented and presently arrived, out of breath but full of importance, to find the house packed and waiting to get on with it.

Without pausing to make inquiries about the deceased, not even knowing whether the departed was a man or a woman, the young man launched upon a beautiful discourse about Death and the Life to Come; but after he had referred to "our transformed loved one," and "the departed spirit," so redundantly that he had begun to feel the urgent need of some more personal pronouns, he edged toward a woman seated within reach of a whisper, and asked, behind his hand, "Brother or sister?" And she replied, "Cousin."

Family Excursion

By Emily Kimbrough

Who can forget the family's first car—what enormous excitement it caused; or the first expeditions in it—the motor which failed to work, the terrified horses along the route, the picnic lunch? One little girl observed it all and remembered such an excursion vividly enough to tell about it with nostalgic detail.

Grandmother Kimbrough called our house one evening about six o'clock. I was washing my hands for supper and I heard Mother answer, because the telephone was in the back hall just across from the bathroom door. It hung so high on the wall that, stretching up to reach the mouthpiece, she always sounded a little breathless. Whenever I talked into it, I had to stand on a chair. All children did. There was a calendar hanging in our kitchen that showed a little girl with yellow curls, and wearing only a pair of panties. She was standing on a chair, and saying into the telephone, so the printing underneath read,

"Is 'oo there, Santa Claus?"

I listened to Mother's conversation, of course, and in a minute or two it was well evident to me that something was going on. I heard her say, "We'll come right up; Hal's home. Don't worry, Mother."

And she hung up. . . .

Mother and Daddy came out the front door, and hurried up the street. I let them get a little ahead of me, and then scuttled after them. It was early Spring, but chilly. Mother had snatched her golf cape off the hat-rack in the vestibule, and was hooking it at the throat as they passed me. I had not stopped to put on any kind of a coat lest I be caught, but I was too excited to feel cold. I knew something was up, and I knew that if I *were* caught I would be given a sharp spank in the rear and sent home. This made the suspense almost unbearable. I passed the Ross's house safely—they were our next door neighbors—and then the Vatets'. After that there was a bad stretch, because there was a vacant field with no protecting shrubbery—nothing to hide behind until clear across Vine Street where Lydia Rich's house stood on the corner.

When Mother and Daddy reached the corner, they saw my two uncles and aunts hurrying along Vine Street, and waited for them. By the time they had all met and started off together, they were so busy talking that it was safe for me to pass the field and cross the street behind them. I was not allowed to cross the street alone, so that if I had been discovered then, I could expect the application of Daddy's bedroom slipper, but not one of them looked back. And by the time we had passed the Richs' and reached the big house itself, I was at their heels like a puppy. They stopped so abruptly in fact, that I very nearly walked up the back of Mother's legs before I could stop myself. She turned around, saw me, and all she said was,

"Out of the way, dear," and pushed me a little, nowhere in particular.

I knew then that whatever had stopped them must be awful, and I raced around in front of them with my heart pounding. I thought it must be something dead on the sidewalk, so I put my hands over my eyes and then looked down between them, but I couldn't see anything. I took my hands away and still I couldn't see anything. I looked back at the family, all of them, and they were staring into the street. There, against the curb, right at the carriage block, was a great, black *thing*. It had a top, with straps at the corners to tie it down. There was a front seat and a back seat. Far in front of the front seat were shining brass lamps. I could not imagine what the contraption was for, unless it was some kind of a couch to go in the Turkish corner of the library, except that it had big wheels.

Grandmother Kimbrough stood on the carriage block, with her back to the *thing*.

Barely five feet two, never weighing more than ninety-six pounds, she was as quick and sharp as a dragon-fly. Her dark eyes were flashing from one member of the family to another. She pushed up her hair off her forehead in a nervous gesture, that soft brown hair which was a constant exasperation to her.

"Why can't it turn gray, the pesky thing?" I heard her demand frequently. "Every respectable woman my age has gray hair. People will think I touch it up."

She folded her arms tight across her chest, a Napoleon on the carriage block I would remember her.

"Your father," she said grimly, "has bought an auto*mo*bile."

Grandfather was standing at the head of the *thing*. He looked very handsome, I thought, and not excited. I had *never* seen him look excited, nor even worried. Once I had heard him say to Uncle Frank, "If you're worrying about that, Frank, then I'll *stop* worrying. One is enough." . . .

Everybody started talking at once. Aunt Huda said you could get coats with bonnets and veils to match. They kept the dust off, and were the latest style. She was going to write to her sister Bertha in New York and ask her to send her an outfit. Aunt Helen was talking to Grandmother, telling her not to be upset, that it would be lovely. She had heard they were very safe, and she knew that Father Kimbrough would be careful. The boys—that is, my father and my two uncles, but I called them that because everyone else did—started over to the automobile itself. They were talking about machinery. Grandfather called out,

"Mr. Lockhart, I would like you to meet my sons, Hal and Frank and Lloyd."

I had not seen that there was somebody on the couch; but a man climbed down from it, and was introduced to us. He had driven the automobile from the factory and was going to stay for two weeks to teach Grandfather, and see that it was all right. . . .

Early in the morning my grandfather rode out to his factory in the machine, the trained expert, Mr. Lockhart, at the wheel. Some time later, about ten o'clock, he telephoned my grandmother and asked if she had been to market. She said that Noah, who was the hired man, was just bringing around Prince. Well, Grandfather told her, if she would care to drive down town in the new auto instead, he and Mr. Lockhart would come for her in about twenty minutes. A mental conflict must have rocked her. There was the danger of the infernal machine, the fact that the night before she had declared she would never set foot in it and Grandfather could go back with it to Kokomo, the knowledge that it was the first one in the town, and the recollection of Aunt Huda saying that it was the most stylish thing you could have, everyone in the East was getting one, her sister Bertha had told her so.

When Grandfather arrived about half an hour later, Prince was back in the barn, and Grandmother was standing on the carriage block. At the sight of him, however, she jumped off and backed away, because *he* was at the wheel and the mechanic from Kokomo was sitting beside him.

"Charles," Grandmother said, "I will not put my foot in this carriage, with you driving. Why, you don't know anything about the crazy thing."

Grandfather told her that he had been driving that morning for two hours, and that Mr. Lockhart considered him extremely apt. Furthermore, he did, after all, build bridges and might therefore be supposed to know something about machinery. The steering contrivance was not unlike driving a horse, once you accustomed yourself to minor differences. But if Grandmother were nervous she had better have Prince brought around again.

Grandmother climbed into the back seat and sat down.

"I will die with you," she said with obscure menace, "and you will always be sorry."

She bounced herself down on the black leather cushion with all the vehemence of her ninety-six pounds and slammed the door, thwarting Mr. Lockhart, who had come round to perform that little courtesy.

Mr. Lockhart reported to Grandfather that she was safely aboard, and Grandfather recited aloud the steps toward putting the machine in motion. The left foot down, the right hand over and back, the right hand then on the steering wheel throttle. And with that a roar convulsed the machine so that it sprang into the air, and stopped dead. Mr. Lockhart got out, went around in front, released an iron bar from a leather loop, ground it a few times and the engine roared again. Grandmother was already out and on her way back to the house. But Mr. Lockhart coaxed her in again. Grandfather called out that he knew exactly the cause of the mishap. It was not the fault of the engine but of his own misjudgment of the allotment of gasoline. The machine moved ahead once more, in jumps, but it kept going. Grandmother grabbed the carriage strap nearest her. They turned the corner on Monroe Street, and she held on with both hands.

A great many people saw them go up Main Street, and witnessed the unusual behavior of Mr. Meeks, the butter and egg man. He was a sturdy man with a round face that was almost as red in the Winter as in the Summer. His hands were red, too, with cracks running up and down across them on both sides. He was a farmer and worked hard but he loved to tell jokes and to laugh, slapping his big red hand down as if he were spanking himself when he was especially tickled. Once a week he brought in butter and eggs to regular customers. When the automobile with Grandfather driving it passed him, he was just getting out of his buggy at the house next to Mr. Bernard's little store. The horse went up over the sidewalk into the yard and one of the shafts of the buggy got stuck between the fence palings. Grandfather called out that he was distressed but couldn't stop. People who didn't see it could scarcely believe what

Mr. Meeks did. He turned around in the yard and shook his fist after Grandfather. Grandmother had her eyes closed in such angry determination that she didn't see it.

Of course Grandmother knew every inch of the way by heart. A railroad track ran along the first cross street beyond Mr. Bernard's little store. This was a branch line of the Pennsylvania Railroad and carried only freight but it did cut right across the town and people always drew in their horses to look up and down before they crossed the track. Grandfather didn't draw in the machine. He was concerned about Mr. Meeks' horse being stuck in the fence and not quite sure, furthermore, of the process of stopping, so he just bumped over the tracks without even slowing down. It jarred Grandmother but she kept her eyes closed. Fortunately there wasn't a freight train coming. . . .

Grandfather came all the way up Main Street with no trouble; none of the horses along the curb shied; he didn't get caught in the trolley track nor have any difficulty about the trolley. The trolley wasn't even in sight. He was very pleased when he got to the corner of Main and Walnut. He even took one hand off the steering wheel to wave at the policeman, whose mouth dropped wide open at the sight of this vehicle. That pleased Grandfather, too. So he turned around and said loudly and cheerfully, "Where do you wish to go, Margaret?"

His voice was so loud and so close that it *made* her open her eyes, and when she saw that his face was turned toward *her*, and not out toward the *road*, she screamed at him,

"Mr. Topps's, Mr. Topps's!"

The shrillness of her tone and her agitation must, in turn, have startled him, for he jumped perceptibly as he turned his head back to the front again. And in the passage he caught sight of Mr. Topps's butcher shop. With a sweep that would have brought around the mighty *Oceanic*, "Greyhound of the Seas," he swung the wheel, and the machine responded. Up over the curb they went, across the sidewalk, and, cleaving a sharp, broad wake, straight through Mr. Topps's plate glass window to the very dot of their destination, the meat counter itself. There, shuddering, the carriage stopped.

Mr. Topps stood on the other side of the counter about two feet away from the front lamps, his cleaver upheld in his right hand, his eyes staring, his teeth bared in an unnatural grin. There *had* been two or three other people in the shop when the conveyance approached the window, but the sight of Mr. Topps's face had caused them to turn and see what was coming upon them. So they too were now on the far side of the counter with him.

When the clatter of falling glass stopped, Grandfather spoke out of the awesome silence.

"This, Margaret," he announced, "is where you said you wanted to come." . . .

Grandmother Kimbrough was not one of the passengers for a long time after her baptism at Mr. Topps's, though all the rest of the family went whenever they had a chance. Grandfather was hurt by Grandmother's prejudice, so he seldom mentioned it. They had always done everything together, and it was inconceivable to him that she should not share this joy as she had all the others. . . .

It was the Fourth of July picnic that broke down Grandmother's resistance. The daughters-in-law had the idea for it during dinner one Sunday noon at the big house. We could get an early start in the morning, they said, and maybe go ten or twelve miles, eat our picnic and then come home in the afternoon. We ought to get back easily by supper time and be ready for the fireworks afterwards that the neighborhood always had at the big house. The boys were pleased with the idea, but Grandfather said he didn't know. He kept looking down at Grandmother at the other end—we were still at the table. I was holding my breath, praying as hard as I could, and saying at the same time eeny, meeny, miney, mo, on my fingers under the table—to see if we *would* go or not. Mother said she would make the Thousand Island dressing, and bring it in a Mason jar. It was her specialty, and she was proud of it. Everyone said that would be lovely, and we could keep the lettuce in a moist towel and mix the salad at the picnic. Then Grandmother spoke.

"You'd better make the coffee too, Lottie," she said. (That was my mother.) "Yours is the best; we can heat it when we get there. You other girls can bring some cake and some fruit, maybe. Your sponge cake is always nice, Helen. But I'll bring the rest of the dinner."

There wasn't a sound for a minute. The sun through the colored glass windows above the sideboard made little red and blue flickering patterns on the embroidered centerpiece, and everybody seemed to be watching them. I stopped saying my prayers, and counting eeny, meeny, miney, mo, and holding my breath, and looked at Grandfather. He had caught my mother's eye and was grinning at her from ear to ear, with his eyes all puckered up almost as if he were going to cry.

Then everybody began to talk at once. But not a mention about Grandmother riding in the automobile for the first time after that terrible other trip of hers. They just said how wonderful it would be to have one of her real picnic meals—fried chicken they hoped. She didn't know why *not,* she told them sharply, and sandwiches, and some deviled eggs. Erna could bake an apple pie, too, just as well as not—Father and the boys always liked that cold. If we went past the Claypool farm we might telephone ahead and ask them to pull some corn fresh, and we could stop and pick it up on our way. We could roast it, but then that might be awfully hot in the middle of the day.

That started a discussion of which way we would go. Aunt Huda said she thought it would be nice to go out towards Winchester. There were pretty places for picnicking along the way. Uncle Lloyd said the only picnicking places there were too near town where they used to go with the horses. If you drove as far as ten miles in that direction it wouldn't be anything. Uncle Frank said he thought the way to Indianapolis was as good as any. Aunt Helen said she could see that road any time she went over on the Interurban. She wanted something new. And Uncle Frank told her the only new thing he didn't want was a road he didn't know about. Mother said she thought it would be lovely to try to find some water, whatever direction it was in. But they all told her you couldn't go round and round just looking for water; you had to aim for something in particular. Grandfather said suppose they all let me decide. It was a very breathless moment for me, but I managed to say, "Let's go to Hartford City."

I had been there once to see my cousins, Inez and Mac, and remembered how I had liked the sidewalk in front of their house; it was wooden and narrow and off the ground so that it was like a bridge. They all said that was as good a direction as any to go, though we couldn't possibly get to Hartford City—at least not there and back in the same day.

"Do you know"—Uncle Lloyd's voice to me was shocked—"that Hartford City is *eighteen* miles away?"

We started on the Fourth about nine o'clock in the morning. Grandmother said that Grandfather had been out since seven, fiddling over the machine, and polishing the monogram. The monogram was a brass CMK in scroll letters, tacked across the radiator, and almost covering it. The boys had given it to them both in June, for an anniversary present.

Grandmother's acknowledgment of the gift had been polite, but certainly not hearty.

I had been out at half-past seven at our own house, but very briefly. Daddy had agreed to buy some firecrackers for me—my very first. Before that I had only seen the ones in the evening at the big house. All the other children had some of their own, and I wanted them, too. So Daddy and I took the package out at half-past seven. He lighted a piece of punk and gave it to me. Then he put one bunch down on the ground, and held my hand, leaned over with it, and touched the string that stuck out. The whole thing shot off with a bang, and jumped into the air. I was back in the house with the screen door shut behind me before the last one went off. I was dizzy with rage, yelling at the top of my lungs,

"I didn't ask for noisy ones!"

And I got sent to my room until time to go to the picnic, for having a bad temper and not counting ten to keep it down.

By the time Mother and I started, everybody else was up at the big house. The food was all packed, which was exactly what I wanted to see done, and they were ready to get in. They had on their dusters, bonnets, veils, and caps. Mrs. Hageman called out from her porch across the street that we all looked very stylish. Grandmother called back that we would be home in plenty of time for the fireworks, and to be sure to come over. She said of course they would, and that Mr. Hageman had some fine, big sky-rockets to bring. Grandmother told Mother privately that they were dangerous, tricky things, and she wouldn't have one around herself. But she waved to Mrs. Hageman and said that would be lovely. Mrs. Little was on her front porch, too, pinching dead leaves off her vines. She was Mr. Hageman's sister, and lived on the corner opposite the Richs'. She called that we had a lovely day for our excursion and God speed to us; she was quite a literary person.

We sailed off down Washington Street with flags flying, the veils from the motor bonnets and my butterfly net, which was hanging outside. I was making a butterfly collection with Betty Ball and wanted to get some more specimens if I could, but there was no place for me to hold the net in the car. I was wedged in the front seat between Grandfather and Uncle Lloyd. We were all of us in rather a tight squeeze. Daddy and Uncle Frank sat in the back seat, with Grandmother between them. Aunt Huda and Aunt Helen sat on little stools. Grandfather had had them made at the factory. Mother started out sitting somewhere between the two little stools, but later she shifted and sat on Daddy's lap. Next to Grandmother and me she was the lightest—she weighed ninety-eight pounds, and was always squeezed in after the other places were taken, but didn't mind a bit, she said. . . .

Pretty soon we were further than we had ever gone with the horses in so short a time, and Grandmother began to be excited.

"Goodness," she said, "this is beautiful country. I hadn't any idea it was such beautiful country."

She didn't mean beautiful country of hills and valleys or mountain streams, of course. She meant fertile, rich country, heavy with corn as far as you could see. "Corn knee high by the Fourth of July," we pray for and boast of. And it *was* knee high that year. Country Gentleman sweet corn, and Golden Dent feed corn, motionless and glistening in the silent heat.

Sometimes the fields were interrupted by a little patch of woods—the trees well apart from one another and with no underbrush below. That is the way they are in Indiana. The sight of one of these with its shade made the boys begin to think of eating.

We didn't know that we were starting that day a refrain which would echo down through all the years of motoring, when Mother said she wished we could find a brook—there must be one a little farther along—and Grandmother said that she didn't like one grove of trees, because it was too close to the road. If people passed by they could see exactly what we were eating, and Aunt Huda said that she wanted a brook, too, like Mother. Aunt Helen was with the boys. It made very little difference to her what she was looking at when she was eating, except that she would just as lief there weren't any cows. Grandfather was very impatient with the idea of dinner. The engine was running along like a bird, he said; it seemed a shame to stop it. Besides, when we stopped we wouldn't have the breeze that the machine was making for us. Just skimming along like this at eighteen miles an hour was his idea of a picnic. Everybody said,

"That's right, Father," and "Certainly, we are all loving it, Father."

Except Uncle Lloyd. He always spoke right up, and he was special with Grandmother Kimbrough—the other boys all laughed about it—because he was the youngest. He just said quietly that he'd hate to think of that beautiful dinner Grandmother had put up for us going to waste. That settled Grandfather. He banged his hand down on the steering wheel.

"Of course we'll stop. I want a piece of that chicken right now, Mother."

And then he slapped the wheel again.

"But we'll let Emily decide where. She told us where to come in the first place."

Mother called out from the back seat,

"Oh, Father, don't."

But the rest of them said,

"Oh, let him, Lottie; it doesn't hurt her."

Grandfather leaned his ear down to me and said,

"Where do you want to eat, Emily? We'll stop there."

"Aren't we going to Hartford City?" I asked him. "That's where I said to go, to Cousin Inez and Mac's with the wooden sidewalk outside."

"That's just where we'll go," Grandfather declared with solemnity. "By jiminy, we'll drive all the way to Hartford City."

There was bedlam all around. The daughters-in-law said they would love to see Inez and Mac, but they didn't think that was the idea of a picnic. Grandmother said Grandfather oughtn't to do that without telling her. If she had known we were going to Hartford City, she would have brought the mustard pickle recipe Inez wanted. The boys were delighted. Would you ever have believed, they kept asking, that you could get into a contraption and drive to Hartford City in the morning, and get there for dinner? And they didn't like sitting on the ground for picnics anyway. The food was fine, but grass was terrible and your knees got stiff. They wouldn't even listen to the daughters-in-law, they were so excited about what the machine could do. And while the argument was still going on we actually came into the town of Hartford City. We turned up the right street, and stopped outside Cousin Inez's own door. The wooden sidewalk was outside just the way it had been before we owned an automobile, up on little planks off the ground like a bridge.

Grandfather put his right hand down outside the car and squeezed the big rubber bulb over and over again. It made a deep doleful sound, something like a bullfrog. Inez and Mac came running out on the porch—everybody on the street came out on their porches, too—but Inez was so surprised that she got dizzy, and had to sit down for a minute, in a rocking chair, before she could come down the steps.

She was very pretty, with blue eyes and dark hair worn in a pompadour. She had the most catching laugh of anybody I knew. She laughed a great deal and I loved to hear it. It was low and full. Mac laughed a good deal, too, but more of a chuckle than a laugh came out. He was short and very fat. They had been married only two years. I had been the ring bearer at their wedding, carrying the ring in a basket of ferns and pink roses. Mother had fastened the ring to the handle of the basket with a piece of darning cotton so that it wouldn't get lost down in the basket. She tied it so tight, too, that the best man couldn't get it off. The minister finally held the basket up in the air, so that he could see it better, and jerked and jerked. The ring came away, but the darning cotton came, too. Inez wore it that way at first, with the long black thread attached. She was superstitious about taking off her wedding ring.

Neither she nor Mac had ever seen an automobile before we drove up. Mac kept walking round and round it just saying, over and over, "Well, sir, what do you think of that? Well, sir."

Everybody was talking at once. You could hardly hear anything that made sense. But Inez hugged me and said it was wonderful for me to bring the picnic there.

After a while we all went into the house. The boys carried the things for the picnic. Inez put the big coffee pot on the stove right away, and all the daughters-in-law helped her set the table. Grandmother unpacked the basket in the kitchen, and mixed up the salad in a bowl with Mother's Thousand Island dressing. The men all sat out on the porch and looked at the machine until Mother sent me out to tell them everything was ready. We ate at the dining room table, but ate with our fingers because it was a picnic. And there were two kinds of cake, because Inez had happened to bake an angel food the day before. Angel food cake was her specialty.

As soon as dinner was over we had to pack up and start right back, though they all said they were too full to move; but we had to, because everybody would expect us for the fireworks that night. Nobody could get over it that we were in Hartford City for dinner, and were going to be back in Muncie for supper. They all kept saying that it didn't seem right somehow; it sort of scared you. Cousin Mac told Grandfather,

"Well, Uncle Charles, I guess nothing will stop you now. One of these days you'll be driving right down to New York City."

Grandfather was so pleased that he let Uncle Lloyd crank.

It was the best start we had made. When Grandfather wouldn't let anyone help, he had to run back from cranking to switch a button over from the magneto to "spark," and pull down the throttle. But sitting in the seat, he could do that the minute the engine caught from Uncle

Lloyd's cranking. The magneto was the only part of the whole automobile that I hated. It made a noise like scraping your nail on a blackboard, and I always put my tongue between my teeth until we were on "spark."

We waved and called back to Inez and Mac until they were out of sight, standing on the wooden sidewalk in front of the house, and then Grandfather began pointing out the sights again that we had just passed on the way in, first with his left hand and then with his right. He showed me a butterfly that I did want for my collection, but no one would let me go after it because the engine might stall if we stopped, and we didn't want anything to hold us back.

We came back over the same road, because the boys thought it was better not to take any chances on a new one, and Grandfather pushed the throttle up to pretty nearly twenty-three miles an hour. He said it was safe on a familiar road. Grandmother begged him not to, but the others talked her out of being nervous. They all loved it, they said. I was quite scared myself because the wind made such a noise. I shut my eyes to slits, which made the scenery exciting and not so scary.

We were coming along lickety-split and not very far from Muncie, when Grandfather saw some cows. They were crossing the road quite far ahead, going from the pasture over to the barn. He didn't want to slow down too much, he said, for fear he might stall the engine, and he wanted to give them warning anyway. So he put his hand down the side and squeezed the bulb as hard as he could, over and over.

Grandmother called from the back seat,

"Father, don't blow it so long. You'll deafen all of us."

He muttered to us,

"I have to blow. My throttle's stuck. I can't slow her down."

And then the cows started to run, up the road and down the road, and back into the pasture, and some streaking across to the barn. The little boy who was driving them was scared at the noise and the stampede. He was taking them home to be milked, so he started running up and down after them, yelling, and trying to coax them. But no one could hear his voice over the horn and the engine. Grandfather was wild, too.

"Holy smoke!" he kept saying.

But he didn't dare stop altogether by turning off the engine, because he didn't know whether he could start again. And the more the horn blew, and the closer we came to them, the worse off the cows were. The boys said,

"Keep on going, Father; keep on going, Father."

I don't think he shut his eyes, and maybe the boys didn't, but certainly the rest of us did. The last I saw we were going into the cows. When I opened my eyes again, we were past them. They were still running, and the horn was still blowing.

"That was a close shave," Daddy yelled.

Grandfather nodded his head proudly. By this time we were coming into the lower end of Walnut Street, making more noise than the whole fire department. Everybody along the sidewalks jumped into the doorways. There were lots of people, too, the way there always are on a holiday, but they scattered.

Grandmother's voice was so high you could hear it above the horn. She was so mortified, she said, she wished she were dead. If anyone persuaded her to set foot in this dratted carriage again, she would know she was crazy. Look at Mrs. George Maring over there, staring at us as if we were a lot of hoodlums. That's what we were too, skiting over to Hartford City and back in a day.

I don't suppose we could hear all of it, but we heard most of it.

We turned the corner on Madison Street, came up Washington, got to the front of the house, and Grandfather stopped the engine, and that stopped the horn, too. All his passengers got out, wriggled and stamped a little to get the stiffness out of their muscles, and said it had been a wonderful day; they would never forget it. Grandmother said nobody in town would forget it either.

Family Reunion

By Wallace Stegner

Wallace Stegner is a Mormon, and the reunion he describes took place at Bountiful, in the Mormon country between Salt Lake City and Ogden, Utah. But as he describes the gooing at new babies, the preparation of potato salad and chocolate cake and ice cream, the small family crises and antagonisms, we realize that this is a celebration which is typical of all America.

Come to a family reunion sometime. It is better than an Iowa picnic at Long Beach, California, and generally almost as populous. Come to one in any of the villages—say Bountiful, between Salt Lake and Ogden. A block down from the Ward House is the old homestead where the patriarch lived with one of his two families not many years ago. In his lifetime he ran the village store and housed and fed itinerant Indians and raised up a numerous progeny by his two wives. The descendants still squabble a little about which family he loved more, and which of his two houses he spent more time in. Up and down the highway are the homes of some of his sons and daughters. Others are scattered around among nearby towns, Ogden, Salt Lake, Farmington, Morgan. The great bulk of the family, however, lives within close range of the old homestead. Mormons are not, except when the Church calls them, a migrant people. They cling to the family patrimony.

One of their most regular wanderings is the annual reunion, and they will come a long way for it. They stream into town by car, on foot, by interurban railroad, some bringing chocolate cakes, some ice cream, some sandwiches, some potato salad or punch. They shake hands, they slap backs, they goo at new babies, they marvel at the growth of the children in the last year. They gather in little knots and talk under their breath about how bad Joe is looking, and about how his wife could do a lot better for him than she does. They kid the girls and talk about the peach crop and holler a welcome as new arrivals fill the Ward House.

Until the festivities start, the women are busy getting food set out and the tables set in the amusement room. They hurry with pursed lips looking for that package of sandwiches that Min brought, they brush the hair back from their faces and open jars of salad, boxes of cake, bottles of olives. Their talk goes up in a high light clatter like the tinkle of knives and forks, and the tables sag under the weight of food. Members of one family whisper together as they examine the whole freezer of store ice cream brought by Aunt Priscilla of the other tribe, and Aunt Mae, who has brought a small freezer of her own homemade ice cream flavored with fresh peaches, guesses that if Father were alive he'd speak to the other family about acting show-offish and spiteful and wanting to be first in everything.

Finally Brother Willard, son of the patriarch, brings the meeting to order in the chapel room, asks Brother Charles to open with prayer. Before Charles can begin, Brother Willard asks Cousin Anne to take her squalling baby outside for a little while. Brother Charles prays for the health and long life of all the family. If there is anything wrong with any member, he mentions that member by name. Remember, Oh Lord, Brother Zeke's wife, who has had a stroke. Shower Thy blessings on Cousin Ed, suffering from cancer. He thanks the Lord for all his blessings and for their membership in His Church, and prays that they may all prove faithful.

Nephew John, the genealogist, reports on the family tree. He has so many names now that the responsibility for vicarious baptisms will have to be shared by all the units of the family. As for the young people, let them begin filling in their family trees in their primary books as soon as possible.

Cousin Walter sings a solo. He is Mary's husband—Mary is Agnes' girl—but Cousin Walter is not supposed to be too faithful in his Church work since he came back from music school. He sings a virtuoso number that thrills the young people and sounds just a little too arty to the old ones. The older ones lean together and suggest to each other that Cousin Walter be brought over to meeting sometime soon.

Now Aunt Peg's daughters troop up on the platform and go through a prepared number, holding up their family coat of arms and taking turns explaining the heraldic symbols. The women applaud vigorously, their eyes full of the cute little figures in pinafores.

Brother Willard leads in singing, takes the whole multitude through a couple of hymns, then through "America" and "Britannia Rules the Waves." Brother Fred, the oldest brother present, then rises to speak, and there are tears in his eyes as he enumerates the blessings that have been visited on the family. He traces the family history down from one great-great-great-great who was a Loyalist during the Revolution and had to flee to Canada. From Canada his descendants worked their way southward and westward through the generations, until now they are safe in the arms of the true Church in the valleys of the mountains. He is an old man now, says Brother Fred, and will not be with them long, but so long as President Grant, in his weakened condition, continues to lead the Church, he himself can only do his part and work as faithfully as he knows how. He hopes the young people present today will always labor in the cause of right as their ancestors have done.

By this time the whole family is ravenous. They adjourn to the amusement hall, and the women rush to get the final preparations made. Every square inch of the long tables is crowded with sandwiches, ice cream, cakes, pies, salads, pickles, dressings, potato chips, olives, preserves. Families are seated together—Hyrum's, Tom's, Fred's, Willard's, Charles'—and the mothers and daughters of each branch flutter around behind, postponing their own meal until the men and children are fed. When all are in their places, Brother Fred raises his hand, surveys the tables with a grave, proud look, bows his head with dignity, and offers up so long a grace that the children snicker and poke each other and steal potato chips.

After the grace the formality breaks down immediately. The tables rock with laughter. Uncle Orson talks incessantly with his mouth full, spinning out yarns about the family, telling how Mamie, riding into Salt Lake with that young Smith fella, got held up, and young Smith was so scared he couldn't walk for an hour afterward. Smith would have got Sister Mamie sure if Bill hadn't come back from his mission right about then and got to work. Brother Joe remarks that he has three daughters in the mission field now and doesn't know how he manages the expenses. The turkeys aren't paying very well, and there was that fire in the barn. But, he says, he pays an honest tithe and the Lord provides for him and his. He has never had a stronger testimony of the gospel.

Sister Ruth, when the eating has begun to dwindle down to half-hearted pecks at tidbits, rises and asks everybody present to report on his occupation. They stand up one by one, grinning, and speak it out, bowing back into their chairs with their napkins clutched in their fists. There are farmers, businessmen, salesmen, a few doctors, a good many school teachers. Women up and down the tables shake their heads at the breadth of the family interests, and lean over toward their neighbors to tell about their children or their Relief Society work.

Nobody comes around with a pot of coffee. No man, no woman, leans back to light cigarette or cigar or pipe. Some of the weaker vessels, like Cousin Walter, may relax with a sigh in their automobiles going home, and reach for the comforting weed, but within the family the Word of Wisdom is rigid law. To light a cigarette at a Mormon family reunion would be the equivalent of cursing aloud in the midst of prayers.

Remember the Sabbath Day

By Bellamy Partridge

The old-fashioned Sunday has almost disappeared. With mixed feelings we remember putting on our Sunday "best" and going to church, where, if we knew what was good for us, we sat straight as ramrods through the long sermon. Then the overpowering Sunday dinner and the interminable afternoon. It was hard for active youngsters, but it must have been wonderful for parents.

Sunday at our house began with breakfast at eight o'clock. How we reveled in this late breakfast, and luxuriated in the knowledge that we would not have to "go on the carpet" before sitting down at table. On weekdays going on the carpet meant a severe military inspection of hands, faces, necks, ears, clothing, and especially shoes. I suppose I was sent back to polish the heels of my shoes oftener than for any other oversight. On Sunday the inspection was doubly stiff, but it came much later since we did not start for church until Father's watch showed the time to be exactly ten twenty-five. It was his custom to snap the case shut on the minute.

The timing of meals was equally exact. We must be there on the tick or take the consequences, which meant a certain loss of privileges. When Father was in the house the bell rang whether the meal was ready or not. We then took our places behind our chairs and waited until grace had been said before sitting down. After we were seated—there we sat until the food was brought in from the kitchen. We were a noisy family, forever talking, teasing, joking, and gibing at each other. But if a meal was slow in coming in Father had little to say and usually sat with his watch in his hand as if he had to catch a train, when really there was nothing more pressing than reading the paper or walking out to look over the garden.

On Sunday morning immediately after breakfast we had family prayers in the library. Father's selections from the Bible were certainly good ones. He did not miss a homicide, a bit of intrigue, an illicit love affair, or any good story having plenty of plot and action. I think Mother used to squirm a little at some of these selections; she could see no good reason for bringing that particular subject up. Grandmother, however, never turned a hair; anything in the Bible was good enough for her.

After prayers we dispersed, went to our rooms, and began a leisurely preparation for church. Immediately following church we came home and had our Sunday dinner. The rest of the day we had to ourselves, except that the older children were expected to attend church in the evening. Mother usually went with them, but Father never stepped out of the house on Sunday evenings. One church service a day was enough for him. He would go once and go willingly; but he was a man who could be pushed just so far and no farther. Mother understood this perfectly, and while she would have derived great comfort from having him attend the evening service, she never made an effort so far as I know to get him to go. Grandmother tried once, but never again. Father told her off in a few well-chosen words. . . .

No secular music was allowed at our house on Sunday. The girls used to play the piano, but they had to confine their music to the hymnbook. We were not supposed to whistle or even to hum anything but religious music. Usually the cover of the piano would remain down all day long, though occasionally on a Sunday one of the girls would go in and pound out a few doleful-sounding Gospel hymns. . . .

For exercise on Sunday we were allowed to take a walk, but it had to be a supervised walk with Father in charge. Mother, presumably because of her child-bearing, was not much of a walker. Our two favorite Sunday walks were to go past the Burdick farm, a stroll of about a mile and a half, or to visit the cemetery. Personally I preferred to go past the Burdick farm, for this took us into the country, across four brooks into which things could be thrown, along shaded country roads, and between pastures and cultivated fields. . . .

All our games and playthings were put under lock and key on Saturday night, all, that is, except the stereoscope. We could look through that as much as we wished on Sunday, for the only pictures that we had were scenes of the Holy Land and views illustrating the life of Christ.

Our Sunday dinner was a meal to reckon with, usually built around a large roast or a platter of fried or fricasseed chicken, but for Sunday night supper we all went into the kitchen to have a bowl of bread and milk, and a piece of cake or a cookie. In those days we all had our individual bread and milk bowls, some with initials and some with nothing but pictures on the sides. My outfit consisted of a wide, shallow bowl and a deep saucer almost as large as a soup plate. The capacity of the bowl was about a pint, and on an average Sunday night I would empty it twice. This bread and milk supper was partly an economy measure, for it made a fine way to get rid of the stale bread which had been accumulating, and partly a religious function designed to release all household help so that they could attend divine worship. In looking back on some of the things I used to hear about the Sunday night adventures of our maids I am not so sure that they did not contribute more to delinquency than to salvation.

As my sisters began to grow up those Sunday night suppers lost some of their austere, meager quality. A single warm supper dish made its appearance, chipped beef on toast, swimming in cream sauce, or perhaps creamed fish of some sort. It was at a Sunday night supper that I tasted my first Welsh rarebit. At the time I thought it a fine way to spoil good cheese, but after a few trials I became and have since remained an enthusiast.

The one thing that I always liked about the Sunday night supper was the complete absence of punctuality. You could come or you could go. You could take it or leave it. The bread was there on the large circular breadboard on the outer margin of which the words "Cut and Come Again" were carved in raised letters. Milk was plentiful, for we kept a cow that furnished us with about twenty quarts a day. You could sit down or you could eat standing. Nobody told you what you could or could not do. There were times when I found the punctuality of our household extremely annoying. Punctuality is, I am told, one of the elements of good conduct. Up to a certain point I heartily approve of it. Beyond that point it can become a nuisance, if not an instrument of torture.

With Father punctuality was the queen of the virtues. He believed in kindness, but there were times when to win a lawsuit he would skin a witness alive. He believed in standing up very straight with the shoulders thrown back; but he was never very erect himself. He believed in telling the absolute truth; though nobody could draw the long bow any more effectively than he. But in the case of punctuality he practiced what he preached, for he never deviated from it by so much as a hairbreadth. I do not believe that he ever missed a train in his life, and in all those years that he started the family for church he was late on only one occasion, and then it was really not his own fault.

It happened one Sunday in the early spring. The garden had just been made, but the cow had not yet been turned out to pasture. The family were all assembled in the library, had all passed muster, and were about to start when the hired girl called down from upstairs and said that the cow was loose and walking around in the yard. Quite naturally Father did not want her walking in his newly made garden, so he sent Thad out to catch her and shut her up.

As Thad went out of the room Father glanced at his watch. When, a few moments later, the church bell began to toll he glanced at it again. From time to time he kept on glancing at it, but Thad did not return. Father became very fidgety, and finally he turned to Mother.

"You start along with the children, Mother," he said, "and I'll go back and see what's happened to Thad. He probably can't catch that cow alone."

He did not wait for an answer, but strode rapidly through the door that led to the kitchen and thence to the back door. But Mother made no move to start for church. She was as anxious as Father to know what was going on in the backyard; and after two or three minutes had passed and he had not come back she went out that way to see for herself. She did not go as Father had gone, striding along and slamming the doors behind him with the abandon of careless haste. It could hardly be said that she went on tiptoe, but at least she made no unnecessary noise. All she wanted was to satisfy her curiosity as to what was going on, and she had no particular desire to be seen.

She found the kitchen quiet, for the hired girl was still engaged with the upstairs work. She listened a moment, and hearing nothing, tiptoed over to the door, slightly ajar, which led into the summer kitchen. Father was crouching and weaving in a most peculiar manner, his fists doubled, and the back of his neck a fiery red. He was making strange motions with his arms suggestive of a boxer. She thought for a moment that he must be out of his head, must suddenly have lost his reason. Then as he crouched far over to one side as if to avoid a blow she saw outside the window what was apparently responsible for Father's pantomime—Thad locked in mortal combat with Red Brower, the boy who lived next door.

Another fight—and on Sunday—! Just an ordinary everyday fight over a sandlot ball game was enough to upset and unnerve her for a whole day, and I never could quite understand why she did not scream and rush out to separate Thad and young Brower. It may have been the responsibility for getting the children to church, or possibly the fact that Red Brower was perennially in need of a thrashing, but in any event she stayed for no more than a glance at what was going on, and without letting Father know of her presence she quietly retraced her steps to the library.

"Has Thad caught her yet?" we asked as she returned to the library.

"Who? Oh, you mean the cow—I don't think so. But Father's there to help him. They'll get her. And we'll go on now and let them come along later. Louise, you come up and walk with Mother. The rest of you can stay in your usual places."

We reached the church on the very last toll of the bell. Father came in almost half an hour late, but apparently so well satisfied with himself that I felt sure he must have caught the cow before she had done any damage to his garden. Thad didn't come at all. When we got home we found that he had been hurt. The story was that Father had met him coming into the house with a black eye, a bloody nose, and several buttons torn from his Sunday clothes. Father instantly guessed what had happened.

"I see the cow has been dragging you around by the rope. I hope you're not hurt."

Thad began to brush himself off. "No, I'm not hurt any—got a few buttons torn off, and I guess I'm kinda dirty."

"There's a little blood on your nose—she must have bumped you somehow."

"Yes, she bumped me two or three times—but I bumped her some pretty good ones, too."

"All right," said Father, "you go in there to the sink and wash the blood and dirt from your face and I'll see if I can handle the cow."

As it turned out he handled her very easily. She let him walk right up to her and take hold of the rope. All the mischief and meanness seemed to have gone out of her. After looking Thad over, however, Father decided that the boy had better stay home from church and hold a piece of raw meat on his eye.

Mother never had liked that cow, and when Thad and Father had finished telling how vicious the animal had been she pretended to believe the story and insisted that the cow must be sold at once. Father protested feebly, but after the gory tale of what had happened to Thad the cow didn't have a leg to stand on, and Father had to let her go. I never could quite square Mother's method of getting rid of the cow with her Christian principles of uprightness and honesty. It is true that she was taking them at their word, but it is also true that she knew their story was a complete fabric of lies. However, the ethics of the transaction never seemed to bother her, and a few years after the cow had been safely disposed of she laughingly boasted to me that she had paid them in their own coin.

It's Thanksgiving Because It's Homecoming

By Henry Beetle Hough

PLYMOUTH, 1621

"And thus they found ye Lord to be with them in all their ways, and to blesse their outgoings & incomings, for which let his holy name have ye praise for ever, to all posteritie.

"* * * All ye somer ther was no wante. And now begane to come in store of foule, as winter approached, of which this place did abound when they came first. * * * And besids water foule, ther was great store of wild Turkies, of which they tooke many, besids venison, &c. Besids they had aboute a peck a meale a weeke to a person, or now since harvest, Indean corne to yt proportion. Which made many afterwards write so largly of their plenty hear to their freinds in England."—WILLIAM BRADFORD (1590–1657), GOVERNOR OF PLYMOUTH COLONY.

Thanksgiving is the holiday of abundance and reverent thanks. It is the traditional American festival of home and family ties, a time of groaning boards, of grandparents and grandchildren. Henry Beetle Hough catches its spirit and its meaning and shows why the holiday will never be transplanted.

Year in, year out, the advent of Thanksgiving brings sentimental references to the Pilgrims and the first celebration of the feast day in the New England wilderness. Thanksgiving remains peculiarly the product of the New England tradition, but you won't be able to catch or define the holiday's spirit by talking about the first Thanksgiving.

That first Thanksgiving is memorable only as an instinctive birth, a spiritual preparation and, perhaps, a faint, warming fragrance of family repasts to come. It was much too early then for the Pilgrims to have grandchildren, though naturally they invited the neighbors, who happened to be Red Men. But many a threshold had to be worn deeply into the grain of the wood, many a winter's snow had to drift the fields and the path from the kitchen to the barn before there could be a real Thanksgiving.

Great-great-grandchildren were needed, as well as uncles, aunts and nephews, with long memories and golden tales to go with the uprush of young anticipation. The fullness of the day never stemmed from colonial times, but from that later period when family and community life had accumulated like wild honey and thriven with the sun, the wind and the soil.

Thanksgiving needed family, although lacking guests with blood ties (as the Pilgrims felt), neighbors could be made to do. It also needed room and scope. A year ahead, at least, Uncle Jared and Aunt Clarissa claimed their turn to entertain. Uncle Jared planted and harvested accordingly, and Aunt Clarissa made the necessary calculations in putting up her preserves. From the first of November she cleaned, scoured and fixed up the spare bedrooms and the cots and patchwork quilts for the children in the chilly, aromatic attic.

The winds of Thanksgiving always blew toward home, and so the course lay from city to town, or from town to village, or from village to country. Even on ordinary days New England dinners were served at noon, and dinner guests were polite if they arrived around 10 for a 12 o'clock meal. For Thanksgiving, early arrival was of the essence, and members of the clan who did not come the day before were expected immediately after breakfast. The men walked around in their good clothes for the sake of better appetites, the women helped in the kitchen, which was large enough to hold them all, with elbow room. The children, hollered at frequently, kept in touch with important matters through a grapevine system of their own.

Then, when the moment came, the extra chairs were lugged into the dining room and every piece of choice china and silverware which Aunt Clarissa owned was displayed on the table. Nothing was held back. Yet the effect was not at all finicky. It was both simple and fine. The generations came to be seated, men first, women next, as they hurried from the kitchen with bright faces, discarding their aprons hastily. Uncle Jared might ask the blessing himself or he might defer to Cousin Luella's husband, who was a deacon, or this might be the year they were having the minister, the minister's wife and their four children.

As grace was spoken, the repose of the Lord and the surcease of labor settled upon the room, and all the New England past seemed to be there also. Then, THEN the company took up its spoons for the preliminary of soup, a trial run of the bounty which was already pressing in from the kitchen as from a great horn of plenty. And the bounty was Uncle Jared's and Aunt Clarissa's own.

If there were turkeys, Uncle Jared had raised them and Aunt Clarissa had roasted them until their skin was golden crisp and shiny. If there were rabbits, Uncle Jared had shot them at the copse over the hill, or if there were canvas-back ducks, he had brought them down at the border of the great pond on a gusty morning. But Aunt Clarissa might have stuffed a brace of barnyard geese, long fed for the occasion, or a young pig, or prepared an enormous eel stifle.

Tradition did not dictate too narrowly. She might have used stuffing of bread, onion and summer savory or sage, or she might have tried a new chestnut dressing or sent Uncle Jared to the cove for oysters. Cranberry sauce might be made from the whole cranberries or strained into the form of jelly. The parsnips might appear in fritters. Each departure would arouse exclamations of enthusiasm, but it was not certain that Uncle Canton's wife would adopt any of them when she entertained next year. She probably had a few of her own in mind, such as whipping quarts of cream for a gigantic charlotte russe.

The one indispensable of the dinner was its roll-call, in plenty, of all the New England vegetables. There could not be one missing, and the heartiest were most important. Begin with the classic white turnip. It had the pungent flavor of something wrung from nature, produced by toil and ordeal through drought, frost and scorching sun. Not everyone liked turnip, but everyone ate it, knowing what was good for him. Then the winter squashes buttered and spiced, onions boiled and creamed, great heaps of potatoes, carrots, parsnips, celery and a flanking of watermelon preserves, pickles and wild grape jelly and beach plum jam.

There was a running supply of Uncle Jared's cider and the ultimate of mince, squash, apple and pumpkin pies and maybe Indian pudding or plum pudding. Except for raisins, sugar and spices, everything of the dinner would have been grown, caught or garnered in the countryside or on the farm itself, and in maritime New England even the spices would have been obtained by barter from some passing vessel or brought in person by Cousin Hosea, just back from the Orient as mate of the clipper Good Return.

Immediately after the main course the younger generation would go outdoors and run around the house in a vain hope of shaking things down and making more room. But there would be room, miraculously, for pocketsful of nuts at the very end as well as for some of Uncle Jared's pears and apples. Then the legendary peace of Thanksgiving became complete, the Lord was praised with distended stomachs and repletion was somehow near to holiness.

While the women were clearing up in the kitchen the men went outdoors again and leaned over the barnyard fence with Uncle Jared to admire the farm animals and the improvements he had made in the place. They had looked around before, but this was official. This was ceremonial.

Then, in due course, the church bells. The women were eager to show themselves in their new dresses, bonnets, ribbons and shawls, and the young men were proud of their homespun and home-dyed coats, wool hats and cowhide boots. No less strongly, the generations of Grandpa and Uncle Jared were drawn to church, too.

Bass viol and fiddle were taken to the singing gallery, and hymns and anthems were never sung with more power and feeling. The minister read out the lesson: "The Lord reigneth; let the earth rejoice, let the multitude of the isles be glad thereof." But when he came to the sermon he was not averse to letting his opinions on the tariff and other timely matters appear. That, too, was New England, and his flock, deeply aware of a superintending Providence and of eternal gratitude for life, safety and the freedom they and their children breathed, sat contentedly and filtered the minister's words.

After church had ended with little sociable talks at the vestry door, and greetings to friends and neighbors driving home, Aunt Clarissa mentioned that she wanted to run over to Josie Hammett's for a minute, and a bevy of relatives went along. So, with calling back and forth, the renewal of friendships, and the sound of voices and laughter in the aisles of browned oak trees along the dirt roads, Thanksgiving drifted gently to a temporary end, an adjournment of a year during which Uncle Jared's hair would turn a little frostier, the youngest scion would grow a couple of inches, and a new crop of white turnips would mature.

So the tradition of Thanksgiving, and in essence the observance, has never changed. It has only contracted, partly because of smaller families and the increasing dominance of town life, and partly because of the pressure of an industrial civilization which tends to pool the bounty of the entire world.

Uncle Lemuel, who as a small boy sat at Uncle Jared's Thanksgiving board, likes to tell the assembled company that he raised the turkey on the place. But these are new times, and everyone knows the turkeys at the bargain store are just as good. Aunt Bertha did not make the watermelon pickles by the almanac, but took them out of a store bottle. Only the cranberry sauce, wild grape jelly and beach plum jam are hers. Soon only the white turnip and other vegetables will be Uncle Lemuel's, the last regional accents of what was once a regional feast.

There is still no day of homecoming in New England equal to Thanksgiving, but with automobiles and, one must say it, with airplanes, the cousins, aunts, brothers, and even the grandchildren, may swish over just an hour before dinnertime. There's no helping to be done in the kitchen and no room for outsiders, either. Aunt Bertha has her electric mixer and range, and so many things come practically ready for the oven or the table.

Yet no stranger could ever mistake the Thanksgiving dinner for any other dinner of the year, not with that array of vegetables, the heirloom china, the representation of all ages, the communing of past and present. Dinner over, the family listens to the football game on the radio, though Aunt Bertha may mention that she wants to run over to Lizzie Hammett's for a minute and won't someone come with her? Long before dark most of the dinner guests are homeward bound in car or plane, and only one or two miscellaneous offspring remain to sleep under ancestral spreads.

Once in a while nowadays one hears of country people going to the city for Thanksgiving, but they are not New Englanders. No matter where their homes, as soon as their cityward journeys start they become members only of that indistinguishable race—moderns. Thanksgiving will never be transplanted. Though diminished, it remains now and forever what it was and what it has to be.

Christmas on the Prairie

By Bess Streeter Aldrich

Many a farmer's wife, fighting drought or loneliness, has found time to bring Christmas cheer to her husband and children. The spirit of such a Christmas is an enduring thing. In the following chapter from Mrs. Aldrich's *A Lantern In Her Hand* it brings the widely scattered members of a devoted family back to the farm after many years.

Every one was in want that year of 1874. In the early fall people began going past the house. "Going home," they all reported. Many times parties of them stayed all night. They had their own quilts and would arrange their beds on the main-room floor. They were beaten, they said. One could stand a few disappointments and failures, but when everything turned against one, there was no use trying to fight.

"Nebraska hasn't turned against us," Will would argue stubbornly. "It's the finest, blackest land on the face of the earth. The folks that will just stick it out. . . . You'll see the climate change, . . . more rains and not so much wind . . . when the trees grow. We've got to keep at the trees. Some day this is going to be the richest state in the union . . . the most productive. I'll bet anything next year . . ."

Always "next year"! It was a mirage, thought Abbie, an apparition that vanished when one came to it. Six times now they had said, "Next year, the crops will be fine."

And so she could not throw off the blue mood that had descended upon her, a horde of worries that had come upon her even as the horde of grasshoppers had come upon the land. The thought that there was nothing to do with; that they could scarcely keep body and soul together; that she probably would never be able now to do anything with her voice; that another child was coming,—they all harassed and tormented her. All fall there was in her mind a tired disinterest over things. In spite of what he said, that surface courage which he pretended had returned to him, Abbie detected that Will, too, was morose. To her keen eye he seemed dull and stoical, underneath an assumption of cheerfulness.

Before cold weather, the old grasshoppers were gone, but first they had taken infinite pains to leave a reminder of themselves in the newly broken prairie everywhere,—holes the size of lead pencils in which they laid one to two dozen eggs in a sack. In a six-inch square of ground, Will testing their number, found a double handful of the next year's hatching. There seemed not even a hope for the following crop.

It was in November that the barrel and box came from the folks back home. Will drove up to the soddie with rattling announcement of their arrival. A letter from Grandpa Deal had been the forerunner of the donations and already Abbie knew that an old brass horn of Dennie's was among the things for Mack. She determined to slip it out without his knowledge and put it away for Christmas. They all gathered around the barrel while Will pried open the top, Mack and Margaret dancing about in an ecstasy of excitement. The first thing to be taken out was an envelope marked "For Abbie," in Grandpa Deal's handwriting. In it was twenty dollars. Abbie cried a little, tears of love and homesickness, happiness and relief, and put it away with secret thoughts of the desired organ. She sensed that Grandpa had slipped it in with his one hand the last thing, so Grandma would not see it.

There were flower seeds and sugar and beans, seed-corn and dried apples in the barrel. Mother Mackenzie had tied and sent two thick comforts. Regina Deal sent an old soiled white silk bonnet with a bead ornament and a cluster of three little pink feathers on it,—"tips," Abbie told the children they were,—and a pair of dirty white "stays" and some old white hoop-skirts. Abbie laughed until she cried at the sight of them.

"Maybe I could put the hoops over some stakes next summer and keep the setting hens in them," she suggested. She put them on over her work dress, the hoops and the stays both, and perched the dirty bonnet on her red-brown hair, dancing about in them, the three noble tips nodding with uncertain dignity as though, like their former owner, they had no sense of humor. She pushed Will and Mack and Margaret into position for a square dance and showed the children how to "whirl your partner" and "alamand left." The four of them pranced around in the impromptu dance, the children in their patched dingy clothing, Will in his denim work things, and Abbie in the foolish soiled cast-offs which Regina had sent with so little thought. The two older children laughed and clapped their hands and shouted that they had never had so much fun in their lives, and little John toddled in and out and between them in an ecstasy of bubbling spirits.

It broke something in Abbie, some tight-bound band around her heart and throat, which had not been loosed for months. She hid the old brass horn of Dennie's in the bedroom. She put away the precious dried apples and popcorn, the seed-corn and the big solid Greenings from the orchard behind Grandpa Deal's house. She hugged the huge warm quilts as though they were the fat pudding-bag body of Maggie Mackenzie. The bad luck was temporary. They were young and well. The children were all healthy youngsters. Why, how wicked she had been! She was only twenty-seven. She mustn't let her voice rust the way she had done this summer. In another year or so she could have an organ and maybe even get to a music teacher. She mustn't let youth slip away and her voice go with it. She was ashamed of herself that she had not sung for months.

"Oh! the Lady of the Lea,
Fair and young and gay was she."

Her voice rose full-throated, mellowed now with tribulations and sympathy. The children clapped their hands that Mother was singing.

"Beautiful exceedingly,
The Lady of the Lea."

She replenished the fire of twisted hay and corn-cobs in the stove with the four holes and the iron hearth in front. She cooked cornmeal mush for supper and set the table. Several times she sang the same verses over.

"Many a wooer sought her hand,
For she had gold and she had land,"

The teakettle sang and the children chattered happily at the window. She lighted the coal-oil lamp with the red flannel in the bowl and washed her hands in the tin basin. The prairie twilight came on. The winds died down.

"Everything at her command,
The Lady of the Lea."

Will came in from doing the chores.

"It's the nicest time of day . . . isn't it, Will . . . the red fire of the corn . . . and the steaming teakettle . . . supper ready . . . and the children all alive and well . . . and you and I together?"

Will put his arm around her for a brief, rare moment.

"It's the nicest time of day, Abbie-girl."

Yes, the coming of the barrel seemed to put something back into Abbie which had been gone temporarily,—laughter and hope, courage and faith. She began planning right away for Christmas. Mack was nearly eight, Margaret six and little John two. They were going to have the finest Christmas they had ever known. To Abbie's pleasure, Will entered into the preparations, too. He was as glad to see Abbie come to life as she was to see him throw off a little of his moroseness.

She told Gus and Christine Reinmueller their plans.

"*Ach!*" Christine snorted. "So? *Gans närrish* . . . voolish."

"A heck of a Christmas we'll have," was Gus's equally enthusiastic response.

But Abbie found sympathy in Sarah Lutz,—Sarah, with her little black beady eyes and her cheerful, energetic way.

"You know, Sarah, I think every mother owes it to her children to give them happy times at Christmas. They'll remember them all their lives. I even think it will make better men and women of them."

"I think so, too, Abbie. We're going to have a cedar tree hauled up from the Platte. Henry can get you one, too."

All day long Abbie worked at the tasks that demanded attention, washing, ironing, patching, mending, baking, churning, caring for the chickens, —all with meager equipment or no equipment at all. Two wooden tubs, three heavy, clumsy flat-irons, a churn with wooden dasher, scissors, needles and thread, and a baking board with a few heavy dishes and utensils. But from them, clean clothes, sweet butter, neatly made-over suits and dresses and food that was palatable. The tapering Mackenzie fingers were calloused and burned and pricked. As tired as all these tasks left her, she would get the children to bed early and then bring out the Christmas things and begin working on them.

She got out the precious paints Mrs. Whitman had given her and worked on a picture for Will when he was away. It was a scene of the prairie with a clump of cottonwoods in the foreground. She tried to get the afterglow of the sunset but even though she worked faithfully, she could not get it. "If I only had some one to help a little," she would say. "Some day I want to take some painting lessons again. If I could just make a picture as I want to,—it would satisfy something in me."

From the barn she got clean husks and made a family of dolls for

Margaret. She made the bodies, heads and limbs from the husks and braided the corn-silk for hair. A man, a lady and a baby, she made, and dressed them in corn-husk clothes. Will built a small bedstead for them. Out of one of the coats in the barrel she made Mack a new suit and concocted a bonnet for Margaret out of the old one Regina had sent, trimming it with a little wisp of the pink tips. With her paints, she marked off a checkerboard for Mack, and Will whittled checkers from the circumference of some small cottonwood branches. She cut a pattern and made a calico dog for little John, stuffing it with corn-husks, and covering it with knotted ends of carpet rags to give it a woolly appearance. She ironed out brown wrapping paper, tied the pieces with yarn and drew waggish-looking cows and horses on it for him, too.

Margaret laboriously hemmed a handkerchief for her father and Mack made him a box for his newspapers. There was a State Journal now, and as scarce as money was, Will had subscribed. "We can't drop out of touch with other parts of the country," he had said. "And we must know what the rest of the settlers are doing."

The children could talk of nothing but the approach of the wonderful day. The word "he" had only one meaning in their vocabulary,—a portly gentleman with a white beard and a sack on his back.

"Are you sure he'll come this year, Mother? Heinie Reinmueller said he wouldn't. He said his mother said so."

"Of *course* he'll come," Abbie assured the three. "Because Father and I are making things, too, to help him when he comes."

With Scotch-Irish cleverness, she could think of a dozen things to do with her meager supplies to add to the festivities. She ran tallow in tiny molds for the candles. She made a little batch of molasses candy and baked cookies in star and diamond shapes. She boiled eggs and painted faces on them and made little calico bonnets for them.

Christine was contemptuous toward the unnecessary festivities.

"For dot . . . no time I haf. You learn 'em vork . . . cows milk 'n' pigs svill . . . 'n' dey for foolishness no time haf."

"Oh, don't let us ever get like Reinmuellers," Abbie said. "We're poor. If we were any poorer we might as well lie down and give up. But we can fight to keep civilized . . . can fight to keep something before us besides the work."

On the day before Christmas the snow lay deep on the prairie and the children's greatest anxiety was whether "he" would find the little house which was half buried. Margaret, with the characteristic ingenuity of the female of the species, suggested tying a piece of bright cloth where "he" would notice it. And Mack, with the characteristic daring of the less deadly of the same, got on top of the low house via a crusty snow bank and tied one of little John's red flannel shirts to the stove-pipe.

At lamp-lighting, they all hung up their stockings, even Will and Abbie. The children were beside themselves with excitement. By their parents' stockings they put the little presents they had made for them. They danced and skipped and sang. They cupped their eyes with their hands, pressing their faces to the little half-window and looking out into the night. The gleam of the stars was reflected in the snow, and the silence of the sky was the silence of the prairie.

"I see the Star."

"So do I. Right up there."

"It looks like it was over a stable."

"Yes, sir. It looks like it was over a manger-stable."

"Now it looks like it's stopping over us."

"Yes, sir, it looks like it's stopping right over *our* house."

Wide-eyed, they went to bed. The three faces in a row on the pillows, with the patchwork quilts tucked under the chins, were flushed with anticipation.

"Always keep the Christmas spirit going," Abbie told them. "Promise me, that when you get big and have homes of your own, you'll keep the Christmas spirit in your homes."

"We will," they promised in glib and solemn accord.

When at last they slept, Will brought in the little cedar tree. The morning found it trimmed with popcorn and tallow candles. And a marvelous flock of butterflies had settled upon it. Their bodies were of dried apples dipped in sugar and their antennæ were pink and feathery, looking surprisingly as though they had once adorned Regina Deal's bonnet. Will had made and painted Abbie a corner what-not with four shelves, secreting it in the stable behind some straw bedding. And he had constructed a monstrous hobby-horse for the children, the body and head of cottonwood chunks, real horse's hair for mane and tail, reins and a bit in the steed's cut-out mouth. The wooden horse of Troy never looked so huge. And then the old brass horn was unwrapped.

"I'm so excited," Mack said, in solemn ecstasy. "I'm so excited . . . my legs itch."

Historians say, "The winter of 'seventy-four to 'seventy-five was a time of deep depression." But historians do not take little children into consideration. Deep depression? To three children on the prairie it was a time of glamour. There was not much to eat in the cupboard. There was little or no money in the father's flat old pocketbook. The presents were pitifully homely and meager. And all in a tiny house,—a mere shell of a house, on a new raw acreage of the wild, bleak prairie. How could a little rude cabin hold so much white magic? How could a little sod house know such enchantment? And how could a little hut like that eventually give to the midwest so many influential men and women? How, indeed? Unless, . . . unless, perchance, the star *did* stop over the house?

It was a half century later and Abbie made her usual extensive preparations for Christmas that year. The daughters and daughters-in-law said a great deal against her using up so much energy. "But you might as well talk to the wind," Grace wrote to Isabelle. "There's something stubborn about Mother. She is bound to go through with all that mincemeat, doughtnut, popcorn-ball ordeal even if she's sick in bed afterward. Margaret wants us to come there to save her all that work, and Emma and Eloise have both offered their homes, too, but she won't listen. 'No,' she says, 'as long as I'm here, the Christmas gathering is here.' I've tried to tell her over and over that conditions have changed, that we don't live out on an isolated prairie any more; that she doesn't make one thing that she couldn't buy, but she just won't catch up with the times. 'They're not so full of the Christmas spirit when you don't fix them yourself,' she says. Isn't that the last word in old-fashioned ideas?"

So the clan came once more to the old farmhouse behind the cedars. Grace was the first to arrive in her own roadster, coming over the graveled highway from Wesleyan University. The others arrived at various times before Christmas eve. Mack and Emma, Donald and Katherine came. Only Stanley was missing from the Mack Deal family. Having married, Stanley had discovered that a wife's people must also be reckoned with. Margaret and Dr. Fred Baker, Dr. Fred, Jr., and his wife and two little boys came. Isabelle and Harrison Rhodes got in from Chicago on the afternoon train, the road boasting a flyer now instead of the old baggage-and-day affair of the time when the children were small. John and Eloise, Wentworth and Laura and Millard, who was eight now, all came over from their home on the other side of Cedartown in time for the evening meal. Every car was loaded to the doors with packages.

Abbie had an oyster supper. That, too, was a hang-over from the days when sea food was scarce and expensive. No matter that the bivalves were on every menu placed before the various members of the Deal family these days, Abbie continued to have an oyster supper each Christmas eve,—bowls of crackers alternating down the long table with celery, standing upright in vase-looking dishes, like so many bouquets from the greenhouse.

Jimmie Buchanan came over later in the evening and brought Katherine a gift. Jimmie was rather astounded at the sight of so many relatives.

"Every one has to be here," Katherine told him. "In all the wedding ceremonies, whenever a Deal is married, the question is asked, 'Do you solemnly promise to spend all your Christmases at Granny Deal's, forsaking all others as long as you shall live?' And if you can't promise,—out you go before you're in."

Abbie Deal was embarrassed beyond words. To speak so to a young man with whom you were keeping company!

Katherine went on, "No, sir,—it wouldn't be Christmas without the wax flowers in the parlor and the patent rocking-chair and the painting of the purple cow and the *whutnut*. Grandma makes us all animal cookies yet. Can you beat it? When I was big enough to read love stories by the dozens, she gave me 'The Frog That Would A-Wooing Go,'—not but that it had its romantic appeal, too. We always stay two nights and we have to have beds everywhere. Granny puts us in corners, on couches, sinks, bath-tubs, ironing-boards . . . and not one of us would miss it. Donald passed up a dance at the Fontanelle for it. You can't tell the reason, but the minute you see those old cedar trees and come up the lane under the Bombarded poplars with snow on 'em, you're just little and crazy over Christmas."

There were some very lovely presents the next morning,—jewelry, a fur, expensive toys and books,—an old musty smelling one for Emma, who had gone in for first and rare editions. Margaret gave her mother the painting of the prairie with the sunshine lying in little yellow-pink pools between the low rolling hills. "For I think you made me love it, Mother, when I was a little girl. I learned to see it through your eyes," she told her.

In the afternoon, Mackenzie Deal, the Omaha banker, in an overcoat and old muffler that had been his father's, spent a large share of his time out in the barn cracking walnuts on a cottonwood chunk. John Deal, the state legislator, went up into the hay-loft and potted a few pigeons with an old half-rusty gun. Isabelle Deal Rhodes, the well-known Chicago singer, called her husband to help her get the old reed-organ out of the storehouse. She dusted it, and then, amid a great deal of hilarity, pumped out, "By the Blue Alsatian Mountains." One of the keys gave forth no sound at all, so that whenever she came to it the young folks all shouted the missing note.

By evening the younger members of the group had gone,—Fred Jr. and his family back to Lincoln, Donald and Wentworth to Omaha, while Katherine was off somewhere with Jimmie Buchanan. But the others, in the early dusk of the Christmas twilight, gathered in the parlor with the homely coal-burner and the lovely floor lamp, with Abbie's crude painting of the prairie and Margaret's exquisite one, with the what-not and the blue plush album and the tidy on the back of the patent-rocker.

"There was one Christmas we had, Mother," Mack said, "that I always remember more than the others. I can see the things yet,—my old brass cornet, a big wooden horse made out of logs, a tree that looked . . . well, I've never seen a tree since look so grand. Where in Sam Hill did you raise all the things in those days?"

"I think I know which one you mean," Abbie was reminiscent. "It was the year after the grasshoppers. Well, my son, your father and I made all of those things out of sticks and rags and patches and love."

It brought on a flood of reminiscences.

"Remember, Mack, the Sunday afternoon we were herding hogs on the prairie and that Jake Smith who kept the store at Unadilla, came along with his girl in a spring wagon, and threw a whole handful of stick candy out in the grass for us?" Mrs. Frederick Hamilton Baker, well-known artist and club woman of Lincoln, was speaking.

"Do I? I can see them yet, red- and white-striped,—and looking as big as barber-poles to me. I wondered how any one in the world could be that rich and lavish," Mackenzie Deal, a vice-president of one of the Omaha banks, was answering.

"And do you remember, John, how scared you were . . . the time we chased the calf and you grabbed it by the tail when it ran by you and the tail was frozen and came off in your hands?"

When they had all laughed at the recollection, Isabelle put in, "But I'll bet he wasn't as scared as I was once, . . . the time a man came to the door and told Father he was drawn on the jury. You all stood around looking solemn, and I took a run for Mother's old wardrobe and hid in behind the clothes and cried."

"Why . . . what did you think?" They were all asking.

"Well, I knew 'jury' had something to do with law and jails and penitentiaries. And I had heard of 'hung,' 'quartered' and '*drawn*' so the inference was that Father was going to be hung in the penitentiary."

"That's as bad as I was." It was John. "Remember that preacher who used to stop at our house, the one with the beard that looked as though it was made out of yellow rope?"

"Who could forget it? He tied it up like a horse's tail when he ate." They were all answering at once.

"The first time he stopped, he said to Mack, 'What's your name, son?' Mack said, 'Mackenzie.' 'And what's yours, little man?' he said to me. I was so scared I said 'Mackenzie,' too. Can you beat it? I'll bet there isn't a kid living to-day as bashful as that."

And so they went on, recalling their childhood days,—days of sunburn and days of chilblains, of made-over clothes and corn-bread meals, of trudging behind plows or picking up potatoes, of work that was interwoven with fun, because youth was youth. Prairie children never forget.

Far into the evening they sat around the old coal burner, talking and laughing, with tears not far behind the laughter,—the state legislator and the banker, the artist, the singer, and the college teacher. And in their midst, rocking and smiling, sat the little old lady who had brought them up with a song upon her lips and a lantern in her hand.

PART II

"Down on the Farm"

Country Days

America began on a farm. The land is our heritage, and the strength of our national character is rooted there. A modern homestead may be as mechanized as a factory, but the old traditions and customs have kept their place not alone in the heart of the farm family, but in the hearts of those of us who, having left the country, find that the country will not leave us.

Once we have considered the pleasures of living on a farm and enjoying the country year, we naturally think of the shared experiences and the people who made them memorable. We remember those tireless people who ministered to the needs of the community: The horse-and-buggy doctor who battled mud and icy weather to visit a sick child; the preacher who came to call not always at a time that suited Mother best; the indispensable hired man who often was almost a member of the family.

We remember the work, for it occupied the major portion of our days. From "can see to can't see" we were busy with chores. A Vermonter knew the excitement of sugaring-off and the syrupy smell of a sugar camp, a Southerner the feel of the hoe in his hands as he chopped cotton. Any farm-bred man or woman has tended the stock, oiled harnesses, or turned the dasher of a churn.

Then there were the places we knew and loved: The country store, where we gazed at such luxuries as hoarhound candy and China bedroom crockery; the old country school where a boy had to make his own way.

There were celebrations, too. The Sunday School picnic with lemonade by the gallon and country ham and declamations and stomach-aches; husking bees and quiltings; hog-calling contests that decided the county champion. And who can forget those necessary standbys, the Sears, Roebuck Catalogue, and the Farmer's Almanac, which took their places next to the family Bible on the parlor table?

On Living in the Country

By David Grayson

Sometimes a man born to farm will also be able to transmit the adventure and fulfillment of planting his own land, fighting a thousand threats to his crop, and finally bringing the harvest home. David Grayson writes of the deep satisfaction he found in farm life in the following passage from *Great Possessions*.

It is astonishing how many people there are in cities and towns who have a secret longing to get back into quiet country places, to own a bit of the soil of the earth, and to cultivate it. To some it appears as a troublesome malady only in spring and will be relieved by a whirl or two in country roads, by a glimpse of the hills, or a day by the sea; but to others the homesickness is deeper seated and will be quieted by no hasty visits. These must actually go home.

I have had, in recent years, many letters from friends asking about life in the country, but the longer I remain here, the more I know about it, the less able I am to answer them—at least briefly. It is as though one should come and ask: "Is love worth trying?" or, "How about religion?" For country life is to each human being a fresh, strange, original adventure. We enjoy it, or we do not enjoy it, or more probably, we do both. It is packed and crowded with the zest of adventure, or it is dull and miserable. We may, if we are skilled enough, make our whole living from the land, or only a part of it, or we may find in a few cherished acres the inspiration and power for other work, whatever it may be. There is many a man whose strength is renewed like that of the wrestler of Irassa, every time his feet touch the earth.

Of all places in the world where life can be lived to its fullest and freest, where it can be met in its greatest variety and beauty, I am convinced that there is none to equal the open country, or the country town. For all country people in these days may have the city—some city or town not too far away; but there are millions of men and women in America who have no country and no sense of the country. What do they not lose out of life!

I know well the disadvantages charged against country life at its worst. At its worst there are long hours and much lonely labour and an income pitifully small. Drudgery, yes, especially for the women, and loneliness. But where is there not drudgery when men are poor—where life is at its worst? I have never seen drudgery in the country comparable for a moment to the dreary and lonely drudgery of city tenements, city mills, factories, and sweat shops. And in recent years both the drudgery and loneliness of country life have been disappearing before the motor and trolley car, the telephone, the rural post, the gasoline engine. I have seen a machine plant as many potatoes in one day as a man, at hand work, could have planted in a week. While there is, indeed, real drudgery in the country, much that is looked upon as drudgery by people who long for easy ways and a soft life, is only good, honest, wholesome hard work—the kind of work that makes for fiber in a man or in a nation, the kind that most city life in no way provides.

There are a thousand nuisances and annoyances that men must meet who come face to face with nature itself. You have set out your upper acres to peach trees: and the deer come down from the hills and strip the young foliage; or the field mice in winter, working under the snow, girdle and kill them. The season brings too much rain and the potatoes rot in the ground, the crows steal the corn, the bees swarm when no one is watching, the cow smothers her calf, the hens' eggs prove infertile, and a storm in a day ravages a crop that has been growing all summer. A constant warfare with insects and blights and fungi—a real, bitter warfare, which can cease neither summer nor winter!

It is something to meet, year after year, the quiet implacability of the land. While it is patient, it never waits long for you. There is a chosen time for planting, a time for cultivating, a time for harvesting. You accept the gauge thrown down—well and good, you shall have a chance to fight! You do not accept it? There is no complaint. The land cheerfully springs up to wild yellow mustard and dandelion and pig-weed—and will be productive and beautiful in spite of you.

Nor can you enter upon the full satisfaction of cultivating even a small piece of land at second hand. To be accepted as One Who Belongs, there must be sweat and weariness.

The other day I was digging with Dick in a ditch that is to run down through the orchard and connect finally with the land drain we put in four years ago. We laid the tile just in the gravel below the silt, about two feet deep, covering the openings with tar paper and then throwing in gravel. It was a bright, cool afternoon. In the field below a ploughman was at work: I could see the furrows of the dark earth glisten as he turned it over. The grass in the meadow was a full rich green, the new chickens were active in their yards, running to the cluck of the hens, already the leaves of the orchard trees showed green. And as I worked there with Dick I had the curious deep feeling of coming somehow into a new and more intimate possession of my own land. For titles do not really pass with signatures and red seals, nor with money changing from one hand to another, but for true possession one must work and serve according to the most ancient law. There is no mitigation and no haggling of price. Those who think they can win the greatest joys of country life on any easier terms are mistaken.

But if one has drained his land, and ploughed it, and fertilized it, and planted it and harvested it—even though it be only a few acres—how he comes to know and to love every rod of it. He knows the wet spots, and the stony spots, and the warmest and most fertile spots—until his acres have all the qualities of a personality, whose every characteristic he knows. It is so also that he comes to know his horses and cattle and pigs and hens. It is a fine thing, on a warm day in early spring, to bring out the bee-hives and let the bees have their first flight in the sunshine. What cleanly folk they are! And later to see them coming in yellow all over with pollen from the willows! It is a fine thing to watch the cherries and plum trees come into blossom, with us about the first of May, while all the remainder of the orchard seems still sleeping. It is a fine thing to see the cattle turned for the first time in spring into the green meadows. It is a fine thing—one of the finest of all—to see and smell the rain in a corn-field after weeks of drought. How it comes softly out of gray skies, the first drops throwing up spatters of dust and losing themselves in the dry soil. Then the clouds sweep forward up the valley, darkening the meadows and blotting out the hills, and then there is the whispering of the rain as it first sweeps across the corn-field. At once what a stir of life! What rustling of the long green leaves. What joyful shaking and swaying of the tassels! And have you watched how eagerly the grooved leaves catch the early drops, and, lest there be too little rain after all, conduct them jealously down the stalks where they will soonest reach the thirsty roots? What a fine thing is this to see!

One who thus takes part in the whole process of the year comes soon to have an indescribable affection for his land, his garden, his animals. There are thoughts of his in every tree: memories in every fence corner. Just now, the fourth of June, I walked down past my blackberry patch, now come gorgeously into full white bloom—and heavy with fragrance. I set out these plants with my own hands, I have fed them, cultivated them, mulched them, pruned them, trellised them, and helped every year to pick the berries. How could they be otherwise than full of associations! They bear a fruit more beautiful than can be found in any catalogue: and stranger and wilder than in any learned botany book!

Why, one who comes thus to love a bit of countryside may enjoy it all the year round. When he awakens in the middle of a long winter night he may send his mind out to the snowy fields—I've done it a thousand times!—and visit each part in turn, stroll through the orchard and pay his respects to each tree—in a small orchard one comes to know familiarly every tree as he knows his friends—stop at the strawberry bed, consider the grape trellises, feel himself opening the door of the warm, dark stable and listening to the welcoming whicker of his horses, or visiting his cows, his pigs, his sheep, his hens, or so many of them as he may have.

So much of the best in the world seems to have come fragrant out of fields, gardens, and hillsides. So many truths spoken by the Master Poet come to us exhaling the odours of the open country. His stories were so often of sowers, husbandmen, herdsmen: his similes and illustrations so often dealt with the common and familiar beauty of the fields: "Consider the lilies how they grow." It was on a hillside that he preached his greatest sermon, and when in the last agony he sought a place to meet his God, where did he go but to a garden? A carpenter you say? Yes, but of this one may be sure: there were gardens and fields all about: he knew gardens, and cattle, and the simple processes of the land: he must have worked in a garden and loved it well.

A Country Year

By Lansing Christman

Slow, inexorable, beautiful, the procession of the seasons cannot fail to stir any perceptive heart. Sometimes the countryman is deeply moved without quite knowing why. Lansing Christman plays unexpected columns of light on long-familiar objects and emotions.

A countryman will always welcome the new year with an anticipation that is made full and rich by all that the past years have given to his hills. The changes that come as the seasons yield, one to another, make a man look forward with eagerness and with hope. The new year, of course, is likely to step across a man's northern slopes through the deepness of snow. Winds may whistle sharply around the house and the barns; they may hum through the boughs of the roadside pines; they may push and bend the limbs of the dooryard elms and the maples. The winds may sing through a winter woods.

But no matter how the new year comes, a man looks ahead to all that the months will bring. The year is a countryman's upland store; the shelves are stocked with songs and blooms, with sunlight and clouds, with wind and placid quietness. The store is stocked with many nights and many days. And all, in turn, will be brought down from the shelves of the year and handed out to a man if he is one to accept from the provident pantry of the hills. The only price he pays is an observing eye and an open heart, an appreciation of birds and flowers, of trees and earth and stone, a love of the land.

A winter wind is invigorating to a countryman. Its sharp keen edges have never chilled his eagerness for long and reflective walks through the uplands. There will be softer April winds. It is fitting, a man thinks, that a northern new year comes when the hills are resting, more or less, resting for their own good season of work. Buds will build into bloom, into leaf and seed. There will be a summer of sun, and a golden harvesting.

The new year comes to a man in all the glory of a rising sun over the morning hills. A countryman cannot enumerate all of the dawns that he has seen. There have been years of them. Yet there is an air of enthusiasm about each new dawn; there is an air of hope. It is deeply instilled into man. And though he has seen the coming of many years to his old farm slopes, there is the same anticipation in each one that assumes its delightful role over the rolling fields and woodlands. It is good for a man to experience the year's close, its full and rich completion. It is good for a man to experience the coming of a year in its vibrant newness. The new year has the freshness of an upland dawn, the hope of a singing and liquid spring. Deep in his winter solitude, a countryman looks to spring, even now, for the new year will point the way of the turning earth to warmer, softer hours.

Spring Outlook

A countryman may well start his outlook for spring long before the season of song tiptoes up from the south to soften his hills. From mid-January on, he has noted that the lengthening hours of sunlight have become more and more pronounced. The sunsets are later, and the dawns come earlier. A man thinks there is more mildness now in the calls and sounds about him, as if the taut winter chords were slackening. The leafless woodlands yield a soft grayness, indicative of swollen buds that will some day come into bloom. The sun, reaching higher, warms the south side of a man's barns and garden walls, and the snow, sheltered from the wind, begins to melt and disappear, even on the sharpest days. Barn roofs and stone walls and south slopes are more receptive to the palms of the warming hands of the sun.

A man thinks of this time of year as a winter pause, the dawn of spring, a prelude to the richer days of thaw and flowing streams, the open fields. He has watched the osiers along the swamp turn brilliantly red as if to point out the course of the swamp's channel which spring will open, and which the muskrats will use. The willows spread a golden hue against the snow-covered slopes, golden as the light of a late afternoon dipped across the land. The catkins of the pussy willow and the alder are soft and swollen. Winter may still hold the reins of the year in its icy hands, but spring is moving in. A man expects it any day, or any hour. A man knows these very hours are building surely and quietly and gently into a day of music and bloom. He relishes the thought that his hills and woodlands are being prepared for the great awakening, readied for the harrow and the plow and the seed.

The air is filled with expectancy and hope. In the stillness of the morning, a man walks along his creek. He listens to the gurgling sound of water under ice. He listens to the seed-pods of the creek-bank's giant ash drop with a clicking sound upon the crusted snow. Purple finches are at work among the propeller-like seeds; a man notes the brilliant purple of the finch against the morning sun; he thinks he sees the beauty of the dawn reflected there. Above the pool, a chipmunk hurries over the snow like a yellow streak, like a child drawing a crayon carelessly over a sprawling sheet of white.

The sun spreads its light longer now over an upland farm, and a countryman is receptive to the milder calls and songs. He is receptive to the wood's soft grayness, to the brilliance of the osier and the willow, to the swollen buds of the lilac and the birch and the maple. In this pause before spring, a man warms his outlook for that delightful country hour ushered in over the hills with a robin's carol or a redwing's flute.

Strawberries and June

Old meadows are a delightful part of an upland farm when June has come again to spread warmth and color and flavor through the weeds and the thinning hay. A countryman knows he will find all that he could ask of the sun-warmed days when he brushes his way with anticipation through the timothy and the daisies and hawkweed to the fields where the wild strawberry grows. The rich aroma, carried on a gentle wind, will lead him to the very spots where the berries are ripening in profusion and quietness. He cannot resist the flavor any more than he can forget the aroma, carried on the soft breeze of every June that he can remember.

A man knows that he will see June at its best. He will spend hours in the old fields, deep in the waving grass and weeds. He will work his hands among the leaves to pick the clusters of ripened berries. The sun will brown his arms; he likes the warmth. He will watch the barn swallows in their swift flight over the flats. He will hear the bubbling song of the bobolink over the high fields. He will hear the cricket and the oriole and the field sparrow. He will watch the rhythmic undulation of the ripening hay across his lands.

A man is glad that June is in song. He will share its symphonic chords, resounding beautifully through the rolling theater of the hills. He feels the pulse of the earth, and the waves of heat moving evenly over his acres. He loses himself in the contentment of the upland slopes where only the sun tells of the passing of the hours, and the wild strawberry tells richly the season of the year.

When his baskets are filled, and he turns his steps once more toward home, a countryman knows full well he has harvested far more than the strawberry, for he has taken in, too, all that is associated with an upland farm and a long June day of song. He has imbued himself with the songs and the chords, with the sun, and the rolling hills. And he knows they will, for all the years to come, be a part of what he sees and hears and thinks; that they will be fluid and clear and pure as the kind summer brook that moistens and cools the roots of the cress and the buttercup. He knows they will, from summer to summer, flavor his philosophy with friendliness and content.

Summer Thundershower

A summer thundershower, moving in at last upon the uplands to break the long dry spell, brings a deep richness to man and his meadows and woods and pasturelands. The shower comes with a moistening comfort to the parched fields. The brown of a summer pasture yields to green again. A man thinks his cows must certainly find the grass more succulent now, and a new green spreads out once more over the meadows where the hay was harvested in June.

At work in his garden, a countryman watches the shower building up in the west. The hour seems as though it were one of a serene silence, with hardly a stir of wind. The thunderheads work higher overhead, and the skies darken over the rim of the western hills. The sun is still hot though, and bird songs have almost come to an end. A man does hear a medley of goldfinch calls in this breathless hour. And he hears the chattering of swallows dipping low in their flights over the gardens and fields.

The faint rumble of thunder gives an almost certain indication that relief is close at hand. The thunder grows louder; there is expectation and hope, and even before the shower is actually upon his own acres, a countryman hears the driving sheets of rain and wind sweeping over the neighboring woods. Leaves rustle and the mullein stalks bend and sway. Moving in to his porch to watch the storm, he sees the hot stone walks steam as the rain falls. Pools form in the hollowed pockets of the stone. The shower is sufficiently long to start a trickle of water in the creek, dried by the rainless weeks since early June.

A man relishes the thundershower and as soon as the rain subsides, he walks out again into the fields. He finds a fresh and cooling atmosphere across the hills. He likes the freshness of the grass and earth, and the aroma of cleanliness that permeates the air. Robins too, have found goodness from the shower; they move almost methodically over the spreading lawns. Goldfinches are back in the creek seeking the liquid shallow pools. Evening comes, and the song of the hermit thrush seems to carry more clearly from the depths of the woodland. It is as though their bell-like notes had been made a little richer by the rain. A countryman sort of hopes that his own songs can ring with the same cadence and clarity as that of the upland hermit thrush after a thundershower has spilled its nourishing moisture upon the rolling meadows and the summer woods.

Through All His Autumns

A man likes to think that the mood of the falling leaf is tempered by the mood of the day, or the night, or by the mood of the hour. The pace is easy in the softness of a rain, in the quietness of sun and stars. But a man, walking with the wind to his back, will find his pace a quickened one. And so will a falling leaf.

He is a true countryman who looks with wisdom and restfulness upon this ever recurring change in the year. He does not mind at all that autumn moves in upon his uplands, for even now he finds a promise in the change.

The leaves may fall in sweeping showers of color before the driving gusts of wind, or they may descend slowly and quietly in the autumn calm, or they may fall softly in a rain. It does not matter. A countryman can forever find a delightful beauty in the leaves, hurried by the wind, seeking their quiet shelter in a dooryard hedge, behind old stone walls, in the woods, in the basins of pools and ponds, and in the streams. Some, he knows, will stay in the shelter they have found. Some will move downstream with the surging currents of water pouring down from the hills after the heavy fall rains; some will wait until March to move with the flow of the rich spring thaw.

Through all his autumns, a countryman is glad that he has detected no sadness in the hour of falling leaves. He likes the season; he likes to watch the leaves fall with the moisture of a rain upon the leafy carpet of a wood. On a still bright day, on a day filled with golden sunlight after frost, a man likes to pause, and to watch and to listen. He can hear the clicking of the crisp and colored leaves, striking upon branches and twigs, striking one another in their spiraling rhythmic fall to earth.

It does a countryman good to feel that his trees, spread across his hills and by his roadsides and lanes, and in his dooryard, have done their year of work, and that they seek now their own sweet night of rest, a rich siesta of quietness. All summer long a man's trees have given beauty and comfort and shade. And certainly, he knows, spring will come again to whisper to the hills. The trees will give their answer, ages old, in a warming morning of opening buds, and unfolding leaves.

Light As a Wing

A countryman appreciates the way that winter settles down at last to a routine of steadiness. He likes the upland winter, the persistence of cold, the snows and strong driving winds. And outside a man's door, his hill farm neighbors sweep in again from thicket and woodlot and slope, to the dooryard bird feeds and the window sills.

There are tree sparrows and juncos, hairy and downy woodpeckers, nuthatches and blue jays. There may be a wintering song sparrow, and a meadowlark or two. Snow buntings move down now and then from the higher wind-swept hills. Sometimes the purple finch and the goldfinch join in a breakfast on the farm lawn's spreading tables. While tree sparrows scratch in the seeds scattered on the crusts of snow, the nuthatches and woodpeckers hammer at the suet hung on the sheltered sides of pear trees and the giant elms. But the most friendly visitor of all, a countryman thinks, is the black-capped chickadee which comes right up to the kitchen window and to a man's hands for the crumbs of fried cakes and broken nut meats that have been provided on the cold clear dawn of each new day.

These are a man's winter neighbors through the weeks of sun and snows, through the long slow hours of driving winds and cold. They etch the stinging days with cheer and friendliness. Some of a countryman's most delightful hours have been spent with the birds. He hears a winter dawn filled with their constant notes and chirps. And it is hard for him to think of a season as too long or too sharp when he can start the day with the pleasing notes of a chickadee's call ringing out through the frost or a dense swirling snow.

Winter loses its heaviness. It becomes as beautiful and intricate as a star-shaped snowflake on a swollen lilac bud. Winter becomes as gentle as the wing of a tree sparrow in the dooryard hedge, as delicate as the touch of a chickadee's toes clinging to the fingers of a countryman's outstretched hand. Winter's sharp ways are turned into a gentleness that befits the friendly little chickadee, ready to take flight after a breakfast of delicacies in the homemade bird house that swings softly in a wind that has worked its way around the corner of the veranda, a wind that never quite reaches to the shelter of the kitchen door. A man who feeds the birds can find the hills of snow as friendly as a summer meadowland of timothy and bloom. Winter's heaviness becomes as light as a wing, and lovely as a song.

Growing Up in the Country

By Alben W. Barkley

From George Washington to the present administration, a reassuring number of men in our government spent their early lives on the farm. Here is a segment from the country boyhood of one of our most popular Vice Presidents, the man who gave affectionate meaning to the word "Veep."

While I am proud, of course, of being a Southerner, I have always taken equal pride in the fact that I have no geographical prejudices. I may beam and lift my more or less mellifluous baritone in song when I hear the strains of "My Old Kentucky Home," but my heart beats fast when "America the Beautiful" is played. This, of course, is the way it should be in this wonderful country of ours.

I have always regarded myself as fortunate in being brought up in a part of Kentucky where no sectional or racial animosities were bred into me. This freedom from prejudices was rather remarkable, since Graves County is in the so-called "Jackson's Purchase" portion of the state, which had strong Southern sympathies during the Civil War.

At any rate, for years after the Civil War, a candidate for political office in our part of Kentucky who had not had at least one limb shot off while fighting for the Confederacy might as well have whistled down a rain barrel. There's the classic story of the hapless candidate for coroner of Graves County who was attending a speaking at Pilot Oak. That is the community which gave McKinley (Rep.) only 4 votes out of 496 when he ran for President in 1896 against Bryan (Dem.). This particular candidate was being opposed by three visibly maimed Confederate veterans. The first one, wearing his gray uniform coat, stood up and proudly called attention to the empty sleeve denoting the arm he had lost in the battle of Cynthiana. The next had lost a leg at Chickamauga; the third, an eye at Perryville.

When the final candidate, hopelessly outclassed, got up to make his appeal, he took the only course. "I never got wounded; I never even fit in the war," he said. "But, if physical disability is to be regarded as an indispensable qualification for the office of coroner, I hereby announce, unqualifiedly and unequivocally, that I am the most completely ruptured son-of-a-gun who ever ran for public office!"

I also remember a Civil War story that I used to hear Irvin S. Cobb tell when he was a newspaper reporter and I was a struggling lawyer in Paducah. It seemed that two Confederate veterans were reminiscing about the days during the war when Paducah was being fought over by the Northern and Southern forces. "I remember," one veteran said, "when we pushed those damyankees all the way across the Ohio and up into Illinois!" The other old soldier regretfully corrected him. "I was there, old friend," he said, "and I'm afraid that wasn't the way it happened at all. Those Yankees drove *us* out of Paducah and almost to the Tennessee line." The first veteran reflected a bit, then sourly remarked, "Another good story ruined by an eyewitness!"

When I was a boy in Kentucky, I would go out and work on the farms of neighboring farmers. Sometimes I would work in the wheat fields as a thresher; then I would labor with shovel, spade, and ax, digging stumps out of the fields so that crops could be planted. Often Negro men and boys would be hired also and would work beside me. In that way I learned that you do not judge a man's character by the color of his skin.

As a matter of fact, I was nine years old before I ever saw a colored person. He was a young fellow named Silas, who showed up at our house one day and told us his folks had worked for Grandfather Barkley when my grandfather had lived in Tennessee. Silas brought his banjo, on which he was expert, and played for us. From then on he came frequently and became a favorite with all of us.

One of the finest, hardest-working men I have ever known was a Negro farmer named Matt Vincent, who lived up the road from us after our family moved to Clinton. Often I worked with Matt at stump-digging, and during the lunch hour we would sit together in the stump hole that we had dug, he eating the lunch which his wife had prepared for him and I eating the sandwiches which my mother had fixed me. He would tell me of his daughters, in whom he took great pride, and of how he intended to give them the best education possible for them to obtain. He did so, and they grew up to become outstanding schoolteachers in the community. As Matt Vincent and I sat there, eating together and talking, there was no question of social equality; it was simply a matter of two persons, one white and one black, getting acquainted and developing a mutual respect for each other.

In the wheat fields I worked with other Negro men, and I learned from them the words and tunes of folk songs which I doubt that you will find written down anywhere. They would make up these songs as they worked, chanting them to monotonous, mournful tunes, and it would provide a rhythm which set a steady pace for the swinging of the scythes which sheared the stalks of wheat. Some of these stanzas have remained in my memory for more than sixty years. One, in particular, began:

See dat dummy, comin' down de line,
(In de evenin'!)
See dat dummy, comin' down de line,
(In de mornin'!)
See dat dummy, comin' down de line,
He had to run sideways to keep from flyin'!
(Mah Baby!)

The pattern was repeated with infinite variations:

Striped-legged britches an' a pigeon-tail coat, Got hair on his chest lak' a damn billy-goat; Catching rabbits ain't no sin, Open yore mouth and shove 'em in; See dat jaybird a-sittin' on de limb, He winked at me an' I winked at him; When I die, won't yuh bury me deep? An' tell all mah wimmen I'se gone to sleep . . .

and, finally, always sung with great feeling, the concluding stanza:

See dese DIA-MONDS on mah breast,
(In de evenin'!)
See dese DIA-MONDS on mah breast,
(In de mornin'!)
See dese DIA-MONDS on mah breast,
An' tell all mah wimmen I'se gone to rest!
(Mah Baby!)

I was about fourteen years old when I began working in the wheat fields. Father and I would go out together at a season when the work on our own farm could be left to my younger brothers. We did it to augment the family's meager income, for we would be paid a dollar a day each for our labor, plus two dollars for the use of our team and wagon. We would stay away from home a week at a time, sleeping either under our wagon, in the farmer's hay loft, or in the new-made straw pile. At an even earlier age I began using an ax and handling my end of a crosscut saw with my father. He was a great woodsman and believed in clearing his fields and hills of trees and stumps. I suppose in my time I have split as many rails as Abraham Lincoln, though I have received less credit for it—and, of course, was never elected to the White House with rail-splitting as a slogan.

For most of my early life in Kentucky our family lived on small farms which my father, John Wilson Barkley, rented. One year Father was renting fifty acres or so on the Martha Sellars place. He was able to employ a hired hand that season—he was a man named Boyd Watson, and Father paid him fifty cents a day and board—and with this extra help he brought in a record tobacco crop that yielded $600 cash. With this money he was able to graduate from the tenant-farmer class by making a down payment on fifty acres of his own, part of a tract near Lowes known as the Coleman place. That purchase of his own farm was one of Father's proudest achievements.

My father was a strong, hard-working man, much like Grandfather Alben in both habits and appearance. He was a farmer most of his life, and, like his father, an elder in the Presbyterian church. He was married at the age of twenty-two to seventeen-year-old Electra Eliza Smith, daughter of a Confederate soldier who died of injuries received with Morgan's cavalry.

Father never had it easy during any of the years on the various farms which he worked. Thinking back on how he toiled, I am reminded of the story of the Negro preacher who called on a hard-working parishioner, a farmer, each year, soliciting increasingly larger contributions for the church. One year, when he got the proposed levy past a point which the farmer thought he could bear, the preacher sought to persuade him by arguing, "Your farm's been good to you, and the Lord's been good to you. Part of this land belongs to the Lord. You're in partnership with Him, so you ought to give Him His share." To which the farmer replied, "I acknowledges that the farm is paying off, that the Lord's been good to me, and that He is my partner. But did you ever see this place when the Lord was looking after it Hisself?"

I think my father would have enjoyed this story, though both he and my mother were highly religious people and they gave us a strict, old-fashioned upbringing. There was lots of fun, but little of what might be called frivolity in our home. I never saw a pack of cards, for instance, in Father's house, and to this day I have never taken up any card games—a circumstance which in later life used to cause such good friends as Vice President "Cactus Jack" Garner to growl at me occasionally.

Father would not work on Sundays unless there was some dire emergency. Stove wood had to be split on the previous day. The only breach of this rule that I remember occurred one Sunday when our tobacco crop, which represented a whole season of work and income, was threatened by a sudden freezing spell. Father, after wrestling with his conscience, asked the neighbors to help him save the crop. If we had lost it, of course, all of us would have gone hungry all winter.

On Sundays my mother would not even touch the cookstove, unless the preacher happened to be coming for dinner; in that case, we figured, as the old country saying goes, that "the ox was in the ditch."

My mother was a fabulous cook. I still get lyrical at memories of her egg custard pie. It was a special sort of egg custard pie, with a delicate and fragrant seasoning; it was not fluffy and airy and void of substance, in the manner aspired to by some of these modern, calory-conscious cooks, but it was a substantial, solid creation that stuck to your ribs and gave strength to the body as well as delight to the gustatory senses. Mommy was equally good on cakes and preserves and many other dishes. In fact, I never think of the table she set without remembering the story I once heard Father tell when I accompanied him on a wagon trip to the store to lay in a winter's supply of goods for the family. Despite Father's devoutness he had a sense of humor and was a good teller of stories, many of which I still remember and use.

As Father told it, it seems that a countrywoman of the same school as my mother had invited the preacher over for an old-fashioned Sunday dinner, not knowing he had what we used to call dyspepsia. The ten-year-old boy of the house—I was about that age myself when I heard Father tell the story—incredulously watched the minister decline helpings of soups, ham, hominy grits, fried chicken, roast goose, sausage, vegetables, biscuits, homemade bread, preserves, cake, and pies. Finally the boy spoke up and said, "Maw, you reckon the old fool would suck a raw egg?"

In such a household as ours the only "likker" permitted past the threshold was a small bottle of corn which had been rendered completely unpalatable, even poisonous, by the liberal addition of camphor balls. This was for external use only: to be rubbed on the chest when "the croup set in."

If there is anything to the old belief that a dram of whiskey is good for snakebite, the lack of it in our ménage almost cost the nation its future Vice President, for at the age of six I was bitten by a copperhead and almost died. We were living at the time in a log cabin; I remember it well, for it was the most primitive cabin we ever lived in—a crude affair with a stick-and-dirt chimney; it was a wonder the place did not burn down every time we lit a fire. Our chickens roosted under the floor of the cabin, and they were being bothered by rats. I was told to crawl under there and chase out the chickens so they would roost in the trees. When I did so, a copperhead, which, of course, we had not known was also lurking under the floor, got me. I did not know exactly what had happened, but, in a short time, I began feeling queer. I opened my mouth to yell for Poppy, but my tongue fell out and hung there like that of a snake, and I lost consciousness.

Luckily "Uncle Jimmy" Breckinridge, who owned the big farm on which my father then rented a tract, lived nearby, and, though a church-going man himself, he happened to be more "liberal" in some respects than my father. Uncle Jimmy just happened to have a pint of whiskey laid by, and Father, putting down his scruples in the face of an emergency, borrowed it, poured most of it down my throat, and I came back to life. That was my first—and last—snakebite. It also was my first, and for many years my last, drink of whiskey. Despite the popular conception of Old Kentucky as a state populated entirely by julep-drinking colonels, with a distillery in every county, there actually is a great deal of dry sentiment in the state, and a large number of counties still exercise local option against the sale of spirits. I was a teetotaler during most of my life.

In addition to the work I have already described I used to help Father with the plowing. As a matter of fact, I rather enjoyed that experience. There is a sort of thrill that comes to a barefoot boy when he plows up the ground, turns it over, and steps into the fresh furrow with his bare feet. There is a good feel and a good smell to the earth. I like to remember the way the birds—all sorts of birds, blackbirds, robins, and bluejays —and the chickens would follow along behind me and pick up the worms as I turned over the dirt with the plow. Our old mule, Nell, was smart, too: when she heard the dinner bell, no matter where we were, Nell would stop her plowing, turn around, and head straight for the barn, where she knew her oats would be waiting.

I also used to work in the tobacco fields with Father, and I liked that less. I can still feel the itchy stickiness of the gum from the tobacco leaves. It pervaded your hands, face, nostrils, eyebrows, ears, and hair. You had to scour it off with ash-and-lye soap. Making that soap was Mother's department: she saved fat drippings and pork scraps from the kitchen and kept an ash hopper out in the yard. That was just one of the many things that she and many other sturdy women of the country did: she also made most of our clothes, and kept geese—and plucked them—to make our feather beds and pillows. A feather bed, of course, was considered the only thing fit to sleep on; my mother would not have had a regular mattress in the house as a gift. As long as I live, I shall never forget the soft, sinking sensation of first settling down on a feather bed. Of course, it was a little hot in the summertime.

This constant tobacco-gum stickiness and the abrasive effects of the lye and ashes must have had considerable effect, not only on my hide, but upon my youthful subconsciousness. I remember the first cake of store-bought soap I ever used. I bought it myself about the time I began noticing the girls: it made me smell a little fancier than Mamma's homemade soap. I used to hide it from my brothers and sisters, and by careful hoarding I could make one cake last me about a year.

I also remember when Father took me into Mayfield to buy my first suit of clothes with long pants. I observed with awe how clean the clerks looked—they dressed better on weekdays than we did on Sundays—and I determined then and there to become a store clerk. Some years later I did clerk briefly in Mr. Jim Rudy's shoe store in Paducah, but I was not a conspicuous success. One day a man with the biggest feet I had ever seen came into the store. As we used to say in the country, he had "about a foot-and-a-half of his leg turned under." He said to me, "I'd like to see a pair of shoes that would fit me." I answered, "So would I." Shortly after Mr. Rudy and I agreed that my future lay elsewhere.

I was twelve years old, by the way, when I got that first long-pants suit. Children get long pants much younger now. I remember it so well, not only because of my being impressed with the neat appearance of the clerks at Mayfield, but because the storekeeper, in recognition of the fact that Father was purchasing a whole suit for me, threw in a pair of red suspenders, a more liberal gift than the stick of peppermint candy which usually accompanied the purchase of a pair of overalls or boots.

Up to that time I had always worn—for dress-up occasions—knee pants and long stockings. The stockings were knitted for me—and for all the other children and Father too—by Mother. She not only carded her own wool and knitted the stockings, but she dyed them as well. They were colored brown from a dye which Momsy made from the juice of sumac berries, which I would be sent into the woods to gather.

I suppose the only garment Mommy ever made for me which I did not appreciate was a certain overcoat. It was of a nice gray herringbone material, but she lined it with yellow Canton flannel, and the boys at school teased me unmercifully about it. They would call me "yellowhammer," after a bird we have down in Kentucky, a sort of gray bird with yellow feathers under its wings. I tried to fight them, then to bribe them with apples, to make them stop their teasing. But there were too many for me to lick, and the bribery, I learned, did not help—a valuable lesson for me, incidentally. At any rate, the trouble I had with it made me despise that coat.

In addition to helping Father with these man-sized chores which I have detailed, I also put in many an hour assisting my mother in taking care of the younger children and helping out with the housework. Even if we could have afforded it, there were no maids in the country in those days. Not only did I rock the younger children to sleep and change their diapers, but I spun yarn, washed dishes and clothes, and even ironed the flatwork. I got to be rather expert at ironing, and even today, if I do not have time to take a wrinkled suit to the tailor before keeping an engagement, I get down the ironing board and iron and do a pretty fair job of pressing. Of course in Mom's kitchen we used a couple of cast-iron flatirons that we heated on top of the wood stove, and the kitchen table served as the ironing board.

Another custom of those days was the system of calling out all the able-bodied male citizens of the community once a year to work on the roads. It was a community enterprise, and no one got paid. A road overseer was appointed for the different districts, and it was his job to see that the men turned out with their own plows, hoes, scrapers, teams, or whatever they could bring, and patch up the dirt roads, which were all we had to serve us.

I began going out with my father on these road-working expeditions as soon as I was old enough to wield the implements. It was a wonderful experience, a sort of a jubilee, or get-together, for the men. Money or station in life meant nothing, as everyone, rich or poor, turned out. The men would fill in the deep holes and wagon ruts with straw, brush, or sod, then scrape over the surface and cover it with fresh dirt. After working a while the men would stop to eat and rest, and they would start swapping stories. I would sit quietly and listen, soaking up the yarns I heard the men tell. It was on occasions such as these, and also at barbecues and political gatherings, that I heard many of the old Kentucky stories which I still use when I address a gathering. A good story is like a fine Kentucky bourbon; it improves with age and, if you don't use it too much, it will never hurt anyone.

I also used to get a chance to absorb stories from my father when I would accompany him on a wagon trip into Paducah or Mayfield. About twice a year we would take our crops into town for sale, and come back with a load of goods that would last us through the winter or summer season. These trips were made in the two-horse wagon, which was our all-purpose vehicle: in it we did our hauling, rode to church, and did what little visiting was in order. Whenever we went into town, if it was too late to return home we would spend the night at a wagon yard, which was an old-fashioned institution, somewhat on the order of a livery stable but with crude rooms where the farmers and teamsters could put up overnight. Father would sit up with the other men, chewing tobacco—his only "vice"—and spinning yarns, and I would be allowed to listen, so long as I stayed in the background and kept quiet.

I tried Father's chewing tobacco once—only once—by the way. It was a brand called "Peach Pie." He would keep huge plugs of it in a bureau drawer, and it was all doctored up with liquids and sweetening that gave it a delicious odor. One time my brother, Clarence, and I—Clarence died of typhoid at the age of twenty—sneaked a plug of Pop's tobacco and took it out behind the smokehouse to try it. It made me sick as a horse, and, after I crawled back into the house, I made a resolution never to try it again. This resolution I have religiously observed.

A Farm Boy Dreams

By Charles A. Lindbergh

As he flew "The Spirit of St. Louis" on that first lonely flight across the Atlantic, one of America's greatest heroes recalled how he had first yearned for wings back on the farm. He remembered, too, that danger is not confined to flying, but is an everyday presence on a farm, in his own time as well as in the days when his grandparents were settlers in the land of the Sioux and the Dakotas.

When I was a child on our Minnesota farm, I spent hours lying on my back in high timothy and redtop, hidden from passers-by, watching white cumulus clouds drift overhead, staring into the sky. It was a different world up there. You had to be flat on your back, screened in by grass stalks, to live in it. Those clouds, how far away were they? Nearer than the neighbor's house, untouchable as the moon—unless you had an airplane. How wonderful it would be, I'd thought, if I had an airplane—wings with which I could fly up to the clouds and explore their caves and canyons—wings like that hawk circling above me. Then, I would ride on the wind and be part of the sky, and acorns and bits of twigs would stop pressing into my skin. The question of danger didn't enter my dreams.

One day I was playing upstairs in our house on the riverbank. The sound of a distant engine drifted in through an open window. Automobiles had been going past on the road quite often that summer. I noticed it vaguely, and went on sorting the stones my mother and I had collected from the creek bed. None of them compared to the heart-shaped agate I'd found at the edge of a pool the week before—purple crystals outlined by stripes of red and white. Suddenly I sat up straight and listened. No automobile engine made that noise. It was approaching too fast. It was on the wrong side of the house! Stones scattered over the floor. I ran to the window and climbed out onto the tarry roof. It was an airplane!

Flying upriver below higher branches of trees, a biplane was less than two hundred yards away—a frail, complicated structure, with the pilot sitting out in front between struts and wires. I watched it fly quickly out of sight, and then rushed downstairs to tell my mother.

There had been a notice in the *Transcript*, my mother said, about an aviator who had come to our town. She'd forgotten to tell me about it. He was carrying passengers from a field over on the east side of the river. But rides were unbelievably expensive. He charged a dollar for every minute in the air! And anyone who went up took his life in his hands—suppose the engine stopped, or a wing fell off, or something else went wrong.

I was so greatly impressed by the cost and danger that I pushed aside my desire to go up in a plane. But I used to imagine myself with wings on which I could swoop down off our roof into the valley, soaring through air from one riverbank to the other, over stones of the rapids, above log jams, above the tops of trees and fences. I thought often of men who really flew. From grown-up conversations, I heard and remembered the names of the Wright brothers, and Glen Curtiss, and Lincoln Beachey—they'd found a way to fly in spite of cost and danger.

As I grew older, I learned that danger was a part of life not always to be shunned. It often surrounded the things you liked most to do. It was dangerous to climb a tree, to swim down rapids in the river, to go hunting with a gun, to ride a horse, to drive my father's automobile. You could be killed as quickly on a farm as in an airplane. I had felt death brush past several times on our farm, and it was not as terrifying as I at first imagined.

I never felt safer, and never came closer to being killed than when a gangplow turned over behind my tractor. It was on one of those May days "when leaves on the oak trees are as big as squirrels' ears," and it was "time to plant corn." I was behind with plowing on the western forty, and working late into evening to catch up. It was an old field, with only a few stones left to hook a plowshare. The furrow lay straight behind, seven inches deep. I had just tripped the plow-lift and started to turn at the field's end when bright steel flashed by my head and thudded heavily on ground. The lift mechanism had jammed, upsetting the entire gangplow. If I hadn't turned my tractor at the moment I pulled the trip-lever, I would have been crushed on the seat. As it was, the share missed my head by less than six inches.

No, farm life isn't as safe as it's cracked up to be. . . .

My grandfather must have found a country like this when he immigrated to America from Skåne in the southern part of Sweden. My father was only a few months old then. Traveling westward, the family settled on Sauk River's bank, in the new state of Minnesota. They built a log cabin in territory through which warpaths of the Chippewa and Sioux had run, only a few years before.

As soon as my father was old enough to carry a gun, it had been his job to keep the family supplied with meat. Since ammunition was scarce, his rounds were counted, and a bird demanded in return for each one fired. When he missed a shot, he tried to hit two birds with the next. My father had spoken of it casually, as part of his daily life in boyhood; but to me, it appeared a miraculous accomplishment—getting two ducks in line to save one charge. Now, as I look down on this game-filled land, I understand his casualness better. It wouldn't be so difficult to kill two birds with one shot when they're as thick as that.

The rule was only for birds and small animals. On days when he brought back a deer, he wasn't asked to account for his ammunition. The woods here must be full of deer, too—and probably bear, porcupine, wildcat, and even moose. Envious of my father's boyhood, I often dreamed of such a country, and here it is, just outside my window—land of the pioneer: forests filled with game; dashing streams of crystal water.

Several small farms line the river ahead—fields walled in by timber. Cattle wade across the water, their shadows falling sharply on its surface. One of my father's stories was about fishing from a riverbank on the homestead. Sioux massacres in the Minnesota Valley and raids northward had left settlers' nerves highly tensed. It had been several years since the uprising, but fear remained in children's minds. Suddenly, my father saw shadows move along the edge of a pool upstream—Sioux warriors! He lunged backward into hazel brush as he looked up to see—no, not warriors, just farm cattle, like those below me now. Everybody feared the Sioux. They'd stretch a man to stakes and build a fire on his belly. They'd cram live children into kitchen ovens and let them roast. So the settlers' stories went.

Once, when my father was very young, a messenger arrived on horseback, warning all farmers to flee for their lives—Little Crow was on the warpath. Hogs and cattle were turned loose, doors locked, homes abandoned. My grandfather harnessed the oxen, and fled with his family to the fort at St. Cloud, about 40 miles away. It was crowded there, with so many people gathered in. There was little to do, and the men quickly grew restless. Two neighboring farmers decided to return to their homes, against the warning of the soldiers. They said the danger of Indians was exaggerated, and that their animals needed care. They left the town on horseback, and were never seen again—probably captured and tortured to death by Sioux, the settlers thought.

That made others at the fort more willing to accept the hardships of a refugee. Complaints lessened. The children even enjoyed their experience, my father said. There were new games to play, new sights to see. It was a welcome change from the isolated life on a homestead. Our family stayed on until my Aunt Linda was born. And what a commotion that caused—men standing around awkwardly outside, women running back and forth, children neglected for the day.

My grandparents were lucky. When they finally returned to their farm, they found everything as they had left it, except for the stock. It was a real job hunting through the woods for pigs and chickens, and rounding up the cows. Grandmother never did get all her chickens back—wild animals, of course.

The warlike Sioux were driven westward into the Dakotas. Red River oxcart trains creaked by the homestead with greater frequency. Father said you could hear them miles away. And more settlers came to set up farms. Only the friendly Chippewa remained—Indians of the forest. Their pointed, birchbark teepees often rose on the banks of Sauk River, near my grandfather's cabin. Many of my father's stories were about them. There was one I asked him to tell over and over again as I lay in bed, looking out at the stars.

They had been trading skins for firewater, those braves who came up to the log farmhouse and demanded food. My grandfather was away. My grandmother was busy baking bread and caring for the children. She had no use for drunken Indians. "Go away," she told them. "I've got nothing for you. See, the bread isn't baked yet." She opened the oven to show them. They muttered and argued for a time outside the door, while Grandmother went on with her work and the children peeked out at them. Finally, they decided to leave. But as they passed the woodpile, one of the braves grabbed my grandfather's axe and carried it off.

My grandmother took time to change her clothes before she ran after those Indians! She put on a silk dress which she had brought from Sweden, and guarded carefully through hard years of frontier life. She knew the importance of dignity in dealing with Indians; it would be unwise to confront them in soiled kitchen garments. When she caught up to them on the road, the brave refused to give up the axe. He shook it at her, scowled, and kept on walking with the others. She followed, arguing and threatening; until one of the squaws snatched the axe from the drunken warrior and laid it on the ground. My grandmother picked it up and returned to the farmhouse, to her work clothes and children, and to baking bread.

Why take such a chance for an axe? Well, that was another story. Grandfather Lindbergh had held a high position in Sweden. He was a leading member of the Riksdag, and a close friend of the King. But he'd gotten into political and business troubles, lost practically everything he had, and sailed to America to start a new life when he was over fifty years of age. In the small log cabin in Minnesota, our family was so poor that my grandfather sold a gold medal he'd been given in "the old country" to buy a breaking plow. Axes, like plows, couldn't be made on the farm; they cost real money, and real money was awfully hard to get. Besides, it was a special axe, weighted and shaped for my grandfather's single-handed use, for he had lost his left arm at the sawmill. He lost that arm trying to earn a little real money to buy things that couldn't be raised on the farm, such as salt, and kerosene, and tools.

Handling logs and lumber was heavy work for a man of my grandfather's age. But he had great physical endurance, and his services were valued. One day he stumbled, and fell against the spinning saw. Its teeth cut through his arm near the shoulder, and ripped open his back. The belt hurled him halfway across the shed. The mill hands claimed that the gash was so deep they could see my grandfather's heart beating. They bound his wounds up crudely and sent for the minister, Reverend C. S. Harrison. Minister Harrison had my grandfather laid on some hay in the bottom of an oxcart and hauled him, bleeding terribly, over the rough roads to the family cabin. A man was started off on the only horse available, with instructions to get relays wherever he could and rush a doctor back. But the nearest doctor lived at St. Cloud—and he was not at home. The messenger eventually found him in a still more distant village, helping a young wife give birth to her child. Meanwhile my grandmother, the minister, and the friends who came to help expected Grandfather to die. They washed his wounds with cold water from a nearby spring, picked out rags and sawdust, and tried to stop the flow of blood.

Three days passed before the doctor arrived. He amputated the arm and stitched together the gaping hole in the back. My grandfather lived despite shock, infection, and loss of blood. Lying on his bed, in great pain, he demanded to see his left arm before it was buried in the garden. It was brought to him in a small, rough-board coffin. Taking the fingers in those of his right hand, he said slowly, in broken English, "You have been a good friend to me for fifty years. But you can't be with me any more. So good-by. Good-by, my friend."

It took months for my grandfather to recover. Then, he had special tools fashioned for his single-handed use. But farming and earning money were more difficult after that, and there were four young children to care for—my father, Linda, Juno, and Frank. Grandmother had to watch each penny spent. Her family couldn't afford to lose an axe.

Horse-and-Buggy Doctor

By Arthur E. Hertzler

"From quack lawyers, quack doctors, quack preachers, mad dogs, and yellow fever, Good Lord deliver us!"

But the old-fashioned country doctor—no specialist—was a very present help in time of trouble. Whether fighting a typhoid epidemic or riding through the night to deliver a new baby, he visited the rich and the poor alike, and the comfort he brought was as healing as his medicines.

No old doctor would want to record his experiences even if he could. Sick scenes have been all but neglected by the painter, yet no subject in human experience offers a more fruitful opportunity to present intense human emotions. A notable exception is the famous painting "The Doctor" which graces the walls of many homes. This picture is typical in that it shows a fine old doctor sitting beside his little patient, lying with her arm flung out, mute evidence of a terminal stage of the disease. The father and mother are shown in the background paralyzed in their helplessness. The old doctor's face is perfectly calm. What thoughts are racing through his mind? Would he like to join the father and mother in their wail of helplessness? The old doctor too is helpless, but he sticks to his task, rendering his ultimate service to his little patient and to the parents. It was this silent faithfulness of the old doctor in the hour of grief that endeared him to the families that he served. The old country doctor was a man of few words because there were no words. . . .

Viewed from the vantage point of the achievements of medicine of the present day, the accomplishments of the old doctor seem pitiably insignificant. Yet the satisfaction one gets out of life is measured by the efforts one exerts in achieving a worthy end, not in the actual achievement. This philosophy touches the very heart of medical practice as it was then; in a measure it is even true of the experiences of today. The question of what the old doctor did is answered by reference to my old case records now covering more than forty-four years. . . .

From what has already been said it is clear that the country doctor's activities had less to do with the saving of life than with relieving a patient's pain and the mental suffering of the family. Whatever one may conclude in retrospect as to the importance of the doctor's ministrations, neither doctor nor patient then doubted the efficacy of the treatment employed. However, the picture must not be painted unduly drab. The patient's sufferings were relieved and in occasional cases the measures employed were unquestionably life-saving.

Let it be remarked that, exalted as are the achievements of the present day, the younger man may well remember that possibly fifty years hence his achievements may seem as puerile as ours do now. Furthermore, what concerns the individual doctor is not so much what medical science can achieve as how much of this he can deliver to his patients. That is the personal element for which each doctor is responsible.

Regardless of what the old doctor was able to accomplish in a therapeutic way, the sense of security inspired by the doctor's arrival affected the patients favorably. The degree of this influence depended on faith, which again was based on personality and previous experiences. The most striking effect was on the family and it became obvious before one even approached the patient or started to render any service. If this be so how did we differ from the quack and the cultist of today? The answer is simple: We had measures capable of relieving suffering even though we could not curtail the disease. . . .

We proceed to the consideration of concrete cases as one met them in country practice. These included just about every disease the human being is heir to; one had to be prepared to meet anything, not only in the nature of disease but also meddlesome neighbors and friends and the dog when he made a country call. It was legal to shoot the dog.

Usually the call was brought by a horseman who dashed up the street on a foaming steed. The movies never produced anything quite so spectacular. The young doc usually answered the call in the same fashion: that is, at first—for he soon came to see how theatrical it was. During the trip he had plenty of time to reflect on the responsibility which awaited him when he reached the patient's bedside. To a young and untried doctor this anticipation was worse than the reality, for a case seldom turned out to be as serious as represented by the messenger. Almost anything from hysteria to postpartum hemorrhage might confront him. The hired man or a boy of the family usually brought the call before there were telephones. Generally, the messenger knew only that there was need for haste and nothing could be learned in advance as to the nature of the illness, though sometimes the hired man would announce that it was about time for an increase in the family. The vulgar might laugh at such a remark but it merely reflected an observant mind.

This lack of preparative information worked a double hardship. The doctor was neither able to take suitable supplies for the condition he was to meet nor to determine which of several calls received simultaneously was the most serious and should be answered first. I always followed this rule: children first, next women, then old men, and finally the adult males. Known cases of hysterics came last. The reason for giving priority to children was that they become violently ill suddenly and require early attention; hours counted. Then too, as it has sometimes been facetiously remarked, if haste was not exercised the child might recover before the doctor arrived. More seriously, the family might have one of those curious compilations, *What to Do until the Doctor Comes,* and might do it too. One hoped to get there before they did. We know now how important haste is in cases of acute abdominal disease, notably in beginning appendicitis and intestinal perforations. In those days the acute intestinal disease of childhood, more than any other disease, justified haste in applying treatment. . . .

The young doctor naturally took things more seriously than the seasoned old doctor, both because of the desire to establish himself in the community and because of the belief that his services always were of great importance. That is to say, his ignorance approached that of the patient. Then, too, the old doctor knew the people, both physically and financially, and if the patient's complaints were negative, he had urgent business elsewhere. One of my first calls will explain why. A boy came galloping to my house, the horse covered with foam, knees shaking and obviously at the point of dropping in his tracks. The boy, eyes bulging, shouted: "Come quick, Doc. Mother's terribly sick." I hastily hitched my horse and made the seven miles in considerably less than one hour—some driving! I rushed into the house only to find an assortment of women solemnly sitting about a stove doing nothing—except talking, of course. I asked, "Who's sick?" The lady of the house calmly answered: "Well, Doc, I reckon it's me. I ain't really sick, but I've been porely since Christmas and so Pa thought I better see a doctor. I didn't feel like ridin' to town so we sent for you because you are the new doctor." The significance of that last remark escaped me at the time, but I soon learned that they never paid any doctor anything and that established doctors turned a deaf ear to them. That is the way with deadheads. They make their call sound urgent in order to break down whatever sales resistance the doctor may have. Another thing this case taught me was that deadheads will call the doctor for minor ailments, whereas in similar circumstances those who expect to pay will go to his office. In this case the patient's family of ten or more children seemed to be the trouble. Any experienced doctor can tell from these remarks what was wrong with her.

This family was interesting in another respect. There were no beds for most of its members. All the boys were sewed into their clothes in the fall when cold weather approached. At bedtime blankets were thrown on the floor and the youngsters lay down on them, clothes and all of course, and were asleep at once. They woke up in the morning all dressed and ready for pancakes and 'lasses. In the spring the clothes were ripped off and the child saw himself, for the first time in a number of months. This was before we learned about the more abundant life. The interesting fact, anthropologically speaking, is that the people did not know they were suffering any hardships. It all depends on the point of view.

Even more trying than the false alarmist were those who invariably called the doctor about eleven at night. Such calls became more numerous after telephones came into use at about the turn of the century. Usually the background was something like this: an ailing child would keep the mother worried all day until Father came home. The hungry father took Mother's report lightly at first. But after a few hours, tiring of the child's lamentations, which interfered with his sleep, the father would send one of the boys after the doctor. One father I knew boasted that he never called a doctor before midnight and thus made him earn his money. Of course, this fellow never paid the doctor, so that phrase "earn his money" was merely a facetious hyperbole. . . . Tiring of this sort of thing one night, I phoned a chronic offender at eleven o'clock that I must see him at once about an important matter that concerned us both, a matter that would not bear discussing over the party phone. He demurred, saying he had been asleep in bed and that he was not feeling well. He had caused me this same feeling many times and I had known he would be in bed when I telephoned. I repeated my message in louder tones and hung up the receiver with a bang. In about an hour I heard a horse clattering, rapidly coming down the road. When he came to my door I feigned sleep but at his second knock I admitted him. Then I told him very calmly that I wanted him to bring me that load of hay he had promised. Being on a party line, one of the neighbors learned the facts and there was much kidding. The result was a greater respect for the doctor's hours of rest throughout that neighborhood. But in a measure he got even, for the hay he brought me was all weeds, wholly unfit for horse feed.

The doctor learned to know his families, and calls from such people as these were usually passed up for a while in the hope that in the meantime a legitimate call might come from the same neighborhood. One could then answer the call without feeling that the expenditure of time and effort was a total loss. Such patients as I have described called the doctor for the most trivial affections, because they never intended to pay him for his trouble. The country doctor cannot bluntly refuse a call just because the patient is a confirmed and joyous deadhead. People of this class do sometimes die, though I cannot at this time recall a case. If such a thing did occur the doctor was censured, even though everybody knew it was good riddance.

I never refused a call, no matter what the condition, or what the chances of remuneration. When I announced that I wished to study medicine my father asked me to promise never to refuse to attend a sick person, whether he could or would pay or not. My father, being a farmer, did not realize how exasperating patients can be or how useless some calls. I have kept the faith: that is, almost. I have always refused to attend a drunk with a headache. I figure that he might as well suffer from the present headache as from the one he will acquire as soon as he is relieved. This may sound complicated to some persons but it will be perfectly clear to others, I am sure.

Thereby hangs a tale. We had in our town a chronic inebriate. One day I saw him zigzagging down the sidewalk. Early that evening the wife called to say that her husband was very ill. I assured her I could substantiate her statement, for I had seen him a few hours before. I advised that she put him to bed, expressing my belief that he would be all right in a few days as had been the case many times before. A few hours later she called again, reporting that her husband was dying. I replied that in that case it was not a doctor she wanted but an undertaker. This gave me an idea. I called the undertaker and informed him that Mr. X was in need of his service. Would he attend? As is the wont with morticians even today, he expressed deep sorrow, but in a tone that indicated grief would not incapacitate him for business.

I thought there might be interesting doings, so I cut down the alley and across lots and hid in the shadows of the house. Soon the undertaker approached in his wagon, with his assistant. There were at that time no mortuaries and a body was "laid out" in the parlor or living room of the late lamented. This undertaker was up-to-date and carried a board and a pair of "horses" on which to place the board. On arrival he found the door slightly ajar, but no one visible. Gently pushing open the door, he entered and quietly arranged the board on the supports ready to receive the relict. Just then the wife came in from the kitchen and, recognizing the undertaker, let out a shriek. This partly aroused the patient and he fixed the undertaker with an uncertain gaze. Spying the board, prepared to receive his remains, he sat bolt upright. He took one good look, and then let out a howl that frightened children four blocks away. The bed stood in front of a screened window. The patient dived through the screen of the very window through which I was peeping, carrying the screen with him. He lit running and after two hours' search his friends found him crouched in the corner of a fence many blocks from home.

He stayed sober for the remainder of his sojourn in our town, some three years. I have always remembered with a devilish chuckle that this man's co-worker was cured of his bibulous habit during a revival, but his cure lasted only nine months while my low-comedy one lasted at least three years. . . .

But to return to our mutton. What the doctor did when he reached the bedside can best be illustrated by citing actual events recorded in my casebooks. Naturally, the diagnostic problems varied greatly. In some cases the probable diagnosis was at once apparent; in many, careful study was needed, and, *voce dulci*, the patient just got well—or else. This was not so bad as it sounds, for as already related, diagnosis or no diagnosis, about all one could do in many cases was to relieve the symptoms, and to do this no pathologic diagnosis was needed. One of my colleagues diagnosed typhoid as malaria in all cases and he had the leading practice in this community: that is, for a while. Most doctors claimed to be able to break up a case of typhoid fever or "typhoid pneumonia"—"if called soon enough." I was too stubborn to follow this policy and boldly declared that if they had it they kept it until they recovered, that the breaking-up claim was all bunk. This cost me heavily, but only for a time. The fates are in the end kind to the stubborn.

The usual procedure for a doctor when he reached the patient's house was to greet the grandmother and aunts effusively and pat all the kids on the head before approaching the bedside. He greeted the patient with a grave look and a pleasant joke. He felt the pulse and inspected the tongue, and asked where it hurt. This done, he was ready to deliver an opinion and prescribe his pet remedy. More modern men had a thermometer and a stethoscope. The temperature was gravely measured, and the chest listened to—or at.

That ritual was followed by every experienced physician. I had ideas of my own. I passed the aged female relatives up, ignored the children and proceeded with the matter at hand. This was not based on bravery on my part, but ignorance. I had not yet learned that most of the things one needs to know in the practice of the art of healing never get into the books. But there were compensating factors. I at least examined my patients as well as I knew how. My puerile attempts at physical examination impressed my patients and annoyed my competitors, which, of course, I accepted as a two-time strike. Word went out that the young doctor "ain't very civil but he is thorough." Only yesterday one of my old patients recalled that when I came to see her young son I "stripped him all off and examined him all over." Members of that family have been my patients for the intervening forty years, so impressed were they. Incidentally, it may be mentioned that in this case I discovered a pleurisy with effusion which had not been apparent to my tongue-inspecting colleague.

The great majority of the country doctor's calls were for trivial and obvious conditions, such as sore throat with or without special involvement of the tonsils, recognizable at a glance. Grandmother might have a renewal of her attacks of bronchitis or asthma, or Father might have lumbago or rheumatiz. These conditions could sometimes be diagnosed while one was driving into the yard. Simple remedies sufficed and one came a day or two later to see how the patient was progressing.

If there was an injury involving the skin one sewed it up without ceremony. The patient was supposed to submit to this without a squawk. If the kids received the injury while up to devilment they stood it heroically, but if they received it in line of duty they did not fancy, there were likely to be loud lamentations. But the ordeal was brief. In case of fracture one went out in the barnyard and hunted himself a suitable board, a loose one if he could find it—otherwise he forcibly removed one from its moorings. From these he fashioned a splint, perhaps with the aid of a bed sheet, if there was such a thing in the house. X-rays were unknown but the results obtained by the country doctor of experience were surprisingly good. At least none died as now sometimes happens when fractures are operated on. Legs, it may be mentioned, in those days were regarded as things to be used, not to look at. Therefore, if a useful limb resulted, everybody was satisfied, even though the result was not a thing of beauty.

Though many of the calls involved trivial and ephemeral diseases, there were many serious and arduous problems to meet such as try the souls of even experienced men. At the top of these stood epidemics of typhoid fever. My introduction to this disease was an epidemic of sixteen cases scattered over a wide territory. This number required a great deal of time, since it was supposed that an attentive doctor would see each patient at least once a day—during the most serious period of the disease sometimes several times a day—and stay all night at the terminal stages.

Happily, no other disease, I can now say, demanded so much of the doctor as typhoid fever. This disease is so insidious and protean in its onset as to try the skill of the most learned. Obviously, it was a great scheme to diagnose any sort of obscure disease as typhoid fever, as my competitors did. For if the diagnosis proved wrong the doctor could say he had broken it up; if it proved correct he got credit for great diagnostic acumen. This worked a great hardship on me, but I stuck to my guns. Word finally went around, "That boy is honest."

The history generally gleaned on the first visit was something like this: headache and backache for a few days with complete loss of appetite. Usually there were general abdominal pains most marked in the appendicial region. Abdominal distention soon followed. Fortunately for our peace of mind, appendicitis was not operated on in those days, and the responsibility of a differentiation was not great. So one just waited to see which it would turn out to be. If there were other cases of typhoid fever in the family, or even in the neighborhood, this was sufficient to make the diagnosis of typhoid fever probable, even in the early stages. Examination showed a distended abdomen, some tenderness and gurgling in the region of the appendix. Later, in many cases, rose spots appeared on the abdomen and, to the practiced eye, clinched the diagnosis; but my eye then wasn't very practiced. The temperature varied usually with the duration of the disease, gradually ascending day by day until the maximum of 104° or 105° was reached. In the early days there were no laboratory tests to be made and observation of the course of the disease was the only means of arriving at a diagnosis.

As the fever increased, the tongue and lips became covered with a dirty crust and there was a low muttering delirium. As the end of the third week approached, the possibility of the dreaded hemorrhage and perforation kept both doctor and family in a high state of dread, and every change that might indicate the advent of these disasters was keenly watched for. If any untoward symptom appeared, a messenger was dispatched for the doctor, though there was nothing he could do when he got there. Irritating occurrences were common. Sometimes a new arrival, usually an ancient relative or the minister, observing the patient for the first time, would express the opinion that the patient did not look right and advise that the doctor be called. This, of course, was to impress the relatives with their great interest in the welfare of the patient. Such solicitude was noted particularly if the patient was a rich uncle. Fortunately ministers always visited the patient in midafternoon and one could answer the call before bedtime. . . .

Those weary trips were galling because one was fully convinced before starting that the call was wholly useless and was instigated by some fool interfering with what did not concern him. One cannot blame the doctor for educating the cleric not to butt in. One could not refuse the call because a complication might actually have developed and, if it had, the death of the patient would be attributed to the negligence of the doctor. . . .

Under certain conditions the doctor was able to be of some service. When the stage of high temperature and delirium was reached cold sponging was demanded, or at least that was the consensus of professional opinion at that time. There being no trained nurse, it fell to the doctor's lot to do the job. It usually required one to two hours of sponging to reduce the temperature to 103°. One was rewarded for his efforts by seeing the patient sleep peacefully, free from muttering, for several hours. I want to say to the young doctors of today that two hours spent bathing a delirious patient seems quite a long time. Occasionally a mother or a neighbor would undertake the task. . . .

Though a typical case of typhoid fever was usually easily enough diagnosed—that is, if one observed it for a week or two—many diagnostic problems presented themselves. An apparently typical pneumonia might end up as a typical typhoid fever. I made such an error which caused me great distress. Just at that time Osler reported three cases in which he made this same mistake. I felt better then. Sometimes a typhoid patient would begin with a sudden severe pain in the region of the appendix. Since, as noted, appendicitis cases were not operated on, a diagnosis was just a matter of professional pride. After appendicitis became an operable disease, many useless operations were performed. Ignorance sometimes saves the doctor from doing foolish things.

The disease sometimes runs a very peculiar course. One of my patients ran a temperature for nearly twenty weeks. Some ran the usual course, were temperature-free for a few days and then started all over again. Most perplexing were two husky young farmers who began their disease on almost the same day and progressed uniformly in a typical way. On about the tenth day one developed a severe headache and neck retraction. I stayed with him through the whole night. Nothing I could or dared to do relieved him. At daylight he died. Spinal punctures were then unknown. I hastened to visit the other patient and found him peacefully eating his breakfast, fever-free.

At the end of this grueling summer I emulated my patients and took typhoid fever myself.

During the summer season digestive-tract diseases were common, particularly among children, and when I was not sponging typhoid patients I was giving enemas to convulsed babies. Doing this, I have no doubt, saved the lives of many children. There was no ice, no sanitation, and there were few screens. Many children died in their second year, that dreaded "second summer."

When word came that a baby was in convulsions, I would drop everything else and hasten to attend. I would find a child in convulsions, with a temperature of 105°. A hasty dose of castor oil was administered, followed by an enema which was perhaps repeated. If the convulsions did not cease the child was placed in a tepid water-filled washtub. After the convulsions ceased it was given salol and bismuth. One of these children that I bathed for six hours one night is now in a penitentiary. At least he is not listed as unemployed, and that is something. Nearly all my babies recovered, whereas those my colleagues treated with Dover's powders or other opiates died. This experience gave me my real start. The word went out, "That young doc stays with them until they get well or die."

In looking back over forty years I am glad to say no branch of medicine has made greater advances than that dealing with the feeding of babies. The young specialists in diseases of children, inheriting the modern knowledge from their teachers, know nothing of the trials of long ago. The art of feeding has now reached such a state of perfection that the acute convulsive diseases are now almost unknown.

If I were a great artist given to paint but one picture I should depict a young mother sitting before the crib of a convulsing baby, with the crushed father in the background. In cases of tragedy the mother nearly always stands up better than the father. No one who knows women as well as the family doctor ever calls them the weaker sex. That phrase was spawned in the parlor by some goof who did not realize that the "weakling" was pulling in the line.

Convulsions in adults, as seen in lockjaw, for example, are terrible to witness, but they are infinitely worse in a child with so-called summer complaint. The cherubic little body is contorted into the most impossible shapes: eyes half open, the balls rolled upward; face twitching and pale or bluish-white. After a few minutes of violent muscular contraction there is slight relaxation and one hopes that it is ended; but not for long, because the contractions soon reappear, perhaps even worse than before. With slight variations this may continue for hours, even days. Usually after a time a diarrhea begins and the child rapidly emaciates, becoming quickly only a skeleton, a mere shadow of its former self. The convulsions are generally absent now, but the temperature rises rapidly, trying the registering capacity of the clinical thermometer. The child lies panting, head buried in the pillow. The limbs grow cold. There is a slight quiver. The emaciated little limbs suddenly straighten, then relax. The child is dead.

I have done many desperate and, I hope, life-saving operations but nothing gives me so much pleasure as the memory of those battles with convulsed babies. To see the contracted limbs relax, the head lift itself from the depths of the pillow; to see the light return to the mother's eyes, and the smile to her lips—that is one of the greatest experiences in life. In that final day when Peter says, "You are one of those bloomin' docs. What did you do?" I shall say, "I did it to even the least of these."

I know of what I speak. I have sat and watched my own little daughter in convulsions for twelve hours, as utterly paralyzed with terror as any layman. After a short sleep she awakened and asked, "Where is my doll?" —the sweetest words ever spoken. I have never attended a sick child since that day. That memory freezes the marrow of my bones after more than thirty years. . . .

Just before I began the practice of medicine many women in this neighborhood died of puerperal fever, chiefly due to one doctor who divided his time between practicing medicine and raising hogs. It was his practice to administer a large dose of ergot in order to hasten labor so he could reach home in time to feed the hogs. He sometimes washed his hands after the completion of labor but never before. After making a digital examination, he used his pants—that is, trousers east of the Alleghenies, as a towel.

I was called to see one of his patients in the very first months of my practice. The following, printed elsewhere, is a better description than I could write now:

A woman in her eighth puerperium had been overcome on the third day after labor by a violent chill and high fever. When I saw her on the fifth day she lay motionless, eyes sunken, wide open, and fixed. Her respiration was labored and rapid and despite this labor her color presented a mixture of waxy pallor and cyanosis, as though some vulgar hand had soiled a marble statue of Distress, or Nature herself was seeking to soften the awful picture to spare the untried sensibilities of the embryo Aesculapian. The distended intestine found little resistance from the lax abdominal muscles and ballooned out to an astonishing degree. My first thought as I saw the patient lying in bed was that a canopy had been formed for her out of barrel hoops to prevent friction from the bed-clothes. My astonishment at finding the whole mass was belly knew no bounds. My eyes at this sight, I am sure, rivaled the patient's in fixity and wideness and my respiration was equally labored. As I sought to feel her pulse the cold clammy skin made me shrink and as I sought the pulse I could find but a quivering string and because of the pounding of my own heart I never knew its rate. As I turned from this scene, standing about the room were the seven older children, the eldest a girl of twelve. These, too, were wild eyed and short of breath. Approaching the cradle I sought to calm myself by viewing the child. Much to my consternation here lay a replica of the mother herself. The infant vainly sought to emulate its mother in girth of abdomen but far exceeded her in rate of respiration. In one particular only was there essential difference. Instead of the waxy gray of the mother it presented a peculiar ochre yellow, the result of cord infection.

Noting my discomfiture, the old doctor with whom I was in consultation said, "Never saw anything like it, did you, boy?" I had not, nor have I since.

I have the greatest pleasure in reporting that no case of puerperal fever has happened to me or any of my assistants. In fact, puerperal infection is rare, really almost unknown, among country doctors. The disease is not so rare, I read, in the hands of specialists in lying-in hospitals. I say this with pride in the country doctor, not in derision of the specialist under ideal surroundings.

There were many trials for the country doctor in attending labor cases. The following stands out. The patient was nearly forty years of age, small, chunky. A glance indicated that a difficult job was ahead. Only the husband was with her. The night was stormy. As soon as I arrived the husband, a half-wit, departed for a destination unknown and I was left alone with the patient. There was a little stove and a basket of corncobs. After a delay of many hours it became evident that instruments would be required. I had no anesthetic. The patient was in great distress. Her intelligence was just one jump ahead of her husband's. It was necessary to get on the bed and hold the patient's legs with my knees while I applied the forceps. I finally got a fine boy who, despite the none too high estate of his parents, grew up to be a fine young man. I felt that he was in a measure my boy, for I had earned him. He died in the war to save democracy, or to end wars, or whatever it was.

In most cases there was some woman about to care for the new arrival. Sometimes there was no one but the husband. A husband in a case of this sort is just one big cipher. In my first cases in such circumstances I attempted to wash the new arrival myself. Trying to wash a new baby is some sleight-of-hand job. Naturally I had no lap, so I would place the object of my efforts on the kitchen table, which was invariably covered with oil cloth. These youngsters are as slick as greased pigs. So, in order to prevent the baby falling to the floor, I was obliged to grasp one leg firmly with one hand, which left only one available for performing the ablutions. After a few such experiences I carried a bottle of sweet oil and just anointed it all over, rolled it in whatever was available and allowed it to await the ministrations of more experienced hands.

Even conducting a labor lone-handed was not the worst that could befall one. Some of the mothers or mothers-in-law were considerably worse than useless. My assistant and I had an experience that illustrates this. It was a case in which instruments would be needed and I worried about how to get rid of that mother. I had no need to worry. That resourceful assistant of mine was seldom at a loss in meeting any situation. He stared at the mother for a moment and asked if she was subject to heart disease. She stammered that she had been, though obviously it was a new thought to her. He stated very solicitously, after he had listened to her heart, that it would be safest for her to go out into the yard, as it might be necessary to give the patient an anesthetic. She not only went into the yard but across the barnyard into the pasture beyond. After everything was attended to she was recalled.

The most common pests were those who urged that something should be done to hasten labor, declaring that their doctor always gave them something to hasten the process. This type I set to boiling water, stating that it might be necessary to give the patient a Sitz bath. It takes quite a while to boil a tub of water in a teakettle. This kept them busy in the kitchen boiling water and out of the way until labor was terminated. Of course, one never intended to make use of the tub of water. . . .

Whether an incident is funny or tragic often depends on the viewpoint. Here is a case. I received a call from a doctor in a neighboring town. He had a patient, a young lady afflicted with a serious heart disease. Would I come? I would. It was a rainy day and the road was a sea of mud. I drove my horse until he became exhausted. Then I importuned a farmer to take me the rest of the way. His outfit was a farm wagon and a very sophisticated span of mules. When I arrived at the house the family doctor was awaiting me. The patient had been employed in a neighboring town. Previously always in the best of health, she had suddenly been taken seriously ill. The symptoms were very confusing to the doctor. Rapid respiration was all he could see and he concluded the trouble was a weak heart. I saw a fine plump girl with pink cheeks. She had been weeping. Her pulse was slower than mine and as regular. Knowing the disposition of the doctor, I asked him and the family to let me talk to the patient alone. It was a risk but necessary. I sat down on the edge of the bed and talked to her like a child, for she was only a child, though nineteen years old. "Now tell me," I began, "now tell me just what happened to him." She burst out weeping. "I don't know," she sobbed. "He just up and married another girl." I inquired in detail all about him, his appearance, his occupation and all that. No occupation, very handsome, with brown curly hair. I evaluated him in my own way. Handsome men, I volunteered, live off either the earnings of their wives or of their fathers-in-law. The commercial value of curly brown hair, figured in terms of buckwheat cakes, I opined, was not very high.

I talked to her at length on how fortunate she was that fate had intervened for her. Mere child, fine figure of a girl, beautiful face, young, she had no need to grieve. In calling a young girl beautiful one runs no risk of offending. One may take a cue from the newspapers. Every female that gets into devilment, if under seventy years of age, is referred to as "attractive." This, I presume, is following the usual newspaper habit of giving the people what they want: to wit, bunk. I explained to her that fate had much better things in store for her. I administered this sort of talk for a while and finally her face began to relax, just as that of a nine-month-old baby does when she is about to reach out her arms to you. I wrapped a blanket about her and said, "Let's go out and tell Mother you are all right." She tripped lightly out of the bedroom, through the living room and into the kitchen where the family doctor and the family were talking. The mother's look as she beheld her smiling daughter walking for the first time in weeks was something you do not see in books. "She will be all right," I assured the doctor. Then I sought the farmer and his mules and made the trip home; elapsed time, fourteen hours for the round trip. Now, is this tale funny or is it tragic? . . .

Another case had a decidedly amusing feature. I was called to see an old Civil War veteran with a chestful of fluid which caused him much difficulty in breathing. That the family doctor had made the correct diagnosis was proved by examination. While I was preparing my apparatus to relieve the old man of his fluid he bawled out, "Say, Doc, you are the homeliest man I seen since I saw Old Abe." "Say, Pa, you better shet up," his wife called from the kitchen. "Old Abe saved your hide onst; maybe this young feller kin now." A death sentence for sleeping on guard when he was a boy in the army had been commuted by the martyred President. Fortunately, the old lady's prediction came true; he promptly recovered. "I oughtn't to have said what I did," he said to his family doctor, who relayed it to me, "I mighta knowed he must be good for something or somebuddy wooda shot him long ago." As an apology without loss of dignity this always has seemed to me a masterpiece. Low comedy such as this between patient and doctor was common in those days. Many of the older men were war veterans first and pioneers afterward—he-men all the while. Fearless and uncomplaining, they fought grasshoppers and drought uncomplainingly, voted their ticket straight and asked no return. We shall not see their like again.

The foregoing may be regarded as in general the business of the practice of medicine followed by all of us, modified by each doctor's idiosyncrasies and by the situations which arose.

The more intimate experiences do not permit telling and the more ridiculous would be out of place. Often, too, they are so intimately blended. The events recounted here are sufficient to give a general idea of the life we old fellows used to lead.

The human side varied much according to the doctor's bringing up and his general view of life. Despite what I have written and what I may write, I have always had close association with many ministers of the gospel and we often compared notes as to our personal point of view. The ministers of the old days were not learned in a book sense, but many were men of great earnestness and high purpose. These men in general had an idea that something notable should take place at the moment of dissolution and seemed to think I should provide pabulum for their discourses. I had to tell them that saints and sinners died alike and that at the time of death, whatever might have been the antecedents, there was no pain. I have seen only one man who looked on death with terror and he was a sanctimonious old sinner, the pillar of his church, at the sight of whom one just instinctively grasped one's pocketbook.

In most cases death is preceded by a dulling of the mental processes as the circulation to the brain lessens due to the failing heart. Those who die just go to sleep. Even in diseases in which consciousness is retained until the last, as in peritonitis, there is no fear. I have sat beside the bed of such cases and talked of things in general, such casual things as the prospect of quail hunting and the like, while the cooling hands denoted the approach of death. Anyone who ever became unconscious during the course of any disease has experienced the sensation of death. Only favorable circumstances brought him back to consciousness again.

In the old days we remained with our patients during their last hours. We saw to it that they did not suffer. The interest in such a situation attached not to the dying but to the living. I can confirm that old saying that in the deepest sorrow there is no weeping. I have sat more than once on the side of a cradle with a mother while a baby died. Our eyes met as the last quiver passed over the little body. She recognized as well as I that life had become extinct. There was no weeping.

The saddest sight I have ever seen was at the deathbed of an old couple who had lived together many years. Both had pneumonia. I watched the passing of the aged wife and then went to see the husband. I made not a sound. "Mother's dead?" he queried. I did not need to answer. He closed his eyes, folded his hands over his chest and in a short time he also was dead. Don't ask me the meaning. The finest scenes I have witnessed have been the serene old age of such couples. As far as I can see, in order to arrive at the same place at the same time it is necessary to travel together. To so travel it seems that the burdens of life must be borne share and share alike. Whatever the more abundant life may be, this, I am sure, is the most abundant death.

Contrary to general belief, husbands are more nearly crushed than wives at the death of the mate. This is confirmed by the number of bereaved husbands who take their own lives on the graves of their departed wives. Such suicides are not unusual among men but are rare among women. I have said again and again, and I say it once more, that whoever it was that first called women the weaker sex certainly was not a country doctor.

Doctors nowadays do not stay with their patients during the last scene. What do they accomplish by remaining? Scientifically nothing; humanly much. I know of what I speak. In the saddest hour of my life, at the deathbed of my daughter, on one side was the magnificent and always faithful Carrie the nurse, on the other side the incomparable Dr. Campbell, calmly applying measures of resuscitation which he and I knew were utterly futile. Yet futile though it was, the battle of these professions inspires an indescribable measure of comfort. I know that my last conscious moments will picture that scene: nurse on one side of the bed, doctor on the other. Though scientifically futile, if my presence in a similar situation ever brought an equal amount of comfort to anyone I am sure it was more worth while than anything else I have ever done. Our mission in life is to lessen human suffering as much as we can.

On the whole those arduous experiences were happy days. When the roads were good and the trip not too long I took my black-eyed little daughter with me. Later on, she had a sister who was anything but black-eyed and another sister halfway between. No one ever achieves more than that, a reasonably assured living and happy children. No music of earth has greater worth than the prattle of a healthy child, it is said. I was established in practice, all school debts paid, eating three meals a day, with a prospect of earning enough to educate my children. Nobody expected anybody to break up typhoid fever or pneumonia and the diagnosis of typhoid fever was often a long and even uncertain procedure. Also there sometimes were diseases that just could not be diagnosed with certainty, and a confession of these facts implied not ignorance but courage and honesty. I had arrived. Beyond this fundamental fact no doctor ever achieves a higher estate.

Preacher Come to Call

By Henry A. Shute

When the minister came to supper the farmer's wife displayed her best china and the family put on company manners. But sometimes, as in this humorous selection from *The Real Diary of a Real Boy*, father was likely to say the wrong thing and the children to giggle during the blessing.

Oct. 16, 186– today the hole town was full of ministers, most of them had long tailed coats and white necktis. Deekon Gooch came down to the house with 2 of them. aunt Sarah was wating in her best dress and when she saw them coming she said Murder Joanna they is 2 of them, what shall we do, and mother said, mercy sakes what will George say. well the bell rung and i went to the door and asked them in and Deekon Gooch said they was Mister Fernald and Mister Robinson, he said they was his brothers. then Deekon he went off and i showed them to the front room up stairs and one of them asked me if i loved the lord and i said yes sir and he said i was a good boy. and then he asked me if i went to church and sunday school and i said yes sir and he asked me what was the tex last sunday and i said i dident know what tex ment and he said what did he prech from and i said he preeched from the pulpit in church and from the platform in sunday school, and Mister Fernald he began to laff and Mister Robinson he said i woodent laff if i was you brother, and then he said what does the minister say after the first prair and i said o yes i know now, he says we will now take up the usual colection and then Mister Fernald laffed again, then Mister Robinson he asked me how many sisters i had and i said 4 and he asked if they went to church and i said Keene and Cele sing in the quire and Georgie goes but Annie and Frankie and the baby was two little and then he asked if father went to church and i said not very often, only when Keene and Cele had to sing a duet, and then he asked me what else he did sundays and i said sometimes he made viniger down celler and sometimes he went over to see John Adams hens or down to Gim Melchers shop or up to Hirum Gilmores, and he said it is very deploorible is it not, brother and Mister Fernald he laffed again and said he gessed he better not ask me any more questions, and perhaps my father woodent like to have me tell all about him, and i said father wasent afrade, and he said he dident give much for ministers ennyway and then Mister Fernald laffed as hard as he cood and Mister Robinson looked mad, then we went down stairs and they shook hands with mother and aunt Sarah and Mister Robinson he set down by aunt Sarah and asked her about the church and prair meetings a why she dident always go and lots of things like that and Mister Fernald he got the baby in his lap and he talked to mother about the children and told us stories and he was jest buly. then bimeby father he came home and he shook hands with them and he said he was glad to see them whitch was a auful lie. then mother said super was ready and we all went in to super and father kept talking and telling stories until mother said George and looked at him, and he shet up and turned red and then Mister Robinson began to pray and all of us kept still but Georgie who began to gigle, and mother looked scowly at her and she shet up two. then father looked at mother and winked and i had to put my hand over my mouth. mother she almost laffed to, and Mister Robinson he kept on praying till bimeby Frankie he said Mama i wish that man wood stop and Mister Fernald he began to coff i bet he wanted to laff. well ennyway Mister Robinson he stoped. then father helped them to chicking and bisket and gelly and coffy and everything and then he helped us and we all begun to eat and bimeby Annie said we have got some napkins tonite, and Frankie said we have got some little plates to put the butter on, and i saw them first, and Annie said we have got some new goblets two, so there, and Frankie run his tung out at Annie and she made up a face at him, and then father told them to stop and they stoped and mother and aunt Sarah turned red and Mister Robinson he looked auful sollum and Mister Fernald looked funny and then he looked at father an begun to laff and father laffed and then we all laffed as hard as we cood, and Mister Fernald he said, dont mind a bit Missis Shute, i have got children of my own, i like Mister Fernald. after super Frankie and Annie were sent to bed and we went into the parlor and father kept us all laffing telling stories, and then Keene and Cele sung now i lay me down to sleep, and there is a bank on which the wild time grows, and Cele sung flow gently sweet Afton and Georgie sung i wood i were a fary queen, and then Mister Robinson wanted us to sing a religious song and we sung shall we gather at the river. then they asked me to sing and i said i coodent and father said before he thought, that boy is bedeviled to play a cornet, then Mister Fernald he said let him play it, it wont hurt him, then father begun to tell some more stories and kept us laffin fit to die, and Mister Fernald he said he hadent laffed so much for years, and he said, to mother, Missis Shute i gess you have a prety good natured husband, and she said yes, and father he said he most never got mad and jest then the bell rung, and Keene went to the door and said that Mister Swane the poliseman wanted to see father and father he went to the door and in a minit we herd him swaring and herd him say it is a dam lie Swane and you know it and then Swane went away and father came in and said that someone had ridden horseback over the concreek sidewalk and they tride to lay it on me. then it was bedtime and Mister Robinson he prayed some more and he prayed for those who took the name of the lord in vane, and then we went to bed.

Oct. 17. Brite and fair, the old ministers has gone. i am glad of it. i liked Mister Fernald but i hated old Robinson. i gess he wont get invited here again. this morning at brekfast he prayed again untl the brekfast was most cold and he prayed a good deal about takin the name of the lord in vane and i cood see that mother looked mad but she dident say anything. bimeby he begun to talk to mother about father having a unfortunate temper, and said his langage was shocking, and Cele she up and said, i gess my father is as good as you are and Keene stuck out her tung and mother sent them away from the table, and then old Robinson he said i am afrade your children are not well brought up, and mother looked rite at him a minit and then she said, i shood feel very badly if my children shood xcept hospitality from another person and crittisise that person to his face, at all events i cannot submit to have my husband or my children crittisised, and Mister Robinson he dident say ennymore you bet. after brekfast they went away, and Mister Fernald he shook hands with us all and he asked mother to let Cele and Keene come down to shake hands and she did. after they had went mother she gave us a peace of mince pie apeace and we all hoorayed for mother. none of us went to church today.

The Hired Man

By Clarence Webster

He was often more friend than farm laborer. He was independent but he never quit in time of harvest or failed to help in a crisis. Sometimes, though he was taciturn and irascible, he taught the boy on a farm as much as his father. To win his approval was a triumph.

Back in those last decades of the nineteenth century, and until almost 1920, there lived in the small Yankee town an unique kind of person, the Hired Man. No civilization or group of folkways save our own could have produced him, and ours could not have existed without his help. Van Wyck Brooks does not know him, O'Neill disdains him, and Frost is only condescending. Nevertheless, this half-forgotten man is as important as any other constructive member of the community. He was not genteel; he was not cultured or social-minded, but he was of the town and the ways of life that built and sustained it. Now, alas, he is out of the picture, gone with the Saybrook Platform, witches, the heath hen, and stern dominies.

There will always be plenty of mercenary yokels who work out on farms, but they are not the hired men I knew thirty years ago. Some were neat, dapper sports who drove a fast horse; others were dirty and always broke. They might be married or single, moral and staid and even church members, or mighty swearers and drinkers with whom no hired girl was safe. About half of them were unimaginative fellows who plodded through a life of hard work; the others labored just as hard and became legendary figures who added zest and color to sedate rural life. Most of them dreamed of how they would farm it for themselves if they had a chance, and a few did get their own places in time; the others died in an ell chamber or a rented room. But no matter what they were like, they were more than just laborers who took wages; they *helped* on a farm, not just worked out.

Those hired men I knew were the best exponents of the social-contract theory the world has ever produced. They knew that of their own free will and accord they had signed an agreement with the men who paid them, an agreement which, through long years of hiring and being hired, had so developed that now it took into consideration the demands of farms, farmers, and helpers, and was more binding than any piece of paper with seals and signatures.

A good hired man might tell his boss to go to hell, but he would not quit in such farm crises as haying or threshing. Changing jobs was no disgrace; in fact, an independent fellow liked to show what he was made of by so doing, but he would not quit because an employer set too fast a pace of work. Mind you, I said, "Set too fast a pace." In other words, the boss was doing as much as he demanded. A hired man could lie all he wanted to about some matters, but he must tell the truth about what happened on the place in the way of crops, cattle, and buildings. He must never steal from the farm, and an employer's family was sacrosanct unless a Mrs. Potiphar was too insistent and Potiphar himself none too moral. All these things a good hand did or did not do, not because he was paid so much money, but because he was helping that family and that farm.

The employer lived up to his share of the contract or he lost a good worker. For instance, a hired man was accepted as part of the family; he usually ate with the folks, called them by their first names, and was listened to when he gave advice. There must be food enough to keep a worker in body and spirit, and he was capable of saying a few words about too much salt pork or dried codfish. As I have said already, a good boss got out and set the pace at working if he were physically capable of doing so. If slight and almost frail, he had to earn the praise of "tryin' his damnedest t' keep up." A farmer could pay as low wages as the market allowed, and he expected a hired man to work overtime in case of emergency, but on the other hand he helped out that hired man if the latter were sick or needed money. Thirty years ago New England farmers had to be gentlemen before they could get along with their help and be given those words of accolade: "A goddam good man to work for."

After the contract of service between the hired man and his boss was drawn, the hired man had to think of his relations to the town. Very seldom, in fact almost never, was he a candidate for any office, but he paid his taxes, went to caucus and town meeting, and voted with more or less thoughtful deliberation. He was not a town father or elder statesman like the man he worked for, and he knew he probably never would be but, just the same, he felt that he was a real part of the town and was helping to make it a better place to live in.

Men like these have almost disappeared. A few of the toughest, bibulous, profane old rascals are still doing chores for their keep on little hill farms, but in another decade the last of them will have been buried by the town, and from our land will have gone another proof that a man can fill a humble role in life and still retain the comforting feeling that he is just as good as the other fellow.

"Sap's Startin'"—Sugaring Off

By Walter Needham

The prediction of the Old Farmer's Almanack in 1798 that maple sugar, the product of our own country, "will ever have the preference of every true American," has not held true. But even today the magic words "Sap's Startin'" bring back memories of the smells and sights and sounds of a sugar camp, the hard work and the fun of making sugar.

They generally start sugaring operations along the first week in March; they begin to wash the buckets. Nowadays they get the buckets out of the sugarhouse and scald them. In grandpa's time they didn't have sugarhouses, to begin with, and at first they didn't even keep buckets from year to year, but made wooden trenchers.

They would cut down a white birch or some other tree with soft wood, and split the tree in half. They would adz out a hollow in the flat side and chop off that section, and then adz out another hollow and chop that off. So the trenchers was a sort of rough oblong chopping bowls, as you might say. They didn't hang them on the trees, but just propped them up on the ground where the sap was handy.

When they got their trenchers made or their buckets tightened up and cleaned and distributed around by the trees, they could start tapping. The Indians used to cut a gash in the tree just as if they was making turpentine. Gramp had got a little beyond that; he used a tapping iron.

A tapping iron looks like a big gouge chisel, and it was used the same way—you simply drove it into the tree at a right angle. Then you put in a steel sap spout. They've come back to metal spouts again now; the oldest and the newest spouts is metal, and the wooden ones that you occasionally see come from the time in between.

The auger to bore a hole for tapping is newer, too; the old-time blacksmiths couldn't make an auger, where they could make a tapping iron. The big old three-quarter-inch augers with a wooden cross handle go along with the wooden spouts. You will find a great many old trees around here that have been bored with an old T-handled three-quarter-inch auger. Now, of course, they only use a half or three-eighths bit, with the small metal spout.

The old steel spouts was made by the blacksmith out of worn-out scythe blades. The blacksmith would cut off the heavy rim on the back to make nails with, and bend the thin part into spouts. That was just one sign of how precious metal was in gramp's time. That was why the blacksmith was such a big man in the community.

The steel spouts they drove into the cut made by the tapping iron. The wooden spouts was whittled out of staghorn shoemake. I've made them myself. You take a piece that is about right for size, and whittle it around to fit a hole the size of your auger. You cut away half of the spout on top, and just left the end that went into the tree round. Then you run a hot iron through the pith and burned out a hole for the sap to flow through.

The science of tapping a tree is something that not many people know. The only results you get from tapping comes from the sap growth, the outer growth. You could bore a hole clear to the center of the tree, and you wouldn't get no more sap than if you just bored two inches under the bark. There is only two inches' depth of sapwood on a tree. You can bore as much deeper as you're a mind to, and all you will do is hurt the tree.

The trees don't seem to be damaged any by tapping. Some of the old holes in a big tree will be ten inches under the bark. Wherever you bore, it makes a kind of an elliptical dead place, and that spot always stays in the tree forever, and the hole doesn't fill up; it grows over, but it won't fill up. You cut any old maple, and you will find the holes far underneath the bark.

In deciding where to tap a tree, you pick out a place that has new growth. It's very hard to tell without you study it, but if you look at the tree, there will be new cracks or openings in the bark. As the tree expands, the bark doesn't expand with it, but keeps splitting open; that is why they are shaggy. If you look around carefully, you will find where the new growth shows on the bark.

The next part of the science is to set your buckets on the side where there is the most limbs or the biggest limbs. The sap goes to the limbs, so you always look up a tree as well as at the bark. You look for the new growth on the side where the limbs will draw the sap. The ideal is to get more or less on the southeasterly exposure, but you tap on any side if the new growth and limbs is right.

Once a tree has been tapped, you mustn't tap directly in line with the old hole, above it or below it. If you tap below it, you will get sap, but it's injurious to the tree. If you tap above it, you won't get any sap. Just move out of line to one side, and it won't matter. The height doesn't matter in itself; you just want a convenient level for handling the buckets.

Well, you tap your trees and you hang your buckets. Then you come back to the weather and the season, the same as gramp done every day of his life. They've got their evaporators and their central-reservoir gathering systems and their state grading nowadays, but the weather is still the only thing that will make the sap run.

To get a good run of sap, it should freeze hard at night and thaw daytimes. For a good sap day there must be a west wind and bright sunshine; it is unusual that sap will run on a south wind.

When the snow goes and the frost gets out of the ground, the minute the buds begin to swell on the tree, the sirup starts to take on a leathery taste. It's like the difference between Scotch and straight whisky. What little sap runs after that is called the bud run; that sugar is generally just sold for tobacco sweetening. The quality of the sap varies from year to year too. Some years it's good and some years it's quite sandy. And some years it's sweeter than other years, so you get more sirup for the same amount of sap.

In a bad year, the sap won't hardly run at all, to do you any good; in a very good year, it may run as long as four weeks. It isn't usually steady. It will run a day or two, and you'll have a freeze-up and it will stop entirely. Then it will start again and run two or three days more. As long as it freezes at night, you're all right; you don't get the buddy taste. During some of these extra runs, the sap may even run all night, and the buckets will be full again in the morning. Then the buckets may start to sour, and instead of drawing sap away, you have to draw water to the buckets and wash them.

Gramp would go around and collect in the morning, and again in the afternoon. Nowadays they use a big gathering tub on a sledge or even run the sap straight from the trees down metal gutters to a reservoir. In gramp's time, you just lugged the buckets in by hand, and they got pretty heavy along toward night, especially if the snow was deep. The modern buckets hold around fourteen to fifteen quarts. The old ones was a lot more awkward, but they had two of the staves on opposite sides prolonged at the top, with a stick running between them for a handle. A lot of people in gramp's time used wooden sap yokes—pieces of wood hollowed out to fit over your shoulders, with a semicircle cut out for the neck and a piece sticking out from the shoulder at each end. You would take two of your wide-bottomed wooden buckets, and hang them by cords on the ends of the yoke, and go to a tree. You could collect from one tree to another until your two buckets was full or, if the ones on the tree was full, you would just swap buckets and go back. In those days you wouldn't pretend to gather a great ways off. Sometimes you see a sap yoke made of two bows fastened together at the ends, with two straps across in between for your shoulders, but I think those mostly come from Canada.

Before the time of the gathering tub, they would just go around and collect the sap, come back and pour it in a big kettle over a fire of maple chunks, and leave it to boil while they went back for more sap. When things got more permanent, they used what they called a sap pan—just an ordinary big iron pan maybe eight feet long and two or three feet wide. That's all I ever knew of gramp's using. After that come the evaporator. There's different kinds of evaporators, but the idea is about the same in all of them. The Bellows Falls evaporator, for example, is a sap pan with crosswise partitions. Each partition connects at one end with the wall of the pan, and at the other end it doesn't. The openings are at alternate ends, so that the cold sap flows in over the fire on the front end, and zigzags through these partitions until it gets to the back end, which has a partition with a gate. You lift up the gate and fill the back end. You shut the gate and start watching your thermometer; the back end boils slowly because it's so far away from the fire, and when you get to the temperature of sirup or sugar—the sugar temperature is higher, of course—you draw the liquid off through a felt strainer into your cans or tubs or whatever you're putting it up in.

In the old days they used to use part of the run to make sap beer. They put the sap in a barrel and let it ferment, just the same as you make cider. I never knew of grandpa's making sap beer, which may be why I never cared much for it. I don't think it's a very appetizing drink myself, but if you go back into the hills around Wardsboro at the right time, you will still get some sap beer, in case you want to try it.

Gramp's sirup was a black molasses, of course, but like I said, he would boil it on down to sugar, and pour it into crocks or tubs. He made wooden sugar tubs specially, and he would pour the liquid sugar right in and let it harden in the tub. When they wanted some sugar, they'd just go in there and crack some out. Sometimes they might melt it. If they wanted it fine, they would pound it up. Ordinarily, they used it in lumps just as they pounded it out, for cooking or in their tea. They didn't drink coffee much in those days, anyway. For sweetening, they put it on the stove and heated it, because when it was melted you could measure it. They melted it for pancakes, too.

Sugaring off is a big occasion around here. The young folks will come in for a party, with doughnuts and coffee and sour pickles. They bring in tubs of snow. They boil the sirup down until it will wax—a little past what the cookbook calls the soft-ball stage—and then they pour it on the snow. It cools right away into sheets or strips, not particularly sticky, and you can pick it straight off the snow with a fork and eat it. The pickles is to cut the sweetness, so as you can eat more sugar.

In the old days they used to sugar off sometimes on the kitchen stove, and they would hang a piece of fat salt pork from the stove shelf. When the sirup got to boiling up, it would hit that salt pork and would flatten right out.

After white sugar got to be common, and maple sugar was something special, it was mostly sold as cake sugar. I remember when they sold a five-pound box of cake sugar for a dollar. That box would probably cost you around six dollars now, if you could find it. I helped put the cakes up in nice clean white basswood boxes with pinked paper. My job was pinking the paper with a toothed iron.

When I was in Indiana I met a girl at Huntington who had what she called maple sugar and pecan nuts, a kind of black stuff. I told her she didn't know what maple sugar was, and I sent her out a box of the best maple sugar I could find. She wouldn't give in, though; she said that was maple candy.

Late years they think they have to have stirred sugar—a very recent invention. You cook it to the temperature marked for stirred sugar on your sugar thermometer, and while it's cooling you beat it with a wooden paddle. It's like warm butter, and never hardens; it grains, but the grains are very fine from being beaten, and that makes it white. It makes a pretty good spread or a frosting, but it don't taste much like maple to me.

Another thing they do in making these little candy hearts and leaves and shapes like that, they dip them in hot sirup while they're fresh.

"Up with the Chickens"— Chores

By U. P. Hedrick

Chores differed with the seasons, but like the weather, they were always with us. Each had his own, Mother and Father directing and taking the heaviest burdens, the children dividing the rest. A boy didn't always get the jobs he thought appropriate. Sometimes he even had to don an apron and churn the butter!

The daily, light work about the house and barn on our farm made up what we called 'the chores.' My chores were mostly about the house. I built the fires in the morning; kept the wood boxes filled; churned butter three times a week; fed the chickens and cleaned the chicken coop; fed the pigs their rations of corn, grain, and slops; and took care of the snow paths in the winter. My brother's odd jobs were all in the barn. He fed and milked the cows and cleaned the cowshed; nursed the calves for the first few months of their lives; and helped Father care for the horses and clean the stable. My sister washed and wiped the dishes; set the table; helped in the cleaning ('redding the house,' as Mother called it) and in making beds; cleaned the lamps and lanterns and kept them filled with kerosene oil. The first two or three winters 'in the woods' we ran short of matches, and my sister made 'spills' to light fires, lamps, and pipes. A spill is a small, tapered roll of paper, six inches long, made with a peculiar twist that leaves it thick as a lead pencil at one end, a sharp point at the other.

What remained for Father and Mother in the way of chores? Father repaired the buildings and tools; gave a hand to my brother in taking care of the horses and cows; smoked and salted hams, shoulders, bacon, side-meat, and sausages in the fall. Mother did the cooking, baking, sewing, knitting, canning, and drying, sewed strips of old cloth for 'carpet rags,' and made quilts and comforters. On Mondays she did the washing, on Wednesdays, the ironing, and on Friday, the baking. She made apple butter and hominy in the fall, a barrel of soft soap in the spring, and every day in the year put away the milk and skimmed the cream, and three times a week madc butter.

There was work for all of us the livelong day. That each task was done cheerfully and as well as any of us knew how were the chief factors of our happy lives in our farm and forest environment.

My day began with building fires. At five o'clock every day in the year, Father called:

'Boys! Boys!' to which we were supposed to answer, usually in chorus: 'Yes!'

If a second call was needed, it came as an ominous:

'Wilbur! Ulysses!'

After the second call, I pattered downstairs in bare feet and shirt tails past Father's bedroom door.

Before even putting on socks, I built the kitchen fire.

All was in readiness. The night before, however late I had gone to bed, or however tired I may have been, preparations for the morning fire were made. In front of the stove, a pile of shavings, whittled from a pine stick, were laid out; in another pile were a dozen kindlings of pine; and in a third heap were sticks of dry maple wood. It took less than a minute to put all in the stove, and touch the shavings with a match.

Our kitchen stove was a small furnace. It was big enough to warm half the house, and had a fire box that burned twenty cords of wood in the course of the year. The oven was commodious enough to bake a small pig. Its back part was a reservoir to heat water. On wash days water was also heated in a washboiler. The stove had three rows of holes, two to a row, over which there were kettles, either on uncovered openings or on the round lids. The lids were removed with a stovehook, a most important implement, which Mother was always losing.

Much of the successes of the coming day depended on my success in making the morning fire. Mother would be down in a minute. Her tea-kettle and coffeepot were ready to boil on the back of the stove. On the kitchen table was a pan of sliced potatoes ready to fry; a jar of buckwheat batter stood on a small stand near the back of the stove from November to May—from May to November, batter for flour or corn-meal pancakes; eggs, sausage, ham, or bacon were ready to fry. At half-past six, we were again at the chores; by seven, all hands must be in the fields.

Before thc kitchen stove much of the life of our family was enacted. There the children of the household came after school, from work, and from doing chores in the icy cold and blizzards of winter. Never was the living room so cheery, nor had one the pleasant smells of cooking, or a singing teakettle. There, one of us on each side of the stove rested our stockinged feet on a stick of firewood, to thaw or toast. Behind the stove and the wood box, Flash, the dog, snored, and the cat purred away her nine lives. No gas, or electric, or any other than a wood stove was ever as dependable and comfortable as our kitchen stove.

In the living room, Father and Mother had special chairs in which we children seldom sat. Father's was a heavy armchair of curly maple; Mother's a low rocking chair, in which she would gently rock back and forth; it, too, was of polished curly maple; both had cushions—once soft. As a tiny child I was permitted to sit in Mother's comfortable rocker. Death had left no vacant chairs in our household, and there were none until my brother and I went to college.

The living-room stove also played its part in the life of the family. By the time supper was ready in winter we had thawed out and toasted our feet, put on our foot wear, and taken our places at the kitchen table. After supper, my brother and I scrambled for the best reading place at the round table in the living room, never taking Father's throne nearest the double-burner kerosene lamp. After the supper dishes were done, Mother and my sister joined us; during winter evenings, we children read or studied. If the kitchen stove was the heart of the family, surely the living-room stove was its brains.

Our living-room stove was an expensive luxury; it cost the enormous sum of $60, as much as our Singer sewing machine. It was in shape a huge acorn and was called the 'Acorn,' made in Dowagic, Michigan, as we were told by the silver letters on the nickel foot rest. It was roomy enough to hold several chunks of wood, from which, through the square of mica in the door of the stove, we could see flames curling from chunk to chunk. This sturdy stove sat on a heavy square of figured zinc, and, since every winter's night it was red-hot, it must never stand too close to wooden walls. Mother kept the body black and the nickel scrollwork shining. At the top, a brightly gleaming spire pointed heavenward. In early morning, when I shook down the fire, the nestled chunks of maple, beech, or birch burst into bright orange-red flames with bluish curls, popping and shooting sparks, each of the three woods burning a different colored flame.

It was always Mother who wound the one-day clock. Its power was heavy iron weights; its works were brass; it struck the hour with a pleasant musical sound, very comforting to sick children lying awake at night. The clock was made in Waterbury, Connecticut, in 1864, and was encased in beautiful mahogany; under the large, Roman figures was a very good picture of George Washington.

The two stoves called for other chores than building fires. Mother reserved May Day and the first day in October for her sons to move stoves and clean stovepipes. Half of our woodshed, all winter wood having been burned, was turned into a summer kitchen, the other half was kept for storage. Into these rooms the stoves were moved. If the weather was bright and sunny, the stoves were moved and stovepipes cleaned one at a time, just after the midday meal, taking two or three hours for each. If the weather was rainy, an afternoon sufficed to move the two.

Our stovepipes did not run straight up and down. From the stove the pipe went up to within a foot of the ceiling, then made a right-angle turn to the middle of the room, then passed into the room above into a large drum which held heat. Father's and Mother's room, and the one in which my sister slept were warmed by drums; the room in which my brother and I slept was pretty close to the temperature outside. It was this complicated system of pipes and drums that had to be cleaned.

The first step was to spread newspapers wherever soot might fall or tracks might go. Next the wires that held the horizontal pipes to the ceiling were untied. Then each of us tackled a right-angle turn. Eventually a strong tug brought the pipes apart, there being no way to prevent soot from dropping below. Next the pipe was taken from the short neck of the stove.

Wood for our house fires came from the forest in thick slabs a foot wide and eighteen inches long, and was corded up to dry through the summer for the next winter. Nothing but straight-grained, knot-free beech, maple, and yellow birch went into our stoves, though several cords of knotty chunks were saved to keep fire over night in the sitting-room stove, which Father regularly chunked before going to bed.

The firewood was split into slabs as it was sawed in the woods, and it was my work to split these slabs for the kitchen stove all through the winter. It was a rather pleasant chore to split slabs of wood into pieces small enough for the kitchen stove. A single blow of an ax split a slab; a tough slab went into the chunk pile. Of all the chores I had to do, day in and day out, splitting wood and filling the wood boxes were as agreeable as any.

The worst chore to befall a country-bred boy in his tender nonage is churning. Three times a week I had to churn. Nowadays churning in country homes is not so bad; electricity or gasoline is often used to turn a crank, and the churn goes round and round and butter is quickly made; but ours was a dasher churn, three feet high, nine inches in diameter at the top, ten at the bottom. The important part of this churn was the dasher, made of a circular piece of wood eight inches in diameter, at the lower end of a round broomstick handle five feet in length. Cream was put into the churn and my job was to raise and lower the dasher up and down, up and down, until butter came. The handle had free play and this permitted small splashes of gurgling cream to slosh through the top.

I had to do the churning in the morning, after breakfast, before going to school. To protect my clothes, one of Mother's aprons fell from my neck down over my feet. Always the hired men jeered at me as I stood in my apron; always other children on the way to school stopped in and saw me thus arrayed; always I wiped the dasher handle, rich with cream, with a finger, and then put the finger in my mouth, which entailed a punishment if Mother caught me in the act.

There was a saying that butter 'went back' if one stopped churning even for a few seconds. Mother would say: 'Keep churning! The butter is going back!'

It was said, also, that butter 'came' more quickly if a stranger took a hand at the churn. No stranger ever was around when I was churning.

There were preliminaries to churning. When the milk came in from the barn it was strained through a strainer, covered with a thin cotton cloth, into milk pans. These pans were set in a cool place in summer and a warm one in winter. By the next morning a thick top layer of cream had risen; this was skimmed off with a skimmer and put in a tall crock to 'ripen.' Before breakfast on churning days the churn was half filled with hot water to warm it up, and the cream was set near the kitchen stove. After breakfast, the water was poured out, the cream put in. When all was propitious, butter came quickly; on some days the cream was stubborn and churning might take an hour.

Eventually, even on bad days, butter 'came' in large golden globules, which were dipped out with the cream skimmer and then worked with a ladle until the milk was squeezed out; the butter was salted, pressed into a round compact cylinder, and stored in a cool place. Some of our neighbors liked unsalted butter; we liked it salted.

Father loved buttermilk and on churning days, if he was not too far away from the house, came in and finished with pleasure the chore I so greatly loathed. Before Mother could take the butter out of the churn,

Father had lifted the lid and with a long-handled dipper brought out a full quart of creamy buttermilk with flakes of butter floating in it. He drank the dipperful to the last swallow. 'That's the drink of paradise!' he would say.

My brother had only one chore as unpleasant as churning; he had to teach newly born calves how to drink milk out of a pail—he became a foster mother of young bovines. The first three days in its life, a calf takes its milk from its mother as nature intended; then it must be taught to drink from a bucket so that humans may have the milk. My brother 'broke' a calf into feeding itself, the belligerent mother bawling her emphatic disapproval. The calves were kept in a calfpen adjoining the cowyard. In this pen my brother began the education of his calves.

The newly born calves got only the skimmed milk and this had to be warm. Mother warmed the milk on the kitchen stove and poured it into a wooden bucket, at which point my brother took over, climbed into the messy, ill-smelling enclosure, and began 'breaking-in.' First he chose the cleanest corner and backed the calf tightly into it; he straddled the infant bovine and called for the milk. This having been handed him, he placed it in front of the calf and forced its mouth down into the pail, all the while keeping an eye on the bawling mother. Lastly he stuck two fingers in the youngster's mouth and pushed its head into the milk so that it drank or suffocated. Meanwhile the calf was anything but quiet; it struggled forward, backward, sideways, up and down. Only strong arms and legs kept the juvenile cow from breaking loose or upsetting the bucket. In as few as three or as many as six lessons the calf's education was completed; at least, fingers were no longer inserted in the mouth. In a week, the calf eagerly awaited the coming of the bucket; in two weeks a little corn meal or wheat 'shorts' was added to the milk diet, all this to be followed in a month by a transfer to the pasture.

Once every two or three weeks, we made ice cream. In our sub-Arctic land, ice was plentiful, summer and winter; with several cows, cream, too, was always on hand. Our freezer was a wooden pail holding three or four gallons, in the middle of which a heavy metal can, holding a gallon, stood upright, supported top and bottom; in this can was a flanged dasher. With the can well covered, an ingenious device permitted a crank to be fastened to the dasher so that it was turned round and round.

First, a smallish cake of ice was brought from the ice house, doused with water to wash off the sawdust, then broken into chunks and put in an old grain bag, in which it was hammered into crushed ice with the woodsman's maul kept in the woodshed. This crushed ice was tamped about the cream container in the freezer with a liberal supply of coarse salt.

Just what Mother's mixture was for ice cream, I cannot say; it may have been pure cream, flavored with coffee, caramel, or vanilla. Chocolate we did not have. I doubt if she used eggs or a custard, as modern cooks do. When a little short of cream, Mother made an ice cream pie, in which pure cream was frozen and put in a pie crust such as she made for lemon or pumpkin pies. This was a favorite pie in our family the year round.

There was never trouble in getting a boy to turn the crank of an ice-cream freezer, especially if, as sometimes happened, he could stay at home from church to do it. Besides, there was always a reward. Whoever froze the cream could 'lick the dasher.' When the crank of the freezer could no longer be turned, ice and salt were carefully removed from the top of the cream container; the dasher, with its four wooden flanges, was pulled out, always thickly covered with ice cream, very delicious an hour before dinner.

My brother gave the cows their hay and grain. Cows gave little milk in winter unless fed some green food; as we had no silo, instead of ensilage our cows were fed carrots, rutabagas, and pumpkins. These had to be cleaned and cut. The pumpkins were easily prepared; we took an ax and cut them in chunks as large as eggs, discarding the seeds, and fed them with a little chopped grain to the animals. But pumpkins lasted only until the middle of December, after which, until spring, the cows had to have carrots and rutabagas.

Cutting these root crops in winter was most disagreeable. The work had to be done in the root cellar, as close and dark as the Black Hole of Calcutta, lighted only with a smoky kerosene lantern. The roots had been cleaned when they were stored, but each one had to be rubbed with a coarse cloth and then cut in pieces small enough to keep the cows from gulping them down and choking. To be sure, we wore grain-bag mittens, but our hands were always cold, always so chapped and cracked that we were ashamed to have them seen in school. This chore had to be done morning after morning all the winter through, before breakfast. What a chore!

Other odd jobs every boy bred in the country had to do before the advent of power machinery were turning a fanning mill, a corn sheller, and a grindstone. There are worse chores than shelling corn and cleaning grain, though few worse than turning a grindstone on a farm that is being carved out of a forest. Shelling corn and cleaning grain with a fanning mill are infrequent chores, not to be dreaded day after day, as is turning the grindstone. We shelled corn and cleaned grain only for seed sowing, and when corn and grain were to be taken to the mill to be chopped into coarse meal.

There were special times for cleaning grain. Wheat had to be run through the fanning mill soon after threshing, to provide clean seed for fall seeding. The second and main time came on cold, rainy days in late autumn when the weather prohibited work out of doors. At this time we usually had a hundred or more bushels of wheat and about the same amount of oats, and some years half that quantity of rye. All grain was cleaned preparatory to grinding at the mill for stock food. Turning the crank of a fanning mill hour after hour was terribly monotonous. Because of poor threshing machines, our grain had much chaff and dust, which covered one from head to foot after even a short turn at cleaning it. One man, more often two, handled the grain, which was brought in grain bags just as it had come from the threshing machine; a second man put the grain in bags to go to the mill. Another operation in cleaning grain was to remove, every hour or two, the chaff, weed seeds, dust, and dirt that the mill had separated from the grain. This refuse was kept for poultry.

Shelling corn was much more pleasant than cleaning grain. It was harder to turn the crank of the sheller than to furnish power for the fanning mill, but there was much less dust and no chaff at all. Besides, it was a rather pretty sight to see husked ears of corn, each ear with exactly as many rows as any other, go into the sheller. The brightly colored bushel box that came with the sheller slowly filled with the golden dented kernels of the dent corns or the reddish-yellow smooth flint corns, each kernel a nugget of gold, either kind the most beautiful of all grains. There were always more bushels of corn than of all other grains put together. Some farmers sent it to the mill to be chopped, cob and all, for cows. This the farm papers of that day told us made fat, sleek cattle.

Another farm chore was oiling the harnesses. Late in the autumn, before steady cold weather came, a day was set, usually a Saturday, for this annual event. The real work was done in the woodshed, but water and oil had to be heated in the kitchen. Father superintended the work and the hired men did the greasing. Mother made an awful fuss over 'harness day,' when four or five males tramped into her kitchen with dirty feet and oily hands to borrow her kitchenware; she scolded one and all, and we all took it meekly.

Father made his own harness oil from a formula that called for tallow and unsalted lard, made black as pitch with lampblack. Always the harness oil was made a day or two in advance, and on the day when operations began was warmed up to a temperature as hot as the hands could stand.

The work on 'harness day' started with taking harnesses apart. Woe betide the person who mixed the parts of sets!

What boy, in these days of automobiles, can name the parts of a harness and tell at sight a single from a double harness, a buggy harness from one used in farm operations? Whatever the kind of harness, there were for the head, bridle, blinds, check reins, bit, lines with numerous buckles; the breast harness included breastband, or a collar and harness with yoke straps and traces for a single or tugs for a double harness; the parts of the body harness were the saddle, bellyband, crupper, hip straps, and breeching. In a double harness there was the complicated crossing of the two guiding lines held in the driver's hands to the four ends attached to the two bits in the horses' mouths. It was quite a task to take a harness apart, and there might be much trouble if the parts of each harness were separated.

Mother's wash tubs were brought into service for the first operation in greasing harnesses. They were half-filled with hot water into which a half pound of soda had been added. The leather parts of the harness then went into the tubs and were scrubbed with a stiff brush on a washboard until all the grease and dirt were removed. When the leather had been hung for a few minutes for the water to drip off, the hot harness grease was rubbed in. Meanwhile, my brother and I had been polishing the metal parts, chiefly buckles, to silver brightness. By the end of the long day the half-dozen harnesses for the farm's horses had been washed, greased, repaired, and put together for another year's service.

Another annual autumn chore, about the last before winter set in, was banking the house. Our earliest houses did not have stone foundations. Their framework rested on pillars of sturdy logs down to the bottom of the cellar, and stood perhaps a foot above the surface of the ground. The part above ground was solidly planked in, but planks, doubled and tripled, could not keep out the searching cold of a northern Michigan winter, and the house had to be 'banked up' to keep frost out of the cellar and from working through into the house to chill feet and legs in spite of red-hot stoves.

For banking some of our neighbors used straw, others manure. We found sawdust cheapest and best. Stakes were driven eighteen inches from the house in sufficient number to support heavy planks a foot wide. When the planks were put in place, and the space so made was filled with sawdust, well tramped down, a second layer of planks was put up and a second filling of sawdust made. With such a covering encircling the house, we could feel comfortable indoors when the days grew short and Arctic gales raged outside.

Asked to name her most arduous work, I am sure my sister would have said 'cleaning lamp chimneys and lanterns,' a daily task as long as she was in her father's house. We burned kerosene oil and lots of it. Lamps and lanterns had to be filled and their globes cleaned, lamps one day, lanterns the next.

There must have been eight or ten lamps in the house. There were three large double-burner lamps: one in the living room, another on the dining-room table, and a third in the kitchen. There was a single-burner for each bedroom. Common items for Saturday's trading in the village stores were a five-gallon can of kerosene oil, a potato stuck on the spout to keep the oil from spattering, and lamp chimneys and lantern globes. As often as lamps and lanterns were filled with oil, the splotches of black smoke on the inside of chimneys and globes had to be cleaned; remnants of old dresses, sheets, aprons, and shirts were always saved for this work.

It was amazing how many lanterns were used on our farm. For eight months in the year every male on the place had to have a lantern to do early morning chores and to finish up in the evening. Whoever drove out at night, except when there was a full moon or in the snow whiteness of winter, hung a lantern beneath the front of the vehicle. Each of the two or three persons who worked about a sick animal in the barn needed a lantern. Whoever went to visit a neighbor on a moonless night carried a lantern. Wherever a flashlight would be used now, a lamp or lantern was needed.

Many a time the sight of a light from a lamp or lantern brought cheer to my heart. A gleaming lantern, coming or going, far down a lonely road was a most welcome sight; and a lantern in hand was a most comfortable companion. When I was coming home late on a dark night, especially in a gale in winter, its tiny wick all aglow warmed me all the way through. There was nothing comparable to lamps and lanterns in our isolated home to raise the morale of its inhabitants, whether they were outside or inside the house.

The Woodshed

By Haydn S. Pearson

A woodshed is far more than the place where an irate father took off his belt to strap a rebellious boy. It is an index of a farmer's industry. In it is stored his insurance against the winter's cold, the neatly cut and stacked fuel which his wife needs to heat the kitchen range. The woodshed testifies to providence and hard work.

There was a time, not so long ago, when it was an axiom of the countryside that you could judge a farmer by his woodpile. A good farmer took pride in his fuel supply. In the winter or early spring it was sawed, split, and stacked in the woodshed.

On frosty, star-studded nights when the cold air hangs like a blanket over hills and valleys, waiting to tuck the earth in for its long, strength-restoring sleep, many a farmer pauses as he comes from the barn. The yellow light of the lantern makes a picture as it plays over the stacked tiers.

A real country woodshed is a place of deep, fundamental satisfaction. It represents honest labor—the cutting, the trimming and hauling; the sawing, as the whirring knife-edged teeth sang through the oak, maple, beech, and hickory; the splitting, as the axe flashed down and hit the exact spot so that a chunk separated along the grain; the stacking, as the symmetrical tiers rose toward the woodshed attic floor.

It's a place of good smells. A woodshed that has been used for years has a tangy, pungent aroma. There's the resinous zip of the pine limbs, which make a quick kindling on zero winter mornings when the hoarfrost is deep on kitchen windows; the nostril-tickling acridness of red oak; the zesty tang of old apple wood; the bland smoothness of sugar maple and beech; the peculiarly pungent odor of hemlock; and the clean, exhilarating smell of cedar. Penetrating through all the other smells is that dry, slightly musty aroma of the inches-deep base of splinters, bits of bark, and debris that is the accumulation of years.

Woodsheds are part of America, the same as johnnycake, two-seated democrats, buck saws, and pancakes and maple syrup.

Holiday Time at the Old Country Store

By Gerald Carson

Men sat around the stove and talked, or played checkers, or whittled. Their wives pondered how to spend the egg money. Macy's and Gimbel's never catered to a wider variety of human wants: Harness parts and salt blocks, dotted swiss for curtains, reading glasses for Grandpa's failing eyes, molasses out of a barrel—the country store had everything, and extra stock for Christmas.

Millions of Americans, reared on a farm or in a country village, still treasure the recollection of December shopping expeditions to the old-time general store as one of life's most permanent and agreeable memories. The crossroads store, around the turn of the century, was still in its full glory. A bazaar for all lines of merchandise required by its trade—which meant, in the words of the firm of Merrill & Hinckley, at Blue Hill, Maine, "Almost Everything"—the old store also provided many other services as community message center, parcel room, informal bank, political forum, male club and reading room. It was also a United States Post Office, fourth class.

A door, wall or pillar served as bulletin board. There were notices about horse thieves, church socials, elections, farm auctions. Here handbills announced in wood-block type that a turkey shoot would be held, or that a Hambletonian stallion "will make the season . . . at the home of Frank Varble . . . at the modest sum of $10." The general store was indeed the communication center of the area it served. The storekeeper, or "merchant" as he was called in the weekly newspaper, presided over the busy scene from the post-office window, or a strategic location behind his old roll-top desk. The office of the town clerk was, like as not, tucked into a pent-roofed room off the rear warehouse. The storekeeper himself was clerk of the town, custodian of the land records. Or perhaps he was justice of the peace, with the power to sit in judgment or perform the marriage ceremony. A man of many talents, he could also doctor a horse, explain the law of replevin, or draw a viable contract.

The arrival of fresh merchandise was an event, noticed with keen interest at any time by the whole countryside, but especially so around November and December when the big dray unloaded large wooden packing cases, barrels, bales, boxes of figs, jute bags of coconuts and English walnuts, crates of oranges—never seen at any other season of the year—and wooden pails which almost certainly contained stick candy with barber-pole stripes winding up each stick. The weekly newspaper over at the county seat took notice of the occasion, commenting editorially on the "large consignment of seasonal goods reasonably priced and well adapted to the local trade, representing one of the finest assortments ever stocked in this part of the state. See large display advertisement on page four."

About this time every country family decided upon a major expedition to the crossroads to inspect the holiday goods and possibly do a little trading. The trip would be made on a Saturday. The whole family went along, the youngsters sitting on a bed of wheat or oat straw in the light spring wagon. Or, more likely, Father would decide to take the heavier Studebaker or Columbus & Weber farm wagon. He would throw in a few live chickens, legs tied together, stash away a can of cream, or load in whatever butter they had on hand. The boys would take along their pelts—not many so early in the season—and Mother would be in charge of the eggs. This last item was of particular importance to her, since it was a firmly established folkway of farm life that "the Missus" kept the egg money for her own personal use.

Fortunately, the hens were usually busy by December, after their moulting season. Egg prices would be on the way up, good for around seventeen cents a dozen in trade, maybe a little less in cash. A basket lunch of fried chicken for the family and oats for the horses, stowed away at the last minute before the team started up, assured that they would make a day of it.

The store was a two-story building of frame construction, painted white, with gable end facing the road, the store itself on the first floor, the G.A.R. Hall upstairs. Warehousing for reserve stock, poultry feed and other heavy bulk items was provided for in an extension at the rear.

There was commonly a porch or raised platform at the front of the store for convenient loading and unloading of farm wagons, with either a hitching rack or shed shelter nearby for the wagons and bobsleds—an early version of "free parking for customers." A bench ran along the store front for accommodation of the local philosophers and those who were either temporarily or permanently disengaged from any gainful occupation.

Here in pleasant weather they sat "from can to can't"—from the time they could see to the time they couldn't. They whittled, assessed the political situation, recollected the great comet of 1881, discussed in detail the more comely women customers, and told tall tales of farming, fishing, fighting and hunting. They would not be visible, however, to a farm family bent on Christmas shopping. Come hog-killing time, the regulars moved inside to the comfort of the "captain's chairs" provided for them around the cherry-red chunk stove, squatting in its bed of sand, with the raised, cast-iron letters on the side "Made by W. P. Ford & Co., Concord, N.H."

"There are more ducks killed around the stoves on the dry goods boxes at the customary haunts of local nimrods every evening between seven and nine-thirty o'clock," wrote an Illinois country correspondent in a sheaf of news notes to the *Carrollton Patriot*, "than are slain in twenty-four hours along the Illinois River from source to mouth. Unless the legislature puts some restriction on this method of wholesale slaughter, the time will soon come when there won't be any duck-shooting stories to tell —that anybody will put any confidence in."

The double doors opened inward. The remainder of the front elevation was thickly covered by tin signs, each a memorial to the industry and aggressiveness of a tobacco drummer with a tack hammer and a line of good five-cent cigars. In the windows were a jumble of spectacles, notions, gilt jewelry, fine and coarse combs. They were just stored there, rather than displayed; but this was not too serious a lapse from alert merchandising, since there was no pedestrian traffic to speak of, no strangers to attract, and usually no other store to visit. Inside, while one adjusted to the change in light, there was a sense of the world's good things in limitless profusion, long counters down either side, with rounded glass show cases spaced along on top of the counters, the whole length of the side walls lined with drawers, bins and shelves. Heavy hardware stood at the rear: rakes, hayforks, adzes, scythes. Buggy whips hung from the ceiling by a thread. The buyer made a careful selection, jerked his whip free, and it was his.

The ceiling was largely used for display, or at least storage. Corn poppers, lanterns, pails and kitchen ware dangled from hooks and wires. Lamp chimneys were racked up on wooden pegs. Festoons of dried apples, harness and horse collars all crowded in between the big oil lamps which went up and down on their chains and balances when it was necessary to light up the store or put out the lamps. The whole effect was rather on the dark side. There were no side windows, which increased the uncertainty of the customer and his sense of confusion. In general, the right side of the store might be called the ladies' department. Here, toward the front, were ribbons, buttons, braids and fringes. On the shelves, piece goods by the bolt. Brass tacks were driven into the time-smoothed counter to mark an exact yard. ("Don't hold it up and guess. Get down to brass tacks.") Here too were hooks and eyes, thread, and long black or white women's hose, the two fashionable colors, year in and year out.

Farther back came the men's wear: jeans, shirts, shoes, celluloid collars, suspenders and red flannel underwear. At the front, to the left side of the double doors, were the drugs and patent medicines, pipes, tobacco, and the knife for cutting off "eating" tobacco. ("Want a five-cent slice, or a ten-cent slice?") Groceries followed in the middle section, with the great wheel of Herkimer County cheese under its wire screen cage, the store fly trap, the kerosene peanut roaster and the coffee grinder. Then came china, crockery, the spice cabinets—with soaps, cartridges and shells, shoe blacking and horse medicine tucked into odd corners and wooden drawers. Often the customers could go more directly to a wanted item than the merchant himself, a first faint suggestion of the future opportunities for the self-service store! The tiny façade of the little post office squeezed in as best it could at front or rear, a source of modest revenue but great personal prestige to the storekeeper. It was also a convenient means for checking up on wayward customers who might be tempted by the catalogue "wish books" ("I wish I had a Daisy Air Rifle") to send a money order off to one of the Chicago mail-order houses.

The first and, over the years, the most lasting impression upon the rural family as it entered the store came through the olfactory nerve. There was a fragrance which still stands out in memory above all else. Perhaps it was not exactly a fragrance, but more of an aroma, mellow and substantial. Considering some of its constituent parts, perhaps it was not so much an aroma as a smell, the general store smell. All diarists and old-timers agree that it was a well-dug-in odor, with lots of authority, a blend made up of the store's inventory, the customers and the cat. Identifiable still, down memory's lane, are the contributions of ripe cheese and sauerkraut, sweet pickles, the smell of bright paint on new toys, kerosene, lard and molasses, old onions and potatoes, poultry feed, gun oil, rubber boots, calico, dried fish, coffee, and "kept" eggs. Kept eggs meant—well, it was sort of a technical term. It meant eggs that should have been shipped off to the city some time ago but weren't.

Tobacco smoke floated through the store in lazy layers. A suspicion of corn whiskey rose from among the gentry sitting stove-side. Or maybe it was just Hood's Sarsaparilla. Taken daily in generous amounts, either before or after meals, sarsaparilla enjoyed a great reputation as a tonic and body-builder. Since it contained sixteen and one-half per cent alcohol, the properties of the medicine were certain to make themselves felt if the patient followed the directions with enough enthusiasm. Only the "general line" store of years ago could have produced so cosmopolitan an odor, permanent the year 'round, yet accented at Christmas time with spicy winter apples, the smell of oranges and toy paint.

All "boughten" things were fascinating to a rural people who saw but little cash money after they had paid their taxes. But surely December was not the month for staples and necessities. There were eleven other months of the year in which to trade for Macbeth Pearl Glass Lamp Chimneys, axle grease, Dr. Price's Baking Powder, wash boards, stove polish, J. & P. Coats' Spool Cotton Thread, an ax helve, or Pearline ("Pearline is never peddled"). This was not even the time for case-lot purchases of those crispy food novelties—the new patented breakfast foods like Egg-O-See or the Shredded Wheat biscuits that came from the sunlit factory at Niagara Falls. Piper Heidsick Plug Tobacco ("Champagne Flavor") might be considered by Father; or the oyster crackers left by the new "cracker man" to go with the Chesapeake oysters, seasonally displayed with the head off the barrel. Peeking in, you could actually see the big succulent oysters, shipped in salt water from the distant port of Baltimore. Jelly by the pail would be a good buy that an indulgent father might consider. A treat for himself would be the popular tie of the year—if the year were 1901, the "King Edward." He would never buy a moustache cup for himself, but he might like to have one if it appeared on Christmas morning, or even a shaving mug, handsomely embellished with an illustration on its side depicting the life of the farmer.

For Mother there were new dimities, delaines, madras, ginghams and calicoes to be seen, with braids, gimps and passementeries to go with her new Russian-style shirtwaist. A set of china bedroom crockery would fit out the "spare room" so nicely, particularly if Grandma were to come to live with them. It was a day of rich adventure. Let imagination soar with horn combs for wings, and a set of yellow nappies for ballast—those cunning little dessert dishes with sloping sides that were all the rage among the polished hostesses of Boston, Cincinnati and St. Louis. It was a big responsibility to raise a daughter who had already showed a strong bent for the decorative arts in saving her father's cigar bands for a whole year —enough to cover a card tray completely with these colorful examples of tobacco lithography. Christmas morning must bring more buttons for her "charm string," already a wondrous long necklace of jet, mother-of-pearl, brass, wooden blanks covered with cloth, enamel buttons with a tiny inset of velvet, and ingenious rakings from the sewing box. Such a daughter could be counted on to pop the Christmas corn and thread it, until the fluffy white garlands were long enough to drape the tree generously with edible snow. She always placed the little wax candles on the tree so that they burned with the prettiest effect. Perhaps a mother with such an artistic daughter would be wise to settle upon the pyrography set, and end all indecision.

Thinking of the younger children, she might use some of the egg money then and there to buy a sack of ginger snaps, or hot peanuts from the fragrant roaster over there. Where, by the way, *are* the children? Looking at the candy display, of course! Pressing against the counter. Numbering every jar, each safely established on the shelf back against the wall. Each top was a stately pleasure dome sheltering peppermint sticks; or horehound; or rock candy, the crystal clear and the pink kind, each on cotton strings; common and "French" kisses; cigars molded in chocolate or maple sugar; lemon drops, the hard kind, good for sucking; mottoes; jawbreakers; cinnamon red hots; "lickerish" shoe strings; belly-burners, one cent each; and glorious Zanzibars, either lemon- or peppermint-flavored, that kept fresh through all weather and in all climates. Chewing gum? Step up and name your brand. Yucatan, Red Beauty, Mint Julep and Red Star were great favorites.

But this was only the beginning. When the holiday time approached, more room had to be made by drastic means. Carriage bolts, nail kegs and egg crates were pushed aside. The oatmeal barrel was rolled into the back room, without regard for the wishes or comfort of the store cat. They just had to make more room—for toys, watches, tiny knives and forks, wooden soldiers, dolls with china heads and kidskin bodies, linen dogs and cats, to be stuffed and sewed up at home. Tiddledywinks were tumbled in alongside the new game of Lotto. Articles of the omnipresent "tin" made a brave show. It was sheet iron, really, brightly plated and painted, fabricated cheaply into millions of horses, rattles, trumpets and trains.

If you were a boy, and older, there were Barlow knives, under glass, unfortunately, with bone handles and two blades, good for mumblety-peg. For young hunters, a Stevens single-shot .22 calibre rifle. For wintering pleasantly in the country there were Winslow's skates, and the light No. 2 steel traps a boy needed to set up his own trap line and grow wealthy. For the musically inclined, the stock offered the simple jew's harp, harmonicas, or a resplendent guitar.

While Mother feasted her eyes on gay colors, and ran a rough hand shyly over a modish fascinator that she might look at but hardly possess, Father was engaged with the possibilities of Christmas giving for his wife. There was "Hallowed Hymns," a sound choice, to balance against the scrapbook she needed for her greeting cards, visiting cards, and her growing collection of trade cards, brightly-colored bits of lithographed cardboard which she pored over on the long winter evenings. Color printing was a novelty. The cards were infinitely desirable, even when frankly commercial. He remembered the one of the Estey Organ Company, showing an angelic but hearty girl-child strumming a harp in a setting not immediately identifiable; but it must have been either Heaven or Brattleboro, Vt. The Estey card was a particular prize because of the Estey reed organ that stood in their own parlor. She had also a choice series of "girls of all nations" put out by Walter A. Wood, who manufactured reapers at Hoosick Falls, New York. Trade cards were all the rage. Willimantic Thread, B. T. Babbitt, J. D. Larkin & Co., of Buffalo—to name just three from among thousands—contributed to this collecting vogue for popular art blended with commercial puffery. There was a beautiful picture card in every package of McLaughlin's XXXX Glazed Coffee. Since there were eighteen designs in the set, the purchase of seventeen more packages of McLaughlin's was a practical certainty.

An album was nice for pasting up newspaper poetry if you had enough. And Mother had enough. Columns and pages of it, such as the favorite about the old tramp, haled into court and addressing the judge:

Whar did I lose my leg? At Spottsylvania.
Perhaps you've read about that bloody fight.

But then I guess the story won't restrain you
From doin' what the law sets down as right.

through

I served as private in the Tenth New Jersey,

down to His Honor's ringing verdict:

The sentence is that all your life your camp'll
Be in the best room in my humble home!

The judge was, inevitably, the crusty old colonel whose life the soldier had saved at Spottsylvania.

Yes, it was a sentimental age, and Mother did not lag behind her times!

Since this was a day of reconnaissance, Father did not make final decisions on major matters. Just to cover the situation to a degree, he purchased a match safe for the kitchen wall, an almanac for the New Year, and a "dressy comb." Such slight purchases did not call for unrolling the heavy brown straw wrapping paper, mounted like a roller towel, with a stationary blade that sheared the paper off in the length wanted. There were bags for small articles, with red and blue stripes on them, magazined in a rack overhead. The clerk reached them down in a single sweeping motion of the arm and tied them up beside the beehive twine-holder, filled with "Tea Twine," a nice handy cotton twine.

Advertising did not play a great part in the fortunes of the country storekeeper. "Advertising don't take the place of dustin'," as one successful rural merchant said, a man who diligently dusted all his foodstuffs, in fact his whole stock, every morning. But the store owner usually had palm leaf fans in the summertime to give away with his name and address imprinted on the fan. And the paper bags that Father got for carrying his little purchases did carry a message of an institutional character, like the bags of F. H. Dean, who conducted a store for forty years at Monkton, Vermont. They were ornamented with an imposing cut of a large fierce eagle, and the legend:

Let the eagle scream
And buy your goods of F. H. Dean
Honest Weight
And Honest Merchandise.

Being a man of rectitude in financial matters, and having shared substantially during the crop year in the McKinley Prosperity he had voted for, Father took the occasion to settle his account. He remembered how he had read in *Willard's Almanac* as a boy the advice to the farmer for December: "Settle all your accounts this month; collect what's due you, *if you can*; and pay what you owe, which will not be difficult if you have the money. Short settlements, it is said, make long friends, and there is nothing like a good start with the year."

It was a deep satisfaction to see written in the store's great ledger in Father's own handwriting, the words: "Settled and made even all Book accounts to this date," followed by the formal ink signatures, the merchant's and his own. Now the new year would begin properly.

By an ancient tradition, it was up to the storekeeper to show his appreciation. He scurried jovially. Jelly beans for children. A length of ribbon for Mother. A cigar for the valued customer who was now in the clear, with no debit balance against his name. A sign over the cigars said "Nine Good Cigars for 25¢" and Father was duly appreciative.

In the simpler country store days, presents ran to something useful, like a pair of warm mittens, or to something eatable—candies, nuts, apples, or an orange. Yes, *an* orange. Family funds were limited, and so were the stocks at the four-corners store. But all the thrill and magic of Christmas were there, in the planning and choosing, and the giving and receiving.

There came a day when the life of each township and hamlet took on a quicker rhythm, and the reason was spelled a-u-t-o. The car brought the city and the farm so close together there was no room left in between for the old-time country store. Small stocks of gift goods grew smaller still, gathering the dust of the passing seasons like Eugene Field's little tin soldier.

There are still stores in the country, of course. Groceries, drugs, hardware and the like can still be bought locally, and in very small towns the post office may still be tucked away in a store corner, while nostalgic traces of the old regime linger along counters and shelves held over from an earlier day. Yet the store is no longer the self-sufficient center of social and commercial life for an isolated community.

But the memory of holiday time at the general store lingers on in fond recollection. To some it is still a warm personal memory. To the rest of us, it is a heritage and a tradition of life in December as it was lived by a majority of Americans before the customers of the general stores had disappeared down the concrete slab that sped like an arrow to the Big Town.

Country School on the Middle Border

By Hamlin Garland

Every farm boy knew the delight of climbing into the wagon and driving to town for new clothes before school started. Hamlin Garland, in a selection from *Son of the Middle Border*, recalls his first real boots with copper toes and the country school where he wore them out playing such games as "Fox and Geese."

One night as we were all seated around the kerosene lamp my father said, "Well, Belle, I suppose we'll have to take these young ones down to town and fit 'em out for school." These words so calmly uttered filled our minds with visions of new boots, new caps and new books, and though we went obediently to bed we hardly slept, so excited were we, and at breakfast next morning not one of us could think of food. All our desires converged upon the wondrous expedition—our first visit to town.

Our only carriage was still the lumber wagon but it had now two spring seats, one for father, mother and Jessie, and one for Harriet, Frank and myself. No one else had anything better, hence we had no sense of being poorly outfitted. We drove away across the frosty prairie toward Osage—moderately comfortable and perfectly happy.

Osage was only a little town, a village of perhaps twelve hundred inhabitants, but to me as we drove down its Main Street, it was almost as impressive as LaCrosse had been. Frank clung close to father, and mother led Jessie, leaving Harriet and me to stumble over nail-kegs and dodge whiffle trees what time our eyes absorbed jars of pink and white candy, and sought out boots and buckskin mittens. Whenever Harriet spoke she whispered, and we pointed at each shining object with cautious care. —Oh! the marvelous exotic smells! Odors of salt codfish and spices, calico and kerosene, apples and gingersnaps mingle in my mind as I write.

Each of us soon carried a candy marble in his or her cheek (as a chipmunk carries a nut) and Frank and I stood like sturdy hitching posts whilst the storekeeper with heavy hands screwed cotton-plush caps upon our heads,—but the most exciting moment, the crowning joy of the day, came with the buying of our new boots.—If only father had not insisted on our taking those which were a size too large for us!

They were real boots. No one but a Congressman wore "gaiters" in those days. War fashions still dominated the shoe-shops, and high-topped cavalry boots were all but universal. They were kept in boxes under the counter or ranged in rows on a shelf and were of all weights and degrees of fineness. The ones I selected had red tops with a golden moon in the center but my brother's taste ran to blue tops decorated with a golden flag. Oh! that deliciously oily new smell! My heart glowed every time I looked at mine. I was especially pleased because they did not have copper toes. Copper toes belonged to little boys. A youth who had plowed seventy acres of land could not reasonably be expected to dress like a child.—How smooth and delightfully stiff they felt on my feet.

Then came our new books, a McGuffey reader, a Mitchell geography, a Ray's arithmetic, and a slate. The books had a delightful new smell also, and there was singular charm in the smooth surface of the unmarked slates. I was eager to carve my name in the frame. At last with our treasures under the seat (so near that we could feel them), with our slates and books in our laps we jolted home, dreaming of school and snow. To wade in the drifts with our fine high-topped boots was now our desire. . . .

The school-house which was to be the center of our social life stood on the bare prairie about a mile to the southwest and like thousands of other similar buildings in the west, had not a leaf to shade it in summer nor a branch to break the winds of savage winter. "There's been a good deal of talk about setting out a wind-break," neighbor Button explained to us, "but nothing has as yet been done." It was merely a square pine box painted a glaring white on the outside and a desolate drab within; at least drab was the original color, but the benches were mainly so greasy and hacked that original intentions were obscured. It had two doors on the eastern end and three windows on each side.

A long square stove (standing on slender legs in a puddle of bricks), a wooden chair, and a rude table in one corner, for the use of the teacher, completed the movable furniture. The walls were roughly plastered and the windows had no curtains.

It was a barren temple of the arts even to the residents of Dry Run, and Harriet and I, stealing across the prairie one Sunday morning to look in, came away vaguely depressed. We were fond of school and never missed a day if we could help it, but this neighborhood center seemed small and bleak and poor.

With what fear, what excitement we approached the door on that first day, I can only faintly indicate. All the scholars were strange to me except Albert and Cyrus Button, and I was prepared for rough treatment. However, the experience was not so harsh as I had feared. True, Rangely Field did throw me down and wash my face in snow, and Jack Sweet tripped me up once or twice, but I bore these indignities with such grace as I could command, and soon made a place for myself among the boys.

I cannot recover much of that first winter of school. It was not an experience to remember for its charm. Not one line of grace, not one touch of color relieved the room's bare walls or softened its harsh windows. Perhaps this very barrenness gave to the poetry in our readers an appeal that seems magical, certainly it threw over the faces of Frances Babcock and Mary Abbie Gammons a lovelier halo.—They were "the big girls" of the school, that is to say, they were seventeen or eighteen years old,—and Frances was the special terror of the teacher, a pale and studious pigeon-toed young man who was preparing for college.

In spite of the cold, the boys played open air games all winter. "Dog and Deer," "Dare Gool" and "Fox and Geese" were our favorite diversions, and the wonder is that we did not all die of pneumonia, for we battled so furiously during each recess that we often came in wet with perspiration and coughing so hard that for several minutes recitations were quite impossible.—But we were a hardy lot and none of us seemed the worse for our colds.

There was not much chivalry in the school—quite the contrary, for it was dominated by two or three big rough boys and the rest of us took our tone from them. To protect a girl, to shield her from remark or indignity required a good deal of bravery and few of us were strong enough to do it. Girls were foolish, ridiculous creatures, set apart to be laughed at or preyed upon at will. To shame them was a great joke.—How far I shared in these barbarities I cannot say but that I did share in them I know, for I had very little to do with my sister Harriet after crossing the school-house yard. She kept to her tribe as I to mine.

Sunday School Picnic

By Della T. Lutes

The entire community gave itself up to feasting and frivolity. Mother packed a basket of her own specialties—buttermilk cookies, beaten biscuits, fried chicken, baked ham. At the long plank table the neighborhood women presided over gallons of lemonade and old-fashioned freezers of ice cream. The annual Sunday School picnic was a summer event second only to the Fourth of July, a time to help yourself until you couldn't hold another bite.

The social and communal life of our small world's summer centred around a few anticipated events. The Fourth of July was still looked upon as a patriotic anniversary and so taught to children. Towns large and small gave due heed to its celebration with speeches, a reading of the Declaration of Independence, much fanfare by local bands, and fireworks in the evening. This outburst of patriotic fervor, however, did not interfere with a little horseplay on the side, such as climbing greased poles, chasing greased pigs, sack races, potato races, and other primitive sports. Our neighbors, the Covells, always went to the celebration.

Scrubbed and clean, but barefooted, since, as my father said, Old Man Covell was too tarnation mean to buy shoes for them until snow flew, they piled into the lumber wagon, father, mother, children, and the hired man,—theirs or someone else's who wanted a ride,—with the basket of vittles, and set off soon after breakfast to see the doin's. Swinging on the gate, I watched them go, envious to the tip of my own bare toes, as the horses jogged dejectedly along in the hot sand, and the wagon trundled cumbrously off to the wonders of the proper observance of a Fourth o' July celebration. For my father did not hold with crowds, nor had he much patience with public performances. "Caperin's" he called them, and said he had something better to do than chase off to town to see somebody show off.

As a matter of fact, he had—according to his own notions. That little ceremony of his own of fingering from the hills of his early potatoes the first small, round fruit, and plucking the first peas from the vines. These he always brought in with an air of proffering gifts *from* the gods, swaggering a little, boastfully benign, as if to say, "There! Now see what you get by staying at home and letting *me* show you how to celebrate the Fourth of July!"

He always made it a point to sow his buckwheat on this day, too, according to a tradition that was observed by many other Michigan farmers. "Sow your buckwheat on the Fourth of July, wet or dry."

The Sunday School picnic came next, usually somewhere between haying and harvesting. Why, in a locality where one could hardly travel three miles in any direction without coming upon a lake, the Sunday School picnic was always held in an upland grove seemed to me, for some time, a mystery; upon more serious reflection in later years, however, I supposed it was because the lake, in those days, was a useful part of the topography for fishing purposes, but beyond this it had no social interests. The boys swam in it sometimes on hot nights after work, but no one had considered developing it for recreational purposes. The shores were muddy, weedy, and infested with snakes and mosquitoes. The grove, therefore, a cluster of oaks usually, with a few maples and an occasional hickory, was the chosen site for the picnic.

Previous to the given day, the big boys would go and clean out the underbrush, put up swings, build a crude platform from which "pieces" would be spoken, with maybe a dialogue given or a tableau shown, and from which the minister would address the flock.

A long table of planks was laid on "horses," and seats erected at the sides for the dinner. And despite the "programme" or any other attractions that may have been offered by teachers or pastor, it was around this long table that the chief interest centred and it was upon this that all eyes were focused as the vehicles bearing whole families, or parts of families, drew up and disgorged both the human element and that which would provide means for its animation.

Better parents than mine or better citizens would, I believe, have been hard to find, but they were not numbered amongst the zealous in the outward semblance of religion. My mother was much more socially-minded than my father and would, I think, have been glad to lend her support to such community interests as the Ladies' Aid and the Sunday

School, and did, so far as she could by contributing to any special cause. Occasionally the Ladies' Aid met with her, but my father drew the line at prayer meetings. "Lot of carpin' ol' hens," he snorted, "settin' round and rippin' someone up the back and then gettin' down on their knees and talkin' t' the Lord as if He's their brother-'n-law and tellin' Him what to do."

It was therefore not until I was about eight years old that I ever attended a Sunday School picnic, and I was actually feverish with excitement for days beforehand. From the young Covells, who invariably attended this or any other function where food was plenteous, and free; from the hired man, who seemed to have pleasing recollections of similar occasions; and from what I could extract from my mother's more conservative store of knowledge, I had managed to build up an illusion of what heaven would be like, reduced to terms of a hickory grove, and a table as long as from here to town, laden with such stores as nothing short of a feast of Heliogabalus could equal.

There would be lemonade by the gallon, so quoth the Covells, "made in the shade, by the old maid" (the humor of which doggerel I failed to see then, nor have I since), and brought by the donors in stone churns or crocks with whole thick slices of lemon floating free for him to grab who could.

There would also be *ice cream!* This I could hardly believe, for ice cream, *real* ice cream frozen with ice, was a rarity such as no child born of these days and fairly cradled in a cone could understand. With a lake or pond on every third farm, more or less, and ice to be had for the cutting, only one farmer in a hundred, or less, had an ice house. He who did, and could have ice cream *every Sunday*, was a Crœsus amongst us.

Sometimes in winter my mother would bring in some freshly fallen snow and mix it with whipped cream or the beaten white of an egg, sweeten and flavor it. That was a toothsome sweet not to be despised, but to have genuine ice cream right in the midst of summer was too imposing a possibility to be easily adjusted to the childish mind.

The vision invoked by the tales of the hundred-and-one different kinds of cakes that would be found on that long table—even *frosted* cakes—was beyond belief, and waiting for the day became an agony and a dread. *If anything should happen!*

But nothing happened except that my father refused flatly to go.

"I *told* you I wouldn't go," he said hotly as we sat at breakfast on the fateful morning, "and I won't! You can take the mare and go if you're set on it," he said, "but you'll get bit with mosquitoes, and prob'ly sit down in poison ivy, and Stib Obart says Collins' Grove is alive with moccasins."

"Anything more?" inquired my mother, mildly derisive. "You don't suppose the mare'll run away with us, do you, and spill the dinner?"

"Huh!" my father snorted as he shoved back the chair, took his hat, and started impatiently for the door.

"I'll leave your dinner," said my mother, "under a pan in the cellarway. Fried chicken and a basin of beans—but I wisht you'd go along and have some ice cream and cake—"

The door of mosquito netting slammed, after which came the sound of sturdy boots stomping their way off the stoop onto the gravel path beyond.

"He wants to go worse 'n a dog," my mother said as she cleared the table, "but he won't give in. There never was such a stubborn man!"

Certainly he hung upon our going. Twenty times he came steaming in at the door to inquire:—

"What time you goin' to get off?"

"Ain't you most ready yet?"

"You got any bakin' sody in, case you get stung?"

Once my mother ventured to urge him. "You better come along, 'Liger," she said. "You got no hay down—nothin' to hender."

"Nothin' to hender!" shouted my father, flinging out his hands, and wheeling upon her as if she had accused him of some heinous offense. "*Why* ain't there nothin' to hender? I suppose I ain't got to—to cut around the wheat field ready for the reaper—"

"You ain't got a thing to do to-day that you couldn't do tomorrow," my mother interrupted spiritedly, "but if you don't want to go you needn't. Here, take these two baskets and put 'em in the back of the buggy."

Silently my father picked up the two baskets, seemed to study them for a moment, then went out the door. One he set down on a bench outside, the other he kept in his hand.

"Don't forget this one," my mother called after him. "It's got the victuals in it. That one's only got the tablecloth and dishes."

"I'll get it," he called back, "when I bring up the mare."

He harnessed the mare to the top buggy and brought her to the horse block. He hitched her to the post and went back to the barn after the linen duster for our laps. My mother and I went out and climbed into the buggy.

"Did you get both baskets in?" my mother asked, taking the reins in her hands and peering out the side.

"I put in what you handed me," he replied shortly, and stood there looking after us as we drove away.

"He'd give his neck to be goin' along," said my mother impatiently, "but he just won't—stubborn ole coot!"

I looked back as we drove out of the yard, feeling sorry for my father, in whom I saw only the little-boy-left-behind, for that is exactly how he seemed. He could never bear to have my mother go anywhere without him, or to go himself and leave her behind. If it was only to town or to the mill, he wanted her along. When he came in even from the field his first word was a call for " 'Miry," and if she was not in sight or in hearing of his voice, "Where's your mother?" he would demand, and set off, without waiting for reply, to find her. And now there he stood, forlorn and lonely, watching her depart for festivities in which he had neither share nor desire to share.

Sympathy for his unhappy state was clouding the brightness of my own joy in anticipation and, seeing this, my mother said:—

"Now don't you worry about him. He would have come if he'd wanted to. It's just his own cussedness, so let him alone." Her impatience was obviously tempered with tenderness for a willful spouse, and so my heart was soothed.

Realization brought no disappointment in the eagerly looked for fête. There was the platform with a background of branches and leaves of green. A bowery, they called it. On its floor was a piece of carpet, and there stood two chairs and a small table, "property," for the dialogue. There were the little girls who were going to "speak pieces," fluttering about in white dresses. (I had a new one myself, of dimity, smocked and ruffled, for I, too, was going to speak a piece!)

There were the swings already occupied by older girls, while some of the big boys "ran under." And there—there was the long table, and on it were baskets, boxes, things done up in white tablecloths, surety for that feast of delicacies so beguilingly foretold.

Women greeted my mother as we drove up.

"Don't unload your things till after the programme, Miz' Thompson," one said; "they're all ready to begin."

One of the boys came and drove our horse off to unhitch and unbridle her in the shade, and give her the measure of oats my father had provided.

"You fetch our things, Johnnie, when they're ready, will you?" my mother said, and, taking me by the hand, led me over to the position of honor occupied by the performers—a bench at the foot of the platform. Others sat on stumps, blankets, or the ground.

First, the minister had to offer a prayer, and then the programme began. A quartette by the choir, a declamation by this same Johnnie Brent who had taken charge of our horse,—"Darius Green and His Flying Machine,"—given with appropriate, if awkward, gestures and pantomime. Then my own name was called, and, pushed by my mother and pulled by a Sunday School teacher whom I had never seen before, I was hauled, shaking and pallid, to the platform, where I was transfixed with fright and could not, with any amount of prompting, utter one word.

Panicky and sobbing, I was allowed to stumble back to my mother's arms, where she doubtless longed to flay instead of to comfort me, as she did.

In time, however, the programme was finished. Women, whose minds had been on melting butter and drying cakes, rose hastily and proceeded to the unwrapping of their stores. Johnnie was sent for our baskets—and returned with one.

"Where's the other?" demanded my mother. "The one with the *dinner*. This is just dishes and things."

Johnnie protested that this was the only basket in the buggy.

"But I put *two* in! That is—are you *sure?* I'll go and see, myself." She went, and returned twisting her fingers together and all but weeping.

"He never put it in," she cried, distracted. "He just set it down somewheres and forgot it. *All our dinner!*"

Friends consoled, assured her there was enough and plenty to spare. She must not worry.

"I'd go back and get it," she exclaimed, "if there was time." But there was not time. The ice was melting in the lemonade, the ice cream must be eaten soon. Butter was softening.

"You just take hold and help set the tables, Miz' Thompson, and don't give it another thought."

But that she was giving it all her thought, that she was chagrined, sick with disappointment, and not a little angry, was evidenced by her nervous jerky movements, the thin line of her lips and the smouldering fire in her eye. "I don't see," she kept saying, "how he *could* have been so careless. I wish I'd put them in myself." Doing a thing yourself, my mother averred, was the only way of being sure it was done at all.

Overcoming, finally, the natural shyness of the lone child, I was led off to the swings to play with other children. But not, wholly, to lose sight of the fascinating performance going on at and around the table.

Cloths of varied assortment were spread over the planks. Plates, cups, knives, forks, and spoons were laid out according to families. Then began the ceremony of placing the food. Unable longer to withstand the enchantment of the scene, I, with other children, deserted the more extraneous entertainment, and hovered about, goggle-eyed and open-mouthed, as one goody after another came to rest upon the cloth.

A whole ham, boiled, as its producer pridefully announced, in cider which was just at the sparkling point—together with a handful of raisins, —until almost tender, and then skinned and baked long enough to set and brown the crust of brown sugar, mustard, and spices. The knife, cutting through the crunching crust, slipped into the rosy meat like the blade of a scythe before ripened grain, while one thin pink slice after another rolled down upon the cutting board.

Pans of beans with generous slabs of salt pork, cross-ribbed in strips of bronze, islanded in the middle.

Platters of cold chicken. "I had two chickens," mourned my mother, "fried in fresh butter, and a pan of raised biscuits and—butter! I put in two pounds to have enough! It'll melt and run all over Kingdom Come."

Mounds of hard-boiled eggs, bottles of homemade chili sauce, pickled beets in quart jars, sweet pickles, sour pickles, loaves of sweet, fine, moist bread with crust buttered and browned.

"I'll be ashamed to eat a thing," murmured my mother, vexed and sore, "but my tongue just *drips*."

"Don't think of it," they told her. "You always bring more'n your share. It won't hurt, once, to eat off'n others."

When, finally, the cakes were unmasked from their covering of milk pans, white paper, or napkins, and set decoratively down the centre of the table, the suspense grew unbearable. Loaves of frosted cake; layer cakes oozing lemon cream; whipped cream cakes; rich brown chocolate which also inundated top and sides; and raisin cake.

"And I had a panful of sour-cream cookies," wailed my mother, "fit to melt in your mouth if I do say it."

"I guess we all know about your sour-cream cookies, Miz' Thompson. I wisht you'd give me the rule for 'em," said Miz' Bouldry as they worked together setting the table. . . . "What's that, Miz' Taylor?" to an approaching matron.

"I said ain't you 'bout ready?" It was the generalissimo, marshaling forces. "If you be, I'll send the boys after the lemonade."

Miz' Bouldry and my mother were ready.

"Here, boys! Boys—*uz!*" The *charge d'affaires* lifted her voice. "You go fetch the lemonade now, and set it here in the shade. And some of you men bring the ice-cream freezer and keep it covered with blankets. Now, *come on, folks!*" raising her voice and brandishing a long-handled spoon which she struck on a milk pan for attention, "let's get set down and begin. These youngsters are starvin' to death."

The lemonade was brought and served by the dipperful to a miscellaneous assortment of handleless cups, mugs, and glasses. Shouts of amusement greeted Johnnie Brent, aged seventeen, as he held up a huge moustache cup for his portion.

The minister rose and made a prayer, mercifully brief. Just before he had reached the final blessing of the food to His cause, and as the last tattered remnant of patience was wrung from hankering tongues, a mighty rumbling of hoofs, and a clack as of loose boards were heard on the rough woods road leading into the grove.

The minister hastily ended his prayer and all eyes were turned toward the sound. Over a little rise of ground appeared the heads of a span of horses—one with a star in her forehead, the other with a piebald face. There was no mistaking them. They were our horses, Star and Baldy.

My mother gasped and rose, dropping her fork while her napkin floated to the ground.

The horses approached and proved to be hitched to an empty hayrick, the timbers of which beat a tattoo upon each other like running a stick along a picket fence. In what you might call the prow of this vehicle, like some old weather-beaten figurehead braving a battling sea, sturdy legs well apart, hands gripping the reins as of fiery steeds and he guiding a chariot of war, his old straw hat pushed back on his head, his short white beard trembling a little from the unsteady action of his foothold, stood my father.

Some of the men shouted a welcome, some rose. The generalissimo crawled out from the bench where she sat and started toward him, incoherently exclaiming.

My mother remained immobile, watching him. He drew his horses to a flourishing stop and sprang out. He took the missing basket from the bed of the wagon and walked around to where she sat.

"Here," he said shortly, "you went off and left this. I thought I better bring it even if I did have to mess up a day's work."

My mother rose without a word, took the basket, and began to distribute its contents. My father was urged to sit.

"Might 's well stay now 't you're here," they said. And, "Come on, 'Lije—Mert Owen and I can lick the hide off'n you pitchin' horseshoes."

He stood uncertainly, glancing a bit wistfully at my mother. Still she said no word.

"You set right down there in 'Miry's place," one of the women told him genially, "and we'll fix a place for her down here."

"Well," said my father, becomingly hesitant, but finally convinced that he would get no encouragement from my mother, "I s'pose I might 's well now 't I've had to spoil the day anyhow."

The only remark my mother vouchsafed was after we had arrived home, she and I having followed dutifully in the wagon's dust.

My father was standing on the stoop watching the clouds, mumbling pessimistic prognostications of rain.

"Ought never to have lost this day," he growled, "and wouldn't if you hadn't gone off half-cocked—"

My mother narrowed her eyes, thinned her lips, and, looking him unflinchingly in the face, said slowly, *"I noticed you took time to shave and put on a clean shirt."*

Caught squarely in a trap of his own setting, my father grinned like the willful old boy he was at heart, took the milk pail, and went to the barn.

Who-ee, Pig-ee!

By Homer Croy

Hog-calling used to be a matter of necessity. Later the craft became an art that combined lung power and imaginative vocalizing. At county and state fairs, the hog-calling contest is a door to fame and fortune if a man can convince the judges—he need not convince the pigs.

When the settlers first came, hog-calling was tremendously important. The land wasn't fenced, the hogs wandered off. When a farmer came out to feed his hogs, he had to call them; if he didn't have a good pair of lungs, his hogs wouldn't get their feed. The hogs that happened to be "up" would get it; the others would suffer.

But after a time the land was fenced; powerful lungs weren't so completely necessary, but still the hogs had to be called. Fence-building continued; hog pastures grew smaller. It even got so women could call. This was considered pretty low.

It became so bad that a farmer didn't even "call" his hogs; he merely pounded on the gate. Those were dark days for hog-calling.

There had always been an element of humor in hog-calling; sometimes two farmers could call their hogs at the same time and, being human, would try to outdo each other. It was nice to be considered the best hog-caller in the neighborhood.

Hog-callers had their "styles" and tricks; in fact, no two hog-callers went about it exactly the same way. It was soon seen that there was more to hog-calling than giving a few lusty whoops. Strangely enough, each man believed in his own "style"; he didn't think the other fellow had anything. He perfected his own method and developed it and put in fancy touches. . . .

As soon as hog-calling got into the contest class, new tricks and appeals were developed—things the poor, early-day farmers had never dreamed of. In fact, he would have been amazed if he had heard a champion turn loose. . . .

You can't tell a champion by his looks; in other words, the little fellow who doesn't seem to have "projection" has more of it than the strapping big man who would, at first glance, seem to have everything. It's not that simple, as you will see as we go along. . . .

The old-fashioned caller, who has not kept abreast of the times, has little chance today. Hog-calling does not stand still.

A trap that many fell into was the belief that volume was the sole requisite. It was, but briefly. Astute judges soon saw there were other qualities. One was "hog appeal." Some callers had it and some didn't. Those who didn't have it soon lost out.

At last rules and regulations were drawn up for contest calling and were officially adopted at Des Moines, Iowa, in July, 1926, by the Swine Growers of America. There have been a few changes in the rules, but the bedrock was laid down then and, for the most part, kept. Callers were to judge contests on the following scores:

1. *Carrying quality.* This has always had the highest score-rating and few have ever questioned its place.

2. *Hog appeal.* The judges decide how the different calls affect the hogs.

3. *Musical appeal.* The judges must decide on the musical appeal that most stirs hogs. Sometimes the judges can no more get together than the Supreme Court.

4. *Distinctness.* This is so hogs will not become confused.

These are the four basic appeals of hog-calling. A caller who departs very far from them will find himself in the loser class. . . .

Boys who have lived on farms appear to have an interest in hog-calling even after they have grown up and moved to other fields. An example is of Alexander W. Graham, the dignified and human postmaster of Kansas City, Missouri. He is a large, slightly stooped, long-faced man with hair going gray, and with a twinkle in his eyes. It developed that he had been born on a farm near Mineola, Montgomery County, Missouri.

"My grandfather raised hogs and I used to practice calling them. Sometimes I would go away quite a distance just to see how quickly I could get their attention. I had a voice which I could project; this, of course, was a tremendous help. Always, since I was a kid, I have kept my hand in just for the fun of it. When I saw in the papers any news about contests, I was always interested and read every line."

There had been a state contest at Unity Farms, near Kansas City. People had come from all over the state. On the fun program was a hog-calling contest, as in most rural events today.

"I decided to enter," continued Postmaster Graham, "so I put my name down. But when I saw how many had entered I was a bit taken 'back. I decided, however, to go through with it.

"Judges were chosen and placed at the required distance. Then we were lined up; I don't mind telling you I was on the nervous side. We looked each other over; there was a good deal of laughing and persiflage, but we were in earnest about winning.

"I asked the judges if I could cup. There was a hurried consultation and they decided I could. The first contestant stepped forward and turned loose. He was not good; I felt pretty confident of myself, at least so far as this man was concerned. Some had fancy calls, with twists and variations, but on the whole these don't pay off. I use only the one word, *Who-ee*. The *Who-* is drawn out twice as long as the *ee*. I never use the word *Pig-ee*, or anything like that. I once heard a man call *Piggie-Wiggie*. I lost respect for him. That is a child showing off. You can project one word better than two or three. The simpler the better. That is the theory I work on. An' I never breathe but once. The two-breathe and three-breathe man is lost. At least, that's the way I see it. A hog either hears instantly, or not at all.

"My name was called an' I stepped forward. I paused a moment to get over my nervousness, breathed deep, and then cupped. That is, I put my hands to my mouth so as to make a sort of megaphone. I gave it all I had. I could tell by the expression on the crowd that I had done fairly well, but, after all, winning is a matter of opinion and anything can happen. Two of us were called back. I opened up again. The judges conferred and I was declared winner. It was all in fun, but I don't mind telling you I was pleased! The thing no one knew was why I cupped. It was not for volume, as I had plenty of that. It was to keep my false teeth in!" . . .

Yes, it's fun. More than that, it is characteristic of the section. It is indigenous, it springs from the soil. The people enjoy it immensely and so do the contestants. No word from the hogs.

Husking and Other Bees

By Thomas Low Nichols

Sometimes there is too much work on a farm for even a big family to handle alone. Then the neighbors come in, and raising a barn or making a quilt or husking the corn becomes a social event, complete with games. Out of this frontier expediency has come one of America's best traditions—the Bee.

When the crops are gathered there is another job to do, best done in company. At least, it is an excuse for an evening gathering, and the settler is able by this time to give a little treat to those who help him. So all the neighbours, and especially the young men and girls, are invited to a "husking." The Indian corn has been gathered into one end of the house, if there is no barn. It is still upon the stalk, and the long yellow ears, or white they may be, with sometimes a red one, are still enclosed in their tough, fibrous husks.

The husking takes place in the evening, by the light of a good fire of pine-knots, or candles, where civilisation has advanced so far. Both sexes join in the pleasant labour, with songs, stories, chaffing, and the pleasant excitement arising from the rule that the fellow who husks a red ear of maize has the privilege of kissing the girl next him. The baskets are filled, the pile diminishes, the stalks and husks are cleared away. Then comes a supper of pork and beans, pumpkin-pie, dough-nuts, apples and cider, if the orchards have grown, or other and perhaps stronger beverages. Then, if the Puritanism is not too strong, a fiddle and a dance; if it is, games of romps and forfeits, supposed to be less objectionable, and a walk home of happy couples in the moonlight. . . .

"*. . . For now, the corn-house fill'd, the harvest home,*
The invited neighbors to the husking *come;*
A frolic scene, where work, and mirth, and play
Unite their charms to chase the hours away.

Where the huge heap lies centered in the hall,
The lamp suspended from the cheerful wall,
Brown corn-fed nymphs, and strong hard-handed beaux,
Alternate ranged, extend in circling rows,
Assume their seats, the solid mass attack;
The dry husks rustle, and the corn-cobs crack;
The song, the laugh, alternate notes resound,
And the sweet cider trips in silence round.
The laws of husking every wight can tell—
And sure no laws he ever keeps so well:
For each red ear a general kiss he gains,
With each smut ear she smuts the luckless swains;
But when to some sweet maid a prize is cast,
Red as her lips and taper as her waist,
She walks the round, and culls one favored beau,
Who leaps, the luscious tribute to bestow.
Various the sport, as are the wits and brains
Of well-pleased lasses and contending swains;
Till the vast mound of corn is swept away,
And he that gets the last ear wins the day . . ."

(*Joel Barlowe*—Hasty Pudding)

When the orchards have grown, then come the "apple-paring bees." They did come, at least, before ingenious Yankees invented paring machines. The apples were pared with sharp knives and rapid hands, quartered, cored, strung on twine, and hung up to dry in festoons over the kitchen ceiling. The paring bee was a milder kind of evening party than the husking, and ended with the same festivities.

The quilting is mostly a feminine arrangement. Its ostensible object is the manufacture of a bed-quilt. This involves a social gathering—talk, tea, probably a little gossip and scandal, and in the evening the accession of masculinity, with more or less of fun and frolic. The upper surface of the quilt is that marvellous result of feminine industry—patchwork; the lower stratum is more modest calico; the interior cotton or wool; and the whole is united by quiltings in elaborate figures, composed of a vast number of stitches, made by as many old and young ladies as can sit around the frame, beginning on the borders, and, as the frame is rolled up, gradually working towards the centre. The reasons for making this a social undertaking are obvious. When the quilt is in the frame it occupies a large space. It would take a long time for one or two persons to do it, and would be a long time in the way. Finally, it is an excuse for a social gathering.

The men have shooting-matches all to themselves. These come off in the autumn, when turkeys are fat and thanksgiving is coming. Turkeys are put up to be shot at so many rods' distance, at so much a shot, and the poor shots pay for the turkeys which the good ones carry home. In my memory good shots were very common. Every man and every boy could shoot. Guns and rifles were in every house; and when I was eight or nine years old, a light fowling-piece, with which I shot at birds or squirrels, or at a mark, was my favourite plaything. I shot with a rifle resting over a rail in the fence, or across the stump of a tree, long before I could hold one out at arm's length. Crack shots did what were considered very handsome feats in those days, before arms of precision and long ranges were invented. These riflemen, who killed their game without injuring their skins, barked squirrels off the trees, and shot wild turkeys in the head, would hold candles in the night for each other to snuff with a bullet without extinguishing the light, drive a nail into a tree without bending it, or split a bullet into equal halves on a knifeblade.

The Nation's Wishbook

By David L. Cohn

The most carefully thumbed book in the farm household next to the Bible is the Sears, Roebuck catalog. The mail-order book of treasures, over which the farm family dreamed on long winter nights, is a wishbook as well as an invaluable record of American customs.

Some years ago, when I was employed by Sears, Roebuck & Company, I used to pass a few minutes occasionally by running aimlessly and dreamily through the collection of catalogs that record the Company's mail-order business from its beginning in 1886 to date. At first, I was merely amused as the buggies, stoves, organs, revolvers, clothes, patent medicines, and cosmetics of another time poured through my fingers in a dun stream already antique. And my amusement was composed largely of that complacency and condescension which a member of one generation feels as he looks back upon the manners, wearables, follies, and foibles of recent generations. Complacency and condescension fell away from me, however, when I suddenly realized that this was not some faraway and long-ago period that the catalog's pages were illuminating, but *my* time—the only time in which I shall ever walk the earth, savor salt, and talk with my fellows; a time, therefore, infinitely more precious to me than all the centuries that have gone before, however broidered with gold they were or immanent with light.

Here, for example, were the buggies of a day already mistily remote, but a day in which I had lived. As a student at the University of Virginia in 1915, I had driven in just such a buggy as this, a young lady at my side, up the mountain to Mr. Thomas Jefferson's home. This is the shotgun with which I killed my first rabbit when I was a boy; these are the shoes I wore to Court School; that is the middy blouse worn by the golden girl who sat across the aisle. (Where is she now?) Here is a graphophone like the one we had in our home, with the blue horn flowering over the parlor and casting a sickly light upon a white, stuffed baby seal (the gift of a Newfoundland relative) that lay upon the floor. I put an Edison record on the talking machine, the cylinder turns, and the strains of "Everybody Works But Father" bring Lucy from the kitchen. There she stands, black and smiling, until the song is ended.

A horseless buggy of 1909, "guaranteed to go 100 miles in 24 hours if good care is taken of it," brightens a catalog page with the red of its body's paint. Seeing it, I become a child again. On a hot summer's day, I am watering with a garden hose the dusty street that runs along our home in Greenville, Mississippi. My bare feet are cooled by the mud of my own making; I turn the nozzle of the hose until it emits a fine spray, point it at the eye of the sun, and hold a trembling rainbow at arm's length. Then suddenly Leroy Wall, a pioneer automobilist of our town, comes thundering across my horizon at twelve miles an hour. Will Butler, the Negro blacksmith in the shop across the way, drops the hoof of the mule he is shoeing and runs to the door to see this latest and most terrifying example of white folks' madness. (He does not dream that it will ever transform him, a skilled craftsman, into a common laborer.) A flock of chickens, dust-bathing in the road, flies squawking in panic; a two-mule team, bringing a load of firewood to town, skitters into a ditch; while I retreat for safety behind the big cottonwoods that line the sidewalk and, with thumping heart, watch Leroy Wall disappear in a cloud of dust and glory.

"This pretty shirtwaist suit," and this "Very nobby suit, nicely tailored" —these are like the clothes worn by my mother and the mothers of my playmates. I see again long-familiar faces down the corridors of time, calm and framed in the windows of Coovert's Photograph Studio, as I loiter lazily before them homeward bound from school.

Here is the mail-order wig (toupee it was called by the elegant) of old man Huntly—a patch of hair more famous in our town than the tresses of Lilith or Lorelei. For once, long ago, in the heat and passion of the ninth inning of the second game of a double-header between Greenville and Pine Bluff, our star catcher, Reisinger, dropped the ball, and old man Huntly lost his wig as Pine Bluff scored the winning run. Despite the laughter of the fans, he did not discover his loss until he had gone home for supper. Then his wife, Miss Alice, accused him of drunkenness, and made him go back to the ball park and rescue his wig. Years later I learn from the catalog how he had got it, by sending a lock of his hair to Sears, along with the ingenious measurements required by the mail-order wigmaker, and a money order for $10 plus 42 cents for a tube of Toupee Paste.

In the catalog's pages, one finds how men lived, and what they lived by, for nearly fifty years. Here are the clothes they wore; the books they read; the medicines they used; the organs they played; the songs they sang; the plows they followed. Here also are the games that amused them; the furniture that stood in their homes; the diapers that initiate civilized man into his lifelong bondage to clothing; the clocks that tick men's lives away, and the tombstones that mark the end. These are the kettles that sang upon the stove; the rods that took the trout; the traps that snared the mink; the seeds that blew as flowers in rural gardens; the Bibles in which the sorrowful took refuge; the veils worn by brides; the iron heaters that glowed red in the parlor. Here, even, are the pistols that American men not so long ago wore as casually as their handle-bar mustaches.

As my now-fascinated eyes stared longer and longer at the catalog pages, and as I delved deeper and deeper into them, it seemed to me that they constituted an invaluable record of American life; that they were a diary of the times created by the people; a measure of the desires and ambitions of millions. I thought, moreover, that if all the records of the catalog's years should be lost, and only the catalog preserved, a scholar stumbling upon it in the remote future could recreate from its pages the way in which men had lived in America for fifty years. It was, therefore, with a shock of pleased surprise that I found my point of view had been anticipated by an English visitor to America more than a quarter century ago.

In 1911, Arnold Bennett visited Chicago and made this entry in his *Journal:*

Friday, November 17th

Went to Sears Roebuck & Co., in their auto. Got on very well with Murkland, head of book and china dept.

8 million dollars business last month.

Over 7,000 employees. Over 4,000 women. 5½ millions of large catalogs sold. Big bill-typing room. 600 clickers.

Gradually on to car-yard, where cars being filled up. This yard of cars sent out every day.

But most interesting thing was glimpses of real life of these outlying communities everywhere, as seen in ugly common simple stuff they ordered.

Thousands of cheap violins. In one basket, ready for packing, all sorts of little cooking utensils and two mugs (fearfully ugly) labelled 'father' and 'mother.' 4 cents curling iron. Most startlingly realistic glimpse of home life. *All the life (cheap music, chairs etc.) of these communities could be deduced from this establishment.* [My italics.]

The catalogs, however, afford even more than "startlingly realistic glimpses of home life." Just as the concentric rings of California's giant redwood trees reveal years of drought and rainfall through the centuries, the pages of the catalog mark the economic booms and depressions of our times. The catalog for fall, 1915, swells to 1,600 pages from the 1,100 pages of the preceding season. Why? The World War is in its second year; Europe clamors for the produce of American farms and factories; farmers prosper almost overnight; their desires increase, and the catalog dealing with millions of families becomes a heavy, chunky book.

The same process operates also in reverse. As depressions descend on the land, as commodities drop to bankrupt prices and farmers patch their last year's overalls, the catalog suddenly omits several hundred pages, reduces its prices, and begins to adjust itself to hard times.

Year after year, it records the progress of invention and technological change in the United States. Thus, shortly after the turn of the century the great mechanic-revolutionists, White, Duryea, Ford, Olds, and others were beginning to change American manners, morals, ways of living, and business almost beyond comparison with earlier periods. Just as the horses of Cortez burst with terrifying impact upon the Indians of Mexico and cleared the path for the Conquest, while uprooting an ancient culture and diverting the people from their centuries' old course, so did the automobile burst upon the American people, to effect a bloodless conquest in some ways not less profound than that wrought by the conquistadors upon Mexico. Even the allegedly astute gentlemen of finance failed at first to understand the significance of the new vehicle. At the moment when the catalog, expressing not the hopes but the wants of the people, was picturing an automobile, that once famous cosmopolitan financier, Chauncey M. Depew, told his nephew that the horseless carriage would never supplant the horse, and kept the young man from investing $5,000 in the business of a visionary mechanic named Henry Ford. A little later, page after page of tires, oil, and automobile accessories come into the catalog. Simultaneously the buggy begins to disappear, and finally vanishes altogether from the catalog, to survive only in a few rural sections, in the collections of museums, and in the property warehouses of Hollywood.

Buggy whips, too, slowly go out of the catalog. On the day when the last buggy-whip manufacturer closed his factory doors and walked out into the blinding light of a new world where he was lost, no bells were tolled and no dirges sung.

What social historian has marked his passing in a learned study, or assessed the importance of his disappearance? Yet who shall deny that he closed his doors not only upon an empty factory but also upon a long era of American history; that the day when he walked into the street was a day fraught with greater significance for the country than the whole administration, say, of President Van Buren, which is noted in all the histories of America?

The life span of the catalog itself is contemporaneous with perhaps the most dynamic fifty years in American life. It begins in 1886 when the United States was just emerging from the Civil War and Reconstruction into a period of agricultural and industrial expansion unparalleled in the world for breadth and vigor. It continues through the years of the centralization of business into giant combines, trusts, and monopolies; embraces the feverish dream era of "manifest destiny" before and after the Spanish-American War; goes on to the time when Kansas boys died in Flanders fields; stumbles into the darkness of the economic depression of the 1930's from which we have not yet emerged, and the fall catalog of 1939–40 appeared precisely at the moment when German troops were marching into Poland.

Two pages in the 1905 edition might almost be taken as a short socio-economic history of the United States, because they embody much of the essence of that history and vividly contrast the old America that was passing with the new America that was emerging. Page 338 contains a sketch of a covered wagon and a description of "White Duck Emigrant Wagon Covers" tailored to fit many sizes of wagons. Page 339 is devoted to a lusty, bitter denunciation of alleged monopoly practices on the part of a giant camera-manufacturing corporation. On the one page the symbol of *laissez faire* and individualism in their most extreme forms; on the other page one of the instruments of the death of *laissez faire* and individualism.

It is an astonishing mark, too, of the newness of America that emigrant wagon covers did not disappear from the catalog until 1924. Throughout the pages of the catalog, as in the pages of American history generally, one is awestruck by the swiftness of change, by the youth of the country, and by the spectacle of men, who were boys in a pioneer society, contributing in their maturity to urbanized, industrialized America. A startling example of this is the life of Paul J. Starrett who built many of the great skyscrapers and some of the subways of New York.

"My brothers and sisters and I," he writes, "were all born in Lawrence [Kansas]. Our early life was lived in an America now completely gone. Through the vista of the years I look back to the prairies which the Indians, with their squaws and papooses, were still crossing on their single-file trails. I remember standing one morning with a group of scared children in the city jail yard, where the six Sioux chiefs captured after the Custer massacre were incarcerated. As clearly as I can see the aeroplane overhead today, I can see the long trains loaded with buffalo hides going through to the East."

The boy Starrett watching Indians crossing the Kansas prairies; the man Starrett erecting the world's tallest building—the Empire State Building in New York. That is America and it is the America whose life span is the catalog's.

The catalog reveals American life changing as we turn its pages. Technology walks into the home to transform it and to transfigure the housewife. In edition after edition, we note the liberation of the housewife through the coming of labor-saving devices; we observe the drudgery once done by her hands transferred to machines; we see the means by which even the servantless woman in the United States has come to have a higher degree of leisure than any other woman of her kind in the world. At the same time, the catalog records the progress of technology on the farm. Wood is sawed by hand, and then by power saws; water is hand-pumped or carried to the hogs, and then it is driven by electric pumps; men follow horses down turnrows for centuries, and suddenly they are riding the steel saddles of gasoline-powered tractors.

If the catalog is rich in revelations of economic life and struggle in the United States, if it is a series of endlessly changing pictures of changing America, it is also a social barometer. Here we find the development of countless new attitudes—toward reading, the use of cosmetics, the virtues of fresh air and of bathing, and the pleasures of sports. We note how the luxuries of one generation become the necessaries of the next generation, and how the clothing of the middle class tends to approximate that of the rich in fashion and materials, even if inferior in design and workmanship.

The catalog as a chronicle of change and a panorama of American life through fifty dynamic years reveals directly, and by implication, countless forces of many kinds that are constantly at work in a virile, restless civilization such as ours. We glimpse something of the age-long struggle against monopoly and price-fixing; the rise of new attitudes toward private debt; changing parent-child relationships, and a radically different conception of sex. The catalog's pages are starred with changes, but among them I can find none more startling than this: in the past few years they list and describe a great number of contraceptives. On the face of it this fact is not at all startling because contraception is nothing new in America. But let us look below the surface. The catalog, it must be remembered, goes to farmers, rural dwellers, and the economic middle classes and lower middle classes of the towns. These folk are the remnant, yet large, of the godly left in America. Evangelism still surges in their souls; their lips are fluent to hymn-singing; their allegiance is to fundamentalism. Here, if anywhere, we should expect the catalog, in the role of Eros bringing gifts of concupiscence, to be ejected from the rural threshold. But, on the contrary, it is welcomed. What strange ferment must then be at work in the souls of the American people if this large group, who are the defenders of the faith and of the old-time religion, now emulates its city brothers and sisters in the use of contraceptives?

The catalog, however, is revelatory of more than social and economic change in this country. It reveals also esthetic change. No one turning its pages can fail to be struck by the tremendous improvement they show in the design of category after category of goods for the person and for the home. And this improvement is highly significant because it reveals the tastes, wants, and desires not of a few wealthy women in the cities, but of millions of simple women living in the small towns and on the farms of America. For—it must be borne in mind—things in the catalog are things people want. They are not things that Sears thinks they ought to have or hopes to sell them.

Flowing out of this is the one fact indispensable to an understanding of this book: the catalog is based not upon hope but upon experience. There is no room in it for guessing, wishing, or, save occasionally and conservatively, experimenting. It does not attempt to cram down the throats of the public its own ideas of taste or merchandise. The catalog never leads; never crusades. It is based purely upon public acceptance of the goods it offers, and not until the public has clearly signified that it wants a thing does that thing appear in its pages. We know, therefore, beyond all doubt, that the catalog's pictures of American life are drawn not from the imagination but from the living model.

The catalog occupies a unique place in American life. It is more than an instrument of business, although it was designed and is maintained solely as an instrument of business. It has become the best-known book in the United States, a part of American folklore, and, passing strange for a tool of business, it has also become the object of widespread affection.

Wherever the traveler goes in the United States, he will find the catalog. It lies dog-eared and finger-smudged on the log-hewn tables of cabins high in the Great Smokies; it is found in the ranch houses of Montana, the cabins of cotton growers in Alabama, the homes of fruit farmers in California, and even in the mansions of the rich. But wherever it is found, a curious affection surrounds it, an expression that arises perhaps out of a subconscious longing for an America which is vanishing but which still continues to be exemplified by the catalog. America is a once pioneer country now approaching maturity, and it is characteristic of such a country, at this stage of its progress, that it looks back to its past. And the past—in a dynamic, fast-moving land such as this—may be no more than twenty-five or fifty years removed from the present. The United States, moreover, has been in breathless transition ever since 1914; it has been lifted up and thrown down; it is staggered by change; worried and harassed. It is certain that it is going somewhere, but no man can say with the slightest pretense to accuracy where it is going. Under these circumstances, it is natural that the people of a hurrying, scurrying, industrialized, worried country should look back wistfully to a more leisurely and serene day when—such is the power of the retrospective imagination—every man in America sat content beneath his vine. The catalog is the symbol of that day, and, as such, it has come to be surrounded with the affection that men lavish on the symbols of happier days.

It must be remembered, too, that millions of city dwellers were born in the country where, as likely as not, the catalog was part of their childhood. It has been the half dreamworld of millions of children as they looked with wonder through its enchanting, picture-starred pages. The following scene described by Marietta Minnigerode Andrews, in her *Memoirs of a Poor Relation* (page 169), is one that must have been repeated with endless variations everywhere in the country for nearly fifty years. It is, in reality, a vignette of American life; the stuff of which a painter might have made a typical *Portrait of An American Mother with*

Her Children. Here Mrs. Andrews is speaking of herself and her children:

Mary Lord Andrews the third is engaged in building a card house of souvenir postcards. Helen Tucker the second is inspecting a large catalogue of Sears, Roebuck & Company, in which a large number of legs with no ladies attached, as advertisements of beautiful silk stockings, cover one page, and lovely ladies without legs, advertising hats and blouses, adorn another page. Helen Tucker . . . being not quite two years old expresses no astonishment at these mutilations, but Mary Lord . . . says it is sad to see these pieces of people, and where are the ladies that belong to these legs? She is interested in the Sears, Roebuck catalogue, and I feel her active little brain is at work upon some scheme to defraud Helen Tucker of it without interference from me.

The catalog is widely known as The Farmer's Bible, The Nation's Wishbook, and, in Texas, as The Panhandle Wishbook. And a wishbook it is. No one will ever know how many thousands of worn farm women have thumbed its pages, their eyes lingering with desire upon the picture of a new stove that the family badly needs but cannot afford to buy, upon a new dress to wear to church, or a washing machine to relieve the back-breaking labor of the tub. Often, however, dreams come true. For months a boy feasts his eyes upon a shiny .22-caliber rifle in the catalog, hoping someday to carry it under his arm as he hunts game in near-by pastures. Then strawberrytime comes and he earns enough picking berries to enable him to make out an order, count out the hard-won dimes over the counter of the post office, get a postal money order, and mail both to Chicago. A day or two later there is a package in his family's mailbox—how often did he look down the road for the carrier's buggy!—and he opens it with trembling hands to find the steel beauty inside. From one season to the next, thousands of farm families pore over the catalog. They discuss the wisdom of buying this or that; finally decide upon what they want, and then, as the crops come in and are sold, are at last able to buy the things they have dreamed of having. To such families the catalog is indeed a wishbook, and, as wishes are crystallized into reality, and long-hoped-for things are at last transferred from the catalog's pages into the possession of Sears' customers, it becomes surrounded with an aura of affection.

The catalog thus has a hold on a vast group of Americans that suave public-relations counsel, for all their wiles and expenditures, cannot ever achieve for their clients. The catalog grew up without a press agent; it has none in its maturity. The function of the corporation press agent is, too often, to present his client not as he is but as he would like to have the public think he is. The catalog, on the contrary, sticks strictly to the business of presenting Sears and its merchandise as they are.

In addition to its other qualities the catalog is, of course, a charming, sometimes picturesque, naïve, and often moving, account of how millions of plain folk have lived for five decades. It is a vast archeological museum containing thousands of exhibits labeled and minutely described. Here one finds such items as goat sulkies for children, stereoscopes and pyrography equipment, flageolets, mourning handkerchiefs, the mustache cup, Prince Albert suits, the solid-gold toothpick with ear spoon combined, the fur derby hat, umbrella stands, hall hatracks, and leather Turkish rockers. Posterity with this record in its possession will not have to send out expeditions to the sites of buried towns of the Middle West, as we now send them to Ur of the Chaldees to learn how the Chaldeans lived and to determine the instruments they used at home and in the fields.

The Greeks, transcendently wise, knew the human and poetic values of the trivia of living; they understood the significance of the simple things by which men lived. In their obituary poetry there appear again and again the youth's hound, the fowler's snare, the fisherman's net, the farmer's plow. These values, too, are in the catalog, and they are not the less poignant because they belong to our times rather than to antiquity. In this spirit the late Julius Rosenwald, the genius of Sears, saw the catalog as more than an instrument of business.

During the World War, the late Newton D. Baker, Secretary of War, telephoned Mr. Rosenwald and asked him to come to Hoboken a day or two later and sail with him for France. Mr. Rosenwald arrived at the ship's dock carrying a small suitcase containing his personal effects. He was followed by a large number of porters struggling with four huge wooden cases which they moved with difficulty. Mr. Baker asked him what they contained. "You'll see," Mr. Rosenwald replied.

Later in the journey, when Mr. Baker was making a tour of American hospitals in France, he asked several hospital librarians what book was requested most often by wounded soldiers. To his astonishment he was told that it was the Sears catalog. It then occurred to Mr. Baker that Mr. Rosenwald must have distributed the catalogs. These were the contents of the heavy cases he had put aboard ship at Hoboken. A few days later the two men met in Paris and Mr. Baker asked his companion why he had taken the catalogs to the hospital.

"I'll tell you why," Mr. Rosenwald said. "This is the reason. Here is a sick or wounded American boy lying in a hospital. Where did he come from? What kind of a home did he have? The chances are that he is a farm boy, or a small-town boy. And that means he is a boy who once hunted, fished, trapped, or played baseball. There is a pretty good chance that his parents kept our catalog around the house. Now here the boy is in a strange country where people talk a strange language. He is thousands of miles from home. He is both sick and homesick.

"I give that boy a catalog. He turns the pages. He sees the shotgun that right now is standing in his room back home in Illinois. He recalls the day when he killed a rabbit in the pasture or shot a lot of crows in the corn. A few pages farther on the boy runs into fishing tackle. From that second it is no longer cold, rainy weather in France, but warm springtime at home. He digs worms behind the barn, puts them in a can, and pretty soon he is pulling fish out of the creek as fast as he drops his line. In other words, the catalog helps our soldier boys to escape the miseries of war and live happily again, if only for a little while, amid the scenes of their childhood at home."

"I see," said Mr. Baker. . . .

The Old Farmer's Almanack

The Old Farmer's Almanack is a repository of practical information and lighthearted nonsense. It directs plantings, forecasts the weather, predicts "lunations," eclipses, and tides. And what an astronomical guide it is! The information may not always have been based on scientific knowledge, but nobody went far wrong in following it. The Almanack neglected no part of farm life and it is still a beloved standby. Here is a sample from the Farmer's calendar for December, 1796.

Very little can be done on a farm, this month to much profit.

Lay in dry fuel, while the snow keeps off.

Prepare and put in order, your sleds and sleighs as they will come in use very soon.

Look well to your barns, and fatting heards.—"Live temperately, and spend frugally."

The cultivation of the earth, ought ever to be esteemed, as the most useful and necessary employment in life. The food, and raiment, by which all other orders of men are supported, are derived from the earth. Agriculture is of consequence; the art which supports, supplies, and maintains all the rest.

"Remember, ye wealthy and affluent, the sons and daughters of affliction and distress! Think of those, into whose shattered dwellings poverty enters to increase the inclemency and the horrours of the present season. Distribute bread to the hungry, and clothes to the naked." Discharge all the debts you have contracted the last year, with mechanics, shopkeepers, labourers, &c. before a new year commences.

The Old Farmer's Almanack

The Old Farmer's Almanack is a [illegible] of practical information and [illegible] [illegible] [illegible], [illegible] the
[illegible] [illegible] [illegible], [illegible], and what an
[illegible] [illegible] of it. The information [illegible] and [illegible] have
been [illegible] [illegible] [illegible] knowledge, [illegible] [illegible] [illegible] [illegible]
in [illegible] it. The Almanack [illegible] [illegible] [illegible] [illegible] [illegible]
[illegible] [illegible]. [illegible], [illegible] [illegible] [illegible] [illegible] the Farmer's
calendar for December [illegible]:

[illegible]

[illegible] [illegible] [illegible] [illegible] the month [illegible] [illegible].

[illegible] [illegible] [illegible] the [illegible] [illegible]

[illegible] [illegible] [illegible] [illegible] [illegible] [illegible] [illegible] [illegible] [illegible] [illegible]
[illegible].

Look [illegible] [illegible] [illegible] [illegible] [illegible] [illegible] [illegible]
[illegible] [illegible].

[illegible] [illegible] [illegible] [illegible] [illegible] [illegible] [illegible] [illegible] the [illegible]
[illegible] [illegible] [illegible] [illegible] [illegible]. The [illegible] [illegible] [illegible]
[illegible] [illegible] [illegible] [illegible] [illegible] [illegible] the [illegible]
[illegible] [illegible] [illegible] [illegible] [illegible] [illegible] [illegible]

[illegible] [illegible] [illegible] [illegible] the [illegible] [illegible] [illegible] [illegible]
[illegible] [illegible] [illegible] [illegible] [illegible] [illegible] [illegible]
[illegible] [illegible] [illegible] the [illegible] of the [illegible] [illegible]
[illegible] [illegible] [illegible] [illegible] [illegible] [illegible] [illegible] [illegible]
[illegible] [illegible] [illegible] [illegible] [illegible] [illegible] [illegible]
[illegible] [illegible] [illegible] [illegible].

PART III

"Back Where I Come From"

Home Town

America is a nation of home towns. To thousands, home is not just a house and a family, but a street, a neighborhood where shade trees and party lines are shared and a cup of sugar is yours for the borrowing. On Main Street—or Elm or Locust—we learned to be members of the community and discovered the satisfaction of belonging to something bigger than ourselves. The home town—its good and its bad—is the heart of America.

The nostalgic words "Back Where I Come From" may even tempt a native to revisit the scenes of his childhood after fifty years' absence. A New Englander's memories will differ from those of a prairie town boy. But underneath the difference there is a sameness bred of living together in a town where the mayor, the butcher and the banker are as equal as thirteen to a baker's dozen. Here we played together in vacant lots and under the street lamps. Here we met at the soda fountain, or found our first job on a paper route or at a shoeshine stand.

There were those occasions when the whole community gathered to celebrate annual events that thronged the sidewalks and swelled the pride of the old home town. There was the day the circus came to town and small boys followed the fabulous parade; the annual Chautauqua when families for miles around sought out the current cultural heroes; revival meeting time when for a while it looked as if the preacher had purified the whole population; the arrival of the steamboat when even the town drunk woke up long enough to share the community excitement; Decoration Day, when the old veterans marched and set us to thinking of dead heroes. And of course the Fourth of July, that greatest day of all, the day the home town loved best. Of all occasions, Town Meeting was the most important. Here was democracy's finest expression.

And, of course, there were the local characters whose memory can never be dimmed. The small town editor whose paper reached around the world; the town lawyer whose justice, more often than not, was tempered with mercy.

Nowhere in the world does home town have the meaning that it has in America. For nowhere else do so many play so large a part in one community. In the following selections we are again reminded that Hometown, U.S.A.—its streets, yards, and porches—is where democracy lives.

Smith Street, U.S.A.

By Elizabeth Hughes

This is a unique address. True, you can find it, or its equivalent, in any American small town. But it is still unique. The life on Smith Street could happen nowhere but in a sprawling, varied, openhearted country like America. On Smith Street, "neighbor" means "friend," even if you move to another address.

Between the years 1912 and 1929, in the United States, in Oklahoma, in a small town named Vinita, and on a street called Smith, more than a hundred children, of whom I was one, learned to be Americans.

We were born Americans, to be sure, but we learned practical, applied Americanism on Smith Street, just as millions of other children were learning it on their own Elm or Third or Walnut Streets in thousands of small towns all over the nation. Smith Street, I believe, was in every major detail typical of American small town life. There was nothing unusual or distinctive about the block on Smith Street where I grew up —and that is its distinction.

Smith Street may not have been beautiful, and it certainly was not perfect. No doubt it had the faults of narrowness, provincialism, and ignorance so often ascribed to it in fiction. But whatever else Smith Street may have been, it was important. We didn't know it then, and perhaps few of the millions who grew up on such a street have thought about it since, but Smith Street was the most significant social phenomenon in America. To have grown up on Smith Street was to have lived in the nearest thing to a pure democracy that this country has ever seen. It was to have been as nearly unconscious of class or economic distinctions as it is possible for humankind to be.

On that block (we called it the neighborhood, and the name meant something) lived employers and employees, tradesmen, professional men, laborers, government workers, schoolteachers, clerks, city and county workers. The most well-to-do did not live on Smith Street, but neither did the families who constantly had to be "helped." There were twenty houses on our block, and, when we moved there, I think every house was owned by the family who lived in it.

Only three houses were two stories high. The rest were one-story, generally five-room, cottages; all frame, and all painted either white or yellow. They had a front room, dining room, kitchen, and two bedrooms. The front porch was for sitting on after supper. The front yard, theoretically, was a lawn, but there were few grass lawns on Smith Street because the trees cast too much shade and the children trampled the grass down in their play faster than it could grow.

There was no nonsense about the back yard. It was for hanging out the wash and raising a vegetable garden and sometimes for keeping a cow or chickens. Nobody had a maid, though from time to time one or more families would have a hired girl, if they could afford it or if someone were sick. The hired girls ate with the family and usually shared a bed with one of the children.

The residents of Smith Street were at least third generation Americans. Probably most of them had had forefathers in the Revolution. Some were of Indian descent. All bore names of English, Scotch, Irish, or German derivation—McKay, Thaxton, Long, Reidemann, Hughes, Sherwood.

Now, after twenty years, I can call up Smith Street as it was in my childhood. I can start at the corner house at the north end of the block on the west side, go down the block, cross over, and come back on the east side, and describe every family, how they made their living, how many children they had. We knew one another that well.

Mr. Cartwright, the home-loan executive, had the highest income of any man on the block, but his wife seldom kept help. She did the work of a two-story house and cooked three meals a day for five people, quite as a matter of course.

Mrs. Rowe, the widow who clerked in a department store, had the lowest income. Her husband died shortly before the birth of her youngest child, leaving her with five children to rear. She owned her five-room house and rented two rooms of it. I can remember hearing my mother and other neighborhood women speaking with the greatest admiration of Mrs. Rowe. She still was poor, even by our modest standards, but she had weathered the danger that her children would starve unless she was "helped," an alternative almost equally intolerable.

Between the Cartwrights and Mrs. Rowe lay a wide scale of economic situations. Almost everyone, from time to time, would have a period of financial distress and worry over debt, but we always had ample clothing and food.

My family, financially, must have been somewhere in the middle range of Smith Street. The two little girls I played with most were Peggy Cartwright and Ellen Rowe. We waded in the gutters when it rained and sewed doll clothes together and went to Sunday school together because we were within two months of the same age, and all the other little girls on the block were noticeably older or younger than we.

Before World War I there was a neighborhood club. Everyone on the block belonged to it. The women met in the afternoon at one of the houses and brought their children. There was no one to leave them with, even if anyone had thought of leaving them. Several times a year the club met at night so the husbands could come. Then it was a dinner party and each wife brought her special dish, the one no one else could make quite as well.

Everyone was solicitous to see that old Major Buford, a Civil War veteran who had been Indian agent at Muskogee, had everything he liked best. He generally had to eat in the room apart, where we children were sent with our plates. If he hadn't eaten with us we would have eaten with him. We adored the Major. He seemed to enjoy our society as much as we enjoyed his, which was a good thing, for he had in his front yard the neighborhood's most desirable tree for climbing.

There were no formal calls of condolence on Smith Street. When there was a death in the neighborhood everyone went in. Already, if there had been need, they had helped care for the dying neighbor. After death came, they divided the night into shifts and sat up, two to a shift, while the family slept. At that time there were no funeral homes to which the dead could be sent, and in the two nights between death and burial the neighbors kept watch in the house that sheltered both the dead and the living. They came in the daytime and brought quantities of food, cakes and pies, roast meat and vegetables. They put it on the table and urged the family to eat, often staying to eat with them. The neighborhood women did the housework. Everyone came, even though they were not close friends.

The unformulated principle was that a woman's place was where she was needed most. If she had small children she stayed at home and took care of them. If she had no children, or her children were in school, and she could be useful working with her husband, she went to town and worked with him. The druggist and his wife and the jeweler and his wife, neither of whom had children, always worked together in the stores. My mother, after I was in school, went more and more often to the photograph studio with my father.

Artificial class distinctions had no meaning to us. When they were brought to our attention by people from larger cities we thought they were funny. I still remember my father's roars of laughter at the remark of a visitor to Smith Street. She had accompanied her hosts to one of the evening parties of the neighborhood club and had recognized immediately the great personal charm of Mr. Prentice, one of the most popular men on the block.

We left the party just after the visiting lady and her hosts and walked down the street not far behind them.

"Mr. Prentice is a delightful man," the visitor remarked. "What does he do?"

"He's a barber," said her resident relative.

"A barber! A barber! Do you know a barber?"

"Well, of course we know a barber," her host snorted. "He lives only two doors from us."

"But socially! He's charming—but I certainly never expected to meet a barber."

My father reached home without bursting, but it was a near thing. For days afterward he was apt to say, "A barber! A barber!" and go off into shouts of mirth.

I would not have you think that Smith Street was Utopia. There were clashes. A coolness would arise between two families occasionally. Politics (which meant Democrat or Republican and nothing else) were often argued with more heat than tolerance. Our moral code was strict, and if the suspicion arose, which happened rarely, that one of the girls on the block had violated it, we gossiped our heads off.

The gossip was exciting and stimulating, even enjoyable. But underneath it lay a genuine kindliness, and we expressed it by action that was eminently practical. The girl was not shunned or ostracized. Girls her own age may have been quietly instructed by their mothers to see less of her, but that was the limit to overt action. We pretended to her parents that we had heard nothing, with a determination which possibly defeated its purpose. When she married, as in the course of time she always did, we not only treated the whole thing as water under the bridge but persuaded ourselves that there probably was never anything to the talk in the first place.

To me, and I suspect to most of the men and women who grew up on Smith Street, the present bitter arguments of the radicals on both right and left sound silly. We know all about a classless society: we lived in one.

We never thought that Mr. Cartwright was necessarily a superior person because he made more money than Mrs. Rowe. They were members of the same church. Their children played together. Mrs. Rowe would have been shocked at the thought of hating Mr. Cartwright because he was a capitalist. He would have been equally shocked at the thought of fearing or distrusting Mrs. Rowe because she belonged to the masses. In fact, he would have been shocked at the suggestion that Mrs. Rowe did belong to the masses. He would have suspected that the observation implied some reflection on Mrs. Rowe, whom he knew well and held in the highest respect.

The children who grew up on Smith Street are not likely to be very sympathetic toward an ideology that would prevent them from talking freely about anything and anybody they want to. They will not take readily, either, to any system that commands them to regard henceforth as enemies the same kind of people who were their friends and neighbors through the formative years.

It has been ten years since I quit the physical environs of Smith Street. Time enough, one would think, for me to lose the idea that life on Smith Street was reality and life among the class conscious an illusion. Yet to this day I am incapable of making distinctions based on wealth or position. They do not exist for me. After a childhood spent on Smith Street people are either individuals of good character and agreeable disposition, hence persons to be admired, or they are not, and are hence persons to be avoided.

We hundred and more men and women who were children together no longer live, geographically, on Smith Street. The millions of others have gone from their Elm or Third or Walnut Streets. But Smith Street has not left us. It never will.

There is good reason to believe that those who worry over American democracy simply do not know about Smith Street. They can't have forgotten it, so they must never have lived there. If the Battle of Waterloo was won on the playing fields of Eton, the battle for the preservation of American democracy was won on Smith Street, or it is already lost.

How Dear to My Heart

By Richard Barnitz

No matter how much you love your home town, it can be a mistake to go back. Richard Barnitz did, only to find the face of his town changed. His memories of Saturday nights on the square, the gang at the ice-cream parlor, and the hangout in front of the undertaker's intensified his homesickness for the town he had known.

As I wandered through the bustling streets I found it hard to believe that this was my town, the drowsy, easy-going place where I grew up half a century ago. The cracker-barrel grocery store was now a supermarket; the cheerful clop-clop of horseshoes had become the grinding of gears and squeal of brakes at traffic lights. Most of the big trees and fine homes near the Square had disappeared. Where once I knew everyone, I was now surrounded by strangers.

I turned away from the hubbub to a side street. Here were houses and pavements where once I raced through open fields. But around a turn I came upon one last meadow and followed a dim path toward the country and springtime. A shadow walked by my side—a small, sunburned boy carrying a bamboo fishing pole and smelling of bruised mint, dried grass and sweat.

I plodded up the rise to Soldiers' Hill, which was unchanged from the old days. Lying on the grass in the warm sun, I looked down upon Hanover, Pennsylvania—the town that once was mine.

When I was a boy here in the '90's, the sunshine filtering down through leaves of buckeye and maple trees was bright on the dusty streets. The houses, red brick and white frame, stood in roomy yards. Within four blocks of the Square were farms and springhouses in which crocks of butter and cream rested in the clear, cold water.

The Square was, actually, a circle. On rainy days you could walk round it and stay dry, for each store had a wooden awning over the wide pavement. Between the outside posts were plank seats where the old men, many of them Civil War veterans, sat whittling, chewing tobacco, gossiping. Beyond were horses tied to hitching rails. You could pat their velvet noses and breathe in the comforting aroma of stable and old leather.

On sparkling spring mornings, when birds talked cheerily among the leaves that brushed the bedroom windows, I scrambled out of bed joyously alive. Good smells from the kitchen pulled me down the back stairs, struggling into torn shirt and patched pants on the way. If there were not oatmeal with thick cream and dark sugar, fried potatoes, ham, eggs and homemade bread, then there were sure to be strawberries, chops, hot cakes and fried mush, and not infrequently pie. Nobody ran for a train, and there were no morning papers. Instead we had laughter, and leisure, and second helpings.

Our parlor had windows that reached from ceiling to floor, stiff draperies resting on the thick Brussels carpet, and a huge mirror set above a white marble mantel. The chandelier's double row of gas jets with cut-glass globes lent further lugubriousness to the dark engravings and oil paintings on the walls. I was awed by this great room and never comfortable in it. When some visitor detained me I sat on the edge of my chair with a rigidity matching the Victorian furnishings, thinking only of escape, and saying "yes, ma'am" when addressed.

The women loved this company room. Smelling of lavender, they twittered and told me how fast I was growing. They wore prim, trailing skirts and sealskin coats with hourglass waists and leg-o'-mutton sleeves. As they drank tea from fragile, tiny cups and nibbled daintily at cake—all this with gloved hands—they conversed with such vigor that the black sequins on their bonnets trembled and sparkled in the gaslight.

Kids today have cars, radios, movies for their pleasures; we had to be resourceful in finding ours. So we were playful as young animals are playful, and wrung every possibility out of commonplace events and things.

When summer came we headed for the ice dam outside of town. Here where the warm water was hemmed about by willows, we would spend the morning, get home for dinner in ten minutes, and return for the long hot afternoon. We built rafts, fished, netted pollywogs and minnows, and hunted frogs.

Every Saturday night I went "on the Square," wandering around, trying to decide how to spend my five-cent weekly allowance. The place was bustling with people and noisy with the rattling of carriages and wagons, and the stomping of horses' hoofs. Farmers in from the country stood on the curbs eating peanuts and gossiping in Plattdeutsch. Often my nickel went for a soda at Ed Harbaugh's new drugstore fountain, but sometimes I spent it at the veterans' setout, a wooden stand with candles illuminating a muslin sign, "Hard Tack and Bean Soup, 5c, Benefit G.A.R." And sometimes I squandered my allowance in the grocery store where candy was kept in large wooden buckets. It was beautiful—one could look for hours at that fairyland of sugary, glittery green, pink, yellow and lavender sweets. There were hard, white mints, chocolate drops, mixed hard candy and horehound drops. Stick candies, my favorites, filled wide-mouthed jars on the shelves. If I had a peppermint stick now, I'd put one end of it in a lemon and suck—I can't forget how tart and refreshing it was.

We drank pop from squat, heavy bottles sealed with a rubber washer on the inside. When you smacked down with the palm of your hand on the top there was a loud hiss. You had to get the bottle to your mouth quickly before the contents foamed out, but most of us had it running down our chins. The flavors were checkerberry, cream soda, sarsaparilla, strawberry and lemon. As for hard drinks, barrels of whisky stood along the grocery store wall and the contents sold for 40 to 80 cents a quart.

Afternoons in summer I scampered down to the old barn on the end of Johnny Moore's lot where he made ice cream. In spite of the heat I vigorously chopped wood for the engine that turned the freezer, and as a reward I got the dashers to lick.

The ice-cream parlor was in the house. I would help Johnny get the ice-cream cans onto the back porch. Townspeople flocked here to have their favorite fresh-fruit flavors. Nothing was served in the dinky portions you get nowadays. Everyone had "healthy helpings," and you helped yourself to crumbled crackers which were always on the table. One farmer who added the contents of the catsup bottle to top off his dish was told not to come any more. No profit, Johnny snorted. But it was gilding the lily that made him mad.

The real hangout, though, was under the awning in front of the undertaker's, where there were long benches always occupied by doctors, lawyers, bankers and others who stopped to rest and talk. Here intimate details of the town's families were related and prophecies offered. Few professional secrets could be kept in such a close-knit community. I never was allowed to loiter here. The men shooed me away saying, "Little pitchers have big ears." Someone had told me that this gathering was a

Sanctum Sanctorum; what I most wanted was to find out what that might be.

Kids like to get away to secret places where no one will disturb them. In the old orchard which was our back yard, two apple trees had arranged their thick limbs conveniently to cradle the tree houses that I built. During spring and summer I slept in these hideaways, awaking amid the greenery of leaves or the pink of fragrant blossoms to lilting bird song and the sun's first fingers poking my eyes. Then I would go on long, before-breakfast walks through the dewy fields. And with me would go my dog, and sometimes the dogs of neighbors. I talked to the dogs and they talked back and trotted along with me.

Lately, from Soldiers' Hill at dusk, I heard dogs talking to one another. Years ago I could have identified them—"That's Judson's dog, Pinky," or, "There's old Waggles a-howlin'." Now the barks were nameless. And as the electric lights of the town flashed on with a self-confident show of progress, only a slight mist preserved the illusion of remembered lamplight.

I felt that somehow I no longer belonged here, and for a time wondered why. Then it dawned on me: "I know what the matter is," I said aloud. "I'm homesick, in my own home town."

Willie White's Home Town

By William Allen White

Before he was ten, the man who made Emporia famous had learned many of the valuable lessons a small town can teach. The pioneer town of Eldorado, Kansas, where White spent his boyhood, offered everything from live Indians to fancy birthday parties. And by the time Willie White became Will, the town was also beginning to grow up.

Indian scares were common in those days. As a baby, my mother took me into a log house across the street from our home where all the women and children of the town, fearing an Indian raid, were gathered while the men did sentry duty. The Indians, of course, were always in my consciousness from babyhood until boyhood. Not that we feared them—much! But stories of Indian uprisings, of murders and kidnapings, of brushes, skirmishes, and battles with soldiers not so far away, from a hundred to five hundred miles, were often told in the town. Naturally, Eldorado boys knew these stories by heart as they played in the woods. Once when I was a little fellow, probably eight or nine years old, half a dozen of us were playing in the underbrush of the timber half a mile from town, maybe swinging on the grapevines, maybe throwing clubs to knock walnuts off the tall trees, filling our hats with wild grapes and gorging ourselves, or if it was fall, and after frost, eating papaws. Whether it was fall or spring or summer, I cannot remember, but the trees were in leaf.

Suddenly, looking into the road, we boys saw a great company of Indians on horseback, halted in the road where it forked a few rods from us. We did not run into the timber, because they were obviously friendly Indians and we were familiar with them. We walked over shyly to look at the red cavalcade in blankets, one or two of them in feathers, men, women, and children. Why they addressed me, I don't know. Maybe I was farther forward in the group of boys, or maybe they addressed us all and I replied. But they asked how far to town, and I told them. And then one of them, a squaw and a leader, said in perfectly good English, "Boy, will you ride with me and show me?"—and I climbed up and the other boys stood envious. We rode into town, I straddling the horn of her saddle, a little fellow whose bare toes toyed with the mane of the Indian's horse. And as we crossed the bridge to ride up Central Avenue and the town turned from its affairs to watch the Indian procession, they saw me. I knew that I was a person of consequence, and I swelled up. Many is the time I moved in pride in later years, but never in such vainglory as when I rode up Central Avenue and the squaw dropped me gently at the town pump and said, "Good boy!" Often bands of Indians like this passed through town, little more than gypsies. These were Sioux going from their Dakota home to visit their comrades, the Comanches, in the Indian Territory. . . .

Prairie fires raged up to the outskirts of Eldorado, and I have no lovelier memory in my heart than the night picture of a prairie fire on the high hill horizon east of town, a great raging fire. We would see in silhouette the little figures of men fighting the fire with wet gunny sacks. . . .

I was a born exhibitionist and loved the applause of the multitude. I seemed to turn everything into song. The little bee song of my babyhood became a long cantata which I made up, perhaps—words and tune and all—as I sat, a solitary only child, in the shade of the morning-glories or, best of all, in the barn at the end of our town lot. That barn was my first enchanted palace. Modern childhood has no equivalent to my barn. I don't know how young I was when I invented the story that it was haunted, and scared the daylights out of other children as I pointed to the barn's high rafters, pretending to see faces and fairies which they also pretended to see; and we scared ourselves and wrestled on the hay of the loft and smelled the nice smell of the horses and the cow. Sometimes we sat in the corncrib and watched the pigs beneath, and the chickens. It was all strange and adventurous. The old pig that woofed at us, and that we were sure would eat us if she caught us, made us feel that we were in the presence of a dragon as authentic as that which St. George went forth to slay.

Of Sunday afternoons, Pa and Ma walked with me to the timber between our creek and its junction with the Walnut River. Pa made me hickory whistles and taught me how to tell different trees by their leaves and bark. It was before they had cut out the buckbrush, the wild raspberries, the blackberries, elderberries, and pokeberries. Above this wood's brush were the one-story trees—the papaws, haws, buckeyes, and the redbuds that I loved. Far above these rose the sycamore, the hickory, the elm, the oak, the walnut, the ash, the coffee-bean tree or locust, and the cottonwoods. Walking with Pa and Ma of a Sunday afternoon, I saw squirrels, rabbits, and once in a while Pa would show me a coon at the river's brim, or a hell-diver. Pa had been born in the Ohio woods and loved timber, and he taught me from earliest childhood to know and love the woods. But the thing that gave the woods their glamour for me was that, only a few years before, the Indians had moved out of this timber onto the prairie lands far to the West and the South. I used to play little games by myself in the woods with mythical little Indian boys. And in some way—I never exactly knew how—I imagined or fancied or dreamed it, and I believed that I turned into a little Indian boy and indeed was one. So I believed, or most seriously fancied, that some day soon the Indians would come back and take me with them. I was scared and happy at the fantasy, which hung about me a long time—maybe a week, a month or half a year.

Then, of course, I had the prairies, the wide illimitable stretches of green in their spring and summer verdure, stretching westward from my front door, with not a dozen rivers or important streams, to the Rocky Mountains six hundred miles away. As a child, I did not know how far they went. To me, they were merely illimitable beyond the horizon and nothing could happen to me except the bite of a rattlesnake; and I never heard of a boy being bitten by a rattlesnake in my childhood. So the woods, the little stream, the prairies, and the dusty road by my door were my playgrounds.

And how I loved the velvety highway dust! It was thick and felt good to my skin, especially to my bare feet. I loved to throw it up in the air, make great clouds of it and feel it fall in my face. And I imagine that no small part of the joy was in being hauled out and scolded by my mother. All mothers along all dusty highways, since little Cain and Abel played in the dust on the road past Eden, have had that problem of children turning primitive in the dust—wallowing in it, kicking it up and heaving it into the air. Like all sweet, forbidden sin, it had its penalties. I had to be scrubbed and scolded at the same time. But it was cheap sin at that.

But I was not entirely unsophisticated in those pre-school years. It was about this time, somewhere late in my third or early in my fourth year, when I made my first public stage appearance. I was always speaking pieces or singing lusty songs for my father at the store. But this time the town went to the courthouse for tableaux, and Leila Heaton and I were dressed to kill—I in a little plug hat with a little black coat and a little high-collared shirt, and she in some long doll dress. We appeared as General and Mrs. Tom Thumb, and I first received the plaudits of the multitude while I first felt the vague sweet pain of love. Leila Heaton, so far as I can remember, was the first object of my adoration. Her mother was a widow and ran the millinery store, and Leila had a big brother—old and very tough, maybe seven or eight years old—of whom I was afraid. And she had lovely gray eyes and dark hair, with corkscrew curls that ranged about her shoulders. I can remember that she called me "Willie" so sweetly that it was a lovely thing to hear. The affair must have been a town scandal. For someone—maybe a big boy or a big girl, it could not within reason have been a grown-up—told me one day that Albert Ewing had taken Leila Heaton into Myer's Candy Store and Ice Cream Saloon. I waited furtively and with the fever of murder pounding in my heart, in the doorway of Ed Ellet's store near by. When the guilty pair appeared, I rushed at them; Albert Ewing fell upon his back, and we rolled together in the board sidewalk dirt—I with the old blood lust of Cain in my heart and he with Abel's fear and amazement in his eyes. The other day Albert and I were talking about it. He insists it was not he, but Theodore Dunlevy, whom I waylaid. I know it was Albert, for I have never quite been able to obliterate the memory of the rage and jealousy with which I pounced upon him—aged four! . . .

My father was then keeping a drugstore and practicing medicine a little. I cannot remember when the store was in the house except that I sat on the grocery scales there. But it must have been two or three years later, probably in '72 or '73, that my father opened his drugstore. It had great bottles of colored water in the window, five- or ten-gallon bottles, shining red or blue or green. On the left hand as one went in was a soda fountain with half a dozen flavors—lemon, strawberry, banana, raspberry and "don't care," which was a mixture of the odds and ends of all of them. In the top of the screen that shielded the prescription case was a huge mortar and pestle. Bottles, gold-labeled with the names of drugs, stood on one side of the store, and an amazing array of patent medicines adorned shelves on the other side. A short counter of stationery and a case of cigars were opposite the soda fountain.

He made money from his drugstore—and, being Yankee, saved it. A story still is told in Eldorado about the man who came into the store one winter day when my father's cronies were loafing around the stove. The man asked for a quarter's worth of powdered sulphur. My father wrapped it up for the customer, who clicked a coin on the counter and walked out. My father walked to the coin, called vainly after the customer, "Hey, this is only a nickel!" started toward the door, looked out, and saw the man hurrying down the street. My father halted, turned back to the crowd, sighed and told the stove-warmers:

"Oh, well, I made four cents profit anyway!"

A barrel of whiskey and several barrels of wine ranged along the sides of the back room beyond the prescription case. It was my father's complaint at home that his clerk, whoever it happened to be, was selling too much whiskey; and the town made much fun of him. The town's two or three good saloons should have supplied its liquor demand, but possibly the winebibbers and those who desired to be knocked about by strong drinks thought his liquor was better than the saloon liquor. For it was an everlasting fight between him and his clerks to keep down the sale of liquor.

One day a town drunk lay in the gutter before his store, and the town wags, one after another, poked their heads into the store with raucous taunting and ribald remarks to rile up the proprietor. My father got two buckets of water at the town pump on the corner, returned with them, sweating, for it was a hot summer day. He stood over the drunk in the gutter and lifted up a bucket, while the whole town up and down the street cried, "My God Almighty, Doc, what are you doing?" *et cetera*, and with variations.

As he soused one of the buckets in the drunk's face, and lifted up the other, the crowd protested. He roared to the multitude:

"Is freedom dead in this country, that a man has no right to water his own liquor?" So he soused down the other bucket. Whereupon the drunk sat up, rubbed his eyes, and walked fairly sober down the street.

The store was so profitable that within a few years my father was able to trade it for a good farm, and have enough capital to run this at a loss for a year or two. . . .

My father had traded his drugstore for the farm. So, when we came back to town, I could no longer go into the store and get a glass of soda water free from his fountain. I had to ask politely for the empty cigar boxes under the counter. I was no longer permitted to take a handful of almanacs and distribute them among my friends. It seemed strange, and the strange seeming still lingers in my memory, that I could not go into that store and make free of it. So came the sense of property to my childhood.

In the meantime, I was sent to school. What a day! Ma started to take me, but Pa objected. He always objected when she coddled me. Of course I liked to be coddled, and I sided with her; but he had his way. The compromise was that he said, "I'll take him!" And so we started out. She was in the doorway, and I left her with her eyes full of tears, for she knew, having taught school, that I would never come back her baby! She knew that I was gone out of her life as a child and would return that noon a middle-aged young person, out in the world for good and all. Pa took me two blocks on my way to the schoolhouse, still three blocks away, and when he was out of sight of Ma and the doorway he prodded me with his cane in pride and affection and said:

"Now, Willie, you are a man. Go to school!" and turned and left me. He could not bear the shame of bringing me into the schoolroom, shame for him and shame for me, and we both knew it. And I trudged on and was glad. And then, for the first time, I remember Albert Ewing coming along the same way, and he and I walked into the schoolhouse together—my first boy friend. After that day we were inseparable for ten years. . . .

The public schools in Eldorado, and all over the West in those days, were the best that money could buy. We had the largest building in town, a two-story stone one with four rooms which soon afterwards became six—the largest edifice in Butler County. The rooms were well equipped, with good seats and desks and blackboards. We had no pioneer hardships in our Kansas schools. All over the Missouri Valley, the settlers first built a sizable schoolhouse and then built their towns around it. But our school, graded from the primary to the high school even in the seventies, was ahead of the civilization about it.

We sang gospel hymns every morning, and the teacher read a chapter in the Bible, and there was no nonsense about that. For we were all little Protestants, and no one thought of objecting to Teacher reading the Bible. She made us say the Lord's Prayer after the Bible reading, and then we were started off right for the day. At noon we sang another gospel hymn and loved it. The words did not mean much, but it was fine exercise for our lungs. And, a few grades higher than the primary, we were taught to read music and were given secular songs to sing.

As for playgrounds, we had everything west of the schoolhouse to Denver. The prairies came within a hundred yards of the building. And sometimes, when prairie fires rose, we boys—the little and big—took our coats off, soaked them in tubs of water from the school well and flopped out the fire, standing with the men of the town. Once the flames almost reached the woodpile that fed the big, potbellied iron stove in every room. Each room had its own water bucket and its own tin cup. And you were supposed to quench your thirst at recess and not bother Teacher between times. At recesses and at noon, we played ball, sometimes one-old-cat, or two-old-cat, town ball and baseball, marbles in season, pull-away, stink base and hide-and-seek. Any new boy had to fight his way into the lodge of boyhood with Byron Snow, Dow Blair, or Ed Dupee, who were ordained to pick a fight for that purpose by the school masonry. A few times—but not often—I was edged into the job; but Albert Ewing, never.

Albert Ewing was held up to me as a little gentleman, which he was. He could do everything better than I could do it. His clothes were always clean, as my mother pointed out—starting me spick-and-span to the schoolhouse every morning. Albert's hair stayed brushed, while mine never did. And he could spell better and write better and draw his geography pictures better than I. We were seatmates and loved each other dearly. And both of us loved Leila Heaton, which was a school scandal. But, being of a wandering and predatory nature in my love life, I again fell away from Leila Heaton and fell head over heels in love with my first teacher, Ida Fitch. I really brought her red apples and really polished them, and really brought her flowers. How fickle I was! The next year I was advanced a grade, and the teacher, Miss Bacon, came to our house to board, and I adored her and hated her beau. And once, very slyly, I dug a deep hole in the path which he passed near our house when he came to see her. I pulled grass and piled on twigs to cover the hole. I hoped in my heart he would fall and break a leg. And this at six! I took love seriously. For me then, it was the greatest thing in the world! It still is!

I was eight years old when I stepped out into society. A note in beautiful Spencerian handwriting, on pink paper with gilt edges—I have it yet—came to me, declaring:

Master Willie White is invited to be present at the birthday party of Miss Alice Murdock at their home on Star Street, March 23, 1876.

And so I was dressed to kill in a little blue suit, bound in black braid, with shiny little golden buttons, white stockings, and black shoes. My hair was wet and pasted down, and my neck washed even behind the ears. It was an afternoon party, bright and gay, and little Alice, with her spinal curvature, was the sunshine of it all. And her grand stepmother in flowing robes—she always affected negligee with loose drooping sleeves—and such red lips and such glowing cheeks and such an alabaster skin, looked like a queen, though she had been a schoolteacher before Bent Murdock married her after his first wife's suicide. We played games (kissing games, I think—post office, clap-in-clap-out, and forfeits) and then went on the lawn, shot arrows at a target, and rather wickedly played hide-and-seek in the barn and had ice cream and cake and lemonade, sitting around like little angels eating their ambrosia. It was all very exciting.

In the meantime, at home things were changing. . . . Eldorado had grown by that time to be a town of nearly a thousand people. It was a self-sufficient community. We had shoemakers who made my father's shoes, although my mother's came from St. Louis, where he traded in his merchant days. The town tailor made Pa's Sunday clothes; my mother made his everyday clothes. She, or other women whom she hired, knitted our socks. The food of the town was mostly raised on the townsite, or near it on the farm. A small packing house put up hams and bacon and cured beef. A wagon shop back of our lot made carriages, and one of the town's most distinguished artists was a wagon painter who striped buggy wheels and painted the elaborate designs—cornucopian, or the seal of Kansas—on the sides of wagons. The town had two or three blacksmith shops, which were busy all day. Ringing anvils woke me in the morning and tolled like bells when I went into the house at dusk. Busy places were those blacksmith shops, which mended and made a score of gadgets for house and farm. We had three harness shops, where I loved to play and listen to the stories of the soldiers who sometimes gathered there; for one harness maker was a noted soldier. A little tannery was established, and a small furniture factory made the chairs, tables, and beds of the pioneers. Native lumber—walnut and oak—stood behind these factories curing, and we boys used to play on the lumber piles and hide between them in our games.

Then the railroad came, and everything was changed. I did not know that the smell of coal smoke, which first greeted my nostrils with the railroad engine, was to be the sign and signal of the decay of a town and indeed of pioneer times, when men made things where they used them—all the things necessary to a rather competent civilization.

In the boy's world, it meant that homemade sleds and little homemade wagons would pass; that the bows and arrows, which boys made by seasoning the hickory behind the stove and scraping and polishing them with glass, would as an art disappear forever out of the life of American boys. The railroad meant that the woodpile would slowly disappear, and that on the far horizon great engines were gathering to wreck the barns, and that the town herd, which I drove for a time, would vanish before the onslaughts of the milk bottles in another fifty years. What a revolution for boys came chugging into the world with that iron horse!

We boys in Eldorado saw colored people for the first time—railroad laborers sweating at their work and singing. We caught their songs and echoed them in our play, building little railroads with whittled ties, imitation rails, grades, and ballast. Our hands were so deft, our imaginations so quick, that we imitated the very thing that would rob boys of their skill and their homely work. . . .

Probably four major influences made this child: the home, where there was reading and considerable intelligent guidance which only later did he perceive, as he recalled certain attitudes of his parents; then came the barn, with its ancient lores and skills, its trapeze swinging from the rafter, its haymows full of somersets, forward and backward, where gangs of boys tried to reproduce circus gyrations; after the barn, the river—swimming, fishing, rowing in summer, and skating in winter; and the roaming through the timber, trapping quail and redbirds and mockingbirds and rabbits, and cutting stick horses in spring. Probably the stick horse has passed out of childhood. But this Willie, who developed his acquisitive faculty early, kept a stick-horse livery stable and was a stick-horse trader before he was seven. The woods also yielded walnuts for all the boys who would go after them, and a few hard hickory nuts and papaws after frost in autumn, and coffee beans and buckeyes, which had a certain commercial value in the primitive swapping commerce of childhood. The woods was a storehouse of all boys' treasures. . . .

Willie learned to skate and was proud of his achievement, cutting Dutch rolls, figure eights, and fancy curlicues. One winter the boys found an old dead mule imbedded in the ice. They grew skillful in jumping over the carcass as they rushed upon it. And many a little tail thumped hard upon that frozen body when a boy failed to clear the hurdle. The river was a great teacher of boys in that day and time.

Probably marbles and fighting were extracurricular activities attached to and surrounding the school—also foot racing and ball. Willie was a fairly good shot at marbles. His mother lived in the pink cloud of innocence that Willie did not play for keeps. Pa knew better and never betrayed him. But here is a curious thing. The little devil had an acquisitive faculty, and he found, watching the wiles of the older boys, that by setting up a fancy marble for boys to shoot at from a hazardous distance and charging two or three commies or a white alley a shot, then giving the prized marble to the man who hit it, he could accumulate marbles faster by running this thing he called a bank than he could by playing for keeps, although he was fairly deft at that. So he set up a bank. But, alas, one day his father discovered that his child had a whole cigar box full of glassies, potteries, and agates which he had accumulated running his bank. That was the end of the bank. Said Pa:

"Now, Willie, whatever you get playing keeps is yours. It's a fair game. But these are dirty marbles. You didn't win them, and you didn't earn them. Your bank was a swindle."

And so the bank was closed, and the career of a future capitalist was nipped in the bud. . . .

I was Will White, not Willie, when I came to my tenth birthday. The town of Eldorado had lost its tough pioneer character. Brick buildings were appearing on Central Avenue and Main Street. Substantial residences, with east and south porches, were rising up on the hill beyond the town. The big stone schoolhouse acquired an addition. It was a six-room grade school with a high school, for which I was headed intrepidly. Because our new grand house, all ornamented with jigsaw jimcracks, had six bedrooms—all fancily furnished with washstands, bureaus, and chairs, and covered with ingrain carpet—my father in his pride always invited people whom he knew from Emporia, Kansas City, Lawrence, or from Leavenworth, where he traded, to stay overnight. And my mother tried to look smiling and hospitable. If she failed, my father would say: "Well, Ma, get a girl to help you!" This was easier said than done, for she felt that "help" was more trouble than service. I am afraid I shared my father's sinful pride in the house—in its grained dining-room wainscoting, in the painted yellow and black squares on the dining-room floor, and in the big kitchen and in the parlor with body Brussels carpet and a gaudy parlor suite, most expensive, in the comfortable living room, crawling with half a dozen rocking chairs, large and small.

The house was heated downstairs with three hard-coal base-burners, each glittering with nickel-plated fenders and fancy doodads—glowing household idols! And the house had such a woodshed as a boy prince could dream of in his palace! There was room even for a trapeze. The worm in the bud was that I could split wood there even when it rained, a drawback but not a major flaw. For on rainy days boys gathered there, and, being host, I acquired some prestige, if not quite leadership. In the woodshed I tied my pet coon and kept my trapped mockingbird, also my little lonely bluebird and my voiceless drooping redbird, until my father persuaded me to let them all go though I could have traded them for a king's ransom.

In the woodshed I assembled from the house and from the barn the various tools of my trade, being a boy, what might be called the hereditary appurtenances of Will White: a thick piece of glass that was used for scraping and polishing cowhorns; a drawknife; skates with runners, rubbed with bacon rind to keep away rust; bits of iron that had no use but were potentially of extreme value, for only boys know what reason; a rawhide quirt—an eight-strand, square-braided whip of my own construction, a priceless treasure; rows and ranks of cigar boxes filled with nails, screws, tops, marbles, and Heaven only knows what of the wampum of boyhood. So the place, indeed the entire woodshed, glowed with the warm and comfortable feeling of great riches in my boy's heart. I was an acquisitive kid, with methodical ways, and stored my treasure there in the woodshed with something like a capitalist's delight in great treasure, good investments.

Two events make me remember my tenth birthday: a sheet-and-pillowcase party, at which all the children who went to Alice Murdock's party, that is to say the nobility and gentry, were assembled; and the glorious fact that on my tenth birthday my parents gave me a Mason & Hamlin Cabinet organ, most ornate, most gorgeous, with a chromo of an autumn field on the centerpiece at the top. The other day, more than sixty years after, among my mother's things I found the bill for it, $240, and a receipt. It came from Chicago and was the town pride. That it was the most splendid organ in town, where not more than three or four pianos rivaled it, of course did not make me humble. And probably I needed that black and shiny eye that Ive Williams gave me for my soul's good the next summer. Music, since I can remember, has always been one of my chief delights. I can recall now, after seventy years, hearing the Eldorado silver cornet band playing down in Burdette's grove by the mill. The strains wafted across our creek to our place. I remember even that I was sitting under the grapevines preparing my little stomach for a gorgeous bellyache, eating the half-green grapes and listening to what I felt was heavenly music. It was the first band I had ever heard. I had a little toy brass trumpet with four notes, and I used to make other trumpets of green pumpkin stems. And Charley Harvey and I, from some whatnot, God knows where, managed to sneak two lovely pink conch shells and used to sing in them, and made what we thought were mellifluous noises that passed for music. From that through the twanging jew's-harp to the mouth organ was but a step; and before I had the organ I could play the mouth organ, put it in a tumbler for resonance or put it in my hand and make a grand fortissimo, as I played. At the school organ I had learned to pick out by ear any tune I knew by one hand, and before I had my own organ I could fake some kind of bass for the two or three notes. And I was singing alto by that time and deeply in love with Agnes Riley.

Baseball and Games under the Street Lamp

By Carl Sandburg

Boys invented games out of their own natural exuberance—on sidewalks, in vacant lots, under street lamps. There was ample opportunity for a future poet to learn his shortcomings as an outfielder.

On the wooden sidewalks of Berrien Street we played one kind of mumble-peg and in the grass of the front yard or the grass between sidewalk and gutter ditch we played the more complicated and interesting kind with jump-the-fence, thread-the-needle, plow-forty-acres, and plow-eighty-acres. On the wooden sidewalks we spun tops, flipped jackstones, chalked tit-tat-toe. On the street we played baseball, two-old-cat, choose-up, knocking-up-flies. In shinny any kind of club would do for knocking a tin can or a block of wood toward a goal, though the fellow with a plow handle had the best of it. And duck-on-a-rock had its points—knocking a small rock off a large rock and then running to pick up your own rock to get back to taw without being tagged.

After we had seen the commencement Field Day on the Knox or Lombard campus, we put on our own field day, barefoot in the summer dust of Berrien Street. Some boy usually had a two-dollar-and-a-half Waterbury watch and timed us as we ran fifty yards, one hundred yards, a few seconds slower than the college runners, and five or six seconds under the world's record. We knew how near we came to the college records in the standing broad jump, the running broad jump, the hop-skip-and-a-step, the standing high jump and the running high jump. Whoever could throw a crowbar the farthest was counted put-and-shot "champeen." We did everything the college athletes did except the pole vault. The mile run we did afternoons, breaking no records except some of our own, yet satisfying ourselves that there is such a thing as "second wind" and if you can get it you can finish your mile.

Straight across the street from the house next east to ours was an average two-story frame house, with a porch. In the street in front of this house was our home base when playing ball. Often we saw on that porch in a rocking chair a little old woman, her hair snow-white with the years. She had a past, a rather bright though not dazzling past. She could lay claim to fame, if she chose. Millions of children reading the McGuffey and other school readers had met her name and memorized lines she had written. For there was in the course of her years no short poem in the English language more widely published, known, and recited than her lines about "Little Things":

Little drops of water,
Little grains of sand,
Make the mighty ocean
And the pleasant land . . .

Little deeds of kindness,
Little words of love,
Help to make earth happy
Like the heaven above.

She was Julia Carney. Her sons Fletcher and James were Universalists and Lombard graduates, Fletcher serving three or four terms as mayor of Galesburg. There she sat in the quiet of her backward-gazing thoughts, sometimes gently rocking, an image of silence and rest, while the air rang with boy screams, "Hit it bang on the nose now!" "Aw, he couldn't hit a balloon!" "Down went McGinty to the bottom of the sea!" Rarely she turned her head to see what we were doing. To us she was just one more nice old woman who wouldn't bother boys at play. We should have heard about her in school. We should have read little pieces about her in the papers. She has a tiny quaint niche in the history of American literature under which one line could be written: "She loved children and wrote poems she hoped children would love."

In early years we would stop our play and follow the lamplighter when he came along before dusk. He carried a small ladder he would set against the lamppost, and we would watch him climb up, swing open the door of the glass case holding a gas burner, turn on the gas, and with a lighted taper put the flame to the escaping gas. Then he would climb down and move on from the corner of Pearl and Berrien to the corner of Day and Berrien, a block east. Then came the electric lights, one arc lamp at every second corner, exactly in the center of the four street crossings, high enough so a man driving a load of hay couldn't reach up and touch the globe. The lamplighter was gone. We missed him.

It wasn't long before the fathers and mothers along Berrien Street had new troubles with their boys. Under that electric light at Day and Berrien the boys had a new playground. They could turn night into day. There was night baseball, night shinny, night duck-on-a-rock, night tug-of-war. There were winners yelling because they had won. There were losers yelling that next time they would make the winners eat dirt. Vehement remarks floated through windows into rooms where honest Q. shopmen and worthy railroad firemen and brakemen were trying for a little sleep.

One of the sleepers who couldn't sleep had a voice like a big-league umpire when one night he clamored from his bedroom window, "You boys shut up and go home with you. If you don't I'll get the police on you." The noise stopped. We sat cross-legged on a patch of grass next to a sidewalk and talked in whispers: "Do you s'pose he means it?" "Aw, we got a right to holler, this is a free country." "Yeah, but what if he means it? We'll get run in." "Yeah, I don't want no patrol-wagon ride." About then came a woman who wanted her sonny-boy; she took him by one ear and led him away and his face had a sheepish look. Then came two men, fathers. They spotted their boys, collared them, and led them away like two sheep for slaughter. Mart and I went home. If we didn't get into the house by nine o'clock we would get scoldings or worse.

On a later night the boys forgot themselves and the hullabaloo they made could be heard a block away. Then as promised, the patrol wagon came. Before it could stop, five or six boys skedaddled. That left five or six of us who weren't going to run and show we were scared. We stood in a huddle waiting. Out of the patrol wagon came two policemen, their nickel-plated stars shining on their coats. One of them, Frank Peterson, weighed about two hundred and twenty pounds, and looked like a battleship coming toward us. We expected hard words from Policeman Peterson. But he spoke in a soft voice like what he was saying was confidential. "Don't you boys know you're disturbing people who are trying to sleep?" What could we say to a quiet intelligent question like that? One boy said, "Yes," another, "Well, you know we were just trying to have some fun." "Yes," said Peterson, again quiet and confidential-like, "but ain't there some way you can have your fun without keeping people awake that's trying to sleep?" We had come to like Policeman Peterson. We saw he wasn't mad at us and it didn't look like we were going to be put in the wagon and hauled to the calaboose. We said yes, we would try to have our fun without making so much noise.

Before walking away Peterson said, "Now that's a promise, boys, and I expect you to keep it. If you don't stop your noise, we'll have to run you in." And his voice got a little hard as he said, "Remember that. We don't like to arrest young fellows like you but sometimes we have to do it." That word "arrest" stuck in our ears. They could have arrested us. When you're arrested that means you're a criminal. And if you're a criminal, where are you?

The patrol wagon drove away. When the rumble of its wheels had died away we sat on the grass and talked in low tones near a whisper. All of us agreed that from now on we had better try to have our fun without yelling. All agreed except the boy who had on another night said, "Aw, we got a right to holler, this is a free country." This boy guessed he'd rather stay away and have some other kind of fun than come around and be a nice boy like the police told him. And he did stay away and later he took to the poolrooms and the saloons and still later put in a year in the Pontiac reformatory for petty larceny.

We went on playing under the electric light and trying to keep quiet but it was a strain. I had a job where I had to report at six-thirty in the morning and had gone home early one night, leaving the boys in a hot game of shinny, back in their old hooting and yelling. They told me next day that a railroad fireman had come out in his nightshirt with a club and a revolver. He shot in the air twice to show the gun was loaded. He sent a bullet into a sidewalk plank and had them look at the bullet. He was wild-eyed, cursed them, slapped one of them, kicked another, then took out a watch and said if every last one of them wasn't gone in two minutes he would shoot to kill. Half the boys ran and the rest went away on a fast walk. From then on not as many boys came to that corner at night; it became reasonably quiet, and decent people could sleep. There was hate for the shooting-iron fireman. And Policeman Frank Peterson we would point out with, "He ain't a bad fellow, do you know?"

Four lots to the east of our house was a vacant double lot where later we laid out a small diamond. At the time a good-natured Jersey cow was pastured there. We never hit the cow but when the ball landed near her and the fielder ran toward her it disturbed her. Also it disturbed the owner of the cow, who said he would have the police on us. So we played in the street till the day the cow was gone and we heard it had been sold. Then we went back to our pasture.

On the narrow lot next to the pasture was Mrs. Moore's house. She was the widow of a Civil War veteran, living alone on a Federal pension. She was a tall woman with dark hair streaked with gray—a quiet woman, smoking her clay pipe, keeping to herself and raising vegetables and flowers. She had the nicest all-round flower garden in our block, the front of her lot filled with hollyhocks, begonias, salvia, asters, and morning-glories climbing the fences. First base was only ten feet from her fence and every so often a fly or a foul ball would go over into her potatoes, carrots, and hollyhocks. A boy would climb the fence and go stomping around hunting the lost ball. At such times as Mrs. Moore stood between the boy and the place where he believed the ball fell it was not pleasant for either party concerned. "Why must you boys do this to my place?" she would ask. When the boy answered, "We'll try never to do it again," her reply would come, "See that you don't do it again. I don't want to make trouble for you boys."

Again and again we sent the ball over into her well-kept yard. She tried scolding but she just naturally wasn't a scold. She quietly hinted she might have to go to the police, but she didn't go to the police or to our parents. She had property rights and we were trespassing on her property, and she forgave us our trespasses even though we went on trespassing. She was a woman of rare inner grace who had gathered wisdom from potatoes and hollyhocks.

In our early games played in the street, the bat was a broom handle, the ball handmade—a five-cent rubber ball wrapped round with grocery string. The home plate was a brick, first base a brick, second base a tin can, third another tin can. We played barehanded till we learned how to stuff a large man-sized glove with cotton, wool, or hair to take the sting out of a fast ball.

The days came when we played in the cow pasture with a Spalding big-league regulation ball. We gathered round the boy who first brought it. "Well, what do you know!" we said, "a dollar and a half." And we told it around as a kind of wonder, "We been playing today with a dollar and a half"—the same ball that Amos Rusie was throwing in the big league, the same ball Big Bill Lange was hitting with the Chicago team. When I carried Chicago newspapers and read sports news I learned about the "elusive pill" thrown by Amos Rusie. I was among those who grieved later to hear of Amos Rusie taking to drink, being dropped from major and minor clubs, and being found one day digging gas mains at a dollar-fifty a day. He was doing ten cents a day better than my father at the Q. shop but still I was more sorry for him than for my father.

When Galesburg played Chillicothe or Peoria or Rock Island on the Knox campus, the Berrien Street kids, lacking the two bits' admission, watched the games through knotholes in the fence. Or we climbed a tree fifty yards from the home plate, found a crotch to sit in, and had as much fun as though we were in the two-bit bleachers.

The most exciting baseball year the town had was when a City League was organized and played one or two games a week. The Main Street clerks had one team, the railroad shopmen another, and there were two other teams. Out of the tall grass around Victoria came a team that had surprises. Galesburg had picked the best nine in the town to meet them and the word was that maybe Galesburg would "goose-egg" them. But the country boys played fast ball, among them the Spratt brothers, Bob and Jack, who later went into minor-league clubs. Their center fielder was a tall gawk wearing a derby! As the game got going Victoria took the lead by one or two runs and kept the lead till near the closing inning, when Galesburg with one out got two men on bases and one of its heaviest sluggers came to bat. He hit the ball high and handsome and sent it sailing away out to deep center field. The tall gawk in the derby made a fast run, made a leap for it, caught it with one hand and threw it straight to second to catch a man off base—and Victoria was victorious in one of the craziest, sweetest pieces of baseball drama I have ever seen.

On many a summer day I played baseball starting at eight in the morning, running home at noon for a quick meal and again with fielding and batting till it was too dark to see the ball. There were times my head seemed empty of everything but baseball names and figures. I could name the leading teams and the tailenders in the National League and the American Association. I could name the players who led in batting and fielding and the pitchers who had won the most games. And I had my opinions about who was better than anybody else in the national game.

An idea began growing in me that if I played and practiced a lot I might become good enough to get on a team. Once on a minor-league team I would have my chance to show what I could do and I might end up in the majors—who knows about a thing like that? It was a secret ambition. In what spare time I could find I played with the boys and did fairly well in left field on a scrub team.

Then came an afternoon in early October when I was sixteen. I had managed to buy secondhand a fielder's glove, a regular big-league affair I was proud of. Skinny Seeley and I went to a pasture and knocked up flies. He hit a high one to me and I was running top speed for it. I believed I would make a brilliant catch, the kind I would make when maybe one of the minor-league clubs had taken me on. Suddenly my right foot stashed into a hole and I fell on my face. When I looked at my foot I saw a gash in the shoe leather and blood oozing from the tangled yarn of the sock. In the hole there was a broken beer bottle, and into this my foot had crashed.

I limped across the pasture, about a block, to the house of Dr. Taggart. Out on his front porch he had me take off the shoe, then slowly the sock. He cleaned the cut, picked out yarn and glass, applied antiseptic. Then he brought out a curved needle and sewed four stitches at about the middle of the foot just below the instep. He bandaged my foot and I limped home. My mother spoke sorrow and pity. My father asked when would I ever learn any sense and quit wasting my time with baseball.

From that day on I was completely through with any and all hopes of becoming a big-time ballplayer. I went on playing occasional games, but those four stitches marked the end of my first real secret ambition.

Paper Route

By MacKinley Kantor

A paper route was a boy's first road to independence, his first contribution as a paying member of the family. Maybe, too, it was his introduction to the peculiarities of next-door neighbors and to the harsh world of commerce. For separating the men from the boys, a paper route is probably second only to the army.

When I graduated to full-fledged possession of a paper route, I was so devoted to duty that my family could not help but exhibit their astonished gratification. . . .

My private area for distribution of the daily *Freeman-Tribune* lay mainly in the business district, and there was color and excitement in delivering papers along those streets. . . . We "paper boys" growled continually about our lot, and pretended to hate the weary task before us, just as the best soldiers are constantly complaining about everything from their mess to their C.O. On the whole, we found considerable charm in our routine; we partook of a series of minor adventures, feuds and satisfactions.

Carrying the *Freeman* was a popular job among young males of that period, as testified by a long waiting list of applicants. . . . There was as much variety to our work as there was to the midwest seasons. On summer afternoons we scampered stonebruised and barefoot on our rounds. Many of us had dogs who went along each day, and soon Rover or Patsy knew the routes as well as we did. My own yellow dog would turn up the proper stairways ahead of me, and ignore the ones where no subscribers dwelt. I carried the most papers of any boy: never less than ninety-eight—sometimes as many as one hundred and sixteen—but the distance which I had to travel was short. I walked a few blocks amid stores and offices on both sides of Second and Des Moines streets, and another few blocks among nearby residences. For deliveries in this latter area I usually kept my bicycle parked handy; but when there was snow on the ground I went on foot.

Routes all over town were apportioned as fairly as possible among some fifteen or twenty boys; the ones who had to walk long distances carried, naturally, fewer papers. We toted our burdens in what were called "paper-bags"—bulky sacks of canvas—and each bag had a wide band by which the sack was suspended over the shoulder.

If we missed a customer—forgot to deliver his paper—we were fined three cents out of our weekly wage of one dollar apiece. Those omissions could be extremely painful if they were frequent; generally speaking, our average of excellence was high.

Other benefits than our wages accrued from time to time. When a street carnival came to town, and pitched its tents in the black-cindered area near the C. & N.W. tracks, the carnival manager would buy a certain amount of advertising space in the paper, requesting and receiving some free publicity in the news columns as well, and generally offering a sheaf of complimentary tickets to old D. L. Hunter. The interest of the Hunter brothers in Bo-Bo the Dog-Faced Boy, Bluey-Bluey the Monkey Man, and Luna the Girl in the Moon was understandably at a low ebb during their middle years. We carrier-boys received the tickets with appreciation when they were passed on to us, and at night we trooped riotously to the carnival precincts, usually with some annoyed old-soldier constable herding us along so that we wouldn't get into too much trouble.

On Saturday afternoons most of us had saved a nickel out of our wage, and for an hour before the paper was printed we would be crumpled happily in a row of seats at the Orpheum theatre, sitting on the backs of our necks, with our bare legs doubled up against the seats ahead. There we rejoiced in the spectacles retailed: we followed Pauline among her Perils, Elaine among her Exploits. We sighed before the blonde fragility of Miss Marguerite Clayton, and screeched our approbation of justice meted out by the stern-faced Mr. G. M. Anderson.

When the screen darkened, we would go racing across the street to the *Freeman* office, pattering along the wooden hall, cavorting down a bumpy stairway into thunder of presses and the sharp clatter of a folding machine. In that gloomy old basement tobacco spit deposited by the pressmen made a slippery peril on the concrete floor, though our soiled and leathery feet were never hurt by it. Henry Ingertson, severe and efficient in his black sateen shirt, would dole out our bundles of papers. We would count them carefully, and rush off to carry the news of the town and the outer world to Dr. Berg the dentist, Miss Merle Smith the milliner, and a thousand other expectant subscribers.

With a flush of responsibility, I gave seventy-five cents of my dollar to Mother each week, and retained the other quarter for myself—minus whatever fines had accrued. The very first winter Mother was so pleased with my assumption of this microscopic portion of family obligation, that she bought me a mackinaw; and she could ill afford to do so at the time. . . .

I swaggered with delight, although a few of the boys whooped when they saw me coming, and called me Joseph for a while. I did not mind in the least. I felt that I was a woodsman now—a lumberjack, a French-Canadian trapper. I almost said "By gar!" as I preened in front of the mirror. The mackinaw was solid wool—and that meant something on sharp February evenings when the mercury sank below the minus-twenty mark in every outside thermometer—and lower than that sometimes: when zero seemed a halcyon springtime temperature.

Often I used to freeze my face while coming home from my paper route. This is no brag of an individual hardship; plenty of other people froze their faces too. Acting under the mistaken formula of pioneer first-aid, Grandma would rub my face with snow when I arrived frost-bitten, until the white spots turned a sore red under this urgent manipulation (and thus my right cheek is still tender whenever I face cold weather in the wintry North). The rest of me, guarded by the mackinaw, was snug.

For four years I lugged those papers, when it was 105 in the shade in late July, or breaking through hard crusts of snow six months later. During that time I earned in total about one-tenth of what I received last year for a brief *Readers' Digest* sketch which it took me two hours to write. It seems that I have remarked before, somewhere in print, that writers are often overpaid and paper-boys not paid enough.

I dramatized whatever affliction lay upon me. I felt the angry kindling of a grim ambition which only the poor can know, and only those of the poor who have a pretension toward self-importance, a native craving for luxury: people who do not and cannot accept their lot dumbly, even in the earliest years when they are conscious of it.

The movement of Webster City hours was punctuated by whistles. Their blast came out of the same deep-toned mechanism that identified the location of fire-alarm zones—that whistle tuned at lower C. It blew at seven in the morning, at twelve o'clock noon, at six in the evening; its curfew cousin screeched at nine p.m.

In solid blackness that followed the gray wintry dusk, it was always my intention to finish my paper route before six; but almost never might I do that if the snow lay deep. Across cold roofs and ice-fruited trees the six o'clock blare would sink against my ears before I had reached the last block of my route; the frosty growl would stumble with me along a path behind the Universalist Church.

. . . The Butlers' house: I put the paper under a brick they always left lying on their steps to weight it down. Then west to the next house . . . no, the people had moved away, I was to leave a paper there no longer . . . the little frame Christian Science Church just beyond, its windows black, its steps solid under icicle drippings . . . the lights in the dwelling of Mr. Ed Brown, the bull-necked photographer with a shock of gray hair and a bass voice that frightened bigger boys than I.

The Whiteman house next door: its windows bloomed with light and laughter; there were always delicious smells when the door was open, and at times Mrs. Whiteman offered a cookie or a piece of the fudge she had made for her son Dick. . . .

Four more papers across the street; the Schraeders' house was last of all. The *Freeman* skimmed across chilly boards of a wide porch . . . my job was done until the next day.

I loped past the U.B. Church out into the ruts of snow in Willson Avenue. Perhaps a bob-sled would be coming; a farmer might be driving to his home south of town . . . it was rather late to expect a sled to come. I peered north toward the few lights of Second Street: no mist of horse-steam, no rattle of chains or crunch of runners. . . .

It was standard behavior for us boys to wait in the snow as close to the trampled track as we dared to stand—to crouch, nerved and ready, as the big sleds thundered past—to leap with skill, planting our feet atop the rear runner in the same split instant that our hands clutched the rim of the sled-box. . . . But when I looked back from the summit of the library hill and observed that no sled approached, I turned to the well-shoveled sidewalk instead . . . cold, the cold. . . .

The lights of our kitchen and dining room shone out long before I reached Webster Street corner. . . . Forgotten now the wind keening down from Sioux City and the bad white spaces beyond. Forgotten too the pressed gaskets of snow between my stockings and my crusted shoes . . . I could only run, and gasp and grin with a stiff face. . . . I had come in now; the door was open on brightness. I saw my grandmother's expectant smile—and maybe Virginia had made popovers again, as she could make them very well: the first thing she ever learned to bake. My mother's voice and the dog's hollering were in my ears. . . . O frost, O desolation—lock them out—we are in our staunch small warmth, we have the trust and security of the well-loved—we have homemade tomato soup on the red-hot range tonight.

"S-t-e-a-m-boat A-Comin'!"

By Mark Twain

When the packet boat arrived at Hannibal, Missouri, the whole town came to life. Even the town drunkard awoke to join the excitement of loading and unloading. In *Life on the Mississippi* Mark Twain immortalized the arrival of the steamboat in a sleepy river town and a young runaway's first disillusionment with the tall tales of river men.

When I was a boy, there was but one permanent ambition among my comrades in our village on the west bank of the Mississippi River. That was, to be a steamboatman. We had transient ambitions of other sorts, but they were only transient. When a circus came and went, it left us all burning to become clowns; the first Negro minstrel show that ever came to our section left us all suffering to try that kind of life; now and then we had a hope that if we lived and were good, God would permit us to be pirates. These ambitions faded out, each in its turn; but the ambition to be a steamboatman always remained.

Once a day a cheap, gaudy packet arrived upward from St. Louis, and another downward from Keokuk. Before these events, the day was glorious with expectancy; after them, the day was a dead and empty thing. Not only the boys, but the whole village, felt this. After all these years I can picture that old time to myself now, just as it was then: the white town drowsing in the sunshine of a summer's morning; the streets empty, or pretty nearly so; one or two clerks sitting in front of the Water Street stores, with their splint-bottomed chairs tilted back against the walls, chins on breasts, hats slouched over their faces, asleep—with shingle-shavings enough around to show what broke them down; a sow and a litter of pigs loafing along the sidewalk, doing a good business in watermelon rinds and seeds; two or three lonely little freight piles scattered about the "levee"; a pile of "skids" on the slope of the stone-paved wharf, and the fragrant town drunkard asleep in the shadow of them; two or three wood flats at the head of the wharf, but nobody to listen to the peaceful lapping of the wavelets against them; the great Mississippi, the majestic, the magnificent Mississippi, rolling its mile-wide tide along, shining in the sun; the dense forest away on the other side; the "point" above the town, and the "point" below, bounding the river-glimpse and turning it into a sort of sea, and withal a very still and brilliant and lonely one. Presently a film of dark smoke appears above one of those remote "points"; instantly a Negro drayman, famous for his quick eye and prodigious voice, lifts up the cry, "S-t-e-a-m-boat a-comin'!" and the scene changes! The town drunkard stirs, the clerks wake up, a furious clatter of drays follows, every house and store pours out a human contribution, and all in a twinkling the dead town is alive and moving. Drays, carts, men, boys, all go hurrying from many quarters to a common centre, the wharf. Assembled there, the people fasten their eyes upon the coming boat as upon a wonder they are seeing for the first time. And the boat *is* rather a handsome sight, too. She is long and sharp and trim and pretty; she has two tall, fancy-topped chimneys, with a gilded device of some kind swung between them; a fanciful pilothouse, all glass and "gingerbread," perched on top of the "texas" deck behind them; the paddle-boxes are gorgeous with a picture or with gilded rays above the boat's name; the boiler deck, the hurricane deck, and the texas deck are fenced and ornamented with clean white railings; there is a flag gallantly flying from the jack-staff; the furnace doors are open and the fires glaring bravely; the upper decks are black with passengers; the captain stands by the big bell, calm, imposing, the envy of all; great volumes of the blackest smoke are rolling and tumbling out of the chimneys—a husbanded grandeur created with a bit of pitch pine just before arriving at a town; the crew are grouped on the forecastle; the broad stage is run far out over the port bow, and an envied deckhand stands picturesquely on the end of it with a coil of rope in his hand; the pent steam is screaming through the gauge-cocks; the captain lifts his hand, a bell rings, the wheels stop; then they turn back, churning the water to foam, and the steamer is at rest. Then such a scramble as there is to get aboard, and to get ashore, and to take in freight and to discharge freight, all at one and the same time; and such a yelling and cursing as the mates facilitate it all with! Ten minutes later the steamer is under way again, with no flag on the jack-staff and no black smoke issuing from the chimneys. After ten more minutes the town is dead again, and the town drunkard asleep by the skids once more.

My father was a justice of the peace, and I supposed he possessed the power of life and death over all men and could hang anybody that offended him. This was distinction enough for me as a general thing; but the desire to be a steamboatman kept intruding, nevertheless. I first wanted to be a cabin-boy, so that I could come out with a white apron on and shake a table-cloth over the side, where all my old comrades could see me; later I thought I would rather be the deckhand who stood on the end of the stage-plank with the coil of rope in his hand, because he was particularly conspicuous. But these were only day-dreams,—they were too heavenly to be contemplated as real possibilities. By and by one of our boys went away. He was not heard of for a long time. At last he turned up as apprentice engineer or "striker" on a steamboat. This thing shook the bottom out of all my Sunday-school teachings. That boy had been notoriously worldly, and I just the reverse; yet he was exalted to this eminence, and I left in obscurity and misery. There was nothing generous about this fellow in his greatness. He would always manage to have a rusty bolt to scrub while his boat tarried at our town, and he would sit on the inside guard and scrub it, where we all could see him and envy him and loathe him. And whenever his boat was laid up he would come home and swell around the town in his blackest and greasiest clothes, so that nobody could help remembering that he was a steamboatman; and he used all sorts of steamboat technicalities in his talk, as if he were so used to them that he forgot common people could not understand them. He would speak of the "labboard" side of a horse in an easy, natural way that would make one wish he was dead. And he was always talking about "St. Looy" like an old citizen; he would refer casually to occasions when he was "coming down Fourth Street," or when he was "passing by the Planter's House," or when there was a fire and he took a turn on the brakes of "the old Big Missouri"; and then he would go on and lie about how many towns the size of ours were burned down there that day. Two or three of the boys had long been persons of consideration among us because they had been to St. Louis once and had a vague general knowledge of its wonders, but the day of their glory was over now. They lapsed into a humble silence, and learned to disappear when the ruthless "cub"-engineer approached. This fellow had money, too, and hair oil. Also an ignorant silver watch and a showy brass watch chain. He wore a leather belt and used no suspenders. If ever a youth was cordially admired and hated by his comrades, this one was. No girl could withstand his charms. He "cut out" every boy in the village. When his boat blew up at last, it diffused a tranquil contentment among us such as we had not known for months. But when he came home the next week, alive, renowned, and appeared in church all battered up and bandaged, a shining hero, stared at and wondered over by everybody, it seemed to us that the partiality of Providence for an undeserving reptile had reached a point where it was open to criticism.

This creature's career could produce but one result, and it speedily followed. Boy after boy managed to get on the river. The minister's son became an engineer. The doctor's and the postmaster's sons became "mud clerks"; the wholesale liquor dealer's son became a bar-keeper on a boat; four sons of the chief merchant, and two sons of the county judge, became pilots. Pilot was the grandest position of all. The pilot, even in those days of trivial wages, had a princely salary—from a hundred and fifty to two hundred and fifty dollars a month, and no board to pay. Two months of his wages would pay a preacher's salary for a year. Now some of us were left disconsolate. We could not get on the river—at least our parents would not let us.

So by and by I ran away. I said I would never come home again till I was a pilot and could come in glory. But somehow I could not manage it. I went meekly aboard a few of the boats that lay packed together like sardines at the long St. Louis wharf, and humbly inquired for the pilots, but got only a cold shoulder and short words from mates and clerks. I had to make the best of this sort of treatment for the time being, but I had comforting day-dreams of a future when I should be a great and honored pilot, with plenty of money, and could kill some of these mates and clerks and pay for them.

Months afterward the hope within me struggled to a reluctant death, and I found myself without an ambition. But I was ashamed to go home. I was in Cincinnati, and I set to work to map out a new career. I had been reading about the recent exploration of the river Amazon by an expedition sent out by our government. It was said that the expedition, owing to difficulties, had not thoroughly explored a part of the country lying about the head-waters, some four thousand miles from the mouth of the river. It was only about fifteen hundred miles from Cincinnati to New Orleans, where I could doubtless get a ship. I had thirty dollars left; I would go and complete the exploration of the Amazon. This was all the thought I gave to the subject. I never was great in matters of detail. I packed my valise, and took passage on an ancient tub called the *Paul*

Jones, for New Orleans. For the sum of sixteen dollars I had the scarred and tarnished splendors of "her" main saloon principally to myself, for she was not a creature to attract the eye of wiscr travelers.

When we presently got under way and went poking down the broad Ohio, I became a new being, and the subject of my own admiration. I was a traveler! A word never had tasted so good in my mouth before. I had an exultant sense of being bound for mysterious lands and distant climes which I never have felt in so uplifting a degree since. I was in such a glorified condition that all ignoble feelings departed out of me, and I was able to look down and pity the untraveled with a compassion that had hardly a trace of contempt in it. Still, when we stopped at villages and wood-yards, I could not help lolling carelessly upon the railings of the boiler-deck to enjoy the envy of the country boys on the bank. If they did not seem to discover me, I presently sneezed to attract their attention, or moved to a position where they could not help seeing me. And as soon as I knew they saw me I gaped and stretched, and gave other signs of being mightily bored with traveling.

I kept my hat off all the time, and stayed where the wind and the sun could strike me, because I wanted to get the bronzed and weather-beaten look of an old traveler. Before the second day was half gone, I experienced a joy which filled me with the purest gratitude; for I saw that the skin had begun to blister and peel off my face and neck. I wished that the boys and girls at home could see me now.

We reached Louisville in time—at least the neighborhood of it. We stuck hard and fast on the rocks in the middle of the river, and lay there four days. I was now beginning to feel a strong sense of being a part of the boat's family, a sort of infant son to the captain and younger brother to the officers. There is no estimating the pride I took in this grandeur, or the affection that began to swell and grow in me for those people. I could not know how the lordly steamboatman scorns that sort of presumption in a mere landsman. I particularly longed to acquire the least trifle of notice from the big stormy mate, and I was on the alert for an opportunity to do him a service to that end. It came at last. The riotous powwow of setting a spar was going on down on the forecastle, and I went down there and stood around in the way—or mostly skipping out of it—till the mate suddenly roared a general order for somebody to bring him a capstan bar. I sprang to his side and said: "Tell me where it is—I'll fetch it!"

If a rag-picker had offered to do a diplomatic service for the Emperor of Russia, the monarch could not have been more astounded than the mate was. He even stopped swearing. He stood and stared down at me. It took him ten seconds to scrape his disjointed remains together again. Then he said impressively: "Well, if this don't beat hell!" and turned to his work with the air of a man who had been confronted with a problem too abstruse for solution.

I crept away, and courted solitude for the rest of the day. I did not go to dinner; I stayed away from supper until everybody else had finished. I did not feel so much like a member of the boat's family now as before. However, my spirits returned, in instalments, as we pursued our way down the river. I was sorry I hated the mate so, because it was not in (young) human nature not to admire him. He was huge and muscular, his face was bearded and whiskered all over; he had a red woman and a blue woman tattooed on his right arm,—one on each side of a blue anchor with a red rope to it; and in the matter of profanity he was sublime. When he was getting out cargo at a landing, I was always where I could see and hear. He felt all the majesty of his great position, and made the world feel it, too. When he gave even the simplest order, he discharged it like a blast of lightning, and sent a long, reverberating peal of profanity thundering after it. I could not help contrasting the way in which the average landsman would give an order, with the mate's way of doing it. If the landsman should wish the gangplank moved a foot farther forward, he would probably say: "James, or William, one of you push that plank forward, please"; but put the mate in his place, and he would roar out: "Here, now, start that gangplank for'ard! Lively, now! *What* 're you about! Snatch it! *snatch* it! There! there! Aft again! aft again! Don't you hear me? Dash it to dash! are you going to *sleep* over it! 'Vast heaving. 'Vast heaving, I tell you! Going to heave it clear astern? WHERE 're you going with that barrel! *for'ard* with it 'fore I make you swallow it, you dash-dash-dash-*dashed* split between a tired mud-turtle and a crippled hearse-horse!"

I wished I could talk like that.

When the soreness of my adventure with the mate had somewhat worn off, I began timidly to make up to the humblest official connected with the boat—the night watchman. He snubbed my advances at first, but I presently ventured to offer him a new chalk pipe, and that softened him. So he allowed me to sit with him by the big bell on the hurricane deck, and in time he melted into conversation. He could not well have helped it, I hung with such homage on his words and so plainly showed that I felt honored by his notice. He told me the names of dim capes and shadowy islands as we glided by them in the solemnity of the night, under the winking stars, and by and by got to talking about himself. He seemed oversentimental for a man whose salary was six dollars a week—or rather he might have seemed so to an older person than I. But I drank in his words hungrily, and with a faith that might have moved mountains if it had been applied judiciously. What was it to me that he was soiled and seedy and fragrant with gin? What was it to me that his grammar was bad, his construction worse, and his profanity so void of art that it was an element of weakness rather than strength in his conversation? He was a wronged man, a man who had seen trouble, and that was enough for me. As he mellowed into his plaintive history his tears dripped upon the lantern in his lap, and I cried, too, from sympathy. He said he was the son of an English nobleman—either an earl or an alderman, he could not remember which, but believed was both; his father, the nobleman, loved him, but his mother hated him from the cradle; and so while he was still a little boy he was sent to "one of them old, ancient colleges"—he couldn't remember which; and by and by his father died and his mother seized the property and "shook" him, as he phrased it. After his mother shook him, members of the nobility with whom he was acquainted used their influence to get him the position of "loblolly-boy in a ship"; and from that point my watchman threw off all trammels of date and locality and branched out into a narrative that bristled all along with incredible adventures; a narrative that was so reeking with bloodshed and so crammed with hair-breadth escapes and the most engaging and unconscious personal villainies, that I sat speechless, enjoying, shuddering, wondering, worshiping.

It was a sore blight to find out afterward that he was a low, vulgar, ignorant, sentimental, half-witted humbug, an untraveled native of the wilds of Illinois, who had absorbed wildcat literature and appropriated its marvels, until in time he had woven odds and ends of the mess into this yarn, and then gone on telling it to fledglings like me, until he had come to believe it himself.

Circus Day in the Nineties

By Booth Tarkington

When the circus wagons rattled down Main Street and the calliope wheezed out its shrill tunes, every boy in town tagged along behind the elephants. At the circus grounds they watched roustabouts raise the big top, and even slipped under the canvas to see the greatest show on earth.

The bright sun of circus day shone on Plattville, and the length of Main Street and all the Square resounded with the rattle of vehicles of every kind. Since earliest dawn they had been pouring into the village. There were great red-and-blue farm wagons, drawn by splendid Clydesdales; the elders of the family on the front seat and on boards laid side to side in front, while, in the deep beds back of these, children tumbled in the straw or peeped over the sides, rosy-cheeked and laughing, eyes alight with blissful anticipations.

There were more pretentious two-seated cut-unders and stout buckboards, loaded down with merrymakers, four on a seat meant for two; there were rattletrap phaetons and comfortable carryalls drawn by steady spans. Every vehicle contained heaping baskets of good things to eat and underneath, where the dogs paced faithfully, swung buckets and fodder for the horses, while colts innumerable trotted close to the maternal flanks, viewing the world with their big, new eyes in frisky surprise.

Here and there the trim side-bar buggy of some prosperous farmer's son, escorting his sweetheart, flashed along the road, the young mare stepping out in pride of blood to pass the line of wagons, the youth, resplendent in Sunday best and his scorched brown face glowing with a fine belief in the superiority of both his steed and his lady; the latter beaming out upon life and rejoicing in the light-blue ribbon on her hat, the light-blue ribbon around her waist, the light-blue half-mittens on her hands, and the beautiful red coral necklace about her neck and the red coral buttons on her gown.

The air was full of exhilaration; everybody was laughing and shouting and calling greetings; for Carlow County was turning out from far and near, and clouds of dust rising from every highway and sweeping into town heralded their coming. Dibb Zane, the "sprinkling contractor," had been at work with the town water cart since dawn, but he might as well have watered the streets with his tears. The Square was heaving with a jostling, good-natured, constantly increasing crowd that overflowed on Main Street in both directions; and the good nature of this crowd was augmented in the ratio that its size increased.

Since nine o'clock every window of the courthouse had been occupied, and here most of the damsels congregated to enjoy the parade, their swains gallantly posting themselves at coigns of less vantage behind the ladies. Some of the faces were pretty; nearly all were rosy-cheeked and all were good to see because of the good cheer they showed. Nearly all of them conversed in tones that might have indicated that they were separated from each other by an acre lot or two.

Here and there on the sidewalk, a father worked his way through the throng, a licorice-bedaubed cherub on one arm, his coat on the other; followed by a mother with the other children hanging to her skirts and tagging exasperatingly behind holding toy balloons and delectable batons of spiral-striped peppermint in tightly closed, sadly sticky fingers.

A thousand cries rent the air; the strolling mountebanks and gypsying booth-merchants; the peanut vendors; the boys with palm-leaf fans for sale; the candy sellers; the popcorn peddlers; the Italian with the toy balloons that float like a cluster of colored bubbles above the heads of the crowd, and the balloons that wail like a baby; the red-lemonade man, shouting in the shrill voice that reaches everywhere and endures forever: "Lemo! Lemo! Ice-cole lemo! Five cents, a nickel, a half-a-dime, the twentiethpotofadollah!"—all the vociferating harbingers of the circus crying their wares.

Timid youths, unalterably hooked by the arm to blushing maidens, bought recklessly of peanuts, of all known sweetmeats, and forced their way to the lemonade stands and silently sipped the crimson-stained ambrosia; still arm in arm, they held their glasses in their outer hands—such are the sacrifices demanded by etiquette.

Above all rose the nasal cadence of the Cheap John, reeking oratory from his big wagon on the corner: "Walk up, walk up, walk up, ladies and gents! Here we are! Here we are! Make hay while we gather the moss. Walk up, one and all. Here I put this solid gold ring, sumptuous and golden, 18 carats, 18 carats of the priceless mother of metals, toiled fer on the wild Pacific slope, 18 guaranteed, I put this golden ring, rich and golden, in the package with the hangkacheef, the elegant and blue-ruled note paper, self-writing pens, pencil and penholder. *Who* takes the lot? Who takes it, ladies and gents?"

His tongue curled about his words; he seemed to love them. "Fer a quat-of-a-dollah! Don't turn away, young man—you feller in the green necktie, there. We all see the young lady on your arm is a-langrishing for the golden ring and the package. Faint heart never won fair wummin. *There* you are, sir, and you'll never regret it. Go—and be happy! Now, who's the next man to get solid with his girl for a quat-of-a-dollah?"

Down the middle of the street, between the waiting crowds, ran barefoot boys, many of whom had not slept at home, but had kept vigil in the night mists for the coming of the show, and, having seen the muffled pageant arrive, swathed and with no pomp and panoply, had returned to town, happy in the pride of knowledge of what went on behind the scenes. Tonight the runaways would face a woodshed reckoning; but now they caracoled in the dust with no thought of the grim deeds to be done upon them.

Now, from far up Main Street came the cry "She's a-comin'! She's a-comin'!" After many false alarms and disappointments, the parade was coming at last. There was a fanfare of trumpets. The boys whooped in the middle of the street; some tossed their arms to heaven, others expressed their emotion by somersaults; those most deeply moved walked on their hands. In the distance one saw, over the heads of the multitude, tossing banners and the moving crests of triumphal cars, where "cohorts were shining in purple and gold."

There was another flourish of music; immediately, all the band gave sound. And then, with a blare of brass and the crash of drums, the glory of the parade burst upon Plattville. Glory in the utmost! The resistless impetus of the march-time music; the flare of royal banners, of pennons on the breeze; the smiling of the beautiful Court Ladies and the great, silken Nobles; the swaying of the howdahs on camels and elephants, and the awesome shaking of the earth beneath the elephant's feet, and the gleam of his small but devastating eye; then the badinage of the clown, creaking along in his donkey cart; the terrific recklessness of the spangled hero in a cage with two striped tigers; the spirit of the prancing steeds that drew the rumbling chariots, and the grace of the helmeted charioteers; the splendor of the cars and the magnificence of the paintings with which they were adorned; the ecstasy of all this glittering, shining, gorgeous pageantry needed even more than walking on your hands to express.

Last of all came the tooting calliope, followed by swarms of boys as it executed, "Wait till the clouds roll by, Jennie," with infinite dash and gusto.

The enormous white tent was filled with a hazy yellow light, the warm, dusty, mellow light that thrills the heart because it is found nowhere in the world except in the tents of a circus—the canvas-filtered sunshine and sawdust atmosphere of show day. Through the entrance the crowd poured steadily, coming from the absorptions of the wild-animal tent to feast upon greater wonders; passing around the sawdust ellipse that contained two soul-cloying rings, to find seats whence they might behold the splendors so soon to be unfolded. Everyone who was not buying the eternal lemonade was eating something.

Here, as in the morning, the hawkers raised their cries, offering to the musically inclined the *Happy Evening Songbook*, or presented for the consideration of the humorous the *Lawrence Lapear Jokebook*, setting forth in full the art of comical entertainment and repartee.

The band began to play, and the equestrians and equestriennes capered out from the dressing tent for the Grand Entrance, and the performance commenced. Through the long summer afternoon it went on: wonders of horsemanship and horsewomanship; hair-raising exploits on wires tight and slack; giddy tricks on the high trapeze; feats of leaping and tumbling in the rings; while the tireless musicians blatted inspiringly through it all, only pausing long enough to allow that uproarious jester, the clown, to ask the ringmaster what he would do if a lady came up and kissed him on the street, and to exploit his hilarities during the short intervals of rest for the athletes.

Some hundreds of the spectators, insatiable and still affluent, stayed for the Grand Concert after the Main Performance and with shouts of wonder and esteem beheld the clog dancing of a tinkling and clinking beautiful gold-haired lady who simultaneously sang "She's my Hanky Panky Danky from the town of Kalamazack"; and when these final pearls of pleasure had been seized from the jeweled day and the last replete groups straggled from the great tent that was now a rosy Mont Blanc in the sunset, all the roads leading into Plattville were dim again with the rising dust of new crowds clopping into town for the Grand Evening Performance.

But when the late moon rose out of the eastern woodland groves, that night, all the farm horses were back home in their barns, drowsily shifting their weight from time to time for better rest; the farmers and their families were in their beds, dreaming contented dreams, and in the Plattville lockup there was not a soul. Under the moon the town lay white and quiet, all silent except for the soothing song of the katydids; children smiled in their sleep and down the long highway of the National Road the shrouded circus wagons creaked through silvered night air toward the next county seat. Show Day in Plattville was over—till another summer came.

Chautauqua

By Gay MacLaren

When the Chautauqua opened near an American town, people from miles around went in search of "culture, education, and inspiration." Gay MacLaren cannot forget a gala if exhausting week when, with his mother and sister, he took in most of what Chautauqua offered. A recitation of "The Maniac" scared the daylights out of his sister, but he was much more impressed by his discovery of the "Chautauqua salute."

We lived in Howard, South Dakota. When our town paper, the *Miner County Democrat,* came out with a long piece telling about the Chautauqua which was to open at Lake Madison, Mother said it was an opportunity for culture that no right-minded person should miss. Daddy didn't care much about culture, but he said Mother could go for a week and take us children.

There was a great deal of excitement when the program was announced and the posters put up in the store windows. Mother said she was going to hear Reverend T. De Witt Talmage if she had to walk. For weeks nothing was talked of but Chautauqua, and it seemed as if every one were planning to go.

The paper told about how the first Chautauqua had been founded by Dr. John H. Vincent in 1874 on the shores of beautiful Lake Chautauqua and how people came from all over the United States to spend their summers at the assembly and hear the great speakers and entertainers. It said hundreds of Chautauquas were being established and we were fortunate to have one "in our midst."

The next Sunday our minister spoke about the Lake Madison Chautauqua in his sermon. He said it would "uplift the community and bring inspiration, education, and pure wholesome entertainment into our starved lives."

When it came time for us to go to Chautauqua, Daddy killed Old John. Mother cooked him a whole day and then packed him in a big basket together with fresh loaves of bread, baked beans, jelly, and cake. We took the ten o'clock train, but before we got to Winfred, three miles away, Vern wanted a drumstick and Mother had to unpack the basket. Madison was only twenty miles from Howard; so we got there before noon.

At the station we took a bus and rode up Main Street. I could see the Normal School at the end of the street with a flag floating from the cupola. It was the largest building I had ever seen. The streets were crowded with people all dressed up as if it were the Fourth of July, and there were flags and banners everywhere. The banners had the word Chautauqua printed across them in colored letters. Farmers' wagons piled high with bedding, cooking utensils, and children rattled along the dusty roads leading out to the Chautauqua grounds. A frying pan fell out of the wagon ahead of us, and the bus horses stepped on it.

A street car ran out to the Chautauqua from town. The bus driver loaded our trunks on the little car, then helped Mother with the basket and valises and lifted Dess and me up the steps. As we came in sight of the Chautauqua grounds, I could see the flag on top of the auditorium waving over the tree tops and the lake beyond. The grounds seemed to be dotted with little white spots which turned out, as we came nearer, to be small white tents set up among the trees.

Mother paid our admission fee, and as soon as we were inside the gates a man from the assembly headquarters showed us which one of the little tents we were to occupy. The springs and mattresses were already down on the dirt floor. The only other furniture was an oil stove, two chairs, and a small pine table. We had brought our bedding from home in a trunk. The tents were rented by the Chautauqua Association to people who could not afford to stay at the hotel by the lake.

As soon as our things were in the tent, we set out for the Administration Building to get the tickets which would admit us to the auditorium for the entertainments.

On our way we came to a rough shack built of pine boards, across the front of which was a large banner announcing, "Headquarters of the C.L.S.C." Mother said the letters meant the Chautauqua Literary and Scientific Circle and she must go in and register, because she intended to organize a reading circle in Howard when we got back.

From the C.L.S.C. we walked down past the hotel. People were sitting on the porches and strolling along the paths by the lake. Some distance farther on there were a number of little tents set up close to the water's edge. Wagons were driving up to the tents and unloading boxes and trunks. The minute the children were set down, they would pull off their shoes and stockings and go wading. We didn't have any lakes at home; so I wished our tent had been pitched by the water, but Mother said those cost more and we couldn't afford it. However, she told us that the lake was free to all, and Vern and I could go wading some day even if our tent wasn't by the lake. . . .

On first sight the auditorium appeared to be a large circular building open all the way around. But on closer inspection it proved to be little more than a dome-shaped roof supported by heavy columns.

The space underneath had been excavated to form a large circular pit, making it possible for the tiers of seats encircling the slanting sides to rest securely in the earth rather than on scaffolding.

The seats, made of rough planks without backs, were arranged in graduated sections divided by sawdust-covered aisles. Each of these groups of seats converged toward a broad path at the bottom like the section of an orange. The level space in the center arena was divided by another sawdust trail leading to the platform. On each side were groups of plank seats.

With such a seating arrangement the building could be filled or emptied in a few moments. In case of rain canvas curtains could be let down to cover the opening all the way around. It was all very crude, but it seemed wonderful to us. Mother said there would be something going on in the auditorium both afternoon and evening and our tickets would admit us to everything.

The Chautauqua was to last two weeks. During that time people would come and go. Some could afford only a day or two and others a week or the entire season. Our stay was limited to one week, but Mother said it was to be a week of "culture, education, and inspiration." It looked like a great deal to me, because most of the shows that came to Howard stayed only one night. Even the Kickapoo Indian Sagwaw Company played but three nights, and the Man with the Bear who came every spring was gone before the bell rang for school.

On the way back to our tent Mother stopped at the Methodist Dining Tent for some fresh milk and doughnuts. All the church ladies had dining tents. There were the Baptist ladies, the Presbyterian ladies, the Methodist ladies, and so on. Vern had a fight with the boy in the tent next to us because he said the Presbyterian doughnuts were better than the Methodist doughnuts.

The Chautauqua wasn't to begin until next day. As soon as we had our supper, Mother said we must go to bed, because we would be at the auditorium every night during the next week and we must have a good sleep. We didn't rest very well, because we had visitors. Some toads hopped into the tent in the middle of the night and thumped around on the dirt floor until Mother had to get up and chase them out with the broom.

We were up early the next morning. Vern went to the well for water while Mother made toast on the oil stove. At ten o'clock we started for the auditorium to hear the morning-hour lecturer. His subject was "Your Boy."

The man talked to parents about how they should raise their boys so they would grow up to be good men. Vern didn't seem very much interested, and about halfway through the lecture he asked Mother if we couldn't go down to the lake and go in wading. Mother said we could if we would go out quietly. When we got outside where no one could see, Vern turned around and made a face at the lecturer. He said he didn't want to be a good boy—that he wanted to chew tobacco and brake on a freight train.

After the lecture Mother went to a round table at the Hall of Science and then to a meeting of the C.L.S.C.; so we had a long time to play. We took off our shoes and stockings and waded in the water and hunted for bright pebbles along the beach.

The afternoon program was given by the Chautauqua Ladies' Quartet. We liked them much better than "Your Boy." One of the ladies had a mustache and a long gold chain and sang bass. When they got through singing the people crowded around the back of the auditorium to shake hands with them. I wanted to go, but there was such a crowd that we couldn't get through.

After supper we went to the auditorium again, and Mother allowed Vern and Dess and me to sit down on the front seat with the other children. The same ladies sang again. One song was called "Sweet and Low." The bass lady kept on going down until it seemed to me she would never get to where she was going. After they got through singing, they went off the platform and a man came on and introduced the chalk talker. The Chautauqua Ladies' Quartet had been the prelude, he said, but the chalk talker was the main entertainment.

His name was Mr. Frank Beard. He had a large easel on which there were big squares of white paper. While he talked, he drew pictures with colored chalk. Then he threw the pictures out into the audience for any one who could catch them. Vern got Abraham Lincoln, but Willie Matson and Jimmy Greely fought over George Washington and tore him all to pieces. The chalk talker said if they didn't behave he wouldn't throw any more pictures. Then he drew the superintendent of the schools and the president of the bank, and everybody laughed.

That evening a company of ladies dressed in white robes gave tableaux, but I didn't like them as well as the family band, because there were no children with them. The next day there was a blind senator from Washington, and a lady in a spangly dress who recited "The Charge of the Light Brigade" and "The Maniac." Dess got so scared that she cried and ran back to sit with Mother.

But every one seemed to be waiting for Reverend T. De Witt Talmage. I remembered how Mother had said she was going to hear him if she had to walk, and I felt sure that the reason Daddy had bought us tickets on the train was because he didn't want Mother to walk all the way to Lake Madison.

Besides the people who were already at Chautauqua, staying at the hotel or camping out, many more came just for Talmage day. He was to speak in the afternoon, and the auditorium was crowded to hear him. It was so terribly hot and so many people were standing around the outside that no air could get in, and we were almost smothered from the dust the horses kicked up. We had gone early because Mother said she didn't want to miss a word. The children were not allowed on the front seat for Talmage day. We had to sit with our parents. The platform manager said Doctor Talmage was very nervous and we would disturb him.

Some of the speakers were cross at us children if we didn't pay attention. One time Freddie Kelly put a peanut in his slingshot and hit the lecturer right in the middle of his watch charm. Freddie's mother came down the aisle and spanked him before everybody and made him go back and sit with her. The music ladies were nice to us, and one time a man who recited pieces said if we would be good he would buy us some ice cream at the Christian Endeavor ice cream tent afterward. When he got through his speaking, he said we were the best children he had ever seen.

We were at the auditorium so early for Talmage day that I got tired. After everybody was in who could get in, we kept on waiting, and every little while people would start clapping their hands. I think the horses hitched outside got tired too, because they began to neigh, and one horse ran away.

After people stopped clapping, they began to whisper, and one woman told Mother that she had heard that Doctor Talmage was in the habit of not coming. "I heard that he left an audience waiting while he went off and got married," she said.

Just then the platform manager came out with a telegram in his hand. He said he was very sorry, but Doctor Talmage couldn't come because he had "missed his connection." The people all began to talk at once, and some of them acted as if they were angry. Mother said she was just sick. The next day, the platform manager announced that Doctor Talmage was coming on Saturday; so they got ready for another Talmage day, and this time he came.

But by that time I was so excited over Opal May that I wasn't interested in Doctor Talmage. I listened as long as I could, but it was so hot that I got sleepy and put my head on Mother's lap and went to sleep. A big horsefly bit me, and I woke up just as he was finishing his speech. He was yelling awfully loud, and I felt sorry for him because his collar was melted down around his neck and he looked all worn out.

"No matter what others may choose," he said, "give me a Christian's life, a Christian's death, a Christian's burial, and a Christian immortality."

Then he took a drink of water, bowed, and went off the platform. I looked at Mrs. Turner and she was crying. Rufus tugged at her dress. "What are you crying for, Ma?" he asked.

"Oh, just because I'm—I'm so happy," she said with a sob in her voice. I thought she meant she was happy because Rufus had stayed awake. After selling her butter and eggs so he could hear "The Winning Man," he had slept all through the lecture.

When I looked at Mother, she was crying too, but she was clapping her hands. Pretty soon Doctor Talmage came out on the platform again. Then the people stopped clapping and began to wave their handkerchiefs. At first there were only two or three, but soon everybody, even the farmers, were waving. Their red handkerchiefs looked pretty among the white ones. I unpinned my birthday handkerchief from my dress and waved it too.

Mother said it was the greatest honor that could be given to a Chautauqua speaker. The handkerchief waving, she said, was the Chautauqua salute.

Old-Time Revival Meeting

By Hartzell Spence

A Methodist preacher thundered out the glory, the choir sang "Just As I Am" and "Rock of Ages," and the most miserable sinner crept to the penitents' rail. Who can forget the reformed drunkard, the neighbors who settled their quarrels at the altar, or the echo of the bass Amens? Despite the hell-fire and damnation they threatened, revival meetings were pretty happy times.

The revival meeting has undergone many changes since its early days. There was a time when the followers of John Wesley were known as "the shouting Methodists" because of their vocal response to religious exhortation.

Even when I was a boy certain preachers had standard phrases they relied on to provoke cries of "Amen," and any evangelist who didn't "raise the roof" was not invited back another year. The old-time revivalists loved spontaneous encouragement. Today a minister would feel heckled if his congregation interpolated loud shouts of agreement during his discourse.

I remember an elderly Methodist bishop who worked for an hour and a half to thaw out a prewar congregation. He tried all his tricks but met only stony silence. Exasperated, finally, he interrupted his sermon to ask, "Are those bald heads I see down there or tombstones?"

No one answered.

"You, brother," he said, pointing to a man in an aisle seat, "have you a voice?"

The man nodded but did not speak.

"Then use it, man, use it," the bishop begged. "How does the Lord know you are a Christian unless you shout out the glory?"

His listener merely looked uncomfortable.

"Praise the Lord!" shouted the bishop. Even that drew no reaction. Again he pointed down the aisle.

"Can you say 'Praise the Lord'?"

"Why, of course."

"Then say it man, say it."

The man said it.

"You whisper!" the bishop roared. "Is that all you think of the Lord? Can't you shout? Come, now, follow me. Praise the Lord!"

This time there was a faint echo.

"That's better. Shout it now, louder."

The man shouted.

"Hallelujah!" cried the bishop. "Everyone in the auditorium, now, repeat after me, and use your lungs! Hallelujah!"

The reaction was half-hearted but promising.

"That's the spirit. Again, with all your might. Hallelujah!"

"Hallelujah!" came the answer.

"Now, after me: Praise the Lord!"

"Praise the Lord!"

"Now once more: Amen!"

"Amen!" This time the answer was tumultuous.

The bishop mopped his brow and smiled. "That's better," he said. "I was afraid for a moment I was addressing heathen."

There is a story told of a circuit evangelist in the early days of Indiana Methodism who spent two solid hours exhorting his backwoods audience to repent. At the altar call only a few timid women came forward. Angered at this lack of faith, the preacher glared about the church, then shouted, "I have a deep impression that some young man or woman in this house will be tramping the streets of Hell before I come again." The penitents' rail filled quickly.

Father was as much responsible as anyone in Methodism for a change in revival technique. He never exhorted anyone to be good lest he roast in Hell. Rather, he made the avenue of Christ so tempting that his congregation wanted to walk it with him.

In his regular sermons father usually chose a New Testament text: one in which the Christian way of life was a thrilling experience. During a revival father continued along this tack, though in his early ministry he usually brought in a professional evangelist to exhort those parishioners who responded only to the threat of brimstone, as had their fathers, when Hell-fire was needed to compete against the worldly excitement of free land and Indian murder.

Father's revival-meeting strategy always was the same on the first night.

He worked on his regular church congregation. Graphically he recalled all the sins, both of commission and omission, of which his flock was guilty.

So profound was his understanding of human frailties, needs, and longings that every sermon he preached was personal. He never referred to an actual case, of course. But many in the congregation thought he did, and, as he was preaching, people would look furtively about to discover how many persons besides the pastor had discovered their secret sin. Sometimes half a dozen members would take personally the same remark and hasten to repent.

"I could tell whom I was hitting by the way they looked over their shoulders to see if the family skeletons were sitting behind them," father said years later. "And sometimes members would become angry and stay away, believing my sermon was aimed directly at them."

At the first revival meeting in the new tabernacle, father emphasized the need for an annual renewal, just as the housekeeper puts her home in order and the businessman takes inventory. Then he hit his parish amidships.

"How many of you," he asked, leaning across his pulpit intimately, "have been uncharitable toward a neighbor or have not settled a quarrel? How many of you have neglected your children's religious training because you were too lazy to get up in time for Sunday school? Do you harbor a grudge against a business competitor? Have you overworked your employees or your hired girl? Can you come to the altar of Christ with a pure heart? Or is your soul so crowded with little sins that there is no room for Christ?"

He let that message sink in while the choir, always augmented for revivals, chanted softly:

Just as I am
Without one plea,
But that Thy blood
Was shed for me
And that Thou bidd'st me
Come to Thee,
O Lamb of God, I come, I come!

Father held up his hand. The singing stopped, but the organ continued the hymn. To its accompaniment father spoke: "There probably is no one here tonight who is not trying to live as Jesus would have us all live. But we are human, and we have sinned. Forgive us, O Lord."

From the retired-ministers' corner came a loud "Amen."

Responding to this reaction, father lifted his voice slightly. "There is probably no one here tonight who deep in his heart doesn't want to let Christ in. Open our hearts, O God."

Again came the "Amen" from several directions.

Father stepped from his pulpit to the altar rail.

"I ask all those who earnestly want to follow Christ to join me here at the altar. Let God and your neighbors know that you humbly repent your sins and that you earnestly desire to live the Christian life. Come!"

The choir sang the hymn again.

Just as I am, and waiting not
To rid my soul of one dark blot,
To Thee, whose blood can cleanse each spot,
O Lamb of God, I come, I come!

Nobody moved. But father knew the courage such a declaration required. He was in no hurry.

"We are assembled here," he resumed, "in a new tabernacle. Before us lies a year that will test our faith. Give us courage, O God."

"Amen!"

"We will need greater faith, greater love than ever before. Give us that faith, O God."

"Amen. Amen."

The congregation was a little restless now under the enchantment of the minister's voice and the repetition of the hymn.

Father walked up and down before the altar, then spoke again.

"I remember a man who once said to me: 'Brother Spence, why should I be saved? I am already saved.' My answer was: 'Brother, conversion redeems a man from the sins he has committed. But many a man thinks that because he is saved he can do no wrong and, thus encouraged, he develops new sins.' I have no doubt that many of you here tonight believe that because once you were saved you will forever remain in grace. That is not true. Salvation must be renewed. You need to cleanse your hearts anew. Your pastor needs to cleanse his own heart. Who will join me as I confess my own weakness?"

Father knelt at the penitents' rail, and again the choir sang. Three retired preachers came forward and knelt beside their pastor. Emboldened, a few church members slipped from their pews. Soon a score or more were kneeling.

The visiting evangelist then stopped directing the choir and stepped to the pulpit. That year he was Wilson Keeler, a famous exhorter who brought his wife as organist and his son as tenor and trombonist.

"'Come unto Me,'" he said softly, "'all ye who are weary and heavy laden, and I will give you rest.' How often you have heard those words. Yet how many of you actually come to Christ? How many of you are so proud of your Heavenly Father that you will publicly declare your desire to renew your Christian faith? Will you come?"

They came. The organ played. Father arose and went in turn to each penitent to whisper a few words. Mr. Keeler continued his persuasion.

"There may be many here tonight who have always tried to live the Christian life but have never publicly declared their Christianity. How often have we heard the words? 'I am not ready yet. Wait a little while.' When I was in Michigan last year a beautiful young mother attended many of our meetings, but she would not come forward. 'I am not ready yet,' she said. This year I returned to her town and asked for her. She was dead. And I was deeply touched. Once too often she had said, 'I am not ready yet.' Now it is too late. We never know when our turn may come. I may be next. You may be next. God grant that we may be ready. Come! Do it now, while the Hand is upon you! Do it now, that your heart may be at peace. Don't let the Devil struggle with your soul. Wrest him out and come to Jesus. Come and see how serene your life will be with God in your heart. Don't put it off. Don't say you are not ready. Come!"

They came.

The choir sang other hymns: "Rock of Ages," "Amazing Grace, how sweet the sound that saved a wretch like me," "My Faith looks up to Thee, Thou Lamb of Calvary," and "O Jesus, I have promised, to serve Thee to the end."

Father and Mr. Keeler alternated at the exhortation, with little anecdotes out of their own experience, simple emotional pleas that touched every kind of sinner. In half an hour, when all the church stalwarts had renewed their faith, father dismissed the congregation with a stirring prayer in which he begged God to lay his hand during the revival on all who needed salvation. Then he kept the penitents a little longer for another prayer, and the three retired preachers saw that all filled out a card detailing their names, addresses, and church affiliation, if any.

Rarely was the first night anything but a renewal of faith for regular church members, although a few stray sheep were rounded up. Father would use those saved on the opening night as an inspirational group that sifted through the audience in the course of the following meetings. During altar calls thenceforth little scenes occurred all over the tabernacle.

Mrs. Welch, who had been fighting with her neighbor over a boundary dispute, but could not sue her because the Discipline forbade Methodists from suing each other, slipped into the pew beside her adversary one night and put an arm around her. The two wept quietly for a minute; then Mrs. Welch led her neighbor to the rail and knelt with her.

Mr. Cambridge, angry for weeks at a parishioner who had bought a piano from a competitor, went to his enemy and shook his hand. The two talked for a moment, then went to the rail.

One night Mrs. Baker saw, sitting alone, a young woman who had applied at her millinery store for a job. Mrs. Baker went to her.

"You are Mrs. Salverson, aren't you?"

She nodded.

"May I help you?" Mrs. Baker whispered. "Perhaps if you tell me what's troubling you, it might help."

Wrought to an intense emotionalism by the repeated altar calls and music, Mrs. Salverson cried bitterly. "I can't do it any longer," she sobbed. "Night after night I have come here, but it does no good. I think of my two little children hungry at home. If God was as kind as these men say, wouldn't He keep my babies from starving?"

Mrs. Baker tried to put an arm around her, but Mrs. Salverson drew away.

"I have tried desperately to get a job," she said. "But nobody needs me."

"Have you no husband?" Mrs. Baker asked.

Mrs. Salverson shook her head. "He died a year ago and left nothing."

Tears filled Mrs. Baker's eyes.

"God bless you," she said, "I am a widow, too, and I have very little, but you are welcome to share it. I will find work for you."

A moment later Mrs. Baker led Mrs. Salverson to the altar.

One night, when the hammering of rain on the tabernacle's wooden roof echoed across many empty seats, Major Cooper spied a vaguely familiar face in the congregation. He finally placed it as that of Reuben Wright, once a regular churchgoer but now never seen. The major hobbled up the aisle and slid into Wright's pew.

"I haven't seen you in some time."

"I haven't been here," Reuben Wright scowled.

"Have you been out of town?"

"No."

"Have you been sick?"

"Let me alone," Wright said.

The major sat silently beside him for a long time. The altar call continued. The music swelled. Mr. Keeler's son played softly on his trombone an old hymn: "Jesus is tenderly calling, today. Calling oh, sinner, come home."

Wright stirred. "I haven't heard that for a long time," he said.

The major nodded.

"I was just thinking that, too."

"Do you remember," Wright asked, "how Wesley Carmichael used to play it on the cornet in Sunday school?"

"So he did," the major recalled. "Why, that's fifteen years ago!"

"Yes," Wright replied, "it's been a long time."

"But it would be good to hear him again," the major said. "I wonder if we could get him to play it Sunday? If we could, would you come?"

Wright hesitated. "The church has outgrown me. It doesn't want me around any more."

The major remembered now. Wright had stopped attending church when the choir had been reorganized eight years before. Wright's voice was gone, they had said. A flicker of sympathy came into the major's eyes.

"They don't need me, either," he said, humbly. "I no longer do anything except attend the Sunday service. And I get mighty lonely, sitting there by myself. Why don't you come out next Sunday and join me? It would help. Maybe we could organize an old duffers' Bible class, and you could teach. You used to discuss the Scriptures wonderfully, I remember."

Reuben Wright looked at the major for the first time. "Do you think we could?"

"Why not?" the major asked. "There must be others, like us, who have grown away."

"There's the Widow Jordan," Wright said. "She hasn't been to church since Albert died. There's Harry Gray—you remember him—"

"And Lizzie Carson," the major added, "whatever happened to Lizzie Carson?"

"We ought to find out," Wright suggested.

"Let's do it."

It was Wright now who sought the major's hand.

"You know," he said, "I've been hoping for years that I could get back to my church. I've missed it."

A moment later they walked up the aisle together. Father knew from their faces that something extraordinary had happened and gave them a special blessing.

Another rainy night brought an entirely different scene. Forester Ross, entering by a side door, hung his wet coat on the end post that supported the altar. The corner was dark, since gas lamps in the tabernacle were centered as much as possible. After the sermon father, as usual, filled the rail with penitents and at the end of the service sent them to their seats. As usual, too, before his benediction he glanced up and down the rail, for sometimes a sinner, wrestling with a particularly heavy sin, remained at prayer after everyone else had gone. This night, in the dim corner by the door, he saw a figure hunched into a coat, head bowed so low it was out of sight.

Quietly father addressed the meeting. "We still have one soul at the altar. If upon his conscience there is a grievous burden, he needs our help. Let us all pray silently that he may recover his faith."

The organ played softly one verse of a hymn.

"Amen," father said, but the penitent did not rise.

Father waited a moment, then prayed aloud for mercy on the sinner. Still there was no response. Again father waited, then gave a broad hint. "Go in peace," he said, "and may the Lord go with thee."

Still nothing happened.

Thinking perhaps the man had fainted, father walked over to the dim corner. He put his hand on what should have been a shoulder and touched a post.

Unabashed, he turned to his flock, which by then realized what had happened.

"Let us not be dismayed," he said quietly, "that we have lifted up our prayers for an empty coat. Now you know how I feel, night after night, praying for living, breathing souls in this tabernacle who could respond and will not."

Decoration Day Parade

By John P. Marquand

Whether you called it Decoration Day or Memorial Day, it was the time to remember our heroes dead in battle. Sometimes it meant carrying wreaths to the cemetery, or flags; sometimes, a parade like the one described in *Melville Goodwin, U.S.A.*, which started a boy to thinking about a career as a general.

"It always beats me," his father had said on one visit, "what made you want to be a soldier. I always sort of hoped you'd be a doctor and take over old Byles's practice. I saved up money for you to go to medical school. It must have been those confounded Decoration Day parades. I guess you're doing all right, Mel, but I wish that you had stayed home."

His father had been right. He never had recovered from a certain Decoration Day when the family had gone to Nashua to visit his mother's parents.

The whole family had been asked to spend the day, and they were leaving at nine in the morning in order to reach Nashua in time for the parade. So many other families were leaving, too, for the day's outing, that the square was very crowded. Mel Goodwin could remember the starched dresses and the big bow ribbons of the little girls, and the billowy sleeves and long skirts of their mothers. He could remember particularly how hot and uncomfortable his own Sunday suit was, and that his father had not wanted to go, and thus leave his clerk, Elmer Thomas, alone in the store.

"It's hot, and there will be a big run on the soda fountain," Mr. Goodwin said, "and Elmer's always dropping glasses."

"Now don't be hard on Elmer," Mrs. Goodwin said. "He can run the store for once, and you can have a good time with the children and me for once. They'll be grown-up and gone before we know it, and besides it's educational for the children."

"What's educational?" Mr. Goodwin asked.

"Why, the parade."

"What?" asked Mr. Goodwin. "Seeing a lot of old men out of step?"

"The militia will be marching, too," Mrs. Goodwin said, "and besides, Father and Mother want to see the children."

The boys were playing tag around the open trolley cars in the square, climbing on the running boards, whistling and yelling and getting ordered off again.

"Robert," Mrs. Goodwin said, "don't you think it would be nice to give the children a soda at the store before they start? They'll all be thirsty before they get to Nashua."

As soon as she asked if it would be nice, Melville knew that his father would agree.

"Well, all right, Mother," he said, "but I don't want the children thinking they can go in any time and get free sodas. I caught Harry yesterday behind the fountain helping himself to Moxie. They'll have to have sarsaparilla today. We're overstocked on sarsaparilla."

Melville still enjoyed sarsaparilla when he could get it, not root beer but regular sarsaparilla, although it was never as good as it used to be in Hallowell.

The store was cool and shadowy that morning, full of the clean smells of perfume, soap and chemicals.

"Sarsaparilla for everybody, Elmer," Mr. Goodwin said, "and you can have one for yourself. Easy, Elmer, on that syrup. Here, I'll fix these up myself."

"Now, Robert," Mrs. Goodwin said, "Elmer is fixing the sodas very nicely."

"All right, Mother," Mr. Goodwin said, "but just remember we have to get a living off this store. Melville, take your drink right down, and don't blow bubbles through the straw."

"Now, Robert," Mrs. Goodwin said, "don't worry over everything. Melville's only trying to make it last."

"By jingo," Mr. Goodwin said, "it's lucky somebody worries in this family. What are you looking at over there, Harry?"

"At the candy," Harry said. "How about a licorice stick, Pa?"

"Oh well," Mr. Goodwin said, "seeing it's a holiday, give them each three pink gumdrops, Elmer, and hurry with your sarsaparilla, Melville. It's time the cars were starting."

Four veterans of the GAR were going to march in the parade, and everyone hung back to let them get on first. They were old men but still able to get around without canes, and their black felt hats and blue uniforms gave them a dignity which they completely lacked at other times of the year. Then Sam Jacques, the motorman, began calling to everyone else to get aboard, and he said the little ones could ride with him up front.

"You, Melly," he said, "you can get up front."

Melville found himself sitting next to Muriel Reece but he did not consider it a privilege. Muriel was a dumpy, fat little girl, with hair the same color as his own.

"Melville Goodwin," Mrs. Reece called to him, "you take good care of Muriel."

"Yes, Melville," Mrs. Goodwin called, "you take good care of Muriel," and then she said to Mrs. Reece loud enough for Melville to hear, "Don't they make a cute little couple?"

"What are you chewing on in your mouth?" Muriel asked.

"It's a gumdrop," Melville said.

"Well, give me one," Muriel said.

It was not fair, having to give up his last gumdrop. As far as he could recall, he did not say another word to Muriel all the way to Nashua. When she said it was nice riding up front, he did not bother to answer, and when she told him to stop squirming, he did not bother to answer. If anyone had told him that Muriel Reece would be his best girl someday, he never would have believed it; but it was nice riding up front in the trolley car to Nashua with the singing and the shouting behind him, with the soft May wind on his face, with the buds of the oak trees reddish pink and with the apple blossoms out and with a dizzying sense of speed. Trolley cars moved very fast in those days.

He hardly recognized his Grandfather Allen in his GAR uniform. The old man had kept his figure and he looked tall and straight in it, and he had spent good money to have it tailored to fit him. Furthermore he wore riding gauntlets which were not regulation, but they were a part of his old cavalry equipment.

"Well, well," he said. "Melville, ask your grandmother to give you a quarter of a dollar, and take your hat off when the flag goes by. I must be getting down the street. Will you have a cigar, Robert?"

"No thanks," Mr. Goodwin said.

"Well, I will," Mr. Allen said, "and there's a little something in the parlor cupboard if you're thirsty, Robert." He walked away down the street with his riding gauntlets stuck in his belt, blowing rank puffs from his Pittsburgh stogie.

"Oh dear," Melville heard his mother whisper, "I'm afraid Father's started drinking."

If he had, Melville often thought, the old man knew how to hold his liquor and it had done him more good than harm that day in Nashua.

Perhaps it was not a good parade according to later standards, but Melville had no basis for comparison that morning. It was the first time he had ever heard a military band—if you could call the Nashua band military, when it played "Marching through Georgia." It was the first time he had ever seen the colors on parade. The beat of the band had put life into the wavering marching columns, even into the GAR. He had no way of knowing then that the volunteer militia company, sweating in their thick dress uniforms behind the veterans of the recent war with Spain, was an unimpressive outfit. He had never seen shouldered muskets. He had never heard an order given. The sight of that uneven marching company took Melville's breath away, and before he knew it he found himself on the street following the parade with other boys from Nashua. The band was like the flute of the Pied Piper playing its tune to childhood. He would have followed the band anywhere and perhaps that band was playing for him still.

He was still "Marching through Georgia" when he sat on the steps of his grandfather's front porch later listening to the old men talk. There was no doubt by then that old Mr. Allen and his contemporaries had been drinking. Their coats were unbuttoned, their hats were off and their tongues were very loose. One of the old men was talking about Malvern Hill and another was speaking of Fredericksburg, and his grandfather was saying that he had personally seen General Grant.

"Well now, Melville," his grandfather said, "maybe you'll go to a war sometime yourself—but maybe you'd better run inside now. . . . Wait a minute. Here's a twenty-five-cent piece for you."

The Glorious Fourth

By Ross Lockridge, Jr.

No other day could compare with the Fourth of July. It was the best. The rockets soared as high as the moon, the brass bands aroused our patriotic fervor, and the yellowjackets buzzed around the picnic watermelon. In *Raintree County* Ross Lockridge described the court house square and the excited crowd that gathered on Independence Day to hear the orators and the hair-restorer salesmen, to bet on the footrace and learn the wonders of phrenology.

July 4— —1854

BIG CROWD OF PEOPLE

HAD POURED INTO THE COURT HOUSE SQUARE

of Freehaven for the Fourth of July Celebration. Among them was Johnny Shawnessy, fifteen years old, bony and angular and beginning to bust out of his kneepants. His head looked too big for his body, his hair was a tangled mat of brightness, his cheeks and chin showed the beginnings of a beard and were sprinkled with little pimples. From a platform erected on the court house yard, a military band blasted out number after number, while the people came streaming from every corner of the County, into the foursided, sunflooded morning of the Square. There they walked with shining eyes, looking over their shoulders, craning their necks, bobbing out from behind buildings as if they were hunting for something. . . .

His brother Zeke was waving from in front of the Saloon. In the middle of a crowd there, a young man stood, white teeth flashing from a brown bearded face. In one hand he held a beermug, and with the other he kept pushing back the brown shag of his hair. His skintight pants showed off the hard length of his legs and the great breadth of his white-shirted chest and shoulders. The young man laughed and said in a harsh, high voice, as Johnny approached.

—I can beat any man or boy in the County, and here's five dollars says I can.

He buried his white teeth in the mug and came up, mouth and beard shining. A gold coin glinted in his free hand. A hush fell on the crowd. Two men removed their hats, perhaps to see better. Johnny joined Zeke on the edges of the crowd.

—I said I can lick any man or boy in this County.

—And he can do it too, a solemn, sharpfaced man confided to Johnny. Just like he says, can't none of 'em touch 'im. Flash Perkins kin outrun 'em all.

From this remark, Johnny gathered that the talk was about the annual Fourth of July Footrace by which the fastest runner in Raintree County was determined.

—Our boy from Prairie Township'll make yuh eat them words this afternoon, a voice in the crowd said.

—Who said that? Flash Perkins said.

His forehead shot up into ridges, his mouth went on smiling, his eyes never changed from the childlike, excited look. He shoved his way into the crowd.

—Hot darn! Zeke said. A fight!

The crowd withdrew leaving one man alone in a ring of red faces. The man, a tall gawky fellow, looked embarrassed and put upon. He extended his arm, his finger almost touching Flash Perkins' nose.

—Take it easy now, brother, he said. Better not start nothin' you cain't finish.

His voice was high and nervous.

—You the man that said that? Flash Perkins asked.

—Yes, I am. I said it, and I stick by it.

—Reckon you wouldn't want to cover that there statement with a little coin?

The man looked relieved.

—I cain't cover it by myself, but they's a bunch of us from Prairie will make up a pot for Pud Foster.

—Git a hat, said a voice.

—Here's a hat, said a voice.

—Who's here'll back Pud Foster from Prairie?

—I'll put in, a man said. He can beat any beersot from town any day.

Several men shoved their way in and began to talk bets. There was a frightful blast of sound. It was the band starting up again. They were playing 'Yankee Doodle.'

—Shucks, Zeke said. No fight.

—But that sure ought to be some race, Johnny said.

—What's going on, boys?

It was T. D. He was taller than anyone else in the crowd. His blond pointed beard was bobbing up and down. He was rubbing his hands together and smacking his lips.

—They're betting on a race, Johnny said.

—That's what I thought, T. D. said.

He pushed his way into the crowd.

—Gambling is a sin before the Lord, gentlemen. Put up your money.

—Put up your lip, you old she-goat, a man said.

The crowd roared.

—Pa's gittin' hisself into something, Zeke said. Looks like they might be a fight after all, and us in it.

—No harm done, Pop, Flash Perkins said. Here, give the old guy a drink.

—Who is that crazy old bastard, anyway? the solemn, sharpfaced citizen said to Zeke.

—That's my pa, Zeke said.

Zeke was seventeen and looked a man. His red hair bristled all directions.

—What's that? the man said.

—I said that's my father.

—O, the man said. Is that a fact?

He looked thoughtful and began to move away through the crowd.

—Young man, T. D. said to Flash Perkins, who was holding his beer-mug in one hand and a hatful of money in the other, don't you know that your body is a temple of the spirit and you defile it and pollute it with that devil's brew you have there?

Flash's forehead made ridges.

—If you say so, Pappy.

—Hello, Johnny.

It was Ellen Shawnessy, her face excited and curious, her small body straining on tiptoes to see over the shoulders of the crowd.

—What's T. D. doing? she asked.

—Pa's preaching a little at them.

T. D. went on talking awhile about the lusts of the flesh and the wages of sin. He clasped his hands behind his back in the usual way and teetered back and forth from heels to toes, smiling amiably at the crowd, his long blue eyes a little absent and noticing things that went on some distance away. His closing remarks were delivered in some haste, like a child's recitation.

—What are they betting about? Ellen whispered to Johnny.

—The Footrace, Johnny said.

—When is it?

—I don't know.

—Be sure not to let me miss it, she said.

—O.K., O.K. Reverend, I get it, Flash Perkins said. We were just foolin'.

T. D. bowed pleasantly, straightened his tie, and walked serenely down the street with Ellen. The crowd went right on arguing and making bets, only now they all moved into the Saloon and got drinks. Johnny could see through the batwing doors how they laughed and swatted each other's backs and how they kept wiping beer out of their mustaches.

—I hope he loses that race, Zeke said.

But Johnny somehow felt that Flash Perkins would win the race. He looked like the winner type.

—Ladies and Gentlemen, spare me a little of your precious time, boomed a rich voice from the court house lawn.

Behind a table loaded with brightcolored bottles, stood a man with noble black mane and heavy beard, unshorn, lustrous, magnificent.

—I trust you all perceive the object which I hold in my hand, the man said, as the boys joined the crowd.

—Yes, we see it, Perfessor.

—What is it?

—Well, what of it?

—It is nothing, the man said, but a bottle, a simple, unadorned, ordinary bottle. And yet, friends, this simple, plain, unadorned, and ordinary bottle contains in it a secret preparation, the miracle-worker of our age. Ladies and Gentlemen, may I have just a little of your precious time to describe to you the extree-ordinary virtues of the elixir contained in this bottle?

—Sure. Go on.

—Get to the point, Perfessor.

—I am getting to the point, the man said serenely, and judging, my good sir, from the condition of *your* scalp and hair, you would be wise to pay special heed to what I have to say.

The man who had said, Get to the point, was standing right beside Johnny. He was a short man, genteelly dressed. Singled out, he put his hand up and smoothed a wreath of hair fitted down on his bare dome.

—Now then, the speaker continued, I trust you will all permit me to indulge in a little personal reminiscence. I am sure that few of you will believe me when I tell you that not many years ago my head was fast approaching the condition of hairlessness that you behold in the gentleman on the front row and in several other domes which I see about me here and which are, in the words of the poet,

Open unto the fields and to the sky,
All bright and glittering in the smokeless air.

Now I think we will agree that the good Lord never does anything without a purpose, and if he meant mankind to go about with his skull naked of hair, why did he bestow upon us this lush and luxuriant foliage that in our natural state starts and stands triumphantly, according to the words of the poet,

With all its fronds in air?

Fellow Americans, the good Lord intended each and every one of us to have his hair and all of it too, for as the fellow said about his wife, She ain't much, but I mean to hang on to her if I can.

The crowd whahwhahed.

—Yes, Ladies and Gentlemen, I was once in the condition of several of you here. For about twenty years, my hair had been turning gray and had become very stiff and unpliant. Bald patches were appearing on my scalp, and the skin scaled off. Each time I brushed my hair, I found the brush matted with dry tufts of hair. I tried all the famous hair restoratives on the market, but they seemed to only aggravate my condition. Then a friend told me about Mrs. Allen's World Hair Restorer and reported to me the marvellous recoveries effected thereby. I will confess to you that I was very skeptical at first, but on the repeated importunities of my friend, I finally gave in and purchased a bottle of Mrs. Allen's World Hair Restorer. Ladies and Gentlemen, need I say more? Within a week or two, a noticeable change was apparent. My hair began to recover the black lustre it had in my younger days when a boy in the hills of western Virginia. My head became entirely clear of dandruff, and new hair grew where the old had been. You see before you today, Ladies and Gentlemen, a man whose pride and hair have been restored together and general health improved. Butler, my acquaintances often remark to me, where did you get the fine wig? But I assure you, friends, it is no wig.

—It looks like a wig to me, friend, the baldheaded man said.

—Pull it, friend, the vender said.

The baldheaded man walked right out of the crowd and carefully examined the speaker's head. He pulled hard.

—No sir, he said, that's no wig.

—You bet it isn't, the speaker said. It's hair, friend, live and lusty, and you can have a head like that too, friend.

—How can I, friend? said the baldheaded man, now standing beside the speaker.

—Very simple, friend. Purchase one bottle of Mrs. Allen's World Hair Restorer for one dollar and fifty cents, and I will personally guarantee that you will have the beginnings of a fine head of hair in a week or two.

—I'll take a bottle of that, the baldheaded man said.

He pulled out a dollar and a half and gave it to the speaker.

—And just to be sure that you get your money's worth, the speaker said, I am going to give away to you free, gratis, and for no extra charge this large bottle of Doctor Hostetter's Celebrated Stomach Waters, guaranteed to cure any and all diseases of the alimentary tract, nervous, respiratory, muscular, and circulatory systems—to wit, stomach ache, heartburn, dyspepsia, diarrhea, dysentery, dizziness, fainting spells, biliousness, piles, pimples, arthritis, lumbago, rheumatism, jaundice, kidney trouble, female complaints, and organic weaknesses caused by youthful indiscretion or the approach of old age. For the next ten minutes, to everyone who can get up here with a dollar and fifty cents, I will make this extra-special-gigantic-double-for-your-money offer of two bottles. Mrs. Allen's World Hair Restorer is also an excellent hair-dressing for the ladies.

—I'll take *two* orders, Perfessor, said the baldheaded man, who was still holding his money and had not yet got his hands on the bottle.

—Here you are, my friend, the man said.

He gave the baldheaded man four bottles and put the money in his pocket.

The baldheaded man opened a bottle of the hair-restorer, shot a little of the brown liquid into the cup of his hand, and rubbed it on his head. There was a silence. A hundred eager faces watched the little man with the shiny bald head.

—It tingles, said the baldheaded man.

—You bet it does, friend, the vender said. It tingles, and that means it's taking already. Use that bottle religiously, friend, and I predict the barbers of this community will get a lot of your money before the year is out.

—But he ain't from this community, a man next to Johnny said.

—Where's he from? another man said.

—I dunno, the first man said, but I never seen him before.

—And, said the vender, let me be the first to congratulate you on the great discovery which you have just made. Your wife will be a happy woman, friend.

—I'm not married, friend, said the baldheaded man.

—You will be, friend, you will be! said the vender magnificently. No woman in town will be able to resist you when you grow the shiny, black, and vigorous head of hair that will spring up in response to the stimulating power of this wonderful hair restorative.

Johnny Shawnessy felt happy because the baldheaded man had discovered the secret for getting back his hair; he was very happy, too, to see how people flocked up and bought bottle after bottle from the vender. He could not remember ever having seen so much money in so short a time.

—How can he make any money, giving that other bottle away? Johnny asked.

—I reckon he does it for fun, Zeke said. Look how he's enjoyed hisself.

—I wish I had a dollar and fifty cents, Johnny said. I'd like to get a couple of bottles.

—But you got all your hair, and you ain't sick, Zeke said.

—Just the same— Johnny said.

Just then the band struck up again, and the two boys moved reluctantly away. They watched the baldheaded man withdraw from the crowd. Moving along close to this person whose scalp now seemed to shine with the promise of reviving hair, they were a little surprised when he stopped at a small tent on the other side of the Square and went in. They waited, and in a moment, he came out again, carrying a large board frame, which he hung over a nail on a maple tree beside the tent. The frame bore a huge picture of a head, seen in profile and with all the upper part, beginning on a level with the eye, divided into sections, in each of which a word was written. Some of the words were Acquisitiveness, Alimentativeness, Amativeness, Cautiousness, Sublimity, Spirituality, Self-Esteem, Approbativeness. Above the picture were the words

PROFESSOR GLADSTONE, WORLD-RENOWNED PHRENOLOGIST

At the bottom were the words

KNOW THYSELF

The little man re-entered the tent and reappeared with a pointer, an armload of small clothbound books, and a cowbell, which he began to ring. A large crowd gathered.

—Allow me, said the baldheaded man, to introduce myself, Ladies and Gentlemen. I am Professor Horace Gladstone. Those of you who may have heard me lecture in the great city of Cincinnati will pardon me if I repeat some of the things I said there to the distinguished company which assembled in the great lecture hall of that metropolis of the West.

Now I have a question to ask each and every intelligent person gathered here. Friend, are you everything today that you would like to be? Are you as rich as you wish? Do you excel in the social graces? Do you radiate that personal magnetism which makes the great to respect you and the humble to acknowledge your superiority? Why, friends, *why* are there so many blighted and unhappy lives, so many stunted souls, so many men and women today in this great and glorious country of ours who are something less than they had hoped to be in the blithe optimism of their youth?

Ladies and Gentlemen, I can answer that question. It is through a simple ignorance of the scientific principles that regulate human life. O, you say, Perfessor, don't go giving me any high-falutin' language about science because I can't understand it. Friends, it is my happy good fortune to have it within my power to open up to each and every one of you all the marvellous secrets of a great new science, by which you can achieve, like thousands before you, complete self-knowledge and self-control. That science, Ladies and Gentlemen, is the great new science of Phrenology.

Now we all agree, do we not, that no man can or does exist in rational society without a brain. May I say that in Kentucky, whence I have lately come, I felt some disposition to modify that statement, but—

The Professor waited for the applause and laughter of the crowd to subside.

—But I see no need to do so for the intelligent and enlightened concourse that I see before my eyes. Now, we all know that the brain is the instrument of every mental act, just as every movement of the body has to be performed by a muscle. Certain areas of the brain control certain human faculties and are large or small in proportion to the development of the faculties they control. Thanks to the great experiments and studies of Professors Gall, Spurheiz, and Fowler, it is now possible to say with the strictest accuracy which part of the brain controls which faculty. These facts are now available to all. Nothing is simpler, once these principles are known, than to apply them.

I have myself become a specialist in the science of Phrenology. I have examined the heads of three Presidents and many other great and distinguished heads here and abroad, not excepting the crowned heads of Europe. By helping people to become better acquainted with their strong and weak points, I have been able to direct them to a fuller exercise or restraint of certain faculties. Many hundreds and thousands of people have already benefited from this instruction. Penniless paupers have become the possessors of uncounted pelf. Timid and backward souls have sought and won the hands of the richest and most ravishing maidens. Old men have recovered the lost joys of their juvenescence. Gentleman and Ladies, I am here in your fair little city of Middletown—

—This ain't Middletown, said a voice in the crowd. It's Freehaven.

—Freehaven, said the Professor. Thank you, friend, for the correction. I am here in this fair little city of Freehaven for a limited time. I have a small stock of books left over from my travels in the great cities of the West, and I should like to get rid of them as rapidly as I can. Now I wish I could give each and every one of you a private and personal analysis of your phrenological faculties. Alas, my friends, due to the small time I have at my disposal, I must forego this signal pleasure. But I have here between my two hands a little book that contains all the advice needful. It is perfectly within the comprehension of every one and each of you. On the inside page of this book is a copy of the chart which you see hanging here, and a table of the phrenological faculties. Now the book is entirely self-explanatory, but I am willing to give a little demonstration here of Phrenological Analysis, if someone in the crowd will be so kind as to volunteer.

There was a silence.

—Come, don't be embarrassed, the Professor said. It's absolutely free of charge, and furthermore I will give to anyone who so volunteers for the instruction of this amiable and enlightened company one of these books at half-price instead of the usual price of one dollar and fifty cents.

Johnny Shawnessy felt himself propelled from behind out of the crowd.

He heard Zeke laughing, and he was about to duck back, but the Professor was tapping him smartly on the shoulder with his pointer.

—Yes, my boy. Step right up here. I am about to do you a great favor, my boy. O, that I had had the inestimable blessing of a Phrenological Analysis when I was your age! How old are you, my boy?

—Fifteen, Johnny said. I didn't mean to—

—Perfectly all right, my boy. Just come up on this platform and sit down here on the edge of this table.

A firecracker exploded, and the band struck up a number. The Professor waved his hands to indicate that nothing could be accomplished until the band was through. For the first time in his life, Johnny had the sensation of being extracted from the crowd and placed above it in naked isolation. The Court House Square was converging upon him; he was being absorbed by its manifold bright eyes. The band stopped playing.

—Ladies and Gentlemen, said the little man, we have an interesting head here, a very interesting head. To you, this may be only another head, more or less, but to the practiced eye of the phrenologist, this boy's character and potentialities—nay, his whole past, present, and future—are legible in the geography of his skull. Now, then, just cast your eyes on this chart a moment, friends, and notice this section of the head below the eye.

The pointer touched the glazed, segmented head and underlined the word LANGUAGE.

—According to phrenological principles, friends, we are to measure the degree of prominence which these various areas of the skull possess and we can determine thereby the capabilities of the person we are dealing with. Now then—

A fat hand touched moistly the region below Johnny's eyes.

—Open your eyes, boy. Don't sit there blinking like an owl.

As usual the sun hurt his eyes; there was much light in the Square.

—Extraordinary, the man said. Very.

The crowd drew closer. People gathered from far back.

—Very, very interesting. Please observe, folks. Very long eyes and set somewhat forward in the head. Cheekbones prominent. In a boy of fifteen, the development is quite unusual. Now, then, let us turn to the book.

The man expertly thumbed the book.

—Here we are. 'Such people are (I quote) exceedingly expressive in all they say and do, have a most expressive countenance, eye, and manner in everything, and thoroughly impress the various operations of their own minds on the minds of others; use the very word required by the occasion; are intuitively grammatical, even without study, and say oratorically whatever they attempt to say at all; commit to memory by reading or hearing once or twice; learn languages with remarkable facility; are both fluent and copious, even redundant and verbose,' and so forth, and so forth.

There was a stir in the crowd.

—Here, the man said, are pictures illustrating these developments. An engraving of the great English author Charles Dickens, whose linguistic characteristics are excessively developed.

—Say, Perfessor, Zeke said from the crowd, you ain't fer wrong about that boy. He's got a head for memorizing like nothin' you ever seen.

—There you are, the little bald man said, Phrenology never lies. And I was about to say that even if the boy hadn't shown any faculty in that direction, it was high time he cultivated his natural aptitude for it. But to pass on.

The Professor went all over Johnny's head, pointing out interesting hills and hollows and putting numbers in a chart that was in the front of one of the books. Finally, the Professor had worked clear over the top of Johnny's head and down to the base of his skull behind.

—Mirthfulness, the Professor said. Very large. This boy ought to be the fiddle of the company.

—Ain't that T. D. Shawnessy's son? a man said.

—Smart little cuss, someone said.

—What a cute boy! a woman said.

The band blew up; it was another march. Everyone began talking very loud and strong. People were laughing violently. Somebody set off a firecracker under a fat man in the crowd and blew his hat off. A horse got scared and began dragging a buggy down the street. The band finished its number, and by that time the Professor had made another discovery.

—Very remarkable! the Professor said in a loud voice. For a boy of his age too. Most extree-ordinary! Unusual, to say the least.

—What is it, Perfessor?

The crowd was now participating freely in the examination.

—Let us in on it, too, Perfessor.

—Has he got lice?

—Ladies and Gentlemen, the Professor said, please observe the remarkable development of this boy's head at the base of the skull. The lump of AMATIVENESS is remarkably distended.

—What does that mean, Perfessor?

—What does that mean, friend? To put it bluntly, this young gentleman is going to be an extra-special catch for the ladies.

The Professor winked and rubbed his hands jovially together. People in the crowd sniggered. Various men felt the back of their skulls.

—Hey, girls, Zeke said, I got a lump back there big as a duck's egg.

—Say, Perfessor, said a little man thrusting forward, and presenting his head for inspection. Feel that there. What do you think of that?

With obliging hand the Professor palped the back of the little man's skull and whistled.

—Hey, Perfessor, how about me? another man said. Feel that.

—Now, wait a minute, folks, the Professor said, suddenly walking back to the platform and grabbing an armload of books. Much as I would like to, I can't subject each and all of you to a personal scrutiny, but this book here will answer all your questions. For those whose various organs and faculties are underdeveloped, rules for enlargement are given. Know thyself, said the great philosopher Socrates to the Athenians in the Golden Age of Greece. And I say to you, Know thyself, fellow Americans, in this great age of Progress and Perfection, in this greatest and fairest republic the world has ever known. God bless her on the day of her birth and glorious founding! One dollar, folks, just one round dollar —reduced from a dollar and a half!

As if by prearrangement, the band exploded with 'Hail, Columbia! Happy Land!' and with moisture in his eyes, the Professor began to distribute books as fast as he could, at the same time dropping dollars into a box on the table. Johnny sat for a while watching from the platform how the people all rushed up and pulled dollars out of their pockets, rudely grabbing for books in their haste.

—While they last! While they last! the Professor said. One dollar, friends, while they last! One hundred and fifty-four illustrations. *Phrenological Self-Instructor*.

People who hadn't even heard what the Professor said fought their way through and bought a book. The pile was almost gone, and Johnny Shawnessy began to feel alarmed.

—Know thyself! Know thyself! One dollar. While they last.

The pile was gone.

—One moment, folks, the Professor said. I have a small reserve supply that I had hoped to save for sale in the great city of St. Louis.

He disappeared in the tent and reappeared immediately with another armload of books. When the last sale had been made, there were still some books left. Johnny went up to the man and put down seventy-five cents.

—It's a dollar, my friend, the Professor said.

—But you said I could have it half-price. Half of a dollar and a half is—

—Unusual development of the bumps of Calculation and Eventuality, the Professor said.

He laughed at his own good joke.

—Here's your book, boy, all marked. You've a good head on your shoulders there, son. What is your name, my boy?

Johnny told him, and the Professor took a pencil from his coat pocket and on the title page where it said THE CHART AND CHARACTER OF he wrote on blank lines provided for the purpose:

John Wickliff Shawnessy

As Marked By

Professor Horace Gladstone,
July 4, 1854

—I predict a great future for you, my boy, the Professor said, tossing the three quarters deftly into the air.

He bit the tip off a cigar.

—Smoke?

—No, thanks, sir.

—Never start it, said the Professor. Filthy habit. Yes, a great future, my boy. Tell me, son, is there a place around here where one can obtain a little liquid refreshment for the stimulation of a jaded physique?

—The Saloon is right over there.

—Good day, boy, the Professor said and walked off briskly, landing smartly on his heels, his toes turned slightly up and out.

—Ladies and Gentlemen, said at that moment a rich, oily voice from the other side of the Square, spare me a little of your precious—

Johnny walked away holding the little book in his hand. For a few bright coins, dropped in a wooden cigar box, a future of wonderful self-mastery had been opened up. In the presence of the people he had become a child of prophecy; his consecration had been sanctified by the majestic adjective 'scientific' and the formidable epithet 'phrenological.' Here, suddenly and by accident on the Court House Square, there had been a confirmation of something Johnny Shawnessy had always secretly believed—that he was destined to be a great man and to find one day the key to all knowledge. For a while, he felt jealous of all the other people who had purchased the same cheap ticket to intellectual beatitude, but when he saw the innocent, shy joy on their faces, as they wandered somewhat confusedly like himself in the Court House Square, clutching their *Self-Instructors*, he was thrilled to think that he was to be one of a whole community of Americans working together toward the creation of a perfect republic.

He didn't have time to look over the book at all, because the Program for the Day was beginning. He and Zeke went over and found seats in a big space in the assembly ground south of the Court House, and all the people sat and listened to a man read the Declaration of Independence. Then the chairman of the program introduced the outstanding boy orator Garwood Jones. Talking in a thundering, artificial way and waving his arms, Garwood brought the crowd down with gems of American oratory, including the peroration of Webster's Reply to Hayne.

Wearing his Mexican War uniform and all his medals, Captain Jake Jackson, Raintree County's war hero, got up and gave a very dramatic speech about the security of the Nation. He was a virile young man, of open, fearless countenance. He stood very straight with one leg slightly forward and spoke with chest expanded. He said that the Union was threatened from within and without, but he reminded his hearers that the last bunch who tangled with the sovereign authority of the United States of America had got one devil of a drubbing, in which he, Jake Jackson, had taken, as they knew, a humble part. And he was there to say that although he was a man who loved peace, he, Jacob J. Jackson, would personally Gird on the Sword and once more Bare his Patriot Breast to the Sleet of Battle ere he would permit one corner of the Dear Old Flag to be Dragged in the Dirt. Johnny applauded violently and was angry when an older man close by said he was getting goddam tired of young Jackson's heroics and fuh Christ's sake, did he think he fought the Mexican War singlehanded?

The Honorable Somebody or Other was introduced for the Address of the Day. He spoke for two hours, beginning in the usual vein but getting louder, hoarser, and more eloquent all the time. . . .

—Fellow Americans, he said, I am addressing you in one of the darkest hours that has confronted our great republic since those glorious days when Washington was nursing the tiny flickering flame of our freedom in a tattered tent in the windy wilderness of Valley Forge. It is a time when, if necessary, a man should put aside wife and child, leave the hearth of his home, and go resolutely forth to do battle for the preservation of those great principles upon which this republic was founded and which we have just heard read to us from that immortal document, the Declaration of Independence.

—Let them alone, and they'll leave us alone, shouted a voice from the crowd.

—Throw that guy out! yelled other voices.

—It is a time, said the speaker, to gird on armor and the sword. Our most pious blessing and our most fervent hopes must go with those courageous spirits who are at this moment giving up all they have to rush into the newly opened territories of Kansas and Nebraska to insure that when those territories are petitioning for membership in the Union of the States, no shadow of that cursed blight whose ancient crime has stained the otherwise perfect beauty of our institutions shall sully the virginal banners of their statehood.

The orator went on and on, and the afternoon waned, and when he finished, the formal program was over. . . .

—The race is starting!

Naked to the waist and barefooted, Flash Perkins stood in the middle of a crowd at a street intersection one block from the Square.

—What do you think this is, Flash—a prize fight? someone yelled as the two boys came up.

For answer, Flash struck a pose, balled fists up. The muscles of his cocked arms bulged circularly. The afternoon bathed his body with a young radiance. He seemed stronger and more real than anything else in the exploding vortex of the Fourth of July.

—God, don't he think he's some punkins! said a man next to Johnny.

—Struttin' aroun' like a damn bull on show, said another man. I hope to hell he gets beat and beat proper.

—Pud Foster'll beat 'im, damn 'im, said the first man. They say this here Perkins has been drinkin' his guts full all day and can't hardly walk.

—Seems to me he walks all right, the first man said.

—Yeh, but can he run?

—If he's drunk, maybe it'd be smart to take some of his money, said the first man.

—Damn right it would be!

It got around the crowd that Perkins was filled to the ears and could hardly stand, and a lot of men began to take some of the Perkins money.

Meanwhile Flash Perkins had gone over to a nearby buggy and then back to the starting line. His hairline jumped up each time he smiled. His eyes, full of drunkenness and goodnatured insolence, had never lost the childlike, excited look.

—They's a young lady over here, he said, wants to bet somebody five dollars a certain galoot name of Orville Perkins, better known as Flash, will win this here race. Person'ly, I respect the sex too much to doubt this young lady's opinion, and I'll add another five dollars to her bet and bet anybody here that I can beat any man in Raintree County—or anywhere else, by God!—and let's see the color of his coin.

—Christ amighty! he's drunk! the first man said.

A rather dowdy girl in the buggy fanned herself vigorously.

—It must be her, that one over there, Zeke said. She's some looker.

—I'll bet he gets her regular, a man in the crowd said.

Those days, there was always someone in the crowd who took a cynical view of things.

All of a sudden a man walked into the street with a pistol in his hand.

—Ladies and Gentlemen, he yelled, the Annual Fourth of July Footrace is ready to start. The contestants are . . .

The runners lined up, the crowd began pushing out of the street, the starter's pistol went off, and everyone yelled and pushed and shoved down toward the Square where the race was to end. Johnny got a passing glimpse of Flash Perkins, white teeth bared, fists churning, far ahead of his competitors as he ran toward a distant string.

There was a vast yelling in the Court House Square, and several cannon crackers blew up simultaneously. The band played 'Hail to the Chief.'

When Johnny and Zeke got to the Square, they saw Flash Perkins on the shoulders of a throng. He was borne toward a platform where a girl sat holding a ring of oakleaves. Bare to the waist, sweating, magnificent, he accepted the circlet of victory and fitted it down over his tangled hair. His teeth were clenched on an unlit cigar.

—Speech! yelled the crowd.

—It was easy, folks, Flash said. They give me a good race, but like I said, I can beat any man in Raintree County. . . .

That night there was a fireworks display on the court house yard. Rockets rose over the dark town, burst into sparks, and went down, feebly flaming, in distant fields. Some exhibition pieces were hung on trees, and the climax of the whole day came with a contraption called 'The Glorious Union.' It was supposed to burn like a lot of stars and stripes in the shape of a shield, but it fizzled at first.

—It ain't goin' to go, everyone said.

Then it did go after all; in fact it caught on fire and blew up all at once with a terrific bang.

As they drove home that night, Johnny told T. D. about the book on Phrenology.

—What do you think about it, Pa? Is it any good?

—Sounds scientific, T. D. said. I seen the man giving you a going-over. Of course, it might of been a fraud. You shouldn't of spent all that money for it, John. You could of looked at someone else's book. . . .

Johnny Shawnessy looked up at the purple night thicksown with stars that brooded warm and yellow over Raintree County. Yes, things would work out all right. He closed his eyes and seemed to see, ascending in a starless night, the thin, bright streaks of rockets. So would the years go speeding through the purple night of time and bring him all good things before they dropped, feebly flaming, in the distant meadows of the future. So would he too some day know fame and fortune and a great love, and the people in the Court House Square would cheer him. Time and the secret earth of Raintree County would bring all good fruits to him who knew the secret. One day, he would be the fastest runner in Raintree County, because he willed it to be so. One day he would stand with breast expanded, bright with medals, and the crowds would cheer the savior of the Nation.

Town Meeting

By John Gould

The annual meeting of voters to choose selectmen and decide weighty issues is the purest example of democracy in action. A man is not only allowed to speak his mind, but accorded the respect of his neighbors even if they disagree with him. In the following account John Gould takes us to a traditional New England town meeting.

Up in the Town Meeting belt we have five seasons. The brief summer is followed by a lingering fall, and the January Thaw settles winter to good sledding. Before spring brings the sap to the maples we have our fifth season. *Mud Season,* we call it, and school is dismissed while roads dry out. Mud Season, like as not, coincides with Town Meeting Time—and horses with blue clay over their gambrels often replace automobiles for the annual trip to town to vote.

The whole family comes—mother and father to vote, and the children to listen and to learn how. Town Meeting Day begins after chores—the moderator is sometimes chosen as early as six-thirty. Events move on with balloting in the forenoon, dinner, appropriations in the afternoon, supper at six, and a Town Meeting dance at night. Commerce, industry, and schooling stop. The entire population—men, women, and children—gather at Town House to deliberate on matters of government for the coming year.

Mud Season is simply the breaking up of a long, hard winter. The frost is coming out of the ground—the beginning of the New England year. Fit time, then, to hold Town Meeting—to examine the accounts of the year past, to elect officers, to appropriate money.

The New England Town differs from community organizations elsewhere in the country. It begins with a geographical boundary and every legal voter within that area enjoys equal rights, whether he lives over his

Main street store or on an eighty-acre piece in the north-end gore. Parishes, districts, townships, and similar distinctions known elsewhere in the nation are unimportant in New England—where even the county is strictly judicial and has few if any administrative functions. Only the state is superior to the Town, and even state legislatures have been set back on their heels occasionally by independent-minded Town Meetings. Also, the Town is uniform throughout New England, but it failed somehow to become established even in adjacent New York. Mattawamkeag, Maine; New Hampton, New Hampshire; Londonderry, Vermont; Williamstown, Massachusetts; Slatersville, Rhode Island; and Southbury, Connecticut, are alike in organization—but different from so-called towns elsewhere in the country. The New England Town arose from the leniency of the old Massachusetts Bay Company that brought settlers to Boston. The citizens are supreme in all matters entrusted to them by the general laws, and so long as matters run smoothly they are answerable to no higher authority than themselves.

Absolute independence characterizes Town Meeting. No one tells a Yankee how to vote, no one dictates; and only another Yankee can persuade. In a world where Democracy perishes, and in a country where self-government occupies every thinking mind, it is startling and refreshing to find New England Town Meeting alive and able and in the hands of a tightfisted people who keep their heritage well.

Just Before the Meeting

Originally Towns assembled at random, whenever problems arose. Later they met only annually and selected leading citizens to handle matters of the meantime. The Selectmen (stress syllables equally, thus—See-lect-men) are assisted by other officers in charge of each municipal department. All are required to make complete reports annually which the Selectmen compiles into printed volumes called Town Report. The basis of competent Town Meeting action is a thorough knowledge of Town Report and New Englanders practically memorize it. Lately a new awareness of Town Meeting importance has led Selectmen to embellish the reports with graphs, tables, and photographs. Appearance as well as information is considered.

Holding town office is not a career. A patriotic enthusiasm induces the candidate and the wages seldom pay expenses. Nor do his official duties interfere too much with his normal vocation. His vocation comes first—his duties in civic affairs often occupy only his Saturday afternoons.

Meeting Day Comes

Town Meeting Day is the climax of a feverish season. The tax collector has sold property on which taxes remained unpaid; Selectmen have printed the Town Report; the warrant has been posted. Caucuses have been held, candidates are lined up. Every item of business to be transacted has had full and complete public discussion. Groups have debated in the store and postoffice. Men have sat by the kitchen stove and considered the reports. Women have talked at sewing circle and Mizpah Class. Children have been holding mock Town Meetings at school. Only Town Meeting itself remains.

The sun, probably, came up red and it will cloud in and be warm. At six o'clock a crust tops the mud and the steps of the Town House creak as a dozen early-comers assemble to elect the moderator. Ollie Brocklebank arrives—first from the Flying Point neighborhood to come and vote for Lin Maybury; Lee Soule hurries in to take part before he goes to the depot to meet the morning train with his express truck; Paul Powers —Freeport attorney—comes in with Roberts' Rules of Order under his arm, all set to be moderator; Al Dyer follows with the Maine Statutes, revised, and the town books—the clerk has to open the meeting. The main body of voters will dribble in all morning—and by noon the Town will be assembled.

Out in the country farmers are hurrying their chores. Women are packing their pots of beans and pies for the trip to town. Village storekeepers are hustling the morning orders. Groups already stand on the street drumming up votes for tax collector. Teachers sketch the morning lessons and close for the day at morning recess. At approximately eight-thirty a highway department truck will rattle out the Wardtown road to dump gravel in a honey-pot near Woodside's—that honey-pot has defeated and elected commissioners many times. By ten-thirty voting is well under way—for "Town Clerk, Selectmen, Assessors and Overseers of the Poor, Road Commissioner, Treasurer, Member of the School Board, and all other necessary Town Officers."

Pretty girls sell dinner tickets. High school students have a tag day for the athletic fund. The Pythian Sisters set up a sandwich booth and jingle *sody* bottles. Everywhere groups with heads together discuss the candidates and afternoon business.

Precisely at noon the moderator hurries out to dinner, and returns to close the polls at one. He names the ballot counters and then calls the

Town to order. While the ballot counters light up cigars and dump the box on a table, the Town settles to a long afternoon. Now they will pass on school funds, highway money, fire protection, street lights, hydrant rental, accept new streets, set the fees for clam licenses, accept bequests for cemetery care, debate pine blister rust control, and maybe argue about parking regulations and zoning ordinances.

Getting Under Way

It takes a minute or two to mark and drop the ballot. After this part of Town Meeting is attended to, the voter has no further duty until afternoon. This leaves the shank of the morning for talk—and the talk is mighty important because it may affect the afternoon voting on appropriations.

". . . and if you remember we raised five hundred dollars. Well now, I watched them, and if they did eighteen dollars' worth of real honest labor all the time I watched, I'll sing. When the fall rains come that culvert snagged up tighter'n a clam and four feet of water stood in my front field. I don't blame Joe s'much as I do the men he had around him, but I'm cussed if I like it, and . . ."

". . . so they come around and unscrewed the light and you couldn't see nothing. I asked how-come, and they told me the see-lectmen told 'em too. Didn't have enough money to keep 'em all going. So we been without lights since July. Economy's all right, but why don't they just take out every other bulb, and leave half of them going—then we can all have *some* light? Every last body on Maple street's here, and . . ."

". . . Hello, Jim, well—glad to see you again. Your wife in? Good! I suppose you'll be asking for another hundred or two on that Beech Hill road? I don't blame you. Tell you what I'll do—you make the motion, and I'll . . ."

". . . if they won't sell them tax-deeds they ought to be made to . . ."

". . . but the best they could do was three per cent. Now if we had the school fund up to date, and could gaffle an extra five hundred for interest from the contingent fund, I'll bet we could go to the very same bank and get two or two-and-a-half . . ."

". . . Vote for him? I did not! Why, when Lillian came home from school that day so itchy the poor child squirmed all night, I went to the health officer and that thing wouldn't say aye, yes, nor no, one way or the other. Just a jellyfish. Nosir! I just left my ballot blank to give me that much satisfaction . . ."

". . . the count of stock showed eighty-five hundred. A revaluation costs money, but people like him would be paying for it, in the end . . ."

"Here comes Hugh now, must be pretty near time to begin. Let's sit over near Margaret, away from that stove . . ."

Chit-chat like this has been going on among small groups all about the hall. A steady stream of other citizens has been coming in, casting ballots, and joining the groups. The warrant has been gone over many times. When Hugh mounts the moderator's platform it is precisely five minutes to one. "Five minutes left to vote," he yells above the hub-bub, "Bring in your ballots!" Five minutes later he brings his claw-hammer gavel down with a final bang. The ballot is closed. It is time to begin the afternoon session.

Hugh clears his throat. "Before proceeding to article six," he says, "I'll call on Reverend Herrick to invoke the blessing of Deity."

Time Out for Dinner

Dinner, in New England, is a noon-day meal. In addition to this special meaning, dinner has an extra significance when applied to one of these baked bean and pie festivals starring the community's best cooks and served for a special occasion. The Granges and Masons have them, and the churches put them on to make money—but of all the New England dinners none can quite touch the Town Meeting dinner. Served in the dining room of a nearby church or Red Men's Hall, it congregates the best food from all the town, not only in quantities but in varieties. The price range is from 25¢ to 35¢, and the menu is not to be attempted by strangers to the climate without the advice of a physician. The Yankee voter just takes it in his stride, and when you feel he must at last be finished—he has another piece of pie.

The dinner is always sponsored by a women's group. Each member brings some part of the meal—a pot of beans, a cake, a pie, a loaf of bread, pickles, cream—until enough is on hand to supply every appetite. It isn't fair to say *beans* and thus dismiss the matter. There are pea beans and yaller-eyes, and kidneys, and Jacob's Cattle, and Soldiers, and Lows Champions, and kinds you don't know. And there are pies; mince and apple and cranberry, raisin and custard and lemon, chocolate and butterscotch and squash, and even that old standby when other pie materials fail—vinegar pie. And there are cakes—all the cakes the Yankee housewife has borrowed, devised, invented, remembered, and thought up, from plain hot-milk cakes to decorated layer cakes with fudge frosting. There are sweet pickles and sour pickles and mixed pickles and mustard pickles and piccalilli; muffins and buns and rolls and bread and crackers; jellies and jams; and whole families of edibles Fannie Farmer never heard of. And while the foregoing may seem a fairish meal to the uninitiated, no mention has yet been made of the meat and potatoes and turnips and squash and beets and carrots and sundry similar edibles with which the really famished may piece out.

The voter sits down before this array, holding his 25¢ ticket, and is served by jolly women who pass with both hands. After concluding the pie courses he returns fortified to Town Hall to give his attention to a cigar and legislation.

Settling Down to Business

Town Meeting is a collection of individualists. When a man arises and cries, "Mr. Moderator!" and is properly recognized, no man living is big enough to make him sit down. So long as he speaks on the subject, uses proper words, and obeys parliamentary procedure he can say what he pleases. And every listening citizen in the hall knows that the same privilege will be extended in turn. So long as anyone wishes to speak, the matter at hand is held open for discussion. Knowing this, the Yankee carries the Town Meeting privileges over into his private life, and likewise into his state and national politics. Town Meeting may have developed the Yankee frame of mind, or the Yankee may have developed Town Meeting, but they go together like pork and beans and one explains the other. Each voter brings his utter independence into the hall, and from the congregation results a majority decision in which unity is attained without anyone's losing the least bit of his own separate self.

A misunderstanding about Town Meeting may be rife throughout the country because of the recent interest in radio and neighborhood forums which have been titled, broadly, *town meetings*. These discussion groups gather to debate problems of the day—indeterminable topics like tariff, unemployment, wars and rumors of wars. Naturally no vote taken can result in definite settlement of the problems, and the forums become merely an intellectual pastime, and clarify public opinion by parading the pros and cons.

The New England Town Meeting is first of all a legislative assembly. Each topic brought up ends in a vote and the result is properly recorded in the books of the Town Clerk. While the argument of the meeting is best remembered, the greater part of the action is taken without debate.

The moderator may go along for two hours without a word from the voters—picking motions out of the air. If a street light costs $12 a year, and the town has a hundred lights, there isn't any point in debating the light bill of $1,200. But after a period of quiet business the town may come to life on an article worth debating.

The debate is to the point, and the moderator will rap for order if a speaker wanders from the text. The variety of the discussion can be a lesson in applied argumentation. The banker will talk from a row of adding machine figures and reduce everything to percentages; the school superintendent will appeal to reason and quote things; the farmers will get to the nub with old sayings and rural similes; the highway workers may swear a bit; the ladies will muckle down to sentiment and the welfare of the children. And if the cross-fire becomes heated the *argumentum ad hominem* is displayed at perihelion.

In its most excited moments, however, Town Meeting is thoroughly dignified. Everyone is wholly serious—although humor may be called in as a hortatory embellishment. It is true that citizens will argue for hours over $50, and then pass a school budget of fifty thousand without a flicker. They will even argue on matters of principle involving no expense whatever—like discontinuing a road. But through it all the voters show a grave concern and display acute awareness—lest someone put something over on them.

The independence of action reaches beyond the town lines, too. In Freeport, one year, the school superintendent was asking for money to make some alteration or other in the system. His speech was to the point, he knew what he was talking about, and he made only one mistake. He concluded: "In the neighboring Town of Yarmouth this plan has been in operation for five years and has proved highly successful—I therefore move that we adopt it in Freeport."

Instantly a farmer up back jumped to his feet and called, "What do we care what they do in Yarmouth?" That was all. The motion was defeated by a thunderous no.

Any article which seeks money with the phrase "in conformity to existing state laws" will start under a handicap. Voters dislike the implication that the state is compelling them to act. Nor has there been any lack of applying this to Federal agencies—the PWA had its first set-back when a New England Town voted unanimously not to have any New Dealings. A Maine Town, offered flood aid by Washington, recorded its decision: ". . . that there may come a time when we need assistance, but until then we will pay our own way and stand on our own feet."

So the moderator drones on, article by article is disposed of. They are small matters, unimportant in the wagging of the world. But they are home matters, the most important governmental problems to those who consider them. And because they view Town Meeting so, the voters carry their independence over to state and national politics. To those with eyes to see it may be significant that Maine and Vermont are the two New England states where Town Meeting survives closest to the form it had when this country was young.

Women Vote Too

The Town Meeting of the old days was a place of cussing and tobacco smoke, with sawdust on the floor. By the time the meeting was really underway the air was so blue that the moderator recognized those in the rear only by voice. Those were the horse days, too, and much of the stable came to meeting. Buffalo and bear coats with a rich country tang rolled in at the front door with a buggy whip in one hand. If the day was brisk, squirrel and 'coon skin caps appeared. The crossroads Cicero used language and spoke from the shoulder—and a spade was always a plain, ordinary, well-handled spade.

The nineteenth amendment jarred these traditions. The next March saw Easter lilies at the moderator's table and the air was pure and sweet. The men hung around outside scarcely daring to come in. The spellbinders were silent, or spoke in fumbling obscurities. The meeting lasted scarce an hour and a half and was heralded as a social failure—albeit the transactions seemed entirely in order.

The years since have changed that, and now some of the ladies use censorable language. They speak with confidence and logic. The women have been known to take meetings into their own hands and contribute outstanding civic improvements. The men still show, by straws in the wind, an unconquerable disapproval, however, even if it means little and gains less. They wear their hats as if the nearest woman were ten miles off, and they frequently mumble together while a woman is speeching.

Women have added sentimentality to Town Meetings. They favor parks and tree planting programs, better school conditions, police protection, and a variety of items the men never worried about. Women will applaud a fine speech—men never did. And a conniving man can often line up the women's vote to his own advantage by sentimental chicanery that would have got him hooted out of meeting twenty-five years ago.

But Town Meeting goes ahead with the women present without any changes in form or effect. The women take to town affairs with interest and enthusiasm, and they are just as independent about it as the men—although they are more inclined to voting as a group than their husbands. Interesting figures should be available, but aren't, on the number of Yankee wives whose votes off-set those of their husbands—and neither party loses sleep over the difference of opinion. A Yankee demands respect for his own frame of mind, and respects that of others.

The women hold office with increasing commonness, discharge their duties efficiently. They do this at a greater sacrifice than the men, too, because there are babies and things. Dishes may stand in the sink, and babies may come in arms, but the average New England wife turns out to vote with laudable enthusiasm.

While Children Learn

Social aspects of Town Meeting hold the interest of children long before they have the slightest knowledge of town affairs. The speeches are fun, and father usually donates a dime for *sody* from the Pythian Sister sandwich booth. At ten the average child knows all but the practical side of Town Meeting. In the next few years, both in school and at meetings, he begins to see the reasons behind the debating and voting. In meeting he watches his elders and in school he participates in mock meetings where the teacher explains *Roberts' Rules of Order*. Whoever Roberts was, he runs New England Town Meeting. Usually the child of eighteen has actually voted in meeting, so well is he grounded. Enthusiasm frequently carries the children away. The discerning moderator will ignore the juvenile hands unless he needs the vote to carry an article in which he is specially interested. If the result is *doubted* the recount simply reveals a forgivable error.

Many men tell of not missing a meeting since they were eight or ten, and since women voted many a baby of tender months has raised his voice in Town Meeting. At twenty-one the new voter is well skilled in Democracy. His youth deters him from arbitrary stands, and his maiden speech falters. But the older folks tell him he did well and show genuine approval of his efforts. Throughout all New England is a kindly attitude toward children at meeting. "The Town's safe as long as the kids take an interest," you'll hear them say.

Another Year Begins

Old Amos Stevens has just jumped at the sound of his name. The whole Town was watching him. Amos always adjourns Town Meeting. Along about article 35 he begins to doze, dropping his beard onto the bosom of his faded pea jacket, and by the time the Town arrives at the last article Amos is sawing them off in grand style. At the end of the meeting the moderator looks at Amos, winks at the Town, and fairly bellows:

"I have a motion to adjourn by AMOS STEVENS!"

As Amos jumps to wakefulness the Town adds with one voice, "Second the motion!" and files slowly out of the hall to bring an end to the meeting. Amos has been adjourning Town Meeting now for years and it brings him his speck of glory in an arena where—twenty or so years ago—he was a dominating figure. It goes in the Town records, too; "Motion to adjourn by Amos Stevens." "Quite a good meeting we had this year," offers Amos as he joins the folks going home.

The folks go home perfectly satisfied. The budget has reached an all-time high of $83,000, making a tax rate of 42 mills—figured, of course, on a very low valuation. The Selectmen are now being sworn in by the Town Clerk and the machinery is already started for the year. If something of unexpected nature comes up—like bridges being washed out in the spring freshet—a special meeting may come during the year, but otherwise the Town will not assemble until another Mud Season comes around.

But matters have been left in good hands. Every cent of the annual budget has been provided by majority concurrence of the voters; every officer is specifically assigned to duties the Town has approved. From Town Meeting the citizen can almost diagram the course of civic matters for the year, allowing only a proper leeway for unpredictables; and if the unpredictable is of major consequence the Town will handle it by a special meeting duly called and convened.

Schools will be operated, roads built, fires put out, the poor clothed and fed; and over all the minor officers the Selectmen will keep a watchful eye. The possibility of malfeasance in office is so remote that citizens scarcely think of it—in the short space of a year the least mis-step would be quickly discovered; and the officers are too familiar to their constituency, an intimacy that deters misuse of trust.

The variety of Selectmen duties is enormous. They must keep within the budget and their lawful duties; but they have all the authority of the Town. They deal with the state and other towns as community representatives; they survey roads and sidewalks; they handle welfare; they license auctioneers; they perambulate the Town bounds; they act as or appoint fire and police chiefs; they listen to minor complaints or defend the Town against legal action; they wind up the year by making full and complete report and arrange the warrant for the next meeting; they remain in office until the next board is sworn in and thus are constantly popping up in meeting to answer questions and make explanations.

Under them the road commissioner carries out his work; the poor farm operates—often at a profit; the collector gathers in the taxes—the clerk records everything in permanent order; the weights and measures are sealed, fences are viewed, dogs licensed, victualers inspected; and throughout the year the affairs of the Town are carried out in an ordered system that is never more than ten days away from a Town Meeting—because any ten citizens can call such a meeting if they mistrust the conduct of affairs.

". . In Conclusion, Mr. Moderator . ."

"And in conclusion," wound up Rufus Lombard on the closing of Potters's Point School, "I hope that things remain in that there status quo." And Town Meeting, so long as the sea washes the Maine coast and the sun drops red behind the Green Mountains, will undoubtedly remain as Rufus wishes his school. Arising from the necessity of applying a workable government to the settling of a rugged and hazardous country, Town Meeting developed with the land and the people—and became not only an inheritance, but an inborn aptitude, almost instinctive.

And New England people value their inheritance with an independent satisfaction. They, of all Americans, are closest to Democracy; and because they have remained the kind of people they are their Town Meetings will remain at least basically the same. Town Meeting in the remote hills of Vermont and Massachusetts, along the down-east coast, and back in the bear and potato country of Aroostook is less than two cents different from Town Meeting in the Boston days when homes were a foot-race away from the block-house. As towns increase in size they sometimes find the system unwieldy and resort to Town Managers or limited Town Meetings in which all may speak, but only elective members from bounded precincts may vote. Some have become cities by change in charter; some have reverted to wild land or unorganized places. Many have appealed to the states to take over impossible finances—mainly because of loss of industry and settled inhabitants. But these changes come to all governments as time unfolds. Probably the greatest hindrance in New England to continued success with Town Meeting is the influx of strangers—which works in two ways. Many mill towns have received outlanders who speak different languages—and whose nationality and make-up is immediately at odds with Town Meeting traditions. French-Canadians, for example, are fine people—but in politics they organize almost solidly. Organization and Town Meeting are, politically, North and South.

Again: the summer people from urban centers, drawn to the countryside as vacationists and remaining as year-'round residents, immediately take delight in Town Meeting participation. In most instances they are willing but unqualified. They allow theory to outweight practicality. And the Town Meeting Yankee is ever as practical as a whiffletree; as empty of modern political theory as a Samson Pole, but equally useful in the proper chore. While the organized groups, if they become large enough, usually gain the balance of power and ruin Town government, the summer people can be assimilated and make splendid Yankees. In a few years they are speeching like old timers—and their broader point of view adds a wholesome quality to their remarks. The discerning American who seriously investigates Town Meeting is first amused at the Yankee *characters* taking part, but remains to praise. Politics have, lately, induced numerous migrations into New England, and Maine and Vermont can quote official figures on remodelled abandoned farms, whose present owners wouldn't miss Town Meeting on a bet.

So New England Town Meeting continues to function as a basic form of democratic government. It will continue to serve only as long as there is a predominance of Yankee determination—either native or acquired—to hold fast to the precept that there are two sides to every question, and that the majority shall rule.

Small Town Lawyer

By Bellamy Partridge

Like the horse-and-buggy doctor, the old-fashioned small town lawyer was equipped with a staggering diversity of knowledge. Bellamy Partridge's father, who hung his shingle on a tree in Phelps, New York, handled everything from the defense of boys who set an Independence Day bonfire to the prosecution of a hog stealer.

Village life in America was at its best when, in the late sixties, my father opened a law office in Phelps, New York. The spirit of family solidarity —that priceless importation of the Pilgrim Fathers, worth far more than all the tables and chairs, real and imaginary, brought over in the *Mayflower*—was still alive in the land. A son of the small town might go off to college in quest of an education, but once he had been graduated he would come home and go into business with his father or open a store or office of his own across the street. The daughter was content to marry the boy next door and set up housekeeping just around the corner. The days of the bond salesman and filling station were happily far beyond the horizon. If a boy went off to the city to live, people used to feel sorry for him because there seemed to be no place for him in the home town.

Phelps was a serene and gracious example of what the small town could be before the coming of the automobile. From end to end the main street was lined by tall elms and maples, with here and there a gnarled locust or a shedding chestnut tree to relieve the monotony. My father's first shingle was hung from the limb of a tree outside his office window. At that time there were shade trees in front of nearly every place of business in the village. Many of these grizzled giants had been there when the street was still an Indian trail; but, alas, they fell before the unsparing ax of progress and were replaced by tie rails and hitching posts at which long rows of horses stood stamping and switching in the summer sun or shivering before the searching blast of a winter's gale.

The town was for the greater part built along a single street. There were, of course, some back streets, but they were known only to the people who lived on them, and the tax assessor. The life of the town was along the main thoroughfare, and had been since the days when the old stagecoaches came rumbling in from the last leg of the Albany run and changed horses for the first leg of the run to Buffalo. . . .

For more than half a century my father practiced there as a country lawyer, occupying the same office and using the same furniture for forty consecutive years. . . .

The period of my father's practice as a country lawyer—the half century of comparatively peaceful times between Appomattox and Sarajevo—seems from the viewpoint of today to have been the golden age of the country town and the country lawyer. I do not mean to say that life was better then or fuller: merely that, more secluded and less regimented than life today, it gave greater scope to the development of the individual and of the flavor of the locality.

My remembrance of my father as a country lawyer dates from the time when I first saw him standing in the light of the evening lamp removing the tape by which the pages of a legal paper were bound together. Having removed the tape, he shuffled the pages and went around the dining-room table, distributing them among the members of the family, who sat with pens in their hands and inkwells before them, ready for an evening of copying.

This was back in the eighties before the typewriter had come into general use. It had been patented in the sixties, but the inventors were still busy trying to make it work, and all legal papers had to be written out by hand.

This particular occasion must have been the first evening that I had been allowed to help with the copying. I had been training for the event for some time; one had to be a fast and accurate penman. The thought of copying papers does not seem so attractive to me now, but then it was the most desirable thing in life, for it meant that I could sit up until ten o'clock, when the rest of the family went to bed. We were eight children—and a lawyer's children were expected to help with the copying of legal papers just as a farmer's children were expected to help to get in the crops.

We used to gather around the table as soon as the supper dishes had been cleared away, and evening after evening we would sit there and write until it was time to go to bed. For a lawyer with a good practice the means of having papers quickly and accurately copied was a matter of great importance. . . .

We lived in a house large enough to be a hotel. It was three stories high, with an unbeautiful mansard roof. I have heard my father describe it as a packing-box type of house. There were four large rooms on the ground floor with a hallway through the middle. The library and dining room were at the left of the front door, and the parlor and back parlor at the right. Double doors connected the four rooms, and when these were all open we had a fine place to dance.

An addition at the back housed ample kitchens, pantries, and storerooms and provided a number of small sleeping rooms on the second floor. The master bedrooms in the main part of the house were always referred to as "chambers." There were the front chamber, the east chamber, the blue chamber. No crowding was necessary in order to find space for the eight children, a grandmother, an aunt or two, and an occasional cousin who would come for a week and stay all summer.

Our lot covered an acre of ground, with a lawn that always seemed unnecessarily large to me, and a garden that, when I had a certain number of rows to hoe on a summer day and there happened to be a ball game, looked bigger than the Great Plains.

We were, I imagine, a rather noisy family when we were not at work on a copying assignment. Nearly all of us could play some musical instrument, and there was endless practicing. Music for dancing could be furnished at almost any time, and, with a nucleus of eight to start with, our house was a magnet for the children of the neighborhood.

The copying of papers that I have been describing was not an isolated occurrence. Sometimes we would work every evening for a week, and a fortnight rarely went by when some of us were not called upon to help out by making copies of this or that. My father had a regular copyist besides. Lawyers had *copyists* in those days—not stenographers or secretaries. He used to pay Libby Weston fifteen cents an hour for her work, and she was very glad to get it. She was accurate, but she was slow, and if father was in a hurry to get things finished he used to bring them home with him at night and turn them over to members of the family.

Libby did a good part of her work at home, though she was usually willing to come and sit in the office with her copying while father was away at court, as he was quite a good deal of the time. He was always in the Surrogate's Court on Mondays with some probate matter, and he rarely missed going on Saturday to the Special Term, the court for motions. And while he was gone, Libby was in charge.

She would sit at the flat-top desk in the front office, with a background of dusty pigeonholes, and smile brightly at anyone who entered the door, though she obviously did not belong there. This was a man's office with masculinity sticking out all over it. A man's old hat and rubber raincoat hung from an iron rack in one corner, and a man's galoshes and umbrella gathered dust underneath. The place reeked of cigar smoke, and there were usually several partially smoked cigars lying on the edge of a desk or bookshelf, cold and clammy, looking like dead mice. Libby always acted as much afraid of these extinct cheroots as if they really were dead mice.

Pigeonhole cabinets crammed with faded papers ran halfway to the ceiling, and a potbellied stove hugged the inner wall between the two rooms. The chairs were heavy, sturdy, uncomfortable—all except one, a low rocker intended for women clients. For thirty years my father tripped over the rockers of that chair almost daily, but never once was he known to sit down in it.

The rear office, my father's study, looked out on the hospitable doorway of a livery stable before which interesting transactions in the horse world were frequently taking place. In the center of this room was a large flat-top table piled with bundles of papers tied with faded pink tapes. These were the papers that were currently active. Behind the table was a stand-up desk at which my father used to work when he was tired of sitting and wanted to rest. A gloomy-looking safe stood in one corner and a mahogany commode in another, and on all sides, the crowded bookshelves reached to the ceiling. There was a large rug in this room, and a scattering of the same sturdy, uncomfortable chairs.

The tradition of the law hung like a cloud over the entire place, which had been built for a law office in the eighteen twenties and had never been used for another purpose. My father had taken a fancy to the place the first time he saw it. He had to wait ten years before it was available, but when he finally got possession he dug in and stayed for nearly half a century.

My father was not a native of Phelps. He had come there from Rochester upon his admission to the bar shortly after the Civil War. There was even at that time a current belief that the cities were overcrowded, and a young man's best chance for advancement was in going to a small place and, in the oft-repeated words of the distinguished journalist, growing up with the country. On that one point my father agreed with Mr. Greeley; and in addition to that he had a strong desire for country life. Though city-born, he had spent much of his boyhood on a farm and had acquired a love of the soil that stayed with him through life. Even before he was admitted to the bar he had been married. One of the eight children had already arrived and another was on the way before he had heard of what was said to be a very good place to hang out his shingle. . . .

The First Case

At the time my father was admitted to the bar his knowledge of the law was entirely theoretical. He had never drawn a deed, he had never framed a complaint or an answer; indeed, he had never even filled out a summons or a subpoena. He realized, of course, that although he was a member of the bar he was not yet equipped to render very valuable legal services to the public, and to make up for his deficiency he spent a few intensive weeks in one of the busiest offices in Rochester trying to grasp something of the practical machinery of the law business. Here he learned to draw simple wills as well as contracts and conveyances, how to start actions and serve papers. He sat in on trials and arguments, but at the time when he hung out his shingle and opened his office in Phelps he had tried only one case in his life—a little skirmish in police court in which he defended a janitor who was facing a charge of petty larceny.

Preparation for the bar in the sixties was much simpler than it is today. Academic requirements were practically nil. Nor were there formal examiners who made it a business to tangle up and trip, if possible, any youth who fondly imagined that he wanted to be a lawyer. Some local jurist was told off to examine a group of candidates, and he examined them according to his own fitness and his own ideas. If he happened to be a probate lawyer they were in for a severe quizzing on the law of wills, whereas if he was a criminal lawyer the questions were more likely to veer toward the distinction between manslaughter and murder, or the theory of reasonable doubt. And there were oral as well as written questions to test the candidate's fitness.

There was little or no supervision of the reading of a law clerk in those old days. The student was expected to read the commentaries of Kent and Blackstone and to familiarize himself with the works of Coke, Chitty, and Story, but there was no prescribed course of study such as is furnished by the law schools of today.

If my father had done a little less reading and a little more of the actual work of a going law office he would have had much less grief over some of the early clients who came to him with questions which puzzled him and which really should have been matters of ordinary routine. For example, the proper way to describe a cow in a chattel mortgage caused him no end of trouble, and the effect of hortatory words written on the outside of a will after it had been properly signed and witnessed had him digging into his books for half the night.

Business began coming to him from old Charley Hobson before my father had chairs enough in his office for the clients to sit down on. And within a week he had been retained as defense counsel in what turned out to be one of the locally famous cases of the season, though it never went further than the justice court. This case was the outgrowth of a desire on the part of the youth of the town to give the advent of the Fourth of July a suitable welcome.

For many years the arrival of the Fourth had been heralded by the lighting of a huge street bonfire on the bank corner. The preceding year, however, the boys had thoughtlessly built their fire so close to the curb that the heat from it had cracked a plate-glass window in the bank, and the Village Fathers had passed an ordinance forbidding all fires in the streets except for the burning of leaves and grass. The Solons had also taken the precaution of warning the merchants and storekeepers that if they should furnish the boys with the materials for a bonfire they would be held accountable for any damages that might result.

But, as was to have been expected, the youth of the town did not propose to have their patriotic zeal curbed by the ukase of Four Old Men, and as soon as night had fallen on the evening of the third they began to scout around for materials that would make a good bonfire. When they found the usual supply missing from the back doors of the stores, they enlarged the scope of their quest, with the result that when, on the stroke of twelve, the match was applied, the astonished villagers beheld on the bank corner a beacon fire, the like of which, both in brilliance and in aftereffects, had not been seen within the memory of the oldest inhabitant. It was such a bonfire as Chic Sales' "specialist" would have appreciated and enjoyed, for it was composed almost entirely of the small though useful structures of which that talented fabricator in wood was an acknowledged master builder.

Whoops of delight arose from the spectators as the flames went crackling upward through the well-seasoned wood which ignited with the speed of tinder boxes and burned with the roar of a forest fire.

Some of the buildings, as they burned, were neatly outlined, the doors, the oddly cut windows, the little wooden chimneys boldly etched in flame. High on top of the pile was a tidy red building with yellow trimmings which matched in color and architecture the barn of the Village President. Before the flames had reached this brilliant red-and-yellow apex of the pile, murmurings of regret were heard that it should have been given so important a position, only to be turned upside down. When, however, it became well ignited and the beholders saw how it burned in three tall pillars of fire reaching far into the sky—two large and one small—their lamentations died on their lips, and a laughter that was Jovian indeed burst in great tumult upon the midnight air.

As a bonfire it was a decided success, but there were, as I have intimated, reverberations. The Village Fathers were outraged, incensed, and insulted. They turned the minions of the law out with instructions to "get" the culprits, and before the end of the week there were arrests. Five young men, four of them scions of the best families, were arraigned before Lysander Redman, a local justice of the peace, charged with malicious mischief and violation of an ordinance—and my father was retained to defend them.

He entered a plea of not guilty for his clients and called for a jury. This required an adjournment, and he took the youths and their fathers to his office for a conference. When the case came on for trial a week later, the Village Fathers showed how much in earnest they were by appearing in court with a prosecutor from Geneva and twenty witnesses. Some of the most indignant of the witnesses were those who had laughed the most loudly on the night of the fire.

The arraignment had been in Justice Redman's office, but the trial was held in the Town Hall. Several times a day my father had passed the rather plain stone building with a wooden portico reaching all the way across the sidewalk, but he had never been inside it before. The entrance to the hall was in the middle of the building, with the town clerk's office on one side and a shoe store on the other. A broad stairway led to the second floor, which was completely occupied by a large barnlike room with recessed windows. Above the stairway a stepped gallery extended all the way up to the raftered ceiling. Across the end of the room opposite the gallery was a sturdy fence. Beyond the fence were two large tables, a number of chairs for the litigants and their lawyers, and a straight-backed bench for the jury. There were a few benches along the walls outside the fence, but for the main part of the crowd, aside from those seated on the hard wooden steps of the gallery, there were no seating accommodations at all.

As the presiding justice walked in with the two lawyers, followed by the five defendants and their fathers, the crowd fell back to let them inside the enclosure. Then the gate was shut, and a constable was put in charge. The justice opened his docket book and called the name of a juryman. A man from the crowd came forward and was admitted through the gate. If he was accepted he remained, but if he was rejected he was led out through the gate. A satisfactory jury was soon found and sworn in, and, after a brief opening by the prosecutor, the examination of witnesses began.

The prosecution had no trouble in proving that all the defendants were on the scene on the night of the fire. Some of them were recognized as persons who had helped to draw the light wagon by which the fuel was brought to the location of the fire. Others were pointed out as members of the party who had piled up the materials in preparation for the conflagration. And one defendant was positively identified by an enraged citizen as the person who had sat on his chest to hold him down while the other boys had carried away certain inflammable parts of his freehold. No evidence was introduced, however, to show who had applied the match.

It was on this ground that my father moved for a dismissal of the complaint. Motion denied. Exception. He then announced that he would call no witnesses and was ready to present his case to the jury.

Though there had been some moments of hilarity during the trial, my father chose to regard his summary to the jury as a momentous occasion. It was his first opportunity to show his new friends and future clients what he was made of. He felt conscious of his youth and inexperience as he stood up before them; but he was unafraid, and he could not have been more serious if he had been addressing the Supreme Court of the United States. If people had come there expecting coarse jokes and broad humor they were doomed to disappointment. Never once did he refer even indirectly to the fuel of which the bonfire had been built. He confined himself strictly to the safe if humorless subject of patriotism. Were these young men to be punished, were they to have their records blackened and their characters besmirched because of a crime which was nothing more than excess of patriotism?

For a full hour he made the eagle scream. This was really no great effort on his part, since he still had fresh in his mind a Fourth of July oration that he had delivered in the little town of Irondequoit only a few days before, and he let the judge and the jury have the whole of it. Packed to suffocation, the Town Hall rang to the rafters with applause when he had finished.

The prosecutor had taken the case as the average lawyer takes justice court litigation. He regarded it as trivial and had made no particular preparation for it. He must have been somewhat surprised at the flight of eloquence displayed by his youthful opponent; but he disregarded it entirely and shouted with indignation over the uncontested evidence in the case. The good men and true, however, were not interested in uncontested evidence. Patriotism was much more important to them than a miscellaneous lot of carpenter's masterpieces, and after all the shouting was over they brought in a verdict of not guilty.

With fifty dollars in his pocket—ten from each defendant—my father walked home, feeling very much on top of the world. He laid the money on the table before my mother where they could both look at it and enjoy it—the first real money he had ever earned at his profession. There was never any other money like it. He remarked that it would pay for the new baby. It did, several months later, with twenty-five dollars left over.

The trial of this case brought my father welcome publicity, but it also brought him a nickname that was not quite so welcome. As he was going out of his front gate the next morning, two of the neighborhood boys went past. They touched their caps respectfully—a little too respectfully, he thought—and said, "Good morning, Judge." My father smiled as he returned their greeting. But he did not smile when the clerk in the post office said, "Well, Judge, I see you won your case."

My father did not look up from his mail. "Better be careful what you put on your bonfires in the future," he said and turned and walked out.

He resented the use of the title, since he felt sure that it was based on a desire to tease him. He hoped that the little joke would soon be forgotten. Perhaps it was. But the title stuck. There were little variations, of course. In time it became "the Judge" and after a good many years, "the Old Judge." And, ironically enough, at no time in his life was he actually a judge. . . .

During his first few years in practice he tried literally hundreds of these minor cases, some of them involving a total amount of no more than fifteen dollars. From the standpoint of cash it was not remunerative business, but in the matter of imponderables it was priceless. All the time he was schooling himself in the selection of jurors, the examination of witnesses, the tactful handling of the court, and the parrying with difficult counsel. It is well known among lawyers that the pettifogger is at his best in the minor courts. He has, indeed, almost ceased to exist in the courts of record. The lower courts in the larger cities are still infested with attorneys of a low order who wrangle and connive, coach witnesses, and even suborn if they dare, but as the bench improves and the bar tightens its regulations, they are being crowded out, or at least kept in hand.

In justice court, however, there is no way to cope with them. Anyone may practice there, and in almost every community there is a shrewd old codger, possibly an ex-justice, who, though not a member of the bar, knows all the tricks and pitfalls of justice court practice. A justice of the peace can make his rulings on the admission of evidence but cannot enforce them. The pettifogger knows this, and over the objection of opposing counsel and the ruling of the court he goes right ahead and introduces any evidence that he thinks will help him win the case. To meet one of the gentry on his own ground, an attorney must be alert and more than ordinarily resourceful. My father's method of fighting the pettifogger was to turn his own weapons against him if possible.

He was once called upon to prosecute a case of hog stealing in a distant corner of the county, far from the beaten track and miles from the railroad. After a long, muddy drive he found himself confronted by a fat, shifty-eyed old pettifogger and knew that he was in for trouble. Theft is never too easy to prove. Thieves are seldom caught in the act, and to prove them guilty, circumstantial evidence is nearly always necessary. My father had a strong case, however, and in spite of the most determined and exasperating opposition, aided and abetted in every possible way by the court, which favored the defense at every opportunity, he drove home his evidence.

After both sides had rested, the defendant's lawyer got to his feet and solemnly intoned to the six-man jury of farmers one Latin quotation after another. "*Nulli est homini perpetuum bonum. Qui desiderat pacem praeparet bellum. O quam cito transit gloria mundi!*"

The counsel for the defense rolled these under his tongue with relish, and the jury seemed much impressed. Then in a low, almost an injured tone he began a discussion of the "ridiculously inadequate" evidence that had been offered against his client. As he went on he gathered force and soon was shouting so that he could have been heard blocks away. But at the end he lowered his voice and fell once more into Latin. "*Ego cogito, ergo sum.*"

After the defense counsel had seated himself my father rose and stood silent before the jury for a time. Then he began to intone in imitation of his opponent all the most common Latin phrases which came readily to mind.

"*Sic semper tyrannus . . . multum in parvo . . . tempus fugit . . . e pluribus unum . . .*"

He paused, looking earnestly from one member of the jury to another. "That, gentlemen of the jury, is Latin. *But,*" he shouted in a thunderous voice, "what has *Latin* got to do with it? This man was arrested for *stealing hogs—!*"

An outburst of laughter greeted this sally, and after that it was all over but the shouting. The defendant was held for the grand jury and eventually sent to Auburn, where he had a long time to reflect upon the maxims quoted by his learned counsel.

All the justices of the peace in a township have concurrent jurisdiction, and it is a favorite trick of the pettifogger to bring his suit before the justice least accessible to the defendant. The more isolated the place the better the pettifogger seems to like it. In an early case of my father's involving the sale of a threshing machine the defendant was summoned to appear before Justice Smith, a delightful old farmer who used to hold court in his own parlor among the framed mottoes on the wall and the wax flowers under glass. The stool of an Esty organ was used as the witness stand, and the opposing counsel sat at opposite ends of a sewing table. My father had brought with him a dozen or more threshing hands who were to be called as witnesses, but there was no room for them in the house, and they stood in the dooryard and listened to the testimony through the open windows.

When dinner time came the justice excused himself and retired to his own dining room to eat, leaving lawyers, litigants, and witnesses to sit in the parlor, where they could smell the tantalizing aroma of roasting meat, the pungent scent of pies baking in the oven. The case had not been completed at six o'clock, and the torture was repeated. There was no place within miles where they could go to eat; so they sat and suffered. The famished jurymen did not get the case until nearly nine o'clock, and at one minute after nine they were back with a verdict. My father never could remember which side won the case. That little detail was apparently not important enough to remain in his memory. But there was one thing he never could forget: the only person foresighted enough to bring his lunch was the pettifogger who brought the case. . . .

Gossip and Slander

Nobody knows better than the country lawyer how little personal privacy is to be found in the small town. For that you must go to the city, where you may live for years in the same house with people and not even know their names—or care. In the country you do care about your neighbors. You want to know who they are and what they are up to.

Gossip is as much a part of country life as the air we breathe, the stars above, the green earth we tread, and the waters under the earth. The word "gossip" is in somewhat bad odor today, but that was not always so. In the beginning the word was "god sibb," denoting a spiritual relationship, such as that of a sponsor in baptism. In Chaucer's day "gossip" denoted a familiar friend, a companion. "My gossip . . . her name was Alisoun." It may have denoted something even closer than a familiar friend. But today, in rural life, the gossip is about on a par with the slanderer. When you call a person *that* you'd better smile.

Much of the gossip floating around the country town is kindly. It is no more than news, and it is not meant to be anything else. The eagerness of newspapers to establish a news beat is no more than the enlargement and incorporation of the idea of being the first to pass on an interesting item about a neighbor. My father used to say that gossip was the boon and the bane of the country lawyer's existence. Without it he could not possibly have known many of the things that it was necessary for him to know; much of the evidence in his cases first came to him in the form of gossip. The successful contest of a will, for example, is almost invariably built on gossip, and, similarly, it is nearly impossible to find the evidence to sustain a contested will without falling back on gossip.

There is some basis of fact behind most of the gossip in a country town, though the lawyer is about the only one who knows how much the fact amounts to, for he is the only one who knows both sides.

"Is that just an ordinary lie, or is it a true lie?" I heard my father ask a man who had brought him an item about a lie that was going around.

The power of the spoken word in the country town was something that my father both feared and respected. He used to tell a story about a man whose standing in the community was completely undermined by a story that, though harmless, was so good that it was repeated over and over again.

The victim was an inoffensive little fellow who had probably killed more men than Jesse James and Billy the Kid combined—for he had been a sharpshooter in the Civil War and by all odds the best one in a regiment of crack shots. He could still obliterate the bull's-eye of a target at a hundred paces, though he was so shy that if a rabbit had turned on him he would probably have dropped his gun and run for his life. His name was Johnny Wright. He was a tinsmith, and a good one. For years he worked as the tinker in a hardware store. When the owner died and he had to do something else he opened up a hardware store of his own. It was a little one-man establishment located next door to a rather ornate saloon run by a gentleman named Tug Wilson.

Tug was a rough-shod fellow who had accumulated a number of enemies, among them a group of rowdies called the O'Brien boys, who lived in Longville, a small though tough community about nine miles away. The O'Brien boys had long been wanting to avenge some grievance against Tug Wilson, but it was not until Tug had refurbished his saloon and installed some large and decorative mirrors there that they saw their chance. They sent word to Tug that they would come down some night and toss a few bricks through his mirrors for him. When he received this warning, Tug came to my father in a panic and asked if there was not something that he could do to stall off the raid.

"Is your glass insured?" asked my father.

"Insured? Against fire, you mean?"

"Against breakage, accidental or otherwise."

Tug shook his head. "Didn't know it could be done. Graves down to Geneva handles my insurance. I'll see him about it today. But, Judge, ain't there any way I can stop those skunks from coming down here and smashing up my place?"

"Do you want to tackle the job of having them arrested and put under bond to keep the peace?" asked my father.

Tug shook his small pointed head. "Is that the only way?"

"It's the only way I know of," said my father, who thought that the threats did not sound very serious. "You don't really think they'll attack your place—after sending you notice?"

"Sure they will."

Tug was right about it. They came the next Saturday night. Two of them entered the swinging front doors at the same moment that the other two entered at the back. All were well armed with rocks and brickbats. The proprietor himself was behind the bar when the barragc began. They could easily have struck him down. But they had no desire to injure him; all they wanted to do was to wreck the place, and after their first salvo there was not an unbroken mirror left.

At the first crash of glass Tug Wilson dropped to the floor behind the bar, where he remained until the battle was over. But the bartender, a hard-looking individual with a cauliflower ear, was made of sterner stuff. He had learned his trade on the old Bowery, where, to survive at all, a man must take care of himself. The initial crash that had sent the proprietor to the floor automatically put the bartender into action. He began to throw bottles—first at the heads of the attacking party—and afterward at any head that raised itself above the level of the table tops. He had a deadly aim and a large supply of ammunition with which he floored everybody in the room. When, suddenly, he saw still another head poke through the swinging door he promptly took a crack at it.

That was how it happened that when the local constabulary finally arrived at the scene they stumbled upon the prostrate form of Johnny Wright lying among the gory O'Briens and the others who littered the barroom floor. Johnny's skull was fractured, and he was bleeding freely from a six-inch scalp wound. They were just carrying him out when my father, hastily summoned by Tug Wilson, entered the door.

People were greatly surprised to find Johnny Wright's name listed among the casualties in a bloody barroom brawl, but Johnny had a perfect explanation. He had heard the noise of the attack from his store next door and had gone to see what the trouble was.

Everybody who heard or repeated that story knew that it was true. Johnny Wright was not a roistering man. He did not use alcoholic beverages in any form. Nobody doubted his word when he said that he had never before been in that saloon or any other. But the picture of good, sweet, pious, inoffensive little Johnny Wright being found with a broken head among a welter of bloody O'Briens after a barroom fracas was more than anybody could resist—and the story was told and retold until it began to get under the skin of the local temperance society of which Johnny had been secretary and treasurer for many years. The temperance people made no scandal about it, but at the end of the year, when Johnny's term expired, they put in a woman to take his place.

He was also dropped from the board of elders of the Methodist Church.

When his name came up for re-election he received only two votes out of the entire congregation—probably his own and his daughter's, people said.

Johnny told my father that he used to wonder about these things. He did not like the idea of being misunderstood, and he did his best to explain to people just how the accident had really happened. He used to tell the story to anybody who would listen. For a while people put up with him as a bore, and then gradually, as the constant repetition of the alibi became a fixation, they began to regard him as being a little cracked, perhaps from that smash on the head.

Old Johnny has been dead these twenty years, and all that people remember about him—just as my father predicted—is that he was somehow mixed up in that raid of the O'Brien boys on Tug Wilson's saloon.

Here was a story that was both true and harmless, but the repetition of it left a picture that was misleading and injurious. Local gossip does not often take on the elements of slander until it passes through the mind of a person who is scheming or malicious. Actual trials for slander are scarce in the rural counties, but rarely a month passed during my father's practice when someone did not come to him with what might have been regarded under a strict interpretation of the law as a cause of action for slander or defamation of character. Almost invariably my father was able to clear up the situation by an explanation of the rural jury's reluctance to interfere with what it considers freedom of speech and by a word of warning to the person accused of uttering the defamatory matter.

But even though slanderous talk did not always end up in court, it often led to other things that did. Perhaps the most prevalent of these was suspicion. Just as a sensationally horrible ripper murder is likely to be followed by other sensational ripper murders, a bit of gossip about the goings-on of a married man was almost certain to arouse the suspicions of a number of women about the doings of their own husbands. "Sympathetic suspicion," my father used to call it. Occasionally these blind suspicions would hit the mark, though usually they accomplished no more than to make the wife a little ridiculous.

One of the most unusual of these cases of groundless suspicion came to my father's attention not through a jealous wife who wanted a divorce but through the robbery of the safe in a wagon factory and a night watchman who wanted an alibi. When he was called upon to account for his presence at the time of the robbery, the watchman told my father, who was investigating the case, that he had temporarily left the factory and was making a call on a housemaid of a family who lived near by. Pressed for details, he gave my father the name of Mrs. Orlow Wilson, the girl's employer, who, he said, had seen him there.

Mrs. Wilson came readily to my father's office in response to a letter, but when she learned his reason for asking her to come she shut up like a clam and said that she had nothing to say. When, however, my father had explained that if the watchman was arrested for the crime he would almost certainly subpoena her into court—whereas, by giving a full explanation in advance, she might be able to clear the man, she gave in and told him her story.

She and her husband had been married for over ten years, she said. They always got along well. Orlow had no bad habits, though he was fond of billiards and poker and was out at night a good deal. In fact, nearly the only evenings when he was at home were those on which they had invited another couple in for a rubber of whist. He was usually home before midnight, and Mrs. Wilson had never dreamed that he was doing anything out of the ordinary until her suspicions were aroused by her best friend, Madge Horton.

It had all come about through the indiscretions of a servant girl that Mrs. Wilson had never spoken to in her life. Her name was Rita Phipps. Rita had become so involved with a married man that the whole town was talking, and Madge had suggested that Mrs. Wilson had better keep an eye on her Sarah, who, she reminded Mrs. Wilson, had formerly been an intimate friend of Rita's.

"And another thing," Madge had added. "Your Sarah is altogether too good-looking to have around the kitchen of any married woman's home. I know I'd never draw an easy breath if she was in *my* kitchen."

Mrs. Wilson had never thought of that before, but after she had gone home and taken a good look at Sarah she began to be a little uneasy herself. Orlow had never, so far as she knew, even looked at Sarah or any other woman. But once the thought had come into her mind she found it hard to get out again. Until this time she had paid little attention to Sarah's comings and goings, but now, without really meaning to, she began to watch her quite closely. But with all her watching she found nothing amiss with her pretty serving maid. It was when she was not watching at all that she made the startling discovery that Sarah was taking a man up the back stairs to her room when she went to bed one night.

Sarah had come into the house just after the clock had struck ten. Mrs. Wilson was already in her room, partly undressed. She never would have known that anybody was with Sarah if she had not stepped into the back hall to tell her something about breakfast. She stood there in the dark waiting for the girl to turn on the light before coming up. There was a switch at the bottom of the stairs and another at the top. But Sarah did not turn on the lights, and Mrs. Wilson was wondering why she had suddenly become so economical about electricity when she heard whispering —and then she realized that Sarah was not alone and that two persons were trying to keep in step as they went up the stairs.

Mrs. Wilson did not see the man—not when she made the discovery, at any rate—but she went into her own closet, which, though in the front part of the house, was next to the wall of Sarah's room, and by putting her ear against the wall she could hear them whispering and giggling in a very suggestive manner.

Her first impulse was to discharge the girl without giving any further reason than, "I guess you know why." But she thought better of the idea and decided that before making up her mind what to do about it she would talk over the situation with Madge to see if Madge had any ideas. Madge certainly had.

In the first place, she thought that she ought to come down and listen through the wall for herself. She wanted Mrs. Wilson to be sure of her ground before taking a leap in the dark. And in her outspoken way she approached another angle about which Mrs. Wilson had hardly dared to think. "By the way," she said, "where was your own perfectly good husband last night?"

"Playing poker with yours."

"But he wasn't! Chauncey said that Orlow promised to come—but didn't show up."

For some moments the two women had sat and looked at each other without a word. Then Madge asked, "How long was it after you heard the visitor go downstairs before Orlow came in?"

"About half an hour."

Madge nodded. "Uh-huh, just about what you'd expect. A good safe allowance. Did you happen to notice what time it was when the caller left?"

"Sarah went down and let him out just before eleven. I remember hearing the clock strike soon after she returned to her room."

"And you haven't said anything about it to Orlow?"

Mrs. Wilson shook her head. "Usually I tell him everything, but this time I didn't. I guess it was because I didn't want him to know the kind of girl Sarah is. You don't really think, do you, Madge—?"

"I don't know what to think. But you better ask Orlow—very casually of course—what he was doing last night. Just ask him whether he won or lost at the poker party."

Mrs. Wilson did ask him after he came home to dinner that night, and he answered casually that he didn't play. He said that he had gone with Bert Van Vranken to look at a litter of Llewellyn pups and that by the time they had returned and played a couple of games of billiards it was too late for poker. And anyway, he added, he had not been feeling very lucky lately.

This explanation satisfied Mrs. Wilson, but Madge thought it very thin. She said the situation would bear watching. And the next time that Sarah entertained her gentleman friend both Madge and Mrs. Wilson were listening in the dark as the lovers came up the stairs. When, after an interval of an hour, Sarah went softly down to let her lover out, the two women posted themselves at a rear window from which they saw a man go skulking out across the garden. It was too dark to recognize his features. All they could make out was that the visitor was not a tall man. Orlow Wilson was not a tall man. They were still standing at the window looking out into the darkness of the garden when they heard the clock strike eleven.

Mrs. Wilson had looked at the clock as her husband's footstep sounded on the porch. It was eleven-thirty to the dot. She thought he looked guilty as he came in the door. She would have liked to accuse him on the spot, but Madge had advised against it. A man could lie out of any accusation, she said. The only way to bring him to time was to catch him red-handed. Mrs. Wilson had suggested that they might switch on the light at the head of the stairs the next time they heard the lovers coming up, but Madge had said that this would not prove anything. He would say they were hunting for burglars or had heard a noise up there or something of that sort. There must be no halfway measures, Madge said. If he was guilty he must be caught in the act in the presence of a witness.

"But how can we catch them in the act?" said Mrs. Wilson. "I always hear them turn the key in the door."

"Well—isn't there a closet in Sarah's room?"

There was, and the next time Sarah entertained her visitor Madge and Mrs. Wilson were hidden in the closet long before it was time for the guilty pair to come. At last, however, they heard Sarah coming up the stairs, and they could tell from the sound that somebody was with her. Then they heard the bedroom door softly close and the click of the key in the lock. They gave Sarah and her visitor plenty of time to undress and get into bed. Then they suddenly rushed out and switched on the light. For days Mrs. Wilson had been nerving herself up for this moment, and as her fingers closed on the switch she was muttering through clenched teeth, "I'll give you the surprise of your life—!"

But as the light flashed on she gasped and drew back. The man in the bed was not her husband! The startled face she beheld peering up out of the bedclothes was that of the night watchman of the wagon factory over on the back street, a low fellow who was constantly becoming involved in new scandals before he could live down the old ones.

"You sure did," he mumbled. Then, when he had seen the expression on her face, he added, "But I guess I wasn't any more surprised than you were. You must have been looking for somebody else."

"I most certainly was—" The words escaped before she could stop them.

She put out her hand to steady herself, and he must have thought that she was going to switch off the lights, for he said:

"Just a minute—" He ran his hand under the pillow and drew out a great, ugly revolver. Mrs. Wilson shrank back. "Oh, you needn't be afraid," he said. "I'm not going to shoot. I was just looking for my watch. I thought as long as the lights were on I might as well see what time it is. I have to be back to punch the buttons at eleven."

The robbery had taken place between ten and eleven, and the constabulary were already in charge when the night watchman came puffing up shortly before eleven.

"What about the alibi?" the president of the wagon company asked my father the next day.

"It's absolutely watertight," my father replied. "He was at Mrs. Wilson's house calling on her maid—just as he said. Mrs. Wilson and Mrs. Horton both saw him there—and they both heard him say that he must soon be getting back to the factory so that he could push the eleven o'clock buttons."

The Ethics of a Country Editor

By William Allen White

The small town newspaper has always been an important influence in the development of our national character. The practical ethics of its editor made the Emporia *Gazette* the best of such papers. News from Emporia, Kansas, was world news.

The only excuse an editor has for being is that his paper shall print the news. The question that comes to every man running a newspaper is: What is news? That he must settle for himself, and, having found a rule, must stick as closely to it as possible. When an editor begins monkeying with his conscience, stretching his rule to shield his friends or to punish his enemies, he is lost. He becomes wobbly, and has no anchor and no direction.

Every day matters come up in every community, big or little, that are disagreeable to print. Nasty stories are always afloat. Gossip is always in the air. An editor in a town of one hundred people could fill a six-column daily every night with gossip alone, if he could keep from being lynched. Much of it would be false and all of it would be unfair. And yet often these matters come up in such a shape that they may not be ignored. And here is where an editor has to set his jaw and go ahead, following his conscience without fear or favor. Such times come to every attorney, to every doctor, to every preacher, to every man in every relation of life. It is a safe rule to follow, that gossip may be ignored, no matter how loudly it buzzes, till it becomes a matter of court record. Then it may not be left out of the paper. If a man has a grievance against his fellow-man that he or she is too cowardly to air in the court, it is safe to say that there are two sides to the question, and the editor who prints the story prints it at his peril. But, on the other hand, when a man takes his grievance into court, when he spreads it upon the record and gives his opponent a chance to answer in an open, public manner, then the quarrel, no matter whom it involves, is a matter that no editor can overlook. And, after a case gets into court, a newspaper should let the courts try it, printing the claims of each side, not trying to convict or acquit either of the parties.

That, it seems to the *Gazette*, is the fair way to treat unsavory matters. No honest editor cares to have scandal and improper stories in his paper, and no one should print such stories in such a way that they may not be read aloud in the family circle. It is the way news is handled that counts for or against decency. A vile story may be handled with care and the readers be no worse for seeing it.

As we live longer in the newspaper business, we see more and more things which shouldn't be in the paper. To print the kind of a paper we printed ten years ago would turn us yellow with mortification; and the *Gazette* of twenty years ago would stink to high heaven. Divorce news, other than the bare statement of the findings of the court, went out early in the game; resolutions of respect followed. Patent medicines stepped on the heels of the resolutions of respect, and advertising of traveling doctors and painless dentists bumped into the patent medicines. The names of first offenders in police court, unless under unusual circumstances, dropped out after the quack doctors, and advertising of unlisted mining and promotion stock followed the first offenders. Now we are going to refuse after today to take any more advertising of the fellow who gives public notice of his refusal to pay his wife's bills. We've been nursing a growing grouch on him for several years. We don't think a newspaper is the place for him to air his family problems. If his wife is spending too much money, he has two perfectly good avenues of publicity; he can telephone the secretary of the Lyon County Retailers Association, and the secretary will notify every store of any importance of the injured husband's intention. Or, if that fails, he can beat his wife within an inch of her life, and we always give wife-beaters' names the fullest publicity.

Speaking generally, when a family row has to be aired in the newspapers, it should be settled in court. We don't want the money of the poor devil with a fool wife, and we don't want the money of a tightwad husband with a good wife. So nix, after today, of the item from the husband who refuses to pay his wife's bills.

An editor can build up his community only by preaching unselfish citizenship. The booster, the boomer, the rizz-razzer who screams in headlines about the glories of the town gets nowhere. But the editor who, by his own practices as well as his own preaching, stands for decent things and encourages unselfish citizenship, glorifies giving and frowns on taking, has a constructive attitude which is sure to help his town. He may not bring more people in; that is as fate wills it. But he certainly can make life better and happier and broader and more comfortable for the people who live in the town. It is better to have 10,000 people living equitably and happy than to have 10,000 people growing fat upon the toil of 90,000 who live lean and sordid lives. The *Gazette* is printed in a community where there are 13,000 people, without a pauper, with every man at work, without a millionaire, with as many telephones as there are homes, as many automobiles as there are families, as many schools as the children need, as many books in the library as the people will read, with a municipal band, a bathtub in nearly every house, no homemade crime. The people in our jails come to town to get there, and we haven't an able-bodied person in the poorhouse.

That's the kind of a town a paper should strive for. From purely selfish motives it pays an editor to stand for justice. Because the more equitably the gross income of the town is distributed, the more money more people will have to buy more papers and patronize more advertisers.

The editor who hollers for more population without regard to the kind of population is a fool who doesn't know his own business.

McGuffey

By Herbert Quick

The Blue Back Speller, the New England Primer, and McGuffey's Readers were the books buckled over many a boy's shoulder. Johnny learned to read and spell or else! Herbert Quick looks back, with affectionate regard, to the five readers in which Mr. McGuffey introduced him to the world of literature.

I have just looked at a copy of a twenty-year-old edition of the McGuffey's First Reader. It has not a single lesson that was in the one I took in my trembling hand when Maggie Livingstone called me to her to begin learning my letters. Mine had a green cover, but it was hidden by the muslin which my mother had stitched over it to save the wear on a book that cost thirty cents. It was filled with illustrations which I now know were of British origin, for all the men wore knee breeches, the girls had on fluffy pantalets and sugar scoop bonnets, and the ladies huge many-flounced skirts. One boy had a cricket bat in his hand, and the ruling passions of the youngsters seemed to be to shoot with the bow and to roll the hoop. "Can you hop, Tom? See, I can hop! Tom, hop to me." How easily does the English language lend itself to early lessons of such simplicity!

These books were intensely moral, soundly religious, and addicted to the inculcation of habits of industry, mercy, and most of the virtues. Lucy was exhorted to rise because the sun was up. "Mary was up at six," she was assured; and then was added the immortal line, "Up, up, Lucy, and go out to Mary," which scoffers perverted to "Double up, Lucy." Most of the words were of one syllable, but "How doth the little busy bee" was in it, I am certain, and "I like to see a little dog and pat him on the head." It was an easy book, and if it fell short of the power in the moral and religious fields of the more advanced volumes—why, so did its students in the practice of the vices and the need for reproof or warning.

My mastery of the First and Second Readers—just the opening of the marvels of the printed page—was a poignant delight. The reading of anything gave me a sort of ecstasy. These books did not, however, set in operation the germinant powers of actual literary treasure hunting. They did give to the mind of the writer and to the world some things of universal knowledge. We learned that George Washington could not tell a lie about the cherry tree and that his father proved to him the existence of God by the device of sowing lettuce in a trench which spelled George's name. "It might have grown so by chance," said the elder Washington in this Second Reader lesson, but George saw clearly that it could not have come by chance. Some one sowed those seeds in that way. And his father assured him that this world of wonderful adaptations could not have come as it has by chance. There were many fables and lessons about insects, birds, and beasts. Most of the scenes were British. Our habits, our morals, and our faith were carefully kept in mind, and we grew to know Mary's lamb by heart.

In the Third Reader Mr. McGuffey began to give to my young mind some tastes of real literature. It had several beautiful selections from the Bible. Croly's description of the burning of the amphitheater at Rome, which I have never run across anywhere since, was one of the lessons. There was an analysis of How a Fly Walks on the Ceiling, which gave me as much of an urge toward natural philosophy as if it had been a correct one—which it was not. One gets a glimpse into the McGuffey character from the treatment which the Indian received in these books. The author, whose father was an Indian fighter of renown and who must have sat entranced at fireside stories of Indian wars, in several lessons in these Readers treated the Indian with great respect. There was Logan's great speech in the Fifth, for instance. I can see it before my eyes still: "I appeal to any white man to say, if ever he entered Logan's cabin hungry, and he gave him not meat; if ever he came cold and naked and he clothed him not." I wonder how much of the persistent sentiment among Americans favoring justice to the Indians comes from these old Readers. It has not saved the race from exploitation and oppression, but it has always persisted and it has done much good.

The Third Reader introduced me to such writers as Croly, Irving, Woodworth, through "The Old Oaken Bucket," Scott, and others, but not by their names. In the Fourth we had William Wirt, Wendell Phillips, Lord Bacon, Eliphalet Nott, Addison, Samuel Rogers in his "Ginevra," Willis, Montgomery, Milton and Shakespeare, Campbell, and a variety of lesser and anonymous authors. The Fifth Reader carried me on to longer and more mature selections, all chosen by the same rules—the rules of gradually introducing the child to the best of English literature with no letting down of the requirements as to morality and religious sentiment. There was more of Shakespeare, some of Byron, Milton, Johnson, Bryant, Addison, more of the Bible, and much British matter now lost—to me at least. Every selection was classic English.

But the old Fifth Reader of 1844 we never used in our school. My brother's copy was a wonderful mine for me. The front cover was gone, and a part of the Rhetorician's Guide, which told us when to let our voices fall, when they should rise, and when the circumflex was required. I never regretted the loss. But the text consisted of some hundreds of pages of closely printed selections made by Alexander McGuffey with all the family judgment and taste. There was Pope with "Hector's Attack on the Grecian Walls," from that version of the Iliad of which a critic said, "A very pretty poem, Mr. Pope, but don't call it Homer!" There was "How the Water Comes Down at Lodore." There was oratory —Pitt, Burke, Fox, Barré, Otis, Adams, Webster, Hayne. I had the volume all to myself. There were months when it was my only resource in my favorite dissipation of reading.

A small ration, these McGuffey Readers, for an omnivorous mind, but by no means a negligible one. I did not use them with any intelligence. I simply enjoyed them. I found a tune to which I could sing Browning's "How They Brought the Good News from Ghent to Aix" and sang it at the top of my voice as I followed my cows or the plow or harrow. I shouted "Ivry" to the vastnesses of the prairie. I deepened my boyish voice to orotund on "Now godlike Hector and his troops descend" and "They tug, they sweat, but neither gain nor yield, one foot, one inch, of the contested field!"

And somehow I was inoculated with a little of the virus of good literature. I gained no knowledge that it was anything of the sort. I got not the slightest glimpse into the world of letters as a world. Nobody ever said a word to me about that. I read nothing about it for years and years afterward. But when I did come to read the English classics, I felt as one who meets in after years a charming person with whom he has had a chance encounter on the train. I had already met the gentlemen.

Farewell, My Lovely!

By Lee Strout White

Days were golden in the American home town when young men cranked their Model T's, and their Gibson girls wore sailor hats swathed in veiling. The Lizzies had their idiosyncrasies but they were well-nigh indestructible, both in memory and fact. Lee Strout White records the palmy days.

I see by the new Sears Roebuck catalogue that it is still possible to buy an axle for a 1909 Model T. Ford, but I am not deceived. The great days have faded, the end is in sight. Only one page in the current catalogue is devoted to parts and accessories for the Model T; yet everyone remembers springtimes when the Ford gadget section was larger than men's clothing, almost as large as household furnishings. The last Model T was built in 1927, and the car is fading from what scholars call the American scene—which is an understatement, because to a few million people who grew up with it the old Ford practically *was* the American scene.

It was the miracle God had wrought. And it was patently the sort of thing that could only happen once. Mechanically uncanny, it was like nothing that had ever come to the world before. Flourishing industries rose and fell with it. As a vehicle, it was hard-working, commonplace, heroic; and it often seemed to transmit those qualities to the persons who rode in it. My own generation identifies it with Youth, with its gaudy, irretrievable excitements; before it fades into the mist, I would like to pay it the tribute of the sigh that is not a sob, and set down random entries in a shape somewhat less cumbersome than a Sears Roebuck catalogue.

The Model T was distinguished from all other makes of cars by the fact that its transmission was of a type known as planetary—which was half metaphysics, half sheer friction. Engineers accepted the word "planetary" in its epicyclic sense, but I was always conscious that it also meant "wandering," "erratic." Because of the peculiar nature of this planetary element, there was always, in Model T, a certain dull rapport between engine and wheels, and, even when the car was in a state known as neutral, it trembled with a deep imperative and tended to inch forward. There was never a moment when the bands were not faintly egging the machine on. In this respect it was like a horse, rolling the bit on its tongue, and country people brought to it the same technique they used with draft animals.

Its most remarkable quality was its rate of acceleration. In its palmy days the Model T could take off faster than anything on the road. The reason was simple. To get under way, you simply hooked the third finger of the right hand around a lever on the steering column, pulled down hard, and shoved your left foot forcibly against the low-speed pedal. These were simple, positive motions; the car responded by lunging forward with a roar. After a few seconds of this turmoil, you took your toe off the pedal, eased up a mite on the throttle, and the car, possessed of only two forward speeds, catapulted directly into high with a series of ugly jerks and was off on its glorious errand. The abruptness of this departure was never equaled in other cars of the period. The human leg was (and still is) incapable of letting in a clutch with anything like the forthright abandon that used to send Model T on its way. Letting in a clutch is a negative, hesitant motion, depending on delicate nervous control; pushing down the Ford pedal was a simple, country motion—an expansive act, which came as natural as kicking an old door to make it budge.

The driver of the old Model T was a man enthroned. The car, with top up, stood seven feet high. The driver sat on top of the gas tank, brooding it with his own body. When he wanted gasoline, he alighted, along with everything else in the front seat; the seat was pulled off, the metal cap unscrewed, and a wooden stick thrust down to sound the liquid in the well. There were always a couple of these sounding sticks kicking around in the ratty subcushion regions of a flivver. Refueling was more of a social function then, because the driver had to unbend, whether he wanted to or not. Directly in front of the driver was the windshield—high, uncompromisingly erect. Nobody talked about air resistance, and the four cylinders pushed the car through the atmosphere with a simple disregard of physical law.

There was this about a Model T: the purchaser never regarded his purchase as a complete, finished product. When you bought a Ford, you figured you had a start—a vibrant, spirited framework to which could be screwed an almost limitless assortment of decorative and functional hardware. Driving away from the agency, hugging the new wheel between your knees, you were already full of creative worry. A Ford was born naked as a baby, and a flourishing industry grew up out of correcting its rare deficiencies and combating its fascinating diseases. Those were the great days of lily-painting. I have been looking at some old Sears Roebuck catalogues, and they bring everything back so clear.

First you bought a Ruby Safety Reflector for the rear, so that your posterior would glow in another car's brilliance. Then you invested thirty-nine cents in some radiator Moto Wings, a popular ornament which gave the Pegasus touch to the machine and did something godlike to the owner. For nine cents you bought a fan-belt guide to keep the belt from slipping off the pulley.

You bought a radiator compound to stop leaks. This was as much a part of everybody's equipment as aspirin tablets are of a medicine cabinet. You bought special oil to prevent chattering, a clamp-on dash light, a patching outfit, a tool box which you bolted to the running board, a sun visor, a steering-column brace to keep the column rigid, and a set of emergency containers for gas, oil, and water—three thin, disklike cans which reposed in a case on the running board during long, important journeys—red for gas, gray for water, green for oil. It was only a beginning. After the car was about a year old, steps were taken to check the alarming disintegration. (Model T was full of tumors, but they were benign.) A set of antirattlers (98¢) was a popular panacea. You hooked them on to the gas and spark rods, to the brake-pull rod, and to the steering-rod connections. Hood silencers, of black rubber, were applied to the fluttering hood. Shock-absorbers and snubbers gave "complete relaxation." Some people bought rubber pedal pads, to fit over the standard metal pedals. (I didn't like these, I remember.) Persons of a suspicious or pugnacious turn of mind bought a rear-view mirror; but most Model T owners weren't worried by what was coming from behind because they would soon enough see it out in front. They rode in a state of cheerful catalepsy. Quite a large mutinous clique among Ford owners went over to a foot accelerator (you could buy one and screw it to the floor board), but there was a certain madness in these people, because the Model T, just as she stood, had a choice of three foot pedals to push, and there were plenty of moments when both feet were occupied in the routine performance of duty and when the only way to speed up the engine was with the hand throttle.

Gadget bred gadget. Owners not only bought ready-made gadgets; they invented gadgets to meet special needs. I myself drove my car directly from the agency to the blacksmith's, and had the smith affix two enormous iron brackets to the port running board to support an army trunk.

People who owned closed models builded along different lines: they bought ball-grip handles for opening doors, window antirattlers, and deluxe flower vases of the cut-glass antisplash type. People with delicate sensibilities garnished their car with a device called the Donna Lee Automobile Disseminator—a porous vase guaranteed, according to Sears, to fill the car with a "faint clean odor of lavender." The gap between open cars and closed cars was not as great then as it is now: for $11.95, Sears Roebuck converted your touring car into a sedan, and you went forth renewed. One agreeable quality of the old Fords was that they had no bumpers, and their fenders softened and wilted with the years and permitted the driver to squeeze in and out of tight places.

Tires were 30 x 3½, cost about twelve dollars, and punctured readily. Everybody carried a Jiffy patching set, with a nutmeg grater to roughen the tube before the goo was spread on. Everybody was capable of putting on a patch, expected to have to, and did have to.

During my association with Model T's, self-starters were not a prevalent accessory. They were expensive and under suspicion. Your car came equipped with a serviceable crank, and the first thing you learned was how to Get Results. It was a special trick, and, until you learned it (usually from another Ford owner, but sometimes by a period of appalling experimentation), you might as well have been winding up an awning. The trick was to leave the ignition switch off, proceed to the animal's head, pull the choke (which was a little wire protruding through the radiator), and give the crank two or three nonchalant upward lifts. Then, whistling as though thinking about something else, you would saunter back to the driver's cabin, turn the ignition on, return to the crank, and this time, catching it on the down stroke, give it a quick spin with plenty of That. If this procedure was followed, the engine almost always responded—first with a few scattered explosions, then with a tumultuous gunfire, which you checked by racing around to the driver's seat and retarding the throttle. Often, if the emergency brake hadn't been pulled all the way back, the car advanced on you the instant the first explosion occurred, and you would hold it back by leaning your weight against it. I can still feel my old Ford nuzzling me at the curb, as though looking for an apple in my pocket.

The lore and legend that governed the Ford were boundless. Owners had their own theories about everything; they discussed mutual problems in that wise, infinitely resourceful way old women discuss rheumatism. Exact knowledge was pretty scarce, and often proved less effective than superstition. Dropping a camphor ball into the gas tank was a popular expedient; it seemed to have a tonic effect on both man and machine. There wasn't much to base exact knowledge on. The Ford driver flew blind. He didn't know the temperature of his engine, the speed of his car, the amount of his fuel, or the pressure of his oil (the old Ford lubricated itself by what was amiably described as the "splash system"). A speedometer cost money and was an extra, like a windshield-wiper. The dashboard of the early models was bare save for an ignition key; later models, grown effete, boasted an ammeter which pulsated alarmingly with the throbbing of the car. Under the dash was a box of coils, with vibrators which you adjusted, or thought you adjusted. Whatever the driver learned of his motor, he learned not through instruments but through sudden developments. I remember that the timer was one of the vital organs about which there was ample doctrine. When everything else had been checked, you "had a look" at the timer. It was an extravagantly odd little device, simple in construction, mysterious in function. It contained a roller, held by a spring, and there were four contact points on the inside of the case against which, many people believed, the roller rolled. I have had a timer apart on a sick Ford many times, but I never really knew what I was up to—I was just showing off before God. There were almost as many schools of thought as there were timers. Some people, when things went wrong, just clenched their teeth and gave the timer a smart crack with a wrench. Other people opened it up and blew on it. There was a school that held that the timer needed large amounts of oil; they fixed it by frequent baptism. And there was a school that was positive it was meant to run dry as a bone; these people were continually taking it off and wiping it. I remember once spitting into a timer; not in anger, but in a spirit of research. You see, the Model T driver moved in the realm of metaphysics. He believed his car could be hexed.

One reason the Ford anatomy was never reduced to an exact science was that, having "fixed" it, the owner couldn't honestly claim that the treatment had brought about the cure. There were too many authenticated cases of Fords fixing themselves—restored naturally to health after a short rest. Farmers soon discovered this, and it fitted nicely with their draft-horse philosophy: "Let 'er cool off and she'll snap into it again."

A Ford owner had Number One Bearing constantly in mind. This bearing, being at the front end of the motor, was the one that always burned out, because the oil didn't reach it when the car was climbing hills. (That's what I was always told, anyway.) The oil used to recede and leave Number One dry as a clam flat; you had to watch that bearing like a hawk. It was like a weak heart—you could hear it start knocking, and that was when you stopped and let her cool off. Try as you would to keep the oil supply right, in the end Number One always went out. "Number One Bearing burned out on me and I had to have her replaced," you would say, wisely; and your companions always had a lot to tell about how to protect and pamper Number One to keep her alive.

Sprinkled not too liberally among the millions of amateur witch doctors who drove Fords and applied their own abominable cures were the heaven-sent mechanics who could really make the car talk. These professionals turned up in undreamed-of spots. One time, on the banks of the Columbia River in Washington, I heard the rear end go out of my Model T when I was trying to whip it up a steep incline onto the deck of a ferry. Something snapped; the car slid backward into the mud. It seemed to me like the end of the trail. But the captain of the ferry, observing the withered remnant, spoke up.

"What's got her?" he asked.

"I guess it's the rear end," I replied, listlessly. The captain leaned over the rail and stared. Then I saw that there was a hunger in his eyes that set him off from other men.

"Tell you what," he said, carelessly, trying to cover up his eagerness; "let's pull the son of a bitch up onto the boat, and I'll help you fix her while we're going back and forth on the river."

We did just this. All that day I plied between the towns of Pasco and Kennewick, while the skipper (who had once worked in a Ford garage) directed the amazing work of resetting the bones of my car.

Springtime in the heyday of the Model T was a delirious season. Owning a car was still a major excitement; roads were still wonderful and bad. The Fords were obviously conceived in madness: any car which was capable of going from forward into reverse without any perceptible mechanical hiatus was bound to be a mighty challenging thing to the human imagination. Boys used to veer them off the highway into a level pasture and run wild with them, as though they were cutting up with a girl. 'Most everybody used the reverse pedal quite as much as the regular foot brake—it distributed the wear over the bands and wore them all down evenly. That was the big trick, to wear all the bands down evenly, so that the final chattering would be total and the whole unit scream for renewal.

The days were golden, the nights were dim and strange. I still recall with trembling those loud, nocturnal crises when you drew up to a sign-post and raced the engine so the lights would be bright enough to read destinations by. I have never been really planetary since. I suppose it's time to say good-by. Farewell, my lovely!

PART IV

"Me and Mamie O'Rourke"

City Sidewalks

If the memories of millions are bound up in the phrase "Down on the Farm," there are increasing numbers who think in terms of "city streets." For every grownup who remembers a childhood of chores and swimming holes, there is another who recalls stickball and marbles and roller coasters.

Brooklyn, Chicago, San Francisco and a score of others—each a metropolis—have added brush strokes to the composite portrait of America. The barefoot boy with fishing pole finds his counterpart in the city kid with hot dog. When Irwin Shaw proclaims "I sing of Brooklyn, city of myth, stone mother, whose cobbled caress shaped me," he waxes as lyrical as any sonneteer of sunsets. This section opens with remembrances of three great cities, written from opposing points of view, but seen through observing and nostalgic eyes. They can be matched with similar recollections by loving sons or daughters of Providence, Atlanta or Salt Lake City.

What do we remember most vividly about our city childhoods? Playing in the streets, for one thing. Brushes with rival gangs—rarely as bloodthirsty as the newspaper accounts. Watching the ships from strange corners of the world, if we were lucky enough to live in seaports. Visiting the livery stable, and inhaling the odor and the lore of horseflesh. And there were more formal social occasions, the urban counterparts of husking bees, such as calls on family friends at New Year's; or taking part, even if it were only so minor as peeping over the top of the stairs, in the evening affairs of the grown-ups.

The life of the city has its special days, its parades and celebrations, its great political and sporting events. Of the latter, the nonpareil is of course the World's Series. Is there a boy in the land who has not imagined himself a Mathewson or a Ruth? Is there one who does not want to be in the box behind third base on opening day? And what city girl has not compared bonnets in The Easter Parade? Then there is the city spectacle of them all—the bejeweled adornment of shops and streets and homes that comes at Christmas time. Here is the summit of urban excitement, a picture that stays with us forever.

Brooklyn: Home of Coney Island, the Dodgers, and the BMT Subway

By Irwin Shaw

It's the butt of myriad jokes, the subject of myriad happy myths. It's a city that could happen only in America—raucous, boisterous, untamed, but with a million homes and a thousand places of worship. In a warm and varied memoir, Irwin Shaw tells what Brooklyn was like in the days of his boyhood and youth.

I sing of Brooklyn, city of myth, stone mother, whose cobbled caress shaped me, for better or worse, into the man I am today. Heroic stepdaughter of the metropolis, water-girdled, iron-voiced, at the far end of all high bridges, subway empire, barracks for the millions, port for the humbler vessels of the seas, bargain playground for the sweltering masses of the city, borough of homes, borough of churches, borough of schools, borough of cemeteries, borough of back gardens, borough of thugs, borough of poets, borough of Capone, borough of O'Dwyer, anybody's borough, everybody's borough, nobody's borough. Who does not know Ebbets Field? Who is ignorant of Jackie Robinson's batting average? Who has not, in his mind's voyaging, sailed the Gowanus? Who has not eaten a hot dog? Who has not seen the dizzy lights of the roller coaster? Who has not heard the bull-larynxed barker calling, "The one and only living half-man and half-woman, it shaves one side and paints the other, all for the price of ten cents, the tenth part of a dollar, one thin dime"? Famous, notorious, overpraised and foully maligned, known and misunderstood, hideous and beautiful, breasting the Atlantic chop with brown, dredged beaches, its flat inland plains pierced by gummy and odorous canals, where can we start and say, "From this point we begin to tell the truth about Brooklyn"?

In the geography of our minds, Brooklyn is a land bounded vaguely on one side by the movies and on the other by the sporting pages of our newspapers. From this ambiguous country come strange, wild figures, making raucous and humorous sounds, comically different from the rest of the citizens of the nation. The truth, of course, must be otherwise, but the myth persists. There are 2,881,000 souls in Brooklyn today and reason tells us that nowhere on the face of the earth could there be that vast a concentration of comedians.

There are two Brooklyns: There is the Brooklyn of the historian and census taker, and there is the private and personal Brooklyn, untouched by statistics, which haunts the memory and shapes the behavior of all her sons, no matter where they roam.

When I first took up residence in Brooklyn, I was about seven years old, and I felt at the time what other new settlers in the borough, of greater years, must have felt at similar moments—that I had been driven into exile. Torn by restless parents from a dear land far away—the Bronx —where all was familiar to me, where every face was known, every retreat mapped out, every schoolteacher measured, I howled with loss and deep self-pity at this irrevocable removal to a strange, wild, half-built, sea-swept place.

Before this, Brooklyn had been a holiday region, where, at Coney Island, we visited my grandparents on fine Sundays. We rattled along in an open trolley, observed by tethered goats, through green fields and strung-out settlements, until we sniffed the bracing air of the nearby sea and alighted. Most of the day was spent in the water, with time out for beach-combing expeditions. The beach was stained by oil, congealed into tar, and littered with thousands of small, three-inch-long capsules of yellow powder, from ships that had been torpedoed off Sandy Hook. The First War was on then, and we took it for granted that the capsules contained gunpowder, and we felt daring and solemn as we made small hoards of our loot, later to be left to the new work of the incoming tide. Until then, the war had been an abstract thing, not easily comprehended, for which one uncle had to eat many pounds of bananas to pass a Navy examination, and in which another uncle had gotten a ride in an airplane in a place called Montgomery, Alabama. Also, at school, we had been told to collect peach and prune pits for use in gas masks, but this was too farfetched a process to enlist a child's imagination. But the bobbing yellow capsules on the tar-stained waves gave us tangible evidence of war, of ships sunk and treasure spread across the waters, and we watched gravely as vessels crossed the horizon on their way to Europe, waiting for them to go down before our eyes.

Later in the day we would walk with our parents along the old Brighton boardwalk, a splintery, weather-beaten structure on mossy and barnacled pilings, that ran alongside once-splendid huge wooden hotels at which, in earlier days, the fashion of the city had put up during the racing season at the nearby Sheepshead Bay track. The splendor was already gone, the boards were weather-beaten and yellowish, and in the frame theater adjoining the hotel, where once great stars had played and famous songs been sung, lowly motion pictures were being shown.

The conviction of disaster was further strengthened when I reported for school. The schoolhouse was on the outskirts of Coney Island, a forbidding ancient pile of smoky brick that looked as though it had been erected by the British for Yankee prisoners during the Revolutionary War. It had narrow windows, gas fixtures arranged for electricity, cavernous wardrobes heavy with dust from the coats of scholars who must have long since ripened and died. All traffic between floors was carried on by rickety outside stairways that poured rain down your collar on wet days, and the students, even at that tender age, seemed wild and leering and not at all like the politely brushed young ladies and gentlemen with whom I had learned to read and write in the airy new building in the Bronx. This lost paradise had been built on a hill among green fields near the border of Long Island Sound, and from it, on sunny days in spring, we used to make short pilgrimages to the grave of Joseph Rodman Drake, the poet in whose honor the school was named; he was buried in a country graveyard nearby and on his stone was carved the first poem I ever voluntarily memorized:

Green be the turf above thee,
Friend of my better days!
None knew thee but to love thee,
Nor named thee but to praise.

The school in Coney Island was clearly not named after any poet. If it had been named in honor of an escaped convict or a hanged spy it would not have surprised me. It bore only a prosaic number, and confirmed my belief that I had been plunged into a blighted neighborhood, neglected even by the otherwise impartial board of education of the City of New York. But it was to this same gloom-ridden school that I was to owe one of the most profound pleasures of my childhood.

One year later, the building was condemned. In the middle of an ordinary workday morning, we were told to collect our things and march downstairs. Quickly the delicious news spread, and among a thousand other cheering and singing children, I paraded gaily around the doomed pile, my faith in the eventual justice of the world around me somewhat restored.

The teachers who labored in this grim institution seemed immune to its mournful vapors. I remember high-spirited maiden ladies of various ages, usually Irish, who conducted their overcrowded classes with infectious zeal and easy good humor, very different from the bleak testiness and fatigue which seem to accompany the business of teaching and learning in our public schools today. Also, since many of them lived in the neighborhood, they would drop in for a cup of tea with the mothers of their charges on the way home (death on truants), all this giving a personal and villagelike air to the process of education which has long since been lost.

The region was rich in two things that go far to make a child happy—boats and horses. Across the horizon came and went a daily procession of ships that called at all the ports of the earth. Closer into shore there were canoes, fishing launches, pleasure craft, a small excursion steamer that docked at Steeplechase Pier and made two-hour runs along the beaches. (The romance of this particular vessel was considerably reduced after we had taken a ride in it on a rough afternoon and my mother and I fell ingloriously seasick.) Then there was the white majesty of the Iron Steamboat that raced down the harbor every day in the summer from the Battery to its dock at Steeplechase Pier, exploding hordes of musliny, sunburnt, distracted mothers and battalions of deliriously screaming children into the delights of Coney Island. And nearby was Sheepshead Bay, a narrow, landlocked finger of water, lined with weathered wooden docks, its gentle water crowded with fishing boats and pleasure yachts trimmed in mahogany and shining brass. Sometimes there would be a Coast Guard cutter tied up alongside and if you were lucky you might see a barefooted crewman carelessly tossing a canvas hood over the one-pounder in the bow, with which rumrunners were policed.

The fishermen threw their catch up on the docks for sale, spreading out the still flopping flounder, mackerel, and bass for inspection by the housewives of the neighborhood. And over it all, through the shifting and bobbing masts with their nets spread out to dry, came the winy smell of the harbor, compounded of salt water, fish, wet rope, fuel oil, mixed with the aroma of steaming chowders and frying clams from the innumerable restaurants that at that time were built on rickety high stilts over the water.

If there was a grownup along whom you could wangle into putting down the money, you got a round-trip ticket for one of the Rockaway ferries. These were small, cabined craft, with benches on top exposed to the sun. They made the trip down Sheepshead Bay and across to Rockaway Beach, chugging bravely around the pale white sand of Oriental Point and into the invigorating chop of the open sea on the way to the spit of surf-battered land on the horizon.

The New York City police force and the owners of the pony tracks at Coney Island gave the small boys of the neighborhood the shining vision of the Mounted Life. Not far away, on Ocean Parkway, the great boulevard that parades tree-lined to the sea from Prospect Park five miles inland, the police department had a stable and ring where they broke in fresh Western horses for use all over the city. From there, troops of mounted policemen, easy and perfect in their polished saddles, each leading a fully equipped and bridled animal, would trot briskly through the streets, night-sticks swinging in holsters against the flanks of the handsome young chestnut geldings, the dance of their hoofs making a breathless music through the traffic they were learning to ignore. It was not hard, seeing them, to think of Jeb Stuart and his riders trotting through a raided town, or Custer and his men, pennants flying, moving in a spray of prairie dust, toward the Little Big Horn battlefield.

And from spring to early fall, going to work from their stables in the morning and returning late at night through the deserted streets, would be the twinkling *remuda* of ponies, herded by two riders whose feet dangled to the ground on both sides of their mounts, an exhilarating confusion of tossing manes, streaming combed tails, flashing heads, flickering hoofs. I would watch with respect the somewhat larger animal, trotting along docilely enough now, but which I knew as a maniac bucker with a rider on his back. If you rode him successfully you were given a prize by the manager. I had watched him perform often and had seen him throw many a bragging cowboy from Bensonhurst and Brownsville rashly attempting to impress his friends with his horsemanship.

In the bright light of morning the passage of the ponies was a gay and spirited thing, but their return at night, with their oversize riders' grotesque shadows under the lamplight, and with the creak of their saddles and the thin clatter of their hoofs echoing and hollow in the surrounding silence, there was something nostalgic and defeated about them, as though gaiety were far behind them and the music of the carnival they had served long since died down, never to come up again.

Coney Island, since it was so constantly available, soon lost a great deal of its charm for most of the children of the neighborhood, although there were some boys who were connoisseurs of the various scenic railways and awaited with keen impatience the opening of new and more harrowing rides, each of which advertised unhesitatingly that this was the most death-defying contraption invented by the mind of man. I had a well-developed taste, of course, for hot dogs and root beer, cotton candy and jellied apples, staple items in my early diet; but aside from the gala week of Mardi Gras, with its huge floats, parading firemen, caparisoned horses, and confetti-throwing crowds, I really preferred Coney Island in the wintertime, when everything was shut down but a carrousel whose mournful calliope greeted you through the bitter air as you came into the sleeping region of joy and whose bejeweled chargers, unmounted, went round and round and up and down in sad and ceaseless splendor. Open, too, were one or two hot-dog stands, where heavily sweatered men in white caps shivered behind steaming grills of frankfurters, potato chips, hamburgers, and frying onions. And the movie houses were open. These dim, enchanting halls, surrounded by a balcony where family groups could sit sedately in screened-off boxes, were run on a kind of free-lunch arrangement, in reverse. That is, you paid for the food, and the sin was supplied by the management. They were furnished with round tables and rickety restaurant chairs, and a waiter would come over through the darkness as soon as you sat down and ask you what you wanted. You always said the same thing, "Hot dog and sass." This came to fifteen cents, by some unwritten covenant the minimum you were allowed to spend in the place. Then, chewing thoughtfully on the frankfurter and sipping slowly from the small glass of sarsaparilla, you settled back to enjoy *The Son of Zoro* or *The Hunchback of Notre Dame*.

Governed by a rigid code, the waiter never came back to embarrass you by asking if you wanted anything else. Occasionally there was the soft touch of a cat against your leg, prowling the obscure floor in search of the mice that ventured out for the crumbs that fell from the tables. But the audience sat in rapt silence, occasionally clinking the ice in their glasses by accident, as they stared unblinkingly at the dim screen at the end of the hall. Sometimes, now, when I go into one of our movie palaces, and sit down on plush for one of our modern epics, surrounded by an audience armed with rustling bags of popcorn, which they destroy with the methodical sound of a herd of cows in a small but rich pasture, I yearn for the old quiet days of the Coney Island movies, with their gliding, night-sighted, untipped waiters, the clink of ice in sarsaparilla glasses, the all-pervading odor of generations of hot dogs, and the feline touch of hunting cats against your leg in the darkness. It was easier to pay attention to the pictures then, and perhaps, too, the pictures were better.

In the summertime we went to the Rocking Chair movies in Brighton Baths. This was a dress-up affair. For it I tried to induce my brother, whom I was forced to take with me as a condition of the expedition, to comb his hair, a long drawn-out and bitterly contested battle of wills.

The oversize screen was set on pilings out in the surf, and there was a circular wooden bandstand off to one side for an orchestra. As the summer sun died on the dunes behind us, and the rows of rockers were filled, the orchestra, under the leadership of a maestro named Harold Stern, who was something of a power in seaside musical affairs for many years, played long, vibrating overtures, *Poet and Peasant* and the *William Tell Overture* being among the most popular selections. Then, in the salty twilight, with the appropriate music of the band vying with the noise of the surf, we would watch the silk-hatted comedian, Raymond Griffith, debonairly outwit his tormentors or Buster Keaton, playing an improbable king, straight-facedly launch a ship down the ways and bleakly, without change of expression, watch it sink straight to the bottom.

The days of summer were of course spent on the beach, where it was taken for granted that every child could swim as naturally as he could walk. Great projects were afoot at this time along the entire ocean front. A magnificent boardwalk, a kingly promenade, a boardwalk to end all boardwalks, was being built, to stretch finally all the way from Manhattan Beach to Sea Gate three and one-half miles away. First, great dredges worked for months, pumping coarse brown sand from the ocean bottom, to enlarge the beaches and push the edge of the sea farther back. Room was being made for millions more cases of sunburn, acres were being added to the United States in which to throw a medicine ball, flirt with your neighbor's wife, drop orange peels, step barefooted on broken glass, misplace your child. We gazed mournfully at the flood of brown mud settling dankly over what had heretofore been comparatively fine white sand, feeling that the price of progress and expansion was sometimes too high to pay.

The pugnacity, suspicion, quick temper, and skeptical pessimism of many Brooklynites might be traced back to early immurement in these infant tenements. The landlord having control of the furnace, and having a natural landlordly interest in buying as little coal as possible, every brisk day was the occasion for passion and discourteous interchange between neighbors, sometimes in the form of eloquent argument with frequent reference to the regulations of the board of health, sometimes, when matters had gone past words, in the form of no less eloquent tappings on the radiators with wrenches and broom handles.

Since the walls were only thick enough to hide one room's nakedness from the next, all arguments, gaiety, music, weeping and laughter became the common property of four families, so that a ten-year-old child practicing Czerny could finally become a raw-nerved obsession with perhaps a score of otherwise sensible citizens.

The demands of culture for the community were met by a small public library in neighboring Sheepshead Bay and the cavernous Brighton Theater, a block from the ocean, where the highly touted artists of the Keith-Orpheum Circuit performed, in season, on the wings of a cool sea breeze. Years later, when I was permitted to go every Saturday for the matinee performance (again with my brother, who by this time combed his hair without protest and who did not fall asleep in the afternoons) I saw, summer after summer, with undiminished joy, the same acts, which included Eva Tanguay, swinging out over the audience in tights, singing hoarsely, a woman who had trained pigeons which pulled a chariot and went through a marriage ceremony, and Pat Rooney in a one-hour review called Rings of Smoke, in which he reflectively smoked a cigarette in an armchair, sang nostalgic Irish melodies and did his famous heel-clicking trick in mid-air.

The walk to the library was a long but rewarding one, by way of an abandoned spur of the Long Island Rail Road. In the old days before the building of the electrified Brighton Line, steam engines and day coaches had made the run to the clapboard station on the edge of Manhattan Beach, but now the embankment on which the track was laid was overgrown with weeds and wild flowers, through which the rusted rails wound in a dull red trail. A brooding, desert silence hung over the tracks and the rich smells of the sea and the rank growth mingled in the heavy afternoon sunlight, and it was easy to imagine, for a boy with a book under his arm, the ghosts of luxurious ancient trains clicking by, filled with strangely dressed ladies and gentlemen, on their way to older amusements at the shore. The tracks ran on a bridge over a salt creek (now long forfeit to the dredging machines, but at that time furnished with a couple of weather-beaten dories and equally weather-beaten fishermen), and by a slight detour you could walk along Sheepshead Bay itself, looking for new craft at anchor and recognizing the old.

The library, although installed in two ordinary stores, with the partition between knocked out, was one of the most agreeable places devoted to books that I have ever seen. Spotlessly clean, its lamps and tables neatly arranged, filled with a gentle whispering silence, broken occasionally by the tap of the librarian's stamp, with a slight fragrance from the bowl of narcissus that always seemed to be on the front desk, it bespoke a deep and orderly love for books and people, especially children, who read books.

At the age of ten I took upon my spreading shoulders the full burden of being a Brooklynite—I started traveling daily in the subway. What drought is to the Oklahoma farmer, famine to the Bengalese peasant, silicosis to the coal miner, the BMT, the IRT, and the newer Independent Subway are to the dweller in Brooklyn.

Worse, it is both his punishment and the prime necessity of his life. Droughts end, there are whole cycles of good crops in India, new methods are constantly being devised to lay the cutting dust of the mines, but the sound of the underground wheels roaring out of the DeKalb Avenue station is the beat of the living heart of Brooklyn. Stop the Sea Beach Express, flag down the Fourth Avenue local, cancel the New Lots run, and two million souls halt in mid-air, as if tranced. Examine, if you can, the nightmares that are dreamed in Brooklyn, and in them all there will be a subway car, packed tighter than the brain can imagine, pulling out of Times Square at 5:30 in the afternoon on a 90° day in summer.

The occasion of my apprenticeship to the five-cent fare was the decision on the part of the school authorities to send me to a junior high school in which it would be possible to do two years' work in one. There was a rash philosophy prevalent in educational circles in those days which skipped slightly precocious children as hurriedly as possible through the badly overcrowded system, trusting to luck that by a process of osmosis the scholars would somehow pick up en route the subjects they had missed. I had already been artificially advanced a year and a half (in the process escaping the term in which the theory of fractions was taught, as a result of which I cannot, to this day, add, divide, subtract, multiply, or do anything but avoid any fraction) and I had no desire at all to be thrust out upon the cold world of commerce and grown-up affairs another full year ahead of my time. This was not due so much to my love of leisurely learning as it was to the fact that I had just begun to play football, and did not wish to try to play tackle for Princeton until I had reached my full growth, which I was fairly certain would not be at the age of fifteen.

But my fate was out of my hands and one charcoal dawn I put the nickel in the slot and started the long ride that for most Brooklynites ends only in death. The school I was bound for was an hour's trip away, in a neighborhood near which Mayor O'Dwyer, then Patrolman O'Dwyer, walked his first beat. The institution was named after Admiral Dewey (the school song went "Do we love our alma mater, yes we do, we do, we do") and was set near the great docks and railroad yards of the Bush Terminal, a gigantic enterprise that handled cities full of freight and cargo daily.

It also housed a cafeteria run by the YWCA. These good ladies on Friday served a fish-cake lunch that was highly thought of in adolescent gourmet circles, and we would flee from the school at the noon recess, running the quarter-mile in very respectable time over the cobbled streets, to get to the head of the line of trays and gorge ourselves on the crisp brown cod flakes soaked in tomato sauce, nestling among mounds of mashed potatoes. Other days, we would eke out our lunches, brought from home, with whole custard pies (price fifteen cents), eaten standing in the Swedish delicatessen that conveniently adjoined the school.

The neighborhood, with certain Italian enclaves, was largely Scandinavian, and the fathers of many of my classmates were called Johnson or Ericsson and seemed most of the time to be visiting foreign ports in merchant vessels. It couldn't be, I realize now, that they were all chief engineers, but at the time that was my impression of all the grown male inhabitants of Bay Ridge.

Since I was too young and too small to play on the school teams (a fulfilled prediction I threw up to my parents in moments of despair), I turned, as so many other handicapped nonheroes have done through the centuries, to the pen. I accompanied the basketball team on its sorties into the lower depths of Brooklyn and reported the games for the school newspaper. This was good training for a war correspondent, in that you accepted the risks of combat without carrying either the arms or the honor of the combatants. If your team lost, all was well; after the game you were permitted to leave in comparative peace, with only verbal taunts from the mobs of local patriots gathered at the gymnasium door to speed you on your way out of Williamsburg or Red Hook. But if you were unlucky enough to win, your retreat had to be planned as strategically as the Battle of Saint Lô. A tight wedge would be formed inside the door, with the largest and bravest at the apex and wings, and the less worthy and durable, which always included myself, protected in the center. Then, at a signal from the captain, the doors would be suddenly flung open to gain tactical surprise and the wedge would hurl itself at the waiting lines of snarling, defeat-haunted youths, all of whom have long since gone to Sing Sing or become colonels in the Marines. Stones, old vegetables, dead cats, and odd pieces of lumber were the usual long-range weapons, with the fist only used for close infantry fighting. Glued together by the strictest discipline, the wedge held until it had pierced through to the enemy's back country, usually half a block from the door, where we fell into a line of skirmishers and dropped back in an orderly manner, firing from time to time to cover our rear. Pursuit stopped at the subway station, this being considered a neutral boundary beyond which hostilities were diplomatically not feasible.

My own athletic activities were conducted, less glamorously, closer to home. At the first dim signs of spring the Montauk Athletic Club, of which I was a member, would forgather on a cindery diamond in the neighborhood to institute pre-season training with a baseball carefully wound with black bicycle tape and thriftily saved from the preceding season. This missile, especially when wet, as it often was, had the weight and resilience of lead shot, and taking the throw at second base from the catcher, who had an arm like a siege gun, was an act of calculated courage. Playing the outfield, which often required leaping up a small, pitted embankment to a concrete sidewalk in chase of a fly ball, likewise presented its difficulties.

During the winter we had met every Friday night, for the sole purpose of contributing our weekly dues, one dime. With the obscene joy of misers, we listened each week to the treasurer's mounting report, and then, with the beginning of good weather, we would reap the fruits of our prudence. En masse, on a Saturday morning, we would ride the subway to Nassau Street, in downtown Manhattan, a hallowed center of sporting-goods equipment, and there select a half-dozen Louisville Sluggers, a catcher's mitt and mask, and a dozen baseballs for the campaign ahead. After a season or two we found ourselves in good enough financial condition to invest in nine red sweat shirts. By a vote, it was decided which players would be considered the varsity and get the prizes, and since there were about twenty boys in the club, there were fiercely aching hearts beating under unshirted bosoms that Friday night. For years afterward, a good part of my clothing was stained pink with the dye of my precious shirt, which persisted, despite 500 washings, in leaking pigment all the days of its existence. Then came the dazzling moment when we had enough money in the treasury to order complete uniforms. There was solemn discussion for days about the color scheme and heated debate about the writing on the chest, and the final vote for gray flannel pants and shirt, with Montauk written across it in flowing maroon script, like the inscription on the chests of the St. Louis Cardinals, was not achieved lightly. The ceremony of being measured in the fitting room of the sporting-goods store had a bridal thrill for us all, and when the uniforms arrived there was a great deal of full-dress posing before long mirrors, with careful bending of the peaks of the maroon caps to impart a big-league look to the headgear. The socks, of maroon wool, had the same wonderful power as the sweat shirts to impart a pink tinge to any other material which they momentarily touched. All this finery, as I remember it, cost us nine dollars each, and, despite the extravagant outlay, was considered well worth it.

We scheduled most of our games through the *Brooklyn Daily Eagle.* This paper has a certain claim to immortality, often being mentioned in literary histories, because Walt Whitman once worked on its staff and, in fact, reviewed his own *Leaves of Grass* in its columns, giving the volume of poems, not unexpectedly, a generous welcome. I read it religiously, not so much for its connection with Walt Whitman, who was but a dim figure to me at the time, as for its exhaustive coverage of the activities, on and off the field, of the Brooklyn Dodgers. The paper ran, free of charge, on its sporting page, several columns in which you could advertise, "Fast club, 13 to 15 class, uniformed, traveling, looking for games. Call Brighton 2033, any evening after six and ask for Al." Certain clubs advertised that they had permits for the Parade Grounds, and these organizations were much sought after, as the Parade Grounds, an enormous public plain facing Prospect Park with forty-five ball fields on it, had backstops, rubber home plates, pitchers' mounds, and real cut-out diamonds. The field at the waterworks near Avenue U was also considered desirable, although it had the drawback of having a deep ravine into which outfielders sometimes dropped going back for fly balls. The embankment and tracks of the Brighton Line, which ran alongside the field, constituted another hazard, as foul balls often fell between the tracks and you would have to send your smallest and most sure-footed player over the fence to hop over the deadly third rail and retrieve the ball. He would also have to be swift and daring enough to avoid capture by the railroad policemen, who would charge down very often in an unsportsmanlike attempt to keep small boys from being electrocuted, or mangled by the Brighton Express.

The arrangements for the game were simple, but strict. At the cry of "Play ball!" each team supplied one brand-new baseball, out of an unopened box, the winning team keeping both balls. There would be a wager of a quarter a man, delivered into the umpire's hand before game time, of which the club would usually supply fifteen cents and the individual player a dime. You could not steal home because there was no backstop and we liked to keep the scores respectable. A wild throw into the railroad tracks was good for one base, and if any of the casual onlookers and players in other games on the field happened to touch a ball or be hit by one, you played it off him as though he were a fence. A ball into the ravine was played for all you could get, and a standard maneuver for outfielders was a long, blind, hand-grenade kind of throw from a thick bed of last year's leaves in the dank bottom of the gully, in the general direction of an unseen third base. The spoils of victory were usually spent in the nearest candy store on ice-cream sodas, and very sweet they were indeed. The club secretary, a bookish and usually non-playing type, kept the box score and figured out batting averages, and if a boy fell below .300 he would be very restive at the next Friday night's meeting when the talk swung around to possible new members for the club. The treasurer kept the baseballs and was held responsible for appearing with them promptly at practice during the week. The secretary also had the duty of sending an account of the game, with the score by innings and the names of the opposing batteries to the *Brooklyn Daily Eagle*, if we won.

During the summer vacation it was impossible to keep the team together, as some parents wantonly took their first-basemen and shortstop sons to the country on holidays with them, and some of the older boys found work in Coney Island as locker-room attendants at the bathhouses and as shills for the games of chance on the Coney Island Bowery, lackadaisically pumping levers to make mechanical rabbits run in cony races from noon till midnight for ten dollars a week, or tossing baseballs at openings in a canvas sheet to make baby pigs come out of their pens and skid down a slide.

Despite the premature termination of the baseball season, the summer was full of delight. I had been given a new bicycle and I tasted for the first time the soaring freedom of being mobile. Delivered for two months from the fell clutch of the BMT, I drifted, two-wheeled and swift, wherever my curiosity led me, to Gravesend Bay, where deserted picnic grounds behind sagging fences fronted mournfully on the polluted funereal water; to Shore Road, where the owners of the neatly painted homes could look out their front windows and watch great ocean liners passing a few feet from their lawns; over the newly cobbled road across Barren Island, later to be made into Floyd Bennett airport, and across the inlet of Jamaica Bay by ferry to Rockaway. This road, running a long distance over rustling marshes, was a favorite spot for lovers' automobiles after dark, until a lady magistrate gained considerable notoriety by having hundreds of couples pinched, dragged out of their sweet back-seat privacy into night court, there to be harangued by the moral lady judge, and have the girls' names registered and forwarded to what the judge obviously hoped would be vengeful parents.

My favorite ride was down Ocean Parkway, wide and tree-shaded against the hot summer sun, past the mansions that bordered it, past the crowded cemetery flanked by tennis courts, past the riding academies with their troops of nervous fat girls bouncing on cynical horses, to Prospect Park. These wide green acres, one of the noblest city parks in the country, with their rough hills, the large, boat-dotted lake, the tall ancient trees, zoo, tennis and croquet and cricket lawns, the wide bridle paths on which could always be observed some doubtful horseman trying to remember whether he had been told to rise in his stirrups when the horse's left or right leg went forward, were, naturally enough, a never-ending source of entertainment for a boy on a bike. But it was not for these pleasures that I came to the park. I was there to follow a lady.

The lady was like no lady I had ever seen before and I have never come across her like since. She would arrive at the park entrance every sunny morning at ten, in a small, open, brightly painted yellow carriage drawn by a glossy bay horse with a high prancing gait. Dressed in a checkered wool jacket of bright design, with a stock at her throat and a derby perched squarely on her bobbed hair, her gloved hands elegantly holding reins and whip, her skin pale and proud in the morning sunlight, she was a vision of old romance among the prosaic automobiles that passed her with plebeian speed.

I did not pass her. I rode behind her, a faithful attendant, as she circled the park, never varying the spirited pace of her steed. She never looked back. She never spoke to me. I never spoke to her. But day after day, we made our double circuit among the old oaks, along the lake's edge, past the wide meadow near the arch. I thought her beautiful, although I am afraid that I would have thought the same of any woman, wearing a tiny round derby, driving in such an equipage, behind so glittering a horse.

In the afternoons I would pedal down to my father's office to visit him. He was a real-estate dealer doing business in a small frame cottage on the edge of a huge tract of land which had just been thrown open and subdivided in what was called the Marine Park area. The boom was on then, and land was not thought of as earth to plow or on which to build, but as something to buy, sell, mortgage and exchange. On the wall of my father's office was a framed editorial of Arthur Brisbane's, endorsing real estate. Land, according to the great editor, was the true investment, because it could not vanish, like the value of stocks and it would not go bankrupt like a business. The land in this vicinity, it is true, sometimes had a tendency to go under water at high tide, and my father, inspecting property he was contemplating buying, once had to be pulled out of a mud flat in which he was fast disappearing. But there were grandiose schemes for the region's future. The Marine Park was to be a combination of the best features of Venice and Yellowstone Park. Schools would be built, theaters erected, shopping centers created, subways dug. As down payment on the promise, streets were laid out and named, though they stretched through what looked like limitless, untenanted acres of scrub grass.

Eventually homes (rather narrow, attached one-family houses in imitation English style rather than the spacious mansions of the prospecti) were built in considerable numbers, and while the subway never made its appearance, bus lines and trolley lines that finally brought you to a subway were put into operation; but the buying and selling suddenly stopped, and with sinking hearts a great many of the citizens of Brooklyn began to realize that payments on mortgages must be met and that there would be no money to meet them with. The boom seemed to end two years earlier in Brooklyn than in the rest of the country, and the depression seemed to start two years sooner. Brooklyn, typically, was impatient.

But that was for the future. Meanwhile, we all collected among the crowds on the handsome new boardwalk for the weekly fireworks shot off a barge half a mile out to sea, crisscrossing the sky with flaming patterns that were prettier then, in that pre-*Luftwaffe* period, than they would seem today. After the fireworks, the older and more daring boys would attempt to pick up girls among the strolling throngs. Egged on by my coarser friends, who also had the advantage of two years of age on me, a cause of constant private sorrow, I walked up behind a girl who was sauntering along at a pace that seemed deliberate invitation. Taking my courage in my two hands, I said, as formally and unprovokingly as possible, "It is a very nice night, isn't it?"

The girl glanced over her shoulder, the beginning of a welcoming smile on her face. Then the smile froze as she stared at me. "How is it, Junior," she asked, "your mother lets you stay up so late?" Then she turned and continued her walk. She must have been at least sixteen. The event had a lasting effect on me. From that day to this, in travels on three continents and several islands, I have never spoken to a woman unless she has spoken to me first.

Nobody can write about Brooklyn without writing about Ebbets Field. I cannot remember when I first saw Ebbets Field. It is as though I have always known it, as though it is a kind of race memory, not in the genes, but subtly introduced into my subconscious, when, a youthful immigrant from another borough, I crossed the Brooklyn Bridge for the first time.

Dazzy Vance seems always to be pitching in my memory of those long, hot afternoons, his purposely-torn sleeve flapping as he rears way up and comes down with the fearful high, hard one that hits DeBerry's mitt so hard you can hear the riflelike report even way out in the bleachers along the left-field foul line where I sit and marvel. Vance always seems to be pitching against the Cubs, somehow, because, by some peculiarity of the game, he did his best work against them, striking out large numbers of them every time he faced them, a spectacle at which I would make sure to present myself. Zach Wheat, the darling of the bleachers, the Dixie Walker of his day, patrolled left field and conversed with the faithful before the game and between innings, and from time to time, with a gesture of unutterable largesse, would throw, as a souvenir, in a lazy, haphazard arc, one of the practice balls into the clutching hands of his admirers.

I would attend all double-headers, filling a canteen with iced tea against the thirst of the unshaded afternoon, putting my fifty-five cents down very early, so that I would miss none of the practice. There, among the taxi drivers, the milkmen, the post-office workers, who did not have to report until nightfall, the unemployed, the truant, I sat, supremely happy, watching with only temporarily dampened spirits when Brooklyn outfielders were hit on the head by fly balls, when infielders collided under pop-ups, when Brooklyn pitchers were shelled for six runs an inning, when Brooklyn base runners stole third with bases loaded.

All discussion at Ebbets Field was carried on in tones that in any other place would have been the prelude to bloody conflict. "Aaah . . . yer mother's mustache. That bum never hit .300 the best year he ever saw. Why, he couldn't get one out of three, for Danville, in the Three I League. Yeah. That's what I said," was a fair sample of the conversation that took place in between such other activities as throwing bunches of penny firecrackers at enemy outfielders waiting for high flies to settle. And, in more confidential tones, about some disappointing athlete, "I tell yuh what's the matter with him. Physically, he got outstanding equipment, but he ain't got it here," with a significant tapping of the left breast. "He got a ladyfinger for a heart." And, "You say he's got a arm? Why, you make me laugh. A arm? Why, that poor feller can't reach home plate from second base in under three bounces. He's a regular cripple, you watch outside the locker room every day after the game, he comes out with his hand in a sling. Listen to him! A arm, he says!"

It was also standard wit in the bleachers to tell newcomers that Old Man Ebbets was so tight that he could be seen on the roof of the stands during games, running after foul balls and thriftily recovering them for use in the next day's game. And legendary was the phrase, "Wait until next year. We'll be in the first division," which, somehow, by the beginning of the following April, we all of us believed, and continued to believe until the first wave of powerful Western clubs had rolled over our prostrate heroes.

Several years later, when, as a member of my high-school football squad, I actually dressed in the same locker room which had once harbored Zach Wheat and Dazzy Vance, I kept touching the walls with holy wonder. And, when in the last game of the season, the other team having decimated or disgraced all our tackles, the coach got down to bedrock and sent me in, my cleats flew over the sacred turf like independent birds. To this day, in dozing moments of the night, between sleeping and waking, the memory of that afternoon comes pleasantly over me, of myself in a golden jersey, pulling on a helmet, running out to report to the referee in the autumn sunshine, feeling that every eye in the great crowd was upon me, fiercely resolved to stand my ground or die. And when we went on to score and win, I felt that life had served me full measure and everything that came after was so much profit. I was fifteen at the time, in my senior year at high school.

The school was newly built, and had the curious capacity of all schools in New York City, of being critically overcrowded from the very first day it opened its doors. Inundating tides of violently healthy boys and girls flooded through the halls, sweeping the overworked teachers before them with good-natured but savage high spirits. It was only occasionally, by virtue of a colorful personality, an unusual charm, an extraordinary power of intellect, that a teacher could make a real impression on the shifting, roaring, ebullient human stuff that flowed so overabundantly by. For the most part, they seemed to wave scraps of education forlornly at us as we rushed through their classes, hoping that some of us, at least, would have sense enough to seize at them as we tumbled through our stormy and hilarious adolescence toward the forbidding goal of maturity.

More than any of the things that were formally offered to me in the name of education, I remember the games, the times my mother was called to school because I had been caught drawing caricatures of French and geometry instructors, the squirming, silent hours I spent in the detention room after school because I had come late (the school was inaccessible and required a nice timing of subways and buses to be reached on schedule), the sinful joys of truancy when, finding ourselves late in front of the ominously quiet school, we would turn tail and take the train downtown and go into the morning show at Loew's Metropolitan, a headquarters for truants from all over the borough. Or, if it was a warm spring day, we would go canoeing off Manhattan Beach or rowing on Prospect Park Lake, out of reach of disciplining authorities. I remember the frosty nights of winter, when the red ball would go up outside the park and we would go skating on the lake's frozen surface, regaling ourselves later with hot chocolate lathered with melted marshmallow. I remember a sarcastic Latin teacher, rebuking me for a stumbling translation of Caesar, by saying, "I know your type. You don't believe in study. I suppose you're one of those young gentlemen who loll around outside the gate after school hours smoking cigarettes and waiting for girls." I remember the warm glow of pleasure that spread over me at this accusation, and the feeling that I would gladly give ten years of my life if it were really true.

I remember the season I played football, weight 155, on the fourth team, which scrimmaged against the first team every day on the rocky field behind the school, which was seeded every year and every year turned into shale after the first practice. There was a giant, well over six feet, weight 220, who played fullback for the varsity, and, in looking back, I seem to have spent three autumn months of my youth clinging to him, calling frantically to other fourth-stringers to collect around him and help bring him to earth as he churned phlegmatically through the line. I remember another substitute tackle, too lowly even to play on the fourth team or be given a uniform, who supplied his own outfit, shining new and quite luxurious, and who could be observed surreptitiously rubbing dirt into the canvas of his pants to give them the look of honorable service. The following season, I read that he had made the first team, a perfect tower of strength, and had been chosen for the all-scholastic team of the city. He came to the same college I attended and served half a season with us, but gave up football because he played the cello and his mother was afraid he would hurt his wrists.

I remember the beginnings of the literary life, after school hours, in a writers' club, where I first observed the artistic temperament in action. Each of us read his or her offering aloud, waiting for criticism, and the criticism was never long in coming, nor did it differ much from the criticism heard in older and more professional circles in later years. It was used with the same intention and much the same effect as the antipersonnel 105-mm. shell, and an expression of intense rejection was cultivated by us all as a sign of our extraordinary taste and as evidence of the grandeur of our standards.

I was graduated after an incomprehensible address by a lank, youngish visiting educator in a badly fitting dinner jacket, who lectured us on the responsibilities of marriage, a subject in which I had no immediate interest at the time. My one regret was that I was getting out so prematurely, as I was sure that I would weigh 165 by the next football season and was confident I could have made the varsity.

My grandiose dreams of Princeton had vanished with the real-estate boom, and I was thankful to get into Brooklyn College, an institution supported by the city, and at that time a branch of the College of the City of New York. The most important thing about Brooklyn College was that it was free. But my heart, nourished on dappled dreams of spreading, ancient campuses and young gods lounging on the steps of fraternity houses with silver beer mugs in their hands, declined sorrowfully at the sight of the office buildings and converted lofts in downtown Brooklyn in which the pure sweet voice of learning had to shout to make itself heard over the clangor of the trucks and trolley cars in the streets outside the windows. Between two of the buildings there was a shabby burlesque house, in which some of the more affluent students spent their idle hours watching fading strip-teasers grind out bumps for the unemployed and homeless who made up the audience. But most of the scholars wasted no time on such distractions. Grimly poor, from overcrowded homes in hideous slums, working at night as soda-jerkers and clerks to pay for their books and carfare, they knew what they were in school for—and they devoured the intellectual diet that was offered them with a hungry avidity that left me, with my more inconsequential and frivolous habits, completely behind. After one term, and a despairing brush with calculus, I was flunked out.

Feeling that all was over, that the seal of failure had been once and for all put upon my life, contemplating suicide (by drowning, naturally, in the conveniently water-girt borough), I made the dread round of the employment agencies, in each one yielding up the damning information that I was young, inexperienced, and uneducated. Finally, I was offered a job as a shipping clerk in a factory at sixteen dollars a week, and I seized it, with the sense that no other job would be offered me in my lifetime.

My working day began at eight in the morning. We had moved, by this time, to one of the English-style homes in the Marine Park section, which my father, according to the custom of the time, had managed to get in exchange for something a little more valuable. Going to work involved a long ride on a trolley car to the end of the Flatbush Avenue subway line and an interminable journey through the bowels of Brooklyn in a train that kept engorging passengers long after it would have been easy to prove scientifically that there was not an inch of space left in the cars in which to put them. I swept the factory, which was a small one, opened crates that had been delivered to us, usually with considerable damage to my hands, and then packed orders all day into cardboard cartons. The final job of the day was to load the packed cartons onto a hand truck and take them over to the post office for mailing, which usually involved an hour's wait in a press of other clerks slowly advancing toward the window. After 6:30 my time was my own. There didn't seem to be unions for anything in those days.

It was at this period that I determined to be a writer or die in the attempt. In the evenings I went to night classes at Brooklyn College, nodding sleepily over Chaucer or the formula for the curve of a parabola, wondering dazedly where my classmates got the energy that drove them so burningly through their books, and stumbling down the subway steps for the long ride home.

On free evenings I would go to the Civic Repertory Theater, in Manhattan, a draughty old barn on 14th Street, not far from where I worked. This was Eva Le Gallienne's greathearted venture in putting the classic and near-classic dramas on the stage for modest prices. I had been going sporadically to the Broadway theater for several years, buying my tickets at Gray's drugstore, where the less popular attractions sold off their seats at half price. The plays I saw were chosen for me by inexorable economic law. . . . nothing over seventy-five cents. I had enjoyed them all mightily (in fact it was not until I had seen about fifty plays that I realized that there could be such a thing as a bad play), but I doubt that the dramatic nourishment I had received from them was very high. But the Civic Repertory Theater, with its shabby proscenium, grotesquely bright green walls and wooden gallery benches, presented Ibsen, Chekhov, Tolstoy, Gorky, and a whole new vision of the world was spread out for me for my seventy-five cents. There is a parking lot where the ancient theater used to stand, and even now when I pass the gaping, ugly space, some of the old feeling of discovery and pleasure comes over me, saddened by the passage and wreckage of time.

In the autumn I took entrance examinations and returned to college. Having tasted the horrors of honest labor, I was careful to do enough work from then on to insure my staying in school until I got my degree.

Weighing an impressive 170, I immediately went out for the football team, the squad of which was made up for the most part of boys who had never played a game in their lives, since, whatever other charges might be leveled against Brooklyn College, it could never be accused of proselytizing athletes. All our practice that year, before our first game, was conducted in the school gymnasium, since no field could be secured. This room was a small, narrow hall in the basement of one of the buildings, with a ceiling only eight feet high. It was dotted with thick pillars, and was a very curious place in which to prepare a football team for a campaign against college teams. It was so low that no passes could be thrown, so small that you could only walk through one play at a time, and of course spread formations, punts and kickoffs could only be explained theoretically to the players.

I had a sense of impending disaster when we got into the bus at nine o'clock of a bright Saturday morning to start to Trenton for our first game, but I tried to put on a cheery front. We made our lunch on dry sandwiches on the bus and some of the athletes washed the sandwiches down with milk shakes in Trenton just before the game, a practice of which I doubt Knute Rockne would have approved.

The boy who played end next to me had been gently reared and was convinced before and during every game he played that he was going to be killed before the final whistle. The opposing quarterback quickly found out about our end's psychological misgivings, and I spent a monotonous afternoon chasing enemy backs on wide, profitable sweeps over his quivering body. We lost by a score of 38–0, which I think our coach took as a moral victory.

I switched to the backfield after that, as I felt too exposed up front. I had my nose broken several times in various towns in nearby Connecticut, but continued playing, as we had a small squad and a Spartan coach who had once gone through an entire game in his own college days with a broken leg. "Run it off" was his sole prescription for all ills and injuries, and he would show you his limp nose, from which all the shattered bone had been removed long ago, and his gnarled and twisted fingers, crushed innumerable times, as evidence that a man could get through life quite happily in not quite the same piece that God made him.

We lost every game that first season, but since they were all played away from home, our shame, while duly reported in the newspapers, was not suffered before our classmates' eyes. We saw a great deal of New

England through bus windows and we all got a lot of exercise, much more than most of the pampered stars of the great teams who were used for a few minutes a Saturday and then put under blankets to rest. We all played sixty minutes a game, unless the coach was convinced we could no longer get up from the turf under our own power. Since he was a man who could get up and run a mile in under five minutes after being run over by a steam roller, he was very hard to convince.

In later seasons the team improved, although never to a point where the supremacy of Army and Notre Dame was seriously jeopardized by us. We won a few games, but every time a boy showed promise of becoming really useful as a passer or in backing up the line, he was flunked out of school by the faculty, who had an unerring eye for such deeds. We also had mother trouble. Since we all lived at home, the ravages of the sport were immediately visible to loving eyes at the fireside and a random black eye or broken collarbone was sure to bring down a concerted family attack on the barbarism of college football. When I came into the sleeping house late on Saturday nights, after coming home from distant games, I would steal, burglarlike, up to my room with my wounds, but I would always be awakened some time in the middle hours by the touch of my mother's fingers on my lips, as she felt to see if my teeth, which she for some reason considered my chief charm, were still there. One of our best linemen, who was Jewish, and whose mother was very devout, had to smuggle his uniform out of the house and pretend he was going to the museum on Saturdays, so as not to offend his mother's religious scruples about breaking the Sabbath. Since he was a boy who cut easily, and would come home with hideous gashes all over his face and hands, which he was not likely to have received at the museum, his mother quickly caught on, and he had to transfer to the boxing team, which fought during the week and at night.

Everybody in school seemed to work at one job or another. Everybody seemed to be poor in Brooklyn during that time and poverty appeared to us all to be the natural and inevitable climate of existence.

Our social life was necessarily modest. If you went to visit a girl you usually managed to arrive there in time for dinner. If a girl lived two carfares away, you had to be certain that you were very fond of her indeed before you asked to take her out. Devotion was measured in terms of mileage. If a boy took an hour or an hour and a half's trek on a succession of trolleys to see his girl, it was adjudged true love. From late Saturday night till the hours of dawn Sunday morning, the sound of pounding feet on the pavements could be heard all over Brooklyn as homeward-bound and lipstick-smeared swains sped along dark streets in pursuit of trolley cars vanishing down the melancholy vistas of Tompkins, Nostrand and Flatbush avenues. A boy whose father owned a car and who was permitted to borrow it on Saturday night was highly prized as a friend, and usually at least four couples would be squeezed in for transportation to parties and school dances. Then, late at night, after the girls had been properly dispatched at their doors, with three or four other boys who had perhaps been unattached for the evening and whom we picked up en route, we would speed, free of feminine restraint, down to Sheepshead Bay, where Lundy's Restaurant, redolent of fish and clams, kept open all night. The room was musical with the sound of the bay lapping at the pilings on which the restaurant was built, and the hospitable interior was brought to a warm glow by a big-bellied coal stove. We would order clam chowder, served in thick, deep bowls, a heady, spiced mixture of generous chunks of clam, potatoes, and tomatoes, steaming hot, and costing only thirty-five cents, a sum we would carefully amass and preserve during the week against all temptation. With the chowder the waiter would bring platters of hot biscuits and all the butter we wanted. With the winter night wind howling across from the ocean at the walls of the restaurant, with the wet tap-tap of the bay underfoot and the rich warmth of body and spirit engendered by the heat of the stove and the chowder and biscuits, surrounded by comrades who had cars and who, besides that, seemed loyal, dashing, and invulnerable, we would speculate on the future. Our ambitions varied. Some were quite modest, entailing college degrees and schoolteachers' licenses. But most of us had more grandiloquent plans. We had our sights leveled on the great city across the river. Like spies for an invading army, we had stolen in and out of its streets, marking its wealth, the temper of its inhabitants, its deceptively nonchalant defenses, its theaters and museums, the beauty of its women. With its domes and spires constantly in our sight, to spur us on with the tantalizing accessibility of the prize, we laid our plans for conquest. We were all optimistic. Privately, we might feel that the others would fail, but we were confident of our own luck. Although we were in the middle of the depression, we were lightheartedly certain of our ability to make a place for ourselves. Fame and fortune were just a nickel subway's ride away from our front doors. We had been to the inner circle of the fortress and we had found nothing there that looked impregnable. None of us foresaw the war that would claim us all. Full of hot biscuits, chowder and dreams, we went home through the cold pre-dawn weather, to wakc early and play touch football at Wingate Field, a Flatbush landmark, whose concrete stands had witnessed our first attempts to run a hundred yards in less than twelve seconds, and, after that, to doze at home listening to the Sunday program of the Philharmonic on the radio.

The Navy Yard, birthplace of many gallant ships, was nearby, and we would walk past the Marines on guard at the entrance, listening to the clangor of drills and presses beyond the walls, sensing the presence of tall masts, great guns, world-shaking battles on seas whose names we had not yet learned. And lining the street facing the Yard were whole rows of sailors' traps, pool rooms and newly legalized saloons, complete with waiting, hard-eyed ladies.

The walk to the museum on Eastern Parkway led through the Botanic Gardens, famous for their lily display at Easter. Resonant with the hum of insects foraging among the blooms, overlaid with the fragrance of plants that had been brought across oceans to blossom here, with a Japanese garden complete with pond and tiny arched bridge, all of it shut off from the world by thick hedges, the only sound that of playing children on the other side of the hedge, this was spring's country and the home of quiet pleasure. The Museum itself, a majestic and rather forbidding Grecian building where we went to listen to free symphony concerts, had two brilliant rooms where were hung the nation's best collections of the water colors of John Singer Sargent and Winslow Homer. Here, so close to home, were the dazzling shimmer of purple shadows on Venetian cathedrals, the hawk look, caught with a stroke, of an Arab prince; here were the Caribbean in storm and West Indians plucking sea turtles from milk-green waters. It seemed footling and meager to have to take a trolley home from the Museum; there should have been a schooner moored just outside the door, or at the very least a sloop, sails up and manned by dark brown sailors with beards.

But none of these glories could hold me. I deserted Brooklyn several years later, with my degree safely tucked away, having failed to pass the oral examination for an English teacher's license in the high-school system (my long years at Ebbets Field had betrayed me; the examiner was quick to note and damn the raucous *ng*'s and gravelly *erl* sounds I had acquired cheering on Dazzy Vance and Jigger Statz). With the prospect of an early production of my first play, I crossed the Bridge, my ears still ringing with a mother's usual remarks to an eldest son breaking away from home, and took a room, like any young man with a manuscript under his arm, in Greenwich Village.

Traveler, never go back. Your childhood is not there. Your teammates, who were so swift and who wore the proud Montauk in leaky maroon across their chests, have died on Mindanao or become lawyers. The girls you loved can no longer be reached by trolley. Less slender than when they walked past Cranberry Street with you, they now wheel baby carriages and go to psychoanalysts to learn how to bring up their sons. The rusty, deserted tracks along which you heard the click of ghostly Victorian wheels have long ago been covered with two-family homes. The rides in Coney Island now seem tame, and nowhere can a hot dog be bought for a nickel. The bay of childhood has been harnessed in angular concrete, and the docks are all of standardized shape and erected by the city. Lundy's is off the water now and is a sprawling stucco Italianate palace, with a parking lot full of cars, and the coal stove was long ago made into shrapnel. Six-story apartment houses now occupy the sand where you sat in rockers and heard the overture to *William Tell*. The Navy and the Coast Guard have taken over Manhattan Beach Baths and the pure broad sand of Oriental Point, and the growl of the chief petty officer is heard now where once only the sound of the gulls broke the silence.

The lady no longer rides in her yellow carriage under the oaks of Prospect Park, and on the remembered fields, where you shagged flies and slid home with the winning run, now stand grocery shops and bowling alleys. The new crop of boys now play softball, and God alone knows what will come of that. Your old college no longer looks across the docks at the holy bronze figure in the harbor; far inland, in stately Georgian buildings of great size, on a spreading campus, the business of learning goes on, and it does not seem possible that these latter-day scholars could be so hungry or fierce or quick as the ones I knew. The football team has a field all its own, with spacious stands, and two years ago won seven out of nine games. All subways now cost a dime. All things change. I do not know Brooklyn any more.

Chicago: Night Diary

By Ben Hecht

At night Chicago has a thousand mysterious shapes. No native will ever forget them—or the drama and motion of the city. In *1,001 Afternoons* Ben Hecht captured the rhythm of the great city by the lake, its night noises, its streets, the "dark windows of the city."

Where is the moon? Gone. This inferior luminary cannot compete with the corset ad signs and the ice cream ad signs that blaze in the night sky. We stand on a bridge that connects State Street and look at the river.

There are night shapes. But first we see the dark water of the river and silver, gold and ruby reflections of the bridge lights. These hang like carnival ribbons in the water. The "L" trains crawl over the Wells Street bridge and the water below them becomes alive with a moving silver image. For a moment the reflection of the "L" trains in the river seems like a ghostly waterfall. Then it changes and becomes something else. What? The light reflections in the dark water are baffling. It is a game to stand on the bridge and make up similes about them. They look like this, like that, like something else. Like golden pillars, like Chinese writing, like monotonous exclamation points.

There are boat shapes. The river docks bulge with shadows. The boat shapes emerge slowly from the shadows. These shapes, unlike the river reflections, do not suggest similes. They bulge in the darkness and their vanished outlines remind one of something. What? Of boats, of ships, of men.

Men and ships. Little lanterns hang like elfin watchmen from the sterns of ships. The bulldog noses of tugboats sleep against the docks. High overhead the corset ad and the ice cream ad blaze, wink and go out and turn on so as to attract the preoccupied eyes of people far away.

Then the bridges count themselves to the west. First bridge, second bridge, third bridge. Street cars, auto lights and vague noises jerk eerily over the bridges.

The sleeping tugboats, launches and lake craft remind one of nothing at all except that there are engines. But as one stares at them they become secret. There is something mysterious about abandoned engines. It is almost as if one saw the bodies of men lying in shadows. Engines and men are inseparable. And these boats that sleep in the river shadows are parts of men. Amputations.

The night shapes increase. There are buildings. They drift along the river docks. Dark windows and faded brick lines. Their rooftops are like the steps of a giant stairway that has broken down. Where is the moon? Here are windows to mirror its distant silver. Instead, the windows sleep. The nervous electric signs that wink and do tricks throw an intermittent glare over the windows.

Do you know the dark windows of the city, you gentlemen who write continually of temples and art? Come, forget your love for things you never saw, cathedrals and parthenons that exist in the yesterdays you never knew. Come, look at the fire escapes that are stamped like letter Z's against the mysterious rectangles; at the rhythmic flight of windows whose black and silver wings are tipped with the yellow winkings of the corset and ice cream signs. The windows over the dark river are like an alphabet, like the keyboard of a typewriter. They are like anything you want them to be. You have only to wish and the dark windows take new patterns.

Wall shapes arise. Warehouses that have no windows. Huge lines loom in the shadows. A vast panel of brick without windows rises, vanishes. Buildings that stand like playing blocks. The half-hidden shapes, the tracks of windows, the patterns of rooftops suggest things—fortresses, palaces, dungeons, wars, witches and cathedrals.

But after watching them they lose these false significances. They suggest nothing. They are the amputations of men. Things, playthings men have left behind for the corset and ice cream ads to wink at. And this is the real secret of their beauty. The night devours their meaning and leaves behind lines; angles, geometries, rhythms and lights. And these things that have no meaning, that suggest nothing, that are not the symbols of ideas or events—these become beautiful.

There are several people standing on this bridge—loiterers. Their elbows rest on the railing, their faces are hidden in their hands. They stare into the scene. A hoarse whistle toots at Wells Street. Bells clang far away. There is a scurry of dim noises in the dark. Something huge moves through the air. It is a bridge opening. Its arms make a massive gesture upward. A boat is coming through, a heavy shape drifting among the carnival ribbons that hang down in the black water.

Noises that have different tones. Boat whistles, bridge bells, electric alarm tinglings and the swish of water like the sound of wood tapping wood. Lights that have different colors. The yellow of electric signs. Around one of them that hoists its message in the air runs a green border. The electric lights quiver and run round the glaring frame like a mysterious green water. Red, gold and silver pillars in the water. Gray, blue and black shadows; elfin lanterns, "L" trains like illuminated caterpillars creeping over Wells Street, waterfalls of silver, Chinese writing in ruby; black, lead and silver windows and a thousand shades of darkness from bronze to strange greens. All these are things that the loitering ones leaning on the bridge rail know.

A group of movie theaters holds carnival at the entrance to the loop. People hurry under electric canopies, dig in their pockets for dollar bills and buy tickets. The buildings sleep along the river. The boats wait in the shadows. Movie signs, crossing cops, window tracks and different colored suits of clothes; odors, noises, lights and a mysteriously tender pattern of walls—these lie in the night like a reward.

We walk away with memories. When we are traveling some day, riding over strange places, these will be things we shall remember. Not words, but lines that mean nothing; and the scene from the bridge will bring a sad confusion into our heads. And we shall sit staring at famous monuments, battlefields, antiquities, and whisper to ourselves:

". . . wish I was back . . . wish I was back. . . ."

San Francisco: Nob Hill

By Lucius Beebe

Almost since American cities began, the House on the Hill has been a symbol of wealth and aristocracy. One of the greatest clusters of such houses, betokening great wealth if not good breeding, was built in San Francisco. Nob Hill became a symbol of the railroad and mining wealth of the newly opened West. Great mansions, grand balls and unembarrassed display were the elements which contributed to a high, wide and handsome era.

Old San Francisco's Most Opulent Neighborhood

When the Psalmist undertook to lift up his eyes unto the hills, the connotation was not altogether an urban one. The hills from whence cometh help are apt, in the general imagining anyway, to be country heights. But for several centuries Americans have been lifting up their eyes to a number of very densely populated hills, and each has come to stand for something in the American way of life. Bunker Hill is a symbol of patriotism; across the harbor, Beacon Hill for decades has been a hallmark of Boston Brahminism; Murray Hill in mid-Manhattan was a symbol of wealth and conservatism in the gaslit era and until very recently was New York's most respected residential *faubourg,* the home of the Morgans, Bakers and Whitneys. In American folklore the house on the hill has come to be a pinnacle of success, gentility and aloofness. It found its most perfect expression in Edwin Arlington Robinson's *The House on the Hill* which was, of course, the legendary Gardiner mansion in Gardiner, Maine.

San Francisco's Nob Hill has a history that is both glittering and dramatic. In the early days of the city, when Telegraph Hill had already come by its enduring name from the marine telegraph on its summit—the telegraph which relayed news of approaching shipping to a city whose life line with "the States" was by sea—Nob Hill was simply "The Hill." Early in the 70's, however, the railroad millionaires started erecting there the vast mansions which were to outrage and at the same time dazzle an entire generation. Railroad rajahs and bonanza kings were in that day called "nabobs," a word as recurrent in the literature of the times as "tycoons" is today, and The Hill became Nob Hill in popular parlance as soon as the nabobs were in residence. Nob Hill it has been ever since.

A precise geographic definition of Nob Hill is impossible, and anyone's guess, or whim, is as good as the next. The eastern boundary might be said to start at Montgomery Street, for from this point to Nob Hill's summit, at California and Mason Streets, the grade is continuous. In similar manner its southern extremity might be placed as far down as the classic dividing line of Market Street. To the west it might be bounded by the so-called Western Addition, a residential district which emerged after the flowering of Nob Hill's own magnificence; and anybody's preference would be reasonable in defining its northern limits.

The inherent implications of Nob Hill's name, however, would greatly diminish this area. A cross section of San Franciscans queried by the author of this article would bound the essential Nob Hill within a rectangle encompassed by Pine, Leavenworth, Washington and Powell streets. In the early 80's this would have included the precincts of most of the nabobs, the Tobins, Fairs, Hearsts, Floods and Stanfords. Today it would include all the Hill's more notable premises, and, for good measure, the Cathedral Apartments, Stanford Court Apartments, Huntington Apartments and a few less worthy edifices.

Railroad Riches

Nob Hill was a geologic fact long before Sir Francis Drake ever nailed a "Plate of Brasse to a Firme Post," declaring that the "future" site of San Francisco was the "Kingdome of Herr Magesty Queen Elizabeth of England and Herr Successors Forever." But Nob Hill as a *faubourg* of wealth and prestige was actually born about a thousand miles away, at a desolate spot called Promontory, Utah. On the now classic date of May 10, 1869, the rails of the Central and Union Pacific Railroads were joined at Promontory and an entire new category of archmillionaires emerged.

The railroad millionaires—Leland Stanford, Charles Crocker, Collis P. Huntington, Mark Hopkins, and, to a lesser degree, David Colton—previously had been moderately successful Sacramento dealers in hardware, groceries and mining supplies. Shrewd, acquisitive and now fabulously rich, they and their wives set about building for themselves residences suitable to their hard-won position in the world. They selected Nob Hill, hitherto a mere shantytown in a waste of sand, as their demesne. The taste of the period was florid and ornate, and so were the residences erected by the nabobs.

The Feudal Era

The mansion which attracted most press notice at the time of its construction in the 70's belonged to Leland Stanford, former governor of California, president of the Central Pacific Railroad, benefactor of Leland Stanford Junior University, a director of Wells Fargo, genius of the California Street Railway and cofounder, co-owner and coadministrator of almost everything in sight during his lifetime. The Stanford mansion was encircled like a medieval castle by a massive thirty-foot wall; and like a medieval castle it dominated the town. Its billiard rooms and libraries, reception halls, conservatories, music rooms, circular marble entrance hall with the signs of the zodiac in black marble in the floor, its amazements of purple fringe, gold-trimmed velvet, marquetry tables, bronzes, chandeliers, portieres, lace curtains, Honduran mahogany, cloisonné, oil paintings and other Victorian oddments delighted the entire Pacific Coast and made breathless reading for a generation of Sunday supplement clients.

Beyond dispute the hallmark of Nob Hill in the morning of San Francisco's youth was the cable car. By 1874 the cars had already come to San Francisco and the operations of the Clay Street Hill Railroad Company had demonstrated their practicability. In that year Leland Stanford conceived the idea that another cable-car system, this one to operate in California Street, convenient to his own Nob Hill residence, was what San Francisco needed. He discussed the possibilities of the project with the town's first citizens, Mark Hopkins, Lloyd Tevis, David Colton and Charles Crocker. Darius Ogden Mills, satrap of the mighty Bank of California, refused to serve as an officer; there was patently no future in an enterprise which derived its income exclusively from nickels. Five years after Stanford proposed the project the California Street line was carrying 8000 passengers a day over its three miles of tracks and the stockholders were congratulating themselves on their sagacity as they sipped Pisco Punches in Duncan Nicol's Bank Exchange. The cable cars boosted the price of Nob Hill real estate even more than the choice of the hill as the favored preserve of the nabobs and made Nob Hill property among the most valuable in the city.

In the course of its dazzling history, Nob Hill has provided many a choice scandal for the enchantment of San Francisco society, but none with the gaudy overtones and national implications of the affair of Mrs. Mark Hopkins' second husband. In 1878, when the railroad baron died and was removed to a $150,000 rose marble vault in Sacramento, public attention naturally centered upon Mrs. Hopkins, hailed by Sunday supplement writers as "America's richest widow." A retiring and altogether domestic woman, Mary Hopkins was upset by newspaper speculation as to the possibility of her remarriage—she was over fifty—and began to exhibit an eccentricity which manifested itself in a passion for costly residences. She spent $2,000,000 to build a château (modeled on Chambord) which still stands at Great Barrington, Massachusetts. She then purchased a house at 60 Fifth Avenue, bought a brace of summer cottages at Methuen, Massachusetts, and at Block Island, and completed her monstrous castle, one of Nob Hill's most fantastic, at California and Mason Streets.

During this extravaganza of construction, Mrs. Hopkins encountered an interior decorator named Edward Searles, little more than half her age and an employee of Herter and Co., New York decorators and furniture merchants. Searles, whose passion for furniture, particularly chairs, amounted to infatuation, danced assiduous attention on the widow and San Francisco gossip columns had a field day, especially since it was known that her adopted son, Timothy Hopkins, emphatically disapproved of Searles. A family quarrel ensued, and the affair ended with Mrs. Hopkins marrying the furniture *aficionado* and going East to live. Four years later she died, and her will disinherited her foster son, and made no bequests to friends or the conventional charities. The entire Hopkins fortune, estimated at $70,000,000, went outright to Searles.

Nob Hill neighbors were delighted when Timothy Hopkins filed suit to break his mother's will, charging undue influence on the part of Searles. The trial was held at Salem, Massachusetts, and the wires to San Francisco's pressrooms throbbed with its details. Searles said the match had been proposed by the widow, and was consented to by him "both for love and money." The trial lasted only a single day—by nightfall the decorator was ready to settle with Timothy out of court for a sum estimated at $10,000,000.

Titled Daughters

Miles of newsprint were devoted in 1874 to the most stylish wedding yet to amaze the Pacific Coast, that of Clara Adelaide Sharon, daughter of powerful Sen. William Sharon, to Francis Griffith Newlands, a Yale man and one of the community's leading attorneys. The *Chronicle* and other papers of the day detailed the buffet to the last terrine of *foie gras* and split of Mumm's and remarked unabashedly on the cost of everything, including pillowcases at $140 the pair and a brace of $5000 consoles.

Another event that amused San Francisco in the golden age was the marriage of the daughters of the pioneer stage driver, "King" Benjamin Holladay to two titled foreigners, the Count de Pourtalès and the Baron de Boussière. Mrs. Holladay achieved these eye popping catches for her daughters while on the Grand Tour of the Continent and brought back her now titled daughters to San Francisco aboard a private car and with suitable ruffles and flourishes in the press. Old Ben, who had faced Indians, prairie fires and perils by flood and from highwaymen in the rougher days of the Old West, heard the news, clapped on his top hat and fled San Francisco in terror, seeking refuge from the nobility in the still secure fastnesses of Oregon.

One of Nob Hill's most vivid memories was the arrival in 1882 of Oscar Wilde, who lectured to fashionable audiences in the best drawing rooms—including those of the Crockers, Tevises, Hagers and Lillie Hitchcock Coit, the town's celebrated lady buff and toast of the fire department—on The Theory of Esthetics Applied to Home Life. His knee-breeched appearances were exciting, but his lectures were reported to be the reverse. Not so, however, his heroic capacity for alcohol. At one Nob Hill dinner where he was guest of honor, Wilde drank all the gentlemen under the table, switched from champagne to gin at two in the morning and at four was still speaking gracefully and with wit to a table of unconscious tosspots. Only the house servants benefited from his wisdom.

The last night of old Nob Hill, April 17, 1906, was almost theatrically opulent. The town was agog over the arrival of the Metropolitan Opera Company; the evening was the high light of the season: Olive Fremstad and Caruso in *Carmen*. The beautiful opera coaches and landaus of Nob Hill's first families, the Floods, Phelans, de Youngs and Haggins, rolled grandly through the streets for dinner at The Palace and then to the Opera itself. Mrs. James Flood aroused the enthusiasm of the *Call's* society reporter by the comparative modesty of her jewels: a diamond tiara, a dog collar of Oriental pearls, diamond shoulder straps for her Worth gown, a stomacher and corsage decorations of diamonds and pearls. The barouche in which Mrs. Flood rode down California Street that fateful night can be seen to this day in the museum at Harold's Club in Reno.

After *Carmen* there were brilliant supper parties in all the great mansions of Nob Hill. Stately old sirs in opera hats and satin-lined, Inverness cloaks handed down their ladies as English butlers bowed them up the steps. House footmen made nimble with foil-topped bottles in silver coolers, and French chefs were in ecstasies of excitement as terrapin simmered and soufflés inflated to dramatic proportions in a score of kitchens.

None was more in his element than the *gros bonnet* who presided over the cuisine of James Ben Ali Haggin, San Francisco's foremost patron of the arts and the most imperial host the town had seen since the death, years before, of William Ralston, ill-fated cashier of the Bank of California. The Haggin chef was working miracles with a truffled galantine of pheasant as his master's guests arrived: Emma Eames, Sembrich and the great Caruso himself. Madame Eames remembered it as the most beautiful supper party of a lifetime of gustatory splendors.

After singing Don Jose, Caruso had paused briefly to refresh himself at the bar of The Palace with Alfred Hertz and other members of the company, and was in spacious form by the time he addressed himself to Mr. Haggin's pheasant in *foie gras*. He sang for the company, his hand dramatically resting on a magnum of Perrier Jouet; and it was the song of farewell, as it turned out, to the old San Francisco of the golden years. Afterwards everyone went out to the stables to admire Haggin's famous horses, which were almost as grandly housed as the bonanza kings themselves. The harnesses on the tackroom walls were ornamented with solid Comstock silver. The gleaming coaches, dog carts, victorias and Beverly wagons sparkled as though for Tiffany's window.

A few blocks away Mrs. William Kohl was bidding a belated good night to her guests, and her maid was standing by to place in the safe her jewels of the evening: "A jeweled headgear, a two-inch dog collar of pearls and diamonds and an assortment of shimmering things on the corsage line."

The Fire

The exact chronicle of the Fire as it overwhelmed Nob Hill is a fascinating study to students of Americana. Scrutiny of the dispatches printed in the neighboring press of Sacramento, Stockton and Oakland during the progress of the conflagration, have the Hill and its properties alternately standing intact and overwhelmed with flame. The fact that the wind shifted continuously during the afternoon of the first day doomed the Hill at one moment and saved it the next, and what with the poor visibility, difficulties of communication with the outside world and the fantasies of rumor, the reporters disagreed chaotically with one another.

According to the official report of the National Board of Fire Underwriters, fire struck at the southwestern slope of the Hill late in the afternoon of the first day, and its crowning glories were destroyed during the course of the night and early hours of the second morning.

At seven in the evening, Acting Fire Chief Dougherty announced that a determined stand would be made at the Fairmount Hotel and more than three quarters of a mile of hose was run from the foot of Mason Street, boosted by steam pumpers along the way.

Elegy

Also on duty at this front so soon to be overwhelmed was Lt. C. C. McMillan of the revenue cutter *USS Bear* and a detachment of soldiers and sailors who impressed civilians, among them reportedly John Barrymore, in an attempt to salvage the summit of the Hill. The Oakland *Tribune* commented on "the cool eye and wicked-looking pistol of the lieutenant and the way men jumped when it was pointed at them." The Flood, Crocker and Phelan houses stood until about midnight, according to the official report, when one after the other, they went to flaming and expensive glory.

An interesting commentary on the Fire was that the complete envelopment of Nob Hill, of the business district and the thousands of modest and unremembered residences, bulked nowhere nearly as large in the wire reports to the outside world as did the burning of the Palace Hotel. Somehow this remarkable and ornate structure stood as a symbol of the city's magnificence, and when it had gone all else seemed trivial. Babylon the Great was falling, and somehow, the Palace was the archetype of all it stood for.

All the mansions of Nob Hill went up in the incredible bonfire of that April day of doom. Gertrude Atherton watched the new Fairmont Hotel as it burned: "The new marble hotel on the highest hill poured up volumes of white smoke from the top alone, while the hundreds of windows were like plates of brass."

From an adjacent vantage point Jack London gazed down California Street and saw "two mighty walls of fire advancing from east and south." From almost the same spot Arnold Genthe trained his camera on the lower city to obtain a photograph that is the classic pictorial record of the catastrophe.

The homes of the nabobs contributed nothing but the best material to the conflagration. Claus Spreckels' French château gave its gold plumbing fixtures and Algerian marbles; Adolph Sutro's library with its 250,000 volumes, many of them priceless and irreplaceable, disappeared in smoke. At the W. H. Crockers', Rubens' *Holy Family* was lost, but loyal house servants—the family was in New York—saved the original of Millet's *Man With the Hoe* and Corot's *Dance of the Nymphs.* Haggin's sumptuous stables blazed brightly after their valuable inmates had been removed. Gone were the vast and by now almost legendary mansions of Lloyd Tevis, the Hobarts, Tobins, Townes, Coltons, Parrots and Phelans.

Every good San Franciscan knows and cherishes the verses of Lawrence W. Harris and their implicit devotion to "the city that was":

> *From the Ferry to Van Ness you're a god-forsaken mess,*
> *But the damnedest finest ruins, nothing more and nothing less.*

After the disaster of 1906 the original nabobs for the most part disappeared from Nob Hill along with their incredible mansions. The site of the enormous Crocker home was given by the family for the Episcopal Cathedral. The town's best and most expensive apartment houses began to appear in Powell and California streets; the Flood home became the Pacific Union Club; and where Mark Hopkins' turreted and crenelated castle had stood the present Mark Hopkins Hotel flung itself skyward.

Probably the last great lady of an older generation to live today on Nob Hill is Mrs. James Flood (just Mrs. Flood to San Francisco as it was once simply "Mrs. Vanderbilt" to New York). Mrs. Flood, who maintains an apartment at the Fairmont, says, "I'm probably the only person alive in San Francisco today whose son was born in a nunnery and whose daughter was born in a gentleman's club." The references, of course, are to the Sacred Heart Convent and the Pacific Union Club, both former Flood residences.

The crowning glory of Nob Hill today is the stately three-story building of Connecticut sandstone that is the premises of the equally stately Pacific Union Club. Its legends are legion. One of them concerns the majordomo who, when a member inadvertently knocked the ashes from his cigar on the deep-pile carpet, murmured reprovingly: "Not so much noise, if you please, sir!"

The brownstone of the Pacific Union was quarried in Connecticut but, metaphorically, the clubhouse was quarried in the depths of the Consolidated Virginia and California Mines on Nevada's Comstock Lode. In 1882, Jim Flood, former coproprietor of the Auction Lunch Saloon and later the most ostentatious of the silver bonanza kings, bought the Nob Hill block bounded by California, Mason, Sacramento and Cushman streets and began building what was to be, in its somber manner, the town's grandest mansion. Its forty-foot reception room furnished as an Indian maharaja's palace, its forty-six-foot dining salon paneled in the finest San Domingan mahogany, its Moorish smoking room and over-all total of forty-two apartments, bugged the eyes of a whole San Francisco generation. But the most celebrated of all the mansion's features was its fence of beautifully wrought bronze which enclosed the structure and its lawns and carriage houses. Residents believed implicitly that this staggeringly costly enclosure, known as "Flood's thirty-thousand-dollar brass rail," was designed by the former saloonkeeper as a reminder of his humble origins. The mansion was gutted in the Fire of 1906, but its thick walls defied destruction and the fence survived intact. San Franciscans say that it was the beautiful fence, not the austere edifice itself, which influenced the Pacific Union to make the purchase.

In May of 1912, stately members of the Pacific Union, eating their stately way through a simple businessman's lunch of terrapin, boned turkey, Prague ham and the best claret, were startled by an alarm of fire from an upper chamber. Ever apprehensive of any potential fire, the members and servants, headed by Pres. William H. Crocker prudently armed with a seltzer bottle, hastened up the broad staircase. The bedclothes in the apartment of Frank Drum, president of Pacific Gas and Electric, were blazing brightly.

Nob Hill's two most spectacular hotels, forming a massive and glittering triangle with the Pacific Union Club, are the Fairmont and Mark Hopkins, perpetuating the memory of a bonanza king and a railroad baron, respectively. The Fairmont, which has what must be the most opulent and largest lobby anywhere, is the scene of many of San Francisco's more stately sarabands which are not conducted at The Palace.

The Mark, as it is almost universally abbreviated, is devoted to the town's more deluxe frivolities and gilded youth.

Built in 1926 by its present manager and president, George D. Smith, the Mark has the world's most spectacular cocktail lounge. Located on the nineteenth floor and walled with enormous plate-glass windows, the Top of the Mark is a perpetual tribute to one of San Francisco's great architects and devoted *viveurs*, Timothy Pfleuger. Its own *décor* is austere in the extreme; its designer felt that the panoramic view it affords would overwhelm the most inspired decorative detail.

Hundreds of thousands of visitors annually make the pilgrimage to Top of the Mark to sip its beverages, marvel at the unrivaled view of the entire San Francisco region and sometimes, when the fog is in, to float, remote and detached from any trace of the metropolis beneath. During the war years it was the mecca of servicemen passing through San Francisco. It has been remarked of the sidewalk Café de la Paix in Paris that sooner or later everyone of consequence in the entire world must pass by it, and the same is true of the Top of the Mark.

Perhaps Nob Hill's apotheosis in the 20th century was the years of the second World War, when the life line of the Pacific campaigns flowed through a darkened yet vital San Francisco. The night swirled coldly through the carriage entrances of the Mark and Fairmont. Taxis arrived and departed deep-laden with youth bound for a rendezvous with history at Sunda Strait or the Coral Sea. Youth bound for the wars wanted its last taste of wine and roses and it found them at the top of a windy Nob Hill under a fog-blown moon. The gray San Francisco dawn found youth, a little frayed at the edges, reluctant to go, headed down California Street for the transport docks at Oakland and the South Pacific.

Boys on City Streets

By Henry Noble MacCracken

Too often we think of boys on city streets as hoodlums, but one grew up to be President of Vassar. Henry Noble MacCracken embellishes his story of boyhood on Gramercy Park with many homely touches, as he tells of playing marbles and spinning tops, of making eyes at a young flirt and of riding on the L.

"Henry, what shall we do with our Gramercy Park key this year?"

"We'll use it as we always have."

"Now, Henry, you know you've hardly been in the Park all these eight years."

"It's nothing but a badge of respectability," says John.

"We aren't really *in* the Park, anyhow," says Fay. "We're Irving Place people. Only people with Park numbers are *in* Gramercy. We're *on* it."

So Fay doesn't want it because she's at Bryn Mawr, and John is sixteen and doesn't like bird-cages, he says, and Geordie won't take it because the string scratches his neck. He's awfully fidgety.

So the key is mine this year. Mamma ties it round my neck with a string and a lot of good advice. I wear it under my shirt. I'm just the right height to unlock the old gates, and I can get em open on the dead run, quicker'n a wink.

But of course I come home from school first, to get a doughnut, and see what Charley's doing.

Charley Caulkins was a lot of fun. He didn't spell his name "Charlie," which was a sissy way to spell it. He was always laughing. Even when he didn't smile, if you looked in his eyes there was a lot of fun in them, as if he had a secret he could tell only it was too funny. He was always doing things, too. He was the cleverest fellow you ever saw. He could make anything, I bet you, just anything. Gee, I hope he's there when I get home from school.

Broadway to Twenty-first, and Twentieth; that is the best way. Don't have to go past Calvary, or the Panorama either. Too many fellows hanging round them, trying to get somebody to buy their way in. Fourth Avenue, and here's the Park, and nobody round. Irving Place, and here's 84, —but I'll dive in the cellar of 82. That's where Charley is.

"Hey, Charley, where are you?"

"Over here in the shop!"

Dark hole, part under the sidewalk, next the coal-bin. One broken gas jet with a sickly round spot of yellow light, and two short candle-ends. Charley, whistling "The Brass Monkey," working on some piece of wood.

"Come on out and play, Charley."

"I can't, I gotta make som'p'n."

"Aw, come on."

"I can't, I tell ya! I gotta work."

"What you makin'?"

"Secret."

"Aw, tell me."

"Nope. You wait an' see. It's goin' to be good."

"C'n I help?"

"You! What can you do?"

"Well, I can watch, can't I?"

"Sure."

"Wait'll I put my books away, and get a sanwidge."

"Hey, get me one, too."

"I dunno if I can. Annie Kleinroth—"

"Sure you can. Just tease her."

"Aw, all right."

Cross over to the 84 cellar, which connects with 82. Mrs. Caulkins leases both houses, and rents us the two lower stories of 84. The upper floors of 84, with the whole of 82, make her boarding-house.

"Hello, Annie dear."

"Ach, du Bodderfritz! I'm busy."

"Annie, c'n I have a sanwidge? Just a little one?"

"Na, Spitzbuby. You spoil your dinner."

"Aw, Annie, plee-uz. Annie dear!"

"Chuss a little vun, den, und keep out of my kitchen."

"And one for Charley?"

"Dot scalawiggle!" Annie had the most wonderful words. Where did she get them?

"Plee-uz, Annie dear."

"Vell, dis vunce, und clear out."

"Why, Annie Kleinroth! You got em already made. Cheese!"

"Take em, und heraus!"

"Say thanks! Dankebissens! Charley, looka here what I got!"

Charley, sprawled on the floor, spreading long thin strips of wood, and a big piece of wrapping paper.

"Gee, willikun! It's a kite!"

"That's what it am."

"Will it fly, Charley?"

"Why wouldn't it?"

"What did you make it for?"

"What do you think? It's kite-time."

"It is?"

"Sure. Din' you feel the wind today?"

"Is that how you tell?"

"Sure. That's what the wind is for, so we fellows can fly em."

"It's mos' done, ain't it?"

"Nope, I gotta nail it and tie it, and varnish the paper, 'n ever'thing."

"Lemme help. Aw, gwan, Charley. Here's your sanwidge."

Good long tail with red muslin twisters every two feet. Eight foot belly strip and four foot crosspiece. Good long tail-strips, too. Fifty yards of fine whipcord on a spool. Whee! Next day it was finished, and was it a beaut'? We took it out to Gram'cy Park, and flew it. The wind was fine. I held it the way he told me, and Charley ran as fast as he could into the wind, and up she went, and got caught in a branch of the horse-chestnut tree. It tore some of the paper off, but Charley didn't care. We fixed it, and glued the paper back on.

"Let's try it out in the street, where the trees aren't so big."

So we did, and a Mick came along from Third Avenue.

"Hey, you. Wat's dat?"

"It's a kite. What didja think it was? A grand piano? Watch us fly it."

"Chee, dat's great. Gimme a try."

"Naw, it's ours. Make one yourself."

"Dis ain't yer street. It's mine, and you can't fly nuttin' 'less'n I say yer can."

"Iz zat so?"

"Yes, 'atso. You'll find out."

He went off, and came back with a gang. Half a dozen kids jumped on us, and the kite was smashed. We got kicked on the shin.

"Oh, darn it. I wish't I didn't live in this burg," said Charley. I was sort of discouraged myself.

Three weeks later, it was top-time. We had made another kite, not so big or so good, but we had flown it in Irving Place, near 82. When the Micks came, we ran in the cellar. It was no fun.

So we played tops. You didn't make tops. You bought em at Hassl's on Third Avenue and Seventeenth Street. They cost five cents for the little ones, and ten for the next size. The big ones were twenty cents. You held the top upside down, and wound a string of white whipcord very carefully. Then, holding the top between thumb and forefinger still upside down, you threw it upon the stone pavement as hard as you could, so it came down spinning. It was a knack. You made a ring in the dirt next the Park fence. Another fellow threw his top, and tried to split yours with the iron point. If he succeeded, you paid him five cents. If he knocked the top out of the ring, it was his.

We lost at first, but we learned, and pretty soon we began to get the other fellows' tops. Then the Micks came along, and broke the game up. We scuffled and scrapped, but no use; there were too many of them.

"Say, look, we gotta do somep'n. Ain't we got any rights here a-tall? Don't we live here? Whose town is this, anyway?"

"We gotta get some other fellas to help us. I'll get Pussy and Bill and Jim."

"I'll get Eliot and Macy and Artie. Yes, and Cy and Ned and Wilford."

They all lived round the Park. They were all about eleven, or maybe a year or two older. We got them to spin tops with us, and we had fun. The Micks came around, but we stuck together, and they let us alone for a while.

"Look, Nibsy, you'n Charley play tops outside the Park, right by the gate. We'll be in the Park right near the fence, like we're doing nothing. Then if the Micks come, we'll sally out and chase em. See?"

"Yeah, but if they hit us first—"

"Sing out, and we'll be right there. We got it all fixed."

I can never say "No" to anything. I just can't. I don't know why it is, I just say "all right." I'm funny, that way.

Charley don't care. He is a regular daredevil, and he loves a scrap. I'm scared, too scared to say "No."

So we play tops, and have a lot of fun. I cracked two of Charley's and knock another out, and along come the Micks. One of em grabbed the top in the ring, and another grabbed me and tried to get the tops in my pocket. I fought him off, and yelled bloody murder. In a jiff of a pig's tail out came the fellows from the Park, and biff, bang, we did em up brown. They ran away hollering.

"Gee, we're pretty good, I bet," crowed Pussy.

"Yep," said Crawford, "we're a pretty good gang ourselves."

"Gosh, that's right," said Wendell, "that's what we are. We're a gang too. The Gram'cy Park gang."

"Hooray," we shouted, "we're a gang."

And that's how the Gram'cy gang began. We had a great time starting in. Crawford was head, because he was the strongest. There was Ed and Cy Field, and Ted Steinway, and Macy and Artie King, and Billy and Jim Lovell, and Pussy and Eliot and Charley and me, and Paul and all the Blagdens besides Crawford, that's Wendell and Arthur and Meredith—Tom was too old—and the Beardsleys and the Swains and a lot more—I could tell you, but I haven't got time.

We had a secret meeting in Eliot Lee's back yard that night, and we agreed always to stick together and chase the Micks, and clean up the neighborhood, just like the other gangs. We got some sticks and stones, and we went around the Park singing

"We're a gang, the Gram'cy gang,
You look out, or you'll get a bang."

We marched around the Park two or three times singing, but there weren't any Micks around, so we went home.

For a long time it was that way; a week, I guess. Always the Micks were there when the other fellows weren't around, and you had to run for the Park, and get out your key from your neck where it hung on a string, and open the gate and slam it before the Micks got there. But when our gang was around there just weren't any Micks. They were awful cowardly.

So we played tops until we got tired of em, and then we played tip-stick. That was a lot of fun. We made a little stick about six inches long, thick in the middle and thinned at both ends. Then we had a bat made of an old barrel stave. The boy that was it whammed the bat down on the end of the tipstick, and bang! it went up in the air, and we whammed it, and ran across the street to Mr. Tilden's house and touched base. If we got there before a boy got the tipstick and put it in the ring, we were safe. Then another boy whammed it while we were on base and we ran to Mis' Clark's house, and then home across the street. Gee, it was fun!

Of course, you had to dodge the express wagons, and the brewery wagons, and the ashcarts. They made an awful lot of noise though, so you could tell when they were coming, except when you got excited. We made a rule about grocery wagons, that if one of them was in the way it was a foul. They went too fast. I got that rule passed, because I had promised Mamma I would be careful in the street, and anyway I was scared of grocery horses. They bit you when you went by, even if you were walking on the curbstone. So you had to look out. So we were all careful, except Lester Walton. He ran right into an ashcart one day when we were playing and broke his leg. So we were especially careful after that.

Then it got warm and we played marbles. First we played at the foot of the big elm tree in the Park, where there were a lot of good holes all scooped out between the roots.

But after a while the Micks came around and called us fraidcats and sweeties, and things like that and a lot of profanity. So we opened the gate and chased them, and then we played against the wall that runs round the Park, under the palings. It made a pretty good place, only there were too many dogs around. But we didn't care, because we were going to show those Micks we weren't afraid of them.

The old men that live around the Park like to come out and watch us play. Some of them play with us, and they're pretty good. You wouldn't think people as old as that could play games. There was old Mr. Cyrus Field, and Mr. Edwin Booth, and Mr. Smith E. Lane, and an old General Wager Swain. And one time Mr. Hewitt that used to be mayor and had two lamp-posts in front of his house, he played too. Not very good,—well, I mean.

One of the best old fellows was General Swain. We were playing ringers one day, when a shadow fell over our ring. We looked up, and there was a one-legged man. He had crutches, but he knuckled down and played a whole game with us. His lay was perfect, and he never said "slips" once. He knocked three out the first burst. His backspin was just wonderful. He could make the shooter go just anywhere—backspin, drawshot, follows—anywhere. One marble right by the lay line he kissed so sweet he stayed right in.

He had all our aggies and glassies in about ten minutes. We were kind of worried until he said, "We're playing for fair, of course, not for keeps." Then he gave em all back. He didn't keep a mib.

Charley asked him, "Where did you learn to play?"

"In the army, where I left this leg of mine. Come in and see me sometime, and I'll tell you stories."

Just then along came old Mr. Cyrus Field, and didn't those two old fellows buy our marbles and start a game of their own.

Mr. Booth was the best, because he let us play tag on his steps, and climb up the porch, and drop off. Tilden tag was more fun, though, because Mr. Tilden had two front doors and a yard between and we could run down one steps and up the other steps and race along the sidewalk, or vault over into the front yard. Anybody walking by got bumped. Pussy was the best in all the games, because he could run fastest.

One time we were all out playing marbles on the Park side of the street, and a big gang of Micks came along. They rushed us all yelling like wild Indians, and mixed it up. We rolled all around, everywhere, sometimes in the gutter, but mostly on the sidewalk. We were getting licked, too, when a cop came around the corner, and the Micks all ran away down Irving Place. So we ran, too, and pretty soon we were chasing em, and we chased em all the way to Fourteenth Street; and we didn't dare go any farther. So we decided Fourteenth Street was our boundary and we couldn't ever chase Micks any farther than that. We didn't either, except in the great Houston Street fight, and I'll tell you about that later on.

I lost my marbles in the Park fight, and I never won back enough for a full bag. But I got some.

Mutton Gravy

It got kind of warm in June. The ailanthus was all sticky. Pedlars were yelling "Strawberries" up and down Irving Place, and flower-pot wagons sold geraniums and little begonias and so on. Vegetable men from Long Island came along, too, with scallions and peas; old clothes, and knife-grinders—it was an awful noisy street, hardly quiet a minute. Of course, the Belgian blocks in the street made an awful racket, and when a two-wheeler grocery cart came tearing round Nineteenth Street the sparks flew all over, banging around.

Mr. Denman Thompson is running at the 'Cademy of Music, down on Fourteenth Street and Irving Place. I know because his oxen exercise up and down the Place in front of our house. They pull a hay wagon up and down. Gosh, they're big oxen, the biggest in the country, I guess. Kind of tan color, with big horns. They could pull a house right over on its side. The driver is an old feller with a fuzzy beard and a big straw hat. I ast him why he had such a funny beard, and he said, "They pay me fur it, so I grew it, like they said. If they think we wear em, we'll wear em." He was goodnatured, and let me drive the oxen a spell. You use a whip with a lash about twenty feet long, and it's awful hard to crack. You yell "Gee," for the right, and "Haw" for the left, and "Gee Haw" when you want to start em, and "Hup" when you want to stop. But mostly it's the whip that steers em. I couldn't get them round a corner if I tried. I did try, but they almost walked right through Gram'cy Park. They would have pulled the fence right out of the ground if the driver hadn't stopped them. He laughed and laughed at me. "You city boys will be the death of me," he said.

I wonder what "The Old Homestead" is about. They got stickers on the haywagon about it, but it's just country people dancing. We were going to the country soon as school is over, but we can't afford it this year. New York is a fine summer resort, but it's sort of sticky most of the time, and the Jersey mosquitoes bite fierce.

We had a great time, though. There was a girl in the Park named Marie Gravet, and we all called her Mutton Gravy for short. Mutton Gravy came from Paris, France, and spoke French. She spoke English, too, but her lips all puckered up and made it sound funny. She held her lips kinda tight like she wanted you to kiss her. She was flirty, all right. She was always talking about boys and girls. She couldn't play any games, because they made her all hot and tired, and she was very delicate. She got powder and put it on so as not to sweat in this terrible American heat. She wore fluffy white dresses, and held a parasol, and gloves. She just sat and talked.

I don't know how she did it, but in a few days she had all the boys hanging around with their tongues hanging out, looking lovesick at her. Gee, it was disgusting. Even my brother George, who was two years older and big for his age, would come around while she made eyes at him sideways. It would simply make you sick to watch it. I didn't stay around much, because Charley was working on a sailboat to sail in Central Park, and I helped him, sandpapering and everything. So I didn't see much of what went on. You just wouldn't believe it, a bunch of fellows that would fight Micks and chase cats and get chased by cops, moaning around while she talked and simpered.

Pussy Leach had a play buckboard, of yellow wood, with a pole, and she actually got Pussy and Ted to hitch up and pull her up and down the walks in the Park, while she drove them with silk ribbons and a little horsehide whip that George gave her. He bought it down at Hassl's in Third Avenue and Seventeenth Street, right under the L station. Hassl's had a lot of whips, made of one piece of twisted cowhide. They hurt when you hit anybody, but Mutton Gravy just touched them. All the girls hated her, but she didn't care. She just said "Allong," and the boys tore around, and acted skittish and jumped and pulled her all over the Park. It was simply sickening. She got Meredith to sit on behind on the flat part, and when she stopped he would jump up and run around and hold her hand, while she dismounted. She would give him her parasol and he would open it, and hold it so as to shade her. Then she would step down like she was a queen or something and walk to a bench and sink down, and say, "T'ank you, my dear. Oh, it is so terreble hot, not?" and pull out her fan and open it, and fan herself, and look over the fan, and look at you. And all this while those two big goons would stand and pant and sweat, and act like they were having a wonnerful time. They didn't care what anybody said, they just stayed and stood. And pretty soon, Mutton Gravy would get up and walk over to them and put chocolates in their mouths, and say, "My good horses, you are hongry, not?" and they would winny and nod their heads up and down like horses do.

You just wouldn't believe it; you had to see it to believe it. It all happened just like I said. And pretty soon George would come around, like a big baboon, and he would kneel and kiss her hand, and then sit down and fan her, while she cooed at him.

I just couldn't stand it. My own brother! So I went up to Central Park with Charley, and we sailed the boat for a while in the Boat Pond. It was a lot of fun. They were mostly younger kids, but they just had store boats and they didn't know anything about sailing. They just pushed em out and they got all tangled up, and the boatman came around with a long polehook and pulled them in to shore. Charley knew all about sailing, because he used to sail with his father in Barnegat before his father died and his mother took boarders. He fixed up the rudder with an alarm-clock spring that he took out of an old alarm-clock, and when the boat had sailed out for a minute and a half the rudder would turn, and the boat would sail right back. We hardly had to move. My gosh, it was more fun! Sometimes he would fix it so the boat would sail out across the lake, and the other boys would get ready to catch it when it hit, so as not to break the bowsprit, and all of a sudden it would turn square to starboard, and sail over the side where we had gone. It would fool them out of their boots. They looked funny, and we would just laugh at them, because their big boats couldn't do that, even if they were all painted and varnished and white sails and everything.

We sailed for quite a while, and when I went out to the Park next time I just couldn't believe what had happened to everybody. Mutton Gravy had just moved in on the whole Park, and the whole gang of boys and girls were just her servants. She was the Queen of Love, and she used to sit on the back of one of the benches in front of the fountain. She had a big shawl, red and blue, that she sat on, over the back of the bench, that was her throne, and she held her parasol. Sometimes one of the boys as a special favor held it for her. The girls all stood around in their best dresses and were her Ladies. They did everything she said, so meek and quiet you wouldn't believe it. It was like a fairy tale. The boys were her knights, and the bigger boys were Brave Knights. They did everything she told them. Nobody laughed any more either; because if you laughed Mutton Gravy would wave her scepter, which was a stick from the towel rack in her bathroom, but painted with gold paint. And the big boys would run and capture you and bring you to the Queen for punishment. You had to kneel down, and you got a paddywhack or two, and say, "I beg your pardon, O Queen, and I will never laugh at you again," and Mutton Gravy would pardon you after a while. It made you sick, but what could you do? Everybody did exactly what she said, and she ruled the Park—really ruled, I mean.

She made laws that you had to obey. She made them wear their best pants. They had to take off knee pads. The garters couldn't show. She even got George to get Mamma to buy him a pair of long pants so he could wear them in the Park. He was Mutton Gravy's favorite Brave Knight, but he was just as crazy as the rest. Some of them wanted to make him the King, but she said, "No, I don't want a King. I might change my mind." And then she would flirt with George, and he would look red and flushed up so he couldn't say a word but just stand around and look foolish.

She held High Court on Saturdays all June. We had to come out in our good clothes and walk around after her carriage of State, which was just Pussy's buckboard, but all fixed up with ribbons. She would make a tour of the Park, and we walked in a procession after her, two by two, Ladies and Knights. I forgot to say that she paired us all off at her High Court one day, after she had got to know us pretty well. She was awful smart, and she knew how to get the girls on her side. She saw what was going on, and she gave the girls a kind of shove, because the boys weren't ever so crazy about the girls as the girls were about the boys. So she gave every Lady a Knight, and they had to walk around together and make love.

Making love was just walking around very politely and making compliments. You had to say "Dear Lady" every other minute, and pick up her handkerchief, and give her your arm, and walk with your toes out, and step like in Dodsworth's, and make eyes and look sick, and say "How fair you are, My Lady," and stuff like that.

We had tournaments, too, instead of those rowdy games like Prisoner's Base. We had prisoners and set them free by conquering the other Knight. You held hands, and stood on both feet, and made the other Knight tip over by twisting your hand and yanking him around. But you couldn't move yourself. The Queen was the judge. Then you ran around the railing around the fountain, and if you won you were crowned. You got a flower from her balcony, or something. Pussy always won the races. Then we walked around with our Ladies some more. It doesn't sound like fun when I write it down this way, but it was a lot of fun at the time. Anyway, we thought it was, but I can see now we were just a lot of fools hanging around a little French girl like that, and doing everything she said. I don't know how she got elected Queen, or anything. The first thing you knew she was elected, and everybody wanted to be her servants.

She gave me to Electra Nilsson to be a Knight. Electra was a girl who lived at No. 1 Gramercy Park on the corner of Twenty-first. I had got to know her one afternoon when I was chased by the Calvary Choir boys one day when they were coming out of rehearsal, and I ran in her yard and slammed the iron door under the steps on them. They stayed around a while and called me names, but I didn't care; and pretty soon Electra opened the basement door and asked me to come in, because she saw how it was. So we played in her dining room awhile, and when the choir boys went off I came out and went home. So I played with her once in a while after that. She could play marbles quite well for a girl, and she didn't care if she got dirty, and so on. But of course I didn't care much for girls, so I didn't see much of her until Mutton Gravy began bossing everybody around.

Mutton made some rules that she called Kissing Rules. If you went on an errand for your Lady, like buying her a three cent bar of molasses, you were rewarded. You could kiss her hand. If you attended her all day, that was the High Court, you could kiss her cheek at the end of the Court, when Mutton went home. And if she got mad, and was rebuked by the Queen, there was a penalty. The penalty was to be kissed by your Knight, smack on the mouth. If she slapped your face, you had two kisses coming to you. Some of the girls like Elinor and Virginia and Mame Cooper and Janet and Christie used to slap the Knights around a lot, but they always had to pay the penalty, because if she ran away two of the Brave Knights ran after her and caught her and brought her back to pay the Penalty.

It was a lot of fun, only there were too many things to remember, and I got tired of it after a while. Electra didn't like it so much as some of the others, either. So as we had got quite well acquainted I asked her if she didn't want to go on Five Cent Saturday with me, and she said she did, so we went off on several Five Cent Saturdays and didn't go to High Court but had more fun by ourselves.

Five Cent Saturdays was something Papa had started. He thought it was our civic duty to know this city we lived in, and when Mamma objected it would cost money he said he could do it for five cents a day. It really cost more than that, but he didn't care. The whole family went to the Statue of Liberty and the Navy Yard and where Alexander Hamilton was killed, and the Battle of Washington Heights, and St. Patrick's and Grace Church, and the slaughter houses in Jersey City, and the museums and so on.

So Lectra and I thought we could do some Five Cent Saturdays. We went down Third Avenue on the L to South Ferry and transferred to the Second Avenue line and went up to Harlem. We got in the front car and watched the little engine. We peeked in the windows of the people living on Second Avenue and made up stories about them. Lectra made up stories good. They were mostly about immigrants coming over in the steerage from Germany. We pretended we were immigrants too, and talked broken English, and the people that sat with us laughed and said, "Vot language you talk, haah?" And we talked gibberish back at them.

Then we rode back again by getting out and turning around, and we rode all day for five cents, on Ninth Avenue and Sixth Avenue. We even rode down Thirty-fourth Street and Forty-second to the ferries. We took lickerish sticks along and got all dirty chewing lickerish. It's black and greasy and sticks to everything you touch. But we had a lot of fun; you almost forgot Lectra was a girl.

Then we'd go back to the Park next day, and Mutton Gravy was bossing everybody and we had to be Knight and Lady and kiss and hold hands and all that stuff. It was fun, too, but we just seemed like somebody entirely different had buttoned on our skins and was making free with ourselves. But we kept it up because everybody else did, and I got so I liked Electra quite a lot, and she liked me, I guess.

Miss Mutton Gravy didn't like us roving around by ourselves, though, and she made us pay penalties. She said if we didn't stop she would change us around and give me another Lady. So we kept quiet, but we stayed out all the more, and Lectra pretended she was sick and couldn't come out, and I told Mutton I had to lick catalogues. So we got off all right.

One Saturday we spent the whole day on the ferries. We walked down to Twenty-third and East River and for three cents we got the ferry to Greenpoint. Then at Greenpoint, we hid in the ferryboat in the stairs to the engine room until everybody had gone out. We ran out then and over to the Fulton Street ferry slip which was just alongside in the same ferry house. When we got to Fulton Street which is just beyond the Bridge we did the same over to Fulton Street in Brooklyn. From there we went all the way around the Battery to Jersey City and from Jersey City to Liberty Street and from Liberty to Hoboken and Hoboken to Forty-second Street and Forty-second Street to Weehawken and back again. That was a pretty good ride for three cents. Nobody bothered us at all. Sometimes the boatmen would tell us to look out or we would get pinched, but we told them we were just doing it for fun and to see how far we could go, and they were goodnatured. But most of the time they didn't see us at all.

We passed a U. S. ship taking immigrants in from Ellis Island down the Bay. It's just been opened, and the immigrants go through every day. They were singing when we passed them, and they looked happy to be here. We waved to em, and they waved back.

We had a lot of fun. We stood in the crowd when the ferryboat bumped against the slip, and we would pretend to lose our balance and fall all over against everybody and then say "I beg your pardon I lost my balance." Then the boat would hit the other side of the slip and we'd do it all over again. One boatman would fix the dock according to the tide, by turning a big wheel around. The other boatman would throw a cog-catcher over and it would bounce on the cogs with a merry sort of clang and pull the hawser tight so as to lock the boat tight against the dock.

Sometimes we pretended to be late and would jump across from the dock when she started. But I almost fell in one time, and the boatman gave me a cuff on the head and told me not to try that again. So I didn't. The water was terribly dirty, and stunk.

We did this all day till lunch time, and then we got off at Liberty Street and went in the back of a saloon that said "Family Entrance" and got a sanwidge and a glass of milk. Lectra had never been in a saloon before, so we peeked around. All there was, was just a lot of commuters getting a quick glass of beer before they went home on the ferry. Then they take a train on the other side and go home, wherever that is. They didn't seem very interesting.

We had big German sanwidges with liverwurst and bologna and pickles. By the end of the afternoon Lectra didn't feel very well, so we went home and Lectra went to bed. Mamma told me she was quite sick, because Mrs. Nilsson came and told her. She said I was a bad influence and must keep away from Lectra. She also told Mamma all about Mutton Gravy which was the first Mamma had heard about it. She said she was shocked; and it was a dreadful thing that contaminating influences like Mutton Gravy could get right in the Park and ruin children's morals.

I was forbidden to go in the Park for a whole week, and Papa went around to see Mr. King and he told Mr. Gravet, and he told Papa to mind his own business or he would fight him. So Papa was very mad, and said Frenchmen were a bad lot, and he was glad only Germans were coming over now, and not Frenchmen.

A couple of days after that Lectra came out in the Park with the nurse and sat on a bench while we played Fox and Geese. Some Micks came around, and as her bench was near the top gate they began to throw stones at her. Then they called her a dirty word and some more talk which made me mad, and I hollered to the fellows to come chase the Micks. They were throwing pretty big stones, but I ran up and opened the gate with my key, and they hit me on the head with a stone. It made a big gash on my forehead just over my eye and I fell flat. The fellows ran out and beat up the Micks and George ran home and told Papa and he came like a wild man and shouted around, and then he carried me home. It took me a while to get my senses, and the doc came and stitched two stitches, and I had to stay in bed. So John let me stay in his bed which was on Irving Place, and Lectra came around and we talked igsnay a lot. We made up a lot of words too that nobody knew, like "ooshwa" which meant "very much indeed" or "more than anything"; and "baloosh" which meant "disgusting" and "balbriggen" which meant "I love you" and all like that, and a lot more words that I forget. Lectra could make up more words, and I had to work them out, but she helped me with signs in deffandum talk. It was a lot of fun.

One night when I was laid up Papa came in and sat on the bed. He was always shy with us boys. He talked with us about history and books and the University, but he never talked about himself or us, much. That was the first time he ever did it, and I was so surprised I could hardly look at him.

He said, "Noble, who is this girl Electra?"

I said, "Oh, she's just a girl in the Park."

"Are you sweet on her?"

"Well, I guess, a little."

"Does she like you?"

"Some, I spose." I told him all about Mutton Gravy, and he laft.

"Well," he said, "it's a kind of measles, and you have a light case. But don't be too heroic. You might get hurt if you got fighting with fellows bigger than you are."

When I got back to the Park, I had a scar that everybody wanted to see and touch, and I felt quite the thing. I found out quick enough that they were getting tired of Queen Mutton Gravy and her High Court like I had. There were two new girls in the Park, Beatrice Bogert and Carrie Comstock, and they were big and strong, and they didn't like Mutton Gravy a little bit. So they started Cops and Robbers, and we played all over the streets and everywhere, and Mutton Gravy just sat in the Park. We hid in coalholes and areaways and everywhere. I used to hide a lot in the coalholes, only one time I jumped in the one on Lexington and Twenty-third Street and I slipped and slid way down the coalchute into the cellar, where there was a bulldog lying by a furnace. He growled and grabbed me by the pants as I was trying to scramble up the coalhole. I yelled murder and the old Irishman was sitting there asleep. He woke up after a while and called off the dog, and he let me out the areaway and I went home. I was all torn, and black as anything, and Mamma gave me the dickens.

The next I heard was that Mutton Gravy's mother was dead. Mutton came out in the Park with a beautiful black dress, and she sat on a bench and cried and carried on, on another girl's shoulder. She was very pale and sad; and we were very sorry for her. So we stood around and told her she could be Queen again, but she said she would never be Queen again, that nobody loved her in America, and she was going home to France. We found out that was true, but it was because her father was going home to marry somebody else he had known a long time. She was a sort of second wife, and Mutton didn't like her. She had to go just the same, though.

She sailed the second of July, and the fellows went to give her a send off. We went to the ship, which was LaBourgogne, and gave her a box of candy to remember us by. So she said we could all kiss her. So we did, and that was all we ever saw of Mutton Gravy, because the ship went out in the Bay, blowing a big steam whistle, and went to France. I told her "Ybdoog, uoy gnilrad," but she didn't understand it. She was kind of dumb, after all. Lectra said she was glad Mutton was gone, and now the boys could be fun again. But if Mutton hadn't given her to me, I would have missed a lot of fun, I told her; but she couldn't see it.

Election's coming. You got to go around and collect barrels for the bonfire. Barrels, or anything else you can get. Slats and boards are good. The groceryman has a lot of stuff. The boys are all hiding it in their back yards. Charley's got a lot already. He knows a factory in Seventeenth Street, back of Huyler's. You can get a lot there. I go with him sometimes. It's fun, but the nails scratch you sometimes.

We go in the Park to find the gang. They're all there. Eliot is planning an election barrel raid.

"All the fellows meet tonight, in front of my house. They're having it at Eighteenth Street and Fourth Ave. There's a lot of barrels there, and some tar. Maybe we can get that. Bring any old express wagon to carry the stuff."

"Gee, that'll be fun."

"We'll need all of you. Macy says we can use his cellar." We talk a lot about the fire. Last year we had the biggest fire ever. It was in the Park, and Mr. Byrne got a policeman and put it out. But we singed one of the trees, way up in the branches.

This year we don't know where we'll have it. Anyway, it isn't going to be in the Park, no matter what anybody says. We got to be quick though, or the police will put it out. There's the Micks too.

It will take a lot of planning.

We got a lot already, though. Lester's got some from the oxygen bottles at his father's plant. The Lovells have been saving everything. So have the others.

Gee, it's a long time to election. Who are you for? I'm for Harrison.

"Gwan, now, drop thet, or I'll run ye in."

"Ah, gwan."

"Gwan yourself. Are ye talkin' back to me?"

"Have a heart. Didn't you ever make an election fire?"

"Sure I did, but I never stole anything. I come by it honest."

"He gave us this. Didn't you, Mr. Blauvelt?"

"Ah, well, take it along. Ye know how it is, officer."

We take the barrel tops and slats, singing

> Arrah, g'wan, ye're only teasin',
> 'Pon me word, ye're sum'tin ahful.
> Lave me alone, ye're mighty plazin,
> Arrah, g'wan, g'way, g'wid ye, g'way, g'wid ye, g'way, g'wan.

Election's fun, but we gotta work, or Stuyvesant will have a bigger fire than we'll have.

Columbus. Columbus. Columbus.

Hallelujah. San Salvador.

We're all wearing Columbus buttons and U. S. flags.

Here comes the schoolboys' parade. It's nearly all public schoolboys, but there's some private schools too. We all go up to Seventy-second Street and march down Fifth Ave. to Washington Square. It's a good long way.

There are twenty-five thousand children, the biggest ever. Lots of people on the sidewalk.

A big fife and drum corps marched just a little way ahead. All we had to do was to keep abreast, and keep the line even.

We halted once in a while to let the bands rest, and the old teachers. Then we marched on again.

Some of the schools had uniforms, but we just had a red, white, and blue ribbon over one shoulder. It looked all right. We had a color-bearer, and a captain. Mr. Lyon marched ahead. He was as straight as a ramrod.

I never saw him that way. Fred Gibson told me he was a lieutenant in the Civil War, in the Third Connecticut. Well, he never told us. How were we to know? He never talked as if he liked soldiering.

There was a reviewing stand at Madison Square on the right side. We saluted when we went past. There was the Mayor and the Governor and Senator Depew. I could see our school when we got to Twenty-third Street. We kept right on down Fifth Avenue, though. When we got down to Washington Arch, there was Papa and Mamma waving a flag. I couldn't believe it, I was so surprised. So we all went home together in the Christopher Street car.

Next day, Naval Parade. We went in a little steamboat up and down the Hudson for miles. There were warships from all the countries.

Then came the big day. The parade went through Waverley Place from Broadway and up Fifth Avenue, so we had a grandstand built outside the University. We were there all day long. We took our lunch there. We had sandwiches and coffee and everything. Sausages and hard boiled eggs and veal loaf and blackberry shrub, and pickles and olives, gee, it was swell.

It started about nine o'clock and we went home at five and it was still going. Every state in the Union sent soldiers. They just kept coming and coming. The people stood just packed in the street. I don't know how they stood it all day long. They would cheer and cheer when the best line went by. We thought the Pennsylvanians were best, but Mamma said that was just because Papa's people had lived in Pennsylvania.

Well, the bands were wonderful, and they played all the time. They played the "Washington Post," and the "High School Cadets" and the "Columbian March," and "Hands Across the Sea." It got so we couldn't hear anything after a while, we were just deaf with all the drums.

The paper said it was the biggest parade in history, but Papa said the Grand Army of the Republic was greater in Washington in '65. Anyway, two million people watched it, so it was the biggest watched parade in history, everybody said so. I got so tired watching it I just went to sleep some of the time, in the corner of the University.

It was warm, and the men got tired. Some of them fainted and had to be carried off. Some women fainted in the crowd, too, so there was always something going on.

At night there was a big pageant with floats and animated statues and torchlights, but I was so tired I only saw the beginning and came home.

It was all so exciting I didn't go to school during three whole days.

When I get excited like that, I don't eat anything, I don't talk, I don't hear. I'm in a daze of excitement. I can't sleep, and Mamma scolds as if I had the cholera or something. She says, "I wish old Christopher Columbus had never discovered America."

I did, too, for a while. I felt all right afterwards and I was glad I had seen it. So many boys in the country will never see anything like it, because of course there never will be any more wars, and the Grand Army will die off, and we won't have any soldiers and what will there be to parade about?

It was funny to see how both sides could forget politics for a whole week, just before election, and work together for the big celebration. The Micks put their best clothes on, and looked as respectable as anybody else. Every street was just crammed with flags and miles of bunting. Irving Place ran the bunting along the balconies in straight lines. We all paid our share. Next week we would go to work fighting each other, but this week we just played together.

The fireworks knocked you off your perch. The finale was Niagara Falls about a mile long and half a mile high. You nearly died with excitement. I guess I'll never have a thrill like that again.

Macy has the biggest haul of barrels you ever saw. His father owns an apartment house with a big back yard. It is piled high with the stuff. The yard has a back entry on Third Avenue, and that is where our best fight of election comes in. I'll tell you about it.

Macy and his brother Arty and Cyrus and I are playing in his basement dining room. There is a mouse hole in the baseboard. You throw a cent at it. If you get the mouse that means you're nearest. Each fellow gets three throws. The one that gets the mouse gets all the pennies, gives them a toss, and all the heads belong to him.

We are sort of interested in this game, and don't hear anything for a while. Then Arty looks out of the window and says, "Hey, do you see what I see?"

We look out and there goes a barrel along by itself, looks like and disappears. Well, we know what's going on, and out we pile. There's a lot of Micks there, so we chase out and catch up with one of them. We pull his barrel away, but the rest shinny down the alley and get away with their plunder. Macy is too mad to talk for a while. Then

"Right in my own back yard," he says. "They'll be back for more. Nibsy, you run to the Park and get help."

I chase up through the cellar and over the iron gate, which is locked. Then into the Park, yelling my mouth off. Reinforcments spring up out of the ground, you might say. We get back just in time. Macy and Arty and Cy are in the alley, battling, but the enemy has pushed them back almost to the yard. What followed is known as the Scrap in the Alley. It was something to see, but nobody saw it.

It was a kind of football rush. We piled up about four high and I am sorry to say that our manners were not quite what Mamma would have liked. We were too mad to think. We had gone to all this extra trouble, first to steal and then to store our bonfire stuff, and now they were sneaking it out the back way.

I can't say we won, because we were pretty banged up. I had bumps all over, I know that. But we did save the barrels, because Mr. King's watchman, Mr. Kelly, came around, and as he had a nightstick the Micks decided to let it alone. Mr. Kelly said he would watch the rest, in between his rounds. He didn't, though, because by morning about half was gone, when we went to look.

"Ah, what do you byes care?" said Mr. Kelly. "Sure the other poor fellies should be havin' a little bonfire of their own, don't ye think? Ye've plenty left, and more."

We thought he had let them take it, but we collected fifty cents, and gave them to him. He promised he'd watch better, and he did, after that.

Election Day came around, finally. We had almost forgotten about it. Our yards were all crammed with so much wood you could have started a mill. It was Nov. 8, which is the latest it can come, for some reason. We had to go to school, because of Columbus Day and the celebration. Mr. Lyon gave us a talk about the ballot box and how it works, and how hard it is in a big city to keep the box safe. I found out a lot of the boys were Democrats, people you'd never suspect. It was a great surprise to me.

In the afternoon, I came home, but was chased part of the way, around Twentieth Street. Papa had voted. He was mad. A fellow had called him "Old Whiskers" and told him to hurry up. When he answered back, another fellow challenged him. That means you're in the wrong voting place, or something. So he had to wait, until the police lieutenant came around that is a friend of his, Lieutenant Maguire, and fixed him up.

"Democratic riffraff!" he says. He sits down and writes a letter to the Tribune about it.

When I got out to the Park I found Eliot fixing everything for the fire.

"Ten o'clock sharp. Everybody ready. Here are the yards. I've divided up these tickets." He had some old cigarette cards with places on them. "Everybody goes to the place I've written. At ten o'clock you be all ready, and bring it as fast as you can. I'll be with Wendell and Crawford in their grandmother's house in the corner of Irving Place and Twentieth. We'll yank out six barrels, pile em, throw in the excelsior and let her rip. It'll be too hot for cops to handle in one minute. From then on it's up to you. Watch the streets and dodge the cops."

He was like a general. You never heard anything like it. We did exactly as he said. It worked out fine.

We started at the stroke of ten. I was with Charley. We rushed the cart and got there about as soon as Eliot. We helped him and Crawford pile the stuff. Eliot poured on some kerosene, and ziff, up she went. It was so hot you couldn't get in six feet of it.

We got about thirty barrels going before a cop came around. By that time he couldn't get near it. It was roaring and crackling. There wasn't any danger, because it was over on the Park side of the street, and no trees, even, were there.

Some of us got him over on one side, talking and scolding about it, and shouting, "I'll run ye in fer this." The rest were shoving in the barrels behind his back. At last he saw he couldn't do anything, and besides another cop told him to come along and patrol the other streets, there was no danger here, except maybe from sparks.

So they let us alone, and it burned till midnight. The Micks came around. They couldn't get near it, or do a thing. They said it was a pretty good fire, but we knew they had finished theirs long ago. It couldn't have been very big.

We sang election songs like,

> *"The train is coming around the bend,*
> *Goodby, old Grover, goodby;*
> *It's loaded down with Harrison men,*
> *Goodby, old Grover, goodby."*

The Micks tried to drown us out, but we sure made a lot of noise. There were some drunks there, but nothing happened. We were all too excited and tired.

The fire kept growing until it was as high as Mrs. Clark's top story, four stories tall. Then it went down again. We had four barrels high one time. The tar didn't make as much smoke or flame as we thought it would.

When it was all over we went home. Papa had just come in. John and George were with him. They had been to Madison Square to read the returns. They hadn't had a good time at all. The returns were from New York and New Jersey, mostly, and it was all Democratic. Gilroy was Mayor and Cleveland was President. They expected that, but what scared Papa was the size of the vote and of Cleveland's majority.

"The country's gone to the dogs, I'm afraid," says Papa. "The true men have been rejected."

The Wharves and the Ships

By Henry Cabot Lodge, Sr.

Long after he grew up and became a noted politician, Henry Cabot Lodge the elder was to remember the days when, as a boy, he watched the clipper ships at the wharves and smelled the fragrance of spices from the East. His was a boyhood in the great New England tradition.

Boston in those days offered for a small boy an opportunity to live contentedly within its limits. We could play in each other's gardens or yards, for generous gardens and large yards still existed, a bequest of the eighteenth century, when there seems to have been more land and more leisure for city gardens than there is to-day. Best of all, we had the Common, where we could disport ourselves as of right. There we played all the games, rising, as we went, on to football and baseball. There in winter we coasted on the "Big Hill" and on the long path running from the Park and Beacon Street corner, very near to the other "Long Path" made memorable by the "Autocrat," but which was less suitable for sleds than for lovers. We skated, of course, on the Frog Pond; and on the Common we also waged Homeric combats with snowballs against the boys from the South Cove and the North End, in which we made gallant fights, but were in the end, as a rule, outnumbered and driven back. What was more serious, the ever-increasing number of our opponents gradually by sheer weight pushed us, and still more our successors, from the Common hills and the Frog Pond to seek coasting and skating in the country. This was luckily not such a heavy infliction as might be supposed, for between 1850 and 1867, when I went to Harvard, the country was reached as soon as one stepped outside the city limits. One had but to cross the mill-dam to attain to the country, for the towns close to Boston were in those days small and rural and had not yet become paved portions of the big, absorbing capital.

But Boston and winter—although I loved the heavy snowstorms and the coasting and skating—Boston and winter and school and what passed for education were not only the lesser but the worser part of life. The joy of living in its full sense was united indissolubly with the summer and the sea. I had something of the sea in Boston, for my father was a China merchant, and, after the fashion of the merchants of those days, had his office in the granite block which stretched down to the end of Commercial Wharf. His counting-room was at the very end in the last division of the block, and from the windows I could look out on the ships lying alongside the wharf. They were beautiful vessels, American clipper ships in the days when our ships of that type were famous throughout the world for speed and stanchness. I wandered about over their decks, making friends with the captains, the seamen, and the ship-keepers, and taking a most absorbing interest in everything connected with them. They brought me from China admirable firecrackers and strange fireworks, fascinating in appearance, but which I could not "make go" at all. From them, too, came bronzes and porcelains and pictures and carved ivories, which I was wont to look at wonderingly, and ginger and sweetmeats and lychee-nuts (then almost unknown here), of which I used to partake with keen delight. For the teas and silks which filled the holds I cared nothing, but the history and adventures of the ships interested me greatly. I was indifferent to those which my father had bought and which rejoiced in such names as the *Alfred Hill* and *Sarah H. Snow*, but I cared enormously for the others, which he had built and named himself. One was the *Argonaut*, his "luckiest" ship, in which he told me I had an interest or share. I still have a stiff picture of her painted by a Chinese artist in the Western manner, and a very beautiful ship she must have been. Second only to the *Argonaut* in my affections were two named for the heroes of one of my father's best-loved books, the *Don Quixote* and the *Sancho Panza*. Then there were still others, crack ships in their day, whose names appealed to my imagination—the *Storm King*, the *Cossack*, and the *Magnet*. But over all was the mystery and the fascination of the sea, and those who have been born at its edge and have fallen under its spell are never happy when long parted from the ocean and the ships. Longfellow has given once for all in verse what many a New England boy, born by the sea, has felt and, having once felt, has never forgotten:

"I remember the black wharves and the slips,
And the sea-tides tossing free;
And Spanish sailors with bearded lips,
And the beauty and mystery of the ships,
And the magic of the sea."

Such I know was my feeling, and I can see now the look of the wharf and the men and the ships as I gazed at them from the window of the counting-room or wandered about their decks.

I am happy to find that I am not alone in my memory of the wharves and ships of those early days. In his charming book about "Boston New and Old," my friend and contemporary Russell Sullivan says: "Here, at Commercial Wharf, too, and at Lewis Wharf, came in the merchantmen. The lofts and ground floors of the buildings were stored with products of the Indies; midway, sunny counting rooms overlooked the water, the loading and discharging vessels. There, where the merchants spent their days, the wide, comfortable spaces fitted with time honored furniture, with paintings of clipper ships upon the walls, had a look of well-ordered repose, and, between cargoes, were, indeed, at times so quiet that the gentle lap of the harbor-waves could be heard against the wooden piers below. There was always a fragrance of mingled spices in the air which tranquil dignity pervaded. They had their rough and tumble days, to be sure, when bags of ginger, cases of nutmegs and flat bales of dusty palm-leaf swung up from the hold so fast that the tally-clerks lost count, confusion reigned and tempers went by the board. The troops of small boys who came collecting foreign postage stamps and the decorative shipping-cards of elaborate design which were in vogue, must have been a pestering nuisance, yet were civilly endured. Only a few ill-natured consignees hung out signs warning off these youthful mendicants."

I remember one product of the Indies discovered by Columbus which Mr. Sullivan fails to mention, although it was an import from which the youth of the period drew an immediate revenue. On India Wharf, and no doubt on others, were frequently gathered in serried ranks lying side by side large groups of great hogsheads filled with West Indian molasses. Those who came to buy not infrequently left the long stick with which they tested the contents standing in the bung-hole of the cask. To draw forth this stick dripping with molasses was simple, then, regardless of dirt and impurities, to run the finger along it and convey the finger to the mouth was the work of a moment. It is not a form of gluttony which would attract me now, but my friends and I enjoyed this black molasses hugely, although not even thcft could add to its intense and cloying, if dirty, sweetness.

Livery Stables

By H. L. Mencken

In Baltimore, says Mr. Mencken, livery stables were places of high decorum, operated by proud and even haughty men. They were more than the counterpart of the modern garage, for they were treasure houses of worldly wisdom for inquiring young minds.

In my boyhood in the Aurignacian Epoch of Baltimore the favorite bivouac and chapel-of-ease of all healthy males of tender years was the neighborhood livery stable. I have since learned, by a reading in the social sciences, that the American livery stables of that era were seminaries of iniquity, with a curriculum embracing cursing and swearing, gambling, cigarette-smoking, tobacco-chewing, the classical or Abraham Lincoln repertoire of lewd anecdotes, the design and execution of dirty pictures, and even the elements of seduction, burglary and delirium tremens. It may have been true, for all I know, in the pathological small towns that all social scientists appear to hail from, but certainly it was not true in West Baltimore. I was a regular student at Reveille's stable in Stricker street from the beginning of my seventh year to the end of my nonage, and as special student at Coblens's stable in Paca street, off and on, for most of the same period, but so far as I can recall I never heard a word uttered in either of them, or beheld any human act, transaction or phenomenon, that might not have been repeated before a bench of bishops.

On the contrary, they were both schools of decorum, operated by proud and even haughty men, and staffed by blackamoors of a generally high tone. No palpably dipsomaniacal or larcenous coon could survive more than a few days in any such establishment: there were too many valuable horses and rigs in hand to be trusted to the former, and too many valuable carriage-robes, buggy-whips, hassocks, etc., to be exposed to the latter. My father's No. 1 whip, hung up by the snapper in Mr. Reveille's office, had a gold band around the handle engraved with the insigne of the Ancient Arabic Order of Nobles of the Mystic Shrine, and in Mr. Coblens's office, where he commonly kept his No. 2 whip and his dayton wagon, there was a buffalo robe that he set great store by, although I should add that its hair had pretty well played out, and that after his death I gave it freely to the poor.

Mr. Coblens was a man of erect bearing, reserved manner, and great dignity. He wore none of the loud checks associated with his vocation, but was always clad in plain colors, and not infrequently appeared in a black cutaway. His only concession to the public expectation was a gray derby hat, very high in the crown. If you can imagine a Jewish colonel of a swagger cavalry regiment, then you have got him to the life. My father had a high regard for him, and often paused to discuss horses with him—a subject about which he knew everything and my father next to nothing. He seldom descended from his heights to speak to my brother or me. He knew us very well, and would indicate by a vague flicker of his eyes that he was aware of our presence, but it was not often that he said anything.

His cousin Felix was a far more cordial fellow. Felix was a bachelor in those days, and apparently a somewhat gay one, for more than once I saw him set out of an afternoon in a buggy shining like a $100 coffin, with sometimes a blonde lady beside him and sometimes a brunette. My brother and I, boylike, regarded his ease and success at gallantry with great respect. He was, indeed, one of our heroes, and also one of our friends. He was never too busy to explain to us, with the use of living models paraded by his blackamoors, the points of a harness horse, and he also had illuminating ideas about buggy architecture. When my father gave my brother Charlie and me the pony Frank, it was Mr. Felix who taught us how to handle him—no mean art, I assure you, for Shetland ponies not only kick like mules, but also bite like dogs, and no doubt would scratch like cats if they had claws. To this day I have a scar on my bosom, often passing for a war wound, that proves how effectively Frank could use his teeth.

In 1890 or thereabout my father traded two cases of Zimmer Spanish leaf tobacco for a gelding bearing the strange name (for a horse) of John. John was a trotter, and supposedly of some speed in harness, but my father could never get it out of him. The two did so badly together, indeed, that my father concluded that John must have rheumatism, and thereafter, for two or three months, the poor beast was the patient of a veterinarian who sent in large bottles of a fiery, suffocating liniment and even larger bills, but never did John any good. Mr. Felix, it appeared, had suspected all the while that the trouble was predominantly in the driver rather than in the horse, and eventually he volunteered to go out with my father some afternoon, and make a scientific review of his driving. He returned downcast. "Your pa," he said to me the next time I dropped in, "is hopeless. It would take him two or three hundred years to learn to drive a cart-horse, let alone a trotter. He holds the lines like a man dealing cards. If he ever got John to really stepping he would fall out of the buggy and break his neck."

A few days later, as if reminded by conscience that he may have been hasty in dismissing his duty to the family, he amazed and delighted me by offering to give *me* a few lessons. It was a colossal opportunity to a boy of eleven, for Mr. Felix was an eminent figure in the trotting world of Baltimore, and seldom condescended to pedagogy. I had, as I recall it, only four or five lessons, but when they were over Mr. Felix was so complimentary that I developed on the spot a complacency which still survives after nearly fifty years, protecting me like an undershirt of concrete from the contumely of mankind. Indeed, he said flatly, and I believe he meant it, that I had the makings of a really smart harness driver. "By the time you begin to shave," he concluded, "you'll be showing 'em."

By that time, alas, I had turned from equestrology to chemistry, and a little while later I abandoned chemistry for the kind of beautiful letters on tap in newspaper offices. But for a couple of years I drove John every day, and so gradually improved and mellowed my technic. On Summer afternoons, when my father and I were driving home to Mt. Washington, and the clomp-clomp of a trotter's scissoring hooves began to sound behind us on the Pimlico road speedway, he would silently hand me the reins, and settle back to be torn between parental pride and personal repining. I seemed to hear him groan now and then, but he never said anything. When John, who was really very fast, had left the other nag behind, and the brush was over, he would quietly relight his cigar and resume the reins. He never complimented me: it was too painful. Despite the unction to my vanity that flowed out of these episodes, there was also melancholy in them, and they implanted in me a lifelong conviction that children, taking one day with another, must be damned pests.

But it was not the Coblens stable but the Reveille stable that was my chief haunt in boyhood. The Coblens stable was downtown in Paca street, a few yards from my father's place of business, but the Reveille stable was only two blocks from our home on Hollins street. My brother and I spent many happy hours there, watching the blackamoors currying, feeding and watering the horses, plaiting their tails, excavating and blacking their hooves, dosing them with Glauber's salts and condition powders, and treating their lampas (pronounced *lampers*) with red-hot pokers. This last was a horrifying spectacle, for lampas is an overgrowth of tissue behind the upper incisor teeth, and burning it out involved thrusting the poker into the poor horse's gaping mouth. But I learned before long that horses have very little sense of pain, if indeed any at all; and years afterward I saw one with a leg cut off in an accident munching the grass between the cobblestones as it lay on a Baltimore street, waiting for a cop to come out of a saloon to shoot it.

Mr. Reveille was a Frenchman who seemed venerable and even ancient to my brother and me, for he wore a long beard and always had on a black coat. He had two grown sons, both stout and hearty fellows, but, like their father, very dignified. There was a period when both the trotter John and the pony Frank (whose stable at the bottom of our backyard was transiently shut down) were quartered in the Reveille establishment, along with two buggies, a pony cart and several other rigs, so my brother and I had plenty of excuse for hanging about. The Reveilles always welcomed us gravely, and let us warm up, in Winter, in their tiny office, which was so filled with robes that there was scarcely room for the stove, always verging on white-hot. We admired especially the rack of whips, which included some virtuoso pieces by the Baltimore master-craftsmen of the time. A good whip might cost as much as $25, and we figured that the whole lot must be worth at least $1000.

The colored brethren who pontificated at Reveille's have all faded, with the flight of the years, into a brown smudge—all, that is, save Old Jim. Jim was the carriage-washer, and a fellow of vast size and unparaleled amiability. He was coal-black and built like a battleship, and when he got into his hip-high rubber boots and put on his long rubber apron he looked like an emperor in Hell. Jim's atelier was a skylighted space at the rear of the carriage-house, paved with cobblestones and always flowing with water. He got to work at six in the morning, and was sometimes still going hard at nine at night. He had the care of fifty or more buggies, and of perhaps as many other vehicles, and he kept them clean and shining. His hardest time came on Sunday morning, when he had to wash and polish all the buggies in preparation for the pleasure jaunts of the afternoon. For this business he brought out his newest sponges and cleanest chamois-skins. Also, he put on a black derby hat, never worn on weekdays.

In the intervals of his washing and polishing, Jim took out rigs to the homes of clients of the stable, and thereby sometimes acquired quiet brannigans, for it was the custom to reward him, not with money, but with drinks. My father kept a special jug for the purpose. It was shared by the ice-man, but Jim got most of it, for in view of his great bulk he was given a much larger drink than the ice-man. He always downed it at a gulp, and after it was down he would blink his eyes, rub his belly, and say "Ah-h-h-h-h-!" This was a Baltimore custom of the time, practised by most of the nobility and gentry and imitated by serving folk. Sometimes Jim also got a cigar. He would light it at once, and stalk back to Reveille's smoking it at an angle of forty-five degrees. When he reached the stable he would choke it carefully and deposit it on a high ledge in the brick wall, out of reach of his less Himalayan and reliable colleagues.

My brother and I greatly admired Jim, and delighted in watching him at work. He had a way of spinning buggy-wheels that was really magnificent, and he worked with larger sponges and broader chamois-skins than any other carriage-washer in West Baltimore.

Open House on New Year's

By Samuel Hopkins Adams

The party on New Year's Eve, where beverages flow like water, is now an American tradition. But when Samuel Hopkins Adams was a boy in Rochester, it was the Open House of New Year's Day that counted; and the center of attraction, much to a boy's delight, was not the punch but the endless array of delectable viands.

As early as the 1880's Rochester's most stiff-and-starchy ward was beginning to be affectionately referred to as "the Old Third." It was the self-appointed custodian of the city's ancient ways. In pioneer days, when the town was growing into its pride and prosperity under the impetus of the Grand Erie Canal, it had been called, in recognition of its aristocracy, the Ruffleshirt Ward. Long after it dropped the ruffles from its shirts, it kept them on its traditions.

The fine flower of local custom was New Year's hospitality. On that day the Old Families kept open house with pomp, circumstance and a lavish prodigality of refreshment equalled today only by a gangster's wake. Young and old, rich and (within decorous limits) poor, native and outlander were welcome. Dressed in their best bib-and-tucker, they made the rounds from high noon to 6 P.M., eating their voracious way like a swarm of social locusts. A few adventurous homes kept going until eight and, one year, there was an unverified scandal to the effect that the Kimball mansion revels were prolonged to the licentious hour of ten under the stimulus of a punch in the back parlor, rumored to have liquor in it.

New Year's was pre-eminently a masculine day. Ladies made no calls. They were cast in the passive role of providers, with the young girls, starched and sashed and beribboned, as assistants. For the small boys it was a kind of debut. A year or so at Miss Quimby's Dancing Class was supposed to form one's manners, and the round of January 1st calls was often the first public try-out. For the ten-year-old boy it was something of an ordeal, the rigors of which were mitigated by the prospect of the richest and most variegated cuisine of the year.

Careful tabs were kept on the entertainments. It is doubtful that the accumulated lore was ever reduced to writing; it was handed down by word of mouth from age to age with all the authority of tribal tradition. Before the boy debutant was launched upon the social waves, he was equipped with the gastronomic wisdom of generations.

It was accepted as an article of faith that the Brewsters should serve five kinds of pie, including Marlborough; that the Rogers' chicken salad was beyond all competition; that the Stedmans could be relied upon for that meatiest of rare luxuries, scalloped oysters; that what was known as Charlotte "Roosh" attained its apex of delicacy at Miss Ada Kent's; and that the Pecks offered not only two kinds of turkey, but also duck and goose. The house that was traditionally a "must" for the young was the Chapin mansion on Fitzhugh Street, in that it set forth a superb assortment of exotic fruits and nuts which could be taken from the premises for future use with impunity, a practice elsewhere frowned upon as unmannerly. The Chapins overtly encouraged it. In consequence, long lines of juvenile Third Warders, their coats and trousers distorted to shapelessness, could be seen filing down the front steps and pausing outside the iron fence to appraise and compare their loot.

There was careful preparation for the day. The neophyte was coached in a formula which could not go wrong so long as he stuck to it.

All this valuable information became mine on the day of my debut, in 1881. My cousins, John and Sireno Adams, who lived on the east side of the river where the strange custom of morning calls was observed, had been invited to join me for the afternoon. Grandfather and his wife drove the two across Court Street bridge behind the venerable Adams nag, Horace G., who as his owner frequently said, was no equine dandiprat but had a sterling character. The sidebar cutter drew up in front of my parents' half of the double house on Troup Street, and the four occupants descended.

"Happy New Year's," said John and Reno in unhappy voices. They were apprehensive of the unknown rites before them.

The greetings having been concluded, we three boys were lined up against the sitting-room wall for scrutiny by our elders. Besides the grandparents, there were my mother and Aunt Sophie Hopkins. Father had withdrawn to work on his sermon.

There was little to criticize in our outer appearance. All of us had undergone baths, no extra hardship as it was Saturday, anyway. We were in our best clothes, John in dark blue with brass buttons, Reno in fuzzy brown and new tight shoes with a lustrous polish, and I in my hitherto unworn pepper-and-salt Norfolk suit from Sibley, Lindsay & Curr's Fashions-for-the-Young department. Grandfather was pleased to express his approval. "You look very macaroni. As we said in my day, 'A collar-and-risband sprig of fashion,' each of you."

Aunt Sophie was not so easily satisfied. Taking me by the arm and spinning me like a tailor's dummy, she yanked correctively at the back of my jacket.

"What makes it hump up like a camel, Hetty?" she demanded of my mother.

"Stand up straight, Sam," Mother ordered. She gave the garment a compensatory tug. "There! That's better."

"Ought to be," my aunt sniffed. She had noted the price tag inside the collar. "Ten dollars for a boy's suit, indeed!"

"Pinchpenny ne'er served any," Grandma quoted placidly. "I daresay it's worth the money."

The preliminary inspection having ended, a communal inquisition followed, led by Grandfather.

"Have you all clean handkerchiefs?"

"Yes, sir." (Producing them.)

"Where are your arctics?"

"In the hall."

"You haven't forgotten your calling cards?" This from Grandmother.

"No, ma'am."

These were handwritten in the mode of Spencerian flourish. A decorative seraph's wing, then the name with accented capitals, then a balancing wing. A list of the houses to be visited was handed to John, as the senior, which he carefully stowed in his pocket. We looked hopefully toward the door but were checked by a command in Grandfather's disciplinary voice.

"Hold out your hands."

Chapped but clean, all six passed muster.

"Flatten your gloves in your top pockets."

We obeyed, fidgeting.

"Stop biting your nails, Samuel." I stopped.

"Why do you shoot your cuffs, John?" John abstained.

"Is that gum you are chewing, Sireno?" Reno shamefacedly discarded his cherished tree-spruce.

Footsteps sounded, descending the stairs, and the face of my Uncle Jack, wearing a sardonic grin, appeared.

"Don't they look sweet!" he said offensively, and recited:

Be kind to all, my little dears,
And always wash behind your ears.

"Aw, chestnuts!" I protested.

"Rats!" John added.

"What manners!" said Aunt Sophie.

"I don't suppose any one of 'em has a notion of proper behavior," Grandma said, shaking her head.

John chose to accept this as a challenge. He stepped forward with a gracious smile for an imaginary hostess. "How do you *do,* Miss Julia Whitney?" he inquired in sugared accents. "I trust this happy New Year's Day finds you in good health."

"Very commendable," Grandfather approved.

A jingle of bells sounded outside. A nobby sleigh and pair from Toogood's Livery drew in at the curb. Three bachelor Third Warders in glad array were seated in it. They whistled shrilly.

"Jack! Jack! Here's your rig," Mother called.

Uncle Jack reappeared in the hallway, drawing a muffler about his neck. He was superb in a Prince Albert coat with satin lapels, white pique shirt, a made-up bow of pearly hue, black trousers, and patent leather button shoes. The family were exclamatory in their admiration, as he eased himself into his long, frieze ulster and waved a courtly good-bye with his sealskin cap. Through the door, as he opened it, came derisive shouts. "Dude! Dude! Get onto the dude!"

Three urchins of the Clarissa Street gang were capering on the sidewalk. Uncle Jack ignored them.

Reno made a jump for the nearest window and threw it up. "You wait!" he yelled at the jeering group. "You just wait! C'mon, fellas."

It was not to be. Aunt Sophie, who was slender but sinewy, got a grip on the challenger's collar which was not to be shaken off. Mother had me by the ear. Grandma spryly blocked off John.

"Fighting! On New Year's Day!" she said reproachfully.

"In your new suit!" Mother added.

"Stand still," Aunt Sophie admonished Reno. "You—you eel."

The Clarissa Streeters vanished up the street, hooting. The festal rig set out upon its social career in a whirl of snow. We would-be belligerents were herded into chairs and our instructions were resumed. Don't track snow into the houses. Be sure to greet the hostess before eating and to say good-bye before leaving. Take off gloves before shaking hands. Keep hands out of pockets. Bow as Miss Quimby taught. Don't start tag-you're-it or any other game indoors. Don't ask for a second helping. Leave cards. Act like little gentlemen everywhere.

It was a large and depressing order.

Grandfather unexpectedly lightened the gloom for us. He turned to my mother.

"Hester, is it the mode for callers to make their rounds by equipage?" He had been impressed by the splendor of Uncle Jack's exit.

"If they can afford it, sir." She explained that several bachelors would chip in a dollar apiece and thus defray the costs of transportation.

"In that case, we shall bow to the fashion," the old gentleman said. "Make ready, boys. I will, myself, act as your coachee for the occasion."

This put another aspect on the matter. The sidebar cutter, drawn by Horace G. might not be as elegant as Uncle Jack's turnout, but, at least, it was in the manner. No other boys in the ward would be transported with such distinction; not Charley Robinson, whose father was a broker, nor the Roby brothers of near-millionaire heritage, nor the visiting nephew of the Mumfords whose family were so rich that they lived in a Saratoga Springs hotel all summer.

We piled into the cutter with whoops of joy. There still loomed before us the acid test of unfamiliar social observance. John ventured the suggestion that Grandfather give us his moral support at the start by accompanying us.

"No, no," he said. "Society's pribbles and prabbles are fifty years and more in my past. You must stand upon your own feet."

"Mine hurt," Reno said. "I wanta go home."

He was squelched, and the three of us discharged on the corner of Plymouth Avenue. We had to make a beginning somewhere. But where? John found a solution by closing his eyes, whirling around several times, and pointing, stiff-armed. The house indicated was the Chamberlains'. Each struggling to be last, we went in.

It was not nearly as bad as we had foreboded. Through this and the next few calls we bumbled without open disgrace, by dint of huddling close together and sticking to the formula. Presently our shyness evaporated in the simple warmth of the day's greetings. By an imperceptible transition, we became polished men of the world. John's comments on the weather were models of ease and felicity. I forgot my jacket's deplorable tendency to bunch up in the rear and achieved a dexterity with gloves and handkerchief that would have done credit to Rochester's contemporary Beau Brummel, Mr. Mahlon Day. By the time we had reached the Stoddards', Reno's aplomb had attained to a point where he treated his hostess to the latest thing in variety-show argot.

"Ah, there!" said Reno to the astonished Mrs. Dr. Stoddard. "Stay there."

John and I, horrified, hustled him out before he could commit any further faux pas. On the sidewalk we met with the first setback of the day from Beekman Little who inquired where we were headed.

"Stedman's," I said. "Oysters." I smacked my lips.

"Over the left," Beek said, and broke the bad news. Chippy Chapin's mother, marketing at Moggridge's grocery the day before, had overheard the grocer address Mrs. Stedman in words which afterward became a Third Ward classic.

"Yes, Mrs. Stedman, I *got* saddlerocks. I got plenty saddlerocks. But, makin' so free and you bein' a steady customer"—Here he daintily clamped his nose between thumb and forefinger—"if I was you, Mrs. Stedman, I shouldn't prefer to put none in."

Mrs. Stedman took his advice and substituted a ham. Something had gone wrong with the railroad shipments. The Third Ward went oysterless that New Year's.

It was a disappointment. But there were compensations, in particular the Whittlesey wine jelly and after that a long stretch of house-to-house hospitality. We ate our happy way along and around the corner into Washington Street where stood the John Rochester mansion, famous for the richness and extent of its refections. It looked bleak. No festoons ornamented its front windows. The steps had not been cleared of snow. Reno was sent forward to investigate. Halfway up the long steps he was met by Boardman Smith, descending. Boardman addressed him with the superciliousness proper to his sixteen years.

"N.G., kid. N.G."

"Why is it no good?" Reno demanded.

"N.G. No grub," the other grinned.

"Why not?"

"Basket."

"What's basket?" Reno asked, gaping.

"You're no Third Warder," said the scornful Mr. Smith, "or you'd know that a basket hung to the door means the family's away or something and you can put your card into it, if you got any, and come back next year."

That block was distressingly prolific of baskets. There and in Plymouth Avenue we dispensed most of our Spencerian pasteboards.

Better things were in store. Livingston Park, we had learned, was wide open. Every house on the upper slope was "receiving." We did well there, but toward the end, had a narrow escape. The scene of near-disaster was the stately George Buell place. Mr. Buell was the leading wholesale grocer of the city, and set a table in conformity with his high status. Here, at least, there would hang no repellent basket. The windows were garnished with holly and a wreath decorated the entry. We toiled up the sloping walk between the snow-festooned rhododendron bushes and had pushed open the outer door when a warning hiss arrested our progress.

"Cheese it!"

Lawrence Fitch and Vernam Fitzsimons were crouched in the shadowy lobby.

"Listen!" Lawrence whispered.

A reedy, little-girlish voice came to our ears.

> "*'We are lotht,' the Captain thouted,*
> *Ath he thtaggered down the thtairth."*

"Oh, Lordy!" John exclaimed in dismay. "What's up?"

"She's speaking a piece," Vern explained below his breath. "The Buell's niece or something. She's only six."

"We've been waiting for her to get through," Lawrence added.

"Can't they stop her?" Reno asked.

"They *like* it. Every time anybody new comes in, they make her do it all over again. Then they clap like everything."

"And we have to listen before we get any grub?" I asked.

"That's what," Lawrence said.

We held a council of war. It simply was not worth it, we decided, and crept forth from the unhallowed place, followed by the two lurkers. Even without the Buell fare, we had by this time put in a solid foundation of edibles. It was time to crown it with the glorious superstructure of

Miss Ada Kent's charlotte russe. We three Adamses climbed back into the cutter. The other two boys attached themselves to the runners, and we were stylishly driven out to Troup Street and around into Washington.

Miss Ada Kent's reputation as a benefactor of youth was ward-wide. She was a small, brisk little cricket of a spinster, already, at twenty-five, a predestined old maid. Her table at Sunday School picnics was always the most lavish. She gave a private strawberry festival in June to which the well-behaved young of the locality were bidden. With the first sufficient snowfall she hired a country bobsleigh and took a chosen few on a hayride. Her popularity in the ward was second only to that of Santa Claus.

A group of our crowd were skylarking in front of the Kent gate when we drove up. The equine pomp of our arrival roused them first to envious hoots and then to good-natured violence. In the free-for-all that ensued, John lost three highly essential buttons from the front of his short pants. It could not have happened more unjustly, or to a more modest and mannerly boy. He was for withdrawing from society in the sheltering depths of the cutter while the rest of us enjoyed the ambrosia of the Kent set-out.

Grandfather vetoed this. A conference was held. Jumbo Emerson contributed a scarfpin to the cause of respectability, a sportive design of a pug-dog's head, set in a bodkin-like shaft. Repairs were made, John was cautioned to move gingerly, and we all trooped up the steps.

Miss Ada's pleasure at our advent was heartwarming. "Dear boys!" she beamed. "How nice of you to come! I do hope that you have brought your appetites with you."

The main parlor and sitting room were full of grown-ups, eating, drinking and chattering. In the side parlor a special trestle had been reserved for youth, with a snowy, damask tablecloth in the center of which towered a massive charlotte russe. Several little girls of our own age were deputed to wait upon us. We seated ourselves on opposite sides of the makeshift table. Miss Ada hovered solicitously. My chair was next to Vern Fitzsimons' and across from John's.

All might have gone well had not John over-extended himself in reaching for a plate of ladyfingers. Something slipped. An expression of acute anguish froze his face into rigid lines. He sank back. His hands fumbled in his lap. Plainly he was making private and desperate adjustments. I noticed the tablecloth twitch slightly, but did not interpret the movement until too late. Vern Fitzsimons also had observed his opposite's maneuvers. Vern was precociously quick-witted and tactful.

He craned his neck to give himself a view through the window back of John. "Say, John!" he exclaimed with well-simulated excitement. "Your horse is getting fidgety. Better get out there."

John caught on at once. "Okay, Vern," he said gratefully. "Thanks."

He rose and started for the door. The tablecloth started after him. A serried array of knives, forks and spoons broke ranks and cascaded to the floor with a silvery crash. Two candy bowls rolled merrily after and, in final catastrophe, the lofty charlotte russe toppled and became a creamy smear on Miss Ada's best carpet. All the little girls shrieked in chorus. Miss Ada did a maidenly faint.

Grandfather, dozing in the cutter, was wakened by Horace G. giving a mighty start against the dashboard. The old horse had reason to be shocked. John, the mild-mannered, John the model for the rest of us, John, the paragon of correct behavior, was stumbling and staggering down the steps, clutching himself amidships, trailing interminable lengths of white damask, and screaming horrid imprecations. After him swarmed a turbulent crowd of his fellows, hysterical with mirth, and shouting the refrain of a popular song made and provided for such occasions.

Whoa, Emma! Whoa, Emma!
Emma, you put me in such a dilemma.

Grandfather scrambled nimbly from beneath his lap robe and intercepted the flight. "Get in, John," he said in a tone of quiet command.

John stared at him glassily, then raised his voice in despairing anathema. "Darn! Darn! *Damn!*" he yelped. "Whaddo I care if I go to hell!"

The old gentleman detached Miss Ada's best napery with a yank, lifted the squirming boy into the cutter, and, with a sharp "Gid-*app*, Horace," drove away, leaving Reno and me to walk home.

A year later, on January 1st, 1882, a basket dangled inhospitably from Miss Ada Kent's doorknob. It may have been the resentful aftermath of John's mischance. Or it may have been a non sequitur. As Grandfather might have said, in his favorite phrase, I don't know. Nobody knows.

Posh Party

By Gretchen Finletter

All of us used to love to watch, from the top of the stairs and with surreptitious glee, the antics of the grown-ups at their parties. But not many have had the chance to observe, as did Gretchen Damrosch, such a gathering of swells as graced the dinners of the famous conductor who was her father.

To observe the human race and be invisible oneself gives one a strange sense of power. It is especially interesting to study another generation and to observe its foibles. There should be more concealed doors and hidden balconies in the world.

We had moved to a larger and taller, high-stoop house on Sixty-first Street which was being improved gradually and with much discussion between my parents, while we lived in it. It possessed among other features a long flight of stairs and from the top of it my sisters and I watched dinner parties. It was a proscenium box and gave an excellent view of a series of good first-act entrances and exits. From our position we could see the front hall and its mirror, the center hall and its mirror, a section of the parlor if the portieres were pulled back far enough, the door and a bit of the dining room, and we had a clear view into the very congested pantry.

What we could not see, we could hear. The voices would at times be obscured; but sounds rise, and by moving down a few steps, we could catch actual dialogue.

Though the play began when the curtain went up on the cast, there was a prologue that we never missed. These fifteen minutes gave an overtone to the performance. As soon as my parents had gone down to the parlor we would seat ourselves in our box. Dressed in easy wrappers, knowing we should eat at certain intermissions, we comfortably waited for the show to start.

My mother had just opened a window, and all the portieres were waving. My father, looking very handsome in a dress suit and big white tie, hurried in.

"Margaret, it's freezing," and he lit the fire. "The papers say snow. This room gets cold enough anyhow with the draft that comes from the front door."

Then started the perennial discussion as to whether the whole house should be altered into what was called English basement. We had heard this argument so often that we turned our attention to the pantry door.

Our regular waitress, a tall lady with a great gray pompadour on the top of which rested a white cap with a black bow, was giving some directions to the hired waitress, who wore a different kind of cap and had a haughty manner. It seemed that at the last dinner party where she had hired out, she had started with the roast and the regular waitress had followed with the gravy. But Jenny, our waitress, was sticking up for her rights.

Behind them was Katy, our friend the chambermaid, who had only recently been raised in status from kitchen-maid. Katy easily broke into wild laughter if she got nervous, and showed a set of teeth that looked like Roquefort cheese. She also was wearing a cap—for the first time. Jenny considered Katy too flighty to go into the dining room, and she was kept concealed in the pantry to "hand things."

My father now appeared at the pantry door and told Katy to go in and light the candles. No matter what distance Katy had to travel, she always ran it in ten seconds flat; so seizing the matches and ejaculating an unhappy "Begorra, I'm wrong agin," she tore through the hall, not forgetting, however, to wave to us. Katy was warmhearted and wanted everyone to have a good time tonight.

There were candles on the piano, at the ends of the mantel, and in two great candelabra on the tops of the bookcases. The whole room took on a gay glow. It looked like a party. To us the depth to which the candles burned was the yardstick of how good the evening had been. If they were down a third it was average. If they burned themselves out it was tremendous.

My father's voice now came from the pantry with a note of real anguish: "Jenny, red wine is never iced! Claret should be the temperature of the room. Are you color-blind?"

There was a "Glory be to God" from Jenny, and my mother called out, "Close the pantry door. There's a smell of fish coming up through the dumb-waiter."

My father, having rectified the disaster to the claret by producing four new bottles, joined my mother again in the parlor, but his face was still flushed.

"Ce domestique est insupportable."

"Cette domestique," corrected my mother. She spoke better French than my father and seldom let him forget it.

My parents now began a slightly depressing discussion about their expected guests.

"The trouble with having asked Madame Henriques," said my father, "is that she spoils general conversation by wanting to tête-à-tête all the time."

My father has always been the enemy of the tête-à-tête. He hated being washed up on a sofa alone with any lady. I was never sure whether he felt that he was missing all the fun in the rest of the room or whether he felt the rest of the room was missing something good that he was saying, but he never let himself be trapped for long. An eager lady who wanted to tell him how she adored musicians never got very far unless she was willing to shout it out in front of a big circle. He wanted six or seven in on the love scene, and in the same way he felt destructive towards other duets. If a man and a woman at the dinner table seemed to be having obvious pleasure talking together, they must want to share this pleasure with everyone else. So my father would tap on his glass, propose a health, and cheerfully and successfully break up the dialogue.

"I'm sorry you asked Charley Robinson," continued my father. "He hates music."

"But I got him to balance what you told me was a French soprano, Mademoiselle Bonnard," answered my mother.

"I misread the letter of introduction. It's a tenor, René Bonnard. They say he sings very well."

"I've put him next Ethel Barrymore. Ethel will be wonderful with an unknown tenor."

"Ethel is wonderful with everyone," declared my father with great conviction, and the bell rang.

The hired waitress determinedly went to the front door and a lady came in.

"Is this Mr. Damrosch's house?" she asked.

Even to our inexperienced ears the answer did not sound quite right: "I'll be going and finding out. I'm thinking that's the name, but then agin, maybe it's not."

Jenny indignantly appeared and ushered the lady to the center hall. The hired waitress opened the front door again to a gentleman with a beard.

"It's begun to snow," he announced in a surprised voice.

We now had the double view of the lady and gentleman each in front of a mirror and both lost in contemplation. The lady finally walked into the parlor.

"Dear Madame Henriques," exclaimed my father. "What a pleasure!"

Polly beckoned us to come to the window and look out. Hundreds of little dark specks were falling by the street lamp. There was that strange soundless sound that seems to belong only to a snowstorm in the city. The pavements were white and some flakes had collected on the window sill. A taxi drew up.

Richard Harding Davis appeared in the hall below with his wife Cecil. He stood in front of the mirror looking at his handsome, ruddy, soldier-of-fortune reflection with an obvious satisfaction which we above shared. Cecil Davis was taking off a long cape. Her hair was the color of her chow dogs and she had the same mysterious eyes.

"Walter, it's begun to snow," she called.

Two other guests walked in, Irene and Charles Dana Gibson. There were loud greetings from the Davises. Dana Gibson took off his coat and hat. He had on an even bigger white tie than my father's and his collar was much higher. He looked seriously into the mirror. Then he winked at himself once and went into the center hall.

Katy, who had somehow escaped the pantry, gesticulated to us not to miss Irene Gibson. If she would only move a little closer to the mirror we could get a clear view. But in that not so very long ago ladies apparently dressed at home and did not have to remake their faces with powder and lipstick. All we could see was the tip of one white shoulder and her blond hair.

"Button this button on my glove, Dick," said Irene Gibson. "I can't get it through the hole."

My father, hearing cheerful sounds from behind the portieres, or perhaps finding himself too enmeshed by Madame Henriques, now burst through the curtains and seized the gloved hand.

"That is the host's privilege," he exclaimed.

"I got her hand first," answered Dick Davis, not letting go.

Katy, with a singular lack of tact, approached with a hairpin and said sure she could do it easy. Katy was palpably searching for any excuse to be of the party.

The doorbell rang again and they all moved into the parlor.

We watched the new arrival with interest. We had never seen him before. He carried a bouquet of roses with a ruffle of paper around it. The flowers must be for my mother. My mother must be nearly forty years old. It was preposterous. He took off his hat. Ah, good, it was an opera hat—the crush kind. We could experiment with it later. He hung up a fur-lined overcoat and unwound a heavy silk scarf from about his neck. Then to our great pleasure he pulled a small comb from an inside pocket and combed his hair carefully on each side of a middle part.

We hung over the balustrade, trying not to breathe too loud. He replaced the comb in a little case and put it back in his pocket. Suddenly he leaned forward, opened his mouth wide, and examined his teeth. Apparently satisfied, he smiled charmingly at himself, picked up the roses, and walked through the middle hall and into the parlor. Then he kissed my mother's hand.

Two more guests came and my father appeared again in the center hall, calling to Jenny to close the front door, everyone was freezing. There was a tap on the glass.

"Are you trying to shut me out?" said a lovely familiar voice.

"Ethel!" exclaimed my father with delight.

"*Ach, mein kleiner* Walter!"

He helped her off with her wrap.

"Did you know it was snowing?" she asked.

Polly signaled up to the third floor to tell Minnie, who was watching from above, to come down and get a good look. Minnie would only observe if she felt it was really worth it. Certain guests she would dismiss after a penetrating glance through her eyeglasses as "Trash!" This time she gave her highest praise.

"Very nice. Who is it?"

"It's Ethel Barrymore. Isn't she beautiful?"

Minnie studied her again. "Akee-kock, why don't they cover up their shoulders!"

Minnie was always chilly and always wore what she called a "yacket." Those who were dressed the warmest were to her the prettiest. She now turned her attention to Katy, with deep disapproval.

"Greenhorn!" Minnie hated the Irish.

From the pantry came Jenny with fourteen very small cocktail glasses in which were fourteen Bronx cocktails—no shaker, no dividends. The hired waitress followed with two plates of little sandwiches. Katy, leaping about them like a setter, opened doors and pulled curtains.

Minnie descended the stairs toward the basement.

"That tramp Antonio calls himself a furnaceman. I'm going to put on some coal myself!"

There was a series of little agony buzzes from the dumb-waiter bell. Katy lit the candles on the dining-room table and at last Jenny announced, "Dinner is served," and we watched them march into the dining room. They were all talking, the gentlemen stepping carefully so as not to walk on the ladies' trains.

Katy, having been instructed by us, partially closed the dining-room door. We ran down the stairs quickly and into the parlor. Then we drank up what was left of the cocktails. We did this because we liked the taste of orange juice and this seemed to have more bite to it than the breakfast kind. We then ate up the sandwiches.

Feeling for some reason released, we proceeded to the front hall to examine the tenor's opera hat. The fifth time that we snapped it open, it would not close. By all of us pressing it very hard together we finally shut it again. Something clicked inside. Without saying so, we knew it would never open again. We next tried on a couple of the silk hats and rubbed them both the right and the wrong way. Then we returned to our position on the stairs.

"Do ye want soup?" asked Katy.

"Skip the soup and the fish unless it's shad roe. Open the door wider into the dining room so that we can hear."

The noise was tremendous. Everyone was talking at once. Then came my father's voice.

"Dick Davis has just asked Dana if he is not a perfect Gibson man. I insist that I have always been the model. The ladies must vote."

"I vote for Dick," cried my mother.

"Margaret, you don't count. You're prejudiced. Ethel, Irene, Cecil, I appeal to you!"

There were sounds of everyone disputing. Katy stood in the door, her mouth wide-open, watching with burning interest.

Minnie came toiling up the stairs again, carrying two plates of ice cream, one for herself and one for little Anita. She halfheartedly suggested that we go to bed.

There was applause from the dining room. Katy wheeled once, regained her sense of direction, and made for the hall.

"Sure it's your father that's won the iliction. Ain't that grand!" she panted to us.

"Hurry up and get us something to eat."

Irene Gibson was telling a darky story, mimicking each voice. There was a loud laugh, but the French tenor had apparently not understood. My father tried to translate.

"Un jour un vieux nègre s'appelait Oncle Rastu disait à son arrière petit-fils—"

"You had better say it in German," urged my mother.

"Es war einmal ein alter schwarzer Mann," obliged my father, *"der bei dem Name Onkle Rastus bekannt war. . . ."*

As the dinner progressed, the noise from the dining room grew louder and louder and sounded like the lions at feeding time. We could no longer distinguish conversation.

We ate sections of the courses as they were brought to us, a mélange of salad, rolls, cake, and Hollandaise sauce. The dessert was an egg shape of yellow ice cream embedded in a nest of spun sugar. The spun sugar did not possess any particular flavor, but, like alligator pears, was a party dish we always hailed with admiration. It scratched the mouth but looked holiday. Polly placed some on her upper lip in a trailing white mustache and signaled to the faithful public, Katy.

"Ye look just like Santa Claus," she called appreciatively.

A pleasant smell of tobacco smoke began to float up the stairs. A little later the ladies left the gentlemen, but Cecil Davis remained in the dining room.

"That's what I'm going to do," I announced. "I'm always going to stay with the men and never join the ladies."

I saw a rosy future—me, in a train, with yellow hair, sitting at a table surrounded by Gibson profiles in white ties.

As the men walked through the center hall looking well-fed and contented, Madame Henriques came through the portieres.

"I think I left my handkerchief in my wrap," she said to my father.

"Let me help you."

Madame Henriques seemed to be in no hurry to find it.

"When I watched you conduct last Friday I was so profoundly moved. There was a certain something—"

"It was the tails of my beautiful new dress suit," replied my father, spreading them out. "Jenny," and he made for the pantry door, "bring in the Scotch."

Madame Henriques was left hunting her handkerchief.

The door upstairs opened and little Anita, eluding Minnie and dressed in a pair of blue flannel pajamas, joined us.

"It's snowing!" she told us.

We went again to the window. An unmistakable sound came from outdoors, the scrape of a wooden shovel. There was no one on the streets, but down the block two men had begun to pile the snow. It was a real blizzard. Already the footprints of the guests on our steps had been obliterated. We opened the windows. The outside world had changed. It was intoxicating watching the white flakes whirl by. We must be the only people awake in the city to see it.

Then we heard my father playing a few soft chords at the piano, and the voice of Bonnard rang out:—

O, mon enfant, ma soeur,
Songe à la douceur
D'aller là-bas vivre ensemble.

The voice was beautiful, with that strange intensity that seems to be the unique possession of French singers.

"He's good," whispered Anita.

He sang on:—

Là, tout n'est qu' ordre et beauté
Luxe, calme et volupté.

Across the street a taxi drew up, struggling through the drifts. Our neighbor, Mrs. Douglas Robinson, was coming home from a party with some friends, and their shouts and laughter echoed across to us as they floundered through the snow.

Up the stairs came the creaking footsteps of the cook, who was carrying a loud ticking clock and groaning to herself. Again we heard the piano, and Monsieur Bonnard sang:—

Voici des fruits, des fleurs,
Des feuilles et des branches,
Et puis voici mon coeur . . .

We knew that the candles would gut themselves tonight.

World Series

By Lloyd Lewis

For every small boy who has now grown to middle age, there was one hero above all others—the incomparable Christy Mathewson. Lloyd Lewis, who was to become a famous newspaperman and writer, was no exception to the rule. Such a hero, and such an event, give "World Series" its uniquely American appeal.

"When the bleacher gates at Shibe Park in Philadelphia were thrown open on the morning of October 24, 1911, I was in the mob that went whooping toward the front seats. I got one in right field because the Philadelphians raced for left field to sit as close as possible to the bench of their worshiped Athletics, for the World Series at that moment stood two games to one for the American League's Connie Mack against the National League's John McGraw, and Philadelphia was loud and passionate in the confidence that now they would get revenge for the bitter dose—four games to one, three shutouts—these same New York Giants had given them six years before.

Me, I wanted to get as close to the Giants as possible, and found a place at the rail close to the empty chairs which would that afternoon become the Giants' bull pen. My whole adolescence had been devoted, so far as baseball went—and it went a long way to an Indiana farmboy—to the Giants and to their kingly pitcher, "Big Six," the great, the incomparable Christy Mathewson. I hadn't had the courage to cut classes in the near-by college and go to the first game of the series at Shibe Park. But today I had. Things were desperate. Up in New York's Polo Grounds to start this, the World Series, Mathewson had won—2 to 1—giving but five hits and demonstrating that with twelve years of Herculean toil behind him he was practically as invincible as when in 1905 he had shut out these same Athletics three times.

It had looked like 1905 over again; then, in the second game, the A's long, lean yokel third baseman, J. Franklin Baker, had suddenly and incredibly knocked a home run off Rube Marquard, the Giants' amazing young pitcher. Baker, who had hit only nine homers all season, had tagged the twenty-two-year-old Giant and two runs had come in—and the final had stood 3 to 1.

The papers which I read in the bleachers, as the morning wore on, were still full of that home run and its aftermath.

From the start of the series the newspapers had been publishing syndicated articles signed by Giant and Athletic stars—the real start of the "ghost writers" whose spurious trade flourished so long but which the better papers in time eliminated. And in the article signed by Mathewson the day after Marquard's disaster it had been said that Rube had lost the game by failing to obey orders. The side pitch he liked, instead of the low fast one he didn't like and which McGraw had ordered.

The rebuke had been a sensation which grew in the third game when Baker had hit another homer off Mathewson himself, and had been the main wrecker of the great man's long sway over the A's. Up to the ninth inning of that third game Matty had kept command. Always when the Athletics had got men on bases he had turned on his magic. As he went to the bench at the end of the eighth, New York had risen and given him a tremendous ovation, for in forty-four innings of World Series play, 1905 and 1911, he had allowed the Mackmen exactly one run—and the A's were hitters, indeed. Their season's average for 1911 had been .297.

Then, in the ninth, Eddie Collins had gone out, and only two men had stood between Matty and his fifth series victory over his victims. Up had come Baker with the American League fans begging him to do to Matty what he had done to Marquard—and, incredible as it seemed, he had done this.

As home runs go, it hadn't been much more than a long fly that sailed into the convenient right-field stand at the Polo Grounds, but it had gone far enough to tie the score and give Baker a nickname for life—"Home Run" Baker.

Snodgrass, the Giants' center fielder, one of the smartest and greatest of base runners, had ripped Baker's trousers almost off him, sliding into third in the first of the tenth inning. With McGraw snarling, railing, jeering from the coaching line, the Giants made no secret of their hatred of Baker. To them he was merely a lucky lout, a greenhorn who had by sheer accident homered off the two top pitchers of the season.

But Baker had hit again, a scratch single, in the eleventh which had been part of the making of the run which had won, and Marquard, in his "ghosted" article, had quipped at Mathewson's advice.

All that was in everybody's mind—and mine—as on October 24 the fourth game came up. The papers had had time to chew the sensation over and over, for it had rained for a week after the third game and now, with seven days' rest, Mathewson was to try again—this time in Shibe Park.

The long delay hadn't cooled excitement. The press box was still as crowded as at the opening game. This was the first World Series to be handled in the modern publicity fashion—the first to wire the game play by play to points as distant as Havana, Cuba—the first to which newspapers in the Far West and South sent their own writers. And though the A's now had a lead of two games to one, the threat of the Giants was still great enough to keep fever high.

It was a little after one o'clock when my long vigil ended. Onto the field came the Giants with their immemorial swagger, chips still on their shoulders—the cocky, ornery, defiant men of Muggsy McGraw—the rip-roaring demons who had, that season of 1911, set a record of 347 stolen bases—a record which would stand for another thirty-five years without any other club's ever coming nearer to it than the Senators' 288 in 1913.

And here at long last they were! I knew them from their pictures as, clad in dangerous black, they came strutting across toward their dugout. McGraw had dressed his men in sable uniforms back in 1905 when he had humbled the Athletics, and he was playing hunches now.

Muggsy was first—stocky, hard-eyed. Behind him came slim, handsome Snodgrass, striding as became a genius at getting hit by pitched balls and in scaring infielders with his flashing spikes. Then came swart, ominous Larry Doyle; lantern-jawed Art Fletcher; Buck Herzog, whose nose curved like a scimitar; lithe little Josh Devore; burly Otis Crandall; flat-faced, mohagany-colored Chief Meyers, the full-blooded Indian; Fred Merkle, all muscles, even in his jaws, a lionheart living down the most awful bonehead blunder ever made in baseball.

Then came Marquard, six feet three, his sharp face and slitlike eyes smiling—his head tilting to the left at the top of a long wry neck—Marquard the meteoric! At nineteen years of age he had been bought at a record price from Indianapolis and had immediately flopped two straight years for McGraw, becoming the nationally goatish "$11,000 lemon." Then, this 1911, he had flamed out, won twenty-four games, and become the "$11,000 beauty."

As the Giants began to toss the ball around, I couldn't see my hero, the Mathewson whom I had come to see, the great one who, from the time I was nine, I had pretended I was, playing ball in the Indiana cow pasture, throwing his famous "fade-away" which, for me, never came off. Then, suddenly, there he was, warming up and growling, "Who am I working for, the Giants or the photographers," as the cameramen not twenty feet from my popeyed head, begged him for poses.

I was let down for a minute. He didn't speak like a demigod, but as I stared, he looked it, all the same. He held his head high, and his eye with slow, lordly contempt swept the Athletics as they warmed up across the field. He was thirty-one, all bone and muscle and princely poise.

Surely he would get those Athletics today and put the Giants back in the running. Surely his unique "fade-away," the curve that broke backward, his speed, his snapping curve, his fabulous brain couldn't be stopped. It had been luck that had beaten him in the last game. Now he'd get them.

My eye never left him till the bell rang and he strode, hard but easy, with the swing of the aristocrat, into the dugout, and little Josh Devore went up to hit.

Josh singled, Doyle tripled, Snodgrass scored Larry with a long fly. Black figures were flying everywhere. The big copper-colored Chief Bender on Mack's mound was wobbling, and when the side was finally out he practically ran for the dugout. Later, we learned, he had run in to cut off bandages from his ribs, tape from a recent injury. After that he was to be unbeatable.

Up came the Athletics, Matty, as though in princely disdain, fanned the first two men. The third man, Eddie Collins, singled. Here came Baker, his sun-tanned face tense, his bat flailing—the air thick with one word from 25,000 throats, "Homer! Homer!"

Matty studied him as a scientist contemplates a beetle, then struck him out! What I yelled, I don't know. All I remember is standing there bellowing and paying no heed to the wadded newspapers the Athletic fans around me threw. It was wonderful!

In the fourth, Baker came up to start it and doubled. Dannie Murphy doubled, Harry Davis doubled. Ira Thomas hit a sacrifice fly—three runs. It couldn't be. Up came Baker again in the fifth with Collins on first, and another double boomed across the diamond. I saw Snodgrass eventually stop the ball, but he didn't really have it in his glove at all. It had stuck in my gullet.

Right in front of me an unthinkable thing happened. Hooks Wiltse, the southpaw, began warming up for the Giants. Was Matty knocked out? Another figure rose from the bull pen. Rube Marquard. He didn't warm up, he only strolled up and down, a great sardonic grin on his face. The fans around me were screaming at him, "You're even with Matty now, Rube! He won't tell you what to pitch any more!" etc., etc. Rube smirked at them.

Matty got by without more scores, but in the seventh, with a man on third, Christy walked Baker on four intentional balls, and Shibe Park's walls waved in a cyclone of "boos." I wished I was dead.

The eighth. A pinch hitter went up for Mathewson. I was sorry I hadn't died in the seventh.

Finally it was over.

I walked out through 24,000 of the most loathsome individuals ever created—all jeering at Mathewson, all howling Baker's virtues. I dragged my feet this way and that trying to escape the currents of fans. At the end of a dolorous mile I stopped at a saloon. I had never had a drink. Now was the time.

"Beer," I said, in the voice of Poe's raven.

"You ain't twenty-one," the bartender rasped. Then he took a second look, saw that I was a hundred, and splashed a great stein in front of me.

I took one swallow. It was bitter, just as bitter as everything else in the world. I laid down a nickel and walked out. Every step of the way downtown I kept telling myself that in my coffin, some day, there'd be only room for one thing besides myself—my hatred of the Athletics.

But what I started out to tell was about my greatest day in baseball. That came three years later, October 9, 1914, when the lowly, despised Boston Braves wallowed, humbled, trampled, laughed at the lofty Athletics to the tune of 7 to 1. Hoarse and happy, I came out of Shibe Park, spent hours hunting that same saloon, but I couldn't find it. It had to be that one. What I wanted to do was to walk in all alone—find nobody else in there—order two beers, and when the bartender looked inquiringly at the extra one, say to him in a condescending voice, "Oh, that? That's for Mathewson."

Easter Parade

By Anne O'Hare McCormick

It's a dress parade, not of the few but of the million; a parade, as Mrs. McCormick points out, in which there are no spectators because all are participants. There is a moral in the spectacle, not only for ourselves, but for all those abroad who underestimate the power of the democratic ideal.

The old lady was in a worn black coat, but she had a new hat with a wreath of red roses around the crown and two corsages of red roses pinned to her shoulder. She was wedged in between two pretty granddaughters, in gray suits just out of the bandboxes, on the steps of St. Patrick's Cathedral as the biggest Easter Parade in history jammed the Avenue. She couldn't move, and didn't want to, for from her vantage point she could look down on the preening crowds that packed the adjoining blocks from wall to wall, so closely that buses and automobiles were shooed out of the way and people could move only in slow waves and eddies, with the effect of a flower garden in the wind.

The garden effect came from the hats. There were miles of flowered hats, it seemed; never were so many piled into one place, at any rate; they bloomed and criss-crossed in a multicolored profusion that made the lilies and fountains in Rockefeller Plaza appear tame and sober. It was a gigantic display of new hats—or, some one remarked, like the free-enterprise system showing off. For this was a dress parade not of the few but of the million. It was a parade in which there were no spectators because all were participants.

Happy, Carefree, Opulent

The girls under the hats were of all ages and all types, but whether they stepped decorously out of St. Thomas's, swarmed up from the lower

East Side, or were visitors from other towns, they looked oddly alike. They looked alike, "standardized" if you like, because you could not distinguish the rich from the poor; they were all dressed up in the latest styles and they were pleased with themselves and what they saw. Compared to any other crowd in the world this Easter, they appeared happy, carefree and opulent.

The old lady with the roses on her hat was not opulent. When she tried to anchor her corsages, her hands showed the scars of hard work. Like many in the throngs she watched with such lively satisfaction, she was an immigrant in the long past and the rhythms of the County Kerry still sang in her speech. But she was not thinking of Ireland, or that on this Easter, anniversary of the Easter rising of 1916, the last tie with the British crown is broken and the Free State becomes in name what it has been in fact for years, an independent republic.

She was thinking of America. "It's a grand sight," she said once, "so many people in all their finery." And later: "I wish he could see it." "Grandpa?" one of the girls murmured sympathetically, in the accents of an East Side finishing school. "No, not grandpa," said the old lady, impatiently. "He has better sights to see. I mean that old Stalin."

Stalin Wouldn't Like It

But Fifth Avenue on Easter Sunday would probably irritate Stalin even more than he is already exasperated with the United States. Moscow is planning to build better skyscrapers than New York's, but they are still on paper. It promises to open superior shops stocked with enough clothes for everybody and that everybody can buy. But mass production for the masses is the invention of the capitalist system; so far it has not been attained by the Soviet state. At the present rate it will take a long series of five-year plans before the Soviet woman can buy a dress, a hat or a pair of shoes for anything near the price the average New York working girl paid for her Easter outfit.

It would not be surprising if Stalin is more annoyed by the Easter dress parade than by Wall Street. The distribution of wealth in this country is far from equable or general, but it is wider than anywhere else on earth, and the distribution more than the accumulation irks the Soviet leaders because it underlines the pregnant fact that there is no communism in the Marxist sense in the Soviet Union and no capitalism in the United States as it was conceived in "Das Kapital."

This must be Stalin's great grievance against this country. He is a logical man, who has studied and interpreted Marx and Lenin with enormous diligence, and is too faithful to their gospel and too enclosed in his own world to understand that both capitalism and democratic socialism have been molded by events into something quite different from the rigid imperatives which shape his outlook. It is more accurate to say they have been molded by people, for it is human forces, people moving, thinking, aspiring, experimenting, that work changes in the systems under which they live. This is why democracies grow, evolve and win by persuasion, while systems in which people have no voice remain sterile and can conquer only by force.

Christmas on Fifth Avenue

By Silas Spitzer

Our biggest city—New York; our greatest street—Fifth Avenue; our most important holiday—Christmas! All combine, in this unforgettable selection, to make a lavish and dazzling display of America's wealth and beauty. Nowhere else on earth is such good fortune to be found.

The spirit of Christmas descends upon Fifth Avenue early in December. It sparkles behind its myriad plate-glass windows, spills out of its bronze doorways, produces a deep-throated roar of excitement in its climactic crowds and traffic.

From the steel-ribbed towers of the Empire State Building to the stately hotels off Grand Army Plaza the holiday glow transforms every familiar façade. This is the golden fortnight, peak of the Avenue's busy twelve-month career. Since early spring, the cleverest minds in the world of retail trade planned its strategy.

You and I, and all the other knowing people, may sense the sharp practical motive behind the Avenue's sentimental dazzle; but the knowledge does not spoil our enjoyment of the show. The custom of bestowing gifts at Christmas is a part of our openhanded national character. And here in New York millions of Americans join in the shining market place of Fifth Avenue to seek things that will make others happy.

There is no building on the Avenue that does not display some jovial symbol of the season. Green garlands wreathe the narrow windows of the Fifth Avenue Bank, unyielding brownstone citadel of old-fashioned family fortunes. At every corner, a frost-bitten Santa in red coat and frowzy whiskers jingles his bell and shouts his hoarse cry of "Merry Christmas!" at mink-coated matrons from Westchester County and parcel-bulging couples from the Bronx. Peppermint candy canes, five feet long, bloom gaily in the windows of the jam-packed emporiums of the five-and-dime. At the aristocratic northern end of the Avenue, the celebrated toy store of Schwartz displays Diesel-motored railroad trains, regiments of Napoleon's grenadiers in battle formation, and a whole fairyland of imported dolls with the sophisticated look of Dietrich and Grable.

But, for me, the most delightful touch of all occurs on the great stone terrace of the Public Library at 42nd Street. Here some genial soul buried in that austere bookish vastness has hung bright green wreaths of holly around the massive necks of the two reclining stone lions, changing their everyday facial expressions from frozen nobility to kittenish and irresistible good humor. Instinctively I peer skyward at the cloud-piercing TV mast of the Empire State Building, half-expecting to see a giant wreath hanging from its tip.

From a window ledge twenty stories high in the Squibb Building, at noon of the clock, the Avenue is a narrow channel cut through solid walls of terraced stone, swarming at its lower level with slow-moving masses of vehicles and humanity. A thick column of sound rises from this spectacle far below, bass in register, but interspersed with the sharp insistence of horns and the scream of brakes. At night, from this same vantage point, the darkness below is brightened by floods of red, green and yellow light —the colors of Christmas—spreading their reflections on sidewalks and pavements dampened by rain or snow. The crowds are still tremendous, for the shops stay open nightly during this hectic homestretch period.

To shopper and sight-seer alike, the most magnetic of the Avenue's attractions are the window displays, illuminated with all the tricks of the professional theater, peopled by lifelike mannequins, and decked out with the treasures of museums and private collections. Their seductive offerings are aimed at all purses and tastes. They range from paper doilies at Dennison's to Bonwit's frothy Parisian gowns and Cartier's knickknacks in platinum and diamonds. Best-remembered of all the displays of recent years were the famous windows of Lord & Taylor, which contained no merchandise at all but only a set of golden bells, which chimed mysteriously and sweetly in the street outside.

Among the vaulting buildings and flag-hung plazas of Rockefeller Center, Christmas achieves a glorious crescendo, with a specially magical appeal to children. The neighboring streets for a mile around are crowded with the cars of families who have come to witness the sight. The great tree, blazing with colored globes, looms at the end of the famous passage of fountains and flower beds, outlined against a building so tall and narrow that it seems to lean backward in its climb to the sky.

Twinkling electric stars hang miraculously overhead, and a muffled music of Christmas carols issues from the papier-mâché throats of choral groups in the windows of Saks Fifth Avenue, across the way.

On the eve of Christmas, a hush falls upon the Avenue. Worshipers fill St. Patrick's Cathedral to overflowing, some kneeling in devotion on the stone steps and sidewalks. The shopping frenzy is finished, the clamor of crowds is stilled. And the queen of city streets, its big moment achieved, is wrapped in a mood of unaccustomed peace.

There are still a few elderly New Yorkers around who remember when Fifth Avenue was a street of private homes, without a single shop. They recall the days when two solid rows of brownstone dwellings swept northward from Washington Square, rolling over the very spot where the Empire State Building now looms, and ending at some point in the upper Fifties.

You could really see the sky in those days, for the brownstones seldom rose higher than three or four stories and the slender spires of neighborhood churches were the only punctuation marks on the horizon. The Avenue was not as wide as it is now. The projecting stoops and Victorian bays and bulges had not yet been sheared away to broaden the path of traffic. On sleepy summer afternoons, an air of protected calm lay like the folds of a dream upon this street of the wealthy and secure.

Everything moved at an unhurried pace. Pedestrians strolled from one side of the street to the other, often in the very center of the block, without fear of sudden death. Nursemaids in starchy uniforms, wheeling their charges in the quaintly ornate conveyances of the period, emerged from the neatly-kept areaways, sometimes pausing for a chat with a friendly patrolman in a pot-shaped gray helmet. The only sound that pierced the low hum of the surrounding city was the clatter of passing carriages, or the occasional clockety-clock of a flashy trotting horse, speeding its owner to the parks and driving courses uptown.

That was the old Avenue as a few sentimental survivors describe it; a semisuburban residential haven for the rich, the fashionable and the celebrated of their time. Today, after the relatively short space of fifty or sixty short years, every vestige of that quiet scene has vanished. The tradesmen have triumphed. The old families are gone. In a mere handful of years, as the life of great cities is usually reckoned, Fifth Avenue has changed from a staid residential neighborhood to a dazzling commercial midway.

The story of that transformation is, in a way, a capsule history of New York.

Unlike its close neighbor, Broadway, which grew like an eccentric weed in the footprints and wheeltracks of the early settlers, Fifth Avenue was a deliberate creation of the city fathers. The commissioners sat down to their planning in 1807, spurred to their task not by any vision of a glorious future but by the desperate need for vastly increased living space. The people of the cramped little community knew the meaning of congestion a hundred years before the first subway train or traffic cop. Nearly all the population of about a hundred thousand was concentrated in the butt end of Manhattan Island, between the Battery and Canal Street.

With salt water lapping at its lower boundary, there was no place to expand but uptown. And uptown was a twelve-mile stretch of lonely country; twelve miles of narrow island which today groans under the greatest weight of stone, metals and humans ever concentrated upon so small a segment of the earth's surface. Except for a few farmers and an occasional country estate, this area was almost as primitive as in the days of that sachem of the Canarsie tribe who sold the island to Peter Minuit, and who lives eternally as the poorest judge of real estate in American history.

On the old map, as today, Fifth Avenue cuts a straight swath through the heart of Manhattan, splitting it into two fairly equal parts. From this central spine, like the ribs of a flounder, side streets point east and west and are bisected by avenues which lie parallel with the rivers on either side.

In 1824, the city's workmen began to dig on a straight line from a point about where Washington Arch now stands. Ignoring the clutching tendrils of the city's romantic past, they cut through farms and wilderness, cow pastures and chicken runs, cleaving their proud new avenue straight through Manhattan and into the heart of the future.

From the very beginning, a Fifth Avenue address bore a special cachet of distinction. The typical house was three stories high, built of red brick which turned a soft rose tint with age. They were simple, unpretentious structures for the most part, except for the striking contrast of shutters painted a fresh green, and immaculate white doors bearing shining brass knockers and nameplates.

Nowadays, an air of residential calm still pervades the Avenue from the Arch to that suddenly clamorous corner where it runs smack into raucous, shirt-sleeved 14th Street. The private dwellings have all but disappeared, but in their places are massive apartment buildings and family hotels. It is a neighborhood smartly in demand among business executives who like living within a short bus or taxi jaunt from their mid-town offices.

At its old familiar spot on the southwest corner of 8th Street, the old Hotel Brevoort awakens tender memories, and looks to sentimental eyes like some ancient *boulevardier* who falteringly sustains a gallant front in an indifferent world. Behind the awnings and sidewalk tables of the summer café, the hotel itself is a hollow shell. The famous dining rooms and the vast, moldy bedrooms on the upper floors are now shrouded and vacant. In the early years of the present century, this internationally famous French hostelry was a rendezvous for Village "Bohemia." Visiting Europeans loved it for its wine and ample cuisine, and they felt at home surrounded by its old-fashioned Continental inconveniences. But the fear haunts me, even as I write this, that the crowbars and drills of the wrecking crew may even now be tearing into these elegant wine-stained walls.

Many of New York's most illustrious names once adorned the doorplates of homes in that low-numbered portion of the Avenue, gentlemen drawn together by neighborly and social ties as well as by the comfortable fraternal feeling engendered by the mutual possession of money. Most of them belonged to the same clubs, which multiplied in such numbers that the lower portion of the Avenue became famous as America's first clubland. Oldest and most aristocratic of these clubs was the Union, which was founded in 1836 in the heart of the present downtown financial district, and moved to Fifth Avenue, at 21st Street, in 1855. The collective prosperity of its members was awesome. Among them were the Livingstons, the Van Cortlandts, Van Rensselaers, Schuylers, Suydams, Griswolds and Stuyvesants—names so prominent in the city's affairs that most of them decorate parks, squares, playgrounds and other public places today. Close to the Union were such clubs as the Athenaeum, the Lotos, the Travellers', the Arcadian, the Calumet and the Knickerbocker—each celebrated for its own particular variety of snobbery and entrenched wealth.

There used to be a little snack shop on William Street, called Delmonico's, which was popular with younger Gothamites for its fine food and drink. The owners decided to follow the tide of wealth and fashion that was flowing into the young Avenue, still doggedly digging its way northward. They moved in the late 1850's to the vacant Grinnell mansion, at the northeast corner of 14th Street.

By 1870, Delmonico's was firmly established as the great social gathering place of the New World. The recreational life of the town then centered nearby. The Academy of Music was within easy reach and 14th Street was booming as the new theatrical district. Delmonico's was so convenient to the fashionable clubs that they didn't bother to serve meals to their members.

In contrast to the smoky chophouses and noisy, bustling public dining rooms of the period, Del's was operated in the European tradition of suave and expert service. There was no boisterous shouting of orders by the waiters; they were perfectly trained phantoms in black and white, who glided smoothly and silently about their duties. Like the Colony or Twenty One of today, Del's maintained close personal relationships with its guests, indulging their most eccentric whims in matters of foods and wines. Members of established society held their most important balls and supper parties there, and the "fast" young men of that day, who wore diamonds on fingers and shirt fronts, drove flashy horses and smoked long cheroots in carved ivory holders, ran up accounts that strained their allowances to the limit. If a man valued his reputation in the smart world, he could afford to economize in everything but the regularity of his appearances in those fastidious rooms.

Nowadays, there is nothing in this once-fine residential section worth noting from a bus window. At 14th Street, the Avenue stumbles into mediocrity. A succession of ugly, time-darkened loft buildings fills both sides of the street. Almost every floor displays the black-and-gilt signs of a manufacturer of men's clothing. At 23rd Street looms the sharp-nosed Flatiron Building, first of New York's skyscrapers, and at one time the marvel of sight-seers. In its younger days, this corner had the reputation of being the windiest in town, and males used to loiter at strategic points, watching passing females struggle as the breeze lifted skirts and petticoats. Once the Flatiron was white as snow, and breath-takingly tall. But when you come downtown to it now on a southbound bus, it has the color of a soiled flannel blanket. The busses rumble by, belching fumes; the converging traffic streams of Broadway and Fifth Avenue are reinforced by another gush of trucks and cabs from crosstown 23rd Street; people hurry past, and the once-imposing cliff of carved and windowed stone seems lost and lonely in the crowds.

From the time the first shovelful of Fifth Avenue dirt was dug in 1824, to the early 1870's, the population of Manhattan had jumped from 200,000 to about 1,000,000. New York had become the political and commercial hub of America. It was the Dollar Era, when mines, railroads, land deals and industrial mergers poured an apparently inexhaustible flood of money into the pockets of the greedy and ambitious. In New York, the overflow of all this wealth poured into the Avenue. A private house upon this queenly street now became the coveted symbol that crowned the careers of the newly rich.

At about the time of McAllister's passing, the Avenue from Madison Square northward was a solid row of brownstones. Delmonico's, always sensitive to trends, had made its third move uptown in 1876, this time taking over the 26th Street corner. The exclusive clubs established new quarters in the vicinity. The "man-about-town," a type long since vanished, patterned himself after such polished frequenters of Del's as Hermann Oelrichs, Freddie Gebhard, Wright Sanford, Nat Goodwin and starchy Berry Wall, who was called the King of the Dudes.

Many New Yorkers today are startled to learn that less than fifty years ago the city once drew its water from a huge reservoir at 42nd Street and Fifth Avenue, now one of the busiest corners in the world. It was erected in 1842 at the crest of Murray Hill and the populace celebrated the first flow of water through iron pipes with the greatest parade the Avenue had seen. People came from all over to see this new wonder. Family groups strolled on sunny afternoons along the promenade that topped the fortresslike walls of dark granite, forty-four feet high, or danced sedately on moonlit nights to the gentle ripple of the water. Many still living recall the days of the faithful old Reservoir. No longer in active use, it loomed in the early 1900's like a gloomy Egyptian tomb, a startling anachronism in the Avenue's increasing mercantile bustle. It was removed, finally, to make way for the new Public Library, which was dedicated in 1911. A spacious and beautiful white marble building, set back from the crowded street by a balconied terrace and wide stone steps, the Library today provides the only variation in the unbroken lines of business buildings that stretch to Central Park.

The upper Avenue rapidly filled up with new homes, nearly all smug brownstones, spreading a pattern of dullness which reflected the conservatism of their owners. Henry James once described them in the following acid terms: "The vista seems too hideous, the narrow, impersonal houses with the hard, dry tone of their brownstone, a surface as uninteresting as that of sandpaper . . . their steep, stiff stoops (I played on them as a child), their lumpish balustrades, porticos and cornices." But the rage for dun-colored uniformity subsided when Mary Mason Jones built in 1871 a series of white apartment houses called "Marble Row," in the modern French manner. From that time forward, marble, granite and limestone became the favored materials of construction. The great architect Stanford White left his inspired mark on a number of handsome structures, some of which still endure. St. Patrick's Cathedral was dedicated in 1879, after twenty-one years of labor. Its sculptured stone façade, gleamingly white, rose tall and gracefully proportioned, a gesture of noble beauty which transformed the Avenue's sky line.

Millionaires' Row

Another architectural sensation of the day was the French château of William K. Vanderbilt at 52nd Street. As a boy, I can remember roller-skating past that other imposing castle of the same family, the home of Cornelius Vanderbilt at the 58th Street corner, complete with formal park and porte-cochere. Its appearance was so grand that I always thought of it as a museum, or some other public edifice. The stretch of manicured white mansions above 60th Street in the 1900's was called "Millionaires' Row." Riding atop a Fifth Avenue bus, through that awesome zone of the rich and mighty, aroused in me a curious impression that nothing human ever stirred behind those frosty walls. In all my trips, I never saw an open door, a face at a window, a delivery wagon at the curb, or any other sign of life. But these ornate marble piles were actually owned and occupied by living beings, I later discovered, even if only for a few months of the year. The roster of their names had the rich gleam of gold bars piled up in a vault. Some of the more prominent ones were: Carnegie and Frick, the steelmasters, whose block-front palaces were built on such an enormous scale that today one has become an educational center and the other a museum of classical art; Astor, Choate, Bull, Fish, Gerry, Gould, Havemeyer, Ryan, Gary, Brokaw, Loring, Guggenheim, Bostwick, Phipps, Lewisohn, Yerkes and Reid—a fair sampling of the financial and industrial figures who dominated the nation.

Fifth Avenue, as we know it today, began to emerge about 1897, when the Waldorf Astoria opened its doors to a dazzled throng, on the site of the former Astor town houses at 34th Street. The Waldorf made the town's older hotels look like shabby antiques. It had more windows, plumbing, flunkies, bellhops and rest rooms than had ever before been assembled under one roof. It was a blend of European luxury and American hustle, a product of the 20th Century, slick as paint and sizzling with newborn promise. The lushly decorated lobby was immediately christened "Peacock Alley"; it swarmed with strutting celebrities, it was alive with fluttering ostrich plumes, diamond chokers and Merry Widow hats. The great hotel accommodated 1400 guests, and the word got around that there were exactly 1400 employees to keep them comfortable. And when the Waldorf announced that ladies without escorts were cordially welcome, New Yorkers felt that the last layer of provincialism had peeled off their city, which now really rated the title of metropolis.

Groups of goggle-eyed citizens loitered in front of the great glass windows on the Fifth Avenue side, to watch guests consume platters of oysters and flagons of champagne. The vast circular bar, invitingly cool on the hottest summer days, was fragrant with the mingled aroma of whisky, lemon peel and bitters. It soon became the haunt of downtown brokers and business executives. I remember visiting there in my youth, on Saturday afternoons, to spend a small fraction of my week's earnings in the company of these prosperous-looking gentlemen. For me, the bar's chief attraction, aside from the flattering worldliness of its patrons, was the most wondrous free lunch of New York's most openhanded age. It was dispensed by an elderly white-coated steward at a silver-laden mahogany table. He carved slices of pink roast beef and Virginia ham, wedged out chunks of cheddar and Stilton cheese, and after heaping my plate to the brim, would accept a ten-cent tip with a respectful little bow, just as though I had been old man Rockefeller himself.

In the space of a few years, the vigorous modernity that radiated from this great hotel permeated the midtown Avenue, and soon began to alter the very pace and substance of its life. Again the center of the town's social orbit swung northward, and once more the great clubs followed, this time anticipating the obvious parade of the future by moving into the upper Forties and Fifties. When Mrs. William Astor, ruling queen of society, gave up the house which had been the setting for so many triumphant parties, the lower Avenue's legend was one for the history books. But a change of far more vital significance than mere displacement of the Four Hundred was taking place. It would eventually eliminate everything that had once seemed permanent in Fifth Avenue's eighty years of aristocratic social supremacy.

The great retail stores of New York were then clustered on 23rd Street and along nearby Sixth Avenue. They had drifted uptown as the city expanded, moving from earlier locations on lower Broadway, Grand Street, 14th Street and Union Square. Prominent among these merchants was Benjamin Altman, whose store at Sixth Avenue and 19th Street was a bulwark of old-fashioned quality in a shopping neighborhood already going to seed. An upper Fifth Avenue location, with all the glamour of its patrician setting, struck Altman as the soundest investment for the future.

When the Altman store at 34th Street was finally built, it reflected its owner's pioneer daring in the monumental grandeur of its size and style. This great store, covering the entire block between 34th and 35th Streets, and Fifth and Madison Avenues, anchored the development of the Avenue as the shopping district of the new century. Soon afterward, wide gaps began to appear in the ranks of the brownstones, and shining new stores rose in their place. Tiffany & Co., the celebrated jewelers, moved into one of Stanford White's most imposing neo-Renaissance creations, crowned by the famous clock which since 1850 had decorated their two earlier shops downtown.

Many old and respected institutions like Best & Co., Gunther, Bonwit Teller, Benson & Hedges, Franklin Simon, Arnold Constable, Knox the Hatter, McCutcheon, Black Starr & Frost, W. & J. Sloane, and Lord & Taylor joined the procession.

The quality tradition of Fifth Avenue was so important to these newly established merchants that they determined to defend it at all costs. They had witnessed the disintegration of fine shopping areas like 23rd Street, Sixth Avenue and Union Square, and they resolved that this time it would not happen again. In April of 1907, a group of leading businessmen founded the Fifth Avenue Association.

New Yorkers are the least city-conscious of all urban dwellers. Most of them accept the wonders of their home town with an almost fatalistic lack of excitement. Among other things, they seem to take for granted the rather wonderful good taste of Fifth Avenue. Yet it must occasionally occur to even the most hard-shelled Gothamite that during his many visits to midtown Fifth Avenue he has never been bothered by panhandlers, peddlers or itinerant bootblacks. He must have noticed, too, that the immaculate ranks of stores and office buildings are free from the alien presence of garages, saloons, gas stations, factories, billiard halls, hot-dog stands or funeral parlors. There are no illuminated signs, and no signs project more than one foot beyond the building line. The absence of these, and many other jarring elements, is not accidental, but the direct result of the Association's vigilance.

Tourists' Mecca

Nowadays, next to its spectacular parades, the Avenue's chief lure for townspeople and visitors alike is Rockefeller Center, with its outdoor skating rink, floral displays, fine restaurants, shops and commercial exhibits. It is like a miniature World's Fair—without popcorn, brass bands or vulgarity. Every year, about 500,000 tourists pay $1.40 apiece to join the guided-sight-seeing groups that penetrate Radio City. On sunny afternoons, the clicking of camera shutters among the flower beds sounds like a convention of crickets. Even busy New Yorkers have learned to pause for a moment to sample the peaceful beauties of this unique oasis. Stenographers and clerks from nearby buildings come at noon to rest amidst the soft glow of spring hyacinths or midsummer roses. "Get a load of these pink-and-white things," says a female voice, in pure Flatbush—"but don't get too close. They put some stuff on it that smells."

Kick Number Two on the city-wide tour is the Empire State Building, world's tallest man-made structure, looming fantastically upon the site of the old Waldorf Astoria, of sentimental memory. It rears upward 102 stories, has space for 80,000 occupants, with 67 passenger elevators to whisk them to their floors. "The High Dive" is what cynical police reporters used to call the dizzy promenade around the tower, but recent precautions have materially discouraged suicidal leaps from this inviting springboard.

The best way to see the Avenue's sights used to be from the top of a double-decker bus. Starting from the charming ivy-clad Colonial houses in Washington Square, you would lurch slowly along in the northbound traffic stream and, on either side, history would unroll before your eyes. But young couples who rode the top deck would be too busy holding hands and whispering to notice the scenery. It was probably the least expensive and most romantic form of transportation ever made available to lovers. For a dime you could travel all the way uptown, past old homes and new apartments, past the Flatiron Building, the Waldorf, the Public Library, the great shops, the clubs, the hotels and monuments of the Plaza, the white stone mansions of the money kings, the green panorama of Central Park, the classical pile of the Metropolitan Museum, and, finally, turn crosstown and head for some secluded glen with a view of the Hudson River. If there happened to be a moon, it was thrown in free, and so, too, was the soft evening air, laden with just enough gasoline exhaust to make it agreeable to the local taste.

It saddens me to recall the passing, among so many other fine institutions, of the old open bus, which brought the young people of an earlier generation so much closer to their city and to each other. The sleek new covered jobs, in my prejudiced opinion, roll no faster in today's spasmodic traffic than the ancient Juggernauts of my youth. The fare is higher, too, and the full glare of interior illumination is discouraging to lovers.

Compared to the brazen, frankly likable humanity of Broadway, Fifth Avenue may seem cold and hard as a diamond. Its well-policed decorum inspires admiration but not affection. But, when you get to know the people who work or shop or stroll along the Avenue, they turn out to be just as human as people are everywhere. The haughty photographer's model who hurries past with her make-up and a cheese sandwich in a gold-stamped leather box—the skinny youngster in a blond chignon who makes quick surreptitious sketches of the gowns in Bonwit's windows—the red-faced forty-dollar-a-week Irish doorman of a famous bank who gallantly helps ancient dowagers of fabulous wealth in and out of their Rolls-Roycean chariots—the sharp-eyed "hairdresser" who has never been east of Rockaway Beach but is full of flattering scraps of French like "*Formidable!*" "*Epatante!*" and "*Voila, Moddom!*"—the young lady in an interesting condition examining the infants' layettes in Lane Bryant's window—the lady in the ballet slippers who exercises a gazelle on a leash and the amiable crackpot who promenades in the dead of winter in white cotton shorts and open sandals—the top-hatted coachman at the Plaza cab rank who gravely feeds his wry-kneed horse a handful of grass from a nearby lawn—these are the Avenue's people.

There are those, like myself, who manage to set foot on the Avenue every day, if only for a few minutes, and rarely for business reasons, but mainly to absorb some of its inspiring vitality, a tonic to jaded town-weary souls. It has moods and moments of matchless beauty which never grow commonplace. Walk into the Avenue from some quiet side street in the Fifties on a day when the long rows of flags are snapping in a breeze. You will be lifted by a spectacle no other city affords. The wide expanse is filled with streams of cars and people moving rhythmically between tall buildings and flashing shop windows. The very air seems to vibrate with light and gaiety. And over all there is a sense of some invisible controlling force that endows every part of the scene with maturity and good taste.

Some of the Avenue's vistas recall the grandeur of Paris and Rome, but with a special character of their own which blends the old and new worlds. I cherish a special affection for Grand Army Plaza, Fifth Avenue's final gesture of magnificence before it loses itself in Central Park. Coming into this wide tree-encircled haven on a fine day, you will suddenly notice the sky, a wide sweep of luminous blue stretching to the western horizon. The sun bounces off the varnished wheels and bodies of the hired hacks, each with its languid steed and dignified top-hatted jarvey. It glitters from the windows of four giant hotels—the Savoy, Sherry-Netherland, Plaza and Pierre, rising majestically in a setting of unequalled splendor. Airily suspended among these lofty gray sentinels is a miracle of light-hearted contrast: Karl Bitter's famous bronze statue of the smiling nymph, tiptoe on her cascading fountains, the very soul and symbol of the feminine heaven along nearby 57th Street. Some hundreds of feet away is the grim equestrian figure of General Sherman, now blackened by the years, but once described by Henry James as "splendid in its golden elegance." Even at the height of the rush hour, there is usually a certain peace in this tranquil oasis in the heart of the metropolis.

If you are attracted by beauty of a more animated sort, I give you the ladies of that same 57th Street neighborhood, who dress smarter, look prettier, and move more gracefully than any ladies you are apt to encounter in a lifetime of travel. Even a Texan might agree with this purely personal opinion, if he will only station himself somewhere between the bronze nymph and the Tailored Woman shop, any afternoon around five, when shoppers, salesgirls, showroom models and needleworkers flow past with a soft homeward-bound hunger in their eyes.

People, even more than architectural grandeur, are Fifth Avenue's chief treasure. I have never met with so cosmopolitan a crowd in any other American city, though San Francisco comes close. The best dressed and most sophisticated people are most noticeable in the upper Fifties, and it is here that you will encounter the world's loveliest women, with that special American bloom of health and youth that is noticeable in every class, from office girl to debutante. Here you will see and hear evidences of foreign influence as well. There is a generous smattering of eccentrics, of elderly bearded gentlemen wearing red buttonhole decorations; of lavender-rinsed ladies leading small, carefully sculptured dogs.

East Indian turbans and *saris* are a fairly common sight, as are the sleek cars of foreign diplomats and delegates to the United Nations. Nobody goggles impolitely when a couple of gentlemen in gray Homburgs embrace each other in the impulsive European manner, or clicks into a double-take when Greta Garbo rounds a corner briskly, in a cone-shaped hat and flat-heeled shoes. On a busy day, visiting stars from Hollywood and Broadway are a dime a dozen in the Chanel No. 5 zone up around the Park. "You'd be surprised if you knew what I know about some of those sweater babes' figures," remarked a fitter I know in one of the more exalted *maisons de couture*. "They need real engineering projects under some of those thousand-buck evening gowns."

These human manifestations are interesting to the casual observer, but it is the double row of shops, thirty-six blocks long, which constitutes Fifth Avenue's foremost attraction to the multitude. The museums, the Library, the mansions and the cultural centers are all impressive, but really only incidental to the main show. The very breath of the fabulous highway is business, and its heartbeat is the rustle of folding money. But on this street, as perhaps nowhere else, business is not a humdrum routine, but a fascinating entertainment, staged with dramatic flourish and conducted with all the arts of modern showmanship. And this holds good not only for the salons where the carriage trade congregates to trifle with mutation-mink wraps, strings of cabochon emeralds or gowns by Jacques Fath, but also for the hustling chain stores that sell rayon panties and cotton house dresses, and the clamorous limestone hives of Woolworth and Kress, where your money buys anything from a corn plaster to a complete kitchen unit.

The average man has a depthless dislike of shopping, feels lost and bewildered in the hectic aisles of a big store, and shies from carrying any parcel bigger than a can of pipe tobacco. He often wonders what sharp urge for punishment lures so many family groups to the Avenue on a blazing Saturday afternoon in August—stout mamma and young married daughter, red-faced and harassed, gripping the slippery hands of two or three small children who somehow manage to break loose at odd moments and dart away like dragonflies when the crowd and traffic are most menacing. But the ladies are full of plans, propelled by mysterious springs of energy, and undoubtedly happy underneath it all. "Don't forget," pants mamma—"two and a half yards of organdy for Mildred's birthday dress—and that sale of shirts dad read about in the paper—and, that reminds me, paper napkins—and you promised the kids waffles and ice cream for lunch!"

It's the enormous variety of merchandise and the concentration of so many shops of all degree that bring the ladies to Fifth Avenue by bus, subway or on foot. The upper Park Avenue matron is only interested in that part of it which is smart, expensive and signs its name in thin gold script on box wrappings. She arrives by taxi or limousine, is greeted deferentially by name, and her visits to the plushier establishments are more like social calls than business transactions. "Just send it tomorrow, please," she says, fingering a cobweb-sheer *robe d'intime* or a love seat in ivory satin—"and I'll see how it looks against the new color scheme."

For the delectation of the feminine nature, the Avenue's high-salaried display artists dream up alluring window compositions that have the sophisticated glitter of a Balanchine ballet. At Lord & Taylor, she is sprayed with perfume as she enters the foyer, and charming young debs wait on her in the flattering accents of Bennington or Vassar. Ambitious matrons respond to the seductive exhibits of stores like Sloane, Georg Jensen, Plummer, McCutcheon and Altman, which bring to life the luscious color pages in those slick patio-and-petunia monthlies that keep you up with the Joneses, the Whitneys and the Windsors. Harassed housewives are soothed and uplifted by a walk through the sybaritic aisles of Saks Fifth Avenue, where mink jostles mink, and the very air smells expensive.

She may lunch on a hot dog at Woolworth's counter or on pompano at the Plaza. She can rest her tired feet at the Brass Rail or slip them into a pair of Delman's deliciously fragile dancing slippers fit to tread the cloud tops. The farther uptown she goes, the more exclusive the fashions, the dizzier the prices. At the Avenue's northernmost shopping point, the ultimate is reached. Here Tiffany looms like a monument of ponderous rectitude; diagonally opposite, Bergdorf Goodman echoes the clever techniques of Paris in its elaborately whimsical presentation of expensive feminine adornment.

To me, the Avenue of today is like a smart woman, clad in the newest and most elegant raiment, perfumed and furred and bejeweled. She is modern and self-assured to her gleaming finger tips, yet, now and again she glances back over her shoulder, with a fleeting pang of regret for the colorful days of her past, and a perhaps tiny hint of concern for her future.

PART V

"From Maine to California"

Across the Nation

America is a nation of contrasts. Her regions differ not only geographically, but as widely as the people who live in them. For it is the people—their differences as well as their alikeness—who make the common character of the nation so rich. In this section we remember some of our most cherished regional characteristics: the people, places, and celebrations whose individualities are intact but still peculiarly American.

Our folkways give abundant evidence of the many sources from which our national character draws sustenance. New England is a small neat world of its own, but even within itself there is variety. Vermonters detach themselves from the pressures of the market place, preferring independence to riches. Rhode Islanders take rightful pride in their clambakes. In Boston—well, Boston is a way of life, and a proper Bostonian takes care that his own son knows how and why things are as they are.

Down the coast and inland live the Pennsylvania Dutch in a land of lush fields, red barns, and hex signs. At holiday time these seemingly sober people celebrate some of our most unique customs.

Then there is the South: Kentucky, where the famed Derby is run; Carolina, where blood ties are strong and kissin' cousins as close as brothers, and where the elaborate pre-Civil war traditions of Christmas are preserved. In New Orleans, you may see the most spectacular Southern festival, Mardi Gras.

From North and South the people moved West. In Indiana they created a new kind of American, the Hoosier. Beyond the Wabash, the woods of Michigan yielded fortunes in timber. The lumberjacks came to town for burling contests and to whoop it up on The Fourth. The farmers in the corn belt made an annual journey that remains the most important occasion of the year—the trip to the State Fair.

In the Southwest the tradition is of space and exaggeration. But in the old days there were play parties and Barbecue Days—homespun celebrations that are more fun than nightlife in the big hotels. Cowboys and rodeos may have come to Madison Square Garden, but they began here. From the beginning, cowboys and miners of the wild West knew how to cut loose with their own brand of "helling."

Out of the regions has come a distinctly American pattern. Thomas Wolfe has said it: "America is a fabulous country, the only fabulous country; it is the one place where miracles not only happen, but where they happen all the time."

America's Folkways

By Duncan Emrich

A story told around a pot-bellied stove, a song composed by dozens of singers down the years, a superstition whispered to small children—folklore, like its first cousin history, is always in the making. It is a living record of the people, a treasury of the wisdom and traditions of the past.

American folklore is as earthy as a Missourian's words for a fellow townsman: "Him? He's so stingy he'd chase a mouse to hell for a punkin seed." It is as rough as a pair of canal-boat men indulging in eye gouging, and as gentle as a lullaby from the Tennessee hills. It is as strong as a Conestoga wagon, and as cool as the slang of beboppers.

American folklore is the sailing ship (". . . before steam took to robbing us of our jobs") bound out from Boston, Savannah, Mobile—and the beat of the halyard chanty:

And what do you think we had for breakfast?
Blow, boys, blow!
The starboard side of an old sou'wester,
Blow, boys, bonny boys, blow!

It is the trail herd winding the long way north out of Texas to Montana, in dust, in heat and storm. It is the food of America—baked beans, chowder, maple sirup on johnnycake; smoked hams, hush puppies, Brunswick stew. It is the bindle stiff and gandy dancer, and the argot of the rails: gondola, reefer, shack, red ball, high ball, ball the jack.

Folklore is the adobe house of New Mexico, the sod shanty of the Kansas and Nebraska frontier, the log-and-clay cabins of Virginia, the strung-together barns and houses of New England. It is the rhymes and games of children—duck on the rock, fox and geese, kick the can, mumblety-peg—and a tongue twister from Massachusetts: How much wood would a woodchuck chuck if a woodchuck could chuck wood? A woodchuck would chuck as much wood as a woodchuck could, if a woodchuck could chuck wood.

And another from North Carolina:

She sells sea shells,
Black bug's blood,
Shoat soup and sheep soup.

Folklore is the hand-whittled lobster buoy of Maine and the branding iron of Wyoming, the hay lifts of Utah, and the rail fences of Kentucky. It is the bawdy story in the smoking room of a Pullman, and the jargon of crapshooters: eighter from Decatur, little Phoebe, snake eyes, box cars, the hard way. It is a juke joint jumping with improvised steps; and a banjo, guitar and dulcimer on the front stoop.

It is the speech of Alabama and the Bronx, and the regional niceties of our land: "If there's anything that makes a Maine man sick to his stomach, it's Northern Vermont." It is a sure statement: "Nobody ain't got no right to throw nothing in nobody's back yard." It is the names of America—Hell for Sartin Creek, Jerked Beef Butte, the Stinking Water, Smith's Corners; and the nicknames—Fourth-of-July Murphy, Slanting Annie, Bughouse McCabe, Rat-trap Perkins, and Four Day Jack.

Folklore is a farmer studying the clouds, and a hardrock miner in Arizona listening to the earth turning over on the graveyard shift. It is copper worn against rheumatism, a ghost, the howling of a dog at night, an entry in a family Bible, a four-leaf clover. American folklore is all the traditional knowledge and way of life of our people passed on from generation to generation.

Folklore includes folk architecture, craft and art; folk industry (lumbering, fishing, farming); folk speech and language, folk literature (tall tales, proverbs, rhymes); folk dances, folk music and song; folk history (local legends, the reminiscences of old-timers); folk medicine and weather lore; folk law (the Western code, vigilantes, kangaroo courts); and folk belief and custom (knock on wood, a handshake, and Fourth-of-July picnics). It is considerably more than Grandma Moses, Burl Ives and Paul Bunyan.

The chief touchstone to folklore is the manner in which it is transmitted: one man tells another, one man shows another. Folklore circulates as easily as breathing, and as unself-consciously. There are no formal controls, no classrooms and professors, no textbooks or printed pages, no sheet music to serve as authority. The only authority is "Joe told me," or "That's the way Tex does it"—and even this much authority is rarely called in question.

Because of the way in which it is transmitted, the touch of the individual is upon every item of folklore. The material is traditional, yes, in the way that speech is traditional; but individual in the way that each man expresses himself. No two adobe houses of folk construction, no two Pennsylvania barns, no two Virginia smokehouses are exactly alike as dwellings are in the pea-pod "developments" of the mass-builder. The individual's mark is upon each.

Essentially, the character of folklore lies in the difference between the hand-made and the machine-made, the nonstandardized and the standardized, the individual and the mass. It is the difference between a pot of stew (meat, parsley, bay, veal knuckle, beef knuckle, celery, carrots, onions, red wine) simmering on the back of a stove, and the standard contents of a tin can; the difference between home-made fudge and a Hotcha Bar of Kandy; between a static page of grammar and the language as she is spoke.

From the way in which folklore circulates, it is easier also to understand who the folk are in America. When the Library of Congress issued in its folksong series two songs by Judge Learned Hand, newspaper reporters were curious: "You don't consider him a member of the folk?" On the recording, Judge Hand himself answers: "That song (*The Iron Merrimac*) I learned about sixty years ago in Elizabethtown, which is a very small village in the Adirondack Mountains, Essex County, New York. It was sung by boys of my own age, and I know nothing more about it than that. I think possibly it was sung by my uncle's hired man, who had been in the Civil War, but of that I'm very uncertain. I don't know where we boys picked it up."

A hired man and a small village, however, are not essentials. Of the second song, *Phil Sheridan*, Judge Hand says: "That song I first heard in the Harvard Law School sometime about eighteen ninety-five or six. It was then sung by a man named George B. Eliot, who was afterward general counsel of the Atlantic Coast Line, and has since died. He was from North Carolina. I know no more of the song, never heard him sing any more of the song, nor have I any idea where it came from or where he got it."

To the extent that we acquire our knowledge and way of life in the hand-me-down manner of folklore, and also believe it, to that extent we are, like Judge Hand, members of the folk. Each of us has something, however little, of accepted folklore in our make-up—remembered rhymes from childhood, a family recipe, an off-color limerick, the jargon of an occupational group, or the fragment of a traditional song.

I have used the term "American folklore," but this needs some qualification. Actually, there is no folklore common to all the people living within a political boundary, and political boundaries cannot enclose or limit folklore. A song or way of speech does not stop at the confines of Ohio or Florida. Rather than political boundaries, the important background is the group. Local and regional differences, geography (desert, mountain, seacoast), language, race, trade and occupation are the chief elements creating the myriad groups. The sum total folklore of all these groups constitutes American folklore, since they exist in America. The roots of much of this folklore, however, are world-wide.

The log cabin came to us from the Swedes who landed in Delaware; the frame houses of New England were the contribution of the English; the branding irons of the Southwest came to us from Spain via Mexico; *The Streets of Laredo* was a song about a dying British soldier (what cowboy was buried to the sound of fifes and drums?); the customs of California tuna fishers came from Yugoslavs who sailed the Adriatic; the Christmas tree was inherited from Germany, and Santa Claus from Holland; Greek children played marbles with the knucklebones of sheep before "aggies" were known; the rhythms of a great segment of our music go back to Africa; and our speech borrows from the languages of the world. In the folk process of transmission, of course, these things take on the local and regional characteristics of our country, and become our own: an English ballad sung with the accent and tempo of the Kentucky hills ceases to be English; a cowboy fashioning a "Quarter Circle U" in Montana is unaware of Spain; and a New York cab driver who beefs, "I'm the patsy," has no knowledge of the Italian word, *pazzi*, pronounced almost the same.

Folklore has, of course, taken a beating in our machine age. It began to take the beating with the advent of the Industrial Revolution in England, and the tempo of it has increased with the stepped-up commercial-industrial character of our society. We are, to put it baldly, the most past-destroying civilization the world has known; even our rear guard carries a banner proclaiming "the brand new." By and large, of course, this destruction has been for the good. Only a confirmed Minniver Cheevy would wish to replace a cold pill with asafetida and goose grease, or send housewives back to the butter churn when the packaged product is available. The folklorist has no desire to do so. His concern is with preserving a record of our past on the folk level, a record of our roots as a people, a complement to the bare facts of history.

The scholar and the museum preserve and study folklore in its own terms. A ship's figurehead in the Mariners' Museum at Mystic, Connecticut, and a folksong in the Library of Congress have been moved out of their natural habitats, of course, but they have not been altered. Similarly, studies of folklore at Harvard, or the Universities of Indiana and California, faithfully preserve the original materials. The scholars and the museums are the custodians of folklore, since the folk cannot be themselves.

On the nonacademic level of our society, also, folklore has, in recent decades, become immensely popular. Collections of folk tales and books on folklore hit the best-seller lists; Burl Ives and Jo Stafford are heard by millions; square-dance groups weekly attract thousands; and folk festivals are on the annual agenda of hundreds of communities from Asheville, North Carolina, to Reno, Nevada. What is happening here, however, is neither a rebirth of folklore, nor its preservation. It is a different kettle of fish. A singer of folk songs, for example, is not the same as a folk singer. Nor is a story reshaped for print by a professional writer the same as a folk tale told around a potbellied stove. A rodeo with chamber of commerce and Hollywood trappings is considerably removed from the roundup celebrations of working cowboys; and an Arthur Murray square-dance party, or a contrived folk festival, bears little relation to a Saturday night gathering in the Kentucky hills.

There is nothing wrong with this borrowing and use of folklore. It has gone on from time immemorial, and will continue. But the distinction between the real article and its borrowed counterpart should be kept in mind: folklore is one thing, the use of folklore is another. Once recognized, the confusion between what folklore is and what it is not—between the folk and the popular—disappears. Also it becomes clear that the present popularity of so-called "folklore" does not return the real folklore of the past to us, any more than an interest in the Crusades or the wild-and-woolly West returns those eras to us.

A similar, and equally natural, transfer of materials works in the opposite direction. The purest items of folklore originate on the folk level, but the folk also constantly borrow from the popular, or mass, segment of our society. As this material is altered through the folk manner of transmission, it loses its original character and becomes, in varying degrees, an item of folklore. To become *folk*lore, however, it must circulate and be subject to folk alteration.

A ready example of this alteration is the folksong *The Dying Cowboy* or *O Bury Me Not on the Lone Prairie*. Non-folk in origin, it had nothing to do with a cowboy. Its ultimate source is a poem, *The Ocean Burial*, by the Rev. E. H. Chapin, who published it in *The Southern Literary Messenger* in 1839. The music for it was written by George N. Allen in 1850. The song dealt with a youth dying at sea:

O bury me not in the deep, deep sea,
Where the billowy shroud will roll over me,
Where no light will break through the dark, cold wave,
And no sunbeam rest upon my grave.

Transferred and adapted (we do not know how or when) to the cowboy and the plains of Texas, it circulated orally and became a folksong. It exists today in a variety of textual and musical versions collected from oldtimers throughout the country.

Because our own folklore is with us as naturally as spitting on bait, we are generally unaware of it. Consciousness of it usually comes when we notice customs and traditions at wide variance with our own.

A trip to Mexico is likely to teach a Kansan more about his own way of life than a decade of living at home. The sharp differences become clear. It is also of the nature of things that Easterners "discover" the West, and Westerners the East.

Consciousness of folklore, however, does not demand travel, nor does one have to leave one's own bailiwick to see it daily: the word folklore itself implies recognizable differences. Folk medicine, for example, implies the existence of the science of medicine; folk literature—oral and casual—implies the existence of a written literature; folk music an art music. Folklore is the lore of the folk existing as part of our society, yet set apart from the cultivated portion of it.

Folklore is deep in us, immemorial. It is a child born with a caul, it is a pine coffin carried down a country road. It lies on the land, the roots and the greatness of a people. It walks with us on the sidewalks under the neon lights. . . .

This letter reached me last year at the Library of Congress. It came from Florida.

Here's one I saw happen although I thought it long out of date. One afternoon when things were quiet I was passing through the sheep division of a large stock yard. I saw two young men in a pen carefully going through the wool on a bunch of sheep. I went to one of the yard watchmen to get the story. He had given them permission to go into the pens. They wanted live sheep lice which they were placing in a bottle. They were going to . . . place the *live* sheep lice in capsules and give them to grandma, who had "yaller jaundice," to swallow. The capsules would dissolve and the lice would eat the "pizen" off grandma's liver.

Although I thought it long out of date. . . .

In New England and Pennsylvania, the towns cluster around the village square. The men came from England and Germany, and they brought established tradition with them. In the West, there are no squares. The main street is a straightaway race track on the road west, not so much a part of the town as it is part of the moving highway—the Santa Fe Trail, the Oregon Trail, the Overland Trail. On the one hand, a tradition brought to the land; on the other, a tradition stemming from the land, and men's restlessness on the land. . . .

Broke?
"Hell, I couldn't make money falling down a shaft at eight and a half dollars a foot. . . ."

I saw a highway sign announcing a hamlet in Southern Indiana: Gnaw Bone. A long time ago the place had been French; but the Kentuckians who came later did not know about Narbonne. . . .

Down East, the weathervanes are ships and sailormen and cod. On the farms of New York, they are trotting horses and fat cows. Men live by the weather, and they say that for every heavy frost in October there will be a heavy snow in winter, and that pigs squeal and run around before a storm, because they see the color of the wind, which is red. . . .

The wooden hotel in the Nevada mining camp had no fire escape. I asked the hotelkeeper what to do in case of fire: "Jump out of the window and turn left. . . ."

They say that when the bugs in the rooming houses south of the Slot in San Francisco are chased out of bed, they resent it, jump up on the chandeliers and bark at the men.

On the ranches of Texas they eat sonuvabitch stew. The *cosi* throws everything into it, but if you can tell what's in it, it isn't any good. And they tell a story about a Kentuckian who was bragging about the wonders of his state to a Texan: "Why, we've got the most beautiful women in the world, and the finest horses, and the best pasture. And we've got more gold than the whole world. We've got enough gold at Fort Knox to build a wall four feet high and a foot thick all around the state of Texas."

"Well, I tell you, you go ahead and do it, and if I like it, I'll buy it. . . ."

In Denver, I knew an old-timer from Missouri who sunned himself in the faded elegance of the Windsor lobby. "I've started a book," he said, "pertaining to my life." I read the opening:

In writing this book I have carictorized it in the best manner posible for me to remember as I am a man of 66 years of age and did nevver keep no dairie of the dayley happinings as I should of did but nevver thinking of writing this book, I just have to go back in memory as fare as posible and give the facts as best I can remember. I whas borne in Chariton County Misouri on January 19th 1869 and whas about 18 mounths old when my mother died. . . .

I gave him paper and notebooks and he carried on:

And as far as a edication whas concirned my grand father awlways had a plow handle ore a chopping ax for us in stead of a school book so our edication whas very mutch limited . . . But at that my stepgrandmother did make my grandfather start us to school and we got to go about two mounths and I lurnt more in that time than I evver had lurnt before in my life. . . . That two mounths in school give me a start and I became interested in books from then on and studyed at home with the help of my younger uncle I got right along fine and all of the edication I evver got whas by own efforts and as I grew older nature and horse sence tought me a great deail and not bragging at all I had a good fore sight on things and I worked out lots of them by self expearence and by whatching others do things. . . .

Three hundred pages later, he finished:

And naw as we proceed to close our subjects we will offer up our heart felt thanks with a prayer as we know that a prayer will not hurt you if evven it dose you no good and as we air just to whire we dont know which way to stepp we feel that the good god will hold us responsible for not just knowing whither we might be right ore rong for its the right way we would like to follow if we just had the knowledge as to whitch way whas the right way naw we will proceed in prayer
Our father in haven hallowd by thy name thy kingdom it will be done in earth as it is in haven and give us this day our daily bread and forgive us our debts as we forgive our debtors and leed us not in to condemnation but bear us from all evil for thine is the glory and the power forevver A, Men

Between the beginning and the end, there was a portrait of an American, fearless and independent in the old way, answerable to himself and the God of his conscience. And there was the Missouri land, the speech of the people. . . .

The children play on the sidewalks in the city: "Step on a crack, break your mother's back; step on a line, break your mother's spine." Their rhymes are surrealistic, beyond Dali, and nobody knows where they come from. They chant:

Harry, Harry ain't no good,
We'll chop him up for firewood,
If the fire does not burn,
Harry is a big fat worm.

They count out:

Fireman, fireman, number eight,
Struck his head against a gate;
The gate flew in, the gate flew out,
And that's the way the fire went out.

Ibbity, bibbity, sibbity, sab. . . .

The people have their beliefs, and half beliefs: Pass a new baby three times around a table leg to bring it good luck. The bite of a dying person is deadly poison. The seventh year in a marriage is the crucial year; if you are going to separate, it will be then or never. To rid yourself of freckles, wash your face with watermelon juice. Fried mouse will cure bed-wetting. To get wind while sailing, stick a knife blade into the mast. If a husband or wife should stray, burn seven sprouts of persimmon in the fire, and the unfaithful one will have seven severe pains and return home. Eat hog jowl and black-eyed peas on New Year's Day, and you will have food through the rest of the year. A blacksnake will milk a cow dry. Never begin anything new or start a journey on Friday. If you want to have good luck at gambling, kiss a strange woman, or carry a bat's heart in your pocket. In order to break a hen from setting, put an alarm clock in the nest and let it go off. An ax in the house means death. Throw salt over your left shoulder . . . wish on a falling star . . . keep your fingers crossed . . . touch wood . . . three on a match. . . .

It gets windy, all right. In Montana, the wagon chains stand straight out with the wind, and occasionally the end links snap off. Harry Oliver says that at Searchlight he saw a chicken with its tail to the wind lay the same egg five times. . . .

The people talk in the way of America. Daniel Boone returned after a two-year trip into the wilderness, and told of his experiences. A listener asked if he'd ever been lost. "Lost? No, I never was lost, but I was bewildered once for three days." Governor Jeff Davis of Arkansas said, "I cain't sing. I ruined my voice a-hollerin' for gravy when I was a young-un." Vance Randolph tells of a farmer who listened to a foul-mouthed politician for a while without any comment. Then he said, "That feller reminds me of the time the skunks littered under our barn." Of an almost impossible enterprise, a Missourian cried, "I'd just as soon shin up a thorn tree with a armload of eels." An old man, about to die, commented beautifully, "It won't be long till they'll be puttin' the green quilt over me."

For some of us folklore is a memory of the American past, and our own past. For others it is a living heritage, as lively as a colt in the south pasture.

For both it is good, as grass roots are good.

Vermonters

By Dorothy Canfield Fisher

How many Vermonts could you put in Texas? A Vermonter couldn't care less. He, perhaps more than any American, is unimpressed by bigness. What he has cared about since Ethan Allen's time is taking care of what belongs to him and letting his neighbor do the same. His independence is like his skin—he's hardly aware of it until it's pinched.

Everybody knows that New York State is a queenly creature, with a gold crown on her head and a purple velvet cloak. The face of Louisiana is as familiar—dark-eyed, temperamental. Virginia is a white-haired "grande dame" with ancient, well-mended fine lace. Massachusetts is a man, a middle-aged man, with a hard, conscientious intelligent face. And if I am not mistaken, Pennsylvania is a man too, a business man, with money in his pockets and the consciousness of his prosperity written large on his indoor face and in his kindly calculating eyes.

These State countenances are familiar to us, and many more; but back of this throng of affluent personalities, conscious of their importance in the world, stands one, known to fewer Americans, rather gaunt compared to the well-fed curves of the others, anything but artistocratic or picturesque. Yet the group of mountaineers who know Vermont from having grown up with it have the most obstinate affection and respect for their State, which they see as a tall, powerful man, with gray hair, rough outdoor clothes, a sinewy hand and arm, a humorous, shrewd mouth and a weather-beaten face from which look out the most quietly fearless eyes ever set in any man's head. There is little money in the pockets of that woodman's coat, but there is strength in the long, corded arm, an unhurried sense of fun lies behind the ironic glint in the eyes, and the strong, unspoiled personality is tinctured to its last fiber by an unenvious satisfaction with plain ways which is, literally, worth a million dollars to any possessor. Not to envy other people is an inheritance rich enough; but Vermont adds to that treasure the greater one of not being afraid. It seems incredible, in our modern world, so tormented with fears about its safety, that a whole Stateful of people have no ground for apprehension; but it is true. The Vermonter, used to the moral freedom of not dreading anything, is hardly conscious of it. This lack of fear is the marrow of his bones. Why should he be afraid of anybody or anything?

What are some of the things that other people fear? Well, most of them are afraid of being poor. This fear, rather more than love, is what makes the modern world go round. The Vermonter is not afraid of being poor because he is poor already and has been for a hundred and fifty years, and it hasn't hurt him a bit. To trade for money this lack of fear of poverty would seem to him the most idiotic of bargains, and he does not like to make poor bargains. This quality makes him by no means a favorite with moderns who try to organize the world along what they call "strictly business lines of industrial efficiency." Most of their operations are based on their certainty that people are afraid to be poor. We Vermonters often notice considerable exasperation in such devotees of industrialism when they encounter the natives of our State. We make no comment on this at the time, taking them in with the silent attentive observation which they furiously dub "bucolic stolidity"; but after they have gone back to the city we laugh to ourselves, and some old fellow among us hits on just the droll, ironic phrase to describe the encounter. For years afterwards, we quote this to the mystification of the outsider.

Another well-known and much-described fear is that of not keeping up with the social procession, of being obliged to step down a rung on the social ladder. This is another fear which stops short before it gets into Vermont. That small section of the country has never kept up with other people's processions and has found it no hardship to walk along at its own gait. And as for social ladders, any glimpse of a social ladder or of purely social distinctions moves a Vermonter to the unaffected, pitying wonder which explorers feel at the sight of the complicated taboos of savage tribes. Of course, the Vermonter pays for his high-handed scoffing at sacred social distinctions by a rough plainness of speech and manner which people from outside do not relish and which they describe in far from complimentary terms. This is a pity. But I dare say you can't have something for nothing morally, any more than materially, and perhaps it is not too high a price to pay for the total absence in our world of servility or any sort of pretentiousness. Every man to his taste. We like it better the way we have it.

Perhaps the most corroding fear known to possessors of material wealth, is the panic alarm at any glimpse of possible changes in the social fabric which may make things uncomfortable for possessors. The Latin poet who many years ago described the light-hearted stride of a poor man across a dark plain infested with robbers described the care-free gait at which Vermont moves through the troubled modern world. Vermont, like some of the remote valleys in the Pyrenees, has always been too far out of the furiously swirling current of modern industrial life to be much affected by it or to dread its vagaries. For generations now, when times get hard, when the mills in the industrial States around us are shut down, and the newspapers are talking about bankruptcies and bread-lines, the Vermont family, exactly as rich and exactly as poor as it ever was, remarks: "Well, we'd better ask Lem's folks up to stay a spell, till times get better. I guess it's pretty hard sledding for them." When times get better, Lem's family leave the small frame farmhouse which has been their refuge, and drive off down the steep stony road which is the first stage of their journey back to wages and movies.

The Vermont kin they leave behind realize shrewdly that already they seem countrified to their mill-town, factory-hand guests, but this does not worry them: rather it makes an ironic quirk come into the corner of their mouths. They continue to stand and wave their hands with undiminished kindliness, this time tinged by an amused humor which would be distinctly unpalatable to the others if they could understand it. I am afraid there is an element of sinful pride in the granite-like comfort they take in the security given them by their plain tastes and ability to deal with life at first hand.

Another problem of which we read occasionally as bothering serious-minded folks in other parts is what to do with accumulated wealth. It bothers us as little as how to fight cobras. For the most part, society in Vermont is organized along the most obviously solid and natural lines, primitive and elemental. Everybody is working. Yes, working, you step-lively outsiders, although Vermonters may not hit up the hectic pace of factory hands and although some leisure for talking things over and reading the papers and cracking jokes about life, and going hunting and nutting is a necessity for Vermonters even if they are obliged to pay for it by the forgoing of sacred dollars. They do not desperately need those dollars. It is very rare when anybody in Vermont fails to secure a fair amount of shelter and clothing and food and education; and it is equally rare when anybody secures very much more than that. There are, so to speak, no accumulated possessions at all.

But perhaps what Vermont is least afraid of, and what other people fear and hate most, is politics. You know as well as I do that most Americans are low in their minds about politics. They feel that politics is really beyond them, that they never will be able to get what they want through political action. The "fatalism of the multitude" weighs like lead upon their hearts. When there are so many, what can one man do? Well, you see in Vermont there aren't so many. There isn't any multitude. Self-government is not perfection there, any more than anywhere else, but it bears the closest, realist relationship to the citizens, and is not at all given over to professional politicians. Vermonters see nothing in self-government (local self-government) inherently more complicated than keeping your bank-book balanced. Perhaps this is because Vermont puts up as little as possible with that lazy substitute for self-government known as the "representative system," under which you tell somebody else to do the governing for you and not to bother you about it lest your money-making be disturbed. There is so little money to make in Vermont that few people are absorbed in making it. Nearly everybody has sufficient strength and time left over, and more than sufficient interest, to give to self-government. The Town Meeting is self-government, direct, articulate, personal. It is the annual assemblage not of the representatives of the governed, but of every one of the governed themselves. Anybody—you who are governed by a non-existing entity called "the County" cannot understand this, but it is true—anybody at all who does not like the way things are going in his town can stand up and say so, and propose a cure, as pungently as his command of his native tongue will allow. And Czar Public Opinion not only lets him do this, but rather admires a man who has something to say for his own point of view.

Every question concerning the welfare of the town, to the last forgotten valley in the mountains, is brought up at this meeting and decided after loud and open discussion. When it is over and the muddy cars and lean wiry men stream away from the Town Hall over the rutted roads in the sharp March air, they are all tingling with that stimulating experience, having spoken their minds out freely on what concerns them. They step heavily in their great shoes through the mud, which on March-meeting Day is apt to be deep, but they hold up their heads. They have settled their own affairs. There is none of that stultifying, bored, cynical, disillusioned conviction that the rogues will beat the honest man again this time, as always. Not on your life! The honest men are on the job, with remarkably big and knotty fists, their dander ready to rise if somebody tries to put something over on them. They probably would not be able to cope with specially adroit political rogues, but there is blessedly so little money involved in most Vermont operations that it is hardly worth the while of specially adroit rogues to frequent town-meetings. The Vermonter has for a century and a half found self-government daunting, and often the highest form of entertainment.

This tradition of looking the world in the eye and asking no odds of it, probably seems to the rest of you a rather curious tradition for a poor, rustic State with hardly a millionaire to its name, no political pull of any sort, and nothing to distinguish it in the eyes of the outside world. But all Vermonters know where it comes from, straight down from our forefathers who did look the world in the eye and made the world back down. With nothing on their side but their fearlessness and a sense of human rights as against property rights, they held out against oppression and injustice, though dressed up in the fine names of "legality" and "loyalty to the organization of society."

Not many people outside Vermont know the dramatic story of the State's early life, but everybody inside the State does. There are fewer people in the whole State of Vermont than in the city of Buffalo, which is not at all huge as cities go now. But even at that, there are a good many men, women, and children in the State, over three hundred thousand. There is hardly one of this number who does not know about the history of the New Hampshire Grants, and how our great-grandfathers stood up for their naked human rights against all the tradition embodied in a powerful neighboring Province,—and won the fight.

I know you are vague on this point, though you probably had it as a lesson one day in high school; so I will give you a sketch of it, compressed to a brevity which ought not to bore you too much. After the end of the French and Indian War, Vermont was safe ground for American settlers and the bolder spirits began to come in from New Hampshire and Connecticut. They settled, went through the terribly wearing toil of pioneers, felled trees, reclaimed land, drained swamps, built houses and mills, braved isolation, poverty, danger, health-breaking labor, and made Vermont a region of homes. They had learned to love it as we love it now, silently, undramatically, steadfastly, detesting any florid, high-flown talk about it, burying our love in our hearts. Vermonters are not sentimental, articulate Celts, but hermetically sealed Yankees. But they live on this love for their homes and they have shown themselves quite ready to die for it.

Back there in the eighteenth century, just when the settlers had definitely proved that they could make homes out of the wilderness, they were informed that by a legal technicality the grants by which they held their land were not valid; and that New York lawyers intended to send officers of the law to take the Vermont land away from the men who had reclaimed it. It was then to be given to soft-handed, well-to-do men, with political influence who had no more rightful connection with that land than did the inhabitants of Peking. The Vermont settlers did not pretend to understand the law of that day. They only knew in their hearts that the land they had so painfully reclaimed, worked over, brought up their children on, was theirs, if anything ever belonged to anybody. A shout went up from Vermont to the New York officers of the law: "Just come and take it away, if you dare!" And they got down their long rifles, ran some bullets, and dried their powder.

The hated "York State men" tried to do this, ventured into the Vermont settlements, were roughly treated, and sent home. They were afraid to try it again and retreated to the Albany courts of law, which summoned the Vermonters to submit the matter to trial. With nothing but their inherent human rights back of them, the Vermonters went down to Albany (no true Vermonter can abide the name of Albany since then!) and there went through the solemn twaddle of a law-trial, where the standards were not those of human rightness and fair-dealing, but were drawn from yellow parchments. Of course the parchments won. That is their habit in law-courts.

Ethan Allen was in Albany through this trial, to help the Vermonters. After the decision was rendered, he walked out of the law-court, on his way home, surrounded by a mocking crowd of York State men. The whole history is so familiar to us Vermonters that any one of us would know just what is coming next in this episode. When, in speaking to a Vermont audience, you begin this story, you can see people lay down their umbrellas and handbags to have their hands free to applaud, and you can see every backbone straighten as you go on in the phrases consecrated by time. "They shouted jeeringly at Allen: 'Now, do you know you're beaten? Now will you lie down and give up?' Ethan Allen drew himself to the full height of his magnificent manhood" (we never use any less fine a phrase than this) "and cried out in a ringing voice, 'The gods of the mountains are not the gods of the plains,' and strode away leaving them silenced." (Here is where the speaker always has to wait for people to get through clapping.) He strode back to Vermont and organized a resistance. Was there ever more absurd, pitiable, pretentious attempt? A handful of rough mountaineers, without a legal leg to stand on, to try and defend themselves against the British law! And their only pretext, the preposterous one that they had earned what they held!

Well, to make a long and complicated story short, the handful of rough men did continue to hold the land they had earned, and we, their descendants, are living on it now. They did more. For fourteen years after that, those men, our great-grandfathers, ruled Vermont, free of any sovereignty, an independent republic on the continent of North America. You never heard that quaint and colorful fact about our little State, did you? Yes, for fourteen years they stood straight and strong on their own feet, owing allegiance to nothing in creation but their own consciences. They stood steady in a whirling, shifting world, and proved to their own satisfaction that to stand steady is not an impossible task.

Down to this day, down to the last corner of our green, wooded, mountain-bedecked State, we all stand steadier because of that memory back of us. Every foot of the land on which we live was held for us by the courage, almost absurd in its simple-heartedness, of our tall, lean, ironic grandfathers, and by their candid faith in the inherent strength of a just cause. They risked their fortunes and their lives on their faith in this principle: that those who work and create have certain sacred rights, no matter what laws may be, more than those who do nothing. With that principle as our main inheritance, we Vermonters can cock our feet up on the railing of the porch and with a tranquil heart read the news of the modern world and the frightened guessing of other folks at what is coming next!

Rhode Island Clambake

By T. E. Murphy

A clambake à la Rhode Island excites your palate, delights your innards and destroys nothing but your appetite. Your dyed-in-the-wool Rhode Islander has nothing but contempt for clambakes à la New York or Long Island or any other part of the country. He knows that only succulent Rhode Island clams, wrapped in moist seaweed and placed on hot rocks, are worthy of a clambake.

Walking along the sandy shores of Narragansett Bay one day, a hungry pioneer saw a group of Indians squatting on their heels around a mound covered by an old blanket. From the edges of the blanket there issued wisps of steam. As the pioneer approached, the soft sea breezes wafted to his quivering nostrils the most pungent, tantalizing and appetite-provoking odor he had ever smelled.

These were friendly Indians, and one of them grunted an invitation just as the entire group leaped to the mound and cast aside the blanket. Clouds of steam arose, and the pioneer thought for a moment that he was witnessing a primitive ceremony. Then he saw a bed of steaming seaweed in the center of which nestled piles of clams, tender ears of corn, sweet potatoes and white potatoes and, peeping from their wrappings of leaves, white flakes of fish.

As legend goes, the hearty pioneer at this point let loose a piercing yell that frightened the wits out of the red men, tore off his jacket, loosened his belt, rolled up his sleeves and waded in. Several hours later, other men from the colony found him lying on his back in the warm white sand; the afternoon sun bathed a cherubic smile on his face. He was snoring gently, and the bulge under his belt rose and fell as quietly and rhythmically as the swell of the ocean at his feet. Then and there was born the first Rhode Island clambake master, now a recognized profession in Rhode Island, with trade secrets handed down from generation to generation.

There have been minor variations in the formula throughout the years, but essentially the clambake is prepared and eaten in Rhode Island today just as it was by the Indians hundreds of years ago. It is prepared with an antique cunning and eaten in an air that is laden with the salt spray of the ocean or the pine scent of the grove.

The first white bake master—the aforesaid gourmet who ate with the Indians—taught the hidden art to his son. And it is an art. He in turn passed it on to his sons. Now, today, the great bake masters of the state are willing to swear on a stack of Bibles that each is a direct descendant of the original white settler. And would they practice their art elsewhere? They would not! California, Kansas, Louisiana will never see a Rhode Island bake master performing his culinary magic. There are isolated cases of bake masters going as far as Hartford, Connecticut, a matter of seventy-five miles, to give the outlanders an idea of what it was all about, but mostly they stick close to their native soil.

There are three general classes of clambakes. First, there are the big commercials, where you may sit down at any time of the day and order a clambake as you would food in a restaurant. These pavilions are scattered all along Rhode Island's ragged seashore, but the largest is at Crescent Park. Here, Bill Crowell, dean of Rhode Island bake masters, has baked for as many as 5000 diners on one sunny Sunday, and for 100,000 within ten weeks. Bill figures that in his sixty years of baking he has used an average of 5000 bushels of clams a year, which is pretty close to 10,000,000 quarts of clams. The surviving clams were happy when Bill retired a couple of years ago.

Next are the private bakes, sponsored by political parties, politicians, political clubs, police and fire departments, sporting and fraternal organizations. These flourish principally during the summer preceding election. Sometimes they are served at the big commercial places, but usually a well-known bake master is hired and he serves it at any desired spot in the state.

Next, and far at the top of the list, are the annual affairs which have become as much a part of Rhode Island life as the seasons or the fall and rise of the tides. They were started anywhere from fifty to seventy-five years ago, usually as small church picnics.

Take the Maple Root Six Principle Baptist Church bake on the third Thursday of every August down in Coventry. Last year more than 1000 persons from all parts of the country sat down to eat in a shady maple grove. There were visitors from all parts of New England, from New York State and from Pennsylvania, from several parts of Florida, and there was a family of five from California. Lewell M. Whitman baked the first clambake there sixty-two years ago, when he was fifteen. It was a small affair, and he had been trained by his father, who had been famous as a bake master throughout the state for many years and practiced his art for three quarters of a century. And this year Lewell is planning for his sixty-second bake in August.

The locale of the clambake is not important, so long as it is Rhode Island or within easy transportation distance from her shores. As a matter of fact, the Hornbine Baptist Church bake in Rehoboth, just over the state line in Massachusetts, will serve its seventy-ninth annual clambake this summer. But it will, as always, be a strictly Rhode Island clambake.

You can take your choice of a white sandy beach, with the surf booming and the tangy salt smell, or a shady pine or maple grove, but unless you use Rhode Island clams it is not a real clambake; it is not authentic and not worth bothering with. The Rhode Island clam is as different from the other varieties found along American shores as champagne from seltzer water.

The Rhode Island clam is small; it is delicate, genteel, refined. The shell is soft and oval in shape, and so fragile that it can be crushed between the fingers. The snout is long and meaty and tender. The shell is filled with an ambrosial nectar. The clam is dug from the sand, usually at low tide. For all its delicacy it is not an intellectual creature, for it discloses where it lies burrowed by emitting a stream of water whenever the sand above it is trod upon. The digger merely notes where the miniature geyser erupted, and with a long-pronged rake he digs quickly about ten or fourteen inches down, and there, usually, will be found a cluster of clams waiting to be harvested.

Ask for a clam in New York and you are served a round, concrete-shelled imitation. The New York clam is merely an undersized quahog, known in Rhode Island as a "little neck." There is no denying its edible qualities when eaten *au naturel* from the shell, but for clambake purposes it is useless according to Rhode Island standards. Some of the old-timers in Rhode Island have told me that they attended clambakes in New York where these small quahogs—or hard-shelled clams—were used. But, they snorted, it wasn't really a clambake.

After the clams have been dug and washed, they are sorted over very carefully and divided into two piles—one for clam chowder and one for the bake. And now we come to a very delicate question: clam chowder. A sea of words has been spilled on cream versus tomato as the catalyst in clam chowder. Nearly every legislature in New England has heard some stentorian-voiced politician air his views on the subject. Harsh words have been spoken; friendships have been broken on the question: tomato or cream?

Some rule-of-thumb gourmets have declared, "North of Boston, cream; south of Boston, tomato."

Let us approach the matter with both discretion and decorum. Of course there must be Rhode Island clams. Of late there has been a tendency to add a few ground-up quahogs for flavor. As to the proportion of clams, it is better to err on the side of liberality. The soft shells are opened easily and the juice is carefully saved and strained through cloth. Then the bellies are removed and the rest of the meat is ground moderately fine. Potatoes are peeled and diced and left to soak in water. Experts soak them overnight.

The next moot point is the question of pork. A recent survey of the recognized great chowder makers of the state disclosed that all of them used fat salt pork, from twenty to twenty-five pounds to ninety gallons of chowder. That would be for a medium-sized bake. The pork is diced small and fried slowly, but not crisped. Then a few chopped onions are added. Bermudas are best, because their flavor does not eclipse the clam.

After the onions have been fried soft in the pork grease—but not brown, mind you—both pork and onions are placed in a big kettle and the diced potatoes are added. Sufficient water to cover the potatoes is then put into the kettle and the ingredients are cooked until the potatoes are done. A Rhode Islander never permits his potatoes to become mushy. Then the clams and the clam broth are added and the chowder is left to cook for ten or fifteen minutes, while the bake master seasons with salt and pepper according to his formula. One old-timer insists that a pinch of sage improves the chowder. And that's all there is to it. Any addition or omission is heresy and not to be countenanced.

Those chowder makers who add tomatoes, and refer to it as "Rhode Island chowder" as compared to Maine's "cream-clouded chowder," are looked upon with rage and scorn by most of the old-timers. In some benighted areas folks even go so far as to add canned tomato soup—particularly in the New York area. Chowder makers consider this in the same category of gastronomic monstrosities as sugar on Boston baked beans. The Maine folks who add cream or milk are regarded somewhat tolerantly with the attitude of "Well, if they don't know any better!"

At the commercial bakes, your first course consists of chowder and clam cakes. The reasoning is simple. The more chowder and clam cakes you eat, the less room you have for the more expensive ingredients. And you eat plenty, unless you are smart. There are records of diners who have consumed eight quarts of chowder at one sitting. But at the private bakes the chowder and clam cakes are served at noon and the bake is served about four hours later, in tribute to civilized inroads on appetite.

Chowder is served in bowls of about a quart capacity, and big tureens are placed at strategic points along the long board tables for those who invariably want more.

Now, though the human capacity for Rhode Island clam chowder is astonishing, eventually that capacity is reached, and at this point the diners straggle away to loll on the beach, or toss horseshoes in the grove, or doze in the sand, or just sit around to talk politics with Nate and Jim.

With the chowder-and-clam-cakes course out of the way, the bake master really gets down to business. There is a base of concrete or concrete and stone. Sometimes it is flat; sometimes it is laid in a slight depression. The base Lewell Whitman uses—he built it twenty-five years ago—down at Maple Root, is thirty feet long and eight feet wide. On this base the workers place two and a half cords of wood in six-foot lengths laid crisscross, then two wagonloads of stones about bucket size. There is first a layer of wood, then a layer of stones, then a layer of wood, and so on, until all is used. Then the entire structure is doused with kerosene and set afire. When the wood has burned away and the stones are white-hot, the ashes are raked out and the stones are pushed around to cover the base. A few red embers are left "to make more flavor."

Moist pungent rockweed, freshly gathered from the ocean, is quickly blanketed over the hot stones. On this steaming bed the clams are spread out in a thick layer—bushels and bushels of them. White potatoes in their jackets, sweet potatoes, tiny white bockwurst, fillets of fish, cloth bags filled with savory stuffing, onions and corn with a thin jacket of husk left on, are piled over the clams. By now the rockweed is sizzling on the hot stones.

When all the food is laid, a huge canvas tarpaulin, or "sail," is placed over all to keep in the steam and heat. Some bake masters use double sails; some seal the edges of their sails with moist earth. At some small bakes, the entire mound is covered with earth. There is nothing to do now but wait and let the hot rocks and the salty steam from the moist weed and the clams do their work. The moist rockweed, scorching against the hot rocks, pushes steamy heat upward through the clams. The clams open their shells and the juice trickles down through the seaweed to the rocks. The increased steam pushes up through the potatoes and other ingredients to the corn on top. Each item retains its own flavor, but takes on some of the commingled flavor of everything. It is simple, but it is cunning. The result is soul-satisfying.

It may be his fiftieth or his five-hundredth bake, but the bake master inevitably wears the worried look of an obstetrician awaiting a difficult case. He glances nervously at his watch and tries futilely to engage in small talk. But his eye invariably turns toward the sail to see if steam is escaping. Occasionally the canvas will rise and fall as if breathing. That means there is too much steam pressure and the food will be overdone.

"She's ablowin'," the bake master says, and immediately the assistants lift one corner of the sail and let out steam until he tells them to seal it up again. It is his judgment against the world.

The worst disgrace a bake master can face is to have his bake come out "raw" because the stones were not hot enough. Bill Crowell has one inviolable rule.

"The rocks have got to be hot enough to scorch the rockweed," he says sagely. And he has never lost a bake in more than sixty years.

Next in enormity is the sin of having someone ask for more of anything and being unable to furnish it in any quantity. Quantity is of the essence of a clambake.

Time stands still when the sail is removed about an hour and fifteen minutes after it has been placed. Hungry watchers gape expectantly and there is an involuntary "Ah-h-h" as the first cloud of imprisoned steam is wafted to their nostrils, laden with an inimitable aroma, and distinguishable by clam eaters at a distance of a half mile. Search the world over and you will find no smell like it.

At this point the watchers scurry to the long tables. Hearty eaters like to have the end seats, and any photograph of a clambake usually will show rather rotund gentlemen occupying these favorite seats. It gives them more elbowroom. On the table the waiters have already placed stacks of fresh white bread—usually home-baked—and round slices of brown bread; great platters of sliced tomatoes, cucumbers and onions, and the usual vinegar, catchup, salt and pepper. At each plate there is a small pitcher of drawn butter.

Men roll up their sleeves and loosen their belts. Napkins are tucked into collars. Glances are directed at the skyhigh column of steam and the hissing, clanking and clatter that come from the general direction of the pile.

Then come the waiters. Waiters or waitresses at clambakes never walk; they always rush down the long corridors of uncarpeted earth with the steamed clams in their temporary keeping. They wait not on ceremony or form. The straight line is their route and the shortest distance is the best. It is as if they were the bringers of good tidings, anxious beyond all common wishing to bring this delicacy of baked clams to the hundreds of literally watering mouths. Round, well-chipped and much-battered enameled pans of about a quart capacity are used invariably. Each diner gets one full of clams and there is at least one refill within easy reach.

If it is your first bake, you sit and wait for a moment to see how the situation is handled. Knives and forks appear to be futile tools, and they are. The man at your right is now working with machinelike precision. Watch him closely, for his every move spells "veteran." With a deft movement he removes the meat from the shell, grasps it at the base of the snout, rolls off the thin covering as though it were a loose glove. The clam is dunked with the fingers into the butter. The entire thing is manual. As the right hand lifts the clam to the mouth, the left hand reaches for another clam. Tiny rivulets of yellow butter drip from chins. Fingers on the right hand are assuming a glistening, well-oiled look, and the table between the diners is littered with empty shells.

If it is your first Rhode Island clambake, after you have eaten a few of them, you will want to stay with the clams. There is no warning in the ever-increasing pile of shells before you, but there's always a friendly neighbor to whisper in your ear, "Easy, bub; there's other things coming."

There is a slight hiatus between the baked clams and the next course, the people killing time by nibbling at buttered pieces of brown bread and sliced tomatoes and onions with vinegar, and so on.

Then comes another rush of waiters bearing down on you with huge platters of fish and bockwurst, corn and potatoes and stuffing, and it is heaped before you as yours join the gang of outstretched hands to help yourself.

The potatoes are neither baked nor boiled. They have been permeated by savory steam from the dripping clams and moist seaweed. They have the consistency of ripe bananas. The bockwurst are not their natural selves either. They have been touched by the enchantment of the ocean-drenched seaweed. They literally melt in your mouth.

Perhaps you have eaten roasted corn or boiled corn. Neither is anything like the corn of the clambake. It is not dry and mealy, nor is it hard, nor is it mushy. It is lush and succulent, and after it has been well doused in melted butter and salted slightly, your teeth merely touch the tiny kernels coaxingly, and they leave the cob and come to you almost with an intake of breath.

There is no schedule, no routine. Each man eats as much as he wants and what he wants, and there is never a lack. Someone is always pushing more food in front of you from the front or from the sides or over your shoulder from the back. Between the rows of earnest, face-to-face eaters, the platters are being replenished constantly. Conversation is virtually at a standstill until satiation is reached.

A pallid aftermath, a sort of tapering off after the main frenzy, comes with the thick slices of watermelon, the heavy mugs filled with steaming coffee. A concession to civilization is this, for the Saturnalia is over. Men wipe their chins—and women do, too—and beam on their neighbors. Men light up cigars and pipes, and women powder their noses and sigh contentedly, and say they don't know what ever came over them. They never ate so much in their lives; must be the salt air or the resinous smell of the pine trees, they say.

And your neighbor will say, "You must think I'm an awful glutton, the way I went at all that food!" And she's told, "Why, I felt the same way myself."

Men are already talking politics. Then, after a while, everyone straggles up to where it all began. More important-looking men with round heads and round bodies and an air of self-sufficiency about them—these are the politicians—actually go inside the inclosure where the bake master and his assistants are dunking a few clams for themselves.

Nate—he's the big fellow with the cigar—says in a loud, self-confident voice, "Nice bake, Bill; clams never tasted better."

Bill, with a buttered clam dangling between his thumb and finger, now relieved of the oppression of an unopened bake, says genially, "Thanks, senator; had pretty good luck today."

Luck! Old Bill is modest. He's been making bakes for more years than the senator has lived, and never lost one of them. Never had a raw one. The senator has been saying the same thing for twenty years at least. It isn't luck, and Bill knows it. It is having a father or an uncle or someone who trained you in boyhood; who impressed upon you the importance of white-hot rocks, fresh seaweed and sweet Rhode Island clams. And plenty of fresh sea air; a soft ocean breeze blowing to whip up the whitecaps down there, and the appetite too. And the seagulls wheeling overhead and the far-off blare of a buoy; white clouds scudding across the sky and the cool shade of trees inshore.

Old Bill goes back to his steamed clams and starts figuring for that party of 400 he has to bake for next Sunday. The crowd is moving away slowly in automobiles. Nobody drives fast. Nobody wants to. Nobody has enough ambition. The Rhode Island clambake is designed for comfort, not for speed. Old Bill peers at the sky and hopes the sun will shine next Sunday.

A "Proper Bostonian"

By John P. Marquand

Your proper Bostonian may seem a stiff-necked, inaccessible person holding membership in highly exclusive clubs. Actually he is just as human as the next man, although the ordinary observer might not suspect it. Marquand knows him better than anyone else, and tells us what lies behind the customs and traditions of Beacon Hill.

Dear John:—

I did not sleep well last night. As one grows older sleep does not come as easily. I put on my dressing-gown and went into your mother's sewing parlour at the front of the house to read, but I could not keep my mind on the pages of my book although it was my Emerson, who I believe is one of the greatest men ever produced by this nation, certainly by Harvard. I could not keep my mind on the book because my thoughts were like a book in themselves. I had taken two cups of coffee last night after dinner in order to fortify myself against Professor Speyer's paper, "Certain Dangerous Modern Tendencies," which he read before the Eight O'Clock Club. Being Secretary of this organization I was obliged to keep alert enough to make an abstract of the speaker's remarks. I have never liked the practice of borrowing the speaker's paper later, which is indulged in by some secretaries I might mention. Of late years this necessity for concentration is apt to give me a bad night afterward.

My mind was like the pages of a book. It fluttered here and there as pages do when the wind blows them, out under the pines at Pequod Island. The house was very quiet. Outside the fronts of Beacon Street, the brick walks and the asphalt shone emptily beneath those new glaring street lights that illuminate our front rooms and disturb our slumber. For one of the first times I can remember it seemed to me that Beacon Street was a trifle sad in its emptiness. It was as though something had left it. It was like that street in Ecclesiastes "when the sound of the grinding is low." I began thinking about you and about the newest and most welcome member of our family. I hoped that you were not bringing our new boy into as changing a world as the one into which I introduced you. I had never thought before that this devastating effect of almost uncalculable change is what has made you different from what I might have expected, but I believe that this is the reason that you are sometimes somewhat of an enigma to me. You are a part of this new Frankenstein-like world which will always be a little bit beyond my powers of comprehension.

Have you ever stopped to think how great this material revolution has been? You have probably not done so any more than I, because we accept the obvious so easily. When I was a boy I went to bed by candlelight. The old candlesticks are still on the shelf by the cellar stairs, and later there were jokes about country bumpkins blowing out the gas. I washed out of a pitcher and a basin. Later there was a single zinc tub for the entire family. I remember how it surprised me even five years ago when a salesman demonstrated to me that it was quite possible to arrange modern plumbing facilities in a place like Pequod Island. The human voice can now reach around the world. It is a simple afternoon's diversion to drive eighty or ninety miles. Our two heroes, Byrd and Lindbergh,—by far the most hopeful, indeed to my mind the only hopeful, human products arising from this chaotic change,—have spanned the Atlantic Ocean. (We are all not a little gratified incidentally that Richard Byrd is among us here in Boston. I proposed him myself for the Berkley Club.) There is no use reciting any more of the obvious. I have given reason enough why you should all be changed. This material change has made you all materialists, and yet it has rendered your grasp on reality uncertain. It has made you rely on the material gratification of the senses. It has made you worship Mammon and in this new material world everything comes too easily. Heat comes too easily and cold. Money comes too easily. Don't forget that it will go as easily too. Romance comes too easily, and success. We have all grown soft from this ease. Position changes too easily. Values shift elusively. When everything is totalled up we have evolved a fine variety of flushing toilets but not a very good world, if you will excuse the coarseness of the simile.

I hope for our new boy's sake that this change is very nearly over. I hope, when he grows up, that those who are comfortably off will begin to realize again their duty to the community. I hope, when he grows up, that he may be able to recognize a lady by her manner and by her dress. I hope that he will see what so many of you have forgotten, that there must be certain standards, that there must be certain formulae in art and thought and manners. There must be a class which sets a tone, not for its own pleasure, but because of the responsibility which it owes to others. In a sense it may be what the demagogues call a privileged class, but it must know how to pay for its privilege.

Such a class must always have its eccentricities, but it should also have its ideals. I think that I am safe in saying that we have such a class here, which is what raises us above mediocrity. We have contrived to maintain something of the spirit in spite of all this change. In my opinion it is the best heritage which we can pass to another generation. I hope that I may not live to see the time when this is swept away. I hope that you may understand this now that you have a son.

Yesterday I bowled at the Province Club and my back is very lame. I have also been reading a book which has made me very sad. It is by a new author named Hemingway entitled "The Sun also Rises." I am not a prude but I do not like it. This Hemingway is obviously not a gentleman nor are his characters gentlemen or ladies, yet I am broad-minded enough to admit that the man has a certain startling and crude power, although I feel that he resorts to artistically unfair sensational and mechanical tricks.

When this book came up before our Beacon Street Circulating Library Committee I stood out against all the others except Mrs. Sill, who always likes to be contradictory, for having it included on our recommended list. I did so because the book, gross, sexual, and unmoral though it be, points a very definite moral. It is that this wretched promiscuity so widely practised does not and cannot pay. It shows the unhappiness of those who practise it. Yet surely Mr. Hemingway must exaggerate somewhat. From what I am able to observe of the new members of the Club in Cambridge these young fellows are of as fine a type as ever, though I do believe they drink more than is good for them. . . .

The Pennsylvania Dutch

By Fredric Klees

"Like Gaul, the Pennsylvania Dutch can be divided into three parts: 'plain people,' 'church people,' and Moravians." They are a hardworking, happy people, whose rich fields, red barns, quaint dress, and beautiful Christmas and Easter customs are a distinctive contribution to the American scene.

Lancaster market on Friday afternoon is a rewarding sight in the Pennsylvania Dutch country. In the central market house, an ugly Victorian structure of red brick, where King Street crosses Queen, is to be found an abundance of food fresh from the farm. Behind the stalls farmers "stand market," some in ordinary clothes, others in the simple, archaic dress of the Mennonites, Amish, and River Brethren.

On stands before them and on shelves behind them are piles of apples: summer rambo, smokehouse, winesap, each according to its season; boxes of little white onions, all peeled and ready to pop into the pot; tender, succulent sugar peas to be boiled in the pod; rich, brown apple butter, smelling of spice and sassafras. There are fat Lebanon bolognas and ropes of smoked sausages; shellbark meats and kernels of black walnuts; sweet-apple *snitz* and dried corn; homemade bread fresh from a farm bake oven; the Dutch coffeecakes in all their glory—crumb cakes, potato buns, shoofly pies, and even *schwenkfelders* and *fastnachts*. At the Good Friday market are baskets of dyed eggs, from the rich chestnut brown of the ones dyed with onion skins, to the purple, pink, and green of those colored with store dyes. At Christmas, the stands are filled with toy candy, clear red and yellow, and the many Christmas cookies so dear to the Pennsylvania Dutch heart—*lebkuchen* rich with citron, sand-tarts thin as paper, Moravian cookies from up Lititz way, shellbark macaroons chewy and delectable, animal cookies gay with red sugar.

There are flowers at market too: pails of daffodils, pots of fuchsia, tubs of madonna lilies—if not in April, then in June. All round the calendar the dressed chickens are a feature of the Lancaster market—young, tender, with not one pinfeather to mar perfection. The heart, liver and gizzard are displayed on a bed of parsley on top of the fowl, like a flower arrangement. Furthermore, everything is spotless; even the potatoes look as though each one had been scrubbed.

No matter how much of an ordeal shopping may be elsewhere, in Lancaster it is a pleasure. The quality and quantity of the food and the cheerfulness of the people will make one envy the inhabitants of this city. One never goes to the Friday market in Lancaster without a basket —Friday afternoon market is the principal one of the week. Even those who don't mean to buy anything go to look upon the farm products of this land of milk and honey and to see the people. Both will do your heart good. To one seeing Lancaster County for the first time, the Mennonites, Amish, Dunkards and River Brethren behind the stands may be even more impressive than the food they offer for sale.

A Mennonite farmer with his bushy beard and broad-brim hat is a never-to-be-forgotten figure as he stands in the market house in a blaze of zinnias, marigold and cockscomb; and so are the two buxom Amish women, the one in blue as bright as a jay, and the other equally vivid in purple, with prayer caps and kerchiefs of white to relieve the brilliance of the colors. This dress of these "plain people," the name often given to these sects, has come down from the 17th and 18th Centuries very little changed.

All the women wear bonnets over their prayer caps when they go outdoors, and often shawls instead of coats. The men wear flat broad-brim hats over hair cropped at the top of the ears. If married, the men wear full, bushy beards, but shave the upper lip. The shaving of the upper lip and the absence of buttons on their clothes are inheritances from times when a bold mustache and shiny buttons on a uniform marked a soldier. Hence the Amish, in an ardor of pacifism, still shave the upper lip and use hooks and eyes instead of buttons.

To most of the women this old-world dress is decidedly becoming. On the men it is odd but picturesque; while on the children it is as captivating a costume as man has ever devised. A tiny Amish boy or girl dressed in a miniature version of the father's or mother's garb is a droll and heartwarming sight. Best of all, however, is the serenity in the faces of these people. A look at them clearly shows that none among them goes cold in winter or hungry anytime, that none ever goes on relief or to the county home.

The "plain people" are well aware that they are their brother's keeper. When the war was at its height the Dunkards laid their plans to raise heifers to restock the depleted herds of the war-stricken countries. Almost as soon as peace was declared the first shipments of these heifers began to move toward Poland and Greece and other lands hard hit by the war.

Finding the "plain people" in their homes is not easy. These people dress as they do because of the dictates of conscience, not to attract tourists. The Amish, most picturesque of these sects, live in the country, not in town and village. Almost to a man they are farmers. A fortunate traveler may come upon children swarming out of a little red-brick schoolhouse; or, even better, may happen to pass an Amish meetinghouse just as church is over. That part of the country to the east and northeast of the city of Lancaster is the section in which most of the Amish live. To the north of the Lincoln Highway near such towns as Fertility, Gap, Bird-in-Hand, Paradise and Intercourse live the "House" Amish, so called because they reject churches as worldly and meet instead in their homes. North of the "House" Amish, near the villages of Hinkletown, Blue Ball, Churchtown, Morgantown, and Honey Brook, live the "Church" Amish, who hold their services in meetinghouses not unlike those of the Quakers. The houses are large and plain; but everything—house and house yard, barn and barnyard—is neat as a pin. Beyond the farms is the unending line of wooded hills, covered with oak, hickory, tulip tree and dogwood.

Amish frown on the use of automobiles as worldly, they prefer dirt roads for their horses. It is on these byways one is likely to encounter the young bloods racing along in their buggies and the settled married folks plodding at a sober pace in their tiny, boxlike wagons. It is the ambition of every Amish youth to own a brisk trotting horse and a shiny topless buggy in which to take his girl for a ride to show her—and the other fellow, too—how his horse can eat up the dust. These young Amish blades drive like demons, but gifted demons. All this sounds suspiciously worldly for a people as pious as the Amish, yet something must be done to placate the young men for the ban on automobiles. Once a man settles down to raise a family, the topless buggy is exchanged for a little boxlike rockaway without mudguards, set high and bare above the four wheels. Into this carriage the whole family is crowded: Pop and

Mom and baby in front, while behind stand Kate and Jacob and Dannie peering over their parents' shoulders, all on their way to meeting.

The "plain people," however, are a small minority of the Pennsylvania Dutch, probably not more than a tenth of the whole. The average Pennsylvania Dutchman belongs to the Lutheran or Reformed churches or to such newer denominations as the United Brethren or the Evangelical Church. As such he is as inconspicuous as his fellow Methodist or Congregationalist or Presbyterian. The more countrified among them are more at home speaking Pennsylvania Dutch than English. The familiar story of the sign on the door where the bell was out of order, sounds too good to be true: "Bell don't make; bump." Equally dubious is the tale of the little boy at a grade-crossing watching a freight train. As the caboose went by the little boy said, "Say, pop, when it gives a little red house, it makes all?" Much more credible is the lament of the Pennsylvania Dutch farmer when a neighbor who spoke only English came to see him one evening: "Ei-yi, such a dog's life! Work hard all day you must, and then at night talk English yet!" Some Pennsylvania Dutch murder the English language, but most do not.

The picturesque features of Pennsylvania Dutch life, whether trials for witchcraft or the seven sweets and sours of food, have been so distorted that what began as truth has ended as fiction. The story of the Amishman painting his gate blue to let the world know that he has a daughter ripe for marriage is almost as well known as the legend of George Washington cutting down the cherry tree, and as fanciful. Even the very name of this people is misleading: they were called Dutch by their English neighbors, who misunderstood the word *Deutsch* which these people applied to themselves. The Pennsylvania Dutch are not Holland Dutch but German and Swiss in blood, with a liberal strain of French Huguenot and English. Strictly speaking, they are not exclusively Pennsylvanian, since they have spilled over into western Maryland and the upper half of the Shenandoah Valley with outposts in North Carolina and Ontario, not to mention Ohio, Indiana, Illinois, and a half dozen other states west of the Appalachians.

The Lutherans and the Reformed, often referred to as the "church people" to set them off from the "plain people," represent the dominant Pennsylvania Dutch culture. These are the people whose Christmas and Easter customs have so enriched American life. Santa Claus and the Christmas tree, the Easter bunny and the Easter egg are old customs which the early settlers of Pennsylvania brought from the Rhineland to the banks of the Swatara and Tulpehocken. They have produced most of the Pennsylvania Dutch folk art. The gaily painted dower chests and bride boxes were theirs, as were the baptismal certificates or *taufscheins*. It is the "church people" who decorate their barns with the curious symbols, sometimes known as witch or hex signs, not because they still believe that such signs will keep the cattle safe from witches but, as they will tell you if you ask them, "just for fancy."

The country between Reading and Allentown is rich in these barn decorations. But the barns—not the witch signs—represent the glory of Pennsylvania Dutch architecture. Their houses the Pennsylvania Dutch borrowed from the English, and in return they taught the English how to build barns. When the younger sons of the Pennsylvania Dutch went west to the Ohio country and beyond they built barns like those back home until in time this Pennsylvania Dutch barn became the classic American barn. The basic design for a cattle stable on the ground floor, with a threshing floor, bins for grain, and mows for hay on the floor above, was established early in Colonial days when many of the roofs were still covered with thatch or red tile. An earth bank leading to the threshing floor enabled the farmer to drive a wagon loaded with hay or grain right onto the second floor. A characteristic of these barns is the extension of the second floor on the front of the barn for five to ten feet over the first floor to form an overhang or forebay. The barnyard, usually flanked by wagon sheds, tool houses, corncribs, and ricks of straw, is invariably to the front of the barn on the south.

This whole broad arc of the Dutch country, as it sweeps through southeastern Pennsylvania from Easton on the Delaware to the Maryland line and beyond, is a land of fat farms, clean brick towns, and small industrial cities.

Except for the Lancaster Plain this is a country of rolling hills and sweeping valleys. Almost always there are mountains in the background, sometimes rising sharply from the farm lands, sometimes only a low misty line on the horizon. The mountains and higher hills are all wooded; only the lowlands have been cleared.

The farms in the valleys are fairly small—often no more than sixty acres. These are family-size farms, the right size to be worked by a man with a son or two to help. The fields are well tilled and fertile. This is good limestone soil. Neat fence rows separate the fields of corn or wheat or potatoes or tobacco from the herds of Guernseys or Jerseys in the meadow where the creek flows under the willows and the buttonwoods. Rarely does one find one of these farms run-down.

It is a land of extreme cleanliness, where women in country towns sweep the streets in front of their houses, probably after they have finished washing their kitchen floors on their hands and knees. It is a land of rich living, as witnessed by all the fat people who ooze their way along the streets. And it is a land of thrift. In Lehigh County is told the story of Betsy Barwell, who was seen out in the pouring rain with a brand-new umbrella, still rolled up, under her arm.

"Why don't you put it up?" people asked.

"Ach, no," she declared. "I worked too hard to earn the money to buy this umbrella to get it spoiled right aways."

For admirers of Pennsylvania Dutch furniture and houses, nearly every other town has an antique shop, and good houses crop up all through this countryside. Some of the best houses are in the Oley Valley, a small beautiful valley tucked behind the hills east of Reading.

The Moravian buildings at Bethlehem, like the Augustus Lutheran Church at Trappe and the cloisters at Ephrata, are Central European in origin rather than English, as the steeply pitched roofs, the small dormer windows, and the diagonal paneling in the doors plainly show. The story of Bethlehem is long and honorable. This old Moravian colony founded by Count Zinzendorf was one of the most truly civilized in America. Nowhere else in the colonies did music flourish as it did at Bethlehem. It was through no accident that Bethlehem gave birth to the Bach Choir; this was merely the last of a long line of musical organizations beginning with the Collegium Musicum in 1744. Bethlehem has never forgotten that it was born in song; it was a Christmas carol sung on the Christmas Eve of 1741 that inspired Count Zinzendorf to name the new settlement after the birthplace of Christ. Symphonies and string quartets by Haydn and Mozart were played in Bethlehem in Colonial days before they were ever heard in the larger and more fashionable towns of Boston, Newport, Philadelphia, and Charleston. In Colonial Bethlehem even the watchman who went his rounds by night called out the hours in song:

"The clock is three! The blessed three do merit
The best of praise from body, soul, and spirit."

The Moravian candlelight service on Christmas Eve, which dates back to 1752, is the oldest of its kind in America. As it is primarily a service for children, it is given over to music and candlelight. It is not at all like the Christmas Eve service of other churches. Instead of the familiar carols, there are Moravian Christmas carols and snatches of Handel, Haydn and Mozart.

The Moravians are the third of the three Pennsylvania Dutch cultures, for, like Gaul, the Pennsylvania Dutch can be divided into three parts—"plain people," "church people" and Moravians. The feature of the Moravian celebration of Christmas which fascinates outlanders is the *putz.* This is a Christmas crib, or crèche, of the Christ child with Mary and Joseph, the shepherds, the wise men, and all the cattle of the stable and often the beasts of the woods and fields. Usually it is placed under the Christmas tree, and often it is completely anachronistic with elephants and jeeps among the shepherds and their sheep, or an electric train dashing madly in a circle around the infant Jesus in the manger. The children, of course, love it. . . .

Easter Sunday isn't so crowded, possibly because the principal service is at dawn. During the early hours of the morning the trombone choir, down in the streets of the town or in the belfry of the church, summons the members of the congregation to the graveyard to greet the dawn of the day on which Christ rose from the dead.

Carolina Kissin' Kin

By Ben Robertson

The South in Ben Robertson's *Red Hills and Cotton,* from which this selection is taken, has remained relatively unchanged for 200 years. These are a proud people—simple, homespun, and ascetic. They work their fields, take care of their kin, support the government they believe in, and have faith in the God by whose grace they were born here. They are the backbone of the South.

By the grace of God, my kinfolks and I are Carolinians. Our Grandmother Bowen always told us we had the honor to be born in Carolina. She said we and all of our kissing kin were Carolinians, and that after we were Carolinians we were Southerners, and after we were Southerners, we were citizens of the United States. We were older than the Union in Carolina, and our grandmother told us never to forget that fact. Our kinfolks had given their personal consent to the forming of the Union, we had voted for it at the polls, and what we had voted to form we had had the right to vote to unform. We knew of course what our grandmother was talking about, for our grandmother was an old Confederate lady—she was reconstructed but she was reconstructed in her own way, so whenever she got to talking about us and the grace of God, we said "Yes, ma'am" to our grandmother.

My grandmother believed the finest country in the world was America and the most precious part of America was Carolina. The sun rose and set in our valley; it hovered between Glassy Mountain in the east and Six Mile in the west, then it dropped into darkness, into the dark night of despair; it sank off to shine for a few odd hours on the heathen down in China. I think my grandmother believed God had chosen us for our country, that he had said to us as He had to Joshua: "Arise and go over this Jordan, thou and all this people, unto the land that has been promised." A hundred and ninety years ago God had brought us into Canaan from eastern Pennsylvania. . . .

I and all the families of my kinfolks lived for nearly two centuries in two old and fertile valleys at the foot of the Blue Ridge Mountains in the northwest part of our paradise—in the foothills, and in the valleys, and in the plains, and in the wilderness, and in the south country. It was a land of smokehouses and sweet-potato patches, of fried pies and dried fruit and of lazy big bumblebees buzzing in the sun—a country of deep dark pools, of the soaring spirit, of little rooms stored with apples, and of old Confederates and tenant farmers and colored people and swarms of politicians and preachers. An ideal country for cotton farmers and dreamers; a brooding great country that had caught the sight of God. . . .

We always grew cotton for our living in our valleys—cotton that in spite of droughts and freshets and boll weevils still yields for us a bale to an acre. A heaven-given crop. We are farmers, all Democrats and Baptists—a strange people, complicated and simple and proud and religious and family-loving, a divorceless, Bible-reading murdersome lot of folks, all of us rich in ancestry and steeped in tradition and emotionally quick on the trigger. . . .

For miles and miles up and down the Twelve Mile and Keowee the land is our land, and the houses are our houses, the white Baptist chapels are our chapels, even the burying grounds are our burying grounds. We own so much land in our foothills that one time when my cousin Enid and I were driving toward Pickens, our county seat, to attend a rural electrification meeting, my cousin Enid said to me: "I think I'd better address Uncle Tom as Mister Chairman—if I call him Uncle Tom then I'll have to say: 'Uncle Tom, Mamma says if you will stretch a power line from Uncle Wight's to Uncle Ross's and by Grandfather O'Dell's to Cousin Cody's and to our house, we all will guarantee two customers a mile.' " . . .

I and my kinfolks are Southerners of the inland and upland South. We and the ten million like us call ourselves the backbone of the Southern regions, the hickory-nut homespun Southerners, who while doing a lot of talking have also done a world of work. We are of Scotch-Irish stock, improved Scots of Ulster extraction, and it has never been said of any of us that we have held back from sounding our horn. We are forthright and outspoken. We are plain people and our houses are plain —you will not find on our front piazzas tall white columns holding up the roof. We are the Southern Stoics. We believe in self-reliance, in self-improvement, in progress as the theory of history, in loyalty, in total abstinence, in total immersion, in faithfulness, righteousness, justice, in honoring our parents, in living without disgrace. We have chosen asceticism because all of our lives we have had to fight an inclination to license —we know how narrow and shallow is the gulf between asceticism and complete indulgence; we have always known much concerning the far outer realms, the extremes. We have tried throughout our lives to keep the Commandments, we have set for ourselves one of the strictest, sternest codes in existence, but our country is Southern and we are Southern, and frequently we fail. In the end we stake our immortal souls on the ultimate deathbed repentance. We put our faith in the promise of Paul the Apostle that in a moment, in the twinkling of an eye, we shall be changed.

We believe in hard day labor, and in spite of all our cooks and bottle-washers we hold that every farmer should take his turn in the field—he should plow and pick cotton and thin corn. All that eat should sweat. Some of us, of course, have never sweated, but always we have thought we ought to. We are formal—we address God in prayer as "Thou" and "Thee." We are intimate—we like to call old married ladies by their lost maiden names, "Miss May Belle," "Miss Minnie Green." We flatter—we call men "Colonel" and "Judge" and "Major." Of all the colonels among my kinfolks, only one ever really held that rank. My Great-Uncle Bob was a real colonel. Once he had commanded a regiment of infantry in the army of General Jackson. The rest of our colonels were like my cousin Colonel Tom, of whom my father said: "He is just a Southern colonel." He looked like a colonel, so we called him one. We honored the distinction of his stately appearance. Many of my kinfolks have charm —if I do say it myself. Like almost all Southerners, white and black, we were born with manners—with the genuine grace that floods outward from the heart. I must add also that many of us, far from home, have learned that we can trade on our Southern manners. We do not hesitate to do so, either—we flatter and charm when we can without a flicker of regret.

As Southerners, it is essential to my kinfolks that they live by an ethical code, that they live their lives with dignity to themselves, that they live them with honor. A Southerner who loses his honor loses all, and he had rather die than live in disgrace. Honor is at the base of our personal attitude toward life. It is not defeat that we fear, it is the loss of our intimate honor. We do not only disgrace ourselves, we disgrace all the others, and we cover our heads, for each of us was born in the image and glory of God.

But in a great house there are not only vessels of gold and of silver, but also of wood and of earth; and some to honor and some to dishonor. We have had trifling low-down kinfolks who whittled and fiddled and fished, a great-uncle who was shot in a brawl, a cousin who wounded his son, and a relative closer than a cousin who had to be bailed from jail by our Great-Aunt Narcissa. We have been hit in our pride, for we have known that all of us have carried weaknesses within. Our Great-Aunt Narcissa said even the shame of Aaron Burr was on us. He was kin to us through the Allstons of Charleston. . . .

The South we belong to is a good country, a valiant country; it always has had valor, and it has had industry and thrift. Our house is painted, our grass is green. For those of us who bend our backs and put our shoulders to the wheel, the South is still Canaan land; it is milk and honey. . . .

Our folks are old and settled in our country; we have a sense of continuity, of the infinite age of time—the history of the United States has been told to us in our valley by kinfolks who have been told it by their kinfolks, and it is a personal epic, a personal saga, and in it from the beginning we have been taking our part. We know why we were fearful of adopting the Federal Constitution—it took from us a part of our power; and we know why we opposed the Civil War in the hill country but fought it anyhow because we were Carolinians and Carolina was Carolina. Time and again the old folks and relations have told us during the talk of the night to stand together, to remember what we are, to remember that blood flows thicker than water, that blood will tell, that we are obligated to our kinfolks, that we must amount to something, we must be somebody, we must never bring disgrace upon the kinfolks. Time and again they have told us we are obligated, we have our duty, we must be willing to fight against whatever it is that threatens. We have been told to ask about everything: Will it leave us free?

We are like kites in the hills of Carolina, like ships riding at anchor—we have our red hills and our cotton fields, our big wooden white houses. Someone is always keeping the home place, someone always is there, and no matter how seldom or unexpectedly we may come in, we know someone will rise to give us our welcome. We can stay for a day, for a week, for a month. We can sit in a corner if we like and read a book, or we can milk the cows or feed the chickens, or shoot squirrels in the oaks along the spring branch. It is a great comfort to a rambling people to know that somewhere there is a permanent home—perhaps it is the most final of the comforts they ever really know. Perhaps that is why one of our favorite hymns is that spiritual: "I got a home in that rock, don't you see?"

We have been since the beginning in our valleys—in the same houses, on the same land. We have driven from the same hilltops to vote for all the presidents—we supported Thomas Jefferson the first time he ran, and from that time on we have voted the straight ticket of the Democratic Party. Some of our lands have never even been divided—they have been passed down from oldest son to oldest son, they have never been wrangled over in the courts. . . .

When we were growing up, our Southern country and all of our older people were still grieving. We had lost the Southern cause . . . Among our own kinfolks our Confederate soldiers could not bear to think that so many of our fine and promising and dear relations had died on the battlefields for nothing more than failure. They could not bear to let the lives of so many of our kinfolks sink into such futility and little use. They could not bear that—so they resurrected all the dead. The Confederates who came home from the war spent the rest of their lifetime telling a generation of Southern children and a generation of Southern grandchildren about the men who had died for the South in the Civil War. They gave those dead young soldiers a new life in a glowing personal legend. I don't suppose there ever was an army that lived on individually as the Confederate army has lived for these last eighty years throughout the South. Today I know a great deal more about my Great-Uncle Joel, who was killed at Fredericksburg, than I know about his namesake, my Uncle Joel—and I knew my Uncle Joel well. My Grandfather Bowen and my Great-Uncle Bob, the one who was shot in the hip at Missionary Ridge—these two veterans sat for years on our wide piazza and told us about the men who had been killed in the battles. We would sit in the warm Southern darkness and the katydids would cry in the oak trees, and the tale would grow and grow. They told us so vividly and in such detail that sometimes I feel I have taken part myself in half the campaigns of the Confederate army.

Like most Southerners, I visit battlefields. Southerners will visit almost any battlefield anywhere, but we are especially fond of the Civil War scenes because we know who fought where and how they did their fighting. Once at Fredericksburg, I heard my Uncle Wade correct a professional guide—a man hired by the government to show visitors about the field. The guide said so and so had happened, my Uncle Wade said he was mistaken. Uncle Wade said: "Uncle Alf said this was the way."

I enjoy walking across battlefields, thinking of other men in other times, facing their trouble. I cannot keep back the tears even now at Chickamauga and at Manassas. I am overwhelmed at Appomattox—I remember how my grandfather said he had felt there, hungry and tired and beaten. How sorry he said he had felt for General Lee. How broken-hearted for the South. . . .

The past that Southerners are forever talking about is not a dead past —it is a chapter from the legend that our kinfolks have told us, it is a living past, living for a reason. The past is a part of the present, it is a comfort, a guide, a lesson. My Grandfather Robertson was captured in 1865 and walked after the war was over from a prison camp on the Hudson River all the way to South Carolina, a hard long journey in those days. He was ragged when he got there. Sixty-two years later, during the depression of 1932, I was working in New York, and I said to myself I need not worry too much if I lost my job—what my grandfather could do in 1865, I could do in 1932. I had the same valley to return to that he had. Both of us had the hills and the fields and home. And when I had to be bombed in England in 1940, I said to myself that I had come to my Gettysburg, and what my grandfather had gone through, I could go through. I feel now about London as my grandfather felt about that town in Pennsylvania—I have fought over every inch of the ground. The past encourages us Southerners at all times of crisis. . . .

Our kinfolks on Pea Ridge are intermarried, webbed and woven like a rug, and in the old days the old folks could recite them all—who begat whom and where, who married the ten boys of Cousin Caline, what happened to the eleven girls of Uncle Forrest. We are interested in our ancestors—they were us in another age, they kept the vineyard, plowed the field, dug the well, and they gave everything to us. For them, the winter is past, the rain is over and gone, but we feel gratitude to them—the teachers of our race. Our divination is theirs and whatever of enchantment is about us came from James Robertson and Aunt Mollie Boone and our Great-great-great-Aunt Narcissa. . . .

We are interested in our kinfolks as kinfolks—in them as persons to whom all of us, present and past, are obligated; but we are further interested in them because being closer to them than to other persons, with less hidden, we had a finer chance to understand them as special personalities—to realize what particularities and peculiarities they possess which make them individual, to sense the inner gifts and freaks which separate them from all the rest of us, and even from their own brothers. We know their transgressions, the iniquity and secret goodness hid within their bosoms, of the thistles and the wheat, and of the cockles in the barley.

In the South, being personal in religion, in our way of living in the cotton fields, in our general attitude toward almost everything, we are endlessly fascinated by man's personality. We are interested in a man's difference; it is the variation that attracts us more than the type, for it is the variation that has a separate characteristic. We value the individuality of all life—the chance and the strangeness in everything, the mystery, the wonder, the infinity of life's mutations. . . .

We like the eccentric, the unusual, the vivid person with the live phrase —a man who tells us he has been squirming in hot ashes, a woman who says her hands look as though she has been digging sweet potatoes, a girl who describes a woman as walking like an old cow on thin ice. We laugh a great deal—perhaps because deep within we are melancholy and brooding and touched with the mystic. We talk—we talk and we talk. . . .

We are absorbed in the loneliness and happiness of men and women, in the degree of their discipline, in their self-control. The reason people live, we think, is to attempt to find happiness and to try to save their souls. . . .

We sit on our piazzas and talk about men fighting and about dusting boll weevils and about trying to grow a crop of cotton. We talk about the pigs getting loose and the cows going dry and about "the goldness of the teeth relieving the plainness of the face" and about the universe as spirit and about eternity and our certainty of there being no beginning and no end, of our being now in eternity. We talk about the will of God and about trying to be honest and simple and sometimes we try to imagine the non-end of time, to conceive a trillion years and a trillion trillion. Sometimes we talk for hours about ourselves. We will spend whole Sunday afternoons on our front piazzas talking about the kinks of the kinfolks.

There are about a thousand persons in our valley who are counted among our kin. . . . Nature, no doubt, has accentuated the eccentricities in our blood line, and then, being Southerners, we have accentuated them deliberately ourselves. We have never wished to be like everybody else. We have tried all our lives to be ourselves, to be different if the spirit so moved us. . . .

My Great-Aunt Narcissa, a wonderful personality in our valley, always wore the same kind of long flowing dresses—season in and season out, she wore them; she said why should she bother about fashion. If she waited long enough fashion would return to her. She said once every twenty years she was dressed in the height of style. My Great-Aunt Unity never sat down to the dinner table at mealtime. She would walk back and forth, a plate in one hand, a fork in the other. She would talk as she ate and make gestures with the fork, and now and then she would lean over and spear a slice of fried ham or a piece of chicken. My Great-Aunt Frances kept her bedroom locked and let no one into it for more than twenty years. She would go down to the spring at sundown, wash her hands, put on a pair of knitted mittens, and after that would touch nothing until it was time to go to bed. My Grandmother Robertson, a great lady named Artemissa, smoked a pipe for twenty years—she said she had catarrh. And Windy Bill, the colored man, told everyone who came to our house that he had been in the penitentiary. . . .

Once Aunt Tempe shot a man, and we think Uncle Alf did, too—Uncle Alf may have shot two men. It was during the Civil War that Aunt Tempe shot. She was by herself in the exiled house with her small child when one night she heard someone fumbling at the door. A hand came in and pulled at the wooden latch and Aunt Tempe fired away with a pistol. When it was light enough to see, there was the finger of a man on the floor. The man we are pretty sure Uncle Alf shot was a scalawag and thoroughly needed shooting. Both Aunt Tempe and Uncle Alf were Baptists and they took their shooting hard and to heart, for the Baptist church is uncompromising and places on every individual the responsibility for himself. Neither of them ever said anything much about his shooting. They were not the sort of people who felt it necessary to make public confessions; they were tough and, as their faith required of them, they dealt with their consciences alone. What we remember about our Aunt Tempe and our Uncle Alf, besides the sorrow of their life, is that when the time came to shoot they shot. We admire that resolution. . . .

During the long Southern summers my sisters and I would stay for weeks at our Grandfather Bowen's house on Wolf Creek, one of the little winding streams that ran cross-country in the Twelve Mile valley. My Great-Grandfather Bowen lived at the top of Wolf Creek, then my

Great-Uncle Reece, then my grandfather, and beyond my grandfather's place was the place of my Great-Uncle Bob. My Grandfather Bowen's house, like all the rest of our houses, had many rooms, for always there were many people to sleep there; and it stood on a hill because we liked the tops of hills for our houses. You were more open to tornadoes on a hilltop than you were in a valley, and lightning was more liable to strike you, but we took those chances. . . .

Our grandfather's house had a high hall that was open at both ends so the west wind could sweep through during the summer, and it had wide piazzas, and the high end chimneys were made of mica-speckled granite and slabs of rocks from our fields, slabs morticed together with red clay and mud. The house had lightning-rods, and there were doorsteps made of solid pieces of granite—it was fine to be a small child in the summertime and to sit on the coolness of those stones. There were conch shells to hold back the hall doors—pink conch shells, the trumpet of the Tritons, and there was a cat-hole in the kitchen door, and in the parlor there was an organ and stereopticon slides and daguerreotypes of dead Confederate soldiers, and furniture upholstered in red and yellow velvet. There was a small cedar-panelled room that always smelt like apples and there were washpans and water buckets on the back piazzas and pegs to hang coats on, and there was a rain barrel—a barrel that my sister and I loved because we could sail paper boats in it without bending over. The kitchen smelt of fresh wood ashes, the cluttered cellar smelt of hams and vinegar and melons that were left there to chill, and the dusty attic was filled with the serene fragrance of many years—with spinning-wheels and old Confederate uniforms and worn-out taffeta dresses and cobwebs and mice. There was a beeswax and cedar smell about our grandfather's house —a smell too of leather. My grandfather had a fine secretary, made and signed by one of our kinfolks—a secretary made from trees cut near Hunters Mill just after the Revolution. There were Waterbury clocks and pictures painted by itinerant Pennsylvanians who wandered through our country, and in the dining-room there was a cupboard and a safe that had panels of tin, decorated with holes driven by a nail. We lived on the piazzas at our grandfather's house during the summertime; in winter we lived in the kitchen.

The house was painted a dazzling white, like all of our houses, and all the high ceilings were blue, the color of the sky. There was space and depth about that house, an atmosphere of repose. That was always what we tried most to create about our houses—a presence of stillness and quiet for we were close to the pioneers in spirit—an outdoor people, farmers who worked all day in the blaze of the open, and the house to us was a resting place. It was the secure place, the shelter. We wanted all of our houses to have the feeling within them of peace—we wanted our country to be peaceful, a haven for everyone in the world who felt oppressed.

There were warm log barns and corncribs and cotton houses in our grandfather's yard and smokehouses and a carriage house and there was a gourd tree for the purple martins, and beehives, and there was a well with an oak bucket. One of the happiest experiences of our lives was to see the stars at night reflected in the depths of that well. We lived in a world of stars on our hilltop at night—with honeysuckle to smell and mimosas, with katydids and crickets for a sort of terrestrial chorus. About us for miles were the splendid darkness and silence—sometimes at night we seemed the only people in existence. At our grandfather's house we had time of our own to find ourselves, time of our own to think. . . .

All of our houses stood in groves of original trees, and all of them had bare sanded yards surrounded by gardens of flowers. We did not care for green grass in our yards, as our country was a Southern country, and white sand to us was more restful and quieter-looking than grass. Besides, there was greenness all about us—the groves were green and so were the cotton fields and the valleys themselves. The white of the sand, shaded by the thick trees, formed an oasis, a solemn thing of contrast. Every Saturday morning, with corn-shuck brooms, we carefully swept the yard.

There was no form at all to our flower gardens. They were never fenced, for somehow there was some quality within us that never went in for a fence. Our gardens were just a mass of myrtles and beautiful roses—the star-of-Holland and the star-of-France, and a yellow rose that bloomed in clusters, and a pink rose that turned pinker and pinker as it opened, one that we called the old-maid's-blush. We had a small blue hollyhock, there were flags and four-o'clocks and bachelor's-buttons and pomegranates and snow-on-the-mountain, and there were high, tossing, silky plumes of pampas grass that gave our gardens a romantic touch. We liked our gardens to look romantic, for we were romantic ourselves—we were a dreaming people, a romantic people because we were lonely, we spent much of our time alone. We lived in a world of our own creation. We planted morning-glory vines and honeysuckles to climb up the porches; and for yard shade, in addition to the original great red and white oaks, we planted mulberries and pecans and mimosa trees that the hummingbirds liked. We swapped flowers with everyone and nearly every time we went visiting we brought back some kind of plant. I don't think we ever bought a flower.

We cared more for fragrance than for color—there was enough natural color around us in South Carolina, in the rich red soil, in the blueness of the lovely mountains, in the wild Southern flowers, in the high south sky. We liked to smell things. So we planted beds of hoarhound and rosemary and lavender and catnip simply because they had such musty sweetness, such rarity in their scent. We also planted trees—it became a hobby, for we had discovered what a satisfaction it can be to watch a tree grow and develop. Sometimes a tree will turn out better than any of a man's children, and a tree will endure—its life will outlast our life. My Grandfather Bowen liked to plant walnut trees and cedars, and one of his rules was "Never cut a cedar." He would not remove a cedar tree from his cotton fields—not even from the land that grew a bale of cotton to an acre. My Great-Aunt Narcissa took a pleasure in planting boxwood hedges, and when she was over seventy years old she set out a hedge of the very slowest-growing variety, a hedge that would take a hundred years to develop. One of my great-grandmothers liked to write about her flowers. She once wrote in violet ink in a flower book: "A garden should connect the solemnity of summer with the cheerfulness of spring, and it should be filled with all kinds of fragile flowers, with seats of cammomile and here and there a peach." You could always tell about the character of our people by our trees and boxwood and by the tangled but ordered flowers that we planted in our gardens.

All of that was a secure world that existed when we were children in our valley. It was hard-working and poor but it was safe. No wonder we, with such a background as that, have not succeeded in the industrial age. We have not chosen to succeed in the mechanical era, in the material universe. It has been our choice to wait. . . .

At our breakfast table we would sit on benches with our stern grandfather at the head of the long table, and we would bow our heads while in one descending breath he would mutter the grace. We had a set blessing that we used in all of our houses: "Lord, make us thankful for these and all Thy blessings." I never heard this invocation varied except once when one of our cousins, who did not care for cowpeas and fatback, bowed his head and said: "Good God, look at this." We had quantities of food on our table; no matter how hard the times were, we always had more than we needed to eat, and even when cotton was down to five cents, there was an air of happiness about our boards. We talked, often all of us at once, and we ate, and somebody stood over us with coffeepots and plates of hot biscuits, and somebody with a long-handled paper brush would shoo flies. Sometimes in the middle of a sentence our grandmother would interrupt her talk to say to one of us: "Wipe your mouth" or "There is something on your foot; go clean it"; and then she would continue her conversation without a pause.

At breakfast we had a big bowl of water-ground hominy grits that had simmered for an hour over a slow fire; we never missed having hominy and we never tired of it, we could eat it and we did eat it, every morning of every year, and we were never able to understand why people in the Middle West, in the corn country, did not eat hominy too. Hominy was such a good food, eaten with butter or with sliced tomatoes or with red gravy, and it was so cheap. We do not know what we would do in the South, white folks or black folks, if there were no hominy grits. We had red gravy in bowls and wide platters filled with thick slices of ham, smoked and cured and fried, and we had fried eggs right from the nests. We had pitcherfuls of rich milk that had been chilled overnight in the spring branch, and we had blackberry jam for the hot biscuits, and preserves made from the little clingstone peaches that grew wild on the terraces in the cotton patches and were sweeter than anything we ever cultivated in the orchards. We liked everything that was wild.

At twelve o'clock the bell rang in the back yard, and we sat down to dinner. We washed our faces and hands, combed our hair, and we ate dinner at all of our houses in the middle of the day until one of our cousins came back from Paris and told us company would be coming for lunch. Very often we had company at our houses—always politicians and preachers were dropping in, and there was a steady procession of arriving and departing kinfolks. We did not care who our guests were—Senator Pitchfork Ben Tillman could stay for dinner if he liked, and so could the presiding elder—no one caused us much trouble as all we had to do was kill another chicken. Everything was placed on the table, and we helped ourselves, and ate.

I remember the time one of my aunts tried to make one of our meals more stylish; it was my Aunt Bettie, and she had decided to serve a dinner in courses, for a famous preacher was coming from one of the biggest cities in the South. She got out all the best china and linen and silver, and when we came in, there was no food at all on the table except a little soup. "Where's the dinner?" inquired my Uncle Wade. "Mattie," yelled he to the cook in the kitchen, "bring on the dinner." My Aunt Bettie was so angry that she got up herself and, going to the kitchen door, said in a very quiet and meaningful voice: "Bring on the dinner." Mattie was so mad that she flung dishes of food on the table. My Uncle Wade burst into laughter. "Putting on airs," said he.

At my grandfather's house at noontime we had soup and two or three kinds of meat, fried chicken, fried ham, or spareribs or liver pudding; and we had four or five vegetables and a dessert or so and fruit. We all were fond of fried chicken, but the chicken had to be very young and small—we did not fry old roosters, we fricasseed roosters. We threatened to send to the cotton patch cooks who fried tough chickens. To fry chickens, to boil coffee, to boil rice, and to make good biscuits were the four requirements we demanded of cooks. I don't think I ever had all the fried chicken I could eat until I was twenty-one years of age. I never got enough because I liked the thigh and the gizzard, and half the others also preferred those pieces. We never expected ever even to taste the liver—the older men were served the liver. My Aunt Bettie always declared she liked the back, and my grandmother took the wing, but I did not believe they liked those scrawny pieces of the chicken. They ate those bits because they loved us and did not want to take what we liked best—that was their charity. We liked ducks next to chicken and we sometimes ate a goose or a turkey, but it never occurred to us to eat guinea fowl. We kept guineas at our houses because they were decorative and because we liked the way they cackled. It astonished us once to read in the newspaper that in New York the President of the United States had been served a guinea for dinner. We kept peacocks, too; we were fascinated by their pride.

We were fond of red-pepper sauce, fiery hot, of sage in sausage, of cloves in peach pickles, of nutmegs on clabber; we liked turnip greens, collards, possum and sweet potatoes, roasting ear corn stewed and thickened with flour, cornbread with chitterlings, ambrosia, stuffed eggs, pound cake. We were required to eat something of everything on the table at our grandfather's house, for our grandfather said it was nonsense to pick and choose, to like this and not to like that. He said we would get to like anything if we tried hard enough and kept trying long enough. Eventually I got so I could eat everything under the sun but it did require discipline and persistence to relish parsnips.

When the cooks among our kinfolks did not fry, they boiled. They believed in long cooking over slow fires, and in all of our kitchens the open fireplaces had cranes to swing iron pots from. Beans to be eaten at noon had to be on the fire by eight o'clock in the morning. So did cabbage. My grandmother said cabbage boiled less than four hours would kill you. We boiled beans, potatoes, cabbage, turnip greens, with a chunk of fatback. Our folks have boiled vegetables like that clear across the United States, from South Carolina to Texas, and up the Texas trail right into southern Montana. Either we boil vegetables or we eat them raw—we have never put any stock in the scalding school of vegetable-cooking.

At dinner time we ate until we felt drowsy; then we would say: "Excuse me, please," and would go out and take a nap. . . .

My grandparents never forgot Lee's surrender and the days of starvation in the South, and neither of them ever allowed any of us at their house to waste rations. "You can eat whatever you like and as much as you like," my grandmother told us, "but what you take on your plate you must finish." My grandmother did not mind if we cleaned our plates with a piece of biscuit. "Don't be dainty," was her motto.

Supper with us was simple. We sat down to it at dusk, tired out from the long greatness of the summer day, and often all we would have would be milk, cool from the springhouse buckets; cornbread, sliced thin and almost sizzling hot; soft salted fresh butter; and sorghum molasses. Soon after supper we washed our feet and went to bed. We believed we slept better if at our last meal we had eaten but little. We did not bother really about sleep, but if for any reason we should lie sleepless we did not much care. Most of us by nature were light sleepers, and we often enjoyed lying awake for an hour or so at night. Sometimes we would stir about in the darkness—in the stillness and coolness we would go to the well for a drink, or we would write down something we had thought of. Mary, the colored woman, says there are times when she sips black coffee at night, deliberately to stay awake. "It is very watchful to lie sleepless through the dead still hours of midnight," Mary often declares. "You will hear many little things, both within and without. Everybody ought to try it." . . .

Our stern Grandfather Bowen was a Southern gentleman, a leader in South Carolina, and he worked in the fields all his life along with the rest of the hands. On week-days except Saturdays he wore linsey-woolsey breeches and a loose blue shirt, open at the neck, and from sunrise to sundown, except for the hour of his nap, he would plow and hoe cotton, pull fodder, thin corn. In the autumn he could pick two hundred pounds of cotton in a day. . . .

Out on the wide quiet piazza, my grandfather always sat in a low straight chair—the chair he turned upside down whenever he took his nap. My grandmother was a lady who liked a rocking-chair; she would sit in a broad hickory rocker and rock. The rest of us would sit on the slabs of granite that composed the front steps. Shortly after dusk, our Great-Uncle Bob would arrive from his house down the creek, and he would drop down on the edge of the porch with one foot on the hard sandy ground. The immense Southern night would descend on us all and then the talk would start—my grandmother would rock, and we would listen, and our grandfather and our Great-Uncle Bob would tell us about the Civil War. We would sit in the tremendous starlight, and sometimes a warm, worn breeze would stir, and we would sit still and listen to the story the two men loved to tell. Thirty years have passed since then, but I can still close my eyes and hear them—hear their Southern voices, hear the katydids in the oak trees, the droning chorus of the crickets; hear a hound dog howling, a lean mourning sound; hear still farther away the lonesome remote rumbling of a train. . . .

Our grandmothers and grandfathers in the South influenced my generation more than all the schools and universities. Sometimes, I think, they had more to do with defining purpose for us than did even our fathers and mothers. They had knowledge and intuition and the power to inspire. And they never gave up, they never lost hope, although to them the land was a land of darkness, as darkness itself, and of the shadow of death, without any order, and where the light was as darkness. . . .

Possum Hunting Days in Georgia

By MacKinley Helm

The Georgia flatwoods were the scene of possum hunts, watermelon feasts, and potillias. There Roland Hayes grew up with the language of the Bible in his ears and the strong hand of his mother to guide him. He remembers the spirituals, the dances, the community festivals, but most of all the dignity of a family whose ancestors had been slaves.

When Father William blew his hunting horn the Flatwoods shivered. Hounds moaned and quivered and strained at their leashes. The huntsmen licked their lips, savoring the roast possum they would be eating come next day's dinner.

Pa's hunting horns were famous in the Flatwoods, the Negro settlement in the north Georgian countryside where I was born. In those days farmers allowed the longhorned cattle to wear the curved horns that Nature gave them, and it was from those bony cores that Pa made horns for the hunt. He shaved them paper-thin, clear through the sheath, with splitting knives and small, well-tempered planes. He polished their pearly, opalescent surfaces until they were as smooth and shiny as oak leaves.

With hunting in prospect, perhaps on the night of the new moon after the corn gathering, Pa would take one of his horns down from its peg on the kitchen wall, about ten o'clock of the evening, and shuffle out into the barnyard to call up the neighboring farmers. He had prodigious lung power. When he called hogs down from Horn's Mountain in the autumn, he could be heard all the way to Little Row, the white village three miles up the road; and when he clasped his horn, puffed out his bronzed cheeks, pursed his lips and strained his breath through the mouthpiece, he produced—you can get out of a cow horn only as much as you blow into it—

loud, windy blasts of protracted and full-bodied tone, melodious and powerful and eerie. This was my first remembered music, my introduction to the quality of sound.

My father's colored cronies soon came streaming into the barnyard, some of them afoot, some of them on their ancient nags, all of them with lanterns and torches and tumbling hounds. For a quarter of an hour Pa would din the Mountain with change of key and agitated tremolo, until, with mounting excitement, he had prepared hounds and hunters alike for the fearful adventures of the night.

Pa was part Indian—a good part Indian, according to his own account of himself—and he never cared very much for life on the farm. He loved the wild freedom of wood and stream. He was something of a man of mystery to his children, my father, William Hayes, of God knows exactly where and whence. When my mother met him on the road from Atlanta to Chattanooga, just after the Surrender, he was carrying in his pocket a document which showed him to be a freeman and entitled to passage through the country. He had a notion that he might have been born in Illinois, but it was from Missouri that he went South, in the days of the reconstruction of Atlanta, to find work.

What a wonderful carpenter and craftsman my father was! He owned, during my childhood in the Flatwoods, a fine set of matched and graded tools, which he kept neatly laid out and shining like silver in a nearly immovable hickory chest. He could work magic with those tools.

Pa claimed to be of Cherokee stock, and often boasted that he could read and write his own language. We children, in our time, lacked the means to test Pa's mastery of the Indian tongue, but we loved to hear him speak and sing the guttural syllables which he taught us to associate with Indians. In my mother's ears, however, the forms of speech which he passed off as the language of his fathers sounded suspiciously like pig Indian, and she warned us that Pa was only fooling.

Clearly, father never liked the ten-acre farm where I was born. Nevertheless he was a good worker—under compulsion. When he had to, he could straddle row upon row of young cotton plants, between daylight and dark, and chop the soil with his hoe in a frenzy of sustained, if impatient, performance. After a day of such passionate labor he felt, I suppose, the need of a durable rest, and the next morning he would find himself a comfortable place in the shade.

Pa taught us children to plow behind an ox named Ned, who wore a bell of a size and bigness of tone which our small farm never quite seemed to require for purely locative reasons. I early suspected my mother of having fixed that bell to Ned's collar so that she might be assured of the continuity of his employment.

One hot midsummer day, when Pa had been put to work with the ox in the cornfield, Ned's bell began sounding out an unusual rhythm. Ma, who ever kept both ear and eye upon the problems of our straitened domestic economy, sharply reminded Pa, across the width of field, of the absolute indispensability of his patriarchal occupation. Presently the bell jingled again with obedient regularity. Ma, thinking to reward Pa with a mollifying dipper of cool water from the spring, went out to him in the heat of the afternoon. She found him taking his ease under a shady tree. There he sat, smoking his pipe and contriving, with a rhythmical motion of his wrist, to produce from a tethered cowbell a convincing imitation of Ned at work.

Years later, in 1926, when I visited Joseph Mann, who had inherited my mother from his father not long before the Liberation, I was reminded of that occasion.

"Roland," said Mr. Mann, "are you that boy of Pony's that got caught settin' down on a plow and ringin' a cowbell?" The story had been told all over the Flatwoods, but it was really Pa, and not I, that got caught.

The forests, not the fields, furnished my father with his substantial contribution to our daily bread. If he liked better to eat than to feed my mother's chickens, he was the man to keep the crafty red fox from the coop. If he had no head for figuring and accounts, he could guess within a few ounces the weight of a treed possum by noting the size of the tree the hounds bayed under: the smaller the tree, the bigger the possum; and he would know at once whether to shake him or beat him down. At break of many a day in the fall of the year he would appear from the hunt with meat to eat and skins to be traded for salt and flour from the outside world.

What with the meat Pa fetched from the hills, to supplement Ma's careful husbandry of the produce of the farm, I do not remember that we children—I had six brothers and sisters—ever went hungry. A few steps from the kitchen door stood a smokehouse, with a pit for curing hams and flitches of bacon and sausages. We stuck our hogs just before Christmas, and through the long month of January we tended a hickory fire whose smoke filled the aromatic chamber where the meat was hung, done up in muslin and wired to the rafters. I cannot remember a season, while my father lived, when there was not a piece of smoked meat to flavor our food—the string beans and fresh corn that we ate in summer, and the rice and potatoes of our scantier winter diet.

A small spring bubbled up from the earthen floor of the smokehouse, providing cold storage for milk and butter and eggs during the hot midsummer weather, when out-of-doors the fierce sun parched our dusty fields; and in a murky corner a twenty-gallon keg of sorghum mounted a pair of concave wooden horses. On warm mornings the sorghum flowed freely into a cavernous pitcher, whence it was poured over our cornmeal mush at breakfast, but in the winter only a little core of syrup remained liquid inside a shell of sugar, and it seemed to me, when Ma sent me out into the chilly darkness of the early morning, that it took forever, drop by drop, simply to sweeten the bottom of the jug.

In my childhood I admired my father's wonderful gift for making music. I believed there was no sound in nature that he could not imitate. His voice brought deer, bear, and partridge within range of his gun. He taught me to identify the songs of birds, himself repeating and answering their melodies, over and over again. I learned to distinguish between "true songs," which the male birds sing when they are establishing their private territorial rights in the spring, and the less highly specialized "recordings," as the songs of lonely females and the wintry choruses of gregarious males are indiscriminately called. At the risk of offending my mother, and sometimes at the cost of being whacked with her whip, I used to stop work in the fields to listen to meadow larks, orchard orioles, and summer tanagers—fancying, in the sympathetic way I learned from my father, that I was a bird addressed by my companions in the trees, and birdlike answering them. . . .

I loved to share my father's secret life in the woods. After a possum hunt I had frequently to carry the victim over my shoulder, and when the angry captive, suspended by his naked, prehensile tail from a split poplar sapling, gave over his natural habit of playing possum long enough to snap at my legs, I was too frightened to hang on to my burden. Old Kirby used to take pity on me and try to teach me to be brave.

"We're all hunters here," he would say. "Hunters ain't skeered, hunters can carry their catch safe home all right."

In the late summer a nocturnal hunt usually came to an end in a watermelon patch. Towards two o'clock in the morning the men would build a bright fire—say on the edge of the big Kemp meadow. They would search the vines for ripe, frosty melons—an experienced thumb and middle finger can detect the sound of honeyed sweetness in the dark

—and then, having called all hands and all hounds, they would sit down to gorge themselves until they fell asleep. At daybreak my father would carry me, the carrier, home, still full as a tick of watermelon flesh.

There are said to be twenty kinds of native trees in our old hunting country, including eight varieties of oak, and I am confident Pa knew them all. Certainly he knew the shape of every piece of timber growing on Horn's Mountain, and estimated accurately the best uses each could be put to. He made splits for chair bottoms from the smooth-grained white oak; sound beds and comfortable rocking chairs of maple; straight-backed seats and sturdy benches of impervious hickory. He had built and furnished with his own hands the cabin I was born in some twenty years after the War Between the States.

It was only a log cabin of two rooms that he had built, at the foot of Horn's Mountain, near the town of Curryville (it was called Little Row in my childhood); but it had certain marks of distinction in comparison with even ruder houses in the neighborhood. There were two chimneys made of stone pulled out of the Mountain, and the timbers of which the walls were built were stopped not with red clay, according to local fashion, but with yellow, after my father's whim. He had discovered a small mound of it in a near-by field.

The fireside in the front room was the center of our family life. Opposite the chimney, in the other end of the room, Pa and Ma and Jesse, my youngest brother, slept together in a big maple bed. Pa's rifle, which hung over the bed, caught the firelight at night and brought the far, dark wall to life. I remember how the bursting lights used to glance upon a circle of Victorian picture frames which encased some family photographs. They were gifts, no doubt, of white people my mother worked for when Pa was doctoring in Chattanooga. They were, of course, absurdly inappropriate, but they introduced a note of elegance of which we children were inordinately proud.

On winter nights Pa told stories in front of the fire for the benefit of the whole family. He was a great raconteur; he could make us laugh or cry and cause our crinkly hair to stand on end. One night he came in from the lane, pallid under his bronze skin, and told us that a headless man had followed him all the way home from the neighborhood of Mt. Zion Church.

"I done shot at dat critter," he said, "and what do you think he done? He blowed up, big as a house, and jumped right up into de sky!"

Perhaps once a year Pa would begin to talk about buried treasure, of which there was supposed to be plenty in the Cherokee country. He would tell us that the Big Chief was coming back pretty soon, to look for gold.

"When he comes," he said, "he will go to dat cone of rocks yonder on de Mountain. When he sees dat cut on de wes' side of ol' white oak, he will know where de gold is buried. He will dig it all up, all right."

And then we knew that in a day or two Pa would disappear. Sometimes he would be gone for weeks. When he came back he would bring us presents, but we never knew where he went.

The hand of Death is never very far removed from the latchstrings of the poor. Only the strong survived the accidents and rigors of our humble Flatwoods life. Still, when sorrow did not press too immediately upon us, we enjoyed our simple sociability. Most of us had too little knowledge of the world to feel that our pleasures were attenuated. Although my mother did not like to have my brothers go to breakdowns, where corn likker and bad girls circulated freely, she was willing to let us enjoy diversions invented by church members. And above all, we learned to make parties of the routine events of our lives.

Occasionally, when I was a boy, I was allowed to watch the dancing at the Garlington house or at the John Tate farm. Will Garlington had been a notorious infidel, and although public opinion had finally obliged him to join the church, he had never quite been able to put the world away. There regularly repaired to his house all the colored people who wanted to make the most of the church and the world simultaneously, a kind of semi-respectable fringe to the more sedate fabric of our Baptist society. Church people could go to those dances without taking part, but frequently they would be moved to give themselves to dancing and rioting. Then they were likely to be reported to the deacons and brought before the elders, who would exhort them to repent. Unrepentant members were turned out of the church forthwith.

Will Garlington blew the quills at the Garlington dances, and Ren, his brother, one of the neighborhood toughs, cracked the bones and called the sets. The elderly intinerant musician, Jim Kerby, who boarded at our house when he was in the Flatwoods,—I called him Uncle Nat,—played the fiddle and beat straws, and Jesse Tate picked the banjo.

Many of the musical instruments and a good deal of the music were of African origin. Quills are joints of bamboo, tied together with string in an arrangement like the pipes of Pan. You blow across the open tubes and produce tones like those of a steam piano or calliope, but mellower.

In Africa a bone-cracker cracks real bones, but in Georgia we used simulacra carved from hickory wood. A good bone-cracker can crack bones with both hands, clacking out the rhythms required for buck-and-wing dancing. I learned to blow quills and my brother Robert beat straws, so that, although we were not often allowed to go to the Garlington house, we could make music of our own when Uncle Nat was stopping with us.

Pete Vaughn, who conducted a seasonal singing-school in the Flatwoods, also used to stay at our house when he came to the village. He taught me to read book music, printed in square notes. That was stylish music, from city hymnbooks. Fortunately, not everybody in our congregation learned to read notes, or our folk songs might have gone unsung.

There were certain community festivals which the whole countryside attended, even the church people. When my mother's brothers, Uncle Wiltsie and Uncle Simon, picked the banjo—it was Uncle Simon who invented a name by which I was called in the family circle, Roland-Come-Mumbling-Come-Tumbling-Come-Paregoric—I was allowed to watch and listen. Even the church members joined in the clapping of hands and the singing, although only unbelievers cut steps and swung their partners.

One of the most popular dance tunes was "Ring Around, Swing and Play," and it went like this:—

Ring all around, Suzanne,
Ring all around, Suzanne,
Swing all around, Suzanne,
Swing all around, Suzanne,
Swing your partners, Suzanne,
Swing all around.

My mother's cousin, Jesse Tate, of the earringed ears and the sensitive hands—he is still cheerful and engaging at eighty—used to spell my Uncle Wiltsie in calling the sets at "potillias," as cotillions were called in our county. A potillia was formed by eight dancers, four men and four women, who cut the steps in sets of three "bars." The music and the laughter, the swaying bodies and the shuffling feet, made your own feet itch if you were a church member and not allowed to dance. . . .

Most of what I know about my ancestors I learned from the man who owned my mother. When I went back to Georgia, in 1926, to buy the farm where Ma had lived in slavery, I found the old gentleman, the last of a great family of planters, in a shanty in Sugar Valley, six or seven miles from the Gordon County plantation which he had inherited from his father. He had been obliged to sell his property many years before, and now he lived in penury with his second wife, a nearly lifeless invalid.

The Big House where my mother worked was not distinguished for the colonial simplicity of the manor houses built in the days of the Georges, but in my eyes, when I was a boy, it had seemed a palace. It was a commodious, two-storied structure, with wide chimneys at either end; and across the full front of it there stretched a veranda with a roof supported by six columns. The bedrooms gave upon a canopied balcony with an elaborately embroidered railing, its lacy scrollwork the epitome of Victorian elegance. And no slave quarters on the farm had been, on the contrary, so mean as the cabin to which the last of the Manns had been finally reduced.

Joe Mann came out into his unkempt yard to talk to me. He spoke of Pony, my mother, his first wife's favorite slave.

"You come of a great family for singin'," he said. "Do you remember that song your great-granddaddy made up? It was a song that went, 'He never said a mumberlin' word.' "

I told him I had sung that spiritual about the Crucifixion in most of the capitals of Europe, and begged him to search his memory for other recollections of my great-grandfather Charles.

Joe Mann remembered a good deal. Charles was called something like Abá 'Ougi out in Africa, where he had been a highborn chief. He was ambushed on the Ivory Coast, transported to Savannah, and auctioned off to a family called Weaver. That was along about 1790. It was the Weavers who gave my great-grandfather the Christian name of Charles and wrote out his pedigree. Then, Mr. Joe Mann reckoned, they put him to stud like a stallion.

Charles was a powerful fellow. Joe Mann said it must have taken ten men to capture him. Aboard the slaving ship, crossing the Atlantic, he lay in chains in a solitary cell. At dock in Savannah, after the other captives were driven from the ship like cattle, he strode down the gangplank alone. He was of such superior bearing, so handsome and so strong, that many plantation owners bid for his possession. The Weavers had to pay high for him.

My great-grandfather gave himself to ordered tasks on the Weaver plantation near Jonesboro, in Georgia, and it was not long before he became an overseer. It seems clear to me that he did not try to incite rebellion amongst his fellow slaves, but he did counsel them to prepare themselves against the day when God should give them their freedom. He appointed secret meeting-places in ravines and marshes. In the morning of the day of congregation he sowed the word across the fields. "Steal away," he would whisper to his neighbor, and the phrase was passed from mouth to mouth through all the plantations in the neighborhood. At length the ritual words were set to music and a new spiritual was born.

Plantation owners were reluctant to allow their slaves to attend camp meeting. They were afraid the Northern missionaries who came down to Georgia to evangelize the slaves would instruct them in the heresy of freedom. But the Negroes were determined to hear the comfortable words of Jesus and went secretly at night to sit at the feet of the Christian teachers.

My great-grandfather continued to improvise musical signals to announce the return of the preachers. On a windy morning he would sing:—

Green trees a-bendin',
Poor sinner stands a-tremblin',
A trumpet sounds within-a my soul,
I ain't got long to stay here.

Or if the meeting were prefaced by an electric storm, he sang:—

My Lordy calls me,
He calls me by the thunder,
A trumpet sounds within-a my soul,
I ain't got long to stay here.

The song by which my great-granddaddy is remembered to this day, in the South, was his personal version of the story of Jesus and the Cross, a tragedy which had moved him because he, too, was a man of sorrows.

"Wasn't it a pity an' a shame," the spiritual begins.

Wasn't it a pity an' a shame,
An' He never said a mumberlin' word,
Wasn't it a pity an' a shame,
An' He never said a mumberlin' word, oh,
Not a word, not a word, not a word!
Dey nailed Him to the tree,
An' He never said a mumberlin' word,
Dey nailed Him to the tree,
An' He never said a mumberlin' word, oh,
Not a word, not a word, not a word!

Dey pierced Him in the side,
In-a the side, in-a the side,
Dey pierced Him in the side,
In-a the side, in-a the side,
De blood came a-twinkalin' down
An' He never said a mumberlin' word,
The blood came a-twinkalin' down
An' He never said a mumberlin' word, oh,
Not a word, not a word, not a word!

He bowed His head an' died
An' He never said a mumberlin' word,
He bowed His head an' died
An' He never said a mumberlin' word, oh,
Not a word, not a word, not a word!

We had neither prayerbook nor hymnal in the Mt. Zion Church. Printed books were too dear. We had a kind of local ritual, however, subject to variation at the hands of itinerant preachers and revivalists who visited us. Service always began, for example, with a hymn which the deacon lined out, two verses at a time:—

Amazing grace, how sweet the sound
That saved a wretch like me.

When we had sung so far, he would line out another pair:—

I once was lost, but now I'm found,
Was blind, but now I see.

With what a joyous burst of song we repeated these evangelical stanzas, set to tunes that everybody knew! Prayers and Scripture reading led at length up to the dramatic climax of the meeting, the pastor's sermon. . . .

We children grew up with the language of the Bible ever in our ears. In church it struck me that the Scriptural words were often warm and comfortable. At home we were more likely to hear the hard sayings of Jesus and the Prophets. In later years my mother used to repeat Jesus' words of consolation, like "Come unto me, all ye that labour and are heavy laden, and I will give you rest." But when we were children, she was more likely to instruct us in harder doctrine. She was unwilling to take chances with our immortal souls.

I am sure that my mother appreciated my father's skillful carpentry and his genius as a cabinetmaker, and that she was grateful for all the food he made the forest yield. But it was a mortification to her that he was not also a good farmer and a man of God. The truth is that Pa, although he became a member of the Baptist Church, cared no more for churchgoing than he did for farming. It was probably because Ma was a pillar of the church that Pa was never excommunicated.

My Uncle Bill Mann was read out of the society of believers by reason of his habitual non-attendance at worship, and Uncle Bill most generally non-attended church with my father. When, as frequently happened, he dropped by to visit Pa on the way to church, more often than not he sent my Aunt Maria to hear the Gospel story in Ma's company, while he stopped on to listen to Pa's accounts of less supernatural wonders.

Under the hickory tree, where on week days Pa rived white oak saplings and wove splits into baskets for the cotton pickers—or in front of a roaring fire on a wintry Sabbath—he sat to the tonsorial ministrations of my brother Robert, whose weekly duty it was to plait Pa's long, straight hair. This ritual inevitably recalled to Pa's mind the days when he had lived the tribal life of the Cherokees, and fiercely entertaining were his recollections (or were they fictions?) of that time.

My mother was a small, slight woman, with a beautiful, erect carriage which hard work never bent. She was scarcely more than five feet tall, and she moved rapidly about on her small feet, quick and sprightly as a bird. Her facial structure was both delicate and strong, and you could see from her sharp, keen eyes that she was able to penetrate a situation in an instant. Her skin was as smooth as an olive.

On weekdays she wore plain ginghams and printed calicos, which she herself made up on lines which were perhaps more practical than fashionable. Her "common-sense" shoes, laced tightly to support her ankles, reached up to the hem of her skirt. On Sundays she dressed like an immaculate deaconess in a good black calico frock, over which she wore a starched white apron. A white ruffled bonnet and high buttoned shoes of soft kid completed the dominical costume. I was proud of her when we went to church together.

When we were children, Mother sometimes seemed cold and hard. She was never unkind, she was never unjust. She simply was thoroughly persuaded of the difference between right and wrong, and she steadfastly refused to relax her moral judgments. My older brothers, if they found her discipline unbearable, took to running away from home. It was hard for us to understand why Ma, who was so jolly when there was no wrong in sight, should be so much more severe with her own children than she was with outsiders.

I remember seeing my mother cry only once, and that was when my sister Mattie, her only daughter, died; and to me, who grew steadily more and more dependent upon the solid rock of her character, she was soft and warm only once. The last time I saw her she broke through her devout reserve for a single moment, after more than fifteen years of resistance to my vocation, and said, "Son, you are the continuation of me."

Pa was hurt in a logging operation on Horn's Mountain, so grievously that his body could not be mended. It was pitiful to watch the dissolution of that strong man. I remember that his body was swollen and that he suffered horribly. He would crawl to the side of his bed and clasp the bedposts, the veins standing out from his powerful hands and wrists. Sometimes he would ask me to scratch his head with a comb, and then he would relax and grow drowsy and fall asleep. When he woke up he would tell me a story.

For many days Pa was nearly helpless. He could not lie quietly and he could not get up out of his bed. Then, not long before he died, he seemed to recover a little. He made deliveries of chairs and baskets which he had made before he was injured, carrying them out of the yard on his lame, aching back, and coming home exhausted. Mother Fannie, worn with tending him and us children and our unyielding farm, put him back to bed.

Pa died in my mother's arms. Stilled utterly, the fine, lusty voice that people stopped to listen to when he called hogs down from the Mountain; cold and quiet in death the nimble fingers that had been quick and skillful to furnish a house for his family; mercifully abated the terrifying pain; and ready for its rest the racked body.

I walked with my mother up the lane to Mt. Zion Church, behind my father's coffin, and I heard her voice ring out clearly, even exultantly, when she joined the mourners' chorus in that triumphant song of faith, "Roun' about de Mountain."

A Plantation Christmas

By Archibald Rutledge

Nowhere is Christmas more romantic than in the plantation South. Every Southerner remembers the joyous cry of "Chris'mas Gif'," and Negro spirituals, but not every American has heard firecrackers at Christmas, or seen a holly tree in the great ballroom of a plantation house. Christmas is a green time on the plantation, a time for frolic and deer hunts.

When to the mystical glamour that naturally belongs to the Christmas season one can add the romance that belongs to the South—especially the old-time South—nothing short of enchantment is the result. I do not think that even in the England of Cavalier days was Christmas more picturesquely celebrated than it is today on those great plantations of the South which have managed to preserve the integrity of their beauty and their charm. . . .

At home I have never seen snow at Christmastime. True, it sometimes falls there, but never seriously. Instead, we have a green Christmas, made so by the prevalence of pine, holly, myrtle, sweet bay and smilax that over the top of many a tree weaves emerald crowns. Always, when I go home for Christmas (and this has been an unbroken habit for twenty-five years), what first impresses me is the freshness of the forest—the apparent livingness of the trees, the vernal balminess of the air. And next to the green of the woods, what heartens me most is the singing of the birds. A plantation Christmas is one of wildwood fragrances and wildwood lyrics, as well as one of roaring open fires and festive boards and ancient carols, consecrated as only the centuries can hallow.

I remember getting a Christmas tree that may be considered typical of the plantation variety. A Negro and I hitched an ox to a cart. In the spirit of the occasion the ox apparently did not share. His aspect was lowering, and motions were physically mournful. Nevertheless, he took us into the plantation pine forest, where dulcet odors were abroad, where the huge pines were choiring dimly, where the mellow sunshine was steeping the coverts in the mute rapture of deep-hearted peace. It was "holly year" that year—that is, the crop of holly berries was unusually good. Under a shadowy canopy of live oaks we came to a holly tree some thirty feet high, heavy-foliaged, perfect in symmetry, cone-shaped, and ruddily agleam with berries. Its clean bole shone like silver. Out of this tree we flushed a horde of robins that had been feasting on the berries. The scarlet birds were not frightened. Many of them, alighting on the immense limbs of the oaks, at once broke into trills of delicate song, of the sort that we hear in the North in early-April twilights.

We cut our Christmas tree and the ox bore it homeward for us. In the old ballroom of the house—a room that, running up two stories, has a prodigious height of ceiling—we set it, directly in front of the vast fireplace, which will accommodate logs seven feet long. There stood the regal tree, all jade and silver and scarlet, dewy and tremulous. It needed no decorations. We didn't have to make a Christmas tree—we just brought one in. I felt sorry to have cut so lovely a thing, but Christmas deserves such a tribute. For decorations of a minor sort we used the red partridge berry, mistletoe, smilax, cedar, pine. He who cares to investigate the druidical history of the mistletoe will discover that it is a symbol of the plighting of love's troth. As such, nothing could be more appropriate at this festival of joy and human affection.

In the South, as perhaps is the case nowhere else in the world, there are many superstitions associated with Christmas. No doubt this fact is due to the Negroes, without whom no plantation can be exactly natural or picturesque. One of their superstitions, which amounts to a genuine belief, is that "Christmas *falls*." Possibly long ago some slave heard his master say, "Christmas falls on Friday this year." But whatever the origin of the expression, plantation Negroes firmly believe that the coming of this great day is heralded by some mighty convulsion of Nature. This belief really has an august source; for we find it in Milton. He describes with what tumult and dismay the powers of darkness fled at the birth of Christ.

On the plantation I used, as a boy, to sit up until midnight on Christmas Eve to hear Christmas "fall." It always fell, somehow or other. True, I never heard it; but the faithful always did. Ears that are attuned to hear something supernatural usually hear it. My hearing was too gross; but I used to be immensely impressed by the spiritual advancement of those of my dusky comrades who declared that they distinctly heard the mystic far-off detonation.

Another superstition that I also used firmly to believe—and it has a poetic beauty that the other lacks—is that on the stroke of twelve on Christmas Eve every living thing of the bird and animal world goes down on its knees in adoration of the newborn Master. Convinced that what the Negores were telling me was true, and not a little impressed by the grandeur of the phenomenon as it was described, I went one Christmas Eve to the stable yard, and there sat drowsily with my Negro comrade Prince, while the stars blazed, and the pines grieved, and the distant surf roared softly on the sea-island beaches. As midnight approached we became restless, and our nervousness was communicated to the various creatures in the ample old barnyard. The roosters crowed with uncommon vigor and assurance, the hogs grunted with unwonted enthusiasm, and the sheep bleated with strange pathos. After a time, clearly in the moonlight we saw an old ox heave himself for a rise. For a moment he assumed a most singular position: his hind quarters were up, but his head was quite low—he was actually kneeling. Prince pointed him out in awed triumph. Nor did I raise any question. . . .

Yes, on a plantation, Christmas *falls*; and likewise, every living thing goes down on its knees in the dust before its Maker.

Awaking one Christmas morning, I remember what a pleasure I experienced from hearing, just outside the window, a Carolina wren caroling like mad. Of course, this bird is not a great singer, but for sheer joyousness and abandonment to gladness I do not know his equal. His ringing call, without a trace of wariness or doubt, carries farther than the note of any other bird of the same size. I have heard it full three hundred yards across a river. Now I heard it coming through my window, the curtains of which were gently stirred by a faint breeze out of the aromatic pinelands. Climbing a pillar under my window was a yellow jasmine vine, and in a festive mood to suit the season it had put forth a few delicious blossoms—golden bells to ring for Christmas, saffron trumpets to sound the Day's welcome. Beyond the window I could see the mighty live oaks, with their pendulous streamers of moss, waving gently like my white curtains; then the imperial pines, towering momentously. Christmas morning, with birds and sunshine and scented sea winds! Going to the window, I looked out. All the dim sweet plantation was steeped in faërie light. The far reaches of bowed and brown cotton field; the golden broom sedge fringing the fields; the misty river rolling softly; the sleeping trees, jeweled with dew; the uncertain pearly sky—all these had a magical look. A silvery silence held the world divinely, in virginal beauty.

But soon the stillness was broken, and by no gentle sound. It did not surprise me, but not many Americans other than plantation dwellers would have expected it. Firecrackers! "What is home without a mother?" queries the old saw. Why, it's like Christmas to the plantation pickaninnies without firecrackers! The Puritan Christmas of New England has something exceedingly snowy and austere about it. In the South it is a day for frolic—at least, on the plantation it is not associated in any way with church services. Nor do I think it less a genuine festival of the hearth and the home because all the little Negroes shoot fireworks, all the plantation belles hang mistletoe (and strangely linger near it), and all the plantation men go deer hunting.

The Negroes do not stay long in the colored settlement, but they repair to the Great House, thronging gleefully across the fields, shouting and singing and exercising that extraordinary power for social affability among themselves that *is* truly a racial characteristic. . . .

Before breakfast we distribute to the Negroes whatever we have for them in the way of Christmas cheer. . . . Then the family gathers for breakfast. I love to think of it; the ample room from the walls of which gaze down faded portraits of the plantation owners of an earlier generation; there gaze down, too, a whole fringe of deer horns, festooned with Spanish moss. A plantation home without its collection of staghorns is hardly to be found; and in passing I may say that some of the collections, dating back almost to the time of the Revolution, are of remarkable interest. I know of one such collection that contains upward of a thousand racks of the whitetail, every one having been taken on that particular plantation. In some families, there is a custom, rigorously adhered to, that no deer horns must ever leave the place; so that the horns of every buck killed find their way into the home's collection. Such a frieze in a dining room seems to fill the place with woodland memories, and serves in its own way to recall the hunts and the hunters and the hunted of long ago. Here on the same wall hang the portrait of a famous sportsman and the antlers of many a stag he took in the old days. Gone now are they all. We have only the dim picture and the ancient antlers.

Christmas breakfast on the plantation makes one think of a wedding breakfast. The table is gay with sprigs of holly, with graceful ropes of smilax. A huge bunch of mistletoe, large enough to warrant the most ardent kissings of whole communities, stands upright in the center of the table, its pale, cold berries mysteriously agleam. Then Martha and Sue bring in the breakfast—wholesome, smiling Negroes they are, devoted to the family, and endeared to it by nearly fifty years of continuous, loving service. Here the breakfaster may regale himself on plantation fare: snowy hominy, cold wild turkey, brown crumbly corn breads, venison sausages, beaten biscuits, steaming coffee, homemade orange marmalade. Unless my observation be at fault, the making of coffee on a plantation is a solemn rite not to be trusted to anyone save the mistress of the house. She loves to make it herself before the ruddy fire in the dining room, its intriguing aroma mingling with the fresh fragrances from the greenery hung about the walls. She loves to carry coffee making to the point of a fine art, and to serve it out of a massive silver coffeepot—the same used when a gentleman named General George Washington visited this home during his Southern tour in those last years of the eighteenth century.

While we are at breakfast, we have evidence that the day is not to be spent in langourous and ignoble ease, for from the yard we can hear the Negro huntsmen tuning up their hunting horns; and in response to the faint mellow blasts we hear the joyous yowling of staghounds. Some of these come to the dining-room door, and there stand, ranged in the order of their temerity, fixing us with melancholy great eyes—more eager, I really think, to have us finish our repast and join them in the woods than envious of us for our festive feast.

On the plantations that I know deer hunting on Christmas Day is as natural as a Christmas tree, or kissing one's sweetheart under the mistletoe.

After breakfast, we gather on the plantation porch, and I smell the yellow jasmine that is tossing her saffron showers up the tall white columns. In the flower garden two red roses are blooming. In the wild orange trees beside the house myriads of robins, cedar waxwings, and a few wood thrushes are having their Christmas breakfast. A hale, dewy wind breathes from the mighty pine forest. The whole landscape, though bathed in sunshine, is still fresh with the beauty of the morning. Now the Negro hunters come round the side of the house, leading our horses, and followed by a pack of hounds. A rather motley crew they are, I think, for few plantations can boast of full-blooded staghounds; but they know their business. What they lack in appearance they supply in sagacity.

There is, I suppose, no grander sport in the whole world than riding to hounds after deer; and this is a sport typical of a plantation Christmas. It is almost a religious rite, and it never fails to supply the most thrilling entertainment for visitors. Indeed, I do not know exactly what the rural South would do without deer hunting as a diversion. Even in the cities, when distinguished guests arrive, the primary entertainment always provided is a stag hunt. . . .

Soon we are astride our mounts, turning them down the live-oak avenue toward the deep pinelands. As we ride down the sandy road, we are on the lookout for deer tracks; and these are seen crossing and recrossing the damp road. The Negro hunters who have charge of the pack have to use all their powers of elocution to persuade the hounds not to make a break after certain hot trails. The horses seem to know and to enjoy this sport as well as the men and the dogs do. No horse can be started more quickly or stopped more abruptly than one trained to hunt in the woods.

We start a stag in the Crippled Oak Drive, and for miles we race him: now straight through the glimmering pinelands, sun-dappled and still; now through the eerie fringes of the "Ocean," an inviolate sanctuary, made so by the riotous tangle of greenery; now he heads for the river, and we race down the broad road to cut him off—down the very same stretch of road that in Revolutionary days the planters of the neighborhood used as a race-track. There is a stretch of three miles, perfectly straight and level, broad and lying a little high. Down this we course. But the crafty buck doubles and heads northward for the sparkleberry thickets of the plantation. I race forward to a certain stand, and just as I get there, he almost jumps over me! The dogs are far behind; and the stag gives the appearance of enjoying the race. Away he sails, his stiffly erect, snowy tail flashing high above the bay bushes. I await the arrival of the dogs, and soon they come clamoring along. I slip from my horse and lead him into the bushes. I love to watch running hounds when they do not observe me. They always run with more native zest and sagacity when they are going it alone. A rather common dog, of a highly doubtful lineage, is in the lead. The aristocrats come last. I am always amused over the manner in which full-blooded hounds perform the rite of trailing. This business is a religion with them. They do not bark, or do anything else so banal and bourgeois; they make deep-chested music, often pausing in the heat of a great race to throw their heads heavenward and vent toward the sky perfect music. Their running is never pell-mell. A good hound is a curious combination of the powers of genius: he is Sherlock Holmes in that he works out infallibly the mazy trail; he is Lord Chesterfield in that he does all things in a manner becoming a gentleman; and he is a grand opera star, full of amazing music. I get a never-failing thrill out of listening to hounds and out of watching them at close hand. To me it appears that the music they make depends much upon their environment for its timbre. And as they course over hills and dip into hollows, as they ramble through bosky watercourses or trail down roads, as the leafy canopies over them deepen or thin, their chorus hushes and swells, affording all the "notes with many a winding bout" that make the best melody offers.

Our stalwart buck makes almost a complete circle, outwits us, enters the mysterious depths of the "Ocean," and is lost. But perhaps—at any rate, on Christmas Day—for us to lose his life is better than for him to lose it. Yet his escape by no means ends our sport. We start two stags next, and they lead us a mad race toward Wambaw Creek. I catch a far-off glimpse of white tails and glinting horns. We horsemen, taking our lives in our hands, essay to race the two bucks to the water. We manage to overtake the hounds but not the deer. Indeed, after almost a lifetime of following deer, I may truthfully say that I have seldom, in our country, seen deer in distress before hounds. Unless wounded, or unless very fat (as they are in September), or unless cornered against wire, deer play before dogs. They pretend that they are going to run spectacularly; but after a show of gorgeous jumping and running, they skulk in deep thickets, dodge craftily, cross water, and in other ways rest themselves and baffle their pursuers. When the hounds do approach them again, the deer are as fresh as ever.

After a few more chases, we return to the plantation house; and if there is a sport that whets the appetite more keenly than deer hunting, I do not know it. To the ancient home we return, to the patriarch live oaks watching before it, to the red roses, to the yellow jasmine; and within to the ruddy fires, the rooms festooned with fragrant greenery. As we enter the dining room almost everyone begins to smile in a most understanding fashion; for on either side of the huge bunch of mistletoe in the center of the table are two decanters—and they are full!

I remember what an old Negro said to my father when he was describing to the old servitor a certain kind of liquor. The Negro, in such matters, had an almost painful imagination. This description was just a little more than he could stand. "Oh, please, boss," he said, "don't tell me about that if you don't have none along with you." His was a sentiment with which I can heartily sympathize. I hate, for example, to describe a plantation Christmas dinner if I cannot offer my readers the dinner itself. And yet I cannot think of it without recalling the snowy pyramids of rice, the brown sweet potatoes with the sugar oozing out of their jackets, the roasted rice-fed mallards, the wild turkey, the venison, the tenderloin of pork fattened on live-oak acorns, the pilau, the cardinal pudding!

And this is a dinner by candlelight, even though the daylight lingers outside. Twilight falls as we come to the nuts and raisins. Then we form a great semicircle before the fire, and we rehunt the chases of that day, and of many of the long ago. One or two of the older hounds have the privilege of the dining room, and their presence on the firelit rug adds reality to our stories. I often think that, had they the power of speech, what they could tell us would be well worth the hearing.

It is late ere our stories are ended. It has been a glorious day. I wander out now on the front porch. The risen moon is casting a silvery glamour over the world. Certain great stars blaze in the velvet void of heaven. Far off I can hear the Negroes singing their spirituals of Christmas—the sweetest melody, I think, of which the human voice is capable. The live oaks shimmer softly in the moonshine. I hear flights of wild ducks speeding overhead, hastening toward their feeding grounds far down the river. The magic of the night is abroad; now, I know, the deer are coming out of their coverts delicately to roam the dim country of the darkness. Over the old plantation the serenity of joyous peace descends—the peace of human hearts at Christmastime. Beauty and love and home—these are of peace, these make that peace on earth that Christmas in the heart alone can bring.

Kentucky Derby Day

By Irvin S. Cobb

Kentucky's favorite son contends that Derby Day is the Southern classic of them all. Everybody comes—from the city, from the backwoods, from the nation. Whether it is to see Man O' War or Citation or Nashua, the excitement is the same. The mint juleps flow, the girls wear their prettiest dresses, and Louisville holds the national spotlight.

Naturally I may be prejudiced, being myself a native son—I'd be a poor sort of native son if I were not—but I risk the assertion that nowhere is there produced so colorable a picture of what the Old South must have been as Derby Day is. It is customary for the sport-writers to refer to the Derby as a classic; no self-respecting sport-writer, in describing the race, would fail to do this. He uses the word in the sporting sense, to describe the annual renewal of a long-established racing event. But by another meaning it surely is a classic, too, for it re-creates and revives, on one day of the year, a simulation of a phase of life which elsewhere practically has vanished already or else is very fast vanishing.

Ghosts walk Churchill Downs on Derby Day. To the old-timer the whole place—paddock, field and track—is crowded with memories. Spirits are there of old dead and gone brigadiers to whom the thoroughbred was the noblest thing that went on four legs; spirits of old trainers, old judges, old owners, old gamesters of the South; spirits, too, of bygone Derby winners forgotten now by the present generations, and remembered only where a dainty racing shoe tarnishes above the sagging mantelpiece of some grizzled veteran's best room, or a name is printed in fading letters over the door of a stall in a tumbledown stable somewhere in the Blue Grass.

All of present-day Kentucky that can get there likewise is there. Louisville, playing the host, turns out in her smartest holiday clothes. Out of every corner of the State the visitors pour in. From small shabby towns on the branch line; from citified communities; from the back districts where folks ride yet in side-bar buggies and chewing tobacco still is the regular salad course; from up in the mountains; from the "Asparagus Bed," where fine old brick houses with white porticos stand on gentle eminences among the black walnuts and the white locusts; from the hemp fields and the tobacco patches and the corn lands of the river bottoms, the Kentuckians come.

They bring their pretty daughters with them, and the pretty daughters bring their prettiest frocks, so that on the big afternoon the grandstand turns to a wide hanging garden of Maytime flowers. Until she has seen a Derby run off, a Kentucky girl feels that she has not been properly launched on her social career. For the current year's débutantes, Derby Day is a sort of universal, free-for-all, coming-out party.

Unless he's sick a-bed, the governor is present along with a former governor or so, both the senators, most of the congressmen, the politicians and the sub-politicians, and colonels, majors, captains, judges, 'squires and other honorables past counting. It has been this way now for nearly fifty years—since 1875, when the first Derby winner won the first Derby.

Neighboring states—Tennessee, Indiana, Ohio, Virginia and West Virginia—send sizable delegations. The strictly sporting groups, headed by those oil kings who of late years have turned horse-fanciers, being the same groups which one sees at the Eastern tracks in the summer and at the far Southern tracks in the winter—are on hand, of course, bringing with them the atmosphere of Belmont track and Saratoga. But it is the sporting side of the proposition which largely draws these last. The haunting romance of the thing, the poetry of it, and the physical loveliness of the settings, mean little or nothing at all to the majority of these aliens.

For most of the assembled natives, though, there is more to this particular day and date than merely an opportunity to win a prize as an owner, or, as a bettor, to win or lose money on the result. The Kentuckian may have his wager down—he's almost certain to have his wager down—but a higher sentiment than the gambling chance is pulling at his heart. Perhaps he has not the words to express it, but down in his soul he is paying homage to his two surviving earthly ideals. Before Prohibition his loudest brag was that Kentucky led the world in the production of three things, namely: good-looking women, fine whiskey, and fast horses. One cause for his boasting has by law been abolished. The distilleries are closed or devoted to other uses, and in some populous districts the Eighteenth Amendment so strictly is enforced that a thirsty stranger may have to walk all of half a block to find a place where he can get a drink. But on Derby Day, of all days, a Kentuckian still may worship at the shrine of his two remaining deities—feminine beauty and The Hoss.

And when, in a scroll of dust and a thunder of hoofs, the winner comes down the stretch and the crowd in the stand goes mad, and the black brother in his place goes madder, and the band, according to ritual, plays "My Old Kentucky Home," the observing onlooker who can sense the feeling which permeates the mass, is made to realize that here, at least, is one spot on the map where for one day, anyhow, the spirit of commercialism runs second to the spirit of an Olden Time. For the moment, he catches the savors and the flavors of intangible essences—the whiffs of Bourbon toddies that were drunk long ago, the smell of prime old burley lingering yet in ancient tobacco barns, the gurgle of the corn juice running out of the jug, the bubble and spit of hot grease as the young spring chicken stirs in the frying pan.

Mardi Gras

By Lyle Saxon

There is the Mardi Gras of the white man and the Mardi Gras of the Negro. Each is unique in America. The little boy who was taken to see them both later became a writer of great talent. No wonder his recollection of the event is filled with flamboyant color, with noises and smells and sights, and people which only old New Orleans could produce.

It is the first hour after sunrise in New Orleans. Tall old houses, not yet awake, are tight-shut and mysterious, and the shadows of their wrought-iron balcony railings lie blue and lacelike in the narrow streets. An old gentleman and a small boy are going together to the French Market for morning coffee. They have come from aboard a Mississippi River steamboat which is tied up at the wharf just outside the levee. Already the boy is intoxicated with the scent of the city, strange after the sweet familiar smell of country lanes and new-turned furrows. He sniffs delightedly, wrinkling his nose.

The uneven cobblestones make it difficult for him to walk sedately beside his grandfather; he slips and stumbles instead. As they approach the market he looks curiously at the squat, slate-covered roof supported by tapering pillars of masonry. Under the arcade he sees a moving mass of men, and the building buzzes like a hive of bees. . . .

"This isn't a bit like the plantation," says the boy.

And there, in the midst of all this confusion, is the coffee-house, tucked away between the stalls of fruit and vegetables. The old gentleman and the boy sit upon stools, drinking hot, black coffee together—and there are little cakes flavored with honey, still warm from the oven. The grandfather smiles and nods contentedly over the rim of his thick cup, but the boy is solemn. His eyes are wide as he watches and listens. Around them the market men drink coffee and discuss the affairs of the day. The boy hears the rapid trilling of French, the soft slur of Italian, and the easy droning of Negroes' voices. It is all new and strange and delightful. . . .

And this is my first impression of the fabulous city, when I went there with my grandfather for Mardi Gras, twenty-five years ago. . . .

We went down some narrow street leading away from the river, toward the center of the old city. . . .

Somewhere in Orleans Street, just off Royal Street, my grandfather paused before a heavy door set flush with the sidewalk in the high façade of an old house. He raised the iron knocker and let it fall. And together we waited in the street, while the echoes died away. Orleans Street was a little wider than the streets which we had just traversed, and the houses stood shoulder to shoulder, each one with balconies of ornate ironwork which repeated themselves in shadows against the gray brick walls. . . .

I heard the shuffling of feet beyond the great door, and I heard, too, the muffled muttering of a voice. I kept my eyes fixed upon the door, expecting to see it move, but to my surprise a small door, cut within the paneling of the larger one, swung smartly open, and framed in the narrow aperture stood an old Negro woman, very trim and trig in her guinea-blue dress, her voluminous apron stiff with starch, and a yellow, red, and blue *tignon* upon her head. She stood aside that we might enter, and in we went, stepping high over the door sill.

The passage into which we had come was fully fifty feet long and perhaps fifteen feet wide. It was paved with blue-gray flagstones and the long unbroken walls were of mouldering plaster which had been tinted green at some past time, but which were now peeling off in places, showing purplish patches, and here and there a space where the bare red bricks could be seen. The ceiling was high above my head and was crossed at intervals by large beams. At the end of the passage, seen through an arch of masonry, was a large courtyard in which bamboo was growing and where tall palm-trees waved in the sunlight. . . .

Across the courtyard, at the back, a narrow flight of stairs rose full three stories, stopping now and then at small landings, then curving and continuing upward. The railing of the stairs was of faded green, and was twined from bottom to top with a magnificent wistaria vine, covered with purple flowers. The whole court was full of color, but so subdued these colors seemed against the vast gray walls that the whole was as dim as some old print that has mellowed with the years.

And near the fountain—I had not seen him at first—sat an old gentleman in black, beside a small breakfast table laid in the open air. The sunlight glimmered on the silver coffee-pot, and upon his crest of white hair, and upon a goblet which stood on the white cloth beside his plate. Upon the edge of the goblet sat a green parrakeet, dipping its bill into the water.

The old gentleman cried out in amazement upon seeing my grandfather, and embraced him—which I thought extremely odd, never having known Creoles before—and in a moment they were deep in talk. I stood looking on, less interested in the man than in the parrakeet, that small and demonlike bird which stood still upon the goblet's rim with cocked head, and regarded me with bright and wicked eye.

The old woman who had let us in came out of the house bringing another chair. She was followed by a very black Negro man who carried a smaller chair for me. He was the very ugliest Negro that I had ever seen; his skin was so black that it seemed almost blue, and the whites of his half-closed eyes were yellowish. His arms hung nearly to his knees and he walked with a shuffling gait that was like the slinking of an animal, but when he spoke his voice was so meek and childlike that I nearly laughed aloud.

"Ah may be wrong," he said, "but doesn't yo' wan' a fresh pot a-coffee?"

The old gentleman answered in French, and to my further amazement the Negro replied in the same tongue, his voice rising and falling like a boy's. In another moment he had gone back across the flagstones and had disappeared into the house. . . .

The old woman who had admitted us was now cleaning the long passage with a mop, and after the Negro man had brought the coffee-pot, the thin cups, and the brioche, he went through an archway and began polishing the head of a brass newel post at the foot of the wide stairs which curved upward into the house proper. . . .

Coming back to the conversation of the two men, I found that they were speaking of me. Something unfortunate had happened, I gathered, which was like to spoil the pleasure of my first Mardi Gras.

"The children and their nurse have been gone for an hour—and they will not be home before dark. I have no way in the world of finding them. Otherwise, of course, he could have gone with them."

And they continued to talk more about the children and their joy in masking for the Carnival, until I began to understand that even now at this early hour the children—whoever they might be—were abroad with mask and domino mingling with the other maskers in the streets, and that

I was left behind. There was some talk of my grandfather taking me to see the parades, but the old man was firm. No, the boy must mask, and he must see the thing in the way it should be seen. Every child should have that pleasure once at least. He himself had masked in his childhood. It meant everything. Give him time to think and he would work out some plan.

As they continued to talk, I looked away, feeling somewhat embarrassed, and found myself looking again into the eyes of the Negro who polished the newel post. And, our eyes meeting, he smiled suddenly, a wide smile which exposed two gleaming rows of white teeth. He rolled his eyes so comically that I nearly laughed aloud. But the next moment —as though nothing had occurred between us—his head was bent again over the shining brass.

Almost at that moment the old gentleman called, "Robert!" trilling the *r* . . . "*R-r-o*-bear!"

"Yassuh!" The Negro dropped the rag and came close to us.

Again the old gentleman spoke in French and again the Negro answered. I gathered that they were talking of me, and soon my grandfather explained that Robert was to take me to the center of the city where I could see the maskers and the parades. He was to have charge of me for the entire day, unless I grew tired and wanted to come back to the house. In that case I was to say so. A costume would be provided for me.

So fascinated was I with this unfamiliar world that I would have agreed to anything, and so, after a few preliminaries and another brioche, I was turned over to Robert for the day. He disappeared for a few minutes and returned minus his apron, but wearing a hat and coat. There were admonitions to which I did not listen, and seeing my inattention, my grandfather repeated them to Robert: he was never to let go of my hand for one instant in the crowds, and he was to see that I had a costume that I liked, and he was to see that I had something to eat at intervals. And last came the instructions which had to do with our return after the night parade. At the end my grandfather handed Robert five dollars—which seemed a fortune to me—and we were ready to go.

Just as we turned away, I heard my grandfather ask if Robert could be trusted, and I heard the old gentleman say:

"But of course! *R-r-o*-bear has been with me for years and years—since he was a child, in fact. It was I who named him for the opera by Meyerbeer, 'Robert le Diable'!"

In less time than I have taken to tell it here, Robert and I were walking down the passage which led to the street, my hand held tight in his. As the door opened I saw before us, in the street, a group of children dressed in gay-colored costumes and wearing masks. They came running by, brushing against us, shouting shrilly and tinkling scores of tiny bells that were worn as ornaments upon their dominoes: "Mardi Gras! Mardi Gras!" they shouted.

And as the door closed behind us a great change came over Robert. His meekness fell from him as though it were a cloak thrown aside. He began strutting down the street as though walking in time to silent music: "Us is goin' tuh have us a *time!*" he said.

Enraptured, I trotted after. . . .

In front of the French Opera House at Bourbon and Toulouse streets, men were carrying great gilded statues up the stairs and a group of maskers stood watching, making comments upon the mysterious, glittering figures as they disappeared one after another into the doorway. But Robert would not stop long to let me observe any of these wonders, and I dragged back hanging upon his hand, eager to go forward, but loath to miss anything by the way. It was not long before we turned into a little shop which seemed quite dark after the sunlit street, but in a moment my eyes had accustomed themselves to the dimness and I was dazed by a hundred new delights. It was a costume shop, and even to-day it seems nearly as bizarre as it appeared then.

There were two rooms opening one into the other by sliding doors; in the first room were counter and shelves, with high-piled green boxes bearing labels. Ghostly figures stood stiffly, wearing doublet and hose and plumed hats—models for displaying costumes. Piled upon tables was a motley mess of armor, shields, sunbonnets, false noses, and women's hats trimmed with daisies. Masks were strung across the shop, masks showing the face of satyrs, clowns, and monks, demons, grinning skulls, and silly fat girls. From the ceiling depended other and more elaborate disguises: gilded horses' heads, purple elephants in papier-mâché, and even a unicorn's head with a silver horn, that could be fitted over one's own head in such a manner that the wearer was transformed immediately into that fabulous animal.

In the room beyond a faded woman in black sewed like mad on a sewing-machine, while another woman ran about waiting upon customers. . . .

At last it came our turn to be served and again I saw black Robert respectful and servile as he had appeared at first. He told the woman in charge that I must be fitted with a red devil costume, something nice and clean, he said. And a moment later I was being forced into a sort of red union suit over all my clothes. There was a hood from which two horns projected, and there was a grinning devil mask. In another minute the thing was done, the suit was snatched off again, and I saw it rolled into a bundle. But Robert had other fish to fry. He began explaining that a second costume was needed for his employer, "dis chile's brother"—which surprised me, more or less, as I had no brother. But I remained silent and waited while Robert looked at this and that, and finally selected some red silk tights and a few other fittings for this mysterious stranger. At last he received a second bundle and we departed from the shop.

"Where are we going now?" I wanted to know, and Robert explained that we must go to his room near-by so that we could dress for the day. I followed him, hugging the bundle to my breast, and thinking that New Orleans was like some strange dream. We went west this time and it was not long before we came to meaner streets. The houses were as old and large as in the streets just quitted, but here Negro women leaned from windows and Negro babies played upon door-steps. And through open doors one could see inner courtyards piled high with dirt and rubbish. At last we reached a dwelling with a driveway extending under the house proper to some court beyond, and into this driveway we turned, almost running. In the rear we climbed endless flights of stairs until we reached a balcony just under the roof, and here Robert stopped, put down his bundle and fished a big key out of his pocket. A green batten door was opened and we crossed the threshold. Then Robert locked the door against the curious.

I looked about. This then was Robert's room. It was scrupulously clean and it was furnished well enough. It was quite large. A bed occupied one corner. The walls were covered with pictures of saints in various agonies of torture: Saint Lucy carrying her eyes on a plate, Saint Roch with his sores, followed by a collie that held a cake in its mouth; Saint Somebody Else being burned at the stake. I thought them all magnificent. . . .

Now it was time for putting on my costume, and Robert helped me to undress. Coat, trousers, and shoes off, I was forced into my devilish disguise. It is true that it puckered rather badly in places and fitted too tightly in others, but what of that? Who was I to care for such trifles? It was not long before I was transformed completely and I stood before the watery mirror highly pleased with my changed appearance. The glass reflected a small red devil, rather lumpy in spots, a devil with a crimson face and a grinning mouth from which crooked teeth protruded, a devil with real, if somewhat wobbly horns, and with a beautiful pronged tail hanging down behind.

And now it was Robert's turn. The mystery of my "brother" was explained, for it was Robert and none other who was to wear the other suit. He had resorted to this device, he told me, because the shopkeeper would not rent a costume to a Negro. . . .

First the black legs squirmed themselves into a pair of red silk tights, a dangerous undertaking as the garments were so extremely close-fitting that I expected to see the seams burst asunder at any moment; but once the legs were encased in these tights, the lower part of his anatomy was something wonderful to see. The silk gleamed bright, and there was no wrinkle to be seen. His own tan shoes were put on again. A sort of red silk undershirt was added, and a pair of pleated red and green trunks liberally trimmed with spangles, a pair of trunks from which depended a wondrous tail, also spangled and ending with a red tassel. A hood of red ornamented with a pair of cow's horns fitted snugly upon his head, and his mask and mine were identical. He finished his tiolet by producing a pair of white cotton gloves which he put on; and now that none of his skin was visible, no one could tell whether he were a white man or a Negro—or a Chinaman or anything else, for that matter. As a final touch of elegance to his attire he took from a wardrobe a woman's silk parasol, baby-blue with many tiny ruffles, which if somewhat frayed still made a brave showing, and with parasol in hand he took various *poses plastiques* before the looking-glass.

A few minutes later two red devils emerged from the courtyard into the street, Robert walking before carrying the umbrella and I walking behind supporting his spangled tail. How grand we were! The Negroes on the sidewalk set up a shout of glee and clapped their hands as we appeared. Emboldened by this success, Robert executed a few dance steps, and then started off at a trot down the street, with many a flirt of the blue parasol and many a roguish backward glance. . . .

As the crowd thickened other maskers came close to us and greeted us. To my amazement I heard Robert reply in a high falsetto voice, which sounded like that of an affected woman, while, to my further astonishment, a large, fat woman, dressed in a trailing gown of white silk, spoke in a deep bass voice like a man. I looked sharply at the woman. Now here was a strange thing! Her dress was elegant—surely she was laced tightly into a corset—and her long golden curls were a wonder to see, as they hung down from under a black hat with purple plumes; but her skirt, held high, exposed a brawny leg encased in a purple silk stocking—and she wore a pair of man's shoes! Also, and this was the strangest of all, through the open lips of her simpering mask, a cigar protruded and from time to time she puffed forth a great cloud of smoke.

"Who's that lady smoking a cigar?" I whispered shrilly to Robert, and the "lady" hearing, responded in her bass voice, "Dearie, I'm your grandmother!" and punched me in the ribs.

Then she cried out: "Ho devils! Whither away?" and took Robert by the arm. We made an imposing picture, I think, the three of us as we entered Canal Street, bounding into the center of a group of maskers who danced while six other maskers with mandolins and guitars played some popular tune. . . .

The sun shone down upon the mass of moving color, lighting a spangle to brilliance here, or shining upon a piece of tinsel there. There were bullfighters, pirates, nuns, and priests. A snake charmer with a large imitation snake was shaking its hideous head into the faces of the passers-by. A group of ten boys and girls dressed in identical black and white clown suits marched one behind the other, hands upon the shoulders of the one before; they threaded their way in and out of the crowd as they approached us, but when the leader came abreast of the two devils he uttered a shout, and in a moment we were surrounded. Hand and hand they danced around us, shouting: "Dance devils! Dance devils!" And Robert, quick to oblige, executed a ribald dance which drew shouts of merriment from all who watched, while I capered after swinging from his tail.

It was over as soon as it had begun, and again we threaded our way along, square after square, all packed with masqueraders and those who had come to see. I wished to linger, but Robert was firm. We would have to hurry, he told me, if we wished to be in time for the arrival of the Zulu King.

Now the Zulu King meant no more to me than the fourth dimension, but he sounded exciting, so I demurred no longer but hurried after the devil who bounded before me. We dodged through groups of maskers, we ducked under ropes, and finally after traversing several squares, turned from Canal Street into another thoroughfare where a group of Negro girls were dancing under an arcade while two Negro men picked on banjos. I saw no white maskers here, but there were many Negroes in costume who seemed to be holding a Mardi Gras all their own. And here I found that the crowd was moving in another direction, away from Canal Street. We went along the street with them, square after square. Past pawnshops with the three golden balls hanging outside, past cafés, where Negroes sat on stools eating while other Negroes served them; past saloons which smelled of stale beer and wet sawdust and from which came shouts and curses. At last we reached an open space with a large red railroad station at one side, and with a canal—or what appeared to be the end of a ship canal—directly before us. The banks of the waterway were lined with Negroes, pushing and shoving about in order to gain some point of vantage. Some of them were in costume but most of them were in their everyday clothes. They were packed so tightly together that it was almost impossible to force a way between them.

Just as we found ourselves wedged into the thickest part of the crowd there came a chorus of shouts:

"Yon' he is!"

"Yon' he come!"

"Gawd a-mighty!"

"Wha' he is?"

"Da' he!"

We pushed and shoved with the rest, and in a moment actually succeeded in making our way to the water's edge, and here Robert lifted me bodily and seated the little devil on the big devil's shoulder, where I sat, legs around his neck, looking with all my eyes.

The sun shone bright on the strip of water, and there in the distance I could see a patch of purple and red which was repeated in the water below. It was the royal barge of the Zulu King approaching.

Now there are a great many people who have been born in New Orleans and who have lived there all their lives, but who have never seen the arrival of the Zulu King; and I feel sorry for them, for surely there is no more characteristic sight to be seen in the South. This custom has continued for many years—a sort of burlesque of the grander Mardi Gras of the white people, and it provides the note of humor which is lacking in the great parades.

The Zulu King and his faithful henchmen were approaching slowly, the barge propelled by a tiny puffing motor-boat. The barge itself looked as if it had been rather hurriedly decorated with whatever scraps happened to be at hand. The canopy over the throne was made of sacking, and was supported by rough poles. A bunch of paper flowers adorned its top, and beneath it, in a tattered Morris chair, the king sat. He represented a savage chieftain, but whether from modesty or from fear of cold, the Zulu King wore, instead of his own black skin, a suit of black knitted underwear. There were bunches of dried grass at throat, ankles, and wrists, and a sort of grass skirt such as hula-hula dancers wear, and he wore a fuzzy black wig surmounted by a tin crown. In his hand he carried a scepter—a broomstick—upon which was mounted a stuffed white rooster. There were some tattered artificial palm-trees at the four corners of the royal barge, and a strip of red cloth was draped from palm to palm. Four henchmen, dressed almost exactly like the king—save that they wore no crowns—were capering about beside him. Some red and purple flags were stuck about here and there. And as the barge approached us, the king opened a bottle of beer and drank a toast from the bottle; while Negro men and women on the bank produced flasks from their pockets and drank their own.

And now came the disembarking. With difficulty the Negroes in evening dress opened a way through the crowd and a wagon drawn by mules was brought close to the barge. The wagon was a large, almost square vehicle without sides; only a flat floor over the wheels. At the moment it was bare. But not for long. The king rose, picked up his Morris chair and climbed aboard. The henchmen followed, each bearing a potted palm. The bunting was stripped from the barge and was nailed into place around the edge of the wagon—and the flags and flowers were distributed about. And, with the king and his four followers aboard, it moved along and another wagon took its place.

The second vehicle was much like the first, except that it had a wood-burning cooking stove in the center—a stove in which a fire burned and from the short stovepipe came a cloud of black smoke. An old Negro woman stood by the stove, frying fish, and from time to time she would remove a steaming morsel from the pan and pop it into some open mouth that was eagerly upheld to receive it. The Negroes crowded around the vehicle, screaming out in delight. Two Negro men were seated in chairs near the stove—also aboard the wagon—cleaning fish. And there was a basketful of catfish beside them. Aside from a garland of flowers which adorned the stovepipe, the wagon was undecorated.

The men who had been waiting on the bank now mounted their steeds —mules—and sat there, making a brave show with their white shirtfronts and red and purple scarves. Two of them carried stuffed white roosters on their shoulders. Like the king's, their faces were blackened and painted with red and green stripes. And as the king's chariot moved off from the side of the canal, these outriders distributed themselves around it—a guard of honor. . . .

Slowly the procession went down Rampart Street—that street which Robert and I had just traversed—and from every store, lunch-counter, billiard hall, and saloon, a crowd came out to see. . . .

The parade progressed at a snail's pace, owing partly to the crowded street and partly to the eccentricities of the drivers of the mules, who stopped here and there to chat with acquaintances along the way. At these stopping points the king rose from his chair, went to the edge of the wagon, and bent down to exchange a resounding smack with some dusky belle who came close, holding up her thick lips. And after each of these salutes, the king would turn about and yell back to the old woman who was frying fish, "Give dis gal a mouf'ful uv fish, sister!" to which the old woman would reply, "Sho' will!" and the damsel would stand beside the second wagon until the morsel of hot catfish was put into her open mouth. And at these signs of royal favor the crowd would cheer afresh. . . .

It was nearly noon before we reached Canal Street again where the great street pageants were to take place; for Robert's return down Rampart Street was interrupted a hundred times. Rampart is the Broadway of New Orleans Negroes and there are many shops, eating houses, and booths which sell those things so dear to the Negro's heart, and to the Negro's stomach. . . .

Canal Street, now so tightly packed with people that it was impossible to move forward at more than a snail's pace, was filled with moving figures. About half of them were masked, the others dressed in everyday garb. High above the streets the balconies were massed with spectators, and in every window and even along the roofs of the buildings there were men and women. Flags fluttered everywhere. . . .

And color, color everywhere: red, purple, blue, arsenic green, and the glitter of metal head-dresses and spangles in the sunlight. There were clowns, of every size and of every color of costume; there were hundreds of ballet girls, often ten or more in a group, all dressed in black and white, exactly alike. There were animal disguises; men wearing purple elephants' heads of papier-mâché; huge donkeys' heads. Sometimes two men would combine in order to represent a comical horse or a violet-colored cow. A man passed by high on stilts, his pink and white striped coat tails blowing out in the breeze. Two men were dressed in black tights, painted with white to imitate skeletons; they were truly terrifying with their skull faces and macabre aspect. Accompanying the skeletons was a fat woman dressed in the uniform of a United States marine; she dragged a squalling child by one arm: "That's only your papa," she said, indicating the taller of the skeletons, but the child, unimpressed by this information, continued to squall.

There was a burst of music near us and a policeman rode by on horseback, clearing a narrow path through the crowd. Robert and I, crushed back against the curb, were almost under the feet of the marching men who came swinging by. It was one of the so-called "little parades" which amuse the crowds before the arrival of Rex, King of the Carnival. On a purple and gilt banner I could read the name of the organization: "The Jefferson City Buzzards"! And with a blare of cornets, they were upon us. First came twelve fat men dressed as little girls, all in white. Their huge stomachs were draped with the widest of baby-blue sashes, and they wore pale blue socks which ended half-way up their fat and hairy legs. All of them wore long flaxen curls surmounted with baby caps trimmed with blue rosettes. Nearly all of them were smoking cigars. They bowed right and left as they marched along and smiled widely, gold teeth glittering in the sunlight. Their "queen" was an unusually fat man who bulged out of a baby carriage, sucking a large stick of red and white striped candy. Another man—this one with a big mustache—was blacked up to represent a Negro mammy, and pushed the carriage, perspiring copiously. The babies were followed by a group of men in white linen suits, each carrying an American flag. They strutted with the music and kept bowing and throwing kisses to the spectators. A Negro band brought up the rear—a band which played the rowdiest and bawdiest jazz that I had ever heard.

The Jefferson City Buzzards had hardly passed before another marching club followed it. This time the marchers were in Oriental costumes—men of the desert and their houris. They carried a banner bearing the name of their organization. A few minutes later another club came by, the men dressed as Negro minstrels.

Suddenly I became conscious of a swelling whisper which ran through the crowd. Necks were craned. Maskers stopped their antics and stood on tiptoe, all looking in the same direction. Robert, with his hand on my shoulder, tiptoed too, shading his devil mask with white gloved hand; and then he turned to me and said—his voice muffled behind his mask—"It's de parade!" And then, almost upon us, I saw twelve blue-coated policemen on horseback riding abreast. They came charging down upon the crowd and we moved back before them, falling over each other in our haste.

If the street had seemed tight-packed before, it was even worse now. Elbows came in contact with my forehead, feet smashed down upon mine; I was buffeted about, almost thrown down as the crowd became more congested around me. But Robert dragged me back to him with an effort, and in another moment I found myself seated with my legs around his neck, high over the heads of the others. And as I emerged from that undercurrent which had seemed to drag me down, I had the feeling of a swimmer rising upon the crest of a wave. And there before me, stretched out as far as I could see, was a mass of maskers, and beyond them a series of glittering mountains were moving toward me. . . . The Carnival King was coming.

First came the mounted policemen who cleared the way, and behind them were masked courtiers riding black horses; they wore gold plumes on their hats, and their purple velvet cloaks trailed out behind them over the flanks of the horses; they wore doublet and hose, and they carried gleaming swords in their hands. There were perhaps twelve of these outriders, gaily dressed except for the fact that they wore black masks which gave a sinister effect. Behind them came a brass band tooting lustily. Two Negroes carried between them a large placard emblazoned with one word, "Rex."

And now the parade was actually upon us. The first float in the procession seemed to me the most wonderful thing that I had ever seen. It was a mass of blue sky and white clouds surmounted by a glittering rainbow, and under the rainbow's bridge were masked figures in fluttering silk, men and women who held uplifted golden goblets. It was the title car and upon its side was written the subject of the parade—a subject which I have wholly forgotten to-day, but which dealt with some phase of Greek mythology. The glittering float towered as high as the balconies which overhung the street from the second stories of the houses, and as this gay-colored mountain came gliding past me I was impressed with the fact that the car was swaying and that it seemed fragile for all its monumental size. It was almost as though the whole were on springs. The car was drawn by eight horses covered in white and with cowls over their heads.

A blaring band followed the title car, then more outriders, dressed this time in green and gold and wearing purple masks; and behind them came a car which was even larger than the first. It was like a gigantic frosted wedding cake and at the top on a golden throne was seated Rex, King of the Carnival. Such a perfect king he was, with his fat legs encased in white silk tights, a round fat stomach under shimmering satin, long golden hair and a magnificent curled yellow beard! His face was covered with a simpering wax mask, benign and jovial. On his head he wore the very grandest crown I had ever seen, all gold and jewels which sparkled in the sun; and he carried a diamond scepter in his hand which he waved good-naturedly at the cheering crowd. Behind him a gold-embroidered robe swept down behind the throne, cascaded over the sloping back of the float and trailed almost to the ground, its golden fringe shaking with the movement of the car. There was gauze and tinsel everywhere and thousands of spangles glittered in the sun. At the feet of the monarch two blonde pages stood, little boys no larger than I, with long golden curls and white silk tights, which were rather wrinkly at the knees. How I envied them!

Robert and I were both screaming with delight, and I clapped my hands. And then a preposterous thing happened—a magnificent thing. The blonde monarch, so high over my head and yet so near me, leaned out and with his scepter pointed directly to me as I sat perched upon the shoulder of the big red devil. He said something to one of the pages, something which I could not hear, and the page with a bored smile tossed a string of green beads to me. It swirled through the air over the heads of the people between us and dropped almost into my outstretched hands; but my clumsy fingers missed and it fell to the ground. Immediately there was a scramble. Robert stooped, I fell from his shoulders, and I found myself lying on the pavement as though swept under a stampede of cattle. Hands and feet were all around me, but somehow in the struggle I managed to retrieve those beads, and triumphant I scrambled up again and Robert put me back on his shoulder. . . .

By the time the last car in the parade had passed the spot in the street where Robert and I were standing, the procession had turned at some distant corner and was returning on the opposite side of Canal Street, and without moving from our position we were able to see the parade again. This time, looking with more scrutinizing eye, I noticed things which had escaped me before—that the beautiful masked women who rode upon the floats were strangely masculine in body, and that the figures of papier-mâché which had seemed so beautiful at first were not quite as realistic as I had imagined. However, I did not look upon the parade with a critical eye, but accepted it for what it was, a gay dream.

The moment that the last car had passed in the street, the crowd began to surge about again. Robert, heaving a sigh of relief, let me slide down his body to the ground, and we tried to make our way into a store where cold drinks were for sale; but every one in the crowd seemed to have the same idea, and we found it impossible to force our way inside. Accordingly we drank pink lemonade which a street vendor was dispensing at the edge of the sidewalk. It tasted only faintly of lemon and sugar, but it was cold and pink and our thirst made us grateful. . . .

Robert urged that we begin further investigation. And now that the parade had disappeared in the distance he caught my hand and began picking his way through the crowds of maskers again. I asked no question and made no objection but I found myself so tired that I could hardly drag one red leg after the other. . . .

At last we came to a street where there were black women hanging out of the windows and where Negro men loitered in the street outside, and after passing for a square or more along this street we came to a café where a big sign announced that this was "The High Brown Social and Athletic Club." And it was into this doorway that we turned.

The High Brown Social and Athletic Club turned out to be a Negro saloon. By this time I was beginning to feel quite at home in such places and thought this one to be in no way remarkable. But Robert did not linger in the bar-room. . . .

Behind heavy doors I could hear the booming of a drum and the whine of fiddles. And when this door was opened the breath of air that came out was so stifling that I fell back for a moment. We went in, but it was like entering an oven.

The room was very large and was tightly closed. Electric lights shone brightly and I saw that the ceiling was a mass of red and green streamers of paper, rather reminiscent of Christmas. The ceiling was all I could see, for the place was thronged with Negroes. We made our way through the crowd around the door, and came out upon the dancing floor, where many couples were moving in a slow, shuffling dance; men and women with bodies pressed together so that they seemed one, and many dancing with closed eyes and lunging hips.

And it was then that I saw the Zulu King again. He was lolling on a throne on a sort of dais at one end of the room. He was laughing very loud and showing all of his magnificent white teeth. He lay back in a chair, and upon his knee was a mulatto girl with a short red dress. She was drinking from his glass.

The room smelled of unwashed bodies and stale beer.

Robert led me to a corner and found a chair for me. Then, after telling me to sit there quietly—and cautioning me not to take off my mask—he was gone, promising to return in a few minutes. A little later I saw his red devil costume and realized that he had joined in the dance. With arms entwined around some dusky damsel he was gyrating with the best of them, and his squirms and bumps were something to see! . . .

It would be impossible for me to tell you of all that happened during that long and gaudy afternoon. It remains a blurred remembrance of mad and futile flights from one part of the city to another. First we went down through the Vieux Carré again and into Frenchmen Street. There the people were having a maskers' contest, and prizes were being offered for the most comical masquerader. . . .

After that Robert took me into the most remarkable places: into the lobbies of big hotels and into sumptuous saloons. At these times he would whisper that I raise my mask, and that, if anyone asked questions, I must reply that we were looking for some one. I obeyed without asking questions—but years later it occurred to me why Robert wanted me to do this. Masked, he could not be distinguished from a white man—if he did not speak—and holding a small white boy by the hand, he could gain access anywhere. It is highly probable that Robert saw places that day that he had never seen in his life before and never saw again. For I remember that we strolled nonchalantly through the lobby of the St. Charles Hotel, where there were but few maskers and where reigned a dignified grandeur that Robert assured me was "genteel." Across the street from the St. Charles was the old Ramos bar, where twelve barkeepers stood in a line, shaking the silver containers which held the famous gin-fizz—now only a memory. In the Ramos saloon there were many women, beautifully dressed, who leaned against the bar with one foot on the brass rail and who imbibed the fizzes or sipped absinthe.

Later I learned that on Mardi Gras all police regulations regarding barrooms were put aside, and on that one day it was permissible for women to go into these places. Many of the most fashionable women of New Orleans went on Mardi Gras to drink gin-fizz at the old Ramos bar—and on that day it was considered a more or less conventional thing to do. One incident remains clearly in my mind, a beautiful, slender girl with a corsage bouquet of orchids called me to her—while Robert stood back modestly—and gave me a sip from her glass. It was the first time I had tasted absinthe, and the flavor made me wrinkle my nose and cry out,

"It's paregoric!" This definition was greeted with shouts of laughter. . . .

Robert kept luring me on from place to place by vague promises of showing me something new. We must have visited half a dozen markets, I am sure, and before each of these markets a neighborhood celebration was in progress. Here was none of the grandeur that I had witnessed in Canal Street, but it was the carnival of the masses—and they seemed to be having as good a time as their more fashionable neighbors.

My feet were lagging and my head hung down by the time we had left the fifth or sixth market and I demanded to be taken home. Robert's pleas were all in vain, for I was firm. My grandfather's admonitions were remembered now—when I had need of them—and finally Robert promised that we should go back to his room and rest for a bit. The night parade was the grandest spectacle of Carnival, he told me, and I must be fresh for that. Accordingly we returned on a street-car to Canal Street and after crossing it—threading our way among the tireless maskers who were still parading about and singing and dancing—we turned into one of those narrow streets of the Vieux Carré and finally arrived at the house where Robert and I had dressed that morning.

Once in Robert's room, I collapsed on the bed, wailing that my feet were killing me and that I didn't intend to stir out of the house again. . . .

I fell asleep, and when he roused me it was twilight and outside I could hear the tramping of feet, an endless shuffling, and the murmur of a crowd moving along. It was time, Robert said, for us to be up and stirring, for he wanted me to see the Comus parade from the base of the Lee Monument, many squares away.

He helped me get dressed again, this time in my own clothes, and the devil suit was laid away in a drawer. I hated to see it go out of my life, and I remember touching it with affectionate fingers while Robert was busy at something else. He too had laid away his disguise, and although the night was warm, he was bundled up in a long overcoat which was buttoned to his chin. When I was ready, we went into the street again.

Twilight was deepening and the narrow street was filled with a moving crowd. Every one was going in the same direction, toward Canal Street. We were forced to fall into step and we went forward slowly. Although many wore costume, there were no false faces in evidence now—for with the first twilight the masks must be laid aside by order of the police. Robert gave me a long and rambling explanation for this in which the words "bad people" occurred over and over. I gathered that the masks had been used to shield criminals in the old days, and that the rule for unmasking with the first twilight was strictly necessary.

Canal Street presented a gay picture. There were strings of electric lights looped from corner to corner, and arches of vari-colored electric bulbs crossed the street at close intervals—yellow, green, and purple lights. From the balconies and from the tops of buildings came long streamers of yellow, green, and purple bunting, doubly noticeable now by the artificial light. Flags fluttered and the bunting billowed in the evening breeze from the river. Waves of pleasant coolness came to our grateful faces. . . .

I thought that we would remain on Canal Street as we had done that morning, but Robert assured me that he knew a vantage point that was far superior, and accordingly we went up St. Charles Street for eight or more squares. All along the street men and women lined the sidewalks. Many of them had brought camp-stools or cushions and were sitting along the curb; others spread out newspspers and sat on them. In front of the stores the shopkeepers' families had gathered and were perched on boxes or tables in order that they could see above the heads of those on the sidewalk. In order to walk, we had to leave the sidewalk and move along the middle of the street. There was no traffic other than the moving crowd; for this was the route of the parade and it had been cleared for the coming of Comus.

At last we reached Lee Circle—an open circular place where St. Charles Street widens out and becomes St. Charles Avenue, and where Howard Avenue crosses. Here the ground has been built up into a sort of round mountain, and at the top of this grass-grown mound there rises a huge fluted column of stone which in turn supports a bronze statue of Robert E. Lee. At the base of the column is a pyramid of stone, like gigantic steps rising one above the other, each step more than a yard high. By scrambling up this giants' staircase, we reached the summit; and there, seated on the edge of the topmost step, we sat leaning back against the stone cloumn which disappeared into the darkness above our heads. We were just in time to secure seats, for many others were there already, and within five minutes after our arrival every available inch was filled. The crowd continued to arrive and in a few minutes more the grassy slope was covered. And still they came, crowding the sidewalks until there was no more room at all.

There came a whisper which turned into a cry. The parade was coming. I looked with all my eyes up the avenue but at first could see nothing but the flickering rows of lights as they converged far away, but then, after a moment, I was conscious of a red glare in the sky—almost on the horizon it seemed, an aura which seemed to rise from the ground, or to emanate from the air itself. It was something apart from life as I knew it. It was magic itself.

As I looked, smaller lights became visible in the red glare, little twinkling lights of yellow and blue and green, bright pinpoints of flame. Then, as the endless stream of lights moved nearer I was conscious of great wreaths of black smoke which swirled upward into the darkness, smoke which held and reflected the flaring lights and which surrounded this glimmering far-off pageant with a rim of fire. I heard music . . . first just a broken bar, then another, finally a melody, faint and sweet.

We were high above the parade, and it was coming directly toward us, down the avenue. Little by little objects became visible, dark shapes against the flare—men on horseback clearing the route. Then below each glowing point of flame I could discern a red figure—men holding the torches. And always the bobbing of these lights and their swirling smoke rising toward the dim stars. In the center of each of these circles of light, masses of pale color became visible—the floats, pale in the night, yet brilliant too. And they seemed to glide noiselessly and effortlessly forward; relentless, like a gigantic dragon bearing down upon the crowd.

Slowly details became clear—men on black horses, courtiers with plumed hats and black masks. The horses reared and pranced as though trying to unseat their riders. Music blared out, muffled as though various bands were trying to outdo each other, which indeed was true. And from far off I could hear cheering and rippling applause as those along the way greeted Comus, the last and most dearly loved of all the kings of Mardi Gras.

Now the torches were nearer and I could see that prancing Negroes were holding the flambeaux. The torches flared, and the red-robed Negroes strutted in time with the music. Possibly thirty torches were ranged around each float in the parade. And in addition there were taller, more brilliant flares of stage fire—red and green and white. These lights were reflected upon the decorated cars—cars which rose high in the air and which were shaped irregularly, mountains moving toward us, undulating as they came.

The night parade is a dream festival. Even now, twenty-five years later, I cannot look upon one of them unmoved; but to the small boy they were more real than reality.

First came the title car, shimmering with tinsel and fluttering with gauzy streamers; the torches burned yellow and blue, and the dancing lights were reflected as though from a thousand tiny mirrors. In black letters on gold I read that Comus's whim this year was "Legends of the Golden Age." Following the title car came Comus himself, riding on his swaying, glimmering throne of white and gold, and to me the king seemed suspended in the air upon his golden chair, suspended there, framed in fire. His crown and jewels sparkled with points of light. He was a blonde and jovial monarch who gestured right and left with his scepter, gestured slowly and with a superb geniality. The sheen of golden satin vied with the glistening of burnished metal. Great golden tassels quivered. And this shimmering, glittering, swaying mass passed slowly by, drawn by eight horses—horses which seemed like mysterious, unknown animals, covered with white—their eyes showing black through eyelets in the cloth. Negro men led the horses, Negroes in red robes and with cowls over their heads. And everywhere the prancing Negro torchbearers, and the blaring of bands. The undulation, the bobbing lights, the quivering masses of changing color, the unending rhythm, seemed to stir a similar quivering in me.

We were far enough away and high enough above the parade to feel the illusion. This was no man-made thing that came out of the darkness; it was magic.

One by one the floats passed by: Ulysses setting sail in a golden boat while his bare-armed followers pulled at long shining oars; Circe and the companions of Ulysses—great, terrible swine—built no doubt of papier-mâché, which groveled before a beautiful enchantress; Jason and the golden fleece. . . . It seemed as though all the beauty and all the riches of the world had been spilt out to make a small boy's paradise. . . .

One after another the cars went swaying past, each one preceded by a band, and each one framed in a fiery ring of bobbing flambeaux. As the procession reached the mound upon which we sat, it turned, circled the base of the statue and continued behind us down St. Charles Street. As the last car passed, we turned to follow it with our eyes—and there, strung out along the street, we saw the gorgeous spectacle again, the backs of the floats this time—almost equally beautiful, and exhibiting another side, decorated, and sometimes filled with maskers who danced upon the swaying vehicle. . . .

At last the parade left Canal Street and entered Bourbon Street, a narrow thoroughfare which led toward the French Opera House. So narrow was the street that the great decorated cars covered it from sidewalk to sidewalk, and the maskers who rode high on top of the cars were almost level with the balconies of wrought iron which overhung the street. . . .

Looking down the street, I saw the great floats lose their fairy-like quality—for as they passed beyond the door of the Opera House the Negroes extinguished their torches, and with the light out, the floats became only dead things—their life and beauty gone. One after another they disappeared into the darkness, gone as utterly as a snuffed-out flame.

Robert and I were turning away, or "fixin' to go," as Robert expressed it, when suddenly some one put a hand on my shoulder. "I was beginning to be worried about you," said my grandfather's voice.

He stood beside me in the crowd, smiling down upon me.

"Have a nice time?"

"Yes, sir."

"See everything?"

"Oh, yes, sir!"

"Enjoy yourself?"

"Yes, sir."

"Ready to go back to the country?"

"No, sir."

"Are you ready to go to bed now, or do you want to see some more?"

A moment before I had been so exhausted that I could hardly stand but at the promise of something else to see, I exclaimed:

"I'm not tired at all."

My grandfather turned to Robert who stood meekly by:

"So you took good care of the young man?"

"Yassuh!"

"And did he give you any trouble?"

"No, *suh!*"

I saw my grandfather hand Robert something, and his face lit up:

"Thank you, *suh!*"

"And now," said my grandfather to the Negro, "go on and amuse yourself. Thank you for taking care of the young fellow and showing him everything. I'll take care of him now."

Robert looked at me as though he wanted to ask something of me, but seemed to think better of it, and turned away.

"Good night," he said.

"Thank you a lot . . . if you ever come to the plantation I'll show you things, too." This was the best I could offer. Again Robert said good night and a moment later he was gone in the crowd.

It was then that I saw that the old Creole gentleman was standing at my grandfather's elbow. He too was smiling at me. "Your face is dirty," he remarked as though he were stating a well-known fact. I scrubbed at it with a grimy handkerchief.

"Oh, never mind," he said, "we're going up into the *troisième*. We'll never be noticed. Come along."

I followed the two old men into the Opera House, up long flights of stairs, through great swinging doors and into a foyer with red carpet on the floor and great gleaming crystal chandeliers and mirrors which reflected the people who were passing before them. We climbed more stairs. I was like a child in a dream; everything was vague and a red haze seemed to hang over the lights. At last we reached a balcony high up in the Opera House, and here, after some trouble, we found our seats almost at the back of it. The two men sat down and I squeezed, somehow, between them, disputing with the chair arm for the right of way.

Far, far below me I saw hundreds of men and women moving about. The theater was filled from pit to dome with a mass of spectators—guests at the ball. In the proscenium boxes were women in evening gowns, glittering with jewels. There were flowers everywhere. Below us lay the horseshoe—we could see part of it—and here again were gaily dressed ladies and black-coated gentlemen. The stage was illuminated and decorated to represent a starry heaven. On a high throne were the King and Queen, as small as dolls, it seemed to me—so high I sat. The proscenium arch curved high above their heads, and before them stretched out a long expanse of dancing floor, a floor which extended out over what had been the parquet of the theater. (It was many years later that I found out that a movable floor was put down over the seats for the Mardi Gras balls, thus transforming the theater into a magnificently large ballroom, and the loges, boxes, and balconies serving for seats for the spectators. But I knew nothing of all this then—and accepted this thing as it was.)

My head drooped sleepily. The red haze around the lights seemed to grow denser. Somewhere an orchestra played softly. The King and Queen were rising and beginning their march around the dance floor. Couples fell in behind them—the men in costume and masked, but the women, with the exception of the court ladies, in conventional evening dress. Behind the King and Queen long gold-embroidered robes swept out—robes supported by pages in white. I recognized, in a dim sort of way, some of the characters that I had seen riding by on the floats earlier in the evening: Ulysses, Circe, and the rest of those masqueraders. But many seemed wholly unfamiliar, as I saw them in that half-trance between sleep and waking.

There had been a series of tableaux before we had entered the theater, my grandfather's friend told me . . . but I did not care that I had missed them. I nodded sleepily, and at last my head went down on my grandfather's shoulder. I must have slept for hours, for when he awakened me it was midnight and the court of Rex had left its ball and had come to join the court of Comus—the climax of the Mardi Gras festivity. I was only conscious of two kings and two queens and two courts . . . more spangles, more glitter, more brilliance. It was too much. I could stand no more.

"I want to go home," I said.

"All right, old sleepy head," said my grandfather, "let us go."

Somehow I staggered down the stairs and somehow I staggered through the dim streets. We went back to the house that I had left that morning—a day, a century ago. The courtyard seemed quiet and ghostly in its peaceful dimness—and the moon shone down on the fountain. Again I climbed many stairs and in a bedroom somewhere in the front part of the house I got undressed and tumbled into a big, four-post bed.

When I awakened it was dawn outside and I could see the red reflection of the sun in the sky. An altercation was going on in the street below and there were bells ringing, church bells, sounding dolefully, mournfully, slow solemn strokes.

I slipped out of bed, went to the window and looked down into the street. Outside a policeman was trying to induce a very tipsy masker to relinquish his hold on a lamp post and go home. But the masquerader insisted that he had to go to Early Mass in the Cathedral. This seemed to disturb the policeman, for he argued long and patiently that such a thing was out of the question. But the masquerader was firm. Finally they departed, the policeman supporting the arm of the tippler.

At the corner this couple came face to face with two nuns who walked at the head of a long procession of little girls—girls all dressed alike in pink dresses—orphans on the way to church. The policeman dragged the reveler to one side and reverently raised his cap as the nuns passed by.

After they had all gone the street was empty again, except for a little woman all in black who hurried along with small, clicking steps following the nuns and orphans toward the church. And the sun of Ash Wednesday rose above the steep roofs of the houses opposite. I yawned prodigiously and turned into the room again. My grandfather lay in another bed, still sleeping. I went back and climbed into my own bed again. How strange New Orleans seemed after the plantation! The day before was a gorgeous dream. It couldn't have happened.

A little later there was a knock at the door and Robert came in, meek and mild, bearing the tray with the cups of early coffee. My grandfather sat up and took his cup, looking sleepily at me. As I sat cross-legged in bed sipping the warm, sweet drink I said to Robert: "Oh, wasn't Mardi Gras grand? Robert, *do* you remember . . ."

But he interrupted me. "Ah don't 'member a thing about it," he said meaningly.

"Oh!" I said, and was silent again.

Hoosiers

By William E. Wilson

> *"O the Moonlight's fair tonight along the Wabash,*
> *From the fields there comes the breath of new-mown hay;*
> *Thro' the sycamores the candlelights are gleaming,*
> *On the banks of the Wabash far away."*

"Wabash" is the magic word that calls up a thousand memories to any Hoosier. Along its banks live men known for their friendliness, their cordiality, the groaning tables their wives set, their respect for hard work and salty humor. The Hoosier and the Wabash belong to each other and both belong to America.

It is evening in Indiana, a summer evening. The supper dishes have been washed, and Mother and the daughter whose turn it was to dry them have just come out on the front porch. Some of the children have gone off to the movies or to linger over a soda fountain on Main Street, but the rest of the folks are there. Father is in the swing, his after-supper cigar sending up tendrils of smoke that curl about the moonvine on the trellis. Grandma is in a rocker, resting her feet and rocking gently, to stir up a little air. On the steps a small boy is nuzzling his second slice of watermelon. From time to time he spits out the slippery seeds that collect in the pockets of his cheeks and wipes the back of his hand across his face from ear to ear.

"Be careful, son," his father admonishes. "Don't swaller any seeds, or you'll have a watermelon vine agrowin' out your ears!"

The boy only grins and digs his nose deeper into the fruit. He knows how to eat a watermelon. He knows a lot of things that his father has probably forgotten. He knows how to make pokeberry ink and where to find the best pawpaws, butternuts, and sassafras root. He can knock the bow and spin in the stern's place with his taw. He knows how to fish for camelworms and catch a bullfrog with a red flannel rag. He knows where to find dewberries and how to catch a coon and the best way to take walnut stains off his hands. He can take care of himself, that boy!

The boy's sister and older brother are on the porch too, and Aunt Mollie, who has come over with a dish of her apple slump; and when Mother and her helper come out, it is truly "quite a getherin' "—as Grandma might say. But it is a quiet, comfortable, Hoosier-fed gathering, and, no matter how small the porch may be, there is still room for a neighbor or two.

Everyone looks up when Mother appears, but no one stirs. It isn't time yet. Mother sighs softly, unties her apron, takes down a palm-leaf fan from the rack, and settles herself in a rocker. "Hot!" she says but that is all and nobody answers. They continue to sit in silence, listening to the drone of the locusts and smelling the deep, rich smells of an Indiana summer evening—honeysuckle and heaven trees and other people's suppers. It is as if they were waiting for something. And they are. The soft Hoosier air itself is breathless, and the gathered family are silent as they wait.

It is the boy who sees it first. He stands up on the steps and points through the ghostly, mottled branches of the sycamores.

"Look!" he cries. "There she comes!"

Mother stops fanning herself, and Grandma's rocking ceases. Father turns slowly in the swing, taking his cigar from his mouth. Aunt Mollie utters a little cry of wonder, and the other children run to the boy's side. Then, for a while, everyone is silent again; for a great red moon is lifting slowly into the sky. Half the heavens it covers, almost, in the first few minutes, before it spills its blood upon the sultry evening air and sails more freely upward; and, no matter how many times they have seen it before, the folks on the porch are awed as they watch.

At last, Father turns to Mother and she nods in answer to his unspoken question. She is cool and rested now from her dishwashing.

"A harvest moon," she murmurs; and Father clears his throat, as if he were about to suggest a wholly new and unimagined thing, although everyone knows what he is going to say. It is what they have been waiting for.

"Well, folks," he says and clears his throat once more, "lets all go down and take a look at the river."

. . . A man who lives near a river cannot go for long without a visit to the riverbank. Anyone who has lived near flowing water—and most Americans have—knows that. The river draws him to it, like a magnet, and on its banks he will stand for hours, simply watching the water glide past.

He cannot tell you what attracts him or what holds him there. Perhaps it is the river's beauty. Perhaps it is the current's symbolism of eternal change within eternal changelessness. Perhaps it is the reassurance that the river gives him of the permanence and stability of his world; for the river is his first and natural boundary, and he knows that a strange place, without a river from which he could take his bearings, would seem to him strange indeed—shapeless, confusing, and without reason for being. Perhaps going to look at the river is not a spiritual ceremony at all, but only the river dweller's excuse for idleness. But whatever the motive and whatever the nature of the river—whether it is the clear, blue water that runs from the mountains to the sea or the yellow stream that winds through thousands of miles of bottom land before it reaches the Gulf, whether it is dotted with rich men's sails or cluttered with poor men's houseboats, whether it is navigable only to canoes or bluntly plowed by barges and paddle-wheelers, whether it yields shad or trout or the sleepy mud cat, swift or slow, turbulent or quiet—it is all the same. A man must go and look at the river now and then.

To know America, you have to take a good, long look at the Wabash River. This is not provincial Hoosier pride. Other rivers in America are just as important. But, on the banks of the Wabash, the shape and size of the United States were determined during the Revolution, setting the southern border of Canada for all time at the Great Lakes, rather than the Ohio, and opening the Far West to American development. And on the banks of the Wabash has been nurtured the rare fusion of southern grace and Yankee industry which, for more than a century, has made the Hoosier one of the finest of American types. . . .

These were the men who settled the Wabash country—Kentuckians, New Yorkers, Pennsylvanians, interloping opportunists with no tradition behind them, Virginians, and ultimately Yankees—and decided that Wabash soil should be free.

They were not always divided among themselves according to their backgrounds. Many of the Southerners came to Indiana because they found the institution of slavery abhorrent; many of the Northerners, like Benjamin Parke, worked for the introduction of slavery into the state. Strangely enough, some of the best Democrats, like James Whitcomb, who was elected governor in 1843 and 1846, were from New England, while some of the ablest Republicans, like Abraham Lincoln, were from the South. Perhaps that is why all Hoosiers are politicans at heart; their pioneer ancestors so often were members of fighting political minorities in the regions whence they migrated.

These were the ingredients poured into the Wabash melting pot in pioneer days. The slavery issue was not settled by them with the constitution of 1816, nor even with the case of the Lasselles' Polly. There were still three slaves in the state as late as 1840, and Article XIII of the new constitution of 1851 excluded the immigration of Negroes into Indiana. Even during the war of 1861–1865, the Wabash was a political, if not a military, battleground. But from these ingredients, after a half century, was ultimately distilled the Hoosier.

Physically, the Hoosier is likely to be tall and rather lean. At one time, there was no taller civilized man in the world. Dr. B. A. Gould of the United States Sanitary Service, studying statistics of the Civil War, discovered that "the Indiana men are the tallest of all the natives of civilized countries." The Hoosier's height was probably the result of his diet; for the cereals of the north central states are richer in proteins and show a larger number of heat units than the cereals of any other region of the world. In recent years, however, with standardized breakfast foods on every table and the consumption of corn, wheat, and rye no longer limited to the region in which they are grown, the Hoosier has lost the distinction of unequaled height.

The character of the Hoosier is not easy to describe, for he is a compound of many contradictory qualities inherited from both his Southern and his Yankee ancestors.

His friendliness and hospitality, however, are universally recognizable. He is easy to meet and quite ready to talk about himself. His eagerness to share his possessions as well as his private life sometimes appears naive to the outsider accustomed to the self-protective reticence and suspicion of more thickly populated regions. But the Hoosier is not naive. He inherits his tradition of cordiality from lonely pioneer days when every stranger was at once a welcome friend and a helpless supplicant; yet, from those same early days, he inherits a talent for quick and accurate appraisal of character. You may think that the Hoosier lays himself wide open on short acquaintance; but the chances are that he knows all there is to know about you long before he tells you a single significant thing about himself. If you think he is an easy mark, just try to skin him once—and see what happens!

The Hoosier is sentimental. His poetry and his flourishing fraternal societies, as well as his speech, are proof of that. And, in such a mellow and generous land as his, it is inevitable that he should be sentimental. But he is humorous also, and over his most saccharine effusions he is likely to sprinkle the salt of shrewd wit. Alone in his isolated cabin, thc pioneer had to fool himself to keep from going crazy; but he also had to know when he was being fooled, in order to stay alive.

The Hoosier is fond of good living. No man eats more heartily than he, and no man had better food to eat. Anyone who has put his feet under a Hoosier table will agree. Fried chicken such as can be found nowhere else, even in the South; perch and pickerel and fiddler catfish in a thick crust of brown batter; hickory barbecue that must be eaten out-of-doors to be fully appreciated; rich burgoo; buttered hominy; hot, flaky biscuits; dry, crisp porkchops; well-seasoned succotash stewed in rich, peppery juice; succulent roasting ears; buckwheat cakes with thick sorghum molasses; and blackberry "mountain pie" under a high crust of golden meringue—they specialize in these dishes in Indiana. And everyone who has ever tasted them comes back for more.

The Hoosier is many other things: shrewd; industrious; quick tempered; ambitious; conservative in politics, but willing to experiment; emotional in religion; and inordinately proud of his land. He is no longer of pure pioneer stock. Since the state was founded, there has been a good admixture of Irish and German blood in his veins. In some sections of the state, the Pole and the Italian have appeared in appreciable numbers. But it is because of these additions to his family, and not in spite of them, that the Hoosier is sometimes called "the typical American"; for he has somehow managed to Hoosierize them all.

As for the origin of the name "Hoosier"—no one is quite sure. Some have tried to trace it to the pioneer greeting from cabin windows when strangers knocked at night. The pioneer asked who was there, and from his question the word "Hoosier" was developed. But that explanation is rather farfetched; for the similarity between "Who's thar?" and "Hoosier" is very faint. Others have discovered that a company of hussars once made a nuisance of themselves in Kentucky and the word "hussar," or "husher," thereafter applied to all boisterous and objectionable outsiders, its application eventually being limited to the hard-drinking and rowdy Indiana men across the river. But such an isolated and largely hypothetical source is not satisfying.

Jacob Piatt Dunn, the historian, seems to know more about it than anyone else. He says that "hoosier" was a slang word once used in the south to denote a "jay" or "hayseed." It came originally from England, where "hoose" is still the common name for a disease of calves, known here as strongylus micrurius, which "causes their hair to turn back and gives them a wild, staring look." Any boy who has worn a stocking cap, the modern equivalent of the coonskin, will understand the condition of the average Indiana pioneer's hair; and any man who has experimented with the kind of Indiana "corn" that is preserved in jugs can explain the "wild, staring look."

Whatever its origin, "Hoosier" is now the name for all Indiana folk alike, of Yankee or of Southern stock or of more recent European background—and they all respond to it proudly.

Michigan Lumber Camp

By Thomas J. LeBlanc

In the winter, there was no greater excitement for a northern Michigan boy than riding by sleigh to visit the lumber camps. In the spring, the whole town looked forward to the time when the lumberjacks came to town. From the first day's burling contests till everyone was broke, the streets were enlivened by the riotous good spirits and vigor of the men.

My boyhood was spent in a small northern lumbering town in the heart of the pine forests that cluster along the Canadian border, and my earliest memories are of the whine of the great whirling disk saws in the mills, the crunch of the logs as they crowded the river that ran through the center of the town, the slap of the boards as they fell into place on the decks of the waiting schooners, and the call of the scalers and tally-men. At night the village was bathed in the radiance of the burners that stood against the dark sky like huge torches, each giving off its own flaming feather of sparks. Always there was the closeness of the bush that jostled the edges of the town and made inroads at some of the weaker spots. Over all was the clean fragrant smell of the pines.

Children were not numerous in such wild settlements and I had few playmates. To the few of us living there winter was a time of dog teams and, if we were lucky, an occasional visit to a lumber-camp. In this respect I was fortunate in having Billy. Billy was a friend of the family whose business I never knew. It was sufficient for me that he would call at our house with his sleigh, load me into the box, buried in bearskins, and whisk me away behind his jangling bells for a two- or three-day visit to a camp. For miles we rode, enveloped in a cloud of vapor from the horses, the bobs of the sleigh ringing on the surface of the snow. Finally we would turn on to the glistening surface of a tote road and I would cautiously raise myself and expose my face to the biting cold. We would be gliding down an icy lane, shining like a mirror, and with the tall snow-shrouded pines rising on either side. I used to liken it to riding down the aisle of a cathedral, a giant cathedral with a polished floor. I had once been in one at Christmas time, when the columns were hung with evergreens. Soon we would swing into the camp, a cluster of long, low log buildings huddled in a small clearing and completely buried in snow. Here we received a boisterous and profane greeting from the cook and cookee, and whoever else happened to be in camp.

At noon I sat proudly on the front seat of the stew sleigh, which was loaded with the noon meal for the men at the cutting. Upon our arrival at some central point the cook beat upon a dishpan with a large spoon and roared at the top of his voice, "Yow! 'S goin' to waste!" The ring of axes would then suddenly cease and answering calls would come from the white depths of the woods. Woolen-clad figures came tumbling in from all directions and soon the sleigh was surrounded by a noisy crowd of cutters, and they were served their noon meal of stew, bread, beans and tea by the cookee, who by the way, was the butt of most lumber-camp humor. The meal finished, the men engaged in various diversions: jacking blue jays, wrestling, or throwing things at the cookee. The noon hour over, they returned their various ways and soon the woods rang with the clear resonant notes of their biting axes, with now and then a call of "Comin' down!" followed by the crash of some old forest giant that shook the great folds of snow from the near-by trees as though a shiver had run through them.

At night the lumberjacks came riding in on loads of logs if the tote road passed near the camp, and it usually did. Supper was served at a long low table in one of the buildings and was a roaring and swashbuckling feast presided over by the foreman. The foreman held his position for the same reason that a leader-dog in a team holds his. If the occasion arose he could lick any one in camp, or at least his side could lick the other. All disputes were settled in this manner, promptly forgotten, and no grudge held. Immediately after supper the men gathered in the bunkhouse, a low cabin heated by a huge cylindrical baseburner stove that glowed cherry red in the dim light of the kerosene lamps. The walls were lined by a layer of double- or triple-decked bunks. There was no ventilation and when twenty or thirty lumberjacks gathered about the stove, all smoking cut plug tobacco, and with the place draped with steaming socks, mittens and mackinaws, the atmosphere was almost tangible. Add to this the melancholy whine of some inspired genius of the Jew's harp and the whole took on the air of a witch's cavern. Truly it was a sinister place.

Here as a boy, I sat silently drinking in every word of the tales that flew back and forth: epic tales of battles against thaws, floods, and log jams; tales of record cuttings, of how Black Bill beat Joe into the water with his logs, of the intense rivalry that existed between camps; tales of smallpox, the only disease that these men knew; of the legendary Paul Bunyan and his famous ox that was sixty feet between the eyes; of how Jean Frechette picked up a three hundred pound cask of chain and loaded it into the box of a sleigh; of Georges St. Pierre, who, upon hearing of this, snorted, and, placing his arms around a small horse that stood near by, lifted it clear off the ground and held it struggling; and, lastly, tales of great fights and great fighters . . . tales of men.

During the night a teamster with a sprinkling sleigh flooded the tote road with water and by morning it was a smooth, unbroken sheet of ice. Getting out at two in the morning in weather that was always ten to twenty below zero required considerable enthusiasm, but one who did venture forth was magnificently repaid. These teamsters, and especially the night men, were the most picturesquely profane fellows that I have ever heard, and I have heard many. They were no ordinary blasphemers, but virtuosi. Their horses were full of spirit, and sprinkling the road at night was always attended by unlooked for contingencies. On these occasions, if you were fortunate enough to be present, you were afforded the treat of hearing an artist perform. There was no ordinary disconnected and unrelated flow of vulgarities, but a symphony of rational and harmonious phrases. Let us suppose that it was the off horse that offended. The teamster began his picture by addressing the horse in a low restrained voice. The main theme was genealogical and concerned the horse's ancestors. This was then amplified by a counterpoint that dealt with the horse's present status. The teamster had a fine feeling for the climax, and as he progressed his voice grew louder and louder, and his harmonies more full and round, finally ending in one completely summarizing and devastating phrase. One unconsciously listened for the rumble of the tympani and the crash of the cymbals. I have heard some of the older artists lecture to a horse on some of its major deficiencies for a full five minutes without once repeating the same phrase. Needless to say, their bark was worse than their bite, and sometimes I suspected that the horses appreciated that fact.

Such visits to the camps were the high lights in the winter season and served to hasten the coming of spring. With spring came the drive and with the drive came the lumberjacks, and with their coming the boys of the town looked forward to days and days of riotous entertainment. When the ice melted, the logs that had been piled along the headwaters of the river and on the shores of the lakes were tumbled into the water and their journey to the mills began. The crews followed the drive along the lakes and slower reaches of the river until the current was fast enough to swing the logs along, with the occasional untangling of a jam. Booms of logs fastened together by chains were thrown across the mouth of the river, and soon the bay was a heaving carpet of pine logs, each branded on the end with the mark of its owner. As the drive neared completion and the last fleet of logs swung into view around the upper bend of the river, the lumberjacks began to appear, at first singly and then in groups. Each rode a log easily and gracefully, his calked boots sunk into the soft bark, and leaning on his pike-pole or peavy. I remember how the sight used to thrill me. These fellows, superb in their disdain for danger, with such an air of complete poise, apparently gliding down the surface of a boiling river, seemed more like gods than mere men. I thought that if the gods ever actually visited the earth they would travel like this.

Across the river, some distance from the mouth and connecting the two halves of the town, was a bridge. During the drive the water level was high enough for the bridge to be reached by a leap from the logs that swirled beneath. This made a natural terminal for the lumberjacks. As each one approached the bridge on his log he let out a howl that would have sent the shivers up and down the spine of a lone wolf. This was to notify the town that it was about to be honored by his presence; it also called his friends to the bridge ends. At the proper time he gave forth another howl, a howl of warning to the passers-by as he hurled his pike-pole up on the floor of the bridge. Then, crouching on his log and measuring his distance accurately, at just the proper instant he leaped, caught the lower stringer of the bridge and like a cat swung himself up over the rail. A third howl, answered by his friends, denoted that he had officially arrived. Sometimes, but only rarely, he misjudged the distance and missed the lower stringer, in which case he never gave the third howl. His friends stood for a few minutes gazing mutely down stream at the pounding logs and then hurried off to tell the town bartenders that so-and-so had missed the bridge. Telling the bartenders was in the nature of a published obituary.

When the drive was finished and the last man in, down to the cook and cookee, the men were paid off. This pay amounted to a considerable sum, since they received three to five dollars a day all winter and had no expenses. Upon receipt of his money each jack hurried to his favorite boarding-house and purchased a ticket which assured him board, room, tobacco and laundry all summer. The last item was merely a concession to gentility. Purchase of his ticket left him a considerable balance and with this thrust in the breast pocket of his shirt he swaggered forth . . . and the fun began.

First came the burling contests. Burling consisted of standing on a log with calked boots and, by running or walking at right angles to the axis of the log, imparting a spinning motion to it, somewhat in the manner of a treadmill. Two men on the same log constituted a burling contest. The river near the bridge was dotted with logs, each supporting a pair of burlers. One man won as soon as the other missed his footing and fell into the water. After this elimination the contest narrowed down to the two most skilful burlers. This ended the first day and the final spin was held over until the next. In the meantime the jacks were usually about evenly divided in opinion as to which was the better man of the two final contestants. Betting went on furiously and it was nothing for a whole camp crew to bet their last cent on one of the burlers if he happened to be from their camp. It made no practical difference whether they won or lost, for the money was spent in any case, the winners spending lavishly because they had won, and the losers accepting their hospitality for the equally good reason that they had lost.

All this occurred late in June. After the burling contest was decided, together with the score of fights that always attended such a public show, the next great social event, as it were, was the series of Fourth of July dances. They were so designated because they began on the Fourth, but they lasted until men and maidens, and especially the last, had been exhausted. They were held in places called boweries erected on vacant lots by the lumberjacks themselves. A bowery consisted of a large square floor, roofed over and buried in fragrant cedar and balsam boughs; it resembled somewhat a band stand or pavilion but it was built of clear, knotless white-pine boards, most of them two feet in width. At one end was a platform for the orchestra and the caller. The music was provided by an organ and a fiddler, not a violinist. The distinction is very real. A violinist clamps a violin between the lower border of his mandible and the prominence of his clavicle. With half-closed eyes he sways with the music, while his fingers flutter up and down the length of the fingerboard as he coaxes out the velvet tones. A fiddler, and especially a lumberjack fiddler, lays a fiddle carelessly against his chest, thumps loudly with one foot, and uses only the middle six inches of the bow and a single position on the keyboard to tear out a melody that sets the calked boots to chewing up the new pine floor. While he plays he stares defiantly at his audience and only lowers his eyes at intervals to expectorate over the edge of the platform with sufficient accuracy to avoid harsh criticism from the dancers.

The dances in favor were the so-called square ones, and the party was continuous. There were halts only at the end of the different sets of figures to change partners or to allow fresh couples to replace jaded ones. The whole thing was full of gaudy color, with the lumberjacks in their brilliant woolens, the girls in their calicoes, and the cedar boughs and festoons of bunting over all. The girls were the town's finest and many were the romances that began to the tune of "Swing Yer Partner" or "All Join Hands." I hope I am not divulging any secret when I observe that some of these same girls, thrilled in those far-off days by a whirl in the arms of a perspiring jack, are now matrons of society in the North. A lumberjack, when he went to a dance, was fascinating in direct proportion to the vigor with which he whirled his partner, while the girls were classified as charming or not according to whether their skirts stood out gracefully when they were whirled through the figures. Undoubtedly some of the matrons that I have mentioned will be furious when I whisper that the girls resorted to the unfair device of sewing buckshot into the lower hems of their skirts. I know this to be a fact because once, in my childish absorption of what was going on at one end of the hall, I was struck over the eye by three whirling shot. The dances stopped when all the girls in town were so exhausted that they had to go home. By this time the bowery had spent its usefulness; the floor was chewed paper-thin by the grinding and stamping of calked boots.

The social activity of the town now moved to the saloons. Four stood at each end of the bridge, and as a boy I posted myself every night to command a view of all eight doors. When a fight started, I could be at the scene of battle in an instant. I never had long to wait. The show began with the sudden bursting open of the swinging doors by the rocketing rush of the two contestants, followed more leisurely by the crowd from within. Sometimes the fighters stopped their mauling upon reaching the road, and then each would regain the proper state of frenzy by reciting in a loud, vivid and profane manner what he intended to do to the other. These announced plans were usually very extravagant and gruesome, such as complete removal of the heart, plucking out an eye, or tearing off a leg to be used as a club. The audience listened attentively, if a little bored, but never interrupted the recital. When the proper pitch of battle fury had been reached the two jacks hurled themselves upon each other, and in an instant became a gyrating, cursing mass of thrashing fists and flying feet. They cursed and clawed, sometimes, for an hour at a time, and ended a half mile from their starting point. Sometimes the oratorical preliminaries were dispensed with and the two jacks set immediately to the task of doing each other bodily harm.

These man-like animals, with the hearts and minds of children, set simple rules to govern their encounters. They operated on the rather logical premise that when one fights one does it in order to mutilate or maim the other fellow. There was no code. The task in hand was to beat the other fellow thoroughly, and the quickest and most efficient method was the best. Therefore, nothing was barred. Clawing, gouging, biting, butting, choking, kneeing and kicking were among the better known maneuvers, and not the least of the finer points of the game was to flop your adversary to the ground, and, just as he landed, to plant your calked boot accurately on his face. Many a jack had intricate if not beautiful designs tattooed on his cheeks by this method. They asked no quarter and gave none. The fight was continuous and ended only when one man could no longer resist. He was then officially out. Usually his opponent was the first to assist him to his feet and it was no uncommon sight to see two such fighters a half hour later arm in arm at the bar, singing each other's praises. A grudge never existed and the difference that caused a fight was considered permanently settled when the fight was concluded.

The favorite refreshment was a quart bottle of rot-gut whisky into which had been stuffed a handful of fine-cut chewing tobacco. The whole was shaken vigorously and was then ready for consumption. A treat on the street consisted in hauling out one's bottle, giving it a shake, drawing the cork with the teeth, running a thumb around the neck (a mark of good breeding, as the ruder members of the guild neglected this charming office) and extending it with the remark, "Have a smile, Jack." A refusal on any grounds constituted an insult, which in turn meant a fight. Very few ever refused.

But life for Jack was not all laughter, dancing and fighting. Sometimes there was a tear in his eye, for underneath his hard surface was a soft sentiment and a heart that could swell. I have seen a whole barroom, including the bartender, sad and tearful when some husky, whisky baritone sang, "The Little Boy in Green" or recited "Father, Dear Father, Come Home With Me Now." When the Widow Monahan's cottage at the edge of town burned early one morning, the whole saloon population swarmed to the scene, and by nightfall, after numerous fights and much profanity, the widow gazed through her tears over a flashing new picket fence at a handsome new cottage, complete even to the chicken-coop full of chickens. On another occasion Smoky Paquette, one of the hardest fighters of the North, was told that Father de Vere, the parish priest, had been pining for years for a stained-glass window for his little church. Though none of the jacks had ever seen the inside of a church, least of all Smoky, he, after a proper mellowing with rot-gut, elected himself collector for the worthy pastor. He mounted a table in the Deerhead Saloon and in a bellow that made the flames of the kerosene lamps quiver announced, "I jest heerd that le bon père d'Vere wants a picture windy fer his church, an' I'm 'nouncing that you lousy log rollers is about to tally in fer it." Then with his round felt bush-hat in a fist like a Smithfield ham, he made the rounds of the eight saloons. His method was simple and to the point. He approached each jack, thrust the hat under the victim's nose with his left hand, cocked back his right, and in a voice like a peevish bear, announced that he was collecting for a picture windy for the church. Since Smoky had proven his ferocity on a hundred occasions, his method brought results, and soon one of the cookees, properly lickered up, was wobbling on his way to the priest's house with the money for a picture windy stuffed in the front of his shirt.

So day followed day, each jammed with action and excitement, until all the cash of the men was spent and the town settled down into its summer doze. Then Jack sat in front of his boarding-house and whittled miniature cant-hooks and peavies for the kids. Or he and his friends strolled along in pairs, and where they walked their calked boots gouged the sidewalk into two parallel troughs. After a summer shower these troughs filled with water, and when the sun reappeared I sat fascinated, watching the men swaggering along the little silvery lanes, their heavy boots throwing out sprays of diamonds at every step. Or sometimes I crouched near the basement window of a saloon in the cool, moist draft that came from the beer coils, and listened to tales by my favorite old jack, Pop Gardener. Once I said to him, "Pop, you're getting old. Some day a tree will get you, or you'll die in a barroom. Why don't you quit?" Pop bristled up in his red arm-chair and, glaring down at me, replied, "Sure thing, bucko, a tree will get me, er I'll turn in my check in a barroom; but what of it? Ain't I pickin' my own way of goin', eh? An' won't I be cashin' in among frien's? 'N that's a hell of a lot mor' 'n some of these soft bellies can say. God a-mighty, kid, think o' peterin' out in a hoss-pee-tal among strangers!"

Jack had no thought of the hereafter. His religion was chance, and chances existed only to be taken. If you were lucky certain things happened to you, and if you were unlucky other things happened. In either case you could do nothing about it. His life was hard. He worked hard, played hard, and fought hard. His liquor was hard, his muscles were hard and so was his voice. Everything about him was hard except his heart, and that was soft, full of rough sentiment, and a capacity for loyalty, friendship and generosity that knew no bounds. Clean, hard and vital, Jack was an honest man. . . .

Iowa State Fair

By Phil Stong

Every family in the corn belt looks forward to the State Fair. Baking contests, where the height of a sponge cake or the flakiness of a crust can win a blue ribbon; livestock judgings, where the carefully groomed hog seems to know he's the center of attraction; horse races; fan dancers; the carnival atmosphere of the midway —all provide enough excitement to last until the next State Fair comes along.

There was a time when "Going to the Fair" meant a night journey in a truck with all the family, and with a hog or a blue-blooded bull or a few show-worthy, bad-tempered fowls crated up beside the baskets of quince jelly and angel-food cake which made up the womenfolk's stake in the rivalry of the Fair. That night you had to keep feeling in your pocket to make sure your pickle money or the extra dollar grandpa had given you for dissipation on the roller coaster had not slipped through a hole; and you had to pretend to be asleep in spite of the jolting, when all the time you were wide-awake and had your eyes fixed on the sky ahead where the first light from the fairgrounds would appear.

There wasn't much talk after the first hour or two, and of course you did fall asleep at last; and when you woke up, there was the Fair, and the campground waiting for you.

That is one way—and perhaps the best way to go. But there are other good ways: by train, for instance, or by bus and by big sedans (76,000 cars were parked at the Fair last year), and even by planes flashing along from all the spokes of the compass toward the fairgrounds. For one week in August each year since 1854 (except for the interruption of war) the State Fair is the capital of America's Corn Belt, the site of the greatest food festival in the world. Last year it was celebrated by more than half a million people, through whose efforts most of America—and a good deal of Europe—eats.

The glow from the Fair warms the returning native long before it can be seen. He can feel it in the club car running westward just out of the grimy suburbs of Chicago. He has had an evening on the New York Central, or perhaps the Pennsylvania, surrounded by stately gentlemen absorbed in *The New York Times* and the *Wall Street Journal* and by cold, correct and lonely women dressed by Sophie Gimbel and Nettie Rosenstein. The radio on the train last night gave stock-market reports, a little soft music, and nothing more.

This morning, on the Rocket, he is already in the Midwest, and the club car is full of other pilgrims to the Iowa State Fair. Not the farmers, who have created the Fair and to whom it belongs, but visitors and acolytes from outside who assist at the ceremonies in every way, from setting up radio stations or selling cotton candy or guessing people's weight or presenting a much-expurgated fan dance to looking over the stock exhibits for the Department of Agriculture or making a survey of the Four-H Clubs for the Farm Bureau. There will be a sprinkling, too, of research men from the eastern agricultural colleges, and probably a breezy young man from *Variety*. If the young woman across the aisle happens to be the fan dancer, she will be just as correct as the ladies of last night, but friendlier—and a lot better-looking.

A poker game will start up soon and a gin-rummy game or two; and as the train nears the Mississippi, drinks will be ordered in a hurry. In Iowa, spirits may be sold only by the bottle on a state liquor license, though beer is plentiful, even on the fairgrounds.

The porter, who has been traveling this road for years with State Fair passengers, knows when to turn the radio on, and at the first words that boom from the loud-speaker, the card players pause and every head in the car goes up.

"Temperature 102. Tomorrow and Wednesday, fair and warmer."

A sigh of relief goes round the car and everybody grins. "Good Fair weather."

Nobody knows why the Fair does its best business in a temperature just under boiling. But a comfortably cool gray day cuts the box-office receipts in half. Without the sun, Iowans just won't make merry.

There are a few air-conditioned hotel rooms in Des Moines, but you have to reserve one months ahead, and then you wonder why you bothered, for the descent to Avernus is twice as awful. The streets shimmer, your collar melts, your shoes stick to the pavements; but out at the end of the long trolley line will be white pavilions and lemonade and iced beer and bands playing in the shade. The mighty race of Iowans will be eating fried chicken, hot roast beef and hickory-smoked Hampshire hams when the foreigner from the East can face only a sliced tomato or a bit of ice cream.

The Iowans are right, of course; for seeing the Fair burns up as much energy per hour as plowing the roughest field. There are 378 acres of grounds—full of stock pavilions, exhibition and industrial buildings, small concessions, the grandstand, and the Midway—something over four million dollars' worth of permanent installations. The judging of livestock begins at eight A.M.; there are harness and running races and rodeos all afternoon, and at night there is a big show in the grandstand with fireworks till eleven. Since there are only eight of these fifteen-hour days, one has to keep moving not to miss anything; and one has to eat every two or three hours, to combat exhaustion.

Probably a European observer in the present state of the world would consider all this eating excessive—if not callous. But he would be forgetting that the tribe of Midwest farmers, reduced one third in numbers by the draft, worked double-time, plowed at night by floodlights, had their twelve-year-old children driving tractors to produce the food that set new records for this country and broke Hitler's grip on the continent of Europe.

An English photographer sent by a New York magazine to cover the Fair in 1946 spent Fair Week in a daze. So much food, and none of it boiled. So many acres of shiny parked automobiles. Farmers buying Piper Cubs and helicopters. "But where are the wagons and bicycles?" he asked. "And why are all these city people here?"

They were not city people, but plain dirt farmers, solid, prosperous, well dressed. If Will Rogers were to play in *State Fair* today, he'd have to spruce up a bit more than he did in 1932—much more than he ever did in private life. His beloved seersucker pants might do around the Fox lot in Hollywood, but they'd look pretty dowdy at the Iowa State Fair.

Though the Fair is strictly a family outing, the visiting family separates after breakfast, each member in a hurry to reach the building representing his special interest. The men and the Four-H youngsters flock to the livestock barns—except for those who already are installed there for the duration, sleeping in the upstairs dormitories or on a cot alongside Blue Boy or Lord Lard, or ox-eyed Jersey Juno, who won the blue ribbon last year for milk production. If a family member is showing any of these lordly creatures, he will be busy all day and every day till his class comes up for judging.

Swine and sheep and cattle and horses have to be curried, fed, watered, cheered up, and above all, kept cool. The stock pavilions are the most carefully designed and solidly built of all the Fair buildings, and the best ventilated. After all, they house for a whole week tenants whose value runs into so many millions that even the State Fair publicity office hesitates to estimate it. "Nobody would believe us," they say. These pedigreed animals are delicate and nervous and when you are showing them you are as worried as the manager of a new soprano before her debut at the Metropolitan. It is not unusual in the cattle barn to see a pretty girl squatting in the straw and sponging the face of a mean-looking bull, while her own face streams sweat that she doesn't bother to wipe away.

The stock people will not soon forget that $5000 Berkshire boar that in 1947 minced daintily around the judging ring, acquired his blue ribbon, cakewalked back to his stall and lay down dead.

On the other hand, hogs are such ornery animals that they are likely to catch cold in the middle of summer and die of pneumonia, a fact which so impressed Henry King, director of the 1933 movie version of *State Fair* that, after paying $5000 for Hampshire Blue Boy at the Iowa Fair, and three thousand for Esmeralda, its Duroc girl friend, he spent several thousand dollars more for understudies. For the same amount of money he could have hired several of the highest-salaried human stars to do the fifteen minutes' worth of acting required of the hogs.

To take care of Blue Boy and Esmeralda and the understudies, the motion-picture company employed for forty-five dollars a week a young man out of the stock pavilion, one Martin Fabricius, who held the degree of Bachelor of Science in Animal Husbandry from the State College at Ames.

Martin was unimpressed by Hollywood, spent all his waking hours beside Blue Boy's mahogany-railed pen, declined to meet Janet Gaynor or any other stars—"Girls are all alike," he said—and after three weeks got homesick. Not for a cent under fifty dollars a week would he stay any longer. It took several conferences and some hot words between executives, but finally even movie officials had to admit that it was a poor gamble to risk $10,000 worth of high-strung hog for five dollars a week for six weeks. Martin stayed. After the picture was finished, the bachelor of science went back to his farm in Iowa and Blue Boy was sent to a model farm in Sacramento, where he died, as *Time* magazine put it, "of overtraining and overeating."

Fabricius was a typical example of the serious-minded, educated younger generation of farmers who come in such numbers to the Fair. You seldom see them in the grandstand or on the Midway, for they congregate in the stock-show buildings and stand in crowds before the industrial exhibits, absorbed in the newest farm inventions. A new machine shown at the Fair may affect the working hours and the production of millions of farmers throughout the whole Missouri Valley.

Scientific mastodons like the combine and the hay baler have revolutionized farm life. But even a minor gadget like the posthole digger has saved untold man-hours in the few years since it was invented and introduced at the Iowa State Fair.

Interior fences in Iowa have to be changed frequently. You may graze cattle on a plot one year, grow wheat the next, raise clover the next and turn cattle on it. This requires two changes of fencing and perhaps a hundred fence posts, for the light brush and barbed-wire fencing that will keep cattle in pasture will not keep them out of growing grain, which they can ruin in a night (at ninety dollars an acre on the current market).

Ten years ago, a man could set about twenty posts a day by hand. Today he takes out his tractor with a squizerroo that looks like a Buck Rogers gimmick for going to the center of the earth. He pulls a lever and his gimlet yanks out a posthole in less time than it would take even the best dentist to drill to one's forebrain.

Then there is the corn-picker. A farmer does not drive his wagon slowly while his children and neighbors heave corn into it. He drives a truck lightly up and down while a machine tosses corn into it as gaily as a pickpocket looting at Mardi Gras.

These machines are what the young men look at, at the Fair, and what they buy with the money they made by nearly killing themselves with work through the war years. And these are the beneficent robots that may save the world by feeding it.

The women at the Fair are also bent on feeding the world, or their section of it. There is no temptation now for them to linger at a bingo game for nylons between the gates and the Women's Building or the Educational Building, where canned goods and other culinary entries are judged, for the Fair has outlawed games of chance. The one ingenious circumvention of this rule—a wheel of fortune with a live mouse which, by popping into one hole or another, picks the winning number—does not attract the girls. Half of them are sorry for the mouse and the other half are afraid of it.

The mouse wheel presumably gets its license by "teaching animal behavior." Another educational exhibit which might conceivably interest women is patronized almost exclusively by men: the display of embryos in bottles which is called *Life Begins*.

Bingo and mice and embryos notwithstanding, the women find ample excitement in the Women's and Children's Building.

It houses the home economics and hobby exhibits, a recreational center, the baby-health contests, and a day nursery, to say nothing of a peaceful dining room where the infant Iowan can have his formula prepared by dieticians trained at Ames, and a mother can recharge her energy with an appetizing meal or glass of iced tea served in the Iowa manner with plenty of sugar and lemon juice.

In the Women's and Children's Building one may learn the newest magic of pressure cookery and home freezing and vitamin juggling. But if, as Ruskin said, "cookery means the knowledge of Medea and of Circe and of Helen . . ." (if Helen needed to know about the cookstove) "and of the Queen of Sheba," there are other sorceries that the girls practice in that sacred building at the Iowa State Fair. A male intruder at these rites is not in actual danger of being torn limb from limb by stout, matronly priestesses, but he may wish he had been before he makes his getaway from their shrine.

Escaping the hissing pressure cookers, he may blunder into a room full of gargantuan, hostile infants competing for the Baby Health prizes. Fleeing from these, he can hardly avoid a fashion show, or a concert of P. T. A. musicians who call themselves the Mother Singers. If he dashes through a doorway across the hall, he is likely to step into a rapt circle of females waving palm fans and staring at a woman on the platform who is making a Flower Arrangement out of two Golden Glows and a stalk of Jimson weed. If he runs from their indignant eyes, he may burst into the auditorium just in time to see the Linn County Pageant or a herd of tunicked ladies doing a determined folk dance.

Outside the temple of Ceres and P. T. A., all is normal and reassuring. The bands play, the midget railroad train careens around the park, the psychological mouse jumps in and out of holes, winning hams for Iowans; and now that the judging of livestock and jams and pickles is over for the day, everybody is heading for the grandstand, to see the bland vaudeville, with nothing more ribald than some Scotch and Irish jokes and some prat falls, the horse and auto races, which are one hundred per cent moral because betting is not allowed.

By half past five, if the fiery sun is not lower, one at least believes that soon it will be (in spite of daylight time); and with nothing to stick to one's ribs since lunch but seven hot dogs, four hamburgers, a cubic foot of cotton candy, three sacks of popcorn and assorted pops, colas and ades, one is beginning to look forward to the big plate of baked ham or fried chicken, mashed potatoes, and the pie à la mode that even now are being served in the dining halls and tents dotted about the fair-grounds.

There won't be time for more than two pieces of pie, because the Midway must be covered before the big State Fair Revue at the grand-stand, which starts at half past seven.

By half past six, with supper over, the sun really has dropped a little; the girls from the Four-H dormitories are coming out in pink and yellow dresses, after a long day in jeans, washing the faces of discontented cows; the Four-H boys and some of their Des Moines cousins are sauntering down the boardwalks in clean white flannels, looking sidewise at the girls; and even the women who have Flower-arranged and Mother-sung and pressure-cooked all day are wearing thin, pale dresses and silly hats over their pink plump faces, and showing a tendency to giggle.

The Midway is always the same, and always new. The dwarfs, the giants, the tattooed men, the hairy apes are here, visible in glory for seven days, like a comet lighting up the dark and quiet night of the sober Midwest.

The Heart of the Fair

Old Fair-goers would be grieved and disappointed if any of the traditional shows were missing. The sudden death in Pittsburgh of the Fat Man en route to the Fair in 1946 drew a two-column front-page headline in the Des Moines *Register*. People could have gone to see his Fat Wife and Fat Daughter, who had bravely come ahead when Papa was taken to the hospital; but it hardly seemed decent, when always, time out of mind, they had been the Fat Family of the Fair.

If the prizes at the rifle galleries and the hoop-la stands were anything but hideous and useless, that would be unfitting too. The Iowan who is a crack shot or hoop thrower expects to go home from the Fair with kewpie dolls and plush pigs and table lamps encursted with polychrome and dripping tassels—and a ham or two, also by way of coals to Newcastle.

The barkers have changed somewhat, it is true. The words and the sleek good looks are the same, but the music is different. Their voices are lower now, and smoother. They have listened to and learned from Frank Sinatra. Either you come in and see Zotz, the What-is-it, or you feel you have broken a nice boy's heart.

The girl shows are right and proper, too, a traditional part of the Fair, though grass skirts and bras and sequined panties may be scantier than ever, and the motions of the dance less inhibited. Still, five inches of ankle in 1902 must have had as startling an effect on the libido as five feet of girl in 1948.

But a new girl show appeared on the Midway in 1947—just one girl. The hot and weary people emerging from the freak show, too languid for hoop-la contests, bored with embryos in bottles, saw and stopped before the pitch of Sally Rand. At a rate of 10,000 every evening, they bought tickets and went in to see her.

The dance is beautiful, and Sally herself, only a lovely clean-cut face above the slowly moving, swathing ostrich plumes, is a new kind of State Fair enchantress. Even the women like her. "She looks like such a *nice* girl," they said.

Sally is an expert showman and press agent for Sally Rand. On the grounds, she lives in her own circus van, air-conditioned, decorated by W. & J. Sloane of New York, fitted with its private telephone. It must be the most un-private private telephone number in the world, for Sally gives it to everybody she meets, with the least flicker of a leer in her blue eyes. "If it gets too hot for you, my wagon is cooled, you know." But she gives it to women and children too.

When she is dancing on the Midway many of the matrons who expected to have to drag father away from her in time for the fireworks have to be dragged themselves.

It was thanks to Miss Rand that the grandstand filled up slowly on those August nights of 1947. Her admirers missed part of the State Fair Revue, the first riotous ensemble, "Tally Ho," with "the entire Ballet, dressed in dashing red-flecked riding costumes," depicting "in a rollicking spirit, a Ride to the Hounds."

When the red-flecked riders gave way to *Treasure Island*, a wonderful and awful mélange of Robert Louis Stevenson, Gilbert and Sullivan's *Pirates*, and the *Arabian Nights*, the audience was larger.

And of course nobody wanted to miss the grand finale, when Miss Victory was shot from the mouth of a cannon *three hundred feet*, or fifty in all, not including the arc, across the race track.

The fireworks that concluded the show in 1947 seemed slightly tame compared to those of the year before, which displayed Bikini under the atom bomb. The fireworks people cannot do without war and disaster. When the Four Horsemen do not ride, rockets and Roman candles and set pieces of F.D.R. or Lincoln or George Washington blossom and fade in the sky, to no quickening of the heartbeat.

An old Fair-goer remembers better spectacles; the Battle of Manila Bay, with Spanish men-of-war sinking fast and furiously and the Stars and Stripes flashing out above the burning sea; between wars, a sortie back into ancient history, with all the colonnades of Pompeii sinking under red lava from a skyhigh Mount Vesuvius; then the fresh sensation from a brand-new war, the Battle of the Argonne Forest.

The atom bomb which has staggered the world delighted rather than dismayed the pyrotechnicians of the Iowa State Fair. The tiny Pacific island outlined in lights rocked, quivered, exploded and burned under its carefully designed mushroom of colored smoke.

The fireworks end at last, and the crowd begins to pick up handbags, gather extra jackets (it might just possibly have turned cool toward midnight) and slip tired feet back into castoff shoes. But the pygmy man on the stage there, under the floodlights, is speaking again into his amplifier.

"Folks, friends, please—a moment. Before we disperse from this glorious celebration, one small request. Will you all, each of you, fish in your pockets and your purses for a match, a cigarette lighter. Wait. When the band blows one big resounding note, light up. Send forth a little candle in a naughty world."

The response is universal. Men dig match books from their pockets, hand some of them to the women beside them who do not smoke. On the lighted stage facing the grandstand the Music Department of the Women's Club, Cedar Rapids, takes a deep breath and a firm grip on its instruments, lets out a tremendous squawk of various sound, and from one end of the long grandstand to the other, tiny lights spring out, pinpointed like a quilt of luminous stitches. Under the long roof, people jerk upright, visible as in daylight. And they sigh, from 30,000 throats.

The Fair, breaking up for the night, flows in two directions at once, like an addled river. The larger current (between 70,000 and 100,000 people) moves toward the outside gates, the parking field, the East Des Moines streetcar lines, or the faint hope of empty taxicabs. At the other end of that long avenue stretching due west toward the river and the city, are the crowded hotel lobbies, the airless boardinghouses, the tumbled suitcases and borrowed electric fans and yesterday's wilted clothes. It is going to be another hot night in town.

For 5000 Iowans, however, there is a shorter, happier path to bed. If you are one of these, you turn left when you leave the grandstand and walk past the Midway and the Old Mill and the roller coaster; past the shuttered dining halls and the lemonade stands; past the little man folding up his scales and grinning at you because for nine hours now he will not have to guess the weight of any fat woman who scowls because he does not miss, or rattle off any more of his old jokes in his hoarsely gentle voice. You will meet members of the bands, lugging their big brass pretzels toward home and rest.

Final Curtain

Far across the park there is the rumble of heavy wheels around the stock pavilions. The real monarchs of the Fair, hog, bull, and stallion, are taken home as soon as their classes are judged, and the young men—and some of the girls—who have shown them ride with them. All night they will trundle over the roads toward the home farms before the hot sun rises.

Your path begins to climb a dark hillside, past the glimmer of 19th Century white gingerbread outlining the old Exposition Building. That is the building you always see in your mind's eye when you think of the Fair. It has always been there since you saw it first from your father's shoulder. You hope it always will be.

The sleepy guard at the entrance to the campground nods at you and turns his stile, and you are almost home. This is the unchanged and the unchanging Fair. The Tama Indian who always has sat there before his tepee, like Buddha, smiling at the passers-by, is there now, rolled up in a thin blanket on the ground. The people ahead of you turn in at their tents, calling soft good nights. The flaps and sides of the tents are fastened up, and some of the cots have been pulled out on the platform before the entrances. Maybe you will pull yours out too, this hot night; but probably you won't have to.

That was a good tent site that grandfather staked out in 1892, near the top of the hill where the breeze could reach it under fine shade trees, and near the spring. The spring has not been so important these forty years since they built the bathhouses and put in faucets everywhere. But it still flows and its water will make the best boiled coffee in the world tomorrow morning.

Bock Beer Days in St. Louis

By Lucille Kohler

The Easter morning trip to Herr Klein's with pail and beer chip was entirely and wonderfully different from any other day in the year. This was the beginning of a celebration; this was bock beer time. While the dark, mellow brew lasted, the festival spirit in the German community of old St. Louis remained at its height. There seemed no end to the miracles that bock could work.

It was Easter Sunday morning, and my sister Hulda and I were dressed for Sunday school. Already we had found our hidden nests of colored eggs under clumps of grass on the front lawn. Now, with a clamor for nickels for the collection box, we wanted to be off to the place where we would hear how many eggs other little girls had found and help ourselves to such assorted mysteries of the day as the *Deutsche Evangelische Kirche* had to offer.

"Wait once," said mama. "Papa has been up since five o'clock making nests for you children. Now he should have his enjoyment, too. You have first time to go to the saloon and get him *bock* beer."

"Bock beer!"

How these words wove joy into our spirits, how they rang like music in our shining ears! Here was a point in the onward course of our childhood from which a few succeeding days would shoot like stars in the firmament. Here was an epoch!

We knew that while bock beer lasted the *eltern* would be gayer, kinder. We knew that while bock beer lasted pretzels would be free at all beer saloon counters, and patrons, moved to song, would grow hoarse in *saengerfests*. We knew that while bock beer lasted there would be many who would marry, some even for a second time; and second weddings were twice as much fun. We knew that with bock beer and pinochle the grown-ups would let the evenings stretch and give us our fill of games and peanuts.

For bock beer was the dark and ripened beverage with which the breweries of old St. Louis hailed the Risen Lord and the end of the Lenten season. All the saloons had it on Easter morning.

Mama took a quart pail from the pantry shelf and filled it with cold water at the hydrant outside the kitchen door. When she had made sure the lid was tight down she went to her handbag.

"Only one beer chip left," she said as she shook up the change in the purse. "Here is a silver dollar." She turned to Hulda, for Hulda was the older. "Buy twenty-four chips from Herr Klein. We shall need that many while he has bock beer. Be sure you bring home twenty-three."

We took the bucket between us and started up the street. "Mind that you ask for bock beer and keep the water in till you get there so the vessel will stay cool," mama*chen* called after us.

In Hermann Klein's saloon Hulda and I stood on the rail and swung our bucket up to the counter. Here we could see well what was going on behind the bar.

Herr Klein, quite as tall as papa and with more waist, was busy hanging dozens of fresh pretzels from a bread basket onto a wooden rod. I nudged Hulda, my mouth watered so. Frau Klein, his wife, had made a border of Easter eggs around the back bar and was now admiring them as they doubled themselves in the mirror.

"*Morgen, kinder*," said Herr Klein.

"Bock beer," said Hulda.

"*Ach mein Je, mein Je!*" wailed the saloonkeeper as his hands went into the air. "It did not come this morning!"

Hulda bit her lip in silence. Then my foot slipped on the polished rail and I went down to the floor.

"For shame on you, Hermann Klein," cried the saloonkeeper's wife as she hurried to our side of the bar. "Always must you tease the children till they won't know how to take you." But the fall and her words were nothing to me, for as she brushed from my clothes the fresh sawdust in which I had lit, my hand was already reaching for the fat pretzel Herr Klein held over the counter.

Hulda had sidled down the bar toward the taproom. Suddenly her face grew bright as she pointed at the brass spigots over the drip pan.

"There you have bock beer!" she exclaimed.

"Where?" asked the saloonkeeper, still trying to be stupid.

"In that new tap," Hulda made known with triumph. "Other days you have but two taps and this morning there are three."

Herr Klein laughed heartily. He poured the water from our pail and handed her a pretzel. His hand was on the spigot, ready to release the magic stream, when Hindenburg stepped around the corner of the tap-room and into the drip pan.

"Back again, you loafer!" shouted the saloonkeeper, shaking his fist. The large brown rooster paid no attention to such comment but dipped his beak deep into the drippings. Hulda and I screamed with joy, for we had heard much of the antics of this pet, when, on special occasions, he was permitted to drink from the beer pan.

"He acts like a Hessian this morning," laughed Herr Klein. "Already he has had one jag on. But what should I do when he finds bock beer? Lock him up?"

Hindenburg went on with his own affairs. His comb stood up red and crisp as he tossed his head back to swallow. When his drinking slackened he eyed my sister and me with contempt. Slowly his feathers rose. Then with a quick movement he flew at the red buttons on Hulda's new shoes. She raised her hands high, holding her pretzel above her head. Otherwise she did not budge.

Herr Klein seized the rooster and buckled down his wings.

"Where you think you are, mister, in the hen yard?" he scolded. "Here you act like a gentleman or out of my saloon you go."

The rooster lowered his tail. When Herr Klein put him on the floor again he remained quite cowed.

"Now march, I tell you, march," the saloonkeeper commanded. The order was repeated several times. "Von, two. Von, two." Hindenburg puffed out his feathers once more. He blinked as if to make sure of things and then raised one foot drowsily and held it under his body. When he set it down the toes were stiff and wide apart. The other foot went up, then down the same way.

Hulda and I laughed until our sides ached. Hindenburg was marching!

"That's just like I used to march in the guard back in Baden," said Herr Klein proudly. "I taught him. See how well he does it on bock beer?"

This reminded us that papa and Sunday school were waiting, so we asked for our pail. Herr Klein touched the spigot again, and the dark, mellow scud flowed gently into the bucket.

"Ja, ja," breathed the saloonkeeper as though watching the foamy stream were reward enough for his exertion. "There is no beer like bock beer. Not even what the Kaiser drinks. And nobody should know that better than me, Hermann Klein." How he chuckled. "Was it not some of my regiment stole the Kaiser's beer once and drank it in the Schwarzwald!" he added.

We were only two little girls in bobtailed dresses, but we hurried toward home as though on us empires were waiting. Papa would have his Easter morning beer without any of the foam lost. But such was not to be. In our haste one of Hulda's supporters broke. This stopped us abruptly.

We set the pail down on the sidewalk, and while Hulda was fixing, I lifted the lid and peeped in.

"How dark it is," I ventured. "Do you think papa would mind if we tasted?" With everyday beer I should not have dared this suggestion to Hulda, who was always custodian. Today was different, and Hulda did not know what to say. After she had peeped she looked at me solemnly.

"You may taste if you will stop when I pinch," she instructed. I raised the pail, and after one full gulp Hulda tweaked the flesh of my arm.

"Um, good!" I answered. "Now you taste and I'll pinch."

Hulda had had her lips to the brim long enough, and just as I made ready to pinch, an intervening hand reached for the bucket.

"So here you are, your noses in your papa's beer."

"Bock beer," said Hulda, releasing the pail and looking up for mercy.

There stood Professor Dietrich, who gave us our music lessons.

"Bock beer?" he repeated. Without saying more he looked into the pail, blew back the foam, and drank. My sister stared in horror as she watched the point in his thin neck move up and down many times.

Pinch him, pinch him, I gestured at her frantically, but all she could do was stare.

Our agony seemed unending, and then the professor made the aspirate sound of satisfaction. He reached for the lid and clapped it back on the pail.

"Tell papa he is a lucky man. Easter and two fine girls to bring him bock beer while he sits at home in his slippers." The professor patted my cheek and hurried on.

Hulda's eyes were filled with tears and her lips quivered as we stood before papa in his great chair. When I saw her sorrow a sudden eagerness to snatch the burden from her loosened my tongue.

"Papa," I said, "Hulda and I only tasted, but Professor Dietrich swallowed much of your beer."

"What!" papa exclaimed, leaning forward and weighing the bucket. "Dietrich drank of my beer? Has the man no honor? First he teaches my children to doodle on the piano and ruins my peace at home and then he waits for Easter to steal my bock beer!" Here papa stopped to take a long drink himself.

Mama*chen* hurried in from the kitchen.

"Ah, I have it," papa went on from behind the pail. "I will make him pay. Mama and I will go over there this afternoon. The Schmidts will go, too, and the Rahrs. He shall play for us, play all the music I have needed since Christmas.

"And you two tasters," papa added, winking at mama, "practice your scales while we are away, and maybe tonight it will give games and something sweet."

Because there was no school on Easter Monday, we were allowed to attend an afternoon performance at the Lyric Theater with other children in the neighborhood.

Hans Knabe, Marta Jaeger, and Carl Kunz stood wide-eyed in our kitchen while mama*chen* explained the play we were to see, "Uncle Tom's Cabin," as it said in the papers. "A woman crosses a river filled with chunks of ice with a young child in her arms," mama was saying. "The woman must pick her way with care, yet she must hurry, for men and police dogs are after her. There is a little girl in the play about Hulda's size. She is called Little Eva. Watch it carefully and learn, for there are those who say this play had much to do with the Civil War."

With mention of the Civil War we were anxious to be off, for that we knew all about. Had not General Carl Schurz won it!

A block from the theater Hans, who was oldest, collected our dimes so he might buy all the tickets. "The window is high," he said.

In the lobby we found many of our schoolmates. It was like Saturday morning at Turnverein Hall. Large pictures of greatly colored scenes from the play stood in easels and hung on the walls.

"See, they are all about Little Eva," cried Marta. Sure enough, in each scene a little girl with yellow hair was right in the middle of things. This seemed odd to us who so often heard our *eltern* say that children's place was to be seen when needed and heard when called upon.

"But look," said Hulda, solver of all perplexities, "in the end she goes to heaven. They let her be the whole show because she is going to die."

We found our seats in the dark balcony, and miles away on a stage not too well lighted the play was on. Hulda and Marta and I were moved almost to jealous tears by the splendid acting of the full-voiced Little Eva.

Then the curtain went down on the second act and Little Eva came right into our midst to sell her picture. Here was end to illusion.

"*Ach mein Herr Gott!* look at her," groaned a woman in the row ahead of us.

"As big as Hulda! She's as big as a brewery horse," whispered Hans.

The play went on, but without its audience. Little Eva had thrown herself away. The last act took her to heaven without a quiver of sorrow going with her from our hearts. Dressed as an angel, she stood on her perch beckoning to Uncle Tom, who remained below. The curtain fell. Quickly it went up again, and down. There was no sound but the bump of the curtain pole hitting the stage.

Up. Something then happened that made the playhouse rock with clapping and shouts. The actor had taken off his wig and was wiping his head with a handkerchief. In his other hand was a large tin pail. "Eva, Eva," he called. "For God's sake come back and get me bock beer!"

A stepladder was shoved from the wings, and Little Eva climbed down, took the pail, and fled.

An early season of warm weather followed Easter and the advent of bock beer. This meant added pleasures, for after supper until dark we might follow a Little German Band from beer saloon to beer saloon in our neighborhood, listen to the singing, and reap pretzels and soda water. With the *eltern* we attended charivaris, pinochle and *klatsch* fests, a concert at Liederkranz Hall, and never did we see our beds before nine, even ten, o'clock.

Then came the day when the bung went out of the last keg of this mellowed brew at Hermann Klein's saloon. The breweries had sent out warning that bock beer was near the end of its season, and Herr Klein made his ritual.

The first twelve steins he gave away with flourishes that frightened Hindenburg out of the drip pan. Then he put out a steaming lunch that was the end of two days' cooking for Frau Klein. He hired the Little German Band for all afternoon and evening and himself led the singing of all the slattern verses of "*Ja, Das Ist Ein Schnitzelbank*," so Uncle

Heinrich explained to papa that evening as together they left for the pinochle contest that was to end Herr Klein's festivities.

All the men in the neighborhood had gone to the saloon but Hans' papa. Herr Knabe was getting along in years and his rheumatism gave him no peace.

Out of doors we children shouted and played with all our might. Martha skinned her knee, and Hans tore his pants in a game of "touchings." He tried to make out that this worried him, but we knew better, for he was fourteen and all winter long had been bragging about the long pants he soon would wear. Then came a long, low whistle from the Knabe porch. We knew what that meant. Hans would be sent for bock beer, and we would all go along, we agreed. We saw Herr Knabe hand his son the pail and chip.

On the way Hans showed us how he could swing the pail around, lid off, and not spill any of the water it held. How we admired him. At the saloon he went in alone, for all of us tracking through might disturb the men at their card playing. We stopped for drinks at the pump in Herr Klein's yard and then started down the street again. We had not gone far when a tall, shambling boy, already in long trousers, passed us.

"See the Dutchies rushing the growler," he remarked slightingly.

Hans reached out to cuff him, but the boy dodged and took to his heels.

"Take this," Hans shouted at Hulda and me, thrusting his papa's beer pail at us.

Before we knew what to make of it all we saw Hans was chasing. Marta and Carl followed, then Hulda and I, holding tight to Herr Knabe's bucket. Past the saloon once more we tagged. Two blocks melted behind us. Ahead we could see that Hans was gaining on the miserable one. They turned a corner. Faster we ran.

"Watch out, the beer is slopping," screamed Hulda.

Carl took my place on the handle, and we reached the corner.

"Hans has him!"

No, the boy had broken away and was cutting across an empty lot. Farther and farther we ran, losing sight of the chase now and then but always finding it again. Dusk was coming on when the boy turned abruptly down an alley. Our breath was giving out and we were frightened, but we must follow.

The turn into the alley was the end of our run, for there was the boy sprawled on the ground and Hans on top, pommeling.

"When you have enough, say so," we heard Hans shout, and we shouted too.

But the return home was long and silent. What would our folks say? What would Herr Knabe say? Apprehension took the soul out of victory. Hans was breathing hard and was tired. Hulda and Carl still carried the bock beer. This, at least, was homage.

Suddenly Hans stopped us.

"Listen, all you," he ordered. We listened.

"Don't one of you dare tell papa I got in a fight. Did you hear?" We heard.

"Cross your hearts and say, '*Soll niemand es wissen als Jesus allein.*'"

We crossed our hearts and repeated, "*Soll niemand es wissen als Jesus allein.*"

A block from home Hans took the pail. Herr Knabe was pacing up and down on his front porch groaning with his rheumatism and worry.

"Hans, Hans, my boy, where have you been?" he cried. "My bock beer! The last night I may ever have it! Let me see!"

Hans walked up with the pail. The rest of us stood back.

Herr Knabe lifted the lid, nervously. "No foam," he shouted. "Flat. All flat!"

Frau Knabe, hearing the commotion, hurried to the door with troubled face. "What is it, papa?" she cried. "Is Hans run over?"

"Run over!" he moaned with contempt. "Such a boy like ours would never get run over. The last night of bock beer, and he lets mine go stale. Look, mama, no foam."

"Wait," said Frau Knabe. In a flash she returned with another bucket. Herr Knabe held the two pails and poured the beer back and forth from one to the other in an effort to work life and foam back into it.

"That the Good Man in heaven should give me such a son!" the old man went on. "Have I not always told you to go by yourself to the saloon to make you hurry?"

Hans stood back silent and sullen.

"To think I can't even trust my own son to get my bock beer when I myself can't get around," Herr Knabe was now sad.

At this came what we would have least expected. Hans was crying. And because it seemed strange to us that big Hans should be whimpering, we all slipped away.

It took the passing of a half decade before Herr Knabe was to learn why his bock beer went stale that night. Hans had left high school to go to France to fight for America in the Great War. The old man turned feeble overnight. Always he called for Hulda, now half-grown, to come over and sit by his chair and tell him about the little boy "Hansie" used to be.

One day when Herr Knabe was lower in spirits than ever before, Hulda uncrossed her heart and told him of that evening in bock beer time when we skimmed over city streets and alleys to follow Hans, who must avenge an insult.

That same afternoon mama called Hulda and me to the front window. She could not conceal her astonishment. "Can I believe my eyes?" she said. "There goes Herr Knabe up the street on his cane. Why, he hasn't been out of his chair for six months!"

Sure enough, there went our old neighbor doddering up the street. Later we learned that he could not contain himself after Hulda's story. He must go himself to the saloon where he had not been for years, and tell it. Tell how his bock beer got flat because his Hansie, now fighting for America across the waters, had smashed a smart aleck's nose for insulting a good old German custom!

From then on Hulda must take time each morning to go over the whole story with him again, and each afternoon he trusted his cane to get him to the saloon to repeat it to anyone who would listen. When there was no other audience he would call for Hindenburg, and the aged rooster, with eyes half closed, stood at the old man's feet and heard.

The time never came for Herr Knabe when he could not tell his story in Hermann Klein's saloon. He was carried to his grave two months before Herr Klein was forced to sell his fixtures and cancel his lease, and with Frau Klein and Hindenburg moved up to Canada.

Play-Party in Texas

By William A. Owens

Much has been made of the fabulous resort hotels and oil millionaires of Texas. So much, in fact, that we've almost lost sight of the fact that many Texans are simple people who indulge in simple pleasures. One of the most popular of these pleasures is the play-party, a sort of square dance without a fiddler. Any neighbor's house in the country is a likely rendezvous. As soon as there are enough voices to raise a tune, the dancing begins. And those who are not in the mood for dancing can take their pleasure from supplying the accompaniment.

The play-party game, or swinging game, as it is more frequently called among the rural people, is even today the chief form of entertainment over a large portion of Texas. Many a youth shouts himself hoarse at play-parties singing such old-time favorites as "Old Joe Clark", "Skip-to-my-Lou", and "Old Dan Tucker", and apparently gets about as much pleasure out of the dances as his father and grandfather did. Almost the only difference between the country party of the present time and that of a generation ago is that the modern youth and maiden have freed themselves from some of the restraints that bound their parents, and allow themselves a little more liberty in the execution of the dance figures. There is perhaps some change in rural home-furnishings and modes of transportation, and the chief topic of religious controversy has changed from predestination to evolution; but the essentials of the song-and-dance movements are practically the same.

The play-party, as has been frequently pointed out, is a characteristic institution of American rural communities. It will be remembered that dancing, which is taboo among many Protestant denominations, is regarded by them as closely associated with instrumental music: the fiddle is the devil's instrument. But young people like to dance. The play-party is an institution which permits most of the satisfactions of the square dance, yet avoids the stigma of the church by dispensing with instrumental music and with the formal nomenclature of square-dance calls. Music is furnished by the singing of the participants themselves and of interested onlookers. The figures, which are called "games", are often almost indistinguishable from those of the square dance, but are usually much simpler, and resemble children's games more closely than they resemble the minuet, or even the Virginia Reel as it was danced in the old days.

A party may be given by any one in the community who wants to see the young people get together for a good time; everyone is invited, and no one feels slighted if he gets only a hearsay invitation. The guests begin arriving about dusk, and the playing starts just as soon as enough people are present to dance the figures. Usually the hostess has removed most of the furniture and rugs from one room and has improvised benches around the walls by placing boards on chairs or boxes and covering them with quilts. The other rooms of the house are reserved for the older people and children: it is surprising how many of these come to watch the young folks play. Naturally the children have their own games, and the old people have their prolonged discussions of weather, taxes, and babies.

In nearly every community there is one young man who takes the lead in the games. To be a good leader he must be able to carry a tune fairly well, and to make himself heard above the din made by the other players. He usually opens the party with an easy game in order to break the ice. A very popular choice for this purpose is "Choose Your Mate":

Here we go 'round in this ring so straight,
Now's the time to choose your mate;
Choose the one that you love best,
And I'll be bound it'll suit the rest.
Great goodness alive, what a choice you've made!
You'd better been dead and in your grave laid.
Great long nose and face like a knife—
Everybody's laughing at your old wife.

If a girl has made the choice they sing the last two lines thus:

Great long nose and face like a pan—
Everybody's laughing at your old man.

This is understood as a game in which someone is to be laughed at, and when the choice has been made the dancers laugh loud and long at the one who has been chosen. This game loses its interest quickly, for there is not enough activity in it. But by the time it is over everyone is feeling at home and is ready for more complex figures.

These follow quickly. One of the more popular is "Get Along Home":

Wish I had a needle and thread
As fine as I could sew,
I would sew my true love to my side,
And down the river I'd go.

Chorus:
Oh get along home, home, home,
Oh get along home, home, home,
Oh get along home, home, home,
Down by the river side.

You go up the new-cut road,
And I'll go down the lane;
If you get there before I do,
You can kiss Miss 'Liza Jane.

Peaches in the summertime,
Apples in the fall,
If I can't get the girl I want,
I won't have none at all.

You go up the new-cut road,
And I'll go down the lane;
Asked that pretty girl to marry me,
She said, "Ain't you ashamed?"

The dance movement to this song is not a full development of a square-dance figure, for less swinging and turning is involved than is ordinarily found in a square dance. Another game which is played in practically the same manner, and which is popular because of its adaptability to situations arising at the parties, is "Shoo-da-la", or as it is called in some places, "All Night Long Mary":

All night long, Mary,
All night long, Mary,
All night long, Mary,
Poor Mary's gone away.

Chorus:
In the middle of the ring,
Shoo-da-la,
Oh, help me swing,
Shoo-da-la,
Around and around,
Shoo-da-la,
Shoo-da-la today.

Or:
Red bird motion,
Shoo-da-la,
Or blue bird march,
Shoo-da-la,
Swing your sweetheart,
Shoo-da-la,
Shoo-da-la today.

The following chorus was apparently made out of a situation at a party where a timid young couple named Ed and Mary by their very shyness let it be known that they were in love with each other, and thus bared themselves to the friendly jests of all those present:

Didn't I tell you,
Shoo-da-la,
Ed loves Mary,
Shoo-da-la,
Ha ha ha ha,
Shoo-da-la,
Shoo-da-la today.

A party would hardly be complete without "Old Joe Clark", which probably leads all of the nonsense songs used at play-parties in the number of its verses. This game follows the regular routine of a familiar square-dance movement. The players, usually four or six couples, choose partners and form a circle. During the singing of the first stanza they march around to the right, reversing and marching to the left during the chorus. Then the boys start swinging once around "right and wrong"; the boy takes his partner by the right hand with his right hand and turns her completely around, each usually taking four steps, though this may vary at the will of the player. He then takes the next girl by the left hand with his left hand and turns her completely around to the right. He alternates thus until he has gone around the ring and is back with his own partner. The next movement follows the same routine except that the boy turns the girl around a time and a half. In some places extra movements are put in at this point, but usually the promenade follows. For this movement the boy and girl cross hands and march around in a circle, each couple following the preceding pair closely. The steps in the promenade vary widely; frequently boys vie with one another in "cutting shines", each trying to introduce more new and intricate steps than does his neighbor. Sometimes they even break away from their partners and dance a sort of shuffling jig, catching in again before the end of the promenade. There is also rivalry in the matter of singing new and funny verses, and to this fact is probably due the abundance of variants, some of which are given here:

Old Joe Clark is dead and gone,
I hope he's doing well,
He made me wear the ball and chain
Till it made my ankles swell.
(Often the second line is sung, "*I hope he's gone to hell.*")

Chorus:
Fare you well, Old Joe Clark,
Fare you well, I'm gone,
Fare you well, Old Joe Clark,
Good bye, Lucy Long.

Used to be a little boy
Playing in the ashes;
Now I am a great big boy
Wearing dad's mustaches.

I went to see my girl last night,
She met me at the door;
Her shoes and stockings in her hand,
And her feet all over the floor.

Old Joe Clark had an old yellow cat,
He would neither sing nor pray;
He stuck his head in a buttermilk jar
And washed his sins away.

The variants of these songs form a very interesting phase in the study of the games. The name Lucy Long in "Old Joe Clark" probably comes from the Lucy Long songs known in Virginia. Another variant calls the young lady 'Liza Jane, but there is no hint as to the origin of this name. In different sections of the state the first line of the chorus varies from "Fare you well, Old Joe Clark" to "Rock-a-rock, Old Joe Clark" and "Fly around, Old Joe Clark". These variations are caused by the fact that there were no written copies of the words: players heard them, memorized them, or remembered them incorrectly, and made up words which sounded right and fitted the rhythm of the song. This led to many unintelligible lines, and to phrases which are merely a succession of meaningless sounds: "U-tang U" and "Choo-do-lum, wind the ball" are good examples. The words of the songs were also frequently influenced by the locality. For instance, in "Weevily Wheat" maple swamps, trading boats, and oxen are mentioned in variants from different parts of the country. The song which is sung as "I wish I were a farmer" in the blackland belt becomes "I wish I were a cowboy" in West Texas.

But the reader will probably want to know more of the play-party in progress. If the players become tired they usually sit out a dance on the bench or in another room among the older people. Sometimes the hostess serves cake or coffee to the guests, but refreshments are the exception rather than the rule: the housewife hostess usually has too much other work to have time for much "fixing" for the party. The urban custom of staying at the party until food is served does not hold in the country. But of course there are frequent trips to the water bucket to moisten throats made dry by singing and exercise.

One must see a play-party in progress to appreciate the activity which goes on in one small farm house while the people are together. The rhythm of the dancers resolves itself into a constant dull beat with a sound unlike any other in the world: the sound of rough shoes beating regularly on a wooden floor, echoed hollowly from the four walls. The voices of the singers rise and fall in a regular cadence, for whatever the songs lack in poetry and music is made up for in solid, moving rhythm. The players themselves become unconscious of the words and music, intent only on following through the intricate dance figures. Their shoulders rise and fall in a peculiar jerking manner. There is no hint of the excitement or frenzy which might mark a ritualistic dance—only the joyous evidence of pleasure in rhythmic physical activity. The lookers-on sometimes become absorbed in conversations, but they show interest in the game in progress by clapping hands, tapping feet, or occasionally bursting into song with those in the game. Sometimes the entire burden of the song falls upon those not playing because the players are too much out of breath to sing.

Most of the girls dress rather near the vogue, but there are some whose mothers allow nothing that is "new-fangled": who must wear clothes ten years behind the times, cotton stockings, and no make-up. The older women present a more varied aspect; hats, coats, dresses, and shoes of any of the styles popular within the last fifteen years may be seen. Yet these women seem not to notice that they are not up-to-date in dress; they are interested in the more important things of community life. The boys dress in anything from overalls to tailor-made suits, and as long as a boy is neat and attractive otherwise, his clothing appears to make no difference to the group. The older men, relics of a rougher day in American life, in overalls and rough shoes, sit about the fire smoking and talking. More interesting than the mode of dress of these people is the spirit of friendliness and goodfellowship which prevails. What does it matter that Joe Sikes is having difficulties financially, or that Bud Thompson is in bad with the authorities because of some liquor traffic? They are all there for a good time, and although the members of the group may not condone the missteps of another, they do not bar him from having fun.

Each of the better dancers in the community knows from ten to fifteen play-party games, and they alternate in contributing from their stores as the evening wears on. Sometimes the group will come back again and again to a universal favorite, which in some localities is called a "meat skin" because it is "plumb wore out". The Virginia Reel has supplied the dance form for many of the more popular games. "Weevily Wheat" follows the movements of the Virginia Reel throughout, and "Brick House" is quite similar to it. Many of the more respectable girls and boys in the community refuse to dance such figures because they feel the Virginia Reel is a wicked dance, but there are enough who have no such scruples to keep the form constantly in use. The words for "Brick House" follow:

In some gentleman's fine brick house,
In some lady's garden;
Dance all night till broad daylight
And go home with the girls in the morning.

Swing lady up and down,
Swing lady around,
Swing lady up and down,
And all get around.

Another version of the first verse is this:

I'm in some gentleman's fine brick house,
I'm in some lady's garden;
If you don't let me out I'll break my neck,
So fare you well, my darling.

The most unusual play-party game which I have run across is one called "Foolin' Roxie". The words, the rhythm, and the tune remind one instantly of a Negro "blues" song. It was probably originated among the Negroes, although its historical background is obscure. The "flirt" is almost unknown in rural America, but this song is devoted to the girl who spends her time trying to "fool some man". The players take the longways dance formation of the Virginia Reel, and follow the figures except that when the couple is supposed to swing, the girl passes the boy by, thus carrying out the idea of "foolin'":

Fool him, Roxie, fool him,
Fool him if you can,
Been a long time foolin', foolin',
Been a long time foolin' that man.

Roxie, she's a daisy,
I tell you she won't do;
Been a long time foolin', foolin',
Been a long time foolin' you.

The listener is impressed by the extreme simplicity of the musical forms employed in these songs. The phrases are short and easy to remember, and there is frequent repetition of entire lines. A four-line stanza is the usual form, and in almost every case the tune for each succeeding stanza is the same as that of the first. Occasionally a song has a chorus, but even in the choruses few new phrases are introduced. A common form is that used in "Brown Jug", which repeats the first line twice and then adds a new line for the fourth, as:

Sent my brown jug down to town,
Sent my brown jug down to town,
Sent my brown jug down to town,
So early in the morning.

The rhythm is so distinct that the song is easily learned. Occasionally when the words do not fit the tune exactly, grace notes are used. Frequently uneven lines are slurred over in the easiest manner possible, and this gives rise to more phrases which have no meaning. The leader is never at a loss if he does not have enough words to finish out a line required by the rhythm; he sings some vowel sounds, and these sometimes become incorporated into the songs. The scales, which at first seem to be largely minors, are really pentatonic scales, probably copied after those used in the English and Scottish ballads. The few minor scales employed are distinct enough to be easily recognized. The players are not concerned with the musical form of the songs; it is enough for them to learn the tune well enough to follow the singing and the words well enough to follow the figures of the dance.

Although old in many respects, the play-party is modern in others. New dances are developed to fit tunes that become popular in certain localities. In one section of the state "It Ain't Gonna Rain No More" ranks as one of the most popular games used at the parties. "She'll Be Comin' 'Round the Mountain", made popular by the Southern Methodist University Mustang Band as "Peruna", has attained equal popularity in another section. Although perhaps these have existed as play-party games for a considerable time, their recent revival seems due to the wide notoriety given them. Modern phrases which have come to be a part of everyday speech are also found in these songs. In "Josey" occur requests to "Chew my gum while I dance Josey" and to "Crank my Ford while I dance Josey".

The play-party is over only when the guests get ready to go home, but they are usually tired and eager to get away by eleven o'clock. A suggestion comes from someone that it is time to go, and then all begin to get coats and wraps in preparation for leaving. This occasions much talk and laughter, because all the wraps have been piled together on one bed and a general scramble must take place before all of the articles are properly identified. During this confusion the host and hostess stand together and accept the goodbyes of their departing guests. They know that everyone has had a good time, and that their next party will be equally well attended. The guests leave as they arrived, in Fords, in wagons, on horseback, or afoot. The boys and girls have made good use of their time, and frequently leave the house walking together, the boy leading his horse. Sometimes the voice of a lone footman may be heard floating back across the fields as he sings:

Oh, the girl, the pretty little girl,
The girl I left behind me;
Rosy cheeks and curly hair,
The girl I left behind me.

Old-Fashioned Barbecue Day

By F. M. Kercheville

Before the days of roadside pig stands, Barbecue was a great tradition of the old Southwest. On Barbecue Day, the populations of ranches, range, and neighboring towns gathered for the spread. Preparations went on for days. The actual roasting took place the night before the celebration—and it was an all night affair—with singing and storytelling around the fire. When the meat was done to a turn, feasting began, and continued throughout the next day.

Barbecue Day

To the Editors of the *Southwest Review*.

Sirs: I mark with regret the passing of the old Southwestern Barbecue Day, for with it will go many of the most picturesque customs of the Old West. Today the barbecue comes all hot and fresh from the pig stand across the street, but in the good old days the family, all fresh and hot, came miles and miles to the barbecue.

The barbecue was real in those days, and the pig stand was as yet unknown. For days and days preparations were made for the feast. For several nights before the banquet, crews of men worked, digging long narrow ditches, piling cord-wood into the ditches after they were done. Then, iron bars and chicken-wire were stretched over the top in final preparation for the roasting.

The day before the feed two or three yearlings and several goats were slaughtered, hung up on the limbs of the trees, and judiciously cut. That night the wood in the ditches was set on fire and burned down to thick masses of live red coals. The meat was then placed on the bars and wire, and the barbecuing had begun. After the meat had cooked the whole night, it was all ready for the crowd.

And the crowd was not long in gathering. All night long the cowboys had been drifting in from the range in small groups, to watch Don Juan Pacheco (or some other Old Mexican), who really knew when meat was done up brown, wandering up and down the rows with a bucket of vinegar sprinkled with salt and pepper. The old fellow swabbed the pieces with the contents of the bucket, and while he turned them over slowly he sang snatches from "La Golondrina", "La Paloma", "La Cucaracha", or some other old canción from Spain or Mexico. Sometimes a coyote or two joined in on the chorus with a high tenor wail, and later came up nearer the fire, watching the barbecue with shining eyes. Often the air was filled with yells and songs of the cowboys coming home from a *baile*. Then all through the night the crowd around the fires sang and told tales, while they sampled the cooking meat.

At about ten or eleven in the morning the barbecuing was ended, and by that time all the people from the neighboring ranches and towns were on hand. They amused themselves with gambling, games, and gossip, until about twelve, when there was a rattling of tin pans from the pits and the shout, "Come on an' get it!" The women folks had brought every kind of pie and cake as well as pickles and bread and butter, and the tables improvised from planks were heavily spread. Over to one side, on its own special fire, was a five-gallon Swift's lard can full of black coffee. Then the eating and drinking began, and went on in full swing until the tables were cleaned up and the coffee pail was empty.

After eating, the crowd turned to amusement. Sometimes there would be a rodeo, with bronco-busting, steer-riding, and bulldogging. At other times there would be a ball game. Political bosses and job-seekers would be in hog heaven, tickling the ears of the listeners, and more than often misleading their minds with flowery speeches on the momentous questions of the day. Shy young couples took advantage of the day for courtship, and slipped in many a kiss between bites of custard pie.

As the sun began to set, all the people began the long trip back home, tired as Walker fox-hounds after a long race, but happy.

Now, under the benign influence of social evolution, the pig stand and the automobile have done their part in causing Barbecue Day to pass out. But with its going (which must be considered inevitable) will depart one of the most colorful customs of the Southwest.

Albuquerque F. M. KERCHEVILLE

Rodeo and "Frontier Days"

By Winifred Johnston

If William Cody had known what he was starting, he would probably have bought a piece of Madison Square Garden. The Wild West show and the "Frontier Days" celebration have become America's favorite tournaments. Here is the success story of that bronc-busting, steer-roping, gun-toting hero—the rodeo cowboy from the wild and woolly west.

In the rodeo, the Wild West show, and the "Frontier Days" celebrations now presented annually throughout the West, America has made its unique contribution to the major entertainments of the world. To Europeans, the most characteristic expressions of the American spirit seem to be speed and syncopation. It has often been observed that Negro minstrelsy is America's one authentic contribution to theater art; syncopation has long been accepted as the New World's characteristic rhythm. But to the Old World nothing that America offers in the way of theater can be at once so strange and so glamorous as the frontier entertainments' flashing representation of a life now passing into history. The essence of these performances is speed—a speed so spontaneous and so lacking in self-consciousness that it seems almost unaware of its own prodigious skill: a speed which arose in the need of outwitting death, and which speaks now in terms of the survival of the fit. Remarkable proof of man's power of adaptation, the feats of frontier life are now taking their place in the cultural storehouse of entertainment, and seem to have a good chance to survive as parts of an art form after their original usefulness is gone. Only in the New World has there been such a coincidence of cultures that the creature of folk-lore has lived to perpetuate his own legend in literature and the theater.

With the passing of the unfenced ranges the cowboy became a legend, a figure of romance, the knight-errant of New-World literature and art.

Much of the glamor cast by sentimentalists about the figure of the cowboy perhaps dates back to the days when John Burke, king of press agents, capitalized the publicity given William Cody by Eastern dime novelists. "It is impossible to exaggerate the influence of Buffalo Bill's Wild West Show on the folk-lore of our country," says Rob Wagner. . . .

Times have changed for the boys who once knew little more of sophisticated life than what could be observed in saloon and honkatonk. Dude-wrangling, rodeos, Wild West shows, and the movies now make money for men who once thought twelve dollars a month adequate pay for long days and nights in the saddle.

It was William Cody who first sensed the value of the Old West as a background for a new profession. When General Sheridan secured Cody to act as guide for a hunting party of New York millionaires, the young scout and buffalo-killer sized up the party correctly as a "nobby and high-toned outfit". "I determined to put on a little style myself," he said. "I curled my front teeth; brushed up a new buckskin toga; put on my Sunday moccasins; combed out the fringe in my trousers and left nothing undone but banging my front hair." By thus doing what was expected of him in looking and acting his part, Buffalo Bill set the style for dude-wranglers and cowboy-showmen of the future.

"Treat 'em gentle, Rob," Will Rogers once told Wagner, the writer; "cowboys are more temperamental than opera singers." More significant than opera singers are some of them today. In the life and the letters of America the cowboy holds his own. . . .

It would be unjust to classify as synthetic all the cowboys now participating in professional entertainments. There are indeed "showhands" who were "never nearer cow than condensed milk". Many real hands, however, still exist: men whose specialty is riding, whose pride in their skill is great, and who pick up what money they can while testing their skill. Most of them now sell their picturesqueness where they may: on Broadway, in Hollywood, or in the frontier entertainments staged throughout the cow towns of the West.

The world may well be grateful that in rodeo, Wild West show, and Frontier Days entertainment something of this old life of the pioneer is being preserved—and that, in the attempt at representing it, Indians, scouts, and cowboys have joined to create a truly indigenous spectacle.

In the evolution of this unique entertainment the rodeo came first, the Wild West show second, and the Frontier Days third. It is true that on circus and carnival lot there is little discrimination among these types of frontier entertainments: the ballyhoo artist is seldom nice in his use of terms. But the rodeo, as properly differentiated from other frontier entertainments, is a contest; it is essentially competitive. Each competitor is rated according to the dexterity and speed displayed in skills developed to meet everyday requirements of the range. These skills are primarily riding and roping, in the practice of which man competes with man by pitting himself against the strength and sagacity of horse or steer. The Wild West show, on the contrary, is not a contest; it is a commercial organization for the display of frontier activities, in which the participants receive regular wages for their roping, riding, or shooting acts. Some of these acts may, and often do, duplicate many of the skills seen in the rodeo. But they include others also, such as trick shooting, the buffalo hunt, and the Indian chase, which arose in stages of pioneer life antedating the cattle-range period. Here the showman displays skills developed in the turkey-shoot or buffalo hunt, in which man pitted himself against nature to wrest from it his food, or those developed in the Indian raids and wars in the long struggle over land. The Frontier Days entertainment partakes of the nature of both rodeo and Wild West show and possesses as well, in its most highly developed form, some elements of the community pageant in the representation of scenes drawn from local history.

Never quite so authentic as the pure rodeo, the Frontier Days is distinctly an entertainment and must be judged as such. Like the Wild West show, it is usually a commercial undertaking. But unlike the Wild West show, it is not produced by a permanent organization which travels from place to place. Considered as an entertainment, the Frontier Days must be distinguished from all such traveling acts. Its unity depends upon the community; its personnel is assembled for and dispersed after each annual performance. Here the West dramatizes itself on its own home grounds.

In its simplest form, the Frontier Days is merely a reunion—the old-timers' somewhat sentimental attempt to withstand the rush of time. At its best it is a historical pageant of no mean quality—and as such deserves to be considered a part of the effort to preserve the past as part of the modern world. At its worst, it is a cheap commercial exploitation of history and tradition. Whatever form it assumes, it is apt to be quite as interesting to future historians of the theater. . . .

There is something peculiarly fitting in the fact that this typical American entertainment should be associated, in the West at least, with the most American of holidays.

All up and down the old cow-trails the rodeo still exists. At any little wayside town of the West the Fourth of July is apt to be commemorated with a barbecue and an extemporaneous riding and roping contest. In the old days the barbecue, the "speaking", and the contests constituted the whole show. Out in Arizona patriotic exercises held on the courthouse steps are still part of Independence Day celebrations. Arizona is a state which even now has to rally forces to fight bear, wolf, lion, coyote, bobcat, and fox. In this old cow country, where even the grasshoppers are said to spit tobacco juice and wear chaps, time is almost forgotten in the immensities of space. Yet even here the years bring changes in custom.

In the 'eighties the people came into Prescott for the Fourth from miles around. Women of the range rode in on cow-horses suffering under the annual indignity of currycombing and mane-decoration. Each girl carried a bulky parcel tied carefully behind her saddle—the dainty "best dress" in which she would presently step out before admiring range men. Town friends set aside rooms in which country visitors might dress, and hotelkeepers too were not indifferent to the needs of the women who rode in for the Fourth.

> The young folks would ride out to the tournament grounds and tie their horses to some convenient pine tree [writes Sharlott M. Hall], or some love-smitten range rider would forswear the saddle for one of Shull's or Hathaway's hacks and take his befrilled lady love "out in style"—to be guyed to a finish later on by his comrades.
>
> Families came in every sort of wagon that the ranchers owned—from the Marrses in their shining double-seated spring wagon to the distant ranchers who brought the chuck-wagon and whole outfit along. . . . The grub box in many a wagon was filled with baked chickens and home-made bread and pies and cake and from many a little fire under the trees the smell of Arbuckle coffee filled the air at noon and neighbor range people picnicked and visited together for one big day of the year.
>
> Not always was it the bright eyes of the country girls that drew noontime visitors; more than one ranchwoman was known as a notable cook and punchers were eager to "horn in" on the spread. Restaurants down town were always overflowing, but "Chiny grub" had small attraction for the cow hand who could get an invite to eat roast ranch chicken with some family.
>
> The sports went with a vim and swing inevitable when the whole contest was crowded into one day—with maybe a hang-over on special betting for the next morning. The years between haven't speeded up the efficiency of the cowmen—these old riders and ropers could have held their own in any tournament today.
>
> But their dress . . . would have made a dull and somber background for

the bright shirts and neckerchiefs that have come in with blue and red and green tin Lizzies on every side. No red shirts and ten gallon hats for the men of old—"Too much Greaser" in all that for them—they rode mostly in dark shirts and trousers—chaps laid aside for the holiday—and the hats which they pulled down on their heads were the old flat Stetsons in gray or pale tan, or sometimes black.

The cowboy contest of today is seldom so simple and unassuming as this contest of the 'eighties. Sport has now grown into business, and one of the most difficult tasks of the Rodeo Association of America is to keep the entertainment free of rackets and rowdyism. . . .

Just where and when the first of the frontier contests was held it is obviously impossible to say. Spanish-American rodeos, originally often associated with celebrations of saints' days, were always more full of color than were those of the Anglo-Americans. Records of Spanish-American celebrations show not only that they were widespread, but also that they antedated Anglo-American rodeos. Among the Anglo-Americans the rodeo began—as one old cowhand has said—"as a private picnic just to blow off steam". After spring and fall round-ups the cowhands would indulge themselves with a little fun: race, do a bit of roping, perhaps bet on a couple of flash riders who had dropped by to break outlaws. Contests of this sort were frequent at ranches and round-ups in all parts of the cattle country. Later, when the raising and selling of horses became a profitable industry of the West, they became just as common in the market centers from which the horses were shipped out. It was when these contests grew large enough to draw competitors from a distance that they became known as "cowboy tournaments". Frank Dobie says that there are accounts of tournaments, bull-tailings, and riding matches in Southwest Texas long before the 'eighties, though they were not promoted for commercial purposes. The staging of rodeo performances by soldiers at the front during the Civil War seems to indicate that in the 'sixties such contests were already established as an amateur sport. . . .

Prescott's claim to "the oldest cowboy tournament in the world" is based on a silver medal now in the possession of the Prescott Frontier Days Association. The medal dates back to 1888. The front of it contains the inscription upon which Prescott's claim rests:

> Citizen's Prize, contested and won by Juan Levias, over all competitors at the Fourth of July Tournament, held in Prescott, A. T., 1888, for roping and tieing steer. Time 1:47½; 100 yards start.

This Prescott celebration of 1888 seems to have been an authentic cowboy tournament. A story told by Charlie Siringo in his *Riata and Spurs* indicates, however, that even as early as 1885 such rodeos were already well enough established elsewhere to attract competitors and spectators from long distances. Siringo's story is of a tournament held at a time when the borderline of Indian Territory was watched by "Boomers" on one side and United States soldiers on the other:

On the first day of May, 1885 [he says], Caldwell [Kansas] put on her Sunday clothes and held a grand cowboy tournament at the fair grounds. Cowboys and cattlemen from all over the Indian Territory were there to witness the sport.

One of the games was catching small rings with a long pole, while the pony was running his best, the prize being a fine ladies' gold ring. I had promised my sixteen-year-old wife that she should wear the ring, and the promise was fulfilled, as I won against the dozens of competitors.

In the steer-roping match I won a fine silver cup, hog-tying the steer in forty-four seconds. The first time I threw him, he jumped to his feet after I had dismounted. Then, springing back into the saddle, I had to throw him again. Even with all this lost time the silver cup was awarded to me, and it is kept as a relic of bygone days. My mount was a "crackerjack", a black pony borrowed from Cattle King John Blair.

There is record of a prize tournament even earlier than this one at Caldwell. In the cowboy contest staged by Buffalo Bill in 1882, North Platte, Nebraska, seems to find just basis for its claim that in 1932 it celebrated the fiftieth anniversary of "the first Western contest ever staged anywhere by an community".

It was this way [an old resident of North Platte once told Acton Davis]. Way back in the early '80's Bill came back from the East where he had been playing in some border drama. Old man M. C. Keetin, one of our leading citizens, had just got together the last herd of buffalo that was ever raised near North Platte. He valued them above rubies, of course; to us they were far, far more valuable than either the last rose of summer or the final run of shad. So as soon as we heard the government was going to buy them for breeding purposes, all the cowboys decided to have a farewell little round-up on Ike Dillon's ranch.

It was a lively little party and it lasted three days. Then Keetin turned to Bill Cody and said: "Say, Bill, I'd rather sell the buffalo to you than to the government. Why don't you buy 'em, take 'em east with a lot of boys and show the tenderfeet a real Western show in the open air?" Well, Bill did. You know the rest.

William Cody's own account of how he promoted this three-day party of fifty years ago states that he came home from the East to find big plans afoot for the Fourth of July celebration. The boys wanted to make it a real "Old Glory blowout". Cody was appointed grand marshal:

"Just the man we want," they said. "You get up a Wild West show. Give us some examples of roping cattle, fancy shooting and such. We'll put up the money."

I got out some handbills and sent them to all the ranches for hundreds of miles and advertised in the paper the prizes that would be given for some fancy cowboy stunts. You never saw such a rush to get in. It seemed as if every cattleman in the West wanted to participate. I made up a lot of contests, arranged the prizes, and the day it came off North Platte had the biggest crowd it has ever had before or since.

This "Old Glory blowout" staged at North Platte in 1882 is not only the earliest American cowboy tournament yet brought to light and the beginning of the Wild West show. It was also the model for the Frontier Days celebrations which afterward absorbed the rodeo and displaced the show.

The Cheyenne Frontier Days, an annual five-day show which attracts notable contestants and thousands of spectators, is famous. But its slogan, "The Daddy of 'Em All", is accurate only if it be limited in its application to Frontier Days celebrations alone. . . .

Cheyenne's Frontier Days started on an afternoon in 1897 when a group of citizens decided to get together a number of old cowhands and ranchers to try their luck in a few races and show their skill in roping steers and riding wild ponies. It merits notice because it was the first annual celebration belonging to the species of entertainment to which it gave its name. The Cheyenne show differed from earlier celebrations already noted mainly in a deliberate fostering of some of the atmosphere made popular by Cody in his Wild West show. One of the old stagecoaches used on the Cheyenne-Deadwood trail was hauled out of the half-forgotten hiding-place where it had rested since its last trip ten years before. Some cavalry were borrowed from Fort Russell. Shoshone and Arapahoe Indians were brought down on flat cars from their reservations.

Cary Abbot tells the story, which marks this definitely as an entertainment possessing those elements that distinguish the Frontier Days as a type:

The prizes for the contests were simple, and the show did not pretend to be more than an afternoon's amusement. As the grandstand was small, people went out very early, to insure getting seats, taking their lunches along. . . .

These early performances had many of the faults of amateurish management. Long delays between races and contests, combined with sudden dramatic climaxes unlooked for by the management, made the afternoons in the grandstand or on horseback in the arena both boring and thrilling. Occasionally a steer would climb over all possible obstacles apparently burning to gore everyone in sight. Sometimes a broncho would insist on kicking his way into the middle of next week. The Indian squaw races were always delightful, as the Shoshone women were immense, while their mounts were thin little things, with a habit of turning corners suddenly and upsetting their huge riders. The climax of the earlier shows was the pursuit of the stagecoach around the track by the Indians, to be finally rescued by the cavalry and cowboys.

From the beginning of the Cheyenne attraction, the Union Pacific Railroad contributed saddles to winners of the bucking contests. As the attraction grew, other merchandise prizes were offered to make it seem worth the cowhand's time to come a long distance. The addition of certain bits of local history soon gave these events the individual interest which made it possible for the Cheyenne celebration to maintain a position of leadership among eager imitators. Now there is something to attract both tourist and old-timer. To spectators the annual parade is of historical interest. A pageant of transportation presents roaming buffalo, wagon trains, stage coaches, the construction of the Union Pacific, and model freight and passenger trains. Among the floats are an old-fashioned parlor with spinning wheel and harpsichord; an old-time bar and dance hall; an episode of history in which the Vigilantes deal out justice in a hanging; a ranch scene showing the branding of a calf; and an Indian tepee and campfire, with bucks, squaws, and papooses. All day long the blue banners of the Frontier Days celebration enliven the streets. In the evening the uninitiated, who cannot always appreciate the skills shown in the speedy contests, may find at Frontier Park enjoyments which require little special knowledge: refreshment and entertainment "identical with those of the early days".

But although the Cheyenne celebration established the type, it is now only one of many such entertainments held annually in the West. Tourists interested in frontier sports are indeed apt to consider the whole country west of the Mississippi as a showhouse for their delight. In the community affairs rodeo events are only part of the larger show. Frontier Days are now promoted by amateur and professional agencies: cattlemen, chambers of commerce, fairs, and out-and-out showmen. The big ones are all alike in utilizing a sense of theater. Towns dress the part. Townspeople as well as cowboy and cowgirl contestants don the bright costumes of the plains. The vernacular of the range replaces the tamed speech of the town. Old-time stage-coaches rumble again over roads now paved for trucks and automobiles. Indians and United States cavalrymen add their bits to the multicolored scene. At night the life of the old cow-towns is reënacted. Through the swinging door of the Last Chance Saloon comes the shrill cry of the fiddle. At the bar, cowboys, bull-whackers, trappers, and prospectors consort with wildcat women. From Calgary to the Río Grande the West has learned the lesson of capitalizing its romantic atmosphere.

In late years an attempt has been made to "stagger" these Frontier Days so that cowboys may participate in more than one contest and tourists may follow the trail from one to another. From the first of July to the last of August many an ancient ritual and many an exciting trial of strength are enacted before crowded grandstands. . . .

The average attendance at the Pendleton (Oregon) Round-Up is estimated at sixty-five thousand. Throughout the long summer months, visitors to the Northwest are reminded of this preëminent celebration by Wallace Smith's stunning poster—a symphony in reds and browns, depicting a cowboy riding a bucking bronc—which appears in conspicuous spots along the roads. All the highway systems of Oregon converge at Pendleton. When the last of August arrives, the city is crowded with people who have ridden or driven in or who have taken advantage of special railway rates or motor-bus accommodations.

For years the world's all-around cowboy championship has been settled at this show, which has been held annually at Pendleton since 1910. Cowboys gather here from all over America. Canada, the United States, Mexico: all are represented. More than two thousand Indians also assemble to participate in events arranged especially for them. More than a thousand head of stock are fed on the Round-Up grounds. During the celebration an Indian village springs into existence. Tepees make a picturesque background for families of the Walla Walla, Cayuse, Umatilla, Nez Percé, Bannock, and Yakima tribes, who take part in the events clad in their finest raiment, many of them wearing the legacies of generations. Twenty-six events make up the daily program. The run-off of competitive numbers is interrupted by the cowboys' and cowgirls' mounted parade, the Indian parade, Indian dances, trick riding, trick and fancy roping. Afternoon events include Pony-Express races, Indian-pony relays, cowboy relays, cowboys' standing races, a bucking free-for-all, and championship contests. "Ridin' Roman" is part of the show side of the rodeo business, and there is something of the same quality in the relays. The girls' relays come in the morning. So too do the steer bulldogging and the calf-roping.

Most showy of the early events is the Chuck Wagon Race. This is run for sixty dollars day money. Two outfits are entered, each consisting of a round-up chuck wagon drawn by a four-horse team, a driver, his helper, and two outriders. Here is a contest made from an essential routine of range life. The object of the outfits is to make camp. But before doing this the contestants must cut a figure-eight around two barrels set up on the field, cross between two parallel marks in the center of the arena, and stop not less than ten feet beyond the wire. At the firing of a revolver the two outfits start in opposite directions around the track. On the seat of each lurching chuck wagon are the driver and his helper; at the sides of the wagon are the mounted outriders. Around the barrels in the center of the field the outfits weave their figure-eights. Now one of the wagons pulls to a stop. Almost before the team halts the "Old Lady" and his helper are off the seat. In an instant the eight-foot fly is stretched and staked with poles and guy ropes. Shelter is secured. By the time the other wagon draws to a halt across the wire, the cook of the first outfit has his stove set; by the time the other outfit has its fly staked, he has a fire made under his coffee pot. In an incredibly short time the smoke shows out of the chimney. First money is won.

The last day of the Pendleton Round-Up brings out a banner crowd. Cowboys and visitors have sampled all that is offered by "Happy Canyon", the night show, with its pageantry of the white man's conquest of the Western world and its reproductions of old dance halls and games of chance. Now the grandstand is full of spectators come to see "Westward Ho", the last great Round-Up parade, to witness the Round-Up Derby, and to see the cup awarded to the Indian beauty queen and the championship belt presented to the all-around cowboy champion.

The cowboys are tired. For three days they have worked hard. But many of them are still ready to take a chance on the five-hundred-dollar purse offered in the Derby. After that fast and hilarious event, sobered and a little conscious of the ritual in their sport, cowboys and Indians line up for the grand finale. Spectators gather along the fence outside the racetrack, crowding the space beyond the grandstand. Onto the track and into the arena comes a rider carrying the Stars and Stripes. After him come four other standard-bearers. Across the arena, printing fluctuant patterns on the hard-beaten sod, comes the long line of Indians, brilliant in feathered regalia. Then another flag, and the cowboys and cowgirls: another line, reprinting the winding patterns traced by Indian riders.

One after another the riders pass. "Westward Ho!" The great Pendleton Round-Up is drawing to a close.

Rose Bowl

By Rube Samuelsen

On the first morning of the New Year, California stages her most spectacular extravaganza. Along Pasadena streets roll gaily bedecked floats, which carry pretty girls tossing flowers at the thousands of visitors to the Tournament of Roses. In the afternoon two of the nation's top football teams battle it out in football's World Series—The Rose Bowl. And in one of these encounters rode the Four Horsemen of Notre Dame.

Outlined against a blue-gray October sky, the Four Horsemen rode again. In dramatic lore they are known as Famine, Pestilence, Destruction, and Death. These are only aliases. Their real names are Stuhldreher, Miller, Crowley, and Layden.

Ten weeks after Grantland Rice wrote those immortal words, Notre Dame's fabled Four Horsemen galloped into the Rose Bowl for their last ride—the most memorable of all—because Stanford's Indians gave battle over every inch of ground.

On that warm afternoon of January 1, 1925, the late Knute Rockne's ballet backfield met head on a single blond bull named Ernie Nevers. It was the brute force of Nevers against the nimble finesse of the Four Horsemen, three of whom—Fullback Elmer Layden, Halfback "Sleepy Jim" Crowley, and Quarterback Harry Stuhldreher—weighed less than 160 pounds. It was also The Man versus The Machine.

Eventually the outcome centered around a showdown between the rival fullbacks, Nevers and Layden. It was doubtful if two football stars, playing the same position in the same game, were ever more dissimilar. Nevers, a hulking giant, returned to action in the Rose Bowl after being sidelined for weeks with two broken ankles. Both of his legs were bandaged to the knees, so tightly, reported Russ Newland of the Associated Press, that circulation was all but choked off. The pain was also deadened by shots of novocain.

Layden, a fancy-dan runner, six feet tall but as thin as a lath, was a whirling dervish, a sprinter-fullback who seemed to fly in a football suit. He was the game's great opportunist.

"He took off like a rocket, as though his whole lean figure was rifling through the air on a line parallel to the turf," said Red Smith, New York *Herald Tribune*, heaping praise upon the original Thin Man. "You'd have sworn, at times, that his feet didn't touch the ground at all."

Layden's own tribute, paid to his adversary, was "Ernie Nevers plowed into our line with as fierce a charge as I have ever known."

But let's turn back to the beginning.

All of the Four Horsemen were seniors. Hard upon their 13 to 6 defeat of West Point on October 19, 1924, popular acclaim singled out Notre Dame, and only Notre Dame, as the bona fide Eastern nominee for the Rose Bowl. The tag of "Four Horsemen" had captured the fans' imagination so completely it was obvious no other candidates need apply. . . .

Rockne, the wizard, opened the Stanford game with his Notre Dame "shock troops," just as he had consistently done in piloting the Irish to nine straight victories and a total of 258 points against 44 during the regular season. The "shock troops" absorbed the enemy's best punch, then retired while the ballyhooed Four Horsemen and Seven Mules took over offensively.

"Time after time," recalled Eddie Scharer, shock-troop quarterback, "Rock would instruct me to call plays which I knew wouldn't work. Did I call them? You bet your life I did. There were at least eight other guys to take my place if I didn't. After two or three plays we would always be right where we started and forced to kick. The sports writers never caught on, either."

The Irish setup was a forerunner of the present-day "two platoon" system, but Rockne, typically, worked it with more finesse.

This time it didn't take Notre Dame long to become acquainted with the Stanford brand of fury. The first time the Four Horsemen carried the ball, Miller fumbled, and Charley Johnston, Stanford's right tackle, recovered on the Notre Dame 17. Two thrusts by Nevers set up a field-goal try, made by the reliable Cuddeback from the 17. Stanford led 3 to 0.

Taking the ensuing kickoff, swift parries by Layden and Crowley, mixed with Stuhldreher's passes and bewildering plays, brought the Irish to Stanford's 9-yard line. Here the men of Pop Warner dug in and wrested the ball from Notre Dame on their own 10. But the exultation which swept over the partisan Stanford crowd was short-lived. As Cuddeback attempted to kick out of danger, the ball squirted off his foot and out of bounds on Stanford's 32. It was the Irish opportunists' turn to cash in on a break.

"Sleepy Jim" Crowley, now with eyes wide open, darted off tackle and then weaved and bobbed 13 yards to the Stanford 19. In three more plays, Miller and Layden charged through the line for a first down on the 7-yard line as the first quarter ended. Crowley picked up four yards, after which Layden, Quick Death of the vaunted Notre Dame backfield quartet, blazed over center for a touchdown. Fred Swan, Stanford guard, blocked the attempted conversion and the Irish went out in front, 6 to 3.

Like the mad bull he was, recoiling from a setback caused by Layden's 72-yard punt over the goal line, Nevers went to work. Sandwiched between his bruising plunges was a 14-yard end-around by Captain Jim Lawson, All-America end, bringing the Indians 49 yards to the Notre Dame 31. On fourth down and 6 yards to go, Quarterback Fred Solomon called for a risky flat pass from Nevers to Ted Shipkey. Almost as the big blond cocked his arm, a streak of lightning flashed in the Irish backfield.

Layden was on the move.

The lithe thin man jumped high to tap the aerial away from Shipkey, waited a split second to gather it in, and then streaked 78 yards to the Stanford goal line. Ed Huntsinger, Irish end and the only man near Layden, convoyed his teammate out of the danger zone. Crowley converted, turning the Palo Altoans' threat into a 13 to 3 Notre Dame lead.

Before the half ended, Nevers paced another Indian drive downfield, 58 yards to the Irish 10, but it came to naught when Jim Kelly, substitute end, fumbled. Captain Adam Walsh recovered for Notre Dame on the 17, and the half ended after one more play.

Notre Dame's third touchdown, scored in the third period, came as another bolt from the blue. This time Layden booted a spiral 50 yards upfield, over the head of Solomon, Stanford safety man. As Solly turned to retrieve the pigskin it slipped from his grasp and, as he was blocked out by Chuck Collins, Huntsinger snatched the ball and scooted 20 more yards, unmolested, to score. Crowley drop-kicked successfully, giving the South Benders a 20 to 3 advantage.

Two sudden breaks had turned a close game into a 17-point deficit. Amplified by the Four Horsemen's reputation, it was enough to curl up any team, but not the fighting tribesmen from Stanford. Hadn't they closed an almost similar gap in less than half the time now remaining, to earn a 20 to 20 tie with California?

Nevers himself opened the attack. The crippled fullback, in his display of Samson might, was to give as severe a physical beating to the Irish forwards as he received. In all he made a record number of 34 bull rushes into the line for a gain of 114 yards. Not only was the blond bruiser relentless on offense but, while backing up the line on defense, he made three fourths of the tackles.

Now it was his turn to even the interception score. Picking off a Stuhldreher pass, he returned the ball to the Irish 29. On the march again, it was Nevers, Nevers, Nevers, except for three yards contributed by Lawson. Then Ernie churned his bandaged legs six times beyond the Seven Mules' best resistance—two, three, and four yards at a crack—until the 7-yard line was reached. Here Notre Dame, expecting more of the same rough treatment, was crossed up. On the fourth down, with a yard to go, Ed Walker rifled a pass to Ted Shipkey in the end zone. Cuddeback booted the extra point, making the count 20 to 10.

Before the spectators had taken another good breath, the Indians were banging again at Notre Dame's goal line. It looked like the Stanford-California game all over again. Following the kickoff, George Baker, Stanford center, plucked a Crowley pass out of the air and returned the ball to the Irish 31. Now in the fourth quarter, the Indians didn't propose to waste any time. Ted Shipkey, Captain Lawson's running mate at end, slam-banged his way to the 26-yard line. Eight yards by the redoubtable Nevers took Stanford to the Irish 18, and four plays later he huffed and puffed for seven additional vital yards to record a first down on the 6. It actually looked as though the blond-thatched bull was carrying the entire Notre Dame eleven on his back.

Tension was high, and Notre Dame took time out. It was Crowley, the team's comedian, who may have saved the day in that spot with his flippant crack:

"Look, you guys," said the not-so-sleepy halfback. "You take this game too seriously."

The tautness relieved, Crowley went on to say:

"They came this far by sending Nevers through the line, didn't they? Now, I say they won't change."

Crowley was right. The next two thrusts, by Nevers, fell a yard short of the goal line. Rockne then sent in John McMullin to replace "Rip" Miller at tackle. Here, the players figured, must be the magic key from the sage himself. It couldn't be learned immediately, however, since the rules then prohibited a substitute from talking, after entering the game, until one play had been run. That meant holding Nevers again through use of their own defense strategy—and muscles. Successfully done a half yard out, the Irish hurriedly gathered around McMullin and chorused:

"What did Rock say?"

"Rock said to hold 'em!" the innocent substitute tackle blurted.

Whether the shrewd Notre Dame coach had this time broken the tension with psychological assistance—or the Seven Mules deserved an accolade—or whether the referee's ruling was the pay-off, the record shows that on fourth down Nevers was held inches short of the goal line.

Maybe the Blond Bull was stopped, but you will never make any Stanford rooter, or Nevers himself, believe it. Nor will you ever persuade any Notre Dame man that he wasn't. And so the half-serious argument has continued without letup whenever the paths of those who were present on January 1, 1925—be they players, spectators, or newspapermen—have crossed.

Referee Ed Thorp's call was of great significance because, had the touchdown been allowed, Stanford would then have trailed by only 20 to 17.

"And the way the game was going," Miller, the opposing tackle, admitted, "Nevers could have come down the field easily for another touchdown. He was really belting us around. As it stood, Stanford remained ten points behind and had to gamble with wild passes, one of which we picked off for another seven points."

Stanford partisans were agitated further by the action of Walter Eckersall, head linesman. Strong pictorial evidence, printed the next day in the San Francisco *Chronicle*, showed Eckersall with hands raised in the air, as though signaling a touchdown, when Nevers dove into the pile. Later, Eckersall declined further comment than:

"I wasn't the referee. It wasn't my decision to make. I just made a mistake in signaling at all."

Years later, while the motion picture *The Spirit of Notre Dame* was being filmed in Hollywood, Crowley, Layden, and Miller, who later became U. S. District Attorney for Northern Ohio, were discussing the disputed play with George T. Davis of the Los Angeles *Herald-Express*.

"I still say Ernie carried the ball over the line," Davis defied. "I was right on the goal line in the press box and saw the play through high-powered glasses."

The three Horsemen good-naturedly argued that he didn't see any such thing.

"You'll never make me believe otherwise," Davis persisted.

Just then a small man, who had overheard the debate, joined the group and addressed Davis:

"You're wrong. Nevers did not score. And I ought to know."

"Where were you sitting?" the annoyed Davis demanded.

"On his neck!"

The "intruder" was the fourth Horseman, Harry Stuhldreher.

Looks conclusive, doesn't it? But wait. Nevers contends that he, too, ought to know. Better than Stuhldreher, in fact.

"I was on the bottom of the pile, looking down at the turf," the great All-America fullback testified. "I had the ball in my arms and it was past the white line. Then they pushed me back."

As Noble Kizer, Irish guard, commented: "Everyone on our team thought it wasn't a touchdown and every Stanford player thought it was." Officially, however, possession belonged to Notre Dame, inches from the goal line, and Layden booted the ball out of danger.

Soon Crowley intercepted a Stanford pass on the Irish 10 and Layden again punted out. Only 25 seconds remained to play. Howard Mitchell, now at quarterback, was unaware of Coach Warner's ban on further use of the flat-pass play, Nevers to Shipkey, and called it only to see the same lightning strike again. This time Layden reached up, grabbed the ball from Shipkey's grasp, and sped 70 yards to the final touchdown. Crowley's successful conversion made the final score 27 to 10.

After the game Rockne kidded, "That pass of Pop's was the greatest scoring medium I have ever seen. Either they scored on it or we did."

Warner fumed about the outcome for years and emphasized that Stanford gained 298 yards from scrimmage to 179 for Notre Dame, made 17 first downs to 7, and had completed 11 passes to 3.

"We spotted Notre Dame 21 points," Warner added, "while they actually earned but 6. We completely outplayed them except for those fatal errors. Notre Dame was great, but I think I had the better team."

The sagacious Rockne, nearing the pinnacle of coaching success which was cut short by a fatal plane crash in a Kansas wheat field on March 31, 1931, had only this simply rejoinder:

"It is one thing to get the breaks and quite another to take advantage of them."

It was Crowley, however, who as usual got in the best needle when talk of the Indians' yardage superiority continued.

"Yeah," he drawled, "and next year they're going to award the American League pennant to the team that has the most men left on bases. Besides, 'Rock' taught us to go for the three-baggers and homers and forget about the bunts."

To Pop Warner, however, Nevers was the star of the day, and he labeled him as "a better player than Jim Thorpe because he always tries to do his best." A legion of disbelieving old-timers, knowing that Thorpe had been Warner's charge earlier at Carlisle, have insisted that he made the statement with tongue in cheek. But on January 1, 1925, at least, there was no doubt about it, even if Notre Dame won the ball game. As for the Four Horsemen, Grantland Rice was right—Famine, Pestilence, Destruction, and Death were only aliases.

It's an Old Wild West Custom

By Duncan Emrich

Perhaps there were a few excesses here and there, but who could blame a cowboy or a miner for cutting loose when he came to town? Actually, he was a fairly harmless character; only greenhorns or dandified strangers were made to dance to the music of his six-shooters. He wouldn't have been a westerner if he hadn't done a little "yelling and helling."

While their saloons provided entertainment in the basic forms of whisky and gambling, the men, nevertheless, out of boredom or from sheer excess of animal spirits, turned their idle hours to other forms of amusement and general hell-raising. The cowboys who had spent months on the range, like the sailor home from sea, turned out to paint the town red. Their approach was one either of war-whooping directness or of ambling innocence. Their arrival, with jingling spurs and purses, was welcomed, and their hungover departure hastened.

Because the towns were so remote, and their populations so essentially clannish in terms of their own experience of cattle or mining life, the men's amusements were rough and, to the outsider, alarming and dangerous. Often enough, the outsider himself was the subject of entertainment. The Westerner's traditional scorn of the tenderfoot frequently assumed the active form of the original hotfoot, with shots accurately placed around the visitor's dancing feet. One unfortunate in Leadville had a can tied by a string to his coat tails. When told to "Git!", he got, and the miners fired at the can as he hightailed it down the street. Plug hats were tossed into the air for target practice. Cowboys invariably reserved the roughest horses for newly arrived greenhorns, and "dudes" were entertained by being forced to drink tumblerfuls of raw, frontier whisky. The "dude" was easily distinguished by his dress and language, was often an Easterner from Boston, Philadelphia, or New York, or a touring Englishman, or was sometimes a remittance man, wearing a monocle, spats, cane, and top hat. In addition to his outlandish and impractical costume, he was ignorant of the customs of the country, staring bug-eyed at gun-carrying cowboys, gambling tables, saloons, miners, and women of the town. He was too inquisitive, asking impertinent questions in a land and at a time when a man's business was his own and questioners were apt to be forcibly discouraged. He adapted himself to the ways of the land with difficulty, and his schooling in the West was often hard.

When a St. Louis drummer put on airs in a New Mexico town, preferring to eat alone in his hotel room rather than with the common folk, he was promptly arrested and clapped in jail on a charge of horse stealing. His case was argued seriously in court, the prosecution demanding that he be hanged forthwith. The defense attorney, assigned by the court, pled for the "culprit's" life. How can anyone believe that this kindly gentleman, this upright drummer, this solid citizen, this fine businessman . . . ?" And with every "this," the defense attorney came down with a resounding, open-palmed thwack on the bald head of the "kindly gentleman" until his crown resembled a shining red beet. The judge, summing up the case, began seriously enough, but after two minutes of haranguing burst forth with a belly-splitting laugh, and ran screaming with laughter from the court, followed by jury, attorneys, and witnesses. The dazed drummer, freed from the halter, learned at least not to snub his equals on the frontier.

Similarly, a greenhorn in Gayleyville, who had heard much of the shooting West, found that Curley Bill, leader of a rough band of cowboys, was relatively friendly. The greenhorn should not, however, have confused barroom friendship with familiarity. He made the error of boasting about town that he was a member of Curley Bill's gang and that other cowboys were, in consequence, afraid of him. Curley Bill heard of it and invited him to drink at one of the saloons, an invitation which the "dude" accepted with alacrity. Once indoors, the newcomer found himself dancing to the tune of six-shooters, his hat riddled with bullets and his pockets emptied over the bar for refreshments for the crowd. He left town suddenly, subdued and wiser. . . .

A like joke was played on another newcomer in Creede, a salesman, who looked forward eagerly to visiting, with a local friend, the two blonde and beauteous daughters of Old Man McClintock, reputedly a devil with a gun in defense of virtue, but coincidentally out of town on the evening in question. Armed with bottles of whisky, the local citizen and the salesman climbed the hillside to McClintock's cabin where, instead of inviting damsels, they were met with a charge of buckshot. The "friend" cried out that he was shot, and the salesman plunged, rolled, and tumbled down the hillside to the nearest saloon, where he gave an account of the terrible shooting. Instead of a sympathetic and excited audience, however, the salesman was horrified to find his listeners looking at him with suspicion. "You mean Joe was shot and you left him up there to die alone?" "Anyone knows McClintock hasn't got two daughters." "You wouldn't have shot Joe yourself, would you now?" While Old Man McClintock, Joe, and others drank the salesman's whisky in the hillside cabin, the salesman himself sweated and trembled under the mounting accusations in the saloon. At last, inching toward the door, a providential opportunity came for him to "escape." He bolted down the main street and out of town, a few scattered shots urging him on his way. He was never seen again in Creede.

Among themselves, the cowboys raised virtually every kind of hell imaginable. They and their horses were inseparable, and they rode them precisely where neither God, man, nor beast had ever intended that they should ride. They spurred them into the big saloons for a drink from the saddle, rode them to the card tables for a quick hand of poker, and played a wild game of billiards from horseback. They even invented a game of "pool polo" with their mounts, turning a single, cavorting horse around on the pool table until the last ball had been pocketed by the horse's hoofs. In Montana, two cowboys terrified staid passengers on a Northern Pacific train by riding their horses through the dining car. And at Missoula, a cowboy wagered that he could ride his horse into every room of Sam Arthur's hotel, and would have and could have if he had not been stopped by fourteen bullets from the outraged proprietor.

Their other amusements were rough. Leadville, which was one of the wildest towns of the West in the '80's, humorously reported a leap-year dance: "Leadville has had a leap-year ball which was conducted in proper style. The girls had three knife fights and then a general shooting affray, while the men huddled together in a corner and yelled." In Elko, Nevada, a madame of the "line" wagered that she could walk three times around town as naked as Godiva and that no one would bother her. Soldiers from a nearby fort entered into the spirit of the occasion and guaranteed her an audience by preceding her with a full band. . . .

It was inevitable that the men should patronize the stronger and more bloodthirsty sports which have since been outlawed. In Leadville, ordinary boxing was varied by fighters who slugged it out on top of a twenty-foot derrick, the loser receiving not only punishing blows but the hazard of the fall. Cripple Creek staged one of the very few bull fights ever held in this country. . . . Cockfighting was brought to the camps by Irish and Cornish miners. Dogfights were traditional, and enlivened on one occasion at Butte by setting two greyhounds and a bulldog against a wolf, the dogs winning easily. Brutal shin kicking and head butting contests were violent departures from classic rules of ring sport.

The glorious Fourth was celebrated with frontier abandon. Introduced with dynamite blasted from anvils or exploded in whole barrels on nearby hillsides, the day and night celebrations progressed from early-morning flag raisings to the utter fatigue of the Fifth. In a mining camp of any size, there was the usual parade of the National Guard in dress uniform and the various volunteer fire companies with gleaming equipment. The parade, with its bands, was followed by foot races of the fire companies, each company spurred on by its supporters who bet lavishly on their favorite. Next came the chief mining-camp contests, the rock drilling competition with prizes running into the thousands of dollars for the champion team—men who could pound the drill inches deep into hard granite in as many minutes—and by the mucking contest, the winner shoveling a huge pile of broken rock into empty ore carts. These contests were a matter not only of brawn but skill as well, and the winners were honored by their community and often represented it in contests involving champion teams from other camps. Even today, where the mechanical has supplanted the doublejack, men still compete in the traditional contest, swinging the four- and eight-pound hammers with a steady, skillful rhythm. The sound of steel striking steel that bites into granite can be heard from Bisbee to Butte and from Virginia City to Cripple Creek on their holidays. It is a sound reminding men of the one-time greatness of the camps, and their mining heritage.

Following the outdoor events, the citizenry moved into the saloons, where enormous quantities of whisky were downed in honor of life, liberty, and the pursuit of happiness. Fiddlers and piano players added to the general gaiety. Where no women were on hand, the men danced with each other, whirling violently and ungracefully about the room, occasionally winding up head over tea-kettle among the clanging spittoons. It was during such celebrations that the men saw "side-hill lancers," an animal half-bird and half-beast, with two short legs on the uphill side and two long, long legs on the downhill side:

You can hear the lancer going round and round,
Chasing the miner on his spree,
For only he can see
This side-hill lancer in this country West.
He cannot catch him on the plain
If only he'd run down quick,
But round and round and round he goes,
So don't go on the hill. . . .

Many a miner went on the hill, however. Axel the carpenter, in a betwixt and between state, drove a rusty nail into his foot. His friends recommended a doctor at once. Axel waved them aside—"Never had a doctor in my life." He headed straight for the Bucket of Blood Saloon, bought two pints of Old Crow, took off his shoe, poured one pint into it and the other into himself, and sloshed around town until cured. On his final spree, he lay down in a snowbank and quietly froze to death. Many miners have waked to find that thoughtful friends had taken care of them in their drunkenness, putting them gently to bed in open graves, in coffins, and beside corpses. . . .

Fred Hart, who was never accused of being a teetotaler, described a morning-after celebrant in his *Reese River Reveille:*

"He came up the street with an unsteady gait, his legs now and again acting contrary, one foot trying hard to cross the path of the other. At last he reached a railing that stood by an open cellarway, and here was a haven of rest for his weary and Fourth-of-July-racked soul. He grasped the railing to steady himself; then gradually his head sank down on the rail, and there was a bending of the knee joints. Slowly, carefully, he slid down the cellar stairs; the bottom step was reached; one long-drawn sigh, ending in a deep bass snore, and, away from the gaze of men and the City Marshal, the tired soul was at rest—a rest so perfect that all the firecrackers on earth could not have recalled him to the scenes of unrest of the day after the Fourth. He was there this morning, lying on his back, with the bright sun shining on his upturned face, and several blue-bottle flies sipping the sweetness from his parted lips. Reader, that man was once a little boy, and went fishing on Sunday, and robbed orchards and birds' nests, just like many and many another innocent boy; and had it not been for the demon of whisky, he might have grown up to be a member of the Legislature."

There were other occasions than the Fourth for celebrating. The spring and fall festivals, traditionally observed by all peoples of the earth, appeared in the West with typical local trappings. The calf roundups of the spring and the beef roundups of the fall brought together from scattered ranches cowboys and "reps" who, for their own amusement and the honor of the brand, competed with each other in bulldogging, bronc riding, roping, and lassoing of running animals. The men were inordinately proud of their mounts and their equipment, often spending every penny earned for saddle, bridle, spurs, sombreros, and chaps. The outfits were made for the cowboy's use: the sombrero to keep off the sun and to scoop up water for his horse; the chaps to protect his legs from mesquite and brush; the high-heeled boots to fit the stirrup and to dig deeply into the ground; and his neckerchief to cover his face against the smothering dust of the herd. But in addition to their being useful, the cowboy made them colorful as well. His chaps were decorated with nickel and silver buttons and leather laces, his neckerchief was a bright red or yellow, his sombrero a white or dust-colored Stetson, and his boots often intricately designed with stitching and embossed leather work. His saddle was his great pride, and for it he might spend several hundred hard-earned dollars. . . .

There were still other occasions for parades and celebrations, including the big annual stockyard celebration in Denver, the Festival of Mountain and Plain, various commemorative Admission Days when the young states joined the Union, the annual meetings of the many Stockmen's and Mining Associations, and the varied fiestas throughout the Southwest on saints' days and religious holidays. The visitor will know of the more obvious ones, those widely advertised and backed by Chambers of Commerce, but he will do well—if he wishes to learn from the life of the region—to ferret out the smaller doings, because there the people meet simply, without the fanfare of publicity and Hollywoodesque shows. At the purely local fairs he will find the working ranchers and cowboys, the farmers and housewives and their children, the natural, unsophisticated way of American life. Instead of a ten-dollar box seat and blaring loud-speakers announcing events, he will find himself perched on a corral fence, his heels hooked over a lower rail and the announcements coming to him from a neighbor who knows each participant and horse. From the Stinkingwater to the Ruidoso, and the Big Sandy to the Gila, the small, unheralded rodeos and fairs will teach him more of the land and its honest gentry than he can learn from half a dozen of the highly organized variety, exciting though they are. And always there will be a bit of Western yelling and helling.

Epilogue: The Promise of America

By Thomas Wolfe

Go, seeker, if you will, throughout the land and you will find us burning in the night.

There where the hackles of the Rocky Mountains blaze in the blank and naked radiance of the moon, go make your resting stool upon the highest peak. Can you not see us now? The continental wall juts sheer and flat, its huge black shadow on the plain, and the plain sweeps out against the East, two thousand miles away. The great snake that you see there is the Mississippi River.

Behold the gem-strung towns and cities of the good, green East, flung like star dust through the field of night. That spreading constellation to the north is called Chicago, and that giant wink that blazes in the moon is the pendant lake that it is built upon. Beyond, close-set and dense as a clenched fist, are all the jeweled cities of the eastern seaboard. There's Boston, ringed with the bracelet of its shining little towns, and all the lights that sparkle on the rocky indentations of New England. Here, southward and a little to the west, and yet still coasted to the sea, is our intensest ray, the splintered firmament of the towered island of Manhattan. Round about her, sown thick as grain, is the glitter of a hundred towns and cities. The long chain of lights, there, is the necklace of Long Island and the Jersey shore. Southward, and inland by a foot or two, behold the duller glare of Philadelphia. Southward further still, the twin constellations—Baltimore and Washington. Westward, but still within the borders of the good, green East, that night-time glow and smolder of hell-fire is Pittsburgh. Here, St. Louis, hot and humid in the cornfield belly of the land, and bedded on the mid-length coil and fringes of the snake. There at the snake's mouth, southward six hundred miles or so, you see the jeweled crescent of old New Orleans. Here, west and south again, you see the gemmy glitter of the cities on the Texas border.

Turn now, seeker, on your resting stool atop the Rocky Mountains and look another thousand miles or so across moon-blazing fiend-worlds of the Painted Desert, and beyond Sierras' ridge. That magic congeries of lights there to the west, ringed like a studded belt around the magic setting of its lovely harbor, is the fabled town of San Francisco. Below it, Los Angeles and all the cities of the California shore. A thousand miles to north and west, the sparkling towns of Oregon and Washington.

Observe the whole of it, survey it as you might survey a field. Make it your garden, seeker, or your back yard patch. Be at ease in it. It's your oyster—yours to open if you will. Don't be frightened, it's not so big now, when your footstool is the Rocky Mountains. Reach out and dip a hatful of cold water from Lake Michigan. Drink it—we've tried it—you'll not find it bad. Take your shoes off and work your toes down in the river oozes of the Mississippi bottom—it's very refreshing on a hot night in the summertime. Help yourself to a bunch of Concord grapes up there in northern New York State—they're getting good now. Or raid that watermelon patch down there in Georgia. Or, if you like, you can try the Rockyfords here at your elbow in Colorado. Just make yourself at home, refresh yourself, get the feel of things, adjust your sights, and get the scale. It's your pasture now and it's not so big—only three thousand miles from east to west, only two thousand miles from north to south—but all between, where ten thousand points of light prick out the cities, towns, and villages, there, seeker, you will find us burning in the night.

Here, as you pass through the brutal sprawl, the twenty miles of rails and rickets of the South Chicago slums—here in an unpainted shack is a Negro boy, and, seeker, he is burning in the night. Behind him is a memory of the cotton fields, the flat and mournful pineland barrens of the lost and buried South, and at the fringes of the pine another shack with mother and eleven children. Farther still behind, the slavedriver's whip, the slave ship, and, far off, the jungle dirge of Africa. And before him, what? A roped-in ring, a blaze of lights, across from him a white champion; the bell, the opening, and all around the vast sea-roaring of the crowd. Then the lightning feint and stroke, the black panther's paw—the hot, rotating presses, and the rivers of sheeted print. O seeker, where is the slave ship now?

On there, in the clay-baked piedmont of the South, that lean and tanfaced boy who sprawls there in the creaking chair among admiring cronies before the open doorways of the fire department, and tells them how he pitched the team to shutout victory today. What visions burn, what dreams possess him, seeker of the night? The packed stands of the stadium, the bleachers sweltering with their unshaded hordes, the faultless velvet of the diamond, unlike the clay-baked outfields down in Georgia. The mounting roar of eighty thousand voices and Gehrig coming up to bat, the boy himself upon the pitching mound, the lean face steady as a hound's; then the nod, the signal, and the windup, the rawhide arm that snaps and crackles like a whip, the small white bullet of the blazing ball, its loud report in the oiled pocket of the catcher's mitt, the umpire's thumb jerked upward, the clean strike.

Or there again, in the east-side ghetto of Manhattan, two blocks away from the East River, a block away from the gas-house district and its thuggery, there in the swarming tenement, shut in his sweltering cell, breathing the sun-baked air through open window at the fire escape, celled there away into a little semblance of privacy and solitude from all the brawling and vociferous life and argument of his family and the seething hive around him, the Jew boy sits and pores upon his book. In shirtsleeves, bent above his table to meet the hard glare of a naked bulb, he sits with gaunt, starved face. And for what? For what this agony of concentration? For what this hell of effort? For what this intense withdrawal from the poverty and squalor of dirty brick and rusty fire escapes, from the raucous cries and violence and neverending noise? For what? Because, brother, he is burning in the night. He sees the class, the lecture-room, the shining apparatus of gigantic laboratories, the open field of scholarship and pure research, certain knowledge, and the world distinction of an Einstein name.

So, then, to every man his chance—to every man, regardless of his birth, his shining, golden opportunity—to every man the right to live, to work, to be himself, and to become whatever thing his manhood and his vision can combine to make him—this, seeker, is the promise of America.

[illegible] the apartment, [illegible] [illegible] [illegible] [illegible] [illegible] [illegible] [illegible] down in Georgia. [illegible]